Children's Book Awards International, 1990 through 2000

ALSO BY LAURA SMITH

Children's Book Awards International:
A Directory of Awards and Winners,
from Inception through 1990
(McFarland, 1992)

Children's Book Awards International, 1990 through 2000

by LAURA SMITH

McFarland & Company, Inc., Publishers
Jefferson, North Carolina, and London

Library of Congress Cataloguing-in-Publication Data

Smith, Laura J., 1957–
Children's book awards international, 1990 through 2000 / by Laura Smith
p. cm.
Includes indexes.

ISBN 0-7864-1288-7 (library binding : 50# alkaline paper) 

1. Children's literature — Awards — Directories. 2. Young adult literature — Awards — Directories. 3. Children's literature — Illustrations — Awards — Directories. 4. Young adult literature — Illustrations — Awards — Directories. 5. Book industries and trade — Awards — Directories. I. Title.
Z1037.A2S46 2003
[PN1009.A1]
809'.89282'079 — dc21 2002007811

British Library cataloguing data are available

Manufactured in the United States of America

McFarland & Company, Inc., Publishers
Box 611, Jefferson, North Carolina 28640
www.mcfarlandpub.com

For Cameron

Table of Contents

Introduction 1
The Organization of This Work 3

AUSTRALIA

Alan Marshall Prize for Children's Literature 5
Australian Christian Book of the Year 5
BILBY (Books I Love Best Yearly) 6
Children's Book of the Year Award 7
Children's Peace Literature Award 9
COOL (Canberra's Own Outstanding List) 9
Crichton Award for Illustration 10
Cross Pen Prize for Young Adult Fiction 11
CROW (Children Reading Outstanding Writers) 11
CYBER Award (Children's Yearly Best Ever Reads) 12
Dromkeen Medal 12
Dymocks Children's Choice Awards 12
Environmental Award for Children's Literature 13
Eve Pownall Award for Information Books 14
Family Award 15
KOALA Award (Kids' Own Australian Literature Award) 15
KROC Award (Kids Reading OZ Choice) 16
Multicultural Children's Literature Award 17
NSW State Literary Award — Children's Book Award 17
Sheaffer Prize for Adult Young Fiction 18
West Australian Young Readers' Book Award 18
Western Australian Premier's Book Award — Children's Section 19
Young Australian Best Book Award (YABBA) 20

AUSTRIA

Jury der Jungen Leser 21
Kinder- und Jugendbuchpreisen der Stadt Wien (Children's Book Awards of the City of Vienna) 22
Österreichischen Würdigungspreis für Kinder- und Jugendliteratur (Austrian Appreciation Prize for Children's and Young Adult Literature) 24
Österreichischer Kinder- und Jugendbuchpreis (Austrian National Children's and Juvenile Book Award) 24
Österreichischer Staatspreis für Kinder- und Jugendliteratur (Austrian State Prize for Children's and Young Adult Literature) 28

BELGIUM

Boekenleeuw & Boekenwelpen (Booklion and Bookcubs) 28
Boekenpauw & Boekenpluimen (Bookpeacock and Bookfeathers) 31
Gouden Uil (Golden Owl) 32
Illustratorenprijs van de Stad Hasselt (Illustration Award of the City of Hasselt) 32
Interprovinciale Prijs (Interprovincial Award for Children's and Youth Books) 33
Kinder- en Jeugdjury Vlaanderen (Children and Youth Jury Flanders Award) 33
Prijs Knokke-Heist (Knokke-Heist Prize) 34
Prijs van de Vlaamse Gemeenschap (Belgium Government Prize) 35
Prix Bernard Versele (Bernard Versele Prize) 35

BRAZIL

Prêmio Jabuti (Jabuti Prize) 36
Prêmio Monteiro Lobato (Monteiro Lobato Prize) 37

CANADA

Amelia Frances Howard-Gibbon Illustrators Award 37
Ann-Connor Brimer Award 38
Arthur Ellis Award 39
Canadian Library Association Book of the Year for Children 39
Canadian Library Association Young Adult Book Award 40
Elizabeth Mrazik-Cleaver Canadian Picture Book Award 40

Geoffrey Bilson Award for Historical Fiction for Young People 41
Governor General's Literary Awards 42
Hackmatack Children's Choice Award 44
Information Book Award 44
International Reading Association Children's Literature Award 45
IODE Book Award — Toronto Chapter 45
IODE Violet Downey Book Award — National Chapter 46
Manitoba Young Reader's Choice Award 47
McNally Robinson Book for Young People Award 47
Mr. Christie Book Awards 48
Norma Fleck Award 50
Ontario Red Maple Award 50
Palme Livromagie de l'Imprimerie Gagné 51
Prix 12/17 Brive 52
Prix Alvine Bélisle (Alvine Bélisle Prize) 52
Prix Cécile-Gagnon (Cécile-Gagnon Prize) 53
Prix Littéraire le Droit (Le Droit Literature Prize) 53
Prix Littéraires Desjardins — Littérature jeunesse (Desjardin Literature Prize) 54
Prix Monique Corriveau (Monique Corriveau Prize) 54
Prix Québec/Wallonie-Bruxelles du Livre de la Jeunesse (Quebec Prize) 54
R. Ross Annett Award for Children's Literature 55
Red Cedar Book Award 55
Ruth Schwartz Children's Book Award 56
Sheila A. Egoff Children's Book Prize 57
Silver Birch Award 57
Vicky Metcalfe Award 58
Vicky Metcalfe Short Story Award 58

COLOMBIA

Premio ENKA (ENKA Prize) 59
Premio Latinoamericano de Literatura Infantil y Juvenil Norma-Fundalectura (Latin American Prize for Children's and Juvenile Literature) 59

COSTA RICA

Premio Carmen Lyra (Carmen Lyra Prize) 60
Premio Joven Creación (Young Creation Prize) 61

CUBA

Premio David de Literatura Infantil (David Award) 61
Premio Ismaelillo (Ismaelillo Prize) 61
Premios Edad de Oro (Golden Age Awards) 62
Premios Pinos Nuevos (New Pines Prizes) 62
Rosa Blanca (White Rose Award) 63

DENMARK

BMF's Bornebogspris (Danish Booksellers Association Prize) 68
Danmarks Skolebibliotekarforenings Bornebogspris (Danish Association of School Librarians Children's Book Prize) 68
Forlaget Gyldendals Boglegat for Bornebogsfattere og Billedkundtnere (Gyldendal Publishers Prize) 69
Klods-Hans Prisen (Clumsy Hans Prize) 69
Kommunernes Skolebiblioteksforenings Forfatterpris (Danish School Library Association Prize) 70
Kulturministeriets Bornebogspris (Ministry of Culture Children's Book Prize) 70
Kulturministeriets Illustratorpris (Ministry of Cultural Affairs Prize for Illustration) 71
Skriverprisen (Skriver's Award) 71

FINLAND

Anni Swanin Mitali (Anni Swan Medal) 72
Arvid Lydeckenin Palkinto (Arvid Lydecken Prize) 72
Finlandia Junior 73
Lasten Oman Kirjakerhon Kuvakirjapalkinto (Finnish Picture Book Prize) 73
Rudolf Koivun Palkinto (Rudolf Koivu Prize) 74
Suomalainen Kuvakirja-palkinto 74
Topelius-palkinto (Topelius Prize) 74
Valtion Kirjallisuuspalkinto (National Awards for Literature) 75

FRANCE

Prix des Incorruptibles (Incorruptible's Prize) 76
Prix des Jeunes Lecteurs PEEP (Young Readers Prize) 76
Prix Lire au Collège 76
Prix Octogones (Octagon Prizes) 76

Prix Sorcières (Witches Prizes) 77
Prix Totem (Totem Prize) 77

GERMANY

Alex-Wedding-Preis (Alex Wedding Prize) 78
Buxtehuder Bulle (Buxtehuder Bull) 79
Deutscher Jugendliteraturpreis (German Youth Literature Prize) 79
Friedrich-Gerstäcker-Preis (Friedrich Gerstäcker Prize) 81
Katholischer Kinder- und Jugendbuchpreis (Catholic Children's Book Prize) 81
Oldenburger Kinder- und Jugendbuchpreis (Oldenburger Children's Book Prize) 82
Peter-Härtling-Preis für Kinder- und Jugendlitatur (Peter Härtling Prize for Children's Literature) 82
Rattenfänger-Literaturpreis (Pied Piper Prize) 83
Troisdorfer Bilderbuchpreis (Troisdorfer Picture Book Prize) 83
Weissen Raben (White Ravens) 85

GREAT BRITAIN

Aventis Prize for Science Books 107
Blue Peter Book Awards 108
Branford Boase Award 108
Carnegie Medal 108
Children's Book Award 109
Earthworm Award 110
Eleanor Farjeon Award 110
Fidler Award 111
Guardian Children's Fiction Award 111
Harvey Darton Award 112
Kate Greenaway Medal 112
Kathleen Fidler Award 112
Kurt Maschler Award 113
Lancashire County Library Children's Book of the Year Award 113
Mary Vaughan Jones Award 114
Macmillan Prize 114
Mother Goose Award 114
NASEN Special Needs Book Awards 115
National Art Library Illustration Awards 115
Nestle Smarties Book Prize 116

North East Book Award 118
Rhone-Poulenc Prize 118
Sainsbury's Baby Book Award 119
Sheffield Children's Book Award 119
Signal Poetry Award 119
Times Educational Supplement Information Book Awards 120
Tir Na n-Og Awards 121
W.H. Smith Illustration Award 123
Whitbread Children's Book of the Year Awards 124

GREECE

Circle of the Greece Children's Book Prizes 124
Gynekia Logotehniki Syntrofia (Women's Literary Society Prizes) 126
Penelope Delta Award 127
State Prize for Children's Literature 128

ICELAND

Islandsafdelings Anerkendelse (Icelandic IBBY Award) 129
Reykjaviks Undervisningsradspris (Reykjavik Board of Education Prize) 129
Verdlaunasjodur Islensku Barnabóka (Icelandic Children's Book Prize) 129

IRAN

Institute for the Intellectual Development of Children and Young Adults Award 130
Ministry of Ershad Award 131
Prize of the Iranian Children's Book Council 131
Soroush Publishing Award 131

IRELAND

Children's Books Ireland/Bisto Awards 131
Eilis Dillion Memorial Award 132
RAI (Reading Association of Ireland) 132

ISRAEL

Ben-Yitzkak Award 133

ITALY

Fiera di Bologna per l'Infanzia e la Gioventù (Bologna Children and Youth Book Prizes) 133
Premio Critici in Erba (Critici in Erba Prize) 134

JAPAN

Mimizuku-sho (Owl Prize) 134
Noma Concours for Children's Picture Book Illustrations 134

LITHUANIA

Lithuanian Children's Book Award 135

MEXICO

Premio Nacional de Literatura Infantil y Juvenil (National Award for Children's and Juvenile Literature) 135

NETHERLANDS

Glazen Globe (Glass Globe) 136
Gouden Griffel and Zilveren Griffel (Golden Plaque and Silver Plaque) 137
Gouden Penseel and Zilveren Penseel (Golden Brush and Silver Brush) 140
Jenny Smelik-Kiggenprijs (Jenny Smelik Kiggen Prize) 142
Nienke van Hichtumprijs (Nienke van Hichtum Prize) 142
Theo Thijssen-prijs voor Kinder- en Jeugdliteratuur (Theo Thijssen Prize for Children's and Youth Literature) 142

NEW ZEALAND

Esther Glen Award 143
Gaelyn Gordon Award 143
Margaret Mahy Lecture Award 143
New Zealand Library Association Young People's Nonfiction Award 144
New Zealand Post Children's Book Awards 144
Russell Clark Award 146
Te Kura Pounamu (Maori Book Award) 146
Tom Fitzgibbon Award 147

NORWAY

Askeladd Prisen (Askeladd Award) 147
Brageprisen (Norwegian Literature Prize) 148

Kulturdepartementets Pris (Award from the Ministry of Culture) 148
Norsk Litteraturkritikerlags (Norwegian Critic's Award) 150
Riksmålsprisen — Barne- og Ungdomsbøker (Riksmalsforenings Children's Book Awards) 151
Skolebibliotekarforeningens Litteraturpris (Norwegian School Librarian Association's Award) 151

POLAND

International Janusz Korczak Prize 152

RUSSIA

Maxim Gorky International Award for Literature for Children and Youth 152

SLOVAK REPUBLIC

Bienále Ilustrácií Bratislava (Biennale of Illustrations) 152

SLOVENIA

Levstikova Nagrada (Fran Levstik Prize) 155
Moja Najljibsa Knijiga (My Favorite Book Award) 156

SOUTH AFRICA

Alba Bouwer Prize 157
ATKV Children's Book Prize 157
C P Hoogenhout Award 159
Katrine Harries Award 159
M E R Prize 160
Percy Fitzpatrick Award 160
Sanlam Prize 161
Scheepers Prize for Youth Literature 162
Tienie Holloway Medal for Nursery School Literature 162
Vivian Wilkes Award 163

SPAIN

Premio Apel–les Mestres (Apel–les Mestres Prize) 163
Premio C.C.E.I. de Ilustración Infantil (C.C.E.I. Prize for Children's Book Illustration) 164

Premio C.C.E.I. para Libros Infantiles y Juveniles (C.C.E.I. Prize for Children's and Young Adult Literature) 164
Premio el Barco de Vapor (Steamboat Prize) 165
Premio Gran Angular (Gran Angular Prize) 167
Premio Internacional de Ilustración (International Illustration Prize) 167
Premio Joaquím Ruyra (Joaquím Ruyra Prize) 168
Premio Josep Maria Folch i Torres (Josep Maria Folch i Torres Prize) 169
Premio Lazarillo (Guide Prize) 169
Premio Lola Anglada (Lola Anglada Prize) 170
Premio Merlín (Merlin Prize) 171
Premio Nacional de Literatura Infantil y Juvenil (Creación) (National Prize for Children's and Young Adult Literature) 172

SWEDEN

Astrid Lindgren Priset (Astrid Lindgren Prize) 172
Augustpriset (August Prize) 173
Bokjuryn (Book Jury) 173
Carl von Linné-plaketten (Carl von Linné Plaque) 174
Elsa Beskow Plaketten (Elsa Beskow Plaque) 174
Expressens Heffaklump (Heffaklumpen Prize) 175
Gulliver Award 175
Nils Holgersson Plaketten (Nils Holgersson Plaque) 176
Peter Pan Award 176

SWITZERLAND

Blaue Brillenschlange (Blue Cobra) 177
Hans Christian Andersen Awards 178
Prix Enfantaisie (Children's Prize) 178
Schweizer Jugendbuchpreis (Switzerland Children's Literature Prize) 179
Vache Qui Lit (Reading Cow) 180

UNITED STATES

Aesop Prize 180
ALAN Award 181
American Booksellers Book of the Year (ABBY) Award 182
Américas Award 182
Anne Spencer Lindbergh Prize in Children's Literature 183

Arizona Young Readers Award 183
Arkansas Diamond Primary Book Award 185
Bill Martin, Jr., Picture Book Award 185
Black-Eyed Susan Book Award 185
Blue Hen Book Award 187
Blue Spruce Award 187
Book Publishers of Texas Children's/Young People's Award 187
Book Sense Book of the Year Award 188
Boston Globe Horn Book Awards 188
Buckeye Children's Book Award 190
California Book Awards 191
California Young Reader Medal 192
Carolyn W. Field Award 195
Carter G. Woodson Book Award 195
Charlie May Simon Children's Book Award 197
Charlotte Book Award 197
Charlotte Zolotow Award 198
Child Study Children's Book Award 199
Christopher Awards 199
Claudia Lewis Award 202
Colorado Children's Book Award 202
Coretta Scott King Award 203
David McCord Award 205
Dorothy Canfield Fisher Children's Book Award 205
Drexel Citation 206
Edgar Allan Poe Award 206
Elizabeth Burr Award 207
Empire State Award of Excellence in Literature for Young People 208
Eva L. Gordon Award for Children's Science Literature 208
Evelyn Sibley Lampman Award 209
Ezra Jack Keats New Writer Award 209
Flicker Tale Children's Book Award 210
Flora Stieglitz Straus Award 211
FOCAL (Friends of Children and Literature Award) 211
Garden State Children's Book Award 212
Garden State Teen Book Awards 214
Georgia Children's Book Award 215
Georgia Children's Picture Storybook Award 215
Giverny Book Award 216
Gold Medallion Book Award 216

Golden Archer Award 218
Golden Kite Awards 218
Great Stone Face Award 221
Helen Keating Ott Award for Outstanding Contribution to Children's Literature 222
Hope S. Dean Award 222
Indian Paintbrush Book Award 223
International Brant Point Literary Prize 223
International Reading Association Children's Book Award 224
Iowa Children's Choice Award 225
Iowa Teen Award 226
Irma S. and James H. Black Award 226
Jane Addams Children's Book Award 227
Jefferson Cup Award 228
Jeremiah Ludington Memorial Award 228
Jo Osborne Award for Humor in Children's Literature 229
John and Patricia Beatty Award 229
John Newbery Award 230
Josette Frank Award 232
Judy Lopez Memorial Award for Children's Literature 232
Keene (New Hampshire) State College Children's Literature Festival Award 232
Kentucky Bluegrass Award 233
Kerlan Award 234
Knickerbocker Award for Juvenile Literature 234
Land of Enchantment Book Award 235
Laura Ingalls Wilder Award 236
Lee Bennett Hopkins Promising Poet Award 236
Little Archer Award 236
Louisiana Young Readers' Choice Award 236
Lupine Award 237
Maine Student Book Award 237
Margaret A. Edwards Award (YASD/School Library Journal Young Adult Author Award) 238
Mark Twain Award 238
Maryland Children's Book Award 239
Massachusetts Children's Book Award 240
Maud Hart Lovelace Book Award 241
Michael L. Printz Award 241
Mildred L. Batchelder Award 242

Missouri Building Block Picture Book Award 242
Mythopoeic Fantasy Award 243
National Book Award for Young People's Literature 243
National Council of Teachers of English Award for Excellence in Poetry for Children 243
Nebraska Golden Sower Award 244
Nene Award 245
Nevada Young Readers Award 246
New England Book Award 248
North Carolina Children's Book Award 249
Nutmeg Children's Book Award 249
Ohioana Book Awards 250
Oklahoma Book Award 251
Orbis Pictus Award 251
Outstanding Pennsylvania Author 252
Pacific Northwest Young Reader's Choice Award 252
Parents' Choice Award 253
Paul A. Witty Short Story Award 257
PEN/Norma Klein Award 258
Pennsylvania Young Reader's Choice Award 258
Phoenix Award 259
Please Touch Book Award 259
Prairie Pasque Award 260
Pura Belpré Award 261
Randolph Caldecott Award 261
Rebecca Caudill Young Readers' Book Award 264
Red Clover Children's Choice Picture Book Award 264
Regina Medal 265
Rhode Island Children's Book Award 265
Sasquatch Book Award 266
Science-Writing Award in Physics and Astronomy for Articles or Books Intended for Children 266
Scott O'Dell Historical Fiction Award 267
Sequoyah Children's Book Award 267
Sequoyah Young Adult Book Award 268
Show Me Readers Award 268
Soaring Eagle — Wyoming Young Adult Book Award 269
Society of Midland Authors Award 269
South Carolina Children's Book Award 270
South Carolina Junior Book Award 271

South Carolina Young Adult Book Award 271
Southern California Council on Literature for Children and Young People Annual Children's Literature Awards 272
Spur Award 274
Sunshine State Young Reader's Award 275
Sydney Taylor Body-of-Work Award 276
Sydney Taylor Book Award 276
Teddy Book Award 277
Texas Bluebonnet Award 278
Tomás Rivera Mexican American Children's Book Award 278
Treasure State Award 279
UNICEF–Ezra Jack Keats International Award for Excellence in Children's Book Illustration 279
University of Southern Mississippi Medallion 280
Utah Children's Book Award 280
Virginia Young Reader's Award 282
Volunteer State Book Award 284
Washington Children's Choice Picture Book Award 286
Washington Irving Children's Book Choice Award 286
Washington Post/Children's Books Guild Nonfiction Award 288
WEMA Golden Archer Award 288
William Allen White Children's Book Award 289
Young Hoosier Book Award 290

Author Index 293
Awards and Sponsors Index 311
Illustrator Index 319
Title Index 326

Introduction

The aim of this directory is to make a record of all awards given for the writing and illustrating of children's and young adult literature. It will introduce users to great literature and illustration from around the world, and enable researchers to identify and locate sponsoring organizations.

While many awards are deservedly given to people working in many capacities within the genre of children's books, only awards given to authors and illustrators are included.

Although every effort has been made to contact sponsoring organizations for information about the awards and to provide accurate translations, information was not always accessible or readily forthcoming. Users are encouraged to submit new or corrected information to the author in care of the publisher for inclusion in subsequent editions of this directory.

The Organization of This Work

The directory is arranged alphabetically, first by country and then by award name. Each award listing provides the formal name of the award, the sponsoring organization, the address and telephone number, a contact person (when available), the date the award was established, and what the award actually consists of. A brief description of the award and any particulars given by the sponsoring organization have been included. For detailed information users are advised to contact the sponsoring organization directly.

Following each award description is a list of the winners from 1990 to 2000. Normally, the information includes the year the award was given, names of the recipients, book titles, an English translation of the book title (when available), the publisher and the year of publication. When an award is given to a recipient for his or her body of work, only the name of the recipient and the year of the award are given. Discontinued awards have been incorporated alphabetically with current awards.

The boldface numbers to the left of each citation are entry numbers, provided to facilitate access via the indexes. Citations in the indexes refer to these entry numbers rather than to page numbers. There are four indexes: authors, awards and sponsors, illustrators, and titles.

In deference to users from a large range of language backgrounds, all parts of the book, but notably the indexes, have been strictly alphabetized, word by word, beginning with the first word; in the Title Index this includes articles at the beginning of titles. Articles have been removed from the names of awards to allow the reader to quickly locate alphabetically any entry. Numerals appear at the beginning of the sequence ordered by first digit, then second, etc. (i.e., "26" follows "20,000").

AUSTRALIA

1 Alan Marshall Prize for Children's Literature

Discontinued. ESTABLISHED: 1985. The award was given to living authors who are Australian citizens or permanent residents. It was made solely on literary merit, so the quality of illustrations is not considered.

2 1990. *Onion Tears.* Diana Kidd. Collins/Angus and Robertson, 1989.
3 1991. *Strange Objects.* Gary Crew. Heinemann, 1990.
4 1992. *The House Guest.* Eleanor Nilsson. Penguin, 1991.
5 1993. *Ariel, Zed and the Secret of Life.* Anna Fienberg. Little Ark Books, 1992.
6 1994. *The White Guinea Pig.* Ursula Dubosarsky. Viking, 1993.
7 1995. *Songman.* Allan Baillie. Penguin, 1994.

8 Australian Christian Book of the Year

SPONSOR: Australian Christian Literature Society. ADDRESS: Box 190, Rundle Mall Post Office, Adelaide, South Australia, Australia. PHONE: 61 8 8364 4643. The annual award is given for a book that presents issues of Christianity or belief in the Australian community.

9 1990. *Wadayaknow!* Denise Lake.
10 1991. *Yonderbeyonder.* Thyrza Davey.
11 1992. *Inigo.* Michael Hansen. *Category:* joint winner.
12 1992. *Tomb Travellers.* Roy Pond. *Category:* joint winner.
13 1993. *Toby's Riddle.* Joan Barlett.
14 1994. *Martin's Mountain.* Colin Thiele.
15 1995. *The Burnt Stick.* Anthony Hill. *Illustrator:* Mark Sofilas. Houghton Mifflin, 1995.
16 1996. *Hello God, It's Me.* Shirley Hearn. Aquila Press.
1997. No award given.
17 1998. *Get More New Life.* John Emmett (editor). Uniting Education.
1999. No award given.
2000. No award given.

18 BILBY (Books I Love Best Yearly)

SPONSOR: The Children's Book Council of Australia (Queensland Branch). CONTACT: Lonnie Rutland. ADDRESS: P.O. Box 615, Palm Beach, Queensland, Australia 4221. ESTABLISHED: 1990. AWARD: a trophy, official certificate and a Bilby T-shirt. The award is given to the authors for the following categories: early childhood, younger reader, older reader. These categories were established in 1998.

19 1990. *Matilda*. Roald Dahl. *Illustrator:* Quentin Blake. Cape, 1988. *Level:* read aloud.

20 1990. *The Secret Diary of Adrian Mole, aged 13¾*. Sue Townsend. Avon 1987. *Level:* secondary.

21 1990. *Superfudge*. Judy Blume. Dutton, 1980. *Category:* primary.

22 1991. *The Outsiders*. Sue E. Hinton. Viking, 1967. *Category:* secondary.

23 1991. *The BFG*. Roald Dahl. *Illustrator:* Quentin Blake. Farrar, 1982. *Level:* read aloud.

24 1991. *The BFG*. Roald Dahl. *Illustrator:* Quentin Blake. Farrar, 1982. *Level:* primary.

25 1992. *Where's Wally*. Martin Handford. *Level:* secondary.

26 1992. *Unreal!* Paul Jennings. Viking, 1986. *Level:* primary.

27 1992. *Charlie and the Chocolate Factory*. Roald Dahl. *Illustrator:* Joseph Schindelman. Knopf, 1985. *Category:* read aloud.

28 1993. *The Witches*. Roald Dahl. *Illustrator:* Quentin Blake. Farrar, 1983. *Category:* primary.

29 1993. *Blabber Mouth*. Morris Gleitzman. Harcourt Brace, 1995. *Category:* read aloud.

30 1993. *Flowers in the Attic*. Virginia Andrews. *Translator:* Jesus Pardo. Plaza & Janes Ed., 1985. *Category:* secondary.

31 1994. *Fantastic Mr. Fox*. Roald Dahl. *Illustrator:* Quentin Blake. Puffin, 1998. *Category:* read aloud.

32 1994. *Undone!* Paul Jennings. Viking, 1993. *Category:* read aloud.

33 1994. *Midnite: The Wild Colonial Boy*. Randolph Stow. *Category:* read Australian.

34 1995. *The Watertower*. Gary Crew. *Illustrator:* Steven Woolman. Accents, 1994. *Category:* read Australian.

35 1995. *The Pagemaster*. David Kirschner. Santillana Pub., 1995. *Category:* read aloud.

36 1995. *The Lion King*. Gina Ingoglio. *Illustrator:* Michael Humphries, Marshall Toomey. Disney, 1995. *Category:* read alone.

37 1995. *Looking for Alibrandi*. Melina Marchetta. Puffin, 1992. *Category:* secondary.

38 1996. *When the Wind Changed*. Ruth Park. *Illustrator:* Deborah Niland. Collins, 1981. *Category:* read aloud.

39 1996. *Where's Wally*. Martin Handford. *Category:* read alone.

40 1996. *Jurassic Park*. Michael Crichton. Knopf, 1990. *Category:* secondary.

41 1997. *Bamboozled*. David Legge. *Illustrator:* David Legge. 1995. *Category:* picture book.

42 1997. *The Hobbit*. J.R.R. Tolkin. Houghton, 1938. *Category:* older readers.

43 1997. *Matilda*. Roald Dahl. *Illustrator:* Quentin Blake. Cape, 1988. *Category:* younger readers.

44 1998. *Polar the Titanic Bear*. Laurie McGaw. *Illustrator:* Daisy Corning Stone Spedder. Little, Brown & Co., 1994. *Category:* younger readers.

45 1998. *The Midnight Gang*. Margaret Wild. *Illustrator:* Ann James. *Category:* early childhood.

46 1998. *Tomorrow, When the War Began*. John Marsden. *Category:* older readers. Pan Macmillan, 1994.

47 1999. *Bumface*. Morris Gleitzman. Penguin, 1998. *Category:* older readers.

48 1999. *GASP!* Terry Denton. *Illustrator:* Terry Denton. Penguin, 1998. *Category:* early childhood.

49 1999. *Detective Donut and the Wild Goose Chase*. Bruce Whatley. *Illustrator:* R. Smith. HarperCollins, 1998. *Category:* younger readers.

50 2000. *Grandad's Teeth*. Rod Clement. *Category:* early childhood.

51 2000. *Looking for Alibrandi*. Melina Marchetta. *Category:* older readers.

52 2000. *Just Stupid*. Andy Griffiths. *Category:* younger readers.

53 Children's Book of the Year Award

SPONSOR: Children's Book Council of Australia. ADDRESS: P.O. Box 28, Hunters Hill, New South Wales, Australia 2110. PHONE: 02 9630 2424. ESTABLISHED: 1946. AWARD: $30,000 Australian is divided between the three categories. The awards are given annually to focus attention on children's books, emphasize literary and artistic qualities, encourage new talent, and reward outstanding achievement.

54 1990. *Came Back to Show You I Could Fly*; Robin Klein. 1989. *Category:* best book of the year older.

55 1990. *Pigs and Honey*. Jeannie Adams. 1989. *Category:* best book of the year younger.

56 1990. *The Very Best of Friends*. Margaret Wild. *Illustrator:* Julie Vivas. Harcourt Brace, 1994. *Category:* picture book.

57 1991. *Finders Keepers*. Emily Rodda. William Morrow, 1991. *Category:* best book of the year younger.

58 1991. *Greetings from Sandy Beach*. Bob Graham. *Illustrator:* Bob Graham. Kane/Miller, 1991. *Category:* picture book.

59 1991. *Strange Objects*. Gary Crew. Heinemann, 1990. *Category:* best book of the year older.

60 1992. *The House Guest*. Eleanor Nilsson. Penguin, 1991. *Category:* best book of the year older.

61 1992. *The Magnificent Nose and Other Marvels*. Anna Fienberg. *Illustrator:* Kim Gamble. Allen & Unwin, 1991. *Category:* best book of the year younger.

62 1992. *Window*. Jeannie Baker. *Illustrator:* Jeannie Baker. Greenwillow, 1991. *Category:* picture book.

63 1993. *Rose Meets Mr. Wintergarden*. Bob Graham. *Illustrator:* Bob Graham. Candlewick, 1994. *Category:* picture book.

64 1993. *The Bamboo Flute*. Garry Disher. Ticknor & Fields, 1993. *Category:* best book of the year younger.

65 1993. *Looking for Alibrandi*. Melina Marchetta. Puffin, 1992. *Category:* best book of the year older.

66 1994. *Angel's Gate*. Gary Crew. Simon and Schuster, 1995. *Category:* best book of the year older.

67 1994. *Rowan of Rin*. Emily Rodda. 1993. *Category:* best book of the year younger.

68 1994. *The Gathering*. Isobelle Carmody. Puffin, 1993. *Category:* best book of the year older.

69 1994. *First Light*. Gary Crew. *Illustrator:* Peter Gouldthorpe. Jarrold, 1994. *Category:* picture book.

70 1995. *The Watertower*. Gary Crew. *Illustrator:* Steven Woolman. Accents, 1994. *Category:* picture book.

71 1995. *Ark in the Park*. Wendy Orr. *Illustrator:* Kerry Millard. A & R, 1994. *Category:* best book of the year younger.

72 1995. *Foxspell*. Gillian Rubinstein. Simon and Schuster, 1995. *Category:* best book of the year older.

73 1996. *The Hunt*. Oliver Narelle. *Illustrator:* Oliver Narelle. Lothian Books, 1996. *Category:* picture book.

74 1996. *Pagan's Vows*. Catherine Jinks. Omnibus Books, 1995. *Category:* best book of the year older.

75 1996. *Swashbuckler*. James Moloney. University of Queensland Press, 1995. *Category:* best book of the year younger.

76 1997. *A Bridge to Wiseman's Cove*. James Moloney. University of Queensland Press, 1996. *Category:* best book of the year older.

77 1997. *Not a Nibble*. Elizabeth Honey. *Illustrator:* Elizabeth Honey. Little Ark/Allen & Unwin, 1997. *Category:* picture book.

78 1997. *Hannah Plus One*. Libby Gleeson. *Illustrator:* Ann James. Penguin, 1996. *Category:* best book of the year younger.

79 1998. *Eye to Eye*. Catherine Jinks. Penguin, 1997. *Category:* best book of the year older.

80 1998. *Someone Like Me*. Elaine Forrestal. Penguin, 1997. *Category:* best book of the younger readers.

81 1998. *The Two Bullies*. Junko Morimoto. *Illustrator:* Junko Morimoto. *Translator:* Isao Motimoto. Random House, 1997. *Category:* picture book.

82 1999. *My Girragundji*. Meme McDonald and Boori Pryor. *Illustrator:* Meme McDonald. Allen & Unwin, 1998. *Category:* best book of the year younger.

83 1999. *The Rabbits*. John Marsden. *Illustrator:* Shaun Tan. Lothian, 1998. *Category:* picture book.

84 1999. *Deadly Unna?* Phillip Gwynne. Penguin, 1998. *Category:* best book of the year older.

85 2000. *Hitler's Daughter*. Jackie French. HarperCollins, 1999. *Category:* best book of the year younger.

86 2000. *Jenny Angel*. Anne Spudvilas. *Illustrator:* Margaret Wild. Penguin, 1999. *Category:* picture book.

87 2000. *48 Shades of Brown*. Nick Earls. Penguin, 1999. *Category:* best book of the year older.

88 Children's Peace Literature Award

SPONSOR: The Psychologists for the Prevention of War. CONTACT: address unknown. ESTABLISHED: 1987. The award is given to Australian writers published within the two previous years.

89 1991. *Dodger*. Libby Gleeson.

90 1993. *The Gathering*. Isabelle Carmody. Dial, 1994. *Category:* joint winner.

91 1993. *Rose Meets Mr. Wintergarden*. Bob Graham. *Illustrator:* Bob Graham. Candlewick, 1994. *Category:* joint winner.

92 1995. *Deucalion*. Brian Caswell. University of Queensland, 1995.

93 COOL (Canberra's Own Outstanding List)

SPONSOR: ACT Library Service. PHONE: (02) 62059000. ESTABLISHED: 1991. AWARD: Certificate. These children's choice book awards are voted for by the young people of the Canberra region.

94 1991. *Round the Twist*. Paul Jennings. 1990. *Category:* primary.

95 1991. *People Might Hear You*. Robin Klein. *Category:* secondary.

96 1992. *Came Back to Show You I Could Fly*. Robin Klein. *Category:* secondary.

97 1992. *The Cabbage Patch Fib*. Paul Jennings. Penguin, 1988. *Category:* primary.

98 1993. *Unreal!* Paul Jennings. Viking, 1986. *Category:* primary.

99 1993. *Del-Del*. Victor Kelleher. Walker and Co., 1992. *Category:* secondary.

100 1993. *Window.* Jeannie Baker. *Illustrator:* Jeannie Baker. Random House, 1991. *Category:* illustrated.

101 1994. *Playing Beatie Bow.* Ruth Park. Kestrel, 1981. *Category:* secondary.

102 1994. *The Eleventh Hour.* Graeme Base. *Illustrator:* Graeme Base. Abrams, 1988. *Category:* illustrated.

103 1994. *Possum Magic.* Mem Fox. *Illustrator:* Julie Vivas. Omnibus, 1983. *Category:* primary.

104 1995. *So Much to Tell You.* John Marsden. McVitty, 1987. *Category:* secondary.

105 1995. *The Gizmo.* Paul Jennings. *Illustrator:* Keith McEwen. Puffin, 1995. *Category:* primary.

106 1995. *Toby.* Margaret Wild. *Illustrator:* Noela Young. *Category:* illustrated.

107 1997. *The Lion King.* Gina Ingoglio. *Illustrator:* Michael Humphries, Marshall Toomey. Disney, 1995. *Category:* secondary.

108 1997. *Belly Flop.* Morris Gleitzman. *Category:* primary.

109 1997. *Billy the Punk.* Jessica Carroll, Craig Smith. *Illustrator:* Jessica Carroll. 1996. *Category:* illustrated.

110 1998. *Grandad's Teeth.* Rod Clement. HarperCollins, 1998. *Category:* picture book.

111 1998. *The Third Day, the Frost.* John Marsden. Pan Macmillan. *Category:* secondary.

112 1998. *Bumface.* Morris Gleitzman. Penguin, 1998. *Category:* primary.

113 1999. *Grandad's Teeth.* Rod Clement. *Illustrator:* Rod Clement. *Category:* picture book.

114 1999. *The Third Day, the Frost.* John Marsden. *Category:* secondary.

115 1999. *Bumface.* Morris Gleitzman. Penguin. *Category:* primary.

116 2000. *Bamboozled.* David Legge. *Illustrator:* David Legge. *Category:* picture book.

117 2000. *Night Is for Hunting.* John Marsden. *Category:* secondary.

118 2000. *Bob the Builder and the Elves.* Emily Rodda. *Category:* primary.

119 Crichton Award for Illustration

SPONSOR: Children's Book Council — Victorian Branch. ADDRESS: P.O. Box 28, Hunters Hill, New South Wales, Australia, 2110. PHONE: 02 9630 2424. ESTABLISHED: 1990. AWARD: Certificate and $1,000 Australian. The award is given to a newcomer in the field of children's book illustration to encourage outstanding style and talent.

120 1990. *Pigs and Honey. Illustrator:* Jeannie Adams.

121 1991. *Bip, the Snapping Bungaroo. Illustrator:* Grace Fielding.

122 1992. *The Magnificent Nose and Other Marvels.* Anna Fienberg. *Illustrator:* Kim Gamble. Allen & Unwin, 1991.
123 1993. *Alitji in Dreamland. Illustrator:* Donna Leslie.
124 1994. *Is it True, Grandfather? Illustrator:* Jenny Sands.
125 1995. *I Wish I'd Gone to the Moon with Neil Armstrong. Illustrator:* Astri Baker. *Category:* joint winner.
126 1995. *Power and Glory. Illustrator:* Geoff Kelly. *Category:* joint winner.
127 1996. *The Race. Illustrator:* Anna Spudvilas.
128 1997. *Fang Fang's Chinese New Year. Illustrator:* Sally Rippin.
129 1998. *I'm in the Sky and I Can't Come Back. Illustrator:* Anna Pignataro. *Category:* joint winner.
130 1998. *The Viewer. Illustrator:* Shaun Tan. *Category:* joint winner.
1999. No award given.
131 2000. *Baby Bear Goes to the Zoo.* Lorette Broekstra. *Illustrator:* Lorette Broekstra. Lothian.

132 Cross Pen Prize for Young Adult Fiction (formerly Sheaffer Prize for Adult Young Fiction)

CONTACT: address unknown. AWARD: $12,000. The award is given to the author for a published work of fiction or collection of short stories written for a readership between the ages of 13 and 20.

133 1999. *Deadly Unna?* Phillip Gwynne. Penguin Books.

134 CROW (Children Reading Outstanding Writers)

Discontinued. ESTABLISHED: 1991. The award was given annually to writers and illustrators of children's books. Children voted for their favorite book.

135 1991. *The Eleventh Hour.* Graeme Base. *Illustrator:* Graeme Base. Abrams, 1988.
136 1991. *Matilda.* Roald Dahl. *Illustrator:* Quentin Blake. Cape, 1988.
137 1992. *The Witches.* Roald Dahl. *Illustrator:* Quentin Blake. Farrar, 1983.
138 1993. *Blabber Mouth.* Morris Gleitzman. Harcourt Brace, 1995.
139 1993. *Jodie's Journey.* Colin Thiele.
140 1994. *Undone!* Paul Jennings. Viking, 1995.
141 1994. *The BFG.* Roald Dahl. *Illustrator:* Quentin Blake. Farrar, 1982.
142 1995. *The Gizmo.* Paul Jennings. *Illustrator:* Keith McEwen. Puffin, 1995.
143 1996. *Babe.* Dick King-Smith. Crown, 1993.
144 1996. *Matilda.* Roald Dahl. *Illustrator:* Quentin Blake. Cape, 1988.
145 1997. *Bamboozled.* David Legge. *Illustrator:* David Legge. 1995. *Category:* years 3–5.
146 1998. *Belly Flop.* Morris Gleitzman. *Category:* years 6–7.

147 1998. *Grandad's Teeth.* Rod Clement. HarperCollins, 1998. *Category:* years 3–5.

148 1998. *WICKED!* Paul Jennings, Morris Gleitzman. Penguin, 1997. *Category:* years 6–7.

149 CYBER Award (Children's Yearly Best Ever Reads)

ADDRESS: P. O. Box 216, Claremont, Tasmania, Australia 7011. ESTABLISHED: 1999. Every year children in Tasmania vote for their favorite books.

150 1999. *Bob the Builder and the Elves.* Emily Rodda. *Illustrator:* Craig Smith. *Category:* younger readers.

151 1999. *Tomorrow, When the War Began.* John Marsden. Pan Macmillan, 1994. *Category:* older readers.

152 1999. *Mr. McGee and the Biting Flea.* Pamela Allen. *Category:* picture book.

153 2000. *Buffy.* Bob Graham. *Category:* picture book.

154 2000. *Just Crazy.* Andy Griffiths. *Illustrator:* Terry Denton. *Category:* younger readers.

155 2000. *Tomorrow, When the War Began.* John Marsden. Pan Macmillan, 1994. *Category:* older readers.

156 Dromkeen Medal

SPONSOR: Court Oldmeadow Childrens Literature Foundation. ADDRESS: Main Road, Riddell's Creek, Victoria, Australia 3431. PHONE: (054) 28 6701. ESTABLISHED: 1982. AWARD: A medal designed by Robert Ingpen and a citation. Given annually to the Australian citizen for their contribution to children's literature in the previous year.

157 1990 Mem Fox.

158 1991 Robin Klein.

159 1992 Julie Vivas.

160 1993 Alf Mappin.

161 1994 Agnes Nieuwenhuizen.

162 1995 Jennifer Rowe.

163 1996 Belle Alderman.

164 1997 Colin Thiele.

165 1998 Graeme Base.

166 1999 Barbara Ker Wilson.

167 Dymocks Children's Choice Awards

ADDRESS: GPO Box 4694, Sydney, New South Wales, Australia 1044. Children and teenagers around Australia are invited to vote for their favorite book in the following categories: Picture Book, Younger Reader, Older Reader, and Teenage Book.

168 1998. *WICKED!* Paul Jennings. Morris Gleitzman. Penguin, 1997. *Category:* older reader favorite.

169 1998. Paul Jennings. *Category:* favorite author.

170 1998. *Burning with Revenge.* John Marsden. Pan Macmillian, 1998. *Category:* teenage book favorite.

171 1998. *Grandad's Teeth.* Rod Clement. *Illustrator:* Rod Clement. *Category:* picture book favorite.

172 1998. *Sink the Gizmo.* Paul Jennings. *Category:* young reader favorite.

173 1999. *The Tomorrow Series.* John Marsden. Pan Macmillian. *Category:* teenage book favorite.

174 1999. Morris Gleitzman. *Category:* favorite author.

175 1999. *Rowan of Rin.* Emily Rodda. *Category:* young reader favorite.

176 1999. *WICKED!* Paul Jennings, Morris Gleitzman. Penguin, 1997. *Category:* older reader favorite.

177 1999. *Possum Magic.* Mem Fox. Omnibus, 1983. *Category:* picture book favorite.

178 2000. *The Hidden Forest.* Jeannie Baker. Walker Books. *Category:* picture book favorite.

179 2000. *Tomorrow Series.* John Marsden. Pan Macmillan. *Category:* teenage book.

180 2000. *Toad Rage.* Morris Gleitzman. Penguin. *Category:* older reader.

181 2000. *Aussie Bites Series.* Penguin. *Category:* young reader favorite.

182 Environmental Award for Children's Literature

SPONSOR: The Wilderness Society. ADDRESS: 130 Davey Street, Hobart, Tasmania, Australia 7000. PHONE: (03) 6234 9799. ESTABLISHED: 1994. AWARD: Trophies and certificates. The award is given to fiction and non-fiction children's books published in Australia. The award is given to authors and illustrators of those books that best encourage an attitude of caring, wonder and understanding of the natural world, or those that promote an awareness of environmental issues.

183 1994. *Life of a Rotten Log.* Kathie Atkinson. *Category:* information.

184 1994. *V Is for Vanishing: An Alphabet of Endangered Animals.* Patricia Mullins. HarperCollins. 1993. *Category:* picture.

185 1995. *The Fisherman and the Theefyspray.* Paul Jennings. *Illustrator:* Jane Tanner. Viking. *Category:* picture.

186 1995. *Australian Animal Series.* Pauline Reilly. *Illustrator:* Will Rolland, Gayle Russell. Kangaroo Press. *Category:* information.

187 1996. *It's a Frog's Life.* Densey Clyne. Allen & Unwin. *Category:* information.

188 1996. *The Story of Rosy Dock.* Jeannie Baker. *Illustrator:* Jeannie Baker. Randon House. *Category:* picture.

189 1996. *Spotlight on Spiders.* Densey Clyne. Allen & Unwin. *Category:* information.

190 1997. *High Valley.* Colin Thiele. Walter McVitty Books. *Category:* information.

191 1997. *Spiders Spin Webs.* Yvonne Winer. *Illustrator:* Karen Lloyd-Jones. Margaret Hamilton Books. *Category:* picture.

192 1998. *Blueback.* Tim Winton. *Illustrator:* Karen Louise. Pan Macmillan. *Category:* senior fiction.

193 1998. *One Child.* Christopher Cheng. *Illustrator:* Steven Woolman. Era Publications. *Category:* picture.

194 1998. *The Incomplete Book of Australian Mammals.* Ronald Strahan. *Illustrator:* Pamela Condor. Kangaroo Press. *Category:* information.

195 1999. *Islands in My Garden.* Jim Howes. *Illustrator:* Roland Harvey. Roland Harvey Books. *Category:* picture book.

196 1999. *Australian Guide to Pondlife.* Gould League of Australia. *Category:* non-fiction.

197 1999. *Australian Guide to Seashores.* Gould League of Australia. *Category:* non-fiction.

198 2000. *Australian Guide to Endangered Animals.* Sharee Marris. *Illustrator:* Trish Hart. Gould League. *Category:* non-fiction.

199 2000. *Oceans, Grasslands, Wetlands and Coasts.* Greg Pyers. Reed International. *Category:* non-fiction.

200 2000. *Mahogany the Mystery Glider.* Jill Morris. *Illustrator:* Sharon Dye. Greater Glider. *Category:* picture.

201 2000. *Sand Swimmers: The Secret Life of Australia's Dead Heart.* Narelle Oliver. Lothian. *Category:* picture.

202 2000. *Dreamcatcher.* Jen McVeity. Lothian. *Category:* fiction.

203 2000. *Encyclopedia of Australian Wildlife.* Pat Slater, Steve Parish. Steve Parish Publishing. *Category:* non-fiction.

204 Eve Pownall Award for Information Books

SPONSOR: Children's Book Council of Australia. ADDRESS: P.O. Box 28, Hunters Hill, New South Wales, Australia, 2110. PHONE: 02 9630 2424. ESTABLISHED: 1993. AWARD: $10,000 Australian. The award is given annually for a book written by an Australian, or a resident of Australia.

205 1993. *Tjarany Roughtail: The Dreaming of the Roughtail Lizard and Other Stories Told by the Kukatja.* Gracie Greene, Joe Tramacci. *Illustrator:* Lucille Gill. Magabala Books, 1992.

206 1994. *V Is for Vanishing: An Alphabet of Endangered Animals.* Patricia Mullins. HarperCollins, 1994.

207 1995. *New Faces: The Complete Book of Alternative Pets.* Robin E. Stewart. 1994.

208 1996. *The First Fleet: A New Beginning in an Old Land.* John Nicholson. Allen & Unwin, 1995.

209 1997. *Killer Plants.* Gordon Cheers. Julie Silk. Penguin, 1996. *Illustrator:* Margaret Crosby-Fairall.

210 1998. *A Home Among the Gum Trees.* John Nicholson. Allen & Unwin, 1997.

211 1999. *Going for Kalta.* Yvonne Edwards, Brenda Day. IAD Press, 1998.

212 2000. *Fishing for Islands: Traditional Boats and Seafarers of the Pacific.* John Nicholson. Allen & Unwin, 1999.

213 Family Award

SPONSOR: New South Wales and Victorian Family Therapy Associations. CONTACT: address unknown. ESTABLISHED: 1987. The annual award honors writers for children that presents a family theme.

214 1990. *Two Weeks With the Queen.* Morris Gleitzman.

215 1991. *Change the Locks.* Simon French.

216 1992. *Crossfire.* James Moloney.

217 1994. *Dougy.* James Moloney.

218 1997. *Lockie Leonard, Scumbuster.* Tim Winton.

219 KOALA Award (Kids' Own Australian Literature Award)

ADDRESS: PO Box 268, Artarmon New South Wales, Australia, 1570. ESTABLISHED: 1987. The annual awards made by young readers in NSW are given to the Australian books they have most enjoyed reading during that year.

220 1990. *Unreal!* Paul Jennings. Viking, 1995. *Category:* secondary.

221 1990. *Where the Forest Meets the Sea.* Jeanie Baker. *Illustrator:* Jeannie Baker. Julia McCrae, 1988. *Category:* primary.

222 1991. *The Red King.* Victor Kelleher. *Category:* secondary.

223 1991. *Unbelievable!* Paul Jennings. Viking, 1995. *Category:* primary.

224 1992. *Unmentionable!* Paul Jennings. Viking, 1995. *Category:* primary.

225 1993. *Looking for Alibrandi.* Melina Marchetta. Puffin, 1992. *Category:* secondary.

226 1993. *Unbearable!* Paul Jennings. Viking, 1995. *Category:* primary.

227 1994. *The Power of One.* Bryce Courtenay. Ballentine, 1996. *Category:* secondary.

228 1994. *Undone!* Paul Jennings. Viking, 1993. *Category:* primary.

229 1995. *Tomorrow, When the War Began.* John Marsden. Pan Macmillan, 1994. *Category:* secondary.

230 1995. *Duck for Cover.* Paul Jennings. Puffin, 1996. *Category:* primary.

231 1996. *Uncovered!* Paul Jennings. Viking, 1996. *Category:* secondary.

232 1997. *Billy the Punk.* Jessica Carroll. *Illustrator:* Craig Smith. *Category:* picture book.

233 1997. *Selby Spacedog.* Duncan Ball. *Illustrator:* Allen Stomann. HarperCollins, 1996. *Category:* primary.

234 1997. *Water Wings.* Morris Gleitzman. *Category:* senior.

235 1998. *The Midnight Gang.* Margaret Wild. *Illustrator:* Ann James. *Category:* picture book.

236 1998. *Selby Speaks.* Duncan Ball. HarperCollins. *Category:* junior book.

237 1998. *Cool School: You Make it Happen.* John Marsden. *Category:* senior book.

238 1999. *Just Annoying.* Andy Griffiths. *Illustrator:* Terry Denton. *Category:* senior book.

239 1999. *Grandad's Teeth.* Rod Clement. *Illustrator:* Rod Clement. *Category:* picture book.

240 1999. *Desert Dan the Dunny Man.* Di Bates. *Illustrator:* Stephen Axelson. *Category:* junior book.

241 2000. *Just Stupid.* Andy Griffiths. *Category:* senior book.

242 2000. *Selby Snowbound.* Duncan Ball. *Category:* junior book.

243 2000. *Sharon, Keep Your Hair On.* Gillian Rubinstein. *Illustrator:* David Macintosh. *Category:* picture book.

244 KROC Award (Kids Reading OZ Choice)

SPONSOR: Northern Territory Library Promotion Council. CONTACT: Viki Chmielewski. ADDRESS: address unknown. Northern Territory, Australia. PHONE: (08) 8982 2563. ESTABLISHED: 1990. The book must be written by an Australian author.

245 1990. *Uncanny!* Paul Jennings. Penguin, 1988.

246 1991. *Unbelievable!* Paul Jennings. Viking, 1990.

247 1993. *Undone!* Paul Jennings. Viking, 1995.

248 1994. *Undone!* Paul Jennings. Viking, 1995.

249 1995. *Tomorrow, When the War Began.* John Marsden. Pan Macmillan, 1994.

250 1995. *The Gizmo.* Paul Jennings. *Illustrator:* Keith McEwen. Puffin, 1995.

251 1996. *Round the Twist.* Paul Jennings. 1990.

252 1997. *WICKED!* Paul Jennings, Morris Gleitzman. Penguin, 1997.

253 1998. *WICKED!* Paul Jennings, Morris Gleitzman. Penguin, 1997.

254 1999. *The Gizmo.* Paul Jennings. *Illustrator:* Keith McEwen. Puffin, 1995.

255 Multicultural Children's Literature Award

SPONSOR: MultiCultural Affairs Office of Australia. CONTACT: address unknown. ESTABLISHED: 1991. The award is presented to encourage authors to deal with issues of cultural diversity in their books for young readers and to present themes of social justice and supportive community relations in a positive way.

256 1991. *The Rainbow Serpent.* Elaine Sharpe. *Illustrator:* Elaine Sharpe. *Category:* picture.

257 1992. *The China Coin.* Alan Baillie. *Category:* senior.

258 1992. *Big Dog.* Libby Gleeson. *Illustrator:* Armin Greder. *Category:* picture.

259 1992. *Do Not Go Around the Edges.* Daisy Utemorrah. *Illustrator:* Pat Torres. *Category:* junior.

260 1993. *The Fat and Juicy Place.* Diana Kidd. *Category:* junior.

261 1993. *Mr. Plunkett's Pool.* Gillian Rubinstein. *Illustrator:* Terry Denton. *Category:* picture.

262 1993. *Looking for Alibrandi.* Melina Marchetta. 1992. *Category:* senior.

263 1994. *Tomorrow, When the War Began.* John Marsden. Pan Macmillan, 1994. *Category:* senior.

264 1994. *Metis, the Octopus and the Olive Tree.* Jena Woodhouse. *Category:* junior.

265 1994. *As I Grow Older.* Ian Abdulla. *Category:* picture.

266 1995. *Princesma.* Naomi Lewis. *Illustrator:* Jenni Overend. *Category:* picture.

267 1995. *Lisdalia.* Brian Caswell. *Category:* junior.

268 1995. *Gracey.* James Moloney. *Category:* senior.

269 NSW State Literary Award — Children's Book Award

SPONSOR: NSW Ministry for the Arts. CONTACT: The Secretary. ADDRESS: Level 23, Governor Macquarie, Tower, 1 Farrer Place, Sydney, New South Wales, Australia, 2000. PHONE: (02) 9228 5533. ESTABLISHED: 1979. The award is given annually.

270 1990. *The Blue Chamel.* Katherine Scholes.

271 1991. *Strange Objects.* Gary Crew.

272 1992. *All in the Blue Unclouded Weather.* Robin Klein.

273 1993. *Tjarany Roughtail.* Gracie Greene, Joe Tramacchi. *Illustrator:* Gill Lucille.

274 1994. *The White Guinea Pig.* Ursula Dubosarsky.

275 1995. *Mr Enigmatic.* Jenny Pausacker.

276 1996. *Johnny Hart's Heroes.* David Metzenthen. *Illustrator:* David Metzenthen.

277 1996. *The True Story of Spit MacPhee.* James Aldridge. *Illustrator:* Belinda Ogden.

278 1997. *A Rabbit Named Harris.* Nan Hunt.

279 Sheaffer Prize for Adult Young Fiction (formerly Alan Marshall Prize for Children's Literature)

Discontinued. ESTABLISHED: 1996. The award was given to living authors who were Australian citizens or permanent residents. It was made solely on literary merit, so the quality of illustrations was not considered.

280 1996. *Sleeping Dogs.* Sonia Hartnett. Penguin 1995.

281 1997. *Pagan's Scribe.* Catherine Jinks. Omnibus Books 1996.

282 1998. *Night Train.* Judith Clarke. Penguin 1997.

283 West Australian Young Readers' Book Award

SPONSOR: School Libraries Section (WA Group) of ALIA. CONTACT: Avis Page. ADDRESS: School Library Section (W.A. Group), Box 251, Mundaring, Western Australia, Australia, 6073. ESTABLISHED: 1980. AWARD: A trophy of jarrah wood designed in the form of a book. Young readers nominate titles which are placed on a master list and rated by the students. The winning title must be published five years preceding the award year.

284 1990. *Redwall.* Brian Jacques. *Illustrator:* Gary Chalk. Putnam, 1987. *Level:* secondary.

285 1990. *Selby Speaks.* Duncan Ball. *Illustrator:* Allan Stomann. Harper-Collins, 1987. *Level:* primary.

286 1991. *Mossflower.* Brian Jacques. *Illustrator:* Gary Chalk. Putnam, 1988. *Level:* secondary.

287 1991. *Redwall.* Brian Jacques. *Illustrator:* Gary Chalk. Putnam, 1987. *Level:* primary.

288 1992. *Mattimeo.* Brian Jacques. *Illustrator:* Gary Chalk. Philomel, 1990. *Level:* secondary.

289 1992. *Uncanny!* Paul Jennings. Viking, 1991. *Level:* primary.

290 1993. *Snotty Bumstead.* Hunter Davies. *Level:* primary.

291 1993. *Del-Del.* Victor Kelleher. Walker and Co., 1992. *Level:* secondary.

292 1994. *Looking for Alibrandi.* Melina Marchetta. Puffin, 1992. *Level:* secondary.

293 1994. *Unbearable!* Paul Jennings. Viking, 1993. *Level:* Primary.

294 1995. *Tomorrow, When the War Began.* John Marsden. Pan Macmillan, 1994. *Level:* secondary.

295 1995. *Undone!* Paul Jennings. Viking, 1995. *Level:* primary.

296 1996. *The Power of One.* Bryce Courtenay. Ballentine, 1996. *Level:* secondary.

297 1996. *The Topsy-Turvy Storybook.* Dick King-Smith. *Level:* primary.
298 1997. *Salamandastron.* Brian Jacques. *Illustrator:* Gary Chalk. Putnam, 1997. *Level:* secondary.
299 1997. *Selby, Supersnoop.* Duncan Ball. *Illustrator:* Allen Stomann. HarperCollins, 1997. *Level:* primary.
300 1998. *Lily and Me.* Moses Aaron. *Level:* primary.
301 1998. *The Third Day of the Frost.* John Marsden. Pan Macmillan, 1998. *Level:* secondary.
302 1999. *The Quicksand Pony.* Alison Lester. Allen & Unwin, 1997. *Level:* primary.
303 1999. *Burning With Revenge.* John Marsden. Pan Macmillian, 1998. *Level:* secondary.
304 2000. *Harry Potter and the Philosopher's Stone.* J.K. Rowling. Scholastic, 1998. *Level:* primary.
305 2000. *The Night Is for Hunting.* John Marsden. *Level:* secondary.

306 Western Australian Premier's Book Award — Children's Section

SPONSOR: The Library and Information Service of Western Australia. ADDRESS: Alexander Library Building, Perth Cultural Centre, Perth, Western Austalia, Australia, 6000. PHONE: (08) 9427 3330. ESTABLISHED: 1990. AWARD: $5,000 Australian. The annual awards are given for children's books and young adult books. Authors must be born in Australia or be a resident. Books must be published in the previous year.

307 1990. *Jesse.* Tim Winton. McPhee Gribble.
308 1991. *Lockie Leonard, Human Torpedo.* Tim Winton. McPhee Gribble.
309 1991. *The Devil's Own.* Deborah Lisson. Walter McVitty.
310 1992. *Dear Mr. Sprouts.* Errol Broome. Allen & Unwin.
311 1993. *Tjarany Roughtail: The Dreaming of the Roughtail Lizard and Other Stories.* Told by the Kukatja. Gracie Greene, Joe Tramacci. *Illustrator:* Lucille Gill. Magabala Books, 1992.
312 1994. *Rosa's Famous Elbow.* Mike Lefoy. *Illustrator:* Peter Kendall. Fremantle Arts Centre Press.
313 1995. *Radical Take-Offs.* Glyn Parry. Allen & Unwin.
314 1996. *Idjhil.* Helen Bell. University of Western Australia Press.
315 1997. *A Place of Safety.* Deborah Lisson. Reed Books.
316 1998. *Red Hugh.* Deborah Lisson. Lothian Book. *Category:* young adult.
317 1998. *Desert Dog.* Pat Lowe. *Illustrator:* Jimmy Pike. Magabala Books. *Category:* children's.
318 1999. *Showtime!* Reg Bolton. Dorling Kindersley. *Category:* children's.
319 1999. *Scooterboy.* Glyn Parry. Hodder. *Category:* young adult.

320 Young Australian Best Book Award (YABBA)

SPONSOR: Young Australian Best Book Award Council. ADDRESS: P.O. Box 23, Kew, Victoria, Australia, 3101. ESTABLISHED: 1986. AWARD: A citation. The award is given to the author which children vote as their favorite.

321 1990. *Paw Thing.* Paul Jennings. 1989. *Category:* fiction for younger readers.

322 1990. *Space Demons.* Gillian Rubinstein. Omnibus, 1989. *Category:* best book of the year older.

323 1990. *The Monster Who Ate Australia.* Michael Salmon. *Illustrator:* Michael Salmon. 1989. *Category:* picture book.

324 1991. *Finders Keepers.* Emily Rodda. William Morrow, 1991. *Category:* best book of the year younger.

325 1991. *Counting on Frank.* Rod Clement. *Illustrator:* Rod Clement. Garth Stevens, 1990. *Category:* picture book.

326 1991. *Round the Twist.* Paul Jennings, Glen Lumsden. *Illustrator:* David De Vries. 1990. *Category:* fiction for older readers.

327 1992. *Unmentionable!* Paul Jennings. Viking, 1992. *Category:* fiction for older readers.

328 1992. *Quirky Tails.* Paul Jennings. Puffin, 1992. *Category:* fiction for younger readers.

329 1992. *Window.* Jeannie Baker. *Illustrator:* Jeannie Baker. Random House, 1991. *Category:* picture book.

330 1993. *Unbearable!* Paul Jennings. Viking, 1995. *Category:* fiction for older readers.

331 1993. *Blabber Mouth.* Morris Gleitzman. Harcourt Brace, 1995. *Category:* fiction for younger readers.

332 1993. *The Sign of the Seahorse.* Graeme Base. *Illustrator:* Graeme Base. Henry H. Abrahams, 1992. *Category:* picture book.

333 1994. *Undone!* Paul Jennings. Viking, 1995. *Category:* fiction for younger readers.

334 1994. *Rowan of Rin.* Emily Rodda. 1993. *Category:* best book of the year younger.

335 1994. *Spooner of Later.* T. Greenwood, Paul Jennings. *Illustrator:* Terry Denton. 1993. *Category:* picture book.

336 1995. *The Gizmo.* Paul Jennings. *Illustrator:* Keith McEwen. Puffin, 1995. *Category:* fiction for younger readers.

337 1995. *Tomorrow, When the War Began.* John Marsden. Pan Macmillan, 1994. *Category:* best book of the year older.

338 1995. *Duck for Cover.* T. Greenwood, Paul Jennings. *Illustrator:* Terry Denton. 1994. *Category:* picture book.

339 1996. *Gizmo Again!* Paul Jennings. *Illustrator:* Keith McEwen. Puffin, 1996. *Category:* fiction for younger readers.

340 1996. *Lockie Leonard, Human Torpedo.* Tim Winton. Macmillan, 1995. *Category:* best book of the year older.

341 1996. *Bamboozled.* David Legge. *Illustrator:* David Legge. 1995. *Category:* picture book.

342 1997. *45 + 47 Stella Street.* Elizabeth Honey. Allen & Unwin, 1996. *Category:* best book of the year older.

343 1997. *Billy the Punk.* Jessica Carroll. *Illustrator:* Craig Smith. 1996. *Category:* picture book.

344 1997. *The Bugalugs Bum Thief.* Tim Winton. *Illustrator:* Carol Pelham-Thorman. 1996. *Category:* fiction for younger readers.

345 1998. *ZAPT!* Terry Denton. *Illustrator:* Terry Denton. Puffin, 1997. *Category:* picture book.

346 1998. *Naughty Stories for Good Boys and Girls.* Chris Milne. 1997. *Category:* fiction for younger readers.

347 1998. *WICKED!* Paul Jennings, Morris Gleitzman. Penguin, 1997. *Category:* fiction for older readers.

348 1999. *Bumface.* Morris Gleitzman. Penguin, 1998. *Category:* fiction for older readers.

349 1999. *Just Annoying.* Andy Griffiths. *Illustrator:* Terry Denton. 1998. *Category:* fiction for younger readers.

350 1999. *GASP!* Terry Denton. *Illustrator:* Terry Denton. Penguin, 1995. *Category:* picture book.

351 2000. *Just Stupid.* Andy Griffiths. *Illustrator:* Terry Denton. *Category:* fiction for younger readers.

352 2000. *SPLAT!* Terry Denton. *Illustrator:* Terry Denton. Penguin. *Category:* picture book.

353 2000. *Toad Rage.* Morris Gleitzman. Penguin. *Category:* fiction for older readers.

AUSTRIA

354 Jury der Jungen Leser

SPONSOR: Literaturhaus. ADDRESS: Seidengasse 13, A-1070 Wien, Austria. PHONE: 01/526 20 44-45. ESTABLISHED: 1995. AWARD: diploma. The award is given annually for a children's book, young adult, and occasionally a special award for an outstanding multi-faceted work. New publications written in German from the previous year are eligible.

355 1995. *Princes in Exile.* Mark Schreiber. Jungbrunnen, 1994. *Category:* youth book.

356 1995. *Original Title:* Die wilden Huhner. Cornelia Funke. *Illustrator:* Cornelia Funke. Cecilie Dressler, 1993. *Category:* children's book.

357 1996. *Letters from the Inside.* John Marsden. Beltz & Gelberg, 1995. *Category:* youth book.

358 1996. *Original Title:* Mig — en pige. Lena Eilstrup. Loewe, 1995. *Category:* children's book.

359 1997. *Original Title:* I et speil I en gate. Jostein Gaarder. Hanser, 1996. *Category:* youth book.

360 1997. *Walk Two Moons.* Sharon Creech. Verlag St. Gabriel, 1996. *Category:* children's book.

361 1998. *Original Title:* Panna Nikt. Tomek Tryzna. Luchterhand, 1997. *Category:* special prize.

362 1998. *The Last Polar Bears.* Harry Horse. *Illustrator:* Harry Horse. Arena, 1997. *Category:* children's book.

363 1998. *Original Title:* Wildwasser. Paulus Hochgatterer. Deutike, 1997. *Category:* youth book.

364 1999. *Harry Potter and the Philosopher's Stone.* J.K. Rowling. Carlsen, 1998. *Category:* children's book.

365 1999. *Original Title:* Die Mitte der Welt. Andreas Steinhöfel. Carlsen, 1998. *Category:* youth book.

366 1999. *Original Title:* Toccata og fuge I D-moll — Rias krig. Unni Nielsen. Gabriel, 1998. *Category:* special prize.

367 2000. *The Mennyms.* Sylvia Waugh. Hanser, 1999. *Category:* children's book.

368 2000. *Original Title:* Shylocks Tochter. Mirjam Pressler. Alibaba, 1999. *Category:* youth book.

369 2000. *Original Title:* Joel Tetralogie. Henning Mankell. Oetinger, 1999. *Category:* special prize.

370 Kinder- und Jugendbuchpreisen der Stadt Wien (Children's Book Awards of the City of Vienna)

SPONSOR: Kulturamt der Stadt Wien. CONTACT: Literaturabteilung. ADDRESS: Friedrich-Schmidt Platz 5, 1082 Wien. PHONE: 1/4000/84716. ESTABLISHED: 1954. AWARD: 30.000,- ATS. The award is given by the city of Vienna to the best books for children published by a Viennese publisher. The categories include: children's book and illustration.

371 1990. *On the Other Side. Original Title:* Auf der anderen Seite. Gerald Szyszkowitz. Neuer Breitschopf, 1990. *Category:* young adult book.

372 1990. *Klicketick. Original Title:* Klicketick. Christine Nöstinger. *Illustrator:* Barbara Waldschütz. Dachs, 1990. *Category:* illustration.

373 1990. *Dina and the Magic Dwarf. Original Title:* Dina und der Zauberzwerg. Gerald Jatzek. *Illustrator:* Wolfgang Lengheim. Jungbrunnen, 1990. *Category:* children's book.

374 1990. *Anna's Fury. Original Title:* Anna und die Wut. Christine Nöstlinger. *Illustrator:* Christine Nöstinger. Verlag für Jugend und Volk, 1990. *Category:* young children's book.

375 1995. *Original Title:* Benni und die sieben Löwen. Heinz Janisch. *Illustrator:* Gabriele Kernke. Annette Betz, 1995. *Category:* children's fiction.

376 1995. *Original Title:* Nurmi, der Bär. Stefan Slupetzky. Picus Verlag, 1995. *Category:* children's fiction.

377 1995. *Original Title:* Der blaue See ist heute grün. Jutta Treiber. Jugend & Volk, 1995. *Category:* children's fiction.

378 1995. *Original Title:* Madisou. Barabara Waldschütz. *Illustrator:* Barabara Waldschütz. Dachs Verlag, 1995. *Category:* illustration.

379 1998. *Original Title:* Die Prinzessin auf dem Kürbis. Heinz Janisch. *Illustrator:* Linda Wolfsgruber. Gabriel, 1998. *Category:* children's fiction.

380 1998. *Original Title:* Alles in Butter, liebe Mutter! Birgit Antoni. *Illustrator:* Birgit Antoni. Dachs Verlag, 1998. *Category:* illustration.

381 1998. *True Stories.* Monika Pelz. *Illustrator:* Linda Wolfsgruber. Jungbrunnen, 1998. *Category:* teenage fiction.

382 1998. *Original Title:* Das Königsspiel. Maria Blazejovsky. Jungbrunnen, 1998. *Category:* children's fiction.

383 1999. *Original Title:* Ein verrückter Tag. Friederike Wagner. *Illustrator:* Friederike Wagner. Picus Verlag, 1999. *Category:* illustration.

384 1999. *Original Title:* Ich schenk dir einen Ton aus meinem Saxofon. Heinz Janisch. Verlag Jungbrunnen, 1999. *Category:* children's fiction.

385 1999. *Original Title:* Lissi im Wunderland. Monika Pelz. Verlag Jungbrunnen, 1999. *Category:* children's fiction.

386 1999. *Original Title:* Warum der Hase lange Ohren hat. Martin Auer. *Illustrator:* Linda Wolfsgruber. Gabriel Verlag, 1999. *Category:* children's fiction.

387 2000. *Original Title:* Es war einmal von A bis Zett. Renate Habinger. *Illustrator:* Linda Wolfsgruber. Bibliothek der Provinz, 2000. *Category:* children's fiction.

388 2000. *Original Title:* Von Gutenberg zum World Wide Web. Holler Berger. Dachs Verlag, 2000. *Category:* children's fiction.

389 2000. *Original Title:* Besuch aus der Vergangenheit. Renate Welsh. Obelisk Verlag, 2000. *Category:* children's fiction.

390 2000. *Original Title:* Zack Bumm! Helga Bansch. *Illustrator:* Helga Bansch. Verlag Jungbrunnen, 2000. *Category:* illustration.

391 Österreichischen Würdigungspreis für Kinder- und Jugendliteratur (Austrian Appreciation Prize for Children and Young Adult Literature)

SPONSOR: Bundeskanzleramt, Sektion für Kunstangelegenheiten. CONTACT: Abteilung II/ 6: Kinder- und, Jugendliteratur. ADDRESS: Schottengasse 1, A-1014 Wien. PHONE: 531 20-7562. ESTABLISHED: 1980. AWARD: 150.000 and 75.000,- ATS. The award is given every three years to Austrian writers and illustrators in apprecation for their contribution of the field of children's literature.

392 1992. Renate Welsh.
393 1995. Lene Mayer-Skumanz.
394 1996. Martin Auer.
395 1996. Wolf Harranth.
396 1998. Lisbeth Zwerger.
397 1998. Heinz Janisch.
398 2000. Linda Wolfsgruber.
399 2000. Monika Pelz.

400 Österreichischer Kinder- und Jugendbuchpreis (Austrian National Children's and Juvenile Book Award)

SPONSOR: Bundeskanzleramt, Sektion für Kunstangelegenheiten. ADDRESS: Abteilung II/6, Schottengasse 1, A-1014 Wien. PHONE: 531 20-7562. ESTABLISHED: 1955. AWARD: 250.000,- ATS. The annual award is given for the best published book in the previous year by Austrian publishers. Living authors and illustrators are eligible. Categories include: children's fiction, children's nonfiction, teenage fiction, and illustration.

401 1990. *Original Title:* Die Fliege am Broadway. Heinz Rudolf Unger. Dachs Verlag, 1989. *Category:* children's book.

402 1990. *The Chimpanzee Family. Original Title:* Das Schimpansen—Kinder—buch. Jane Goodall. *Illustrator:* Michael Neugebauer. Neugebauer Press, 1989. *Category:* non fiction.

403 1990. *Original Title:* Meister Joachims Geheimnis. Sigrid Heuck. Thienemanns, 1989. *Category:* youth book.

404 1990. *Original Title:* Hanniel kommt in die Stadt. Lene Mayer-Skumanz. Herder, 1989. *Category:* children's book.

405 1990. *Original Title:* Gans ganz groß. Sylvia Bengs, Thomas Buttkus. *Illustrator:* Thomas Buttkus. Neuer Breitschopf, 1989. *Category:* picture book.

406 1990. *Original Title:* Die Guck-Gucks-Bande. Robert Dörfler. *Illustrator:* Robert Dörfler. Neuer Breitschopf, 1989. *Category:* illustration.

407 1991. *Original Title:* Der Hacht hat's gesagt! Arnica Esterl. *Illustrator:* Gennadij Spurn. Österreichischer Bundesverlag, 1990. *Category:* illustration.

408 1991. *Original Title:* Ich und Jonna. Torill Ende. St. Gabriel, 1990. *Category:* children's book.

409 1991. *Original Title:* Der Junge ohne Namen. Peter Seeberg. Obelisk Verlag, 1990. *Category:* children's book.

410 1991. *Original Title:* Max, der Unglücksrabe. Walter Wippersberg. *Illustrator:* Susan Opel. Obelisk Verlag, 1990. *Category:* children's book.

411 1991. *Original Title:* Die Hexenkralle. Peter Utton. *Illustrator:* Peter Utton. Annette Betz, 1990. *Category:* children's book.

412 1991. *Original Title:* Mein Wienbuch. Reingard Witzmann. Jugend & Volk, 1990. *Category:* children's non-fiction.

413 1992. *Original Title:* Niños del mundo. Peter Wesely. St. Gabriel, 1991. *Category:* children's book.

414 1992. *Original Title:* Ein Sehnen nach etwas. Torill Eide. St. Gabriel, 1991. *Category:* children's book.

415 1992. *Let's Go Home, Little Bear. Original Title:* Gehen wir heim, kleiner Bär. Martin Waddell. *Illustrator:* Barbara Firth. Annette Betz, 1991. *Category:* children's book.

416 1992. *Original Title:* Kunst-Mal-Buch. Heide Kaps-Gabler. Neuer Breitschopf, 1991. *Category:* children's book.

417 1992. *Original Title:* Der kleine Blumenkönig. Hans Gärtner, Michael Neugebauer. *Illustrator:* Pacovska Kveta. Neugebauer Press, 1991. *Category:* illustration.

418 1992. *Original Title:* Die Kinder der Prärie. Käthe Recheis. Herder, 1991. *Category:* children's book.

419 1993. *Original Title:* Kinderbibel. Werner Laubi. *Illustrator:* Annegert Fuchshuber. St. Gabriel, 1992. *Category:* children's non-fiction.

420 1993. *Original Title:* Fünf Minuten vor dem Abendessen. Iva Procházková. *Illustrator:* Vaclav Pokorny. Thienemanns, 1992. *Category:* children's book.

421 1993. *Original Title:* Der tapfere Theo. Erhard Dietl. *Illustrator:* Erhard Dietl. Thienemanns, 1992. *Category:* children's book.

422 1993. *Original Title:* Tanz in die Hölle. Tor Fretheim. Herder, 1992. *Category:* children's book.

423 1993. *Original Title:* Dinosaurier gibt es nicht. Hanna Johansen. *Illustrator:* Hanna Johansen. Obelisk Verlag, 1992. *Category:* children's book.

424 1993. *Original Title:* Hasenmond. John A. Rowe. *Illustrator:* John Rowe. Neugebauer Press, 1992. *Category:* illustration.

425 1994. *Original Title:* Das Land der Ecken. Irene Ulitzka. *Illustrator:* Gerhard Gepp. Picus Verlag, 1993. *Category:* illustration.

426 1994. *Original Title:* Eines Morgens war die Chomreh leer. Hushang Moradi-Kermani. Jungbrunnen, 1993. *Category:* children's fiction.

427 1994. *Original Title:* Mustafa mit dem Bauchladen. Ghazi Abdel Qadir. Obelisk Verlag, 1993. *Category:* children's fiction.

428 1994. *Original Title:* Das Lügennetz. Lene Mayer-Skumanz. Dachs Verlag, 1993. *Category:* children's fiction.

429 1994. *Original Title:* Als Viktoria allein zu Hause war. Martin Auer. *Illustrator:* Simone Klages. St. Gabriel, 1993. *Category:* children's fiction.

430 1995. *The Peach Pit Lives in the Peach. Original Title:* Im Pfirsich wohnt der Pfirsichkern. Wolf Harranth. *Illustrator:* Christine Sormann. St. Gabriel, 1994. *Category:* illustration.

431 1995. *Baby Crow. Original Title:* Raben-Baby. John E. Rowe. *Translator:* Peter Baumann. Michael Neugebauer, 1994. *Category:* children's fiction.

432 1995. *The Secret Knowledge of Penguins 2. Original Title:* Das geheime Wissen der Pinquine 2. Reinhardt Jung. Dachs, 1994. *Category:* children's fiction.

433 1995. *Wolf Saga. Original Title:* Wolfsaga. Käthe Recheis. *Illustrator:* Karen Hollander. Herder, 1994. *Category:* children's fiction.

434 1995. *Good Night Stories for Maria Carolina. Original Title:* Gutenachgeschichten für Maria Carolina. Barbara Frischmuth. *Illustrator:* Dusan Kállay. Dachs, 1994. *Category:* children's fiction.

435 1995. *Sing Again My Brother. Original Title:* Sing noch einmal, mein Bruder. Louis Kruger. *Translator:* Miriam Pressler. Tafelburg, 1994. *Category:* children's fiction.

436 1995. *King and Fool. Original Title:* Konig und Narr. Ernst A. Ekker. *Illustrator:* Linda Wolfsgruber. Herder, 1994. *Category:* illustration.

437 1996. *Original Title:* Der Sohn des Hauptlings. Erich Jooß. *Illustrator:* Antoni Boratynski. St. Gabriel, 1995. *Category:* illustration.

438 1996. *Original Title:* Neun Leben. Neun Danyan. St. Gabriel, 1995. *Category:* children's fiction.

439 1996. *Original Title:* Rot, blau und ein bißchen. Bjørn Sortland. *Illustrator:* Lars Elling. Kerle, 1995. *Category:* children's non-fiction.

440 1996. *Original Title:* Finger hat es aufgeschrieben. Erlend Aas. Kerle, 1995. *Category:* children's fiction.

441 1996. *Original Title:* Der blaue See ist heute grün. Jutta Treiber. Dachs Verlag, 1995. *Category:* children's fiction.

442 1996. *Original Title:* Ein Baum für Mama. Sophie Brandes. *Illustrator:* Sophie Brandes. Kerle, 1995. *Category:* children's fiction.

443 1997. *I Was a Teenage Warrior. Original Title:* Boys, Pickel und andere Megasorgen. Ros Asquith. *Illustrator:* Ros Asquith. Ueberreuter, 1996. *Category:* children's fiction.

444 1997. *The Wizard of Oz. Original Title:* Der Zauberer von Oz. L. Frank Baum. *Illustrator:* Lisbeth Zwerger. Neugebauer, 1996. *Category:* illustration.

445 1997. *Children in the Dark. Original Title:* Kinder im Dunkeln. Julio Emilio Braz. St. Gabriel, 1996. *Category:* children's fiction.

446 1997. *Timeout or the Lion of Kauba. Original Title:* Auszeit oder der Lowe von Kauba. Reinhardt Jung. Jungbrunnen, 1996. *Category:* children's fiction.

447 1997. *Jacob Under the Cherry Tree. Original Title:* Wenn Jakob unterm Kirschbaum sitzt. Sigrid Laube. *Illustrator:* Susanne Wechdorn. Jungbrunnen, 1996. *Category:* children's fiction.

448 1997. *Days of the Thistles. Original Title:* Disteltage. Renate Welsh. Obelisk, 1996. *Category:* children's fiction.

449 1998. *Original Title:* Der dreckige Prinz. Martin Auer. *Illustrator:* Joachim Luetke. K. Thienemanns Verlag, 1997. *Category:* children's fiction.

450 1998. *Original Title:* Donna & Dario. Barbara Frischmuth. Sauerlander, 1997. *Category:* children's fiction.

451 1998. *Original Title:* Indie Underground. Adelheid Dahimène. Grosser, 1997. *Category:* teenage fiction.

452 1998. *Original Title:* Apo Stroph. Heide Stöllinger. *Illustrator:* Heide Stöllinger. Grosser, 1997. *Category:* illustration.

453 1998. *Original Title:* In der Nacht über die Berge. Mahmut Baksi, Elin Clason. St. Gabriel, 1997. *Category:* children's fiction.

454 1998. *Original Title:* To Je Ernest. Mojca Osojnik. *Illustrator:* Mojca Osojnik. Drava-Verlag, 1997. *Category:* children's fiction.

455 1999. *Original Title:* Herr Novak und die Mausfrau. Stefan Slupetzky. Middelhauve, 1998. *Category:* children's fiction.

456 1999. *Original Title:* Als die Steine noch Vögel waren. Marjaleena Lembcke. Obelisk, 1998. *Category:* children's fiction.

457 1999. *True Stories.* Monika Pelz. Jungbrunnen, 1998. *Category:* teenage fiction.

458 1999. *Original Title:* Bananenrot und Himbeerblau. Heinz Janisch, Luise Kloos. Medienfabrik Graz, 1998. *Category:* children's non-fiction.

459 1999. *Original Title:* … von wegen … caminhos … Ruth Gschwendtner. Eigenverlag, 1998. *Category:* children's non-fiction.

460 1999. *Original Title:* Die Prinzessin auf dem Kürbis. Heinz Janisch. *Illustrator:* Linda Wolfsgruber. Gabriel, 1998. *Category:* children's fiction.

461 1999. *Original Title:* Wenn das Licht ausgeht.… Jung von Reinhardt. *Illustrator:* Sonja Vandenberk. Jungbrunnen, 1998. *Category:* illustration.

462 2000. *Caretta Caretta. Original Title:* Caretta Caretta. Paulus Hochgatterer. Deuticke, 1999. *Category:* teenage fiction.

463 2000. *Original Title:* Warum der Hase lange Ohren hat. Martin Auer. *Illustrator:* Linda Wolfsgruber. Gabriel Verlag, 1999. *Category:* children's fiction.

464 2000. *Original Title:* Lucie im Wald mit den Dingsda. Peter Handke. Suhrkamp Verlag, 1999. *Category:* children's fiction.

465 2000. *Original Title:* Es war einmal von A bis Zett. Renate Habinger. *Illustrator:* Linda Wolfsgruber. Bibliothek der Provinz, 1999. *Category:* illustration.

466 2000. *Original Title:* Lieblich klingt der Gartenschlauch. Martin Auer. *Illustrator:* Jutta Bucker. K. Thienemanns Verlag, 1999. *Category:* children's fiction.

467 Österreichischer Staatspreis für Kinder- und Jugendliteratur (Austrian State Prize for Children's and Young Adult Literature)

SPONSOR: Bundeskanzleramt, Sektion für Kunstangelegenheiten. CONTACT: Abteilung II/ 6: Kinder- und, Jugendliteratur. ADDRESS: Schottengasse 1, A-1014 Wien. PHONE: 531 20-2382. ESTABLISHED: 1985. The award is given annually to honor outstanding author's of children's and young adult literature written in German.

468 1993. Hans Manz.
469 1995. Frantz Wittkamp.
470 1997. Josef Guggenmos.
471 1999. Friedl Hofbauer.

BELGIUM

472 Boekenleeuw & Boekenwelpen (Booklion and Bookcubs)

SPONSOR: Fortis Bank. CONTACT: Mr. Wim de Mont. ADDRESS: VBVB, Hof ter Schriecklaan 17, 2600 Berchem, Belgium. PHONE: 032-3-230.89.23. ESTABLISHED: 1962. AWARD: Booklion: 100.000 BEF = 2479 euro and a golden pin. Bookcubs: silver pin. These are annual awards: one Booklion goes to the best children or youth book in Dutch by a Flemish author (considering literary quality and pleasure of reading); there can be four Bookcubs, of which one can go to a translation by a Flemish translator. The bookcubs are a sort of encouraging awards.

473 1990. *The Mountain Guide Talks. Original Title:* De berggids vertelt. Dirk Musschoot. *Category:* bookcubs.

474 1990. *No Wonder Mother Talks to the Goldfish. Original Title:* Geen wonder dat moeder met de goudvissen praat. Ed Franck. *Category:* bookcubs.

475 1990. *The Cloud. Original Title:* De wolk. Gudrun Pausewang. *Translator:* Ernst van Altena. *Category:* bookcubs.

476 1990. *Later, I Want to Be a Stuntman. Original Title:* Later wil ik stuntman worden. Detty Verreydt. *Category:* booklion.

477 1990. *Afraid in Beirut. Original Title:* Bang in Beiroet. Walter Gansemans. *Category:* bookcubs.

478 1991. *My Aunt Is a Whale. Original Title:* Mijn tante is een grindewal. Anne Provoost. *Category:* booklion.

479 1991. *Trijntje Gunpowder. Original Title:* Trijntje Buskruit. Bea de Koster. *Category:* bookcubs.

480 1991. *A Hole to Live in. Original Title:* Een kuil om in te wonen. Bart Moeyaert. *Category:* bookcubs.

481 1992. *Kiss me. Original Title:* Kus me. Bart Moeyaert. *Category:* booklion.

482 1992. *Until the 13th Moon. Original Title:* Tot de 13e maan. Arnulf Zitelman. *Category:* bookcubs.

483 1992. *The Shadows of Pluckley. Original Title:* De schimmen van Pluckley. Ron Langenus. *Category:* bookcubs.

484 1992. *The Teacher is a Sweetheart. Original Title:* De meester is een schat. Bettie Elias. *Category:* bookcubs.

485 1992. *Across the River. Original Title:* Aan de overkant van de rivier. Jaak Dreesen. *Category:* bookcubs.

486 1993. *The Secret of Teacher Joachim. Original Title:* Het geheim van meester Joachim. Sigrid Heuck. *Category:* bookcubs.

487 1993. *Pongwiffy. Original Title:* Pongwiffy. Kaye Umansky. *Category:* bookcubs.

488 1993. *Goose of Wilds. Original Title:* Wok van de Wilden. Sylvia van den Heede. *Category:* bookcubs.

489 1993. *Hotel Hoteldebotel. Original Title:* Hotel Hoteldebotel. Ronni Hermans. *Category:* bookcubs.

490 1993. *For Ever, Always. Original Title:* Voor altijd, altijd. Bart Moeyaert. *Category:* bookcubs.

1993. Award not given. *Category:* booklion.

491 1994. *Selftanned. Original Title:* Bruin zonder zon. Diane Broeckhoven. *Category:* booklion.

492 1994. *Down. Original Title:* In de put. Gregie de Maeyer. *Category:* bookcubs.

493 1994. *Rudi the Running Pig. Original Title:* Rudi Renvarken. Uwe Timm. *Illustrator:* Gunnar Matysiak. *Category:* bookcubs.

494 1994. *A Five and Nine Zero's. Original Title:* Een vijf met negen nullen. Marita de Sterck, Klaas Verplancke. *Category:* bookcubs.

495 1995. *The Granny-complot. Original Title:* Het oma-komplot. Anthony Horowitz. *Category:* bookcubs.

496 1995. *Falling. Original Title:* Vallen. Anne Provoost. *Category:* Booklion.

497 1995. *Summer's Starting, Little Bear. Original Title:* Het wordt zomer, Kleine Beer. Henri van Daele. *Category:* bookcubs.

498 1995. *The Skin of the Bear. Original Title:* De huid van de beer. Sylvia van den Heede. *Category:* bookcubs.

499 1996. *Acceleration in a Current. Original Title:* Stroomversnelling. Lieve Hoet. *Category:* bookcubs.

500 1996. *Miracle Man. Original Title:* Mirakelman. Tim Bowler. *Category:* bookcubs.

501 1996. *Scared or Angry. Original Title:* Bang of boos. Bettie Elias. *Category:* bookcubs.

502 1996. *Bare Hands. Original Title:* Blote handen. Bart Moeyaert. *Category:* booklion.

503 1996. *For Pauline. Original Title:* Voor Paulien. Paul Kustermans. *Category:* bookcubs.

504 1997. *How We Nearly Got Stina Killed. Original Title:* Mansoor, of Hoe we Stina bijna doodkregen. Bart Moeyaert. *Category:* bookcubs.

505 1997. *The Revenge of the Marble Farmer. Original Title:* De wraak van de marmerkweker. Willy van Doorselaer. *Category:* booklion.

506 1997. *A Butterfly at the Window. Original Title:* Een vlinder aan het raam. Jamil Shakely. *Category:* bookcubs.

507 1997. *I'm Doing Fine. Original Title:* Met mij gaat alles goed. Jan Simoen. *Category:* bookcubs.

508 1997. *When the World Was Still Young. Original Title:* Toen de wereld nog jong was. Jürg Schubiger. *Category:* bookcubs.

509 1998. *Love Letters from 0 to 10. Original Title:* Liefdesbrieven van 0 tot 10. Susie Morgenstern. *Category:* bookcubs.

510 1998. *The Rose and the Swine. Original Title:* De Roos en het Zwijn. Anne Provoost. *Category:* booklion.

511 1998. *Salted Water. Original Title:* Water van zout. Bettie Elias. *Category:* bookcubs.

512 1998. *The Letter Rosie Found. Original Title:* De brief die Rosie vond. Bart Moeyaert. *Illustrator:* André Sollie. *Category:* bookcubs.

513 1998. *It's Slippery in June. Original Title:* Het ijzelt in juni. André Sollie. *Category:* bookcubs.

514 1999. *Who. Original Title:* Wie. Dirk Nielandt, Marjolein Pottie. *Category:* bookcubs.

515 1999. *The House of the Tides. Original Title:* Het huis van eb en vloed. Ed Franck. *Category:* bookcubs.

516 1999. *Prince of Emptyness. Original Title:* Prins van de leegte. Karel Verleyen. Davidsfonds/Infodok. *Category:* bookcubs.

517 1999. *Secret Sacrament. Original Title:* Geheim Sacrament. Sherryl Jordan. *Translator:* John Riedijk. *Category:* bookcubs.

518 1999. *Fox and Hare. Original Title:* Vos en haas. Sylvia van den Heede. *Illustrator:* Thé Tjong-Khing. *Category:* booklion.

519 2000. *Jules's Granny. Original Title:* De oma van Jules. Annemie Berebrouckx. *Category:* bookcubs.

520 2000. *The Snowman Who Did Not Want to Melt. Original Title:* De sneeuwman die niet smelten wou. Henri van Daele. *Category:* bookcubs.

521 2000. *Sheepskin and Goosefeathers. Original Title:* Schapenvellen en ganzenveren. Katharina Smeyers. *Category:* bookcubs.

522 2000. *It's the Love We Don't Understand. Original Title:* Het is de liefde die we niet begrijpen. Bart Moeyaert. *Category:* booklion.

523 2000. *A Bridge to Wiseman's Cove. Original Title:* De veerpont. James Moloney. *Translator:* Bea de Koster. *Category:* bookcubs.

524 Boekenpauw & Boekenpluimen (Bookpeacock and Bookfeathers)

SPONSOR: Fortis Bank and Mr. Ludo Gillé. CONTACT: Mr. Wim de Mont. ADDRESS: VBVB, Hof ter Schriecklaan 17, 2600 Berchem, Belgium. PHONE: 032-3-230.89.23. ESTABLISHED: 1989. AWARD: Bookpeacock: 100.000 BEF = 2479 euro and a golden pin. Bookfeathers: silver pin. The awards are given for the most beautifully illustrated book of the year.

525 1990. *Ice Creams. Original Title:* Ijsjes. Gerda Dendooven. *Illustrator:* Gerda Dendooven. *Category:* bookpeacock.

526 1991. *With Little Respect. Original Title:* Met weinig eerbied: een museumgids voor jongeren. Roland Vandenbussche. *Illustrator:* Pierre van Rompaey. *Category:* bookpeacock.

527 1992. *Point, Point, Point. Original Title:* Puntje puntje puntje. Geert de Kockere. *Illustrator:* Geert Vervaeke. *Category:* bookpeacock.

528 1993. *Curious Lotje. Original Title:* Nieuwsgierige Lotje. Lieve Baeten. *Illustrator:* Lieve Baeten. *Category:* bookpeacock.

529 1994. *Auntie Nans Sat on a Goose. Original Title:* Tante Nans zat op een gans. An Debaene. *Illustrator:* Kristien Aertssen. *Category:* bookpeacock.

530 1995. *Rushes in the Bushes. Original Title:* Strikjes in de struiken. Gerda Dendooven. *Illustrator:* Gerda Dendooven. *Category:* bookpeacock.

531 1996. *A Biscuit for Blackie. Original Title:* Een koekje voor Blekkie. Agnes Verboven. *Illustrator:* Anne Westerduin. *Category:* bookpeacock.

532 1997. *Muu. Original Title:* Muu. Geert de Kockere. *Illustrator:* Marjolein Pottie. *Category:* bookpeacock.

533 1998. *The Letter Rosie Found. Original Title:* De brief die Rosie vond. Bart Moeyaert. *Illustrator:* André Sollie. *Category:* bookpeacock.

534 1999. *Tell Me It's Not Going to Snow. Original Title:* Zeg me dat het niet zal sneeuwen. Jaak Dreesen. *Illustrator:* Goele Dewanckel. *Category:* bookpeacock.

535 2000. *The Prince in Love. Original Title:* De verliefde prins. Ron Langenus. *Illustrator:* Gerda Dendooven. *Category:* bookfeathers.

536 2000. *Willy. Original Title:* Willy. Geert de Kockere. *Illustrator:* Carll Cneut. *Category:* bookpeacock.

537 2000. *Happy with Myself. Original Title:* Blij met mij. Leo Timmers. *Illustrator:* Leo Timmers. *Category:* bookfeathers.

538 Gouden Uil (Golden Owl)

SPONSOR: Standaard Uitgeverij (Standard Publishers). ADDRESS: Belgiëlei 176 a. 2018 Antwerpen, Belgium. PHONE: 032-3-760 32 11. ESTABLISHED: 1995. AWARD: 750.000 BEF = 18.592,5 euro. Each year, three books (one fiction, one nonfiction and one children's books) win the prize of 750.000 francs. The award is given to authors of Flanders (Belgium) and the Netherlands.

539 1995. *Falling. Original Title:* Vallen. Anne Provoost. Standaard Uitgeverij. *Category:* Flemish.

540 1996. *The Book of Bod Pa. Original Title:* Het boek van Bod Pa. Anton Quintana. Standaard Uitgeverij. *Category:* Dutch.

541 1997. *Eep. Original Title:* Iep. Joke van Leeuwen. Standaard Uitgeverij. *Category:* Dutch.

542 1998. *Mariken. Original Title:* Mariken. Peter van Gestel. Standaard Uitgeverij. *Category:* Dutch.

543 1999. *Happy Toes. Original Title:* Jubeltenen. Rita Verschuur. Standaard Uitgeverij. *Category:* Dutch.

544 2000. *The Recovery of the Cricket. Original Title:* De genezing van de krekel. Toon Tellegen. Standaard Uitgeverij. *Category:* Dutch.

545 Illustratorenprijs van de Stad Hasselt (Illustration Award of the City of Hasselt)

SPONSOR: City of Hasselt and Publisher Clavis. ADDRESS: Culturele Dienst, Stadhuis. 3500 Hasselt, Belgium. PHONE: 032-11-23.95.53. ESTABLISHED: 1996.

AWARD: 300.000 BEF = 7437 euro + the winner gets a contract at publishing house Clavis. This award is given every two years. Every illustrator (of every nationality) can participate in the contest. They have to create a book for young children between the age of 2 and 7.

546 1996. *Box Full of Monsters. Original Title:* Doosje mon. Riske Lemmens. *Illustrator:* Riske Lemmens. Clavis.

547 1998. *Different. Original Title:* Anders. Van Genechten Guido. *Illustrator:* Van Genechten Guido. Clavis.

548 2000. *Cuddle Cow. Original Title:* Knuffelkoe. Heylen Ilse. *Illustrator:* Heylen Ilse. Clavis.

549 Interprovinciale Prijs (Interprovincial Award for Children's and Youth Books)

SPONSOR: Vlaamse Interprovinciale Commissie voor Letterkunde (Flemish Interprovincial Board for Litterature). CONTACT: Ms. Pluym-Wuyts. ADDRESS: Cultuurdienst, Koningin Elizabethlei 22, 2018 Antwerpen, Belgium. PHONE: 032-3-240 64 01. ESTABLISHED: 1932. AWARD: 200.000 BEF = 4958 euro each. Every four years, this award is been given to the best Flemish children's book and youth book. The award money is raised by the five Flemish provinces.

550 1991. *Grandpa's Kite. Original Title:* De vlieger van opa. Jaak Dreesen. *Category:* children's book.

551 1991. *My Aunt is a Whale. Original Title:* Mijn tante is een grindewal. Anne Provoost. *Category:* youth.

552 1995. *Falling. Original Title:* Vallen. Anne Provoost. *Category:* youth.

553 1995. *A Fruit of Silver. Original Title:* Een fruitje van zilver. Geert de Kockere. *Category:* children's book.

554 1999. *Bare Hands. Original Title:* Blote handen. Bart Moeyaert. *Category:* youth.

555 1999. *Fox and Hare. Original Title:* Vos en haas. Sylvia van den Heede. *Illustrator:* Thé Tjong-Khing. *Category:* children's book.

556 Kinder- en Jeugdjury Vlaanderen (Children and Youth Jury Flanders Award)

SPONSOR: Kinder- en Jeugdjury Vlaanderen. CONTACT: Ms. Liesbeth Vreys. ADDRESS: p/a Villa Kakelbont, Meistraat 2, 2000 Antwerpen, Belgium. PHONE: 032-3-202.83.69. ESTABLISHED: 1998. AWARD: a piece of art. The award is given to the author of the most popular book choosen by thousands of Flemish children.

557 1999. *Oh, Those Spikes. Original Title:* O, die stekels. Guy Daniëls. *Illustrator:* Elsbeth Fontein. *Category:* less than 6 years old.

558 1999. *Fliks and Flora. Original Title:* Fliks en Flora. Marc de Bel. *Category:* 6–8.

559 1999. *Fire in the Woods. Original Title:* Brand in de Tikkebossen. Willy Schuyesmans. *Category:* 8–10.

560 1999. *The Beast of the Canigou. Original Title:* Het beest van de Canigou. Patrick Lagrou. *Category:* 10–12.

561 1999. *The Curse of Visions. Original Title:* De visioenenvloek. Anne Rutyne. *Category:* 12–14.

562 1999. *In the Hands of the Devil. Original Title:* In de klauwen van de duivel. Patrick Lagrou. *Category:* 14+.

563 2000. *Time Is a Circle. Original Title:* De tijd is een cirkel. Malika Oulad-Chaâra. *Category:* 12–14.

564 2000. *Peter's Little Secret. Original Title:* Het kleine geheim van Pieter. Bettie Elias. *Illustrator:* Anne Westerduin. *Category:* less than 6 years old.

565 2000. *The Quarters Club. Original Title:* De kwartjesclub. Pierre Coran. *Category:* 10–12.

566 2000. *Miss Bugger. Original Title:* Juffrouw Verdorie. Patricia David. *Category:* 8–10.

567 2000. *Splinters. Original Title:* Splinters. Marita de Sterck. *Category:* 14+.

568 2000. *Fox and Hare. Original Title:* Vos en haas. Sylvia van den Heede. *Illustrator:* Thé Tjong-Khing. *Category:* 6–8.

569 Prijs Knokke-Heist (Knokke-Heist Prize)

SPONSOR: Davidsfonds/Infodok Publishing. ADDRESS: Blijde Inkomststraat 79-81, 3000 Leuven, Belgium. PHONE: 332-16-31.06.00. ESTABLISHED: 1970. AWARD: 250.000 BEF = 6197,5 euro + the winning story is to be published by Davidsfonds/Infodok. Every two years this award is given to an author from Belgium (Flanders) or the Netherlands for a manuscript (not published) for children between 12 and 16 years.

570 1990. *Jonas, Painter or Rebel? Original Title:* Jonas, schilder of geus? Walter Gansemans. Davidsfonds/Infodok.

571 1993. *Six Times One Is Seven. Original Title:* Zes maal een is zeven. Gerda van Erkel. Davidsfonds/Infodok.

572 1996. *In the Sign of the Ram. Original Title:* In het teken van de Ram. Patrick Bernauw, Guy Didelez. Davidsfonds/Infodok.

573 1998. *Prince of Emptyness. Original Title:* Prins van de leegte. Karel Verleyen. Davidsfonds/Infodok.

574 2000. *White Pain. Original Title:* Witte Pijn. Ina Vandewijer. Davidsfonds/Infodok.

575 Prijs van de Vlaamse Gemeenschap (Belgium Government Prize)

SPONSOR: Ministerie van de Vlaamse Gemeenschap. CONTACT: Mr. Jan Vandenabeele. ADDRESS: Letteren en Podiumkunsten, Parochiaanstraat 15, 2000 Brussels, Belgium. PHONE: 032-2-553.68.83. ESTABLISHED: 1971. AWARD: 300.000 Belgium francs (BEF) = 7437 euro. Every third year this award goes to a children's book. (The other two years the award goes to other forms of art.).

576 1992. *Summer Seventeen. Original Title:* Zomer zeventien. Ed Franck.

577 1995. *Cycling. Original Title:* Fietsen. Gregie de Maeyer.

578 1998. *Bare Hands. Original Title:* Blote handen. Bart Moeyaert.

579 Prix Bernard Versele (Bernard Versele Prize)

SPONSOR: League of Families. CONTACT: Yvette Brainez. ADDRESS: 127 rue de Trône. 1050 Brussels, Belgium. PHONE: 02 507 72 06. ESTABLISHED: 1979. AWARD: 20,000 Belgium francs. Annual awards are given in five categories to encourage intellectual development, pleasure in reading and to stimulate creativity. Winners are chosen by a jury of children who select their favorite books.

580 1990. *Last of the Vampires. Original Title:* Le dernier des vampires. W. Hall. Flammarion. *Category:* to 9 years.

581 1990. *Little Poil, Big Wind. Original Title:* Petit Poil veut grandir. Irina Korschunow. École des Loisirs. *Category:* to 7 years.

582 1990. *Madame Trompette Goes out Tonight. Original Title:* Madame Trompette sort ce soir. Jill Murphy. Centurion. *Category:* to 3 years.

583 1990. *Princess Finemouche. Original Title:* Princesse Finemouche. B. Cole. Gallimard. *Category:* to 5 years.

584 1990. *Rascal. Original Title:* Rascal. Sterling North. École des Loisirs. *Category:* to 11 years.

585 1991. *Matilda. Original Title:* Matilda. Roald Dahl. *Illustrator:* Quentin Blake. Gallimard.

586 1991. *Quicksilver. Original Title:* Vif Argent. Josep Vallverdú. Flammarion.

587 1992. *Baby-sitter* Blues. Original *Title:* Baby-sitter blues. Marie-Aude Murail. École des Loisirs.

588 1992. *Marie Martin. Original Title:* Marie Martin. Gudrun Mebs. Gallimard.

589 1993. *Madame Bigote-Gigote. Original Title:* Madame Bigote-Gigote. Betty MacDonald. École des Loisirs.

590 1993. *The Witch of Midday. Original Title:* La sorcière de midi. M. Honaker. Rageot.

591 1994. *Save This Phantom. Original Title:* Sauvez ce fantôme. S. Reit. *Illustrator:* Quentin Blake. Calligram.

592 1994. *Man of the Waves. Original Title:* Homme des vagues. H. Veromme. *Illustrator:* Marc Lagarde. Gallimard.

593 1995. *Three Running Dogs. Original Title:* Trois chiens pour courir. Elizabeth van Steenwyk. *Illustrator:* Hierry Chrismann. Flammarion.

594 1995. *The Tiny Ones. Original Title:* Les minuscules. Roald Dahl. *Illustrator:* Patrick Benson. Gallimard.

595 1996. *Fifteen Million for a Phantom. Original Title:* Quinze millions pour un fantôme. Jean-François Ménard. École des Loisirs.

596 1996. *White Bottom. Original Title:* Cul-Blanc. Dick King-Smith. *Illustrator:* Henri Fellner. Gallimard.

597 1997. *Small Advertisement. Original Title:* La petite annonce. Brigitte Peskine. École des Loisirs.

598 1997. *Original Title:* Félix Têtedeveau. Anne-Marie Desplat-Duc. *Illustrator:* Gérard Franquin. Flammarion.

599 1998. *Love Letters. Original Title:* Lettres d'amour. Susie Morgenstern. École des Loisirs.

600 1998. *The Mystery of Greenwood. Original Title:* Le mystère de Greenwood. Malika Ferdjoukh. *Illustrator:* J. Howe. Bayard poche.

601 1999. *Friend! Friend? Original Title:* Ami! Ami? Chris Raschka. La joie de lire.

602 1999. *My Dreadful Dad. Original Title:* Mon affreux papa. Chris Donner, Alex Sanders. École des loisirs.

603 1999. *The Secrets of Faith Green. Original Title:* Les secrets de Faith Green. J.F. Chabas, Christophe Blain. Casterman. *Category:* 10 years plus.

604 1999. *The Wolf and the Titmouse. Original Title:* Le loup et la mésange. Muriel Bloch, Martine Bourre. Didier jeunesse.

605 1999. *Jingo Django. Original Title:* Jingo Django. Sid Fleischman. École des loisirs. *Category:* to 9 years.

BRAZIL

606 Prêmio Jabuti (Jabuti Prize)

SPONSOR: Cámera Brasileira do Livro. ADDRESS: Al. Santos, 1000—, 10° andar, 01418-100 Sao Paulo, F P Brasil. PHONE: (11) 229-7855. ESTABLISHED: 1958. The annual award is given to the best book for children published in the previous year.

607 1999. *Original Title:* Nadando Contra a Morte. Lourenço Cazarré. Formato. *Category:* young adult.

608 1999. *Original Title:* Cavalhadas de Pirenópolis. Roger Mello. Agir. *Category:* illustration.

609 1999. *Original Title:* De Frente Para o Sol. Demóstenes Vargas. Moderna. *Category:* illustration.

610 1999. *Original Title:* Dez Sacizinhos. Roberto Weigand. Paulinas. *Category:* illustration.

611 1999. *Original Title:* Dezenove Poemas Desengonçados. Ricardo Azevedo. Ática. *Category:* young adult.

612 1999. *Original Title:* A Outra Enciclopédia Canina. Ricardo Azevedo. Cia. das Letras. *Category:* young adult.

613 2000. *Original Title:* O teatro. Raquel Coelho. Formato. *Category:* illustration.

614 2000. *Original Title:* A revolta das palavras. José Paulo Paes. Cia. das Letras. *Category:* young adult.

615 2000. *Original Title:* ABC doido. Ângela Lago. Melhoramentos. *Category:* young adult.

616 2000. *Original Title:* Exercícios de ser criança. Diniz. Salamandra. *Category:* illustration.

617 2000. *Original Title:* Pindorama terra das palmeiras. Mar Castanha. Formato. *Category:* illustration.

618 2000. *Original Title:* Fiz voar o meu chapéu. Ana Maria Machado. Formato. *Category:* young adult.

619 Prêmio Monteiro Lobato (Monteiro Lobato Prize)

SPONSOR: Fundação Biblioteca Nacional, Departamento Nacional do Livro. ADDRESS: Rua da Imprensa, 16—11º andar, 20030-120 Rio de Janeiro, Brazil. ESTABLISHED: 1965. The biennial award is given for a published book or unpublished manuscript for children. The author should be from Brazil.

620 1993. *complete works.* Ruth Rocha. *Illustrator:* Raquel Coelho.

621 1997. *Original Title:* A terra dos meninos pelados. Graciliano Ramos. *Illustrator:* Roger Mello. Nagel & Kimche.

CANADA

622 Amelia Frances Howard-Gibbon Illustrators Award

SPONSOR: Canadian Library Asssociation. CONTACT: Brenda Shields. ADDRESS: 602-200 Elgin Street, Ottawa, Ontario, Canada K2P 1L5. PHONE: (613) 232-9625.

ESTABLISHED: 1971. AWARD: A silver gilt medal. The annual award is presented to the illustrator of an outstanding children's book published during the previous calendar year. The illustrator must be a Canadian citizen or permanent resident of Canada, and the book must be suitable for children up to age fourteen and be published in Canada.

623 1990. *'Til All the Stars Have Fallen: Canadian Poems for Children.* Kady MacDonald Denton. *Illustrator:* Kady MacDonald Denton. Kids Can Press, 1989.

624 1991. *The Orphan Boy.* Tololwa Marti Mollel. *Illustrator:* Paul Morin. Oxford, 1990.

625 1992. *Waiting for the Whales.* Sheryl MacFarlane. *Illustrator:* Ron Lightburn. Orca Books, 1991.

626 1993. *The Dragon's Pearl.* Julie Lawson. *Illustrator:* Paul Morin. Oxford, 1992.

627 1994. *Last Leaf First Snowfall to Fall.* Leo Yerxa. *Illustrator:* Leo Yerxa. Groundwood, 1993.

628 1995. *Gifts.* Jo Ellen Bogart. *Illustrator:* Barbara Reid. North Winds Press, 1994.

629 1996. *Just Like New.* Ainslie Manson. *Illustrator:* Karen Reczuch. Groundwood, 1995.

630 1997. *Ghost Train.* Paul Yee. *Illustrator:* Harvey Chan. Groundwood, 1996.

631 1998. *The Party.* Barbara Reid. *Illustrator:* Barbara Reid. Scholastic Books, 1997.

632 1999. *A Child's Treasury of Nursery Rhymes.* Kady MacDonald Denton. *Illustrator:* Kady MacDonald Denton. Kids Can Press, 1998.

633 2000. *The Dragon New Year: A Chinese Legend.* Zhong-Yang Huang. *Illustrator:* Zhong-Yang Huang. Raincoast Books, 1999.

634 Ann-Connor Brimer Award

SPONSOR: Nova Scotia Library Association. CONTACT: Heather MacKenzie. ADDRESS: PO Box 36036, Halifax, Nova Scotia, Canada B3J 3S9. PHONE: (902) 490-5822. ESTABLISHED: 1991. AWARD: $1000 CDN. The prize is given to the author of a children's book which has made an outstanding contribution to children's literature in Atlantic Canada. The winning author must be alive and residing in Atlantic Canada at the time of nomination.

635 1991. *Pit Pony.* Joyce Barkhouse. Gage Educational Publishers, 1990.

636 1992. *Eating Between the Lines.* Kevin Major. Doubleday, 1991.

637 1993. *Oliver's War.* Budge Wilson. Stoddart, 1992.

638 1994. *Good Idea Gone Bad.* Lesley Choyce. Formac, 1993.

639 1995. *Mabel Murple.* Sheree Fitch. *Illustrator:* Maryann Kovalski. Doubleday, 1995.

640 1996. *Of Things Not Seen.* Don Aker. Stoddart, 1995.

641 1997. *To Dance at the Palais Royale.* Janet McNaughton. Tuckamore Books, 1996.

642 1998. *The House of Wooden Santas.* Kevin Major. *Illustrator:* Imelda George. Ned Pratt. Red Deer College Press, 1997.

643 1999. *Make or Break Spring.* Janet McNaughton. Tuckmore Books, 1998.

644 Arthur Ellis Award

SPONSOR: The Crime Writers of Canada. ADDRESS: 3007 Kingston Road, P.O. Box 113, Scarborough, Ontario, Canada M1M 1P1. PHONE: (416) 466-9826. ESTABLISHED: 1993. The annual award is given for best juvenile mystery published within the preceding year by a Canadian resident, regardless of nationality, or a Canadian writer living abroad. In 1993, a category for best juvenile mystery was included.

645 1994. *Abalone Summer.* John Dowd. Raincoast Books, 1993.

646 1995. *Torn Away.* James Heneghan. Viking, 1994.

647 1996. *Mistaken Identity.* Norah McClintock. Scholastic, 1995.

648 1997. *How Can a Frozen Detective Stay Hot on the Trail?* Linda Bailey. Kids Can Press, 1996.

649 1998. *The Body in the Basement.* Norah McClintock. Scholastic, 1997.

650 1999. *Sins of the Father.* Norah McClintock. Scholastic, 1998.

651 2000. *How Can a Brilliant Detective Shine in the Dark?* Linda Bailey. Kids Can Press, 2001.

652 Canadian Library Association Book of the Year for Children

SPONSOR: Canadian Association of Children's Librarians. CONTACT: Chairperson. ADDRESS: 602-200 Elgin Street, Ottawa, Ontario, Canada K2P 1L5. PHONE: (613) 232-9625. ESTABLISHED: 1947. The award is presented annually to the author of an outstanding children's book published during the previous calendar year. The book must be suitable for children up to age fourteen and have been published in Canada by an author who is a Canadian citizen or permanent resident of Canada.

653 1990. *The Sky Is Falling.* Kit Pearson. Penguin, 1989.

654 1991. *Redwork.* Michael Bedard. Lester & Orpen Dennys, 1990.

655 1992. *Eating Between the Lines.* Kevin Major. Doubleday, 1991.

656 1993. *Ticket to Curlew.* Celia Lottridge. Groundwood, 1992.

657 1994. *Some of the Kinder Planets.* Tim Wynne-Jones. Groundwood, 1993.

658 1995. *Summer of the Mad Monk.* Cora Taylor. Greystone Books, 1994.

659 1996. *The Tiny Kite of Eddie Wing.* Maxine Trottier. *Illustrator:* Al van Mil. Stoddart, 1995.
660 1997. *Uncle Ronald.* Brian Doyle. Groundwood, 1996.
661 1998. *Silverwing.* Kenneth Oppel. HarperCollins, 1997.
662 1999. *Stephen Fair.* Tim Wynne-Jones. Groundwood, 1998.
663 2000. *Sunwing.* Kenneth Oppel. HarperCollins, 1999.

664 Canadian Library Association Young Adult Book Award

SPONSOR: Canadian Library Asssociation. CONTACT: Chairperson. ADDRESS: #602-200 Elgin Street, Ottawa, Ontario, Canada K2P 1L5. PHONE: (613) 232-9625. ESTABLISHED: 1980. AWARD: a leather bound book with the Award seal embossed on the cover. This prize is awarded to the author of an outstanding English language book for young adults (ages 13–18) published in the preceding calendar year. The winning book must be a work of fiction (novel or collection of short stories) written by a Canadian citizen or landed immigrant published in Canada.

665 1990. *Bad Boy.* Diana Wieler. Groundwood, 1989.
666 1991. *The Leaving.* Budge Wilson. 1990.
667 1992. *Strandia.* Sandra Lynn Reynolds. HarperCollins, 1991.
668 1993. *There Will Be Wolves.* Karleen Bradford. HarperCollins, 1992.
669 1994. *Nobody's Son.* Sean Stewart. Maxwell Macmillan, 1993.
670 1995. *Adam and Eve and Pinch Me.* Julie Johnson. Lester Publishing, 1994.
671 1996. *The Maestro.* Tim Wynne-Jones. Groundwood, 1995.
672 1997. *Takes: Stories for Young Adults.* R.P. MacIntyre (ed.). Thistledown Press, 1996.
673 1998. *Bone Dance.* Martha Brooks. Groundwood 1997.
674 1999. *Janey's Girl.* Gayle Friesen. Kids Can Press, 1998.
675 2000. *Alone at Ninety Foot.* Katherine Holubitsky. Orca Book Publishers, 1999.

676 Elizabeth Mrazik-Cleaver Canadian Picture Book Award

SPONSOR: IBBY Canada. CONTACT: Mariella Bertelli. ADDRESS: 35 Spadina Rd., Toronto, Ontario, Canada M5R 2S9. PHONE: (416) 652-3775. ESTABLISHED: 1986. AWARD: A scroll and $1,000.00 CDN. The recipient is a Canadian illustrator of a picture book published in Canada in English or in French during the previous calendar year. The book must be a first edition and contain original illustrations. All genres are considered: fiction, non-fiction, poetry, folk and fairy tales.

677 1990. *The Name of the Tree.* Celia Barker. *Illustrator:* Ian Wallace. Lottridge. Groundwood, 1989.

678 1991. *The Orphan Boy.* Tololwa Marti Mollel. *Illustrator:* Paul Morin. Oxford, 1990.

679 1992. *Waiting for the Whales.* Sheryl MacFarlane. *Illustrator:* Ron Lightburn. Orca Books, 1991.

680 1993. *Two by Two.* Barbara Reid. *Illustrator:* Barbara Reid. North Winds Press, 1992.

681 1994. *Last Leaf First Snowfall to Fall.* Leo Yerxa. *Illustrator:* Leo Yerxa. Groundwood, 1993.

682 1995. *Josepha: A Prairie Boy's Story.* Jim McGugan. *Illustrator:* Murray Kimber. Red Deer College Press, 1994.

683 1996. *Selina and the Bear Paw Quilt.* Barbara Smucker. *Illustrator:* Janet Wilson. Lester Publishing, 1995.

684 1997. *Ghost Train.* Paul Yee. *Illustrator:* Harvey Chan. Groundwood, 1996.

685 1998. *Rainbow Bay.* Stephen Eaton Hume. *Illustrator:* Pascal Milleli. Raincoast Books, 1997.

686 1999. *A Child's Treasury of Nursery Rhymes. Illustrator:* Kady MacDonald Denton. Kids Can Press, 1998.

687 2000. *Stormy Night.* Michele Lemieux. *Illustrator:* Michele Lemieux. Kids Can Press, 1999.

688 Geoffrey Bilson Award for Historical Fiction for Young People

SPONSOR: Canadian Children's Book Centre. ADDRESS: 35 Spadina Road, Toronto, Ontario, Canada M5R 2S9. PHONE: (416) 975-0010. ESTABLISHED: 1988. AWARD: $1,000.00 CDN. The annual award is given to the author of an outstanding work of historical fiction for young people. The author must be Canadian, and the book must have been published in the previous calendar year.

689 1990. *The Sky Is Falling.* Kit Pearson. Penguin, 1989.

690 1991. *The Sign of the Scales.* Marianne Brandis. The Porcupine's Quill, 1990.

1992. No award given.

691 1993. *Ticket to Curlew.* Celia Lottridge. Groundwood, 1992.

692 1994. *The Lights Go on Again.* Kit Pearson. Viking, 1993.

693 1995. *The Dream Carvers.* Joan Clark. Viking, 1995.

694 1996. *The Rebellion: A Novel of Upper Canada.* Marianne Brandis. Porcupine's Quill, 1996.

695 1997. *To Dance at the Palais Royale.* Janet McNaughton. Tuckamore Books, 1996.

696 1998. *Good-Bye Marianne.* Irene N. Watts. Tundra Books, 1998.

697 1999. *The Wreckers.* Iain Lawrence. Delacorte Press, 1998.

698 Governor General's Literary Awards

SPONSOR: The Canada Council. ADDRESS: 350 Albert Street, PO Box 1047, Ottawa, Ontario, Canada K1P 5V8. PHONE: (613) 566-4414. ESTABLISHED: 1987. AWARD: $10,000.00 CDN each. Formerly the Canada Council's Children's Literature Prizes, the four annual awards are given to writers and illustrators of books in English and French. The winners must be Canadian and the books must be published in the previous calendar year.

699 1990. *Uncle Henri's Dinner Guests. Original Title:* Les fantaisies de l'oncle Henri. Benedicte Froissart. *Illustrator:* Pierre Pratt. Annick, 1990. *Category:* illustration.

700 1990. *The True Story of Clara Vic's Dog. Original Title:* La vraie historie du chien de Clara Vic. Christiane Duchesne. Éditions Québec/Amérique, 1990. *Category:* text.

701 1990. *Redwork.* Michael Bedard. Lester & Orpen Dennys, 1990. *Category:* text.

702 1990. *The Orphan Boy.* Tololwa Marti Mollel. *Illustrator:* Paul Morin. Oxford, 1990. *Category:* illustration.

703 1991. *Original Title:* Deux heures et demie avant Jasmine. François Gravel. Éditions du Boréal, 1991. *Category:* text.

704 1991. *A Champion. Original Title:* Un champion. Roch Carrier. *Illustrator:* Sheldon Cohen. Tundra Books, 1991. *Category:* illustration.

705 1991. *Dr. Kiss Says Yes.* Teddy Jam. *Illustrator:* Joanne Fitzgerald. Groundwood, 1991. *Category:* illustration.

706 1991. *Pick-Up Sticks.* Sarah Ellis. Groundwood, 1991. *Category:* text.

707 1992. *Victor. Original Title:* Victor. Christiane Duchesne. Éditions Québec Amérique, 1992. *Category:* text.

708 1992. *Simone and the Cardboard Town. Original Title:* Simone et la ville de carton. Gilles Tibo. *Illustrator:* Gilles Tibo. Tundra Books, 1992. *Category:* illustration.

709 1992. *Hero of Lesser Causes.* Julie Johnston. Lester Publishing, 1992. *Category:* text.

710 1992. *Waiting for the Whales.* Sheryl MacFarlane. *Illustrator:* Ron Lightburn. Orca Books, 1991. *Category:* illustration.

711 1993. *Original Title:* Le monde salon Jean de … Andre Vandal. *Illustrator:* Stéphane Jorisch. DV editeurs, 1992. *Category:* illustration.

712 1993. *Sleep Tight, Mrs. Ming.* Sharon Jennings. *Illustrator:* Mireille Levert. Annick Press, 1993. *Category:* illustration.

713 1993. *Some of the Kinder Planets.* Tim Wynne-Jones. Groundwood, 1993. *Category:* text.

714 1993. *The Road of Chlifa. Original Title:* La route de Chlifa. Michèle Marineau. Édition Quebec/Amérique, 1992. *Category:* text.

715 1994. *A Beautiful Day to Die. Original Title:* Une belle journée pour mourir. Suzanne Martel. Fides, 1994. *Category:* text.

716 1994. *Adam and Eve and Pinch Me.* Julie Johnson. Lester Publishing, 1994. *Category:* text.

717 1994. *Josepha: A Prairie Boy's Story.* Jim McGugan. *Illustrator:* Murray Kimber. Red Deer College Press, 1994. *Category:* illustration.

718 1994. *My Dog Is an Elephant. Original Title:* Mon chien est un éléphant. Rémy Simard. *Illustrator:* Pierre Pratt. Annick, 1994. *Category:* illustration.

719 1995. *The Maestro.* Tim Wynne-Jones. Groundwood, 1995. *Category:* text.

720 1995. *The Last Quest of Gilgamesh.* Ludmila Zeman. *Illustrator:* Ludmila Zeman. Tundra, 1995. *Category:* illustration.

721 1995. *Like a Skin of Sorrow. Original Title:* Comme une peau de chagrin. Sonia Sarfati. Les Éditions de la courte échelle, 1995. *Category:* text.

722 1995. *Sho and Water Dragons. Original Title:* Sho et les dragons d'eau. Annouchka Gravel Galouchko. *Illustrator:* Annouchka Gravel Galouchko. Annick Press, 1995. *Category:* illustration.

723 1996. *The Rooster's Gift.* Pam Conrad. *Illustrator:* Eric Beddows. Groundwood, 1996. *Category:* illustration.

724 1996. *Noemy: Mrs Lumbago's Secret. Original Title:* Noémie: le secret de Madame Lumbago. Gilles Tibo. *Illustrator:* Louise-Andrée Laliberté. Éditions Québec Amérique, 1996. *Category:* text.

1996. No award given. *Category:* illustration.

725 1996. *Ghost Train.* Paul Yee. *Illustrator:* Harvey Chan. Groundwood, 1996. *Category:* text.

726 1997. *Hair of Snake, Tooth of Spider. Original Title:* Poil de serpent, dent d'araignée. Danielle Marcotte. *Illustrator:* Stéphane Poulin. Les 400 Coups, 1996. *Category:* illustration.

727 1997. *Awake and Dreaming.* Kit Pearson. Viking, 1996. *Category:* text.

728 1997. *Pien. Original Title:* Pien. Michel Noël. Éditions Michel Quintin, 1996. *Category:* text.

729 1997. *The Party.* Barbara Reid. *Illustrator:* Barbara Reid. Scholastic Books, 1997. *Category:* illustration.

730 1998. *Original Title:* Monsieur Ilétaitunefois. Rémy Simard. *Illustrator:* Pierre Pratt. Annick Press, 1998. *Category:* illustration.

731 1998. *Original Title:* Variations sur un même & laqn t'aime. Angèle Delaunois. Éditions Heritage, 1998. *Category:* text.

732 1998. *A Child's Treasury of Nursery Rhymes. Illustrator:* Kady MacDonald Denton. Kids Can Press, 1998. *Category:* illustration.

733 1998. *The Hollow Tree.* Janet Lunn. Alfred Knopf, 1997. *Category:* text.

734 1999. *Charlotte and the Island of Destiny. Original Title:* Charlotte et l'île du Destin. Stéphane Jorisch. *Illustrator:* Stéphane Jorisch. Éditions les 400 Coups, 1999. *Category:* illustration.

735 1999. *A Screaming Kind of Day.* Rachna Gilmore. Fitzhenry & Whiteside, 1999. *Category:* text.

736 1999. *The Great Poochini.* Gary Clement. *Illustrator:* Gary Clement. Groundwood Books, 1999. *Category:* illustration.

737 1999. *Freedom? I Do Not Know… Original Title:* La Liberté? Connais pas … Charlotte Gingras. Éditions de la courte échelle, 1999. *Category:* text.

738 Hackmatack Children's Choice Award

SPONSOR: Nova Scotia Provincial Library. ADDRESS: 3770 Kempt Road, Halifax, Nova Scotia, Canada B3K 4X8. ESTABLISHED: 2000. The award allows children to choose their favorite Canadian and Atlantic Canadian books. The children read from ten fiction and ten non-fiction titles presented as the short list. The books are selected on their literary, cultural and enjoyment factors. The books should be published within two or three years of the selection process.

739 2000. *Sunwing.* Kenneth Oppel. HarperCollins, 1999. *Category:* fiction.

740 2000. *If You Could Wear My Sneakers.* Sheree Fitch. Doubleday, 1997. *Category:* non-fiction

741 Information Book Award

SPONSOR: Children's Roundtables of Canada. CONTACT: Ronald Jobe. ADDRESS: Univ. of British Columbia, Dept. of Language Education, 2125 Main Mal, Vancouver, British Columbia, Canada V6T 1Z5. PHONE: (604) 822-5233. ESTABLISHED: 1987. AWARD: $500.00 CDN. The award is given to recognize an outstanding information book for children and young people 5 to 15 years of age, written in English, by a Canadian citizen. The book will be drawn from the following types: cultural, concept, life cycle, science, biography, history and geography. The book must have been published in Canada during the previous year by a Canadian citizen or landed immigrant.

742 1990. *Wolf Island.* Celia Godkin. Fitzhenry & Whiteside, 1989.

743 1991. *Hands On, Thumbs Up.* Camilla Gryski. *Illustrator:* Pat Cupples. Kids Can Press, 1990.

744 1992. *A Tree in a Forest.* Jan Thornhill. Greey de Pencier, 1991.

745 1993. *The Story of Canada.* Janet Lunn, Christopher Moore. *Illustrator:* Alan Daniel. Lester Publishing, 1992.

746 1994. *On the Shuttle: Eight Days in Space.* Barbara Bondar, Dr. Roberta Bondar. Greey de Pencier, 1993.
747 1994. *Cowboy: A Kid's Album.* Linda Granfield. Douglas and McIntyre, 1993.
748 1995. *A Pioneer Story: The Daily Life of a Canadian Family in, 1840.* Barbara Greenwood. *Illustrator:* Heather Collins. Kids Can Press, 1994.
749 1996. *In Flanders Fields: The Story of the Poem by John McCrae.* Linda Granfield. *Illustrator:* Janet Wilson. Stoddart, 1995.
750 1997. *On Board the Titanic: What It was Like When the Great Liner Sank.* Shelley Tanaka. *Illustrator:* Ken Marschall. Scholastic, 1996.
751 1998. *The Buried City of Pompeii: What It Was Like When Vesuvius Exploded.* Shelley Tanaka. *Illustrator:* Greg Ruhl. Scholastic, 1997.
752 1999. *The Last Safe House: A Story of the Underground Railroad.* Barbara Greenwood. *Illustrator:* Heather Collins. Kids Can Press, 1998.
753 2000. *Wow Canada! Exploring This Land from Coast to Coast to Coast.* Vivien Bowers, *Illustrator:* Dan Hobbs. Diane Eastman. Owl Books, 1999.

754 International Reading Association Children's Literature Award

SPONSOR: Ottawa Valley Council of the International Reading Association. ADDRESS: 1705-211 Wurtemburg St., Ottawa, Ontario, Canada K1N 8R4. PHONE: (613)-241-7917. Also known as Prix Littéraire de la Jeunesse de L'Association Internationale pour la Lecture. The prize is given annually and alternatively to French or English author or illustrator.

755 1991. *The Human Lawsuit. Original Title:* Le procès des humains: comédie en deux actes. Ginette Proulx-Weaver. *Illustrator:* Michel Blanc. Éditions du Vermillon, 1990.
756 1992. *Covered Bridge.* Brian Doyle. *Illustrator:* Alan Daniel. Groundwood, 1990.
757 1993. *Powder Magic. Original Title:* La poudre magique. Jean-Pierre Guillet. *Illustrator:* Gilles Tibo. Éditions M. Quintin, 1992.
758 1994. *The Story of Canada.* Janet Lunn. Lester, 1992.
1995. No award given.
759 1996. *The Maestro.* Tim Wynne-Jones. Groundwood, 1995.
760 1996. *The Bubbles Machine. Original Title:* La machine à bulles. Jean-Pierre Guillet. *Illustrator:* Gilles Tibo. Éditions M. Quintin, 1994.
1997. No award given.
1998. No award given.

761 IODE Book Award — Toronto Chapter

SPONSOR: International Order of Daughters of the Empire. CONTACT: Mrs. B.K. Willard. ADDRESS: 40 St. Clair Avenue East, Toronto, Ontario, Canada M4T 1M9.

PHONE: (416) 925-5078. ESTABLISHED: 1974. AWARD: $1,000.00 CDN. The annual award is given to a Canadian author or illustrator, resident in Toronto or the surrounding area, for the best children's book for audiences ages 6 to 12 years. The book must be published in Canada.

762 1990. *Voices on the Wind.* David Booth (ed.). *Illustrator:* Michele Lemieux. Kids Can Press, 1990.

763 1991. *The Nightingale.* Michael Bedard. *Illustrator:* Regolo Ricci. Oxford University Press, 1991.

764 1992. *The Story of Canada.* Janet Lunn, Christopher Moore. *Illustrator:* Alan Daniel. Key Porter Books, 1992.

765 1993. *Ten Small Tales.* Celia Barker Lottridge. *Illustrator:* Joanne Fitzgerald. Groundwood Books, 1993.

766 1994. *The Dream of Aengus.* Joanne Findon. *Illustrator:* Ted Nasmith. Lester Publishing, 1994.

767 1995. *In Flanders Fields: The Story of the Poem by John McCrae.* Linda Granfield. *Illustrator:* Janet Wilson. Stoddart/Lester, 1995.

768 1996. *The Dust Bowl.* David Booth (ed.). *Illustrator:* Karen Reczuch. Kids Can Press, 1996.

769 1997. *A Winter's Tale.* Ian Wallace. *Illustrator:* Ian Wallace. Groundwood Books, 1997.

770 1998. *Fog Cat.* Marilyn Helmer. *Illustrator:* Paul Mombourquette. Kids Can Press, 1998.

771 1999. *The Clay Ladies.* Michael Bedard. *Illustrator:* Les Tait. Tundra Books, 1999.

772 IODE Violet Downey Book Award — National Chapter

SPONSOR: International Order of Daughters of the Empire. ADDRESS: 40 Orchard View Boulevard, Suite 254, Toronto, Ontario, Canada M4R 1B9. PHONE: (416) 487-4416. ESTABLISHED: 1985. AWARD: $3,000.00 CDN. The award is given to the best English language book published in the previous calendar year by a Canadian and published in Canada. The work must contain at least 500 words of text, be suitable for children aged 13 and under and may be in any category, with the exception of fairy tales, anthologies and adaptations.

773 1990. *Tales from Gold Mountain.* Paul Yee. *Illustrator:* Simon Ng. Groundwood, 1989.

774 1991. *Incredible Jumbo.* Barbara Smucker, Viking, 1990.

775 1992. *Waiting for the Whales.* Sheryl MacFarlane. *Illustrator:* Ron Lightburn. Orca Books, 1991.

776 1993. *Hero of Lesser Causes.* Julie Johnston. Lester Publishing, 1992.

777 1994. *The Lights Go on Again.* Kit Pearson. Viking, 1993.

778 1995. *Out of the Blue.* Sarah Ellis. Douglas & McIntyre, 1994.

779 1996. *His Banner Over Me.* Jean Little. Viking, 1995.
780 1997. *To Dance at the Palais Royale.* Janet McNaughton. Tuckamore Books, 1996.
781 1998. *Wings to Fly.* Celia Barker Lottridge. *Illustrator:* Mary Jane Gerber. Groundwood, 1997.
782 1999. *Janey's Girl.* Gayle Friesen. Kids Can Press, 1998.
783 2000. *Alone at Ninety Foot.* Katherine Holubitsky. Orca Book Publishers, 1999.

784 Manitoba Young Reader's Choice Award

SPONSOR: Manitoba School Library Audio Visual Association. CONTACT: Sheila Duprey. ADDRESS: 115 Brock St., Winnipeg, Manitoba, Canada R3N 0Y5. PHONE: (204) 477-5863. ESTABLISHED: 1991. This award is presented for the Canadian children's book that receives the most votes by children from grades 4–8 involved in the program. Participants must read at least 3 titles from a pre-selected list.

785 1991. *The Zucchini Warriors.* Gordon Korman.
786 1992. *Five Days of the Ghost.* William Bell. Stoddart, 1989.
787 1993. *Can You Teach Me to Pick My Nose?* Martyn Godfrey. Avon, 1990.
788 1994. *Looking at the Moon.* Kit Pearson. Viking, 1991.
789 1995. *The Mystery of the Missing Will.* Jeri Mayer. Thistledown Press, 1992.
790 1996. *Daniel's Story.* Carol Matas. Scholastic, 1993.
791 1997. *Bring Up Beauty.* Sylvia McNicoll. Macmillan, 1994.
792 1998. *Mystery at Lake Placid.* Roy MacGregor. McClelland & Stewart, 1995.
793 1999. *Awake and Dreaming.* Kit Pearson. Viking, 1996.

794 McNally Robinson Book for Young People Award

SPONSOR: McNally Robinson Booksellers. CONTACT: Carlene Rummery. ADDRESS: #206-100 Arthur St., Winnipeg, Manitoba, Canada R3B 1H3. PHONE: (204) 942-6134. ESTABLISHED: 1995. AWARD: $1500 CDN. The award is given to celebrate the best in Manitoba writing and publishing. The categories are Young Adult and Children. Eligible authors will have been a resident in Manitoba for three of the last five years as well as one of the past two years.

795 1995. *The Dark Garden.* Margaret Buffie. Kids Can Press, 1995.
796 1996. *Tiktala.* Margaret Shaw-MacKinnon. *Illustrator:* Laszlo Gal. Stoddart Kids, 1996.
797 1997. *By the Hanukkah Light.* Sheldon Oberman. *Illustrator:* Neil Waldman. McClelland & Stewart, 1997.
798 1998. *Ran Van: Magic Nation.* Diana Wieler. Groundwood Books, 1998.

799 1999. *Smarty Pants.* Colleen Sydor. Lobster Press, 1999.
800 1999. *Being with Henry.* Martha Brooks. Groundwood Books, 1999.

801 Mr. Christie Book Awards

SPONSOR: Christie, Brown and Company. CONTACT: Marlene Yustin. ADDRESS: 2150 Lakeshore Blvd. West, Toronto, Ontario, Canada M8V 1A3. PHONE: (416) 503-6050. ESTABLISHED: 1990. AWARD: Six awards of $7,500.00 CDN each. The award is given for excellence in the writing and illustrating of Canadian children's books. Initially awards were given in the categories of text and illustration for books written in French and in English, for a total of four awards. In 1992 the categories for text were divided into books for ages 8 and under and books for ages 9 to 14 to increase the number of awards to six. In 1994 the number of age groups was expanded to three (7 years and under; 8–11 years; and 12 years & up). In addition, it was decided that books should be judged on their content of text and illustration combined, i.e. Best Children's Book for each age group in each official language. Eligible books are those published in the previous calendar year written and/or illustrated by a Canadian.

802 1990. *What Do the Fairies Do with All These Teeth? Original Title:* Mais que font les fées avec toutes ces dents. *Illustrator:* Phillippe Béha. Editions du Raton-Laveur, 1989. *Category:* illustration.
803 1990. *The Sky Is Falling.* Kit Pearson. Penguin, 1989. *Category:* text.
804 1990. *Original Title:* Rosalie s'en va-t-elle en guerre. Ginette Anfousse. Éditions la courte échelle, 1989. *Category:* text.
805 1990. *The Name of the Tree.* Celia Barker Lottridge. *Illustrator:* Ian Wallace. Groundwood, 1989. *Category:* illustration.
806 1991. *Zamboni. Original Title:* Zamboni. François Gravel, 1990. *Category:* text.
807 1991. *The Story of Little Quack.* Katy MacDonald Denton. *Illustrator:* Katy MacDonald Denton, 1990. *Category:* illustration.
808 1991. *Uncle Henri's Dinner Guests. Original Title:* Les fantaisies de l'oncle Henri. Benedicte Froissart. *Illustrator:* Pierre Pratt. Annick, 1990. *Category:* illustration.
809 1991. *The Covered Bridge.* Brian Doyle. Groundwood, 1990. *Category:* text.
810 1992. *There Were Monkeys in My Kitchen!* Sheree Fitch. Doubleday, 1992. *Category:* ages 8 and under (text).
811 1992. *The Story of Canada.* Janet Lunn, Christopher Moore. *Illustrator:* Alan Daniel. Lester Publishing, 1992. *Category:* ages 9–14 (text).
812 1992. *A Prairie Alphabet.* Joanne Bannatyne-Cugnet. *Illustrator:* Yvette Moore. Tundra, 1992. *Category:* illustration.
813 1993. *A Little Tiger in the Chinese Night.* Song Nan Zhang. Tundra, 1993. *Category:* ages 8–11.

814 1993. *Brewster Rooster.* Berny Lucas. *Illustrator:* Russ Willms. Kids Can Press, 1993. *Category:* ages 7 and under.

815 1993. *Last Leaf First Snowfall to Fall.* Leo Yerxa. *Illustrator:* Leo Yerxa. Groundwood, 1993. *Category:* ages 8–11.

816 1993. *RanVan the Defender.* Diana Wieler. Groundwood, 1993. *Category:* ages 12 and over.

817 1994. *A Pioneer Story: The Daily Life of a Canadian Family in 1840.* Barbara Greenwood. *Illustrator:* Heather Collins. Kids Can Press, 1994. *Category:* ages 8–11.

818 1994. *Thor.* W.D. Valgardson. *Illustrator:* Ange Zhang. Groundwood, 1994. *Category:* ages 7 and under.

819 1994. *Out of the Blue.* Sarah Ellis. Douglas & McIntyre, 1994. *Category:* ages 12 and over.

820 1994. *My Dog Is an Elephant. Original Title:* Mon chien est un éléphant. Rémy Simard. *Illustrator:* Pierre Pratt. Annick, 1994. *Category:* ages 7 and under.

821 1995. *The Dream Carvers.* Joan Clark. Viking, 1995. *Category:* ages 12 and over.

822 1995. *How Smudge Came.* Nan Gregory. *Illustrator:* Ron Lightburn. Red Deer College, 1995. *Category:* ages 7 and under.

823 1995. *Jacob Two-Two's First Spy Case.* Mordecai Richler. *Illustrator:* Norman Eyolfson. McClelland & Stewart, 1995. *Category:* ages 8–11.

824 1996. *Discovering the Iceman: What Was It Like to Find a 5,300 Year Old Mummy?* Shelley Tanaka. *Illustrator:* Laurie McGaw. Scholastic, 1997. *Category:* ages 8–11.

825 1996. *The Fabulous Song.* Don Gillmor. *Illustrator:* Marie-Louise Gay. Stoddart, 1996. *Category:* ages 7 and under.

826 1996. *Uncle Ronald.* Brian Doyle. Groundwood, 1996. *Category:* ages 12 and over.

827 1997. *Biscuits in the Cupboard.* Barbara Nichol. *Illustrator:* Philippa Béha. Stoddart, 1997. *Category:* ages 7 and under.

828 1997. *Silverwing.* Kenneth Oppel. HarperCollins, 1997. *Category:* ages 12+.

829 1997. *The House of Wooden Santas.* Kevin Major, *Illustrator:* Imelda George. Ned Pratt. Red Deer College Press, 1997. *Category:* ages 8–11.

830 1997. *Jean Baptiste, coureur des bois. Original Title:* Jean Baptiste, coureur des bois. Francis Back Davidts.

831 1997. *Hair of Snake, Teeth of Spider. Original Title:* Poil de serpent, dent d'araignée. Danielle Marcotte. *Illustrator:* Stéphane Poulin. Les 400 Coups, 1996. *Level:* ages 7 and under.

832 1998. *Fog Cat.* Marilyn Helmer. *Illustrator:* Paul Mombourquette. Kids Can Press, 1998. *Category:* ages 7 and under.

833 1998. *The Nose from Jupiter.* Richard Scrimger. Tundra, 1998. *Category:* ages 8–11.

834 1998. *Zack.* William Bell. Doubleday, 1998. *Category:* ages 12 and over.

835 1999. *Fog Cat.* Marilyn Helmer. *Illustrator:* Paul Mombourquette. Kids Can Press, 1998. *Category:* English 7 years & younger.

836 1999. *The Nose From Jupiter.* Richard Scrimger. Tundra Books, 1998. *Category:* English 8–11 years.

837 1999. *Zack.* William Bell. Doubleday Canada, 1998. *Category:* English 12 years & up.

838 2000. *Sunwing.* Kenneth Oppel. HarperCollins Publishers, 1999. *Category:* English 8–11 years.

839 2000. *Time Flies. Original Title:* Le temps s'enfuit. Stanley Pean. La courte échelle, 1999. *Category:* French 12 years & up.

840 2000. *The Black Eyes. Original Title:* Les yeux noirs. Gilles Tibo, Jean Berneche. *Illustrator:* Gilles Tibo. Soulieres Editeur, 1999. *Category:* French 8–11 years.

841 2000. *Stella Starfish. Original Title:* Stella étoile de la mer. Marie-Louise Gay. *Illustrator:* Marie-Louise Gay. Dominique et compagnie/Héritage, 1999. *Category:* French 7 years & younger.

842 2000. *Claire's Gift.* Maxine Trottier. *Illustrator:* Rajka Kupesic. North Winds Press, 1999. *Category:* English 7 years & younger.

843 2000. *Being with Henry.* Martha Brooks. Groundwood Books, 1999. *Category:* English 12 years & up.

844 Norma Fleck Award

SPONSOR: The Canadian Children's Book Centre. ADDRESS: 35 Spadina Road, Toronto, Ontario, Canada M5R 2S9. PHONE: (416) 975-0010. ESTABLISHED: 1999. AWARD: $10,000 CDN. The award is to be presented annually to an author and illustrator of Canadian non-fiction for children.

845 1999. *By Truck to the North: My Winter Adventure.* Andy Turnball. *Illustrator:* Debora Pearson. Annick Press, 1999.

846 Ontario Red Maple Award

SPONSOR: Ontario Library Association. ADDRESS: 100 Lombard St., Ste. 303, Toronto, Ontario, Canada M5C 1M3. PHONE: (416) 363-3388. ESTABLISHED: 1998. The annual award is given for a fiction book, written by a Canadian within the last two years for the Grade Level 7–8.

847 1998. *After the War.* Carol Matas. Scholastic, 1996.

848 1999. *Janey's Girl.* Gayle Friesen. Kids Can Press, 1998.

849 2000. *What They Don't Know.* Anita Horrocks. Stoddart Kids, 1998.

850 Palme Livromagie de l'Imprimerie Gagné

SPONSOR: Communication-Jeunesse. ADDRESS: 4388, rue Saint-Denis, bureau 305, Montreal, Quebec, Canada H2J 2L1. PHONE: (514) 286-6020. The award is given for the best book in three categories: ages 6–9, 9–12 and over 12 years.

851 1993. *Sophie Counts. Original Title:* Sophie lance et compte. Louise Leblanc. *Illustrator:* Marie-Louise Gay. Les éditions la courte échelle, 1991. *Category:* 9–12 years.

852 1993. *The Cinema with Dad. Original Title:* Au cinéma avec papa. Dominique Jolin. *Illustrator:* Dominique Jolin. Éditions du Raton Laveur, 1991. *Category:* 6–9 years.

853 1993. *Original Title:* Sauve qui peut l'amour. Marie-Francine Hébert. Les éditions la courte échelle, 1992. *Category:* 12+ years.

854 1994. *Why Cows Have Spots? Original Title:* Pourquoi les vaches ont des taches? Geneviève Lemieux. *Illustrator:* Julie Garneau. Éditions du Raton Laveur, 1993. *Category:* 6–9 years.

855 1994. *Original Title:* Toto la brute. Dominique Demers. *Illustrator:* Philippe Béha. Les éditions la courte échelle, 1992. *Category:* 9–12 years.

856 1994. *The Evergreens Will Never Die. Original Title:* Les grands sapins ne meurent pas. Dominique Demers. Québec Amérique, 1993. *Category:* 12+ years.

857 1995. *The White Light. Original Title:* La lumière blanche. Anique Poitras. Québec Amérique, 1994. *Category:* 12+ years.

858 1995. *They Dance in the Storm. Original Title:* Ils dansent dans la tempête. Dominique Demers. Québec Amérique, 1994. *Category:* 12+ years.

859 1995. *The Park with the Magic Spells. Original Title:* Le parc aux sortilèges. Denis Côté. *Illustrator:* Stéphane Poulin. Les éditions la courte échelle, 1994. *Category:* 9–12 years.

860 1995. *Original Title:* Qu'est-ce que vous faites là? Dominique Jolin. *Illustrator:* Dominique Jolin. Éditions du Raton Laveur, 1994. *Category:* 6–9 years.

861 1996. *An Extra Teacher. Original Title:* Un prof extra. Dorothée Roy. *Illustrator:* Dominique Jolin. Éditions du Raton Laveur, 1994. *Category:* 6–9 years.

862 1996. *Second Life. Original Title:* La deuxième vie. Anique Poitras. Québec Amérique, 1996. *Category:* 12+ years.

863 1996. *The New Mistress. Original Title:* La nouvelle maîtresse. Dominique Demers. Les éditions la courte échelle, 1994. *Category:* 9–12 years.

864 1997. *Original Title:* Bi Bop et que ça saute. Raymond Parent. Mille-Illes, 1996. *Category:* 9–12 years.

865 1997. *Long Silence. Original Title:* Le long silence. Sylvie Desrosiers. Les éditions la courte échelle, 1996. *Category:* 12+ years.

866 1997. *Cruel Cruellina. Original Title:* Cruelle Cruellina. Carole Tremblay. *Illustrator:* Dominique Jolin. Les 400 coups, 1994. *Category:* 6–9 years.

867 1998. *Stephanie's Ponytail. Original Title:* Les fantaisies d'Adèle. Robert Munsch. *Illustrator:* Michael Martchenko. Courte échelle, 1997. *Category:* 6–9 years.

868 1998. *The Match of Stars. Original Title:* Le match des étoiles. François Gravel. Québec Amérique, 1996. *Category:* 9–12 years.

869 1998. *Song for Frederic. Original Title:* Chanson pour Frédéric. Tania Boulet. Québec Amérique, 1996. *Category:* 12+ years.

870 Prix 12/17 Brive

SPONSOR: Salon du livre de Montréal. ADDRESS: 480 St. Laurent, Montreal, Quebec, Canada H2Y 3Y7. PHONE: (514) 397-4879. ESTABLISHED: 1991. The prize is given to two writers, one from Quebec and one from France, for a book for children ages 12 to 17 years.

871 1991. Denis Côté, Claude Gutman.

872 1992. Daniel Sernine, Yves Heurté.

873 1993. Michèle Marineau, Jean-Paul Nozière.

874 1994. Raymond Plante, Élie-Georges Berreby.

875 1995. Jean Lemieux, Hubert Mingarelli.

876 1996. Sylvie Desrosiers, Alain Korkos.

877 1997. Jacques Lazure, Valérie Mathieu.

1998. No award given.

1999. No award given.

878 Prix Alvine Bélisle (Alvine Bélisle Prize)

SPONSOR: ASTED Association pour l'avancement des sciences et des techniques de la documentation. CONTACT: Micheline Patton. ADDRESS: 3414, avenue du Parc, bureau 202, Montreal, Quebec, Canada H2X 2H5. PHONE: (514) 281-5012. ESTABLISHED: 1975. AWARD: $500.00. The award is given to a Canadian author or illustrator for the best children's book published in Canada in the French language. The book must be published in the preceding year.

879 1990. *Rescue. Original Title:* Sauvetages. Sonia Ssarfati. Québec Amérique, 1989.

880 1992. *Full Crisis. Original Title:* Pleine crise. Claudine Farcy. Éditions Héritage, 1991.

881 1993. *The Road to Chlifa. Original Title:* La route de Chlifa. Michèle Marineau. Québec Amérique, 1992. Canada.

882 1994. *Klonk. Original Title:* Klonk, ou, Comment se débarasser des adolescents. Françoise Gravel. *Illustrator:* Pierre Pratt. Québec Amérique, 1993.

883 1995. *A Boat of the Mist. Original Title:* À propos d'un bateau à vapeur. Jean Belisle. *Illustrator:* Jean Belisle. Éditions Hurtubise, 1994.

884 1996. *The Sixth Stop. Original Title:* Le sixième arrêt. Hélène Vachon. *Illustrator:* Yayo. Editions Heritage, 1995.

885 1997. *The Dream Color of Orange. Original Title:* Le rêve couleur d'orange. Jacques Lazure. Québec Amérique, 1996.

886 1998. *The Bear Cub Who Wanted a Juliette. Original Title:* L'ourson qui voulait une Juliette. Jasmine Dubé. Les Éditions de la Courte échelle, 1997.

887 1999. *The Trap Line. Original Title:* La ligne de trappe. Michel Noël. Hurtubise HMH, 1998.

888 2000. *Edmond and Amandine. Original Title:* Edmond et Amandine. Christiane Duchesne. Éditions Dominique et compagnie, 1999.

889 Prix Cécile-Gagnon (Cécile-Gagnon Prize)

SPONSOR: Association des écrivains québécois pour la jeunesse. ADDRESS: 4282-C, rue Fullum, Montreal, Quebec, Canada H2H 2J5. PHONE: (514) 525-4565. ESTABLISHED: 1997. The prize is given for the first work of an author of children's literature.

890 1997. *Prudence, the Bold Princess. Original Title:* Prudence, la princesse téméraire. Michel Grenier. Héritage, 1997.

891 1998. *Free the Wolves. Original Title:* La liberté des loups. Richard Blaimert. Vents d'Ouest, 1998.

892 1999. *Blinking Charlotte. Original Title:* Une charlotte en papillote. Hélène Grégoire. *Illustrator:* Linda Lemelin. Éditions P. Tisseyre, 1999.

893 2000. *A Story Pulled by the Tail. Original Title:* Une histoire tirée par la queue. Élaine Turgeon. Éditions Québec Amérique Jeunesse, 2000.

894 Prix Littéraire le Droit (Le Droit Literature Prize)

SPONSOR: Association des auteures et auteurs de l'Ontario français et de l'Outaouais québécois. ADDRESS: 255, Chemin Montreal, bureau 202, Vanier, Ontario, Canada KIL 6C4. PHONE: (613) 744-0902. ESTABLISHED: 1985. The annual prize is given one year for a work of fiction and the following year for a work of non-fiction published in French. The author must live in Western Quebec or Ontario and must be published during the two calendar years preceding the prize.

895 1997. *Masks. Original Title:* Masques. Marie-Ève Lacasse. Vents d'Ouest, 1997.

896 1998. *Original Title:* Paris-Hanoi. Jean-Louis Grosmaire. Édition du Vermillon, 1998.

897 1999. *Vladimir and Company. Original Title:* Vladimir et compagnie. Claudine Bertrand-Paradis. Éditions Pierre Tisseyre, 1999.

898 Prix Littéraires Desjardins — Littérature jeunesse (Desjardin Literature Prize — formerly Prix Monique Corriveau)

SPONSOR: Salon du livre de Québec. ADDRESS: 480 St. Laurent, Montreal, Quebec, Canada H2Y 3Y7. PHONE: (514) 397-4879. Given for the best work of fiction for children by an author who has published one or two books only.

899 1994. *Marélie of the Sea. Original Title:* Marélie de la mer. Linda Brousseau. *Illustrator:* Leanne Franson. Éditions P. Tisseyre, 1993.

900 1995. *Tales of the Gray Cat. Original Title:* Contes du chat gris. Jean-Pierre Davidts. Éditions Boréal, 1994.

901 1996. *Original Title:* Le plus proche voisin. Hélène Vachon. Éditions Héritage, 1995.

1997. No award given.

1998. No award given.

902 Prix Monique Corriveau (Monique Corriveau Prize)

SPONSOR: see Prix littéraires Desjardins — Littérature jeunesse.

903 1992. *Original Title:* Drôle de moineau. Marie-Andrée Boucher-Mativat. Éditions Héritage, 1991.

904 1993. *Hens Teeth. Original Title:* Les dents de la poule. Raymond Plante. *Illustrator:* Pierre Pratt. Éditions Boréal, 1992.

905 Prix Québec/Wallonie-Bruxelles du Livre de la Jeunesse (Quebec Prize)

SPONSOR: Ministère des Affaires internationales, Direction générale de l'Europe. ADDRESS: 525, boulevard René-Lévesque Est, Quebec City, Quebec, Canada G1R 5R9. PHONE: (418) 649-2330. ESTABLISHED: 1992. AWARD: $2000 CDN. The prize is given annually and alternatively to an author or illustrator from Belgium or Quebec.

906 1992. *The Field Without Eyes. Original Title:* Le domaine des sans Yeux. Jacques Lazure. Québec Amérique, 1989. *Category:* Québec.

1993. No award given.

907 1994. *The Evergreens Will Never Die. Original Title:* Les grands sapins ne meurent pas. Dominique Demers. Québec Amérique, 1993. *Category:* Québec.

1995. No award given.

908 1996. *The Keeper of Horses. Original Title:* La bergère des chevaux. Christiane Duchesene. Québec Amérique, 1995. *Category:* Québec.

909 1997. *The Voyage From Oregon. Original Title:* Le voyage d'Orégon. Rascal. *Illustrator:* Louis Joos. Pastel, 1993. *Category:* Belgium.

910 1998. *Two Friends in the Night. Original Title:* Deux amis dans la nuit. Louise Leblanc. *Illustrator:* Philippe Brochard. La Courte échelle, 1996. *Category:* Québec.

911 1999. *Uncle Rene and Aunt Gilberte. Original Title:* Tonton René et Tante Gilberte. Caroline Grégoire. *Illustrator:* Caroline Grégoire. Pastel, 1999.

912 2000. *The Red Scarf. Original Title:* L'écharpe rouge. Anne Villeneuve. *Illustrator:* Anne Villeneuve. Les 400 coups, 1999.

913 R. Ross Annett Award for Children's Literature

SPONSOR: Writers Guild of Alberta. CONTACT: Miki Anderjevic. ADDRESS: 3rd Floor, Percy Page Centre, 11759 Groat Rd. N.W., Edmonton, Alberta, Canada T5J 0A8. PHONE: (403) 422-8174. ESTABLISHED: 1982. AWARD: $500.00 CDN and a leather-bound copy of their book. The award recognizes excellence in writing by an author who has been a resident of Alberta for at least twelve of the previous eighteen months.

914 1990. *Dawn Rider.* Jan Hudson, 1990.

915 1991. *Cat of Artimus Pride.* Hazel Hutchins. Firefly Books, 1991.

916 1992. *The Crystal Drop.* Monica Hughes. HarperCollins, 1992.

917 1994. *The McIntyre Liar.* David Bly. Tree Frog Press, 1993.

918 1995. *Mission Impossible.* Beth Goobie. Red Deer College Press, 1994.

919 1996. *Big Boy.* Tololwa Mollel. *Illustrator:* E.B. Lewis. Stoddart, 1995.

920 1997. *The Tuesday Cafe.* Don Trembath. Orca Books 1996.

921 1998. *The Prince of Tarn.* Hazel Hutchins. *Illustrator:* Ruth Ohi. Annick Press, 1997.

922 1999. *What They Don't Know.* Anita Horrocks. Stoddart, 1998.

923 2000. *Willa's New World.* Barbara Demers. Coteau Books, 1999.

924 Red Cedar Book Award

SPONSOR: Young Reader's Choice Awards Society of British Columbia. ADDRESS: P.O. Box 35023, Victoria, British Columbia, Canada V8T 5G2. PHONE: (250) 477-9398. ESTABLISHED: 1998. The annual award is given to one fiction and one non-fiction author. The book must be written by a Canadian citizen or landed immigrant who has lived in Canada for at least two years; published two calendar years before the nomination date; published by a recognized publisher; recognized by other reviewers of Canadian children's literature; recognized as being of general interest to students in grades 4 to 7.

925 1998. *Amy's Promise.* Bernice Thurman Hunter. Scholastic, 1995. *Category:* fiction.

926 1998. *In Flanders Fields: The Story of the Poem by John McCrae.* Linda Granfield. *Illustrator:* Janet Wilson. Stoddart, 1995. *Category:* non-fiction.

927 1999. *Anastasia's Album.* Hugh Brewster. Madison Press, 1996. *Category:* non-fiction.

928 1999. *Awake and Dreaming.* Kit Pearson. Viking, 1996. *Category:* fiction.

929 2000. *The Great Race.* Dave Bouchard. Raincoast Books, 1997. *Category:* non-fiction.

930 2000. *Silverwing.* Kenneth Oppel. HarperCollins, 1997. *Category:* fiction.

931 Ruth Schwartz Children's Book Award

SPONSOR: Ontario Arts Council. ADDRESS: 151 Bloor Street, 5th floor, Toronto Ontario, Canada M5S 1T6. PHONE: (416) 969-7403. ESTABLISHED: 1976. AWARD: $2,000.00 CDN for an author, $3,000.00 CDN shared between author and illustrator. The prize recognizes authors and illustrators who demonstrate artistic excellence in Canadian children's literature. The winning book must be published in Canada during the previous year and the author must be a Canadian citizen.

932 1990. *Bad Boy.* Diana Wieler. Groundwood, 1989.

933 1991. *Forbidden City.* William Bell, 1990.

934 1992. *Roses Sing on New Snow: A Delicious Tale.* Paul Yee. *Illustrator:* Harvey Chan. Groundwood, 1991.

935 1993. *Something From Nothing.* Phoebe Gilman. North Winds Press, 1992.

936 1994. *The Hunter's Moon.* O.R. Melling. HarperCollins, 1993. *Category:* young adult/middle reader.

937 1994. *Northern Lights: The Soccer Trails.* Michael Arvaarluk Kusugak. *Illustrator:* Vladyana Krykorka. Annick, 1993. *Category:* picture book.

938 1995. *A Pioneer Story: The Daily Life of a Canadian Family in 1840.* Barbara Greenwood. *Illustrator:* Heather Collins. Kids Can Press, 1994. *Category:* picture book.

939 1995. *Adam and Eve and Pinch Me.* Julie Johnson. Lester Publishing, 1994. *Category:* young adult/middle reader.

940 1996. *Out of the Dark.* Welwyn Wilton Katz. Groundwood, 1995. *Category:* young adult/middle reader.

941 1996. *The Killick: A Newfoundland Story.* Geoff Butler. *Illustrator:* Geoff Butler. Tundra Books, 1995. *Category:* picture book.

942 1997. *Awake and Dreaming.* Kit Pearson. Viking, 1996. *Category:* young adult/middle reader.

943 1997. *Ghost Train.* Paul Yee. *Illustrator:* Harvey Chan. Groundwood, 1996. *Category:* picture book.

944 1998. *Jeremiah Learns to Read.* Jo Ellen Bogart, Rick Jacaobson. *Illustrator:* Laura Fernández. North Winds Press, 1997. *Category:* picture book.

945 1998. *Bone Dance.* Martha Brooks. Groundwood, 1997. *Category:* young adult/middle reader.

946 1999. *Tsar of the Sea: A Russian Wonder Tale.* Celia Barker Lottridge. *Illustrator:* Harvey Chan. Groundwood, 1998. *Category:* picture book.

947 1999. *War of the Eagles.* Eric Walters. Orca Books, 1998. *Category:* young adult/middle reader.

948 2000. *Stella Star of the Sea.* Marie-Louise Gay. *Illustrator:* Marie-Louise Gay. Groundwood Books, 1999. *Category:* picture book.

949 2000. *Sunwing.* Kenneth Oppel. HarperCollins, 1999. *Category:* young adult/middle reader.

950 Sheila A. Egoff Children's Book Prize

SPONSOR: West Coast Book Prize Society. ADDRESS: 1033 Davie St., Ste. 700, Vancouver, British Columbia, Canada V6E 1M7. PHONE: (604) 687-2405. ESTABLISHED: 1987. AWARD: $2,000.00 CDN. The award is given annually to the best children's book published in the previous year written by a writer who has been resident in British Columbia (or the Yukon) for three of the previous five years, published anywhere in the world.

951 1990. *Tales From Gold Mountain.* Paul Yee. Groundwood, 1989.

952 1991. *I Heard My Mother Call My Name.* Nancy Hundal, 1990.

953 1992. *Siwiti: A Whale's Story.* Alexandra Morton. Orca Book Publishers, 1991.

954 1993. *My Name is Seepetza.* Shirley Sterling. Groundwood, 1992.

955 1994. *White Jade Tiger.* Julie Lawson. Beach Holme Publishing, 1993.

956 1995. *The Old Brown Suitcase: A Teenager's Story of War and Peace.* Lillian Boraks-Nemetz. Ben-Somon Publications, 1994.

957 1996. *How Smudge Came.* Nan Gregory. *Illustrator:* Ron Lightburn. Red Deer College Press, 1995.

958 1997. *Back to Beyond.* Sarah Ellis. Groundwood, 1996.

959 1998. *Wish Me Luck.* James Heneghan. Farrar Straus Giroux, 1997.

960 1999. *Driftwood Cove.* Sandra Lightburn. *Illustrator:* Ron Lightburn. Doubleday, 1998.

961 Silver Birch Award

SPONSOR: Ontario Library Association. CONTACT: Stephanie Parcher. ADDRESS: 100 Lombard St., Ste. 303, Toronto, Ontario, Canada M5C 1M3. PHONE: (416) 363-3388. ESTABLISHED: 1994. The award is given for recent Canadian children's fiction and non-fiction book.

962 1994. *Daniel's Story.* Carol Matas. Scholastic, 1993. *Category:* grades 4–6.

963 1995. *Polar, the Titanic Bear.* Laurie McGraw. *Illustrator:* Laurie McGraw. Little, Brown & Co., 1994. *Category:* grades 4–6.

964 1996. *Bring Up Beauty.* Sylvia McNicoll. Macmillan, 1994. *Category:* fiction.

965 1996. *Sho and the Demons of the Deep.* Annouchka Gravel Galouchko. *Illustrator:* Annouchka Gravel Galouchka. Annick, 1995. *Category:* non-fiction.

966 1997. *On Board the Titanic: What It was Like When the Great Liner Sank.* Shelley Tanaka. *Illustrator:* Ken Marschall. Scholastic, 1996. *Category:* non-fiction.

967 1997. *Stars.* Eric Walters. Stoddart, 1996. *Category:* fiction.

968 1998. *Anastasia's Album.* Hugh Brewster. Madison Press, 1996. *Category:* non-fiction.

969 1998. *Silverwing.* Kenneth Oppel. HarperCollins, 1997. *Category:* fiction.

970 1999. *Funny You Should Ask.* Marg Meikle. *Illustrator:* Tina Holdcroft. Scholastic, 1998. *Category:* non-fiction.

971 1999. *Trapped in Ice.* Eric Walters. Penguin, 1997. *Category:* fiction.

972 Vicky Metcalfe Award

SPONSOR: Canadian Authors Association. ADDRESS: P.O. Box 419, 320 South Shores Road, Campbellford, Ontario, Canada K0L 1L0. PHONE: (705) 653-0323. ESTABLISHED: 1963. AWARD: $10,000.00 CDN. The annual award is given to a Canadian writer (citizen or landed immigrant) who has produced a body of work (more than three books) with appeal for children aged 7 to 17.

973 1990. Bernice Thurman Hunter.

974 1991. Brian Doyle.

975 1992. Kevin Major.

976 1993. Phoebe Gilman.

977 1994. Welwyn Wilton Katz.

978 1995. Sarah Ellis.

979 1996. Margaret Buffie.

980 1997. Tim Wynne-Jones.

981 1998. Kit Pearson.

982 1999. Joan Clark.

983 2000. Sheree Fitch.

984 Vicky Metcalfe Short Story Award

SPONSOR: Canadian Authors Association. ADDRESS: P.O. Box 419, Campbellford, Ontario, Canada K0L 1L0. PHONE: (705) 653-0323. ESTABLISHED: 1979. AWARD: $3,000.00 CDN. The annual award is given to a Canadian writer (citizen or landed immigrant) of the best children's short story published in Canada in the previous year.

985 1990. *Choose Your Grandmother.* Patricia G. Armstrong. 1989.
1991. No award given.

986 1992. *Adventure on Thunder Island.* Edna King, John Wheeler. Lorimer, 1991.

987 1993. *The Rink.* Rod McIntyre. Thisledown Press, 1992.

988 1994. *The Hope Bakery.* Tim Wynne-Jones. Groundwood, 1993.
1995. No award given.

989 1996. *The Seasons are Horses.* Bernice Friesen. Thistledown Press, 1995.
1997. No award given.

990 1998. *Chicken Lady.* W.D. Valgardson. Groundwood, 1997.

991 1999. *Leaving the Iron Lung.* Anne Carter. PrairieFire. vol. 19 no. 3, 1998.

992 2000. *Sun Dogs.* Rick Book. Red Deer Press, 1999.

COLOMBIA

993 Premio ENKA (ENKA Prize)

SPONSOR: Enka de Colombia S.A. ADDRESS: Edificio Camacol Carrera 63 no. 49 A-31 A.A. 5233, Medellin, Colombia. PHONE: 57 (4) 260 0900. ESTABLISHED: 1976. The prize is given every 3 years to a writer from Colombia, Venezuela, Ecuador, Peru, Bolivia and Panama with the promise of publication by that organization.

994 1992. *Carabela, Skull. Original Title:* Carabela, Calavera. Luis Carlos Neves.

995 1995. *Aymará Dream. Original Title:* Sueño Aymará. Eduardo León Zamora.

996 1998. *Michael's Pen: An Adventure in the Andres. Original Title:* La Pluma de Miguel: Una aventura en Los Andes. Isabel De Mesa de Inchauste.

997 Premio Latinoamericano de Literatura Infantil y Juvenil Norma-Fundalectura (Latin American Prize for Children's and Juvenile Literature)

SPONSOR: Fundación para el Fomento de la Lectura, Fundalectura y por la Editorial Norma de Colombia. CONTACT: Silvia Castrillón. ADDRESS: Av Cll 40 Nº

16-46, Bogotá, Colombia. PHONE: (571) 3201511. ESTABLISHED: 1995. AWARD: A diploma, a sum of money, and the book is published by Editorial Norma de Colombia. The author must be a citizen of a Latin America country. The manuscript must be unpublished.

998 1996. *As Far As I Want. Original Title:* Lejos como mi querer. Marina Colasanti.

999 1996. *The Only Thing in the World. Original Title:* Lo único del mundo. Ricardo Mariño.

1000 1997. *The Prince of Snow White. Original Title:* El príncipe de Blancanieves. Juan Antonio Ramos.

1001 1998. *The Empire of the Five Moons. Original Title:* El imperio de las cinco lunas. Celso Román.

1002 1999. *Black Horseman. Original Title:* Caballero Negro. Lilia Lardone.

1003 2000. *Blade. Original Title:* Cuchilla. Evelio José Rosero.

COSTA RICA

1004 Premio Carmen Lyra (Carmen Lyra Prize)

SPONSOR: Editoral Costa Rica. ADDRESS: Guadalupe de Goicoechea, Apdo 10010-1000, San José, Costa Rica. PHONE: (506) 253-5354. ESTABLISHED: 1974. AWARD: ¢60.000 and a certificate. The award is given irregularly to Costa Ricans or to a five-year resident of Costa Rica for stories and poetry for children. Stories must be more than 50 pages in length and poetry more than 500 lines.

1005 1990. *Original Title:* Pedro y su teatrino maravilloso. Carlos Rubio.

1991. No award given.

1992. No award given.

1993. No award given.

1994. No award given.

1995. No award given.

1996. No award given.

1006 1997. *Original Title:* Cuentos con alas y luz. Ana Cecilia Brenes Herrera.

1007 1998. *Wings and Light. Original Title:* El cuento Alas y luz. Annie Brenes. Editoral Costa Rica.

1008 1999. *Moon Song for Duende. Original Title:* Canto de lunas para un duende. Máinor Arias. Editoral Costa Rica.

1009 Premio Joven Creación (Young Creation Prize)

SPONSOR: Editoral Costa Rica. ADDRESS: Guadalupe de Goicoechea, Apdo 10010-1000, San José, Costa Rica. PHONE: (506) 253-5354. ESTABLISHED: 1976. AWARD: ¢25.000.oo. The annual award is given to Costa Ricans, or to a five-year resident of Costa Rica, under 30 years of age, for stories, novels, and poetry written for children.

1010 1990. *Original Title:* A medida que nos vamos conociendo. Alí Víquez.

1011 1991. *Original Title:* El Libro del Minotauro. Johnny Mora Delgado.

1992. No award given.

1993. No award given.

1994. No award given.

1012 1995. *Original Title:* El Dios de un Poeta. Eduardo García Rodríguez.

1013 1995. *Original Title:* Una Sombra en el Hielo. Laura Quijano.

1014 1996. *Original Title:* Juegos Infinitos. Heriberto Rodríguez.

1015 1997. *Original Title:* Tatuaje Giratorio. Alejandra Castro Bonilla. Editoral Costa Rica.

1016 1998. *Original Title:* Tatuaje Giratorio. Alejandra Castro Bonilla.

1999. No award given.

CUBA

1017 Premio David de Literatura Infantil (David Award)

SPONSOR: La Asociación de Escritores de la UNEAC. ADDRESS: 17 esquina a H, El Vedado, Ciudad de La, Habana, Cuba. PHONE: 32-4152. AWARD: 1000 pesos. The award is given to an unpublished Cuban writer living in Cuba. A current list of awards was unavailable at the time of publication.

1018 1995. *Looking for a Lost Time. Original Title:* En busca de un tiempo perdido. Ariel Ribeaux Diago. *Illustrator:* Sandro de la Rosa. Edic. Unión 1996.

1019 Premio Ismaelillo (Ismaelillo Prize)

SPONSOR: La Unión de Escritores y Artistas de Cuba. ADDRESS: calle 17 no. 351 Vedado, Havana, Cuba. PHONE: (537) 553112. ESTABLISHED: 1962. AWARD: $1000.00. The annual award is given to works of poetry, novels, plays or stories written for children and young adults by Cuban writers. A complete list of winners was unavailable at the time of publication.

1020 1993. *My Bicycle Is a Fairy and Other Secrets of That Sort. Original Title:* Mi bicicleta es un hada y otros secretos por el estilo. Antonio Orlando Rodríguez.

1021 1994. *The Dream. Original Title:* El Sueño. Antonio Orlando Rodríguez. Artemis-Edinter.

1022 1995. *Original Title:* Un elefante en la cristalería. Antonio Orlando Rodríguez. *Illustrator:* Liisa Helve. Edilux, 1995.

1023 1997. *Images. Original Title:* Imágenes. Aramís Quintero. Ediciones UNION.

1024 1997. *The Age of Gold. Original Title:* El oro de la edad. Ariel Ribeaux Diago. Ediciones UNION.

1025 1998. *Little School of Horrors. Original Title:* Escuelita de los horrores. Pérez Díaz.

1026 1998. *Original Title:* Brujas, hechizos y otros disparates. Nelson Simón González. Ed. Betania, 2000.

1027 Premios Edad de Oro (Golden Age Awards)

SPONSOR: Dirección de Literatura, Instituto Cubano del Libro. ADDRESS: Palacio del Segundo Cabo, O'Reilly No. 4, Ciudad de La, Habana, Cuba 10100. ESTABLISHED: 1971. AWARD: $500.00. The award is given in the following categories: stories, poetry, novels for children and others to authors who live in Cuba. A complete list of winners was unavailable at the time of publication.

1028 1990. *Dreams. Original Title:* Los sueños. Aramís Quintero. *Illustrator:* Rita Gutierrez Varela. Edit. Gente Nueva, 1994.

1029 1994. *Dreams. Original Title:* Los sueños. Aramís Quintero. Gente Nueva.

1030 1998. *Original Title:* Brujas, hechizos y otros disparates. Nelson Simón González. Ed. Betania, 2000.

1031 2000. *Original Title:* Poemas, tantanes y adivinanzas dificilísimas. Andrés Manuel Pi Andreu. Gente Nueva.

1032 Premios Pinos Nuevos (New Pines Prizes)

SPONSOR: La Dirección de Literatura del Instituto Cubano del Libro. ADDRESS: Instituto Cubano del Libro, Palacio del Segundo Cabo, Ciudad de La, Habana, Cuba 10100. PHONE: 32-4152. The award winning story is published in a collection each year. A current list of awards was unavailable at the time of publication.

1033 1993. *Dear Diary. Original Title:* Querido diario. Iliana Prieto. *Illustrator:* David Rodríguez Hernandez. Edic. Unión, 1994.

1034 1993. *The Soul of a Cloud. Original Title:* El alma en una nube. Emma Artiles. *Illustrator:* Alejandro Campos Garcia. Edit. Gente Nueva, 1994.

1035 1995. *Do the Fairies Retire? Original Title:* Se jubilan las hadas? Enrique Perez Diaz. *Illustrator:* Daniel Zorrilla. Edit. Gente Nueva, 1996.

1036 1995. *The Horrible Story Without Remedy. Original Title:* Este libro horroroso y sin remedio. Alberto Yanez. *Illustrator:* Raul Castillo. Edit. Gente Nueva, 1996.

1037 1995. *The Shadows Walk Alone. Original Title:* Las sombras andan solas. Olga Marta Perez. *Illustrator:* Ariel Baro. Edit. Gente Nueva, 1996.

2000. No awards given.

1038 Rosa Blanca (White Rose Award)

SPONSOR: La Unión de Escritores y Artistas de Cuba, and the Cuban Section of IBBY. CONTACT: Enrique Perez Diaz. ADDRESS: calle 17 no. 351 Vedado, Havana, Cuba. PHONE: (537) 553112. ESTABLISHED: 1985. AWARD: Diploma and art work. The annual award is given to writers and illustrators for an individual work or their entire body of work in children's literature. In 1993, the award was opened to Cuban writers and illustrators who published their works outside the country.

1039 1994. *The Soul of a Cloud. Original Title:* El alma en una nube. Emma Artiles. *Illustrator:* Alejandro Campos Garcia. Edit. Gente Nueva, 1994. *Category:* text/illustration.

1040 1994. *Original Title:* Tres lechuzas en un cuento. Dora Alonso. *Illustrator:* Osvaldo Chong. Edit. Gente Nueva.

1041 1994. *Dreams. Original Title:* Los sueños. Aramís Quintero. *Illustrator:* Rita Gutierrez Varela. Edit. Gente Nueva, 1994.

1042 1994. *Someone is Watching Us. Original Title:* Alguien nos está observando. Joaquín Borges Triana. *Illustrator:* Oscar F. Chuyn. Edit. Gente Nueva.

1043 1994. *The Old One that Flies. Original Title:* La vieja que vuela. Froilán Escobar. *Illustrator:* Bladimir González Linares. Edit. Gente Nueva.

1044 1994. *Gold Rain. Original Title:* Lluvia de oro. Jose R. Marco. *Illustrator:* Ubaldo Ceballos. Edit. Gente Nueva.

1045 1994. *Dear Diary. Original Title:* Querido diario. Iliana Prieto. *Illustrator:* David Rodríguez Hernandez. Edic. Unión, 1994. *Category:* text/illustration.

1046 1994. *Songs of the Country. Original Title:* Cantos de camino. Luis Caissés Sánchez. Ed. Holguin.

1047 1994. *The Country of a Thousand Umbrellas. Original Title:* El pais de los mil paraguas. Carlo Calcines. *Illustrator:* Osmani Simanca, Arístides Hernández. Edit. Gente Nueva.

1048 1994. *My Friend John. Original Title:* Mi amigo Juan. Alberto Domingo González. *Illustrator:* Juan Carlos Reloba. Edit. Gente Nueva.

1049 1994. *Secrets of the Palace. Original Title:* Secretos de palacio. Yanitzia Canetti. *Illustrator:* Raquel Díaz. Edit. Gente Nueva.

1050 1994. *Offering Link. Original Title:* Ofrenda linca. Lorenzo Suárez Crespo. *Illustrator:* David Rodríguez Hernandez. Edit. Gente Nueva.

1051 1995. *Tatari, the Gang and I. Original Title:* Tatari, la pandilla y yo. Magaly Sánchez. Edit. Gente Nueva. *Category:* text.

1052 1995. *Moon. Original Title:* Lunar. Omar Felipe Mauri. *Illustrator:* Vicente Rodríguez Bonachea. Ed. Universidad de La Habana. *Category:* illustration.

1053 1995. *The Night. Original Title:* La Noche. Excilia Saldaña. Edit. Gente Nueva. *Category:* text.

1054 1995. *The Stories of the Magician. Original Title:* Los cuentos del mago y el mago del los cuentos. Joel Franz Rossell. Ed. de la Torre. *Category:* text.

1055 1995. *Maria Virginia is on Vacation. Original Title:* Maria Virginia está de vacaciones. Gumersindo Pacheco. *Illustrator:* Nelson Dominguez. Casa de las Americas, 1994.

1056 1995. *Ponolani. Original Title:* Ponolani. Dora Alonso. *Illustrator:* Maria Teresa Sánchez. Edit. Gente Nueva. *Category:* text/illustration.

1057 1995. *Letters of Julio Orlando. Original Title:* Cartas a Julio Orlando. Dulce Maria Loynaz. Edit. Gente Nueva. *Category:* text.

1058 1995. *By Then. Original Title:* Para entonces. Juana Barrio, Carlos Pio Urbach. *Illustrator:* Olga Marta Perez. Edit. Gente Nueva. *Category:* illustration.

1059 1995. *Things of the Heart. Original Title:* Los cosas del corazón. Roberto Fernandez Retamar. *Illustrator:* Roberto Fabelo. Edit. Gente Nueva. *Category:* illustration.

1060 1996. *Dreams and Stories of the Bad Little Girl. Original Title:* Sueños y cuentos de la niña mala. Julio M. Llanes. Ed. Luminaria, Sancti Spiritus. *Category:* text.

1061 1996. *The Small Prodigies. Original Title:* Los pequeños prodigios. Norge Espinosa. *Illustrator:* Osvaldo Chong. Edit. Gente Nueva. *Category:* illustration.

1062 1996. *Do the Fairies Retire? Original Title:* Se jubilan las hadas? Enrique Pérez Díaz. *Illustrator:* Daniel Zorrilla. Edit. Gente Nueva, 1996. *Category:* text.

1063 1996. *Ship of Dreams. Original Title:* Barco de sueños. José Manuel Espino. *Illustrator:* Rosa Salgado. Edic. Unión, 1996. *Category:* text.

1064 1996. *The Adventures of Rose. Original Title:* Las aventuras de Rosa se los vientos y Perico el de los palotes. Joel Fanz Rossell. Ed. Grijalbo-Mondadori. *Category:* text.

1065 1996. *Foolish Tales. Original Title:* Los cuentos bobos. Raul Martinez. *Illustrator:* Raul Martinez. Ed. Abril, 1996. *Category:* text.

1066 1997. *The Postman Called Three Times. Original Title:* El cartero llama tres veces. José Manuel Espino. *Illustrator:* Rubén Iglesias. Edic. Unión. *Category:* text/illustration.

1067 1997. *Searching for a Time Past. Original Title:* En busca de un tiempo perdido. Ariel Ribeaux Diago. *Illustrator:* Sandro de la Rosa. Edic. Unión, 1996. *Category:* text/illustration.

1068 1997. *It Flies, Ertico, It Flies. Original Title:* Vuela, Ertico, Vuela. Joel Fanz Rossell. *Illustrator:* Ajubel. Ed. SM, Madrid. *Category:* text/illustration.

1069 1997. *Advice of the Grandfather Rabbit. Original Title:* Consejos del Abuelo Conejo. Jorge Timossi. *Illustrator:* Eduardo Muñoz Bachs. Edit. Gente Nueva. *Category:* text/illustration.

1070 1997. *Through the Eyes. Original Title:* A través de los ojos. Ernesto Alshuler. Edit. Gente Nueva. *Category:* text.

1071 1997. *Platero and I. Original Title:* Platero y yo. Juan Ramón Jiménez. *Illustrator:* Esteban Llorach Ramos. Edit. Gente Nueva. *Category:* text.

1072 1997. *The Fisherman of the Moon. Original Title:* El pescador de la luna. José Antonio Gutierrez. *Illustrator:* David Rodríguez. Edit. Gente Nue. *Category:* illustration.

1073 1997. *Somebody Flock the Stars. Original Title:* Alguien borra las estrellas. Omar Felipe Mauri Sierra. Edit. Gente Nueva. *Category:* text.

1074 1997. *The Vegetarian Lion. Original Title:* El león vegetaliano. Felipe Oliva Alices. *Illustrator:* Perla González Marinello. Edic. Unión. *Category:* text/illustration.

1075 1998. *Anthology of a Cuban Child. Original Title:* Antologia de la narrativa infantil cubana. Antonio Orlando Rodríguez. Edit. Gente Nueva. *Category:* text.

1076 1998. *White Magic. Original Title:* Magica blanca. José Manuel Espino. Edic. Unión. *Category:* text.

1077 1998. *That Sailor Am I. Original Title:* Que marinéro soy yo. Rafael Alberti. Edit. Gente Nueva. *Category:* text.

1078 1998. *Ismaelillo. Original Title:* Ismaelillo. José Martí. Edit. Abril. *Category:* text.

1079 1998. *The Book of Anton Pirulero. Original Title:* El libro de Antón Pirulero. Antonio Orlando Rodríguez, Sergio Andricain. Edit. Panamericana. *Category:* text.

1080 1998. *My Bicycle is a Fairy and Other Secrets of That Sort. Original Title:* Mi bicicleta es un hada y otros secretos por el estilo. Antonio Orlando Rodríguez. Ed. Rondalera. *Category:* text.

1081 1998. *Invented Friend. Original Title:* Inventarse un amigo. Enrique Pérez Díaz. Edit. Gente Nueva. *Category:* text.

1082 1998. *Original Title:* Mucho cuento! Enrique Pérez Díaz. *Illustrator:* Miriam González Giménez. Edic. Unión. *Category:* text/illustration.

1083 1998. *The Book of the Oregano. Original Title:* El libro del orégano. Esther Suárez Durán. Edic. Unión. *Category:* text.

1084 1998. *Images. Original Title:* Imágenes. Aramís Quintero. *Illustrator:* Miriam González Giménez. Edic. Unión. *Category:* text/illustration.

1085 1998. *The Picture Princess and the Dragon King. Original Title:* La princesa del retrato y el Dragon – Rey. Iliana Prieto. Ed. Norma-Colombia. *Category:* text.

1086 1998. *Original Title:* Como el zunzun era su corazón. Mercedes Santos Moray. *Illustrator:* Rosa Salgado Hurtado. *Category:* text/illustration.

1087 1998. *My Friend Mozart. Original Title:* Mi amigo Mozart. Esther Suárez Durán. Edit. Gente Nueva. *Category:* text.

1088 1999. *Oh Time. Original Title:* Oh, tiempo! Aramís Quintero. *Illustrator:* Bladimir González Linares. Edit. Gente Nueva. *Category:* text/illustration.

1089 1999. *Labyrinth. Original Title:* Laberinto. José Manuel Espino. Edit. Gente Nueva. *Category:* text.

1090 1999. *Musical Stories. Original Title:* Cuentos musicales. Olga de Blanck. *Illustrator:* Rita Gutierrez Varela. Edit. Gente Nueva. *Category:* text/illustration.

1091 1999. *Maisa. Original Title:* Maisa. Nersys Felipe. Edit. Gente Nueva. *Category:* text.

1092 1999. *Men at Play. Original Title:* Hombres en juego. Edgar Montiel. Edit. Gente Nueva. *Category:* text.

1093 1999. *Ikebana. Original Title:* Ikebana. Emma Artiles. Edit. Gente Nueva. *Category:* text.

1094 1999. *House in the Clouds. Original Title:* Casa en las nubes. Ivette Vian. *Illustrator:* Roberto Fabelo. Edic. Unión. *Category:* text/illustration.

1095 1999. *Then Gentleman, This is a Circus. Original Title:* Pues señor, este era una circo. Antonio Orlando Rodríguez. *Illustrator:* Manuel Tomás González. Edit. Gente Nueva. *Category:* illustration.

1096 1999. *In the Coffer of a Pirate. Original Title:* En el cofre de un pirata. Nelson Simón. Edic. Loynaz. *Category:* text.

1097 1999. *Gold in the Hill. Original Title:* Oro en la loma. Samuel Feijoo. Edit. Gente Nueva. *Category:* text.

1098 1999. *The Lines Speak and Play. Original Title:* Las lineas hablan y juegan. Oscar Morriña. Edit. Gente Nueva. *Category:* text.

1099 1999. *That Boy of the Golden Age. Original Title:* Ese niño de La Edad de Oro. José Antonio Gutierrez. Edit. Gente Nueva. *Category:* text.

1100 1999. *Stories Without Age. Original Title:* Cuentos sin edad. Enríque Pérez Díaz. Edit. Gente Nueva. *Category:* text.

1101 1999. *Raul, Grandmother and Spirit. Original Title:* Raul, se abuela y los espiritus. Luis Cabrera Delgado. Edit. Gente Nueva. *Category:* text.

1102 1999. *A Possible Place. Original Title:* Un lugar posible. Olga Marta Pérez. *Illustrator:* Miriam González Giménez. Edic. Unión-Febilibro. *Category:* text/illustration.

1103 1999. *With the Children of Old Havana. Original Title:* Con los niños por la Habana Vieja. Rafaela Chacón Nardi. Edit. Gente Nueva. *Category:* text.

1104 1999. *Letters to the Sky. Original Title:* Cartas al cielo. Teresa Cardenas Angulo. *Illustrator:* Bladimir González Linares. Edit. Gente Nueva. *Category:* illustration.

1105 1999. *Dafnis and Cloe. Original Title:* Dafnis y Cloe. Lázaro Enríquez. *Illustrator:* Lázaro Enríquez. Edit. Gente Nueva. *Category:* illustration.

1106 1999. *Stories Not to Believe. Original Title:* Cuentos para no creer. Omar Felipe Mauri. Edit. Gente Nueva. *Category:* text.

1107 1999. *Just in Case. Original Title:* Por si las moscas. Julia Calzadilla. *Illustrator:* Miriam González Giménez. Edict. Unión. *Category:* text/illustration.

1108 1999. *The Age of Gold. Original Title:* El oro de la Edad. Ariel Ribeaux Diago. Edic. Unión. *Category:* text.

1109 1999. *Against Your Naked Chest. Original Title:* Contra tu pecho desnudo. Esteban Llorach. Edit. Gente Nueva. *Category:* text.

1110 2000. *The Valley of the Pinto Pajara. Original Title:* El valle de la Pajara pinta. Dora Alonso. *Illustrator:* Luis Bestard Cruz. Ed. Pueblo y Educacion. *Category:* illustration.

1111 2000. *Fangoso. Original Title:* Fangoso. Enid Vian. *Illustrator:* Enid Vian. Edic. Unión. *Category:* text/illustration.

1112 2000. *A Fairy and a Magican on the Bottom Floor. Original Title:* Un hada y una maga en el piso de abajo. Magaly Sánchez Ochea. Edic. Unión. *Category:* text.

1113 2000. *Original Title:* El libro de los pecesitos. Nieves Fernández. *Illustrator:* Alexis Lago. Edic. Unión. *Category:* text/illustration.

1114 2000. *Juan Ligero and the Enchanted Rooster. Original Title:* Juan Ligero y el gallo encantado. Dora Alonso. *Illustrator:* Eduardo Muñoz Bachs.

1115 2000. *Slow Sun. Original Title:* Sol sin prisa. Emilia Gallego Alfonso. Ed. de Esteban Llorarch Ramos.

1116 2000. *Original Title:* Guaminiquinaje. Pedro Peglez González. *Illustrator:* Tomás Eskola. Ed. De Libresa Ecuador.

1117 2000. *Little School of Horrors. Original Title:* Escuelita de los horres. Enríque Pérez Díaz. *Illustrator:* Miriam González Giménez. Edic. Unión. *Category:* text/illustration.

DENMARK

1118 BMF's Bornebogspris (Danish Booksellers Association Prize)

SPONSOR: The Danish Booksellers Assistants Association. CONTACT: Lisa Albertson — Chairperson. ADDRESS: Siljangade 6-8, DK-2300 Kobenhavn S, Denmark. PHONE: (45) 31 74 2168. ESTABLISHED: 1980. AWARD: D. Kr 10.000. The award is given annually to honor the author of the best children's book written in the Danish language. Only books published in the specific year can be considered.

1119 1990. Ib Spang Olsen.
1120 1991. Gerd Rindel.
1121 1992. Kim Fupz Aakeson.
1122 1993. Johannes Møllehave.
1123 1994. Bent Rasmussen.
1124 1995. Svend Åge Madsen.
1125 1996. Halfdan Rasmussen.
1126 1997. Vita Andersen.
1127 1998. Hanne Hastrup.
1128 1999. Thomas Winding.
1129 2000. Bjarne Reuter.

1130 Danmarks Skolebibliotekarforenings Bornebogpris (Danish Association of School Librarians Children's Book Prize)

SPONSOR: Danish Association of School Librarians. ADDRESS: Boelskilde 44, Bredballe, DK-7120 Vejle Ost, Denmark. PHONE: (45) 75 81 5634. ESTABLISHED: 1978. AWARD: D. Kr. 8.000 and a diploma. The annual award is given to honor the best Danish author of children's literature or specialized literature including educational materials.

1131 1990. Bjarne Reuter.
1132 1991. Lene og Pierre Bourgeat.
1133 1992. Cecil Bødker.
1134 1993. Sally Altschuler.
1135 1994. Anders Sørensen.
1136 1995. Jørn Mathiassen.
1137 1996. Dorte Karrebæk.
1138 1997. Torben Weinreich.
1139 1998. Louis Jensen.
1140 1999. Ken Denning.
1141 2000. Kim Fupa Aakeson.

1142 Forlaget Gyldendals Boglegat for Bornebogsfattere og Billedkundtnere (Gyldendal Publishers Prize)

SPONSOR: Gyldendal Publishers. ADDRESS: Klareboderne 3, 1001 Kobenhavn K, Denmark. PHONE: (33) 75 55 55. ESTABLISHED: 1982. AWARD: D. Kr 10.000. The annual award is given for outstanding contributions in the field of children's literature.

1143 1990. Flemming Jarlskov.
1144 1991. Kåre Bluitgen.
1992. No award given.
1145 1993. Nils Hartmann.
1146 1994. Bente Olesen Nyström.
1147 1995. Mats Letén.
1148 1996. Sally Altschuler.
1149 1997. Cato Thau-Jensen.
1150 1998. Charlotte Blay.
1999. No award given.
1151 2000. Dorte Karrebæk.

1152 Klods-Hans Prisen (Clumsy Hans Prize)

SPONSOR: IBBY Denmark. CONTACT: Olaf Winsløw, Den Danske, Boghandlerforening. ADDRESS: Siljangade 6, 2300 København S., Denmark. PHONE: (32) 54 22 55. ESTABLISHED: 1984. AWARD: A drawing with figures from Hans Andersen fairy tales. The annual award is given to contributors of PYLS, an annual of Danish children's literature.

1153 1990. Ejnar Agertoft.
1154 1991. Hannah Malling.
1155 1992. Christian Winnem.
1156 1993. Susanne Vebel.

1157 1994. Eva Glistrup.
1158 1995. Lisbeth Knudsen.
1159 1996. Majken Jørgensen, Gitte Vejlby.
1160 1997. Søren Kragh Jacobsen.
1161 1998. Jens Andersen.
1162 1999. Karen Margrethe Fromberg.
1163 2000. Bent Rasmussen.

1164 Kommunernes Skolebiblioteksforenings Forfatterpris (Danish School Library Association Prize)

SPONSOR: Danish Association of School Librarians. ADDRESS: Norrebrogade 159-5, DK-2200 Kobenhavn. N, Denmark. PHONE: (45) 31 81 1666. ESTABLISHED: 1981. AWARD: D. Kr. 20.000. The annual award is given to a Danish author for books of fiction and non-fiction for children and young adults.

1165 1990. *Original Title:* Sommeren er ikke forbi. Kirsten Mejlhede Krog. Thode, 1989.
1166 1991. *Original Title:* Sabers udsendinge I & II. Kåre Bluitgen.
1167 1992. *Original Title:* Læse-let bøger. Hans Chr. Hansen, Bent Nielsen.
1168 1993. *Original Title:* Den plettede tiger. Charlotte Blay.
1169 1994. *Original Title:* Samlede Rim. Thorstein Thomsen.
1170 1995. *Original Title:* Fu Ling's testamente i serien: Alex på Eventyr. Knud Holten.
1171 1996. *Original Title:* Hjertebåndet. Jacob Clausen.
1172 1997. *Original Title:* Arkitektur med andre ord. Jesper Clement, Anne von Holck.
1173 1998. *Me—Becoming A Young Woman. Original Title:* Mig en pige Mig—bli'r kvinde. Lena Eilstrup.
1174 1999. *Original Title:* Lotte og Larsen på campingtur. Mats Letén.
1175 2000. *Original Title:* Billedtid. Jane Kristensen, Jørgen Riber Christensen.

1176 Kulturministeriets Bornebogspris (Ministry of Culture Children's Book Prize)

SPONSOR: Ministry of Cultural Affairs. ADDRESS: Nybrogade 2 Post Box 2140, DK-1015, København K, Denmark. PHONE: 33 92 33 70. ESTABLISHED: 1954. AWARD: D.Kr 30.000. The annual award is given either for an individual work or the entire work of the author. It is awarded for Danish children's literature of high literacy and artistic quality.

1177 1990. *Original Title:* Dengang min onkel Kulle blev skor. Kim Fupz Aakeson.

1178 1990. *Original Title:* Stor og stærk. Kim Fupz Aakeson.
1179 1991. *Original Title:* Min lille hund Mester. Thomas Winding.
1180 1991. *Original Title:* Mester, min lille hund i natten. Thomas Winding.
1181 1992. *The Well. Original Title:* Brønden. Jens Peder Larsen. Fremand, 1991.
1182 1993. *Gina. Original Title:* Gina. Lotte Inuk.
1183 1993. *Gina I Love You. Original Title:* Gina je t'aime. Lotte Inuk.
1184 1994. *Original Title:* Kærlighedens labyrint. Anders Johansen.
1185 1995. *Original Title:* Kragevig-serien: Krageungen, Eddi, Tink og Alek. Bodil Bredsdorff.
1186 1996. *The Girl Who Was Good at Many Things. Original Title:* Pigen der var go' til mange ting. Dorte Karrebæk. *Illustrator:* Dorte Karrebæk. Foreum, 1996.
1187 1997. *Sikka's Tale. Original Title:* Sikkas Fortælling. Cecilie Eken. Gyldendal, 1997.
1188 1998. *Angels Don't Cry and Other Stories. Original Title:* Engle græder ikke og andre historier. Wivi Leth. Host, 1998.
1189 1999. *Under Fire. Original Title:* Med ilden i ryggen. Martin Petersen. Host, 1999.

1190 Kulturministeriets Illustratorpris (Ministry of Cultural Affairs Prize for Illustration)

SPONSOR: Ministry of Cultural Affairs. ADDRESS: Nybrogade 2 Post Box 2140, DK-1015, København K, Denmark. PHONE: 33 92 3040. ESTABLISHED: 1979. AWARD: D.Kr 20.000. Given annually to a Danish illustrator for his or her outstanding contribution to literature for children of young adults.

1191 1990. Dorte Karrebæk.
1192 1991. Palle Bregnhøi.
1193 1992. Irene Hedlund.
1194 1993. Pia Thaulov, Lille Kong Magnus.
1195 1994. Bente Olesen Nystrøm.
1196 1995. Anne Pedersen.
1197 1996. Mats Leténfor.
1198 1997. Bente Bech.
1199 1998. Birde Poulsen.
1200 1999. Mette-Kirstine Bak.

1201 Skriverprisen (Skriver's Award)

SPONSOR: Undervisningsministeriets. CONTACT: Birgitte Glass. ADDRESS: H.C. Andersens Boulevard 43, 1553 København V, Denmark. PHONE: 3392 5389. ESTABLISHED: 1995. AWARD: D.Kr 10.000. The award is given annually.

1202 1997. Jørn Jensen.
1203 1998. Bent Faurby.
1204 1999. Hans Chr. Hansen.
1205 2000. Kirsten Mejlhede Krog.

FINLAND

1206 Anni Swanin Mitali (Anni Swan Medal)

SPONSOR: The Finnish Section of International Board on Books for Young People. CONTACT: Maija Korhonen. ADDRESS: Urheilukatu 16 B 31, FIN-00250 Helsinki, Finland. PHONE: 3589 241 72 27. ESTABLISHED: 1961. AWARD: A silver medal designed by Wäinö Aaltonen. The award is given every three years to a book for children or young people which has a high artistic level and original style.

1207 1991. *The Book of Vladimir. Original Title:* Vladimirin kirja. Hannele Huovi. Gummerus, 1988.
1208 1994. *The Sea Monster. Original Title:* Järvihirviö. Tuula Kallioniemi. Otava, 1991.
1209 1997. *A Boy with Big Legs. Original Title:* Isojalkainen poika. Asko Martinheimo. WSOY, 1996.
1210 2000. *Original Title:* Suvi Kinos ja elämän kevät. Jukka Parkkinen.

1211 Arvid Lydeckenin Palkinto (Arvid Lydecken Prize)

SPONSOR: The Association of Finnish Writers for Children. CONTACT: Ms. Raili Mikkanen. ADDRESS: Palomäentie 13 B, 02730 Espoo, Finland. PHONE: (09) 852 2176. ESTABLISHED: 1969. The award is given annually for the best children's book.

1212 1990. *Original Title:* Yön lintu ja siivetön. Eeva Tikka. Gummerus, 1990.
1213 1991. *Straw Hat, Blanket Shoe. Original Title:* Heinahattu, Vilttitossu ja vauva. Sinikka Nopola, Tiina Nopola. *Illustrator:* Markus Majaluoma. Tammi, 1990.
1214 1992. *Original Title:* Yksisarvinen ja sadepuu. Leena Laulajainen. Tammi, 1992.

1215 1993. *The Dance of the Quadrupeds. Original Title:* Tanssi neljällä jalalla. Annukka Järvi. Karisto, 1993.

1216 1994. *Original Title:* Kirjolohikäärme. Kari Levola. Tammi, 1994.

1217 1995. *Original Title:* Nelli löytää kätkön. Veikko Rissanen. WSOY, 1995.

1218 1996. *Original Title:* Lasiaurinko. Hannele Huovi. Tammi, 1996.

1219 1997. *Original Title:* Ella luokkaretkellä. Timo Parvel. Tammi, 1997.

1220 1998. *Original Title:* Sakun lintukesä. Mari Mörö. Tammi, 1998.

1221 1999. *Original Title:* Kirpun matka maailman ääriin. Jukka Itkonen. Otava, 1999.

1222 2000. *Original Title:* Elsan ja Eetun erikoistapaukset. Tittamari Marttinen. Tammi, 2000.

1223 Finlandia Junior

SPONSOR: Suomen Kirjasäätiö (Finnish Book Foundation). ADDRESS: PL 177 (Lönnrotinkatu 11 A), 00121 Helsinki, Finland. PHONE: 09-228 77 250. ESTABLISHED: 1997. AWARD: 150.000 marks. The award is given annually for the best children's book.

1224 1997. *Original Title:* Gondwanan lapset. Alexis Kouros. *Illustrator:* Alexander Reichstein. Lasten Keskus, 1997.

1225 1998. *Original Title:* Kultamarja ja metsän salaisuude. Leena Laulajainen. *Illustrator:* Anna-Liisa Hakkarainen. Tammi, 1998.

1226 1999. *Original Title:* Tahdon. Kari Levola. *Illustrator:* Kari Levola. Tammi, 1999.

1227 2000. *Original Title:* Keväällä isä sai siivet. Tomi Kontio. *Illustrator:* Tomi Kontio. Tammi, 2000.

1228 Lasten Oman Kirjakerhon Kuvakirjapalkinto (Finnish Picture Book Prize)

Discontinued. ESTABLISHED: 1982. The prize was given annually by a publisher to a praiseworthy book for children. It was discontinued in 1992.

1229 1990. *Original Title:* Aasi ja Morso. Tuula Kallioniemi. *Illustrator:* Riikka Juvonen. Sanoma, 1989.

1230 1991. *The Bird and the Reindeer. Original Title:* Lintu ja poro. Esko-Pekka Tiitinen. *Illustrator:* Tuula Tiitinen. Tammi, 1990.

1231 1992. *Original Title:* Apinakuninkaan juhlat. Ritva Toivola. *Illustrator:* Mika Launis. Sanoma, 1991.

1232 1992. *Original Title:* Koirien Kalevala. Mauri Kunnas. *Illustrator:* Mauri Kunnas. Otava, 1992.

1233 Rudolf Koivun Palkinto (Rudolf Koivu Prize)

SPONSOR: Suomen Kirjasäätiö (Finnish Book Foundation). ADDRESS: PL 177 (Lönnrotinkatu 11 A), 00121 Helsinki, Finland. PHONE: 09-228 77 250. ESTABLISHED: 1949. AWARD: A plaque designed by Tapio Tapiovaara and 30,000 marks. The award is given every two years for the best illustrator of children's books in the previous two years.

1234 1991. *Angel Kid. Original Title:* Ängelungen/Enkelimuksu. Margareta Thun. *Illustrator:* Cris af Enehielm. Tammi, 1990.

1235 1993. *Original Title:* Heinähattu ja Vilttitossu Ioman tarpeessa. Sinikka Nopola, Tiina Nopola. *Illustrator:* Markus Majaluoma. Tammi, 1992.

1236 1995. *Original Title:* Suomen Lasten runotar. Leena Lumme. *Illustrator:* Leena Lumme. Otava, 1994.

1237 1997. *Original Title:* Antti Puuhaara. Jukka Virtanen. *Illustrator:* Mika Launis. Tammi, 1996.

1238 1999. *Original Title:* Nykytaide suurin piirtein. Marjatta Levanto. *Illustrator:* Julia Vuori. Otava, 1998.

1239 Suomalainen Kuvakirja-palkinto (formerly Lasten Oman Kirjakerhon Kuvakirjapalkinto)

ADDRESS: Palomäentie 13 B, 02730 Espoo, Finland. PHONE: (09) 852 2176. ESTABLISHED: 1993. AWARD: 10.000 marks. The award is given annually for the best children's picture book written and illustrated in Finland.

1240 1993. *The Snow Goose. Original Title:* Lumihanhi. Pirkko Vainio. *Illustrator:* Pirkko Vainio. Lasten Keskus, 1993.

1241 1994. *Original Title:* Tomppa tahtoo. Kristiina Louhi. *Illustrator:* Kristiina Louhi. Tammi, 1994.

1242 1995. *Original Title:* Älä ankka aivasta. Eppu Nuotio. *Illustrator:* Markus Majaluoma. Tammi, 1995.

1243 1996. *Original Title:* Paratiisin lintu. Riikka Juvonen. *Illustrator:* Riikka Juvonen. Kirjapaja, 1996.

1244 1997. *Original Title:* Metsän poluilla: luontokirja lapsille. Riitta Pouttu. *Illustrator:* Riitta Pouttu. WSOY, 1997.

1245 1998. *Original Title:* Kultamarja ja metsän salaisuudet. Leena Laulajainen. *Illustrator:* Anna-Liisa Hakkarainen. Tammi, 1998.

1246 1999. *Original Title:* Korvatunturi. Pekka Vuori. *Illustrator:* Pekka Vuori. Otava, 1999.

1247 Topelius-palkinto (Topelius Prize)

SPONSOR: The Association of Finnish Writers for Children and Youth. ADDRESS: Palomäentie 13 B, 02730 Espoo, Finland. PHONE: (09) 852 2176. ESTABLISHED: 1946. The award is given annually for the best youth novel.

1248 1990. *Taivaansavut-series. Original Title:* Taivaansavut-sarja. Lasse Raustela. Tammi, 1989.

1249 1991. *Angel Nights. Original Title:* Enkeliyöt. Riitta Jalonen. Tammi, 1990.

1250 1992. *Original Title:* Tiitiäisen pippurimylly. Kirsi Kunna. WSOY, 1991.

1251 1993. *Original Title:* Salaisuuksia. Leena Krohn. Kirjayhtymä, 1992.

1252 1994. *Stone Angel. Original Title:* Kivienkeli. Inka Nousiainen. Otava, 1993.

1253 1995. *Original Title:* Jonakin toisena päivänä. Maria Vuorio. Otava, 1994.

1254 1996. *Original Title:* Pönttölän väki. Hannu Mäkelä. Tammi, 1995.

1255 1997. *Original Title:* Pikku sammakkoprinssi. Hellevi Salmine. Otava, 1996.

1256 1997. *Original Title:* Asfalttisoturi. Tuija Lehtinen. Otava, 1997.

1257 1998. *Original Title:* Jääsilmä. Taru Väyrynen, Tarmo Väyrynen. Tammi, 1998.

1258 1999. *Original Title:* Rakas Mikael. Marja-Leena Tiainen. Tammi, 1999.

1259 2000. *Original Title:* Näytän hyvältä ilman paitaa. Kari Hotakainen. WSOY, 2000.

1260 Valtion Kirjallisuuspalkinto (National Awards for Literature)

Discontinued. ESTABLISHED: 1969. The annual awards were given to outstanding writers whose works were published in the previous year. It was discontinued in 1992.

1261 1990. *Original Title:* Matkalippu Mostariin. Mirjami Hietala. Tammi, 1989.

1262 1990. *Original Title:* Yön lintu ja siivetön. Eeva Tikka. Gummerus, 1989.

1263 1991. *Original Title:* Kesätukka ja muita juttuja Kukkulan korttelista. Maija Larmola, Leena Lumme. SKS, 1990.

1264 1991. *Original Title:* Iira. Anna Heinämaa. Art House, 1990.

1265 1992. *Original Title:* Kuu taskussa. Sirpa Kähkönen. Otava, 1991.

1266 1992. *Original Title:* Parempi valita susi. Esko-Pekka Tiitinen. Tammi, 1991.

FRANCE

1267 Prix des Incorruptibles (The Incorruptibles' Prize)

SPONSOR: Association du prix des incorruptibles. ADDRESS: loi 1901—13, rue de Nesle, 75006 Paris, France. PHONE: 01 44 41 97 20. ESTABLISHED: 2000. Children vote on their favorite books. The list of winners was unavailable at the time of publication.

1268 Prix des Jeunes Lecteurs PEEP (Young Readers Prize)

SPONSOR: La Fédération des parents d'élèves de l'enseignement public (PEEP). CONTACT: Maitre Cabour. ADDRESS: 160, rue du Temple, 75003 Paris, France. ESTABLISHED: 1985. AWARD: A trophy. The award is given annually for an original work for children ages 9–12 years.

1269 1990. *Original Title:* Les étoiles cachées. Soszewicz.
1270 1991. *Original Title:* Les compagnons de l'ombre. J-P Kerloc'h.
1271 1992. *Original Title:* Une amitié bleue outre-mer. Yvon Mauffret.
1272 1993. *Original Title:* Samira des quatres-routes. J. Benameur.
1273 1994. *Original Title:* La guerre des marrons. G. Senger.
1274 1995. *Original Title:* L'enfant à l'étoile jaune. A. Toupet.
1275 1996. *Original Title:* Les oubliés de Vulcain. D. Martinigol.
1276 1997. *Original Title:* Le Grimoire d'Arkandias. E. Boisset.
1277 1998. *Original Title:* Un grand-père tombé du ciel. Yaël Hassan.
1278 1999. *Original Title:* Les Secrets de Faith Green.
1279 2000. *Original Title:* Le souffle de la Pierre d'Irlande. Eric Simard. Magnard, 2000.

1280 Prix Lire au Collège

SPONSOR: CRDP. ADDRESS: 11, avenue Général-Champon, 38031 Grenoble, France. It is awarded to a work of literature for youth that is a subject of a reading in the classroom.

1281 2000. *Original Title:* A la vie à la mort. Paule du Bouchet. Gallimard.

1282 Prix Octogones (Octagon Prize)

SPONSOR: CIELJ (Centre International d'Etudes en Littérature de Jeunesse). ADDRESS: 25, rue du Petit Bois, 08000, Charleville-Mézières, France. PHONE:

03.24.56.56.46. ESTABLISHED: 1990. Each year the award is given for the best works for youth books for both illustration and writing.

1283 1991. *Original Title:* Zoum au jardin — Zoum au zoo — Zoum au cirque. Claire Nadaud. *Illustrator:* Claire Nadaud. Ed. Syros Alternatives, 1991.

1284 1999. *Original Title:* Tout un monde. Katy Couprie. *Illustrator:* Antonin Louchard. Thierry Magnier, 1999.

1285 1999. *Original Title:* Boogie Woogie. Page Bianchi. Gallimard Jeunesse, 1999.

1286 Prix Sorcières (Witches Prize)

SPONSOR: l'Association des Libraires Spécialisés Jeunesse. ADDRESS: 48 rue Colbert, 37000 Tours, France. PHONE: 02 47 66 95 90. ESTABLISHED: 1999. The award is given in five categories; toddlers, album, first reading, novel, documentary.

1287 1999. *Original Title:* Au cinéma Lux. Janine Teisson. Syros, 1998. *Category:* adolescent.

1288 1999. *Original Title:* Harry Potter à l'école des sorciers. J.K. Rowling. Gallimard, 1998. *Category:* 9-11.

1289 2000. *Original Title:* L'enfant océan. J.C. Mourlevat. Ed. Pocket, 1999. *Category:* 9-11.

1290 2000. *Original Title:* Sombres citrouilles. Malika Ferdjoukh. Ed. Ecole des Loisirs, 1999. *Category:* adolescent.

1291 Prix Totem (Totem Prize)

SPONSOR: Salon du livre de Montreuil. ADDRESS: 41, av. du Roule, 92200-, Neuilly-sur-Seine, France. PHONE: 01 55 86 86 65. ESTABLISHED: 1987. AWARD: statue. The prize is awarded by a jury annually.

1292 1990. *Original Title:* La grande muraille des caractères. Pierre Aroneanu. *Illustrator:* Cheng Dehong. Syros-Alternatives.

1293 1990. *Original Title:* Little Lou. Jean Claverie. Gallimard.

1294 1991. *Original Title:* L'hôtel du retour. Claude Gutman. Gallimard.

1295 1991. *Original Title:* Un dimanche avec Léonard de Vinci. Rosabianca Skira. Skira jeunesse.

1296 1991. *Original Title:* Les quatre fils de la terre. Jacques Cassabois. *Illustrator:* Jósef Wilkón. La Farandole.

1297 1992. *Original Title:* Fil de fer, la vie. Jean-Noël Blanc. Gallimard.

1298 1992. *Original Title:* L'infiniment petit. Nina Canault. Hachette Jeunesse.

1299 1992. *Original Title:* Les derniers géants. François Place. Casterman.

1300 1993. *Original Title:* Croisière en meurtre majeur. Miche Honaker. Rageot Éditeur.

1301 1993. *Original Title:* La vallée des roses. Frank Le Gall. Dupuis.

1302 1993. *Original Title:* Au bonheur des ours. Gabrielle Vincent. Casterman.

1303 1993. *Original Title:* L'invention de la peinture. Gallimard.

1304 1994. *Original Title:* Marcel et André. Pierre Pratt. Le Sourire qui mord.

1305 1994. *Original Title:* Horologiom. Fabrice Lebeaultl. Delcourt.

1306 1994. *Original Title:* La fille du canal. Thierry Lenain. Syros Éditeur.

1307 1994. *Original Title:* Le soleil de Diogène. François Kérisel. *Illustrator:* Agnès Audras. Hatier.

1308 1995. *Original Title:* L'oeil du chat. Fabio. euil.

1309 1995. *Original Title:* Le chien invisible. Claude Ponti. L'école des loisirs.

1310 1996. *Original Title:* Pichenettes. Lewis Trondheim. Dargaud.

1311 1996. *Original Title:* Navratil. Oliver Douzou. *Illustrator:* Charlotte Mollet. Éditions du Rouergue.

1312 1996. *Original Title:* Lettres d'amour de 0 à 10. Susie Morgenstern. École des loisirs.

1313 1996. *Original Title:* Les religions du monde. Larousse.

1314 1997. *Original Title:* Le jour où papa a tué sa vieille tante. Hélène Riff. Albin Michel jeunesse.

1315 1997. *Original Title:* Nakusha, Femmes d'Asie opprimées. Laurence Binet. Syros jeunesse.

1316 1997. *Original Title:* Allez ! Allez ! Xavier Deutsch. L'école des loisirs.

1317 1997. *Original Title:* La révolte d'Hop-Frog. David Blain. *Illustrator:* Christophe Blain. Dargaud.

GERMANY

1318 Alex-Wedding-Preis (Alex Wedding Prize)

SPONSOR: Minister fur Kultur der Deutschen DDR. ADDRESS: Molkenmarkt 1-3, DDR-1102 Berlin, Germany. AWARD: 10.000 DM. Awarded every two or three years for children's and adolescent's literature.

1319 1990. Walther Petri.

1320 1993. Peter Hacks.

1321 1997. Hannes Hüttner.
1322 1998. Klause Kordon.
1323 2000. Benno Pludra.

1324 Buxtehuder Bulle (Buxtehuder Bull)

SPONSOR: Stadt Buxtehude. ADDRESS: Stadt Buxtehude, Stavenort 5, D-21614 Buxtehude, Deutschland. PHONE: 0 41 61 501-344. ESTABLISHED: 1971. AWARD: A steel sculpture of a bull and 10.000 Mark DM. The award is given for the best German book of fiction for young adults, written in the previous year. Children ages 14 to 17 years and a jury of adults choose the winning book.

1325 1997. *Original Title:* Das Museum der gestohlenen Erinnerungen. Ralf Isau.

1326 1998. *Original Title:* Die Mitte der Welt. Andreas Steinhöfel.

1327 Deutscher Jugendliteraturpreis (German Youth Literature Prize)

SPONSOR: IBBY. CONTACT: Ursula Lehr. ADDRESS: Schlörstraße 10, D-8000 München 19, Deutschland. PHONE: (0 89) 168 4052. ESTABLISHED: 1956. AWARD: 15,000 DM for each category. The award is given annually to promote the development of German children's and youth literature. The prize is divided into four categories: picture book, children's book, youth book and non-fiction. Seals are affixed to the winning book. All books must be written by a German author or translated into the German language. Books must be published in the previous year.

1328 1990. *Rudi the Running Pig. Original Title:* Rennschwein Rudi Russel. Uwe Timm. *Illustrator:* Gunnar Matysiak. Nagel & Kimche, 1989. *Category:* children's book.

1329 1990. *Animal Revolt. Original Title:* Aufstand der Tiere. Jörg Steiner. *Illustrator:* Jörg Müller. Sauerländer, 1989. *Category:* picture book.

1330 1990. *How Do the Words Get Into the Book? Original Title:* Wie kommt der Wald ins Buch? Irmgard Lucht. *Illustrator:* Irmgard Lucht. Ellermann, 1989. *Category:* non-fiction.

1331 1990. *Jan, My Friend. Original Title:* Jan, mein Freund. Peter Pohl. Otto Maier, 1989. *Translator:* Birgitta Kicherer. *Category:* youth book.

1332 1990. *Original Title:* Meines Bruders Huter. Israel Bernbaum. *Illustrator:* Israel Bernbaum. Roman Kovar Verlag, 1989. *Category:* non-fiction.

1333 1991. *We Cuckoo Children. Original Title:* Wir Kuckuckskinder. Anatoli Pristawkin. *Translator:* Thomas Reschke Verlag Volk und Velt, 1990. *Category:* youth book.

1334 1991. *Dove Klar. Original Title:* Taube Klara. Wolf Spillner. Erika Klopp Verlag, 1990. *Category:* children's book.

1335 1991. *One, Five, Many. Original Title:* Eins, funf, viele. Kvéta Pacovská. *Illustrator:* Kvéta Pacovská. Ravenburger Buchverlag Otto Maier, 1990. *Category:* picture book.

1336 1991. *The Iron Lark. Original Title:* Die eiserne Lerche. Michail Krausnick. Signal Verlag, 1990. *Category:* non-fiction.

1337 1993. *Safari Into the Empire of the Stars. Original Title:* Safari ins Reich der Sterne. Helmut Hornung. Oetinger, 1992. *Category:* non-fiction.

1338 1993. *Jack.* A.M. Homes. *Translator:* Hans-Georg Noack. Arena, 1992. *Category:* youth book.

1339 1993. *The Bear Miracle. Original Title:* Das Bärenwunder. Wolf Erlbruch. *Illustrator:* Wolf Erlbruch. Hammer, 1992. *Category:* picture book.

1340 1993. *The Dog That Was on Its Way to a Star. Original Title:* Der Hund, der unterwegs zu einem Stern war. Henning Mankell. *Translator:* Angelika Kutsch. Oetinger, 1992. *Category:* children's book.

1341 1994. *Can You Whistle, Joanna? Original Title:* Kannst du pfeifen, Johanna. Ulf Stark. *Illustrator:* Anna Hogland. *Translator:* Brigitta Kicherer. Carlsen, 1993. *Category:* children's book.

1342 1994. *Original Title:* Sofies Welt. Jostein Gaarder. *Translator:* Gabriele Haefs. Hanser, 1993. *Category:* youth book.

1343 1994. *Original Title:* Macker. David Hughes. *Illustrator:* David Hughes. *Translator:* Abraham Teuter. Alibaba, 1993. *Category:* picture book.

1344 1994. *Original Title:* Anne Frank. Ruud van der Rol. Rian Verhoeven. *Translator:* Mirjam Pressler. Oetinger, 1993. *Category:* non-fiction.

1345 1995. *Original Title:* Die Zeit ist kaputt. Klaus Kordon. 1994. *Category:* non-fiction.

1346 1995. *Original Title:* Wenn das Glück kommt muss man ihm einen Stuhl hinstellen. Mirjam Pressler, 1994. *Category:* children's fiction.

1347 1996. *When the World Was New. Original Title:* Als die Welt noch jung war. Jürg Schubiger. Beltz Verlag, 1995. *Category:* children's fiction.

1348 1996. *Original Title:* Feuerland ist viel zu heiß! Anna Höglund. Carlsen Verlag, 1995. *Category:* picture book.

1349 1996. *Original Title:* Winterbucht. Mats Wahl. Anrich Verlag, 1995. *Category:* youth book.

1350 1997. *You Big, and I Small. Original Title:* Du groß, und ich klein. Grégoire Solotareff. Moritz, 1997. *Category:* picture book.

1351 1997. *Original Title:* Königskinder—eine wahre Liebe. Reinhard Kaiser. Schöffling, 1996. *Category:* non-fiction.

1352 1997. *Original Title:* So Lonely. Per Nilsson. Oetinger, 1996. *Category:* youth book.

1353 1997. *Karel, Jarda and That Was Life. Original Title:* Karel, Jarda und das wahre Leben. Sheila Och. Arena, 1996. *Category:* children's book.

1354 1998. *Original Title:* Blosse Hände. Bart Moeyaert. Carlsen Verlag, 1997. *Category:* youth book.

1355 1998. *Original Title:* Haus der Kunst—ein Gang durch die Kunstgeschichte. Susanna Partsch. Verlag, 1997. *Category:* non-fiction.

1356 1998. *Original Title:* Zwischen zwei Scheiben Glück. Irene Dische. Verlag, 1997. *Category:* children's book.

1357 1998. *Original Title:* Hat Opa einen Anzug an? Amelie Fried. *Illustrator:* Jacky Gleich. Verlag, 1997. *Category:* picture book.

1358 1999. *Original Title:* Bruder. Ted van Lieshout. Middelhauve, 1998. *Category:* youth book.

1359 1999. *Original Title:* Der rote Wolf. Friedrich K. Waechter. Diogenes, 1998. *Category:* picture book.

1360 1999. *Original Title:* Eine Insel im Meer. Annika Thor. Carlsen Verlag, 1998. *Category:* children's book.

1361 1999. *Original Title:* Tibet. Das Geheimnis der roten Schachtel. Peter Sís. Verlag, 1998. *Category:* non-fiction.

1362 2000. *Original Title:* Eins zwei drei Tier. Nadia Budde. Peter Hammer Verlag, 1999. *Category:* picture book.

1363 2000. *Original Title:* Hodder der Nachtschwärmer. Bjarne Reuter. Dressler Verlag, 1999. *Category:* children's book.

1364 2000. *Original Title:* Blueprint. Charlotte Kerner. Beltz & Gelberg, 1999. *Category:* youth book.

1365 2000. *Original Title:* Fräulein Pop und Mrs. Up. Antje von Stemm. Rowohlt Taschenbuch Verlag, 1999. *Category:* non-fiction.

1366 Friedrich-Gerstäcker-Preis (Friedrich Gerstäcker Prize)

SPONSOR: Kulturinstitut der Stadt Braunschweig. ADDRESS: Steintorwall 3, 38100 Braunschweig, Deutschland. PHONE: 0531/470-4820. ESTABLISHED: 1951. AWARD: 12,000 DM. The biennial award is given to books which portray youth in adventurous and challenging situations. The book must have been published within the last three years. The author must be a German resident. A current list was unavailable at the time of publication.

1367 1990. *Ben Markis, or The Trip to the West. Original Title:* Ben Markis, oder die reise in das Abendland. Kurt Wasserfall.

1368 1998. *Wolf Years. Original Title:* Wolfsjahre. Günther Bentele.

1369 Katholischer Kinder- und Jugendbuchpreis (Catholic Children's Book Prize)

SPONSOR: Zentralstelle Medien der Deutschen Bischofskonferenz. ADDRESS: Kaiserstraße 163, D-53113 Bonn, Deutschland. PHONE: 0228/103-236. ESTABLISHED:

1979. AWARD: DM 15.000. The award is given every two years for children's and young adult books with a Christian theme.

1370 1991. *The Book of Cropping. Original Title:* Das Buch der Schopfung. Max Bolliger. Herder, 1989.

1371 1991. *Gabriel and the Master Players. Original Title:* Gabriel und der Meisterspieler. Geraldine McCaughrean. Anrich Verlag, 1989.

1372 1993. *Ink Bird. Original Title:* Tintenvogel. Maretha Maartens. Verlag St. Gabriel, 1992.

1373 1995. *The Burning Thorn Shrubs. Original Title:* Der brennende Dornbusch. Peter Dickinson. Verlag St. Gabriel, 1993.

1374 1995. *Oregons Journey. Original Title:* Oregons Reise. Louis Joos. *Illustrator:* Rascal Joos. Arena, 1993.

1375 1997. *Only One Little Thing. Original Title:* Nur eine Kleinigkeit. Robert Cormier. *Illustrator:* Hanno Rink. Sauerlander, 1995.

1376 1999. *The Secret of Fire. Original Title:* Das Geheimnis der Feuers. Henning Mankell. Oetinger, 1997.

1377 Oldenburger Kinder- und Jugendbuchpreis (Oldenburger Children's Book Prize)

SPONSOR: Stadtbibliothek Oldenburg. ADDRESS: Peterstraße 1, 26105 Oldenburg, Deutschland. PHONE: (0441) 235 2692. ESTABLISHED: 1977. AWARD: 15,000 DM. Information and a current list of winners was unavailable at the time of publication.

1378 Peter-Härtling-Preis für Kinder- und Jugendlitatur (Peter Härtling Prize for Children's Literature)

SPONSOR: Verlag Beltz & Gelberg. ADDRESS: Postfach 10 01 54, 69441 Weinheim, Deutschland. PHONE: 62 01 9056 0. ESTABLISHED: 1984. AWARD: 10,000 DM. The award is given to a German author for an unpublished fiction manuscript for children 8–14 years. The winning entry is published and a seal is placed on the book.

1379 1990. *The Wind and the Stars. Original Title:* Der wind und der sterne. Reinhard Burger. Beltz & Gelberg, 1991.

1380 1992. *Original Title:* Der rote Nepomuk. Josef Holub. Beltz & Gelberg, 1993.

1381 1994. *Original Title:* Ein Schmetterling aus Surinam. Ingrid Möller. Beltz & Gelberg, 1995.

1382 1996. *Original Title:* Die Regentrinkerin. Nina Petrick. Beltz & Gelberg, 1997.

1383 1998. *Original Title:* Arabella oder Die BienenKönigin. Irma Krauß. Beltz & Gelberg, 1999.

1384 Rattenfänger-Literaturpreis (Pied Piper Prize)

SPONSOR: Stadt Hameln. ADDRESS: Rathausplatz 1, 31785 Hameln, Deutschland. PHONE: (0 5151) 2 02 0. ESTABLISHED: 1986. AWARD: 10,000 DM. The award is given every two years for an author, illustrator, editor or translator. The theme must be of fairy tales, modern myths or books with a theme from the middle ages. The story of the Pied Piper is the inspiration for the prize. The book must be published in the last two years.

1385 1990. *Original Title:* Erzähler der Nacht. Rafik Schami. Beltz & Gelberg Verlag, 1989.

1386 1992. *Original Title:* Der Rabe Alfons. Erwin Moser. Beltz & Gelberg Verlag, 1990.

1387 1992. *Original Title:* Däumling. Alfred von Meysenbug. Eichborn-Verlag, 1991.

1388 1994. *Original Title:* Kindergedichte und Galgenlieder. Lisbeth Zwerger. *Illustrator:* Christian Morgenstern. Michael Neugebauer Verlag, 1993.

1389 1994. *Original Title:* Der Zwerg Nase. Lisbeth Zwerger. *Illustrator:* Wilhelm Hauff. Michael Neugebauer Verlag, 1993.

1390 1996. *Original Title:* Die letzten Riesen. François Place. C. Bertelsmann Verlag, 1995.

1391 1998. *Original Title:* Die Insel der Möwen. Roberto Piumini. Carl Hanser Verlag, 1997.

1392 2000. *Original Title:* Der Hund mit dem gelben Herzen oder die Geschichte vom Gegenteil. Jutta Richter. Hanser, 1998.

1393 Troisdorfer Bilderbuchpreis (Troisdorfer Picture Book Prize)

SPONSOR: Bilderbuchmuseum der Stadt Troisdorf. ADDRESS: Burg Wissem, 53840 Troisdoef, Deutschland. PHONE: 02241 884111. ESTABLISHED: 1982. AWARD: 15,000 DM. This picture book prize is given for outstanding illustration of children and youth books ages up to 13 years. Additionally there is a prize for an unpublished picture book.

1394 1990. *Sara Wants to Go to the Circus. Original Title:* Sara, die zum Zirkus. Gudrun Mebs. *Illustrator:* Quint Buchholz. 1990. *Category:* second.

1395 1990. *Come Along, Moritz. Original Title:* Komm mit, Moritz. Dieter Wiesmüller. *Illustrator:* Dieter Wiesmüller. 1988. *Category:* first.

1396 1990. *Original Title:* Zylindergeschichten. Sophie Brandes. *Illustrator:* Sophie Brandes. *Category:* unpublished.

1397 1990. *The New King. Original Title:* Der Frischkönig. Binette Schroeder. *Illustrator:* Binette Schroeder. 1989. *Category:* second.

1398 1992. *Original Title:* Der gestiefelte Kater. Stasys Eidrigevicius. *Illustrator:* Stasys Eidrigevicius. 1990. *Category:* second.

1399 1992. *Each to Its Own. Original Title:* Jeder nach seiner Art. Klaus Ensikat. *Illustrator:* Klaus Ensikat. 1991. *Category:* first.

1400 1992. *The Fruit Versus the Seed. Original Title:* Die Früchte-u. Samenuhr. Una Jacobs. *Illustrator:* Una Jacobs. 1992. *Category:* third.

1401 1992. *Original Title:* Koschka. Gert Haucke. *Illustrator:* Katherina Lausche. 1991. *Category:* third.

1402 1992. *Original Title:* Mirre Marre. Heidrun Boddin. *Illustrator:* Heidrun Boddin. *Category:* unpublished.

1403 1994. *Original Title:* Der Möhrenfresser. Christiane Pieper. *Illustrator:* Christiane Pieper. 1993. *Category:* first.

1404 1994. *Ernst Stand and August Remain Seated. Original Title:* Ernst stand auf und August blieb liegen. Karoline Kehr. *Illustrator:* Karoline Kehr. 1993. *Category:* first.

1405 1994. *The Bet. Original Title:* Die Wette, wer zuerst wütend wird. Italo Calvino. *Illustrator:* Susanne Janssen-Mechler. 1994. *Category:* third.

1406 1994. *Original Title:* Okino und die Wale. Marek Zawadzki. *Illustrator:* Marek Zawadzki. 1994. *Category:* children's choice.

1407 1994. *Original Title:* Hans mein Igel. Dieter Krüll. *Illustrator:* Dieter Krüll. *Category:* unpublished.

1408 1996. *Alfred the Bear and Samuel the Dog. Original Title:* Alfred der Bär u. Samuel der Hund steigen aus dem Pappakarton. Ragnar Hovland. *Illustrator:* Peter Schössow. 1996. *Category:* first.

1409 1996. *Berta's Boat. Original Title:* Bertas Boote. Wiebke Oeser. *Illustrator:* Wiebke Oeser. 1996. *Category:* second.

1410 1996. *Edward Dreams. Original Title:* Koch Eduard träumt. Juliane Plöger. *Illustrator:* Juliane Plöger. 1995. *Category:* second.

1411 1996. *Original Title:* Schlaft gut, liebe Trere. Susanne Riha. *Illustrator:* Susanne Riha. 1995. *Category:* children's choice.

1412 1996. *Original Title:* Fratz. Julia Kaergel. *Illustrator:* Julia Kaergel. *Category:* unpublished.

1413 1998. *The King of Colours. Original Title:* Die Konigin der Farben. Jutta Bauer. *Illustrator:* Jutta Bauer. Beltz & Gelburg, 1998. *Category:* first.

1414 1998. *Original Title:* Pin Kaiser und Fip Hauar. Dieter Wiesmüller. *Illustrator:* Dieter Wiesmüller. 1998. *Category:* children's choice.

1415 1998. *Potpourri. Original Title:* Allerleirauh. Henriette Sauvant. *Illustrator:* Henriette Sauvant. Nord-Sud Verlag, 1997. *Category:* first.

1416 2000. *Original Title:* Komm, ich erzahl dir was vom Ferd. Stefanie Harjes. *Illustrator:* Stefanie Harjes. *Category:* unpublished.

1417 2000. *Emile—Eine bunte Katzengeschichte.* Kurt Futterer. *Illustrator:* Ralf Futterer. Eigenverlag, 2000. *Category:* children's choice.

1418 2000. *The Princess Comes Around Four. Original Title:* Die Prinzessin kommt um vier. Wolfdietrich Schnurre. *Illustrator:* Rotraud Susanne Berner. Aufbau Verlag, 2000. *Category:* second.

1419 2000. *Pozor. Original Title:* Pozor. Anne Maar. *Illustrator:* Bernd Mölck-Tassel. Bajazzo Verlag, 2000. *Category:* first.

1420 2000. *A New ABC Book for Children. Original Title:* Neues ABC-Buch für Kinder. Karl Philipp Moritz. *Illustrator:* Wolf Erlbruch. Kunstmann Verlag, 2000. *Category:* first.

1421 2000. *Sad Tiger Toasted Tomatoes. Original Title:* Trauriger Tiger toastet Tomaten. Nadia Budde. *Illustrator:* Nadia Budde. Hammer Verlag, 2000. *Category:* second.

1422 Weissen Raben (White Ravens)

SPONSOR: Internationale Jugendbibliothek (International Youth Library). ADDRESS: Schloß Blutenburg, D—81247 München, Deutschland. PHONE: 49 89 891211 0. ESTABLISHED: 1963. The awards are given annually to newly published books of international interest having a universal theme and/or books that are exceptional and often innovative artistically.

1423 1996. *Original Title:* No Bahamas. Dagmar Chidolue. Dressler, 1995. *Category:* Germany.

1424 1996. *The Rooster and the Fox. Original Title:* Hanen og reven. Peter Christen Asbjørnsen, J. E. Moe. *Illustrator:* Silje Granhaug. Cappelen, 1995. *Category:* Norway.

1425 1996. *Put Your Nose in Your Armpit. Original Title:* Neuzen in je oksel. Midas Dekkers. *Illustrator:* Angela de Vrede. Leopold, 1995. *Category:* The Netherlands (Dutch).

1426 1996. *Mummy! Mummy! Original Title:* Mammie! Mammie! Jaak Dreesen. Altiora, 1995. *Category:* Belgium (Dutch).

1427 1996. *Blah-Blah: Stories and Games for Tigers Large and Small. Original Title:* Blabla: pesmi in igre za male in velike tigre. Boris A. Novak. *Illustrator:* Marjan Mancek. DZS, 1995. *Category:* Slovenia.

1428 1996. *Legends and Myths of the Old Slavs. Original Title:* Báje a mýty starych Slovan. Ivan Hudec. *Illustrator:* Karol Ondrejcka. Slovart, 1995. *Category:* Slovakia.

1429 1996. *The Adventures of Gingerbread Liza: A Fairy Tale. Original Title:* Prikljucenija sdobnoj Lizy: Povest'-skazka. Viktor Lunin. *Illustrator:* Elena Muchanova. Slovo, 1995. *Category:* Russia.

1430 1996. *The Grandma from Paris or The Nightingale from Zarasai: Poems. Original Title:* Bobute iš Paryziaus arba Lakštingala Zarasuose:

Eilerašciais. Juozas Erlickas. *Illustrator:* Nadezda Gultiajeva. Alma Littera, 1995. *Category:* Lithuania.

1431 1996. *Latvian Folk Legends. Original Title:* Latviešu tautas teikas. Gunta Leja. *Illustrator:* Karlis Dobrajs. Spriditis, 1995. *Category:* Latvia.

1432 1996. *Seka's Little Village. Original Title:* Sekino seoce. Mirjana Stefanovic. *Illustrator:* Dušan Otaševic. Ginko, 1994. *Category:* Serbia.

1433 1996. *Tales from the Bohemian Forest. Original Title:* Baje Českého Pošumaví. Adolf Danek. *Illustrator:* Erika Bornová. Kentaur/Polygrafia, 1994. *Category:* Czech Republic.

1434 1996. *Stories from Zagreb. Original Title:* Zagrebacka prica. Blanka Dovjak-Matkovic. *Illustrator:* Vladimir Kirin. Znanje, 1994. *Category:* Croatia.

1435 1996. *A Sunday with Cézanne. Original Title:* Un dimanche avec Cézanne. Alain Madeleine-Perdrillat. *Illustrator:* Florian Rodari. Skira, 1995. *Category:* Switzerland (French).

1436 1996. *The Friday Surprise. Original Title:* Fredagsöverraskningen. Rose Lagercrantz. *Illustrator:* Rebecka Lagercrantz. Bonnier Carlsen, 1995. *Category:* Sweden.

1437 1996. *Original Title:* Grutte Giele & Lytse Loer. Riemkje Pistra. *Illustrator:* Marianne van Tuinen. Afûk, 1995. *Category:* The Netherlands (Frisian).

1438 1996. *Personally It Did Me No Harm to Grow Up. Original Title:* Personlig tog jeg ikke skade af at vokse op. Roald Als. *Illustrator:* Roald Als. Høst & Søn, 1995. *Category:* Denmark.

1439 1996. *It's Not My Fault. Original Title:* Ce n'est pas de ma faute! Linda Brousseau. *Illustrator:* Claire Maigné. Editions Pierre Tisseyre, 1994. *Category:* Canada (French).

1440 1996. *The Lord of Light. Original Title:* El dueño de la luz. Ivonne Rivas. *Illustrator:* Irene Savino. Ekaré, 1995. *Category:* Venezuela (Spanish).

1441 1996. *An Aymará Dream. Original Title:* Sueño Aymara. León Zamora, Aníbal Eduardo. *Illustrator:* Mariluz Meza. Universidad Pontificia Bolivariana, 1995. *Category:* Columbia (Spanish).

1442 1996. *Poor, Bald Corinthians Fan. Original Title:* Pobre corintiano careca. Ricardo Azevedo. *Illustrator:* Ricardo Azevedo. Melhoramentos, 1995. *Category:* Brazil (Portuguese).

1443 1996. *The History of an Exaggerated Love. Original Title:* Historia de un amor exagerado. Graciela Montes. Colihue, 1995. *Category:* Argentina (Spanish).

1444 1996. *Good-night Story for Mary Caroline. Original Title:* Gutenachtgeschichte für Maria Carolina. Barbara Frischmuth. *Illustrator:* Dušan Kállay. Jugend & Volk, 1994. *Category:* Austria.

1445 1996. *Mother of God: A Book for Well-Behaved Children. Original Title:* Boza majka: Knizka za dobri deca. Dora Gabe. *Illustrator:* Dimitar Lalev. Zanet-45, 1995. *Category:* Bulgaria.

1446 1996. *Fred Hollows. Leaving the World a Better Place.* Mark Butler. Cardigan Street Publishers, 1995. *Category:* Australia.

1447 1996. *Hotfoot.* Tom Richards. Basement Press, 1995. *Category:* Ireland.

1448 1996. *Francis of Assisi. Original Title:* Furanchesuko. Takehide Harada. *Illustrator:* Takehide Harada. Suemori Books, 1992. *Category:* Japan.

1449 1996. *Metro Manila.* Ma. Michelle Kuhonta. *Illustrator:* Dindo A. Llana. Cacho Publishing, 1995. *Category:* Philippines.

1450 1996. *Home Run.* Paula Boock. Longacre, 1995. *Category:* New Zealand.

1451 1996. *Her Story. Women Who Changed the World.* Ruth Ashby (ed.). Viking, 1995. *Category:* U.S.A.

1452 1996. *The Prince of Venice. Original Title:* To basilopullon tes Benedias. Kosta Sylloge Pruse. *Illustrator:* Champes Tsangares. Tsangares Champes, 1995. *Category:* Cyprus (Greek).

1453 1996. *The Other Side.* Alejandro Aura. *Illustrator:* Julia Gukova. Annick Press, 1995. *Category:* Canada.

1454 1996. *The School We Made.* André Proctor. *Illustrator:* Hannie Koch. Baobab Books, 1992. *Category:* Zimbabwe.

1455 1996. *The Car with Three Wheels.* Gillian Leggat. *Illustrator:* Marjorie van Heerden. Macmillan Boleswa Publishers, 1995. *Category:* Swaziland.

1456 1996. *The Boy Who Counted to a Million.* Lawrence Bransby. Human & Rousseau, 1995. *Category:* South Africa.

1457 1996. *Etosha Experience.* Anna Louise Marais. *Illustrator:* Christine Marais. Gamsberg Publishers. *Category:* Nambia.

1458 1996. *Ananse and the Golden Drum.* Mohammed ben Abdallah. Woeli, 1994. *Category:* Ghana.

1459 1996. *Yuanyuan's Dream of Getting Rich. Original Title:* Yuanyuan de facai meng. Yangqing Ceng. *Illustrator:* Zonghui Liu. Xinyi Jijin, 1994. *Category:* China.

1460 1996. *Gandhi. The Man of Peace.* Manorama Jafa. *Illustrator:* Deepak Harichandan. Ratna Sagar, 1995. *Category:* India.

1461 1996. *The Ghost of Portitsas. Original Title:* To phantasma tes Portitsas. Basiles Anagnostopulos. Kastaniotes, 1994. *Category:* Greece.

1462 1996. *Micki and the King. Original Title:* Micí Agus An Rí. Gwyneth Wynn. *Illustrator:* Gwyneth Wynn. An Gum, 1995. *Category:* Ireland (Gaelic).

1463 1996. *A Different Globe, Please. Original Title:* Un alt glob, va rog! Monic Savulescu-Voudouris. Ion Creanga, 1992. *Category:* Romania.

1464 1996. *The Little Mermaid. Original Title:* A sereiazinha. Hans Christian Andersen. *Illustrator:* Manuela Bacelar. Afrontamento, 1995. *Category:* Portugal.

1465 1996. *Olympos. Diary of an Adolescent Goddess. Original Title:* Olympos. Diario di una dea adolescente. Teresa Buongiorno. *Illustrator:* Grazia Nidasio. Salani, 1995. *Category:* Italy.

1466 1996. *The Witch Pulls the Sleeping Bag Tighter. Original Title:* Die Hexe zieht den Schlafsack enger. Hanna Johansen. *Illustrator:* Käthi Bhend. Nagel & Kimche, 1995. *Category:* Switzerland.

1467 1996. *Counting Verses to Nibble On. Original Title:* Comptines à croquer. Corinne Albaut. *Illustrator:* Serge Ceccarelli. Actes Sud Junior, 1995. *Category:* France.

1468 1996. *The Tree of the Ravens. Original Title:* L'arbre aux corbeaux. Stibane. *Illustrator:* Stibane. Pastel, 1995. *Category:* Belgium (French).

1469 1996. *Theseus & the Minotaur.* Jules Cashford. *Illustrator:* Daniel De'Angeli. Barefoot Books, 1995. *Category:* Great Britain.

1470 1997. *The Twin Brother. Original Title:* Tvillingbror. Liv Marie Austrem. *Illustrator:* Akin Düzakin. Det Norske Samlaget, 1995. *Category:* Norway.

1471 1997. *Safran. Original Title:* Safran. Bodil Bredsdorff. Høst & Søn, 1996. *Category:* Denmark.

1472 1997. *Tales Told by the Old Maiasaura. Original Title:* Was die alte Maiasaura erzählt. Martin Auer. *Illustrator:* Christine Sormann. St. Gabriel, 1996. *Category:* Austria.

1473 1997. *Forbidden Girls. Original Title:* Zakázané holky. Hana Borkovcová. Albatros, 1995. *Category:* Czech Republic.

1474 1997. *Another Kind of Monday.* William E. Coles. Atheneum, 1996. *Category:* U.S.A.

1475 1997. *Original Title:* Tick-tack. Lena Anderson. *Illustrator:* Lena Anderson. Eriksson & Lindgren, 1996. *Category:* Sweden.

1476 1997. *The Dwellers Beneath.* Mary Arrigan. Attic Press, 1996. *Category:* Ireland.

1477 1997. *The Oxford Children's A to Z of the Human Body.* Bridget Ardley. *Illustrator:* Neil Ardley. Oxford, 1996. *Category:* Great Britain.

1478 1997. *Keri.* Jan Andrews. Groundwood, 1996. *Category:* Canada.

1479 1997. *The Nutcracker and the Mouse King. Original Title:* Hrestac in mišji kralj. E.T.A. Hoffmann. *Illustrator:* Marija Lucija Stupica. DZS, 1996. *Category:* Slovenia.

1480 1997. *Matike, the Street Child. Original Title:* Matike, l'enfant de la rue.

Désiré Onana. Editions Akoma MBA, 1995. *Category:* Cameroon (French).

1481 1997. *The Knights of the Round Table. Original Title:* Rycari Kruglogo Stola. Ekaterina Vjaceslavovna Balobanova, Ol'ga Michajlovna Peterson. *Illustrator:* Denis Dmitrievic Gordeev. Argus, 1995. *Category:* Russia.

1482 1997. *Hello, Prehistoric Lizards. Original Title:* Ahoj, praveké jaštery. Emília Cincurová. *Illustrator:* Vladimír Cáp. Q111, 1996. *Category:* Slovakia.

1483 1997. *Betty and Bala and the Proper Big Pumpkin.* Lorraine Berolah, Lilyjane Collins. *Illustrator:* Noel Cristaudo. University of Queensland Press, 1996. *Category:* Australia.

1484 1997. *The Long Silence. Original Title:* Le long silence. Sylvie Desrosiers. La courte échelle, 1996. *Category:* Canada (French).

1485 1997. *Mrs. Windyflax and the Pungapeople.* Barry Crump. *Illustrator:* Murray Ball. Hodder Moa Beckett, 1995. *Category:* New Zealand.

1486 1997. *Squeaky Henry. Original Title:* Piepheini. Peter Abraham. Ellermann, 1996. *Category:* Germany.

1487 1997. *Lonely Islands and an Orchid. Original Title:* Samotne wyspy i storczyk. Anna Onichimowska. Filipinka, 1994. *Category:* Poland.

1488 1997. *That's Enough. Original Title:* Jetzt reicht's. Ute Diebold. *Illustrator:* Ute Diebold. Neugebauer, 1996. *Category:* Switzerland.

1489 1997. *Original Title:* Keloglan. Atila Çakiroglu. *Illustrator:* Nermin Keskin. Kültür Bakanligi Milli Kütüphane, 1996. *Category:* Turkey.

1490 1997. *The Magic Coach. Original Title:* Volšebnyj vozok. Viktor G. Krotov. *Illustrator:* Anna Vlasova. Dva slona, 1995. *Category:* Ukraine (Russian).

1491 1997. *The Paradise of the Innocents. Original Title:* Le défilé des innocents. Joël Koné Doh Fandanh. Edilis, 1996. *Category:* Ivory Coast (French).

1492 1997. *My Fingers Aren't Long Enough. Original Title:* Mijn vingers zijn niet lang genoeg. Heide Boonen. *Illustrator:* Gerda Dendooven. Altiora, 1996. *Category:* Belgium (Dutch).

1493 1997. *My Baby, I Love You. Original Title:* Moro mu sagapo. Rula Akalestu. Ammos, 1996. *Category:* Greece.

1494 1997. *The Voyages of Tsjam. Original Title:* De reizen fan Tsjam. Willem Tjerkstra. *Illustrator:* Luuk Klazenga. Afûk, 1996. *Category:* The Netherlands (Frisian).

1495 1997. *The Land of Dreams. Original Title:* Le pays du rêve. Anne Brouillard. *Illustrator:* Anne Brouillard. Duculot, 1996. *Category:* Belgium (French).

1496 1997. *A Crime Is Easy? Original Title:* Un crime est-il facile? Michel Amelin. *Illustrator:* Gilles Frély. Epigones, 1996. *Category:* France.

1497 1997. *To Miss with Love. Original Title:* Alla signorina Elle con tanto affetto. Marcello Argilli. *Illustrator:* Alessandra Cimatoribus. Fatatrac, 1996. *Category:* Italy.

1498 1997. *The Woolen Socks. Original Title:* Gurab-i pašmi. Furuzanda Hudagu. *Illustrator:* Hušang Muhammaiyan. Kanun-i, 1994. *Category:* Iran.

1499 1997. *Fables. Original Title:* Fábulas. Jean de La Fontaine. *Illustrator:* António Modesto. Edinter, 1995. *Category:* Portugal.

1500 1997. *Ngoma and Click. Namibian Detective Stories.* Jaspar Utley. Gamsberg Macmillan, 1995. *Category:* Namibia.

1501 1997. *Original Title:* Chumba la cachumba. *Illustrator:* Carlos Cotte. Ekaré, 1996. *Category:* Venezuela (Spanish).

1502 1997. *The Toddler's Dictionary. Original Title:* Het kleuterwoordenboek. Nannie Kuiper. *Illustrator:* Philip Hopman. Piramide, 1996. *Category:* The Netherlands(Dutch).

1503 1997. *Colored Treasury of Folktales from China. Original Title:* Caihui ben zhongguo minjian gushi. Jun Gu. *Illustrator:* Yongli Tang. Zhejiang-Shaonian-Ertong-Chubanshe, 1990. *Category:* China.

1504 1997. *Images in Waiting. Original Title:* L'attente des images. S. Corinna Bille, Maurice Chappaz. La Joie de Lire, 1996. *Category:* Switzerland (French).

1505 1997. *Wild Fables. Original Title:* Fábulas salvajes. Marcelo Birmajer. *Illustrator:* María Gabriela Forcadell. Ed. Sudamericana, 1996. *Category:* Argentina (Spanish).

1506 1997. *The Magic Drum.* Bridget King. *Illustrator:* Robin Miranda. Jacaranda Designs, 1996. *Category:* Kenya.

1507 1997. *The Lure of the Girl Shaking Ice Tea. Original Title:* Zhenzhu naicha de youhuo. Jiaqi Guan. Youshi, 1995. *Category:* China.

1508 1997. *Knocks on the Door at Night. Original Title:* Cando petan na porta pola noite. Xabier P. Docampo. *Illustrator:* Fran Jaraba. Ed. Xerais de Galicia, 1994. *Category:* Spain (Galician).

1509 1997. *Liliana, the Urban Witch. Original Title:* Liliana bruja urbana. Carmen Posadas. *Illustrator:* Enrique Martínez. Fondo de Cultura Económica, 1996. *Category:* Mexico (Spanish).

1510 1997. *Suma Went Walking.* Nana Dadson. *Illustrator:* Ralph Sutherland. Afram Publications, 1996. *Category:* Ghana.

1511 1997. *The Daghur People. Original Title:* Dawo'er zu. Wen Ruo. Zhejiang-Shaonian-Ertong-Chubanshe, 1990. *Category:* China.

1512 1997. *Zizi & !Xau. The Eagle Calls.* Carlos Carvalho. *Illustrator:* Carlos Carvalho. Human & Rousseau, 1996. *Category:* South Africa.

1513 1997. *What's for Supper? Original Title:* Què hi ha per a sopar? Teresa Durán. *Illustrator:* Max. Publ. de l'Abadia de Montserrat, 1996. *Category:* Spain (Catalan).

1514 1997. *The Cucu Will Get You. Original Title:* A cuca vem pegar. Regina Chamlian. *Illustrator:* Helena Alexandrino. Ática, 1996. *Category:* Brazil (Portuguese).

1515 1997. *How Thopo Became a Great N'anga.* Stephen Alumenda. *Illustrator:* Stephen Alumenda. Baobab Books, 1996. *Category:* Zimbabwe.

1516 1997. *The Age of Dreams. Original Title:* La era del sueño. Alicia Morel. *Illustrator:* Thomas Gerber. Dolmen Ed. 1996. *Category:* Chile (Spanish).

1517 1997. *Who Likes Old People Anyway? Original Title:* Quién quiere a los viejos? Ricardo Alcántara. *Illustrator:* Gusti. Vives, 1996. *Category:* Spain.

1518 1997. *The Terror of Class 6B. Original Title:* El terror de sexto B. Yolanda Reyes. *Illustrator:* Daniel Rabanal. Santillana, 1995. *Category:* Columbia (Spanish).

1519 1997. *In the Sky. Original Title:* Sorani. Kanna Funakoshi. *Illustrator:* Yôji Izawa. Suemori Books, 1995. *Category:* Japan.

1520 1997. *The Yao People. Original Title:* Yao zu. Chuan Yi. *Illustrator:* Shourong Hu. Zhejiang-Shaonian-Ertong-Chubanshe, 1990. *Category:* China.

1521 1998. *Mambrú went to War. Original Title:* Mambrú se fue a la guerra. *Illustrator:* Gloria Calderón. Ekaré, 1997. *Category:* Venezuela.

1522 1998. *The Iron Ring.* Lloyd Alexander. Dutton, 1997. *Category:* U.S.A.

1523 1998. *Original Title:* Emma Pippifilippi. Maria Blazejovsky. *Illustrator:* Maria Blazejovsky. Jungbrunnen, 1997. *Category:* Austria.

1524 1998. *The Filthy Prince. Original Title:* Der dreckige Prinz. Martin Auer. *Illustrator:* Joachim Luetke. Thienemann, 1997. *Category:* Germany.

1525 1998. *Books are Liars. Original Title:* Knjige lazu! Darko Macan. *Illustrator:* Stjepan Bartolic. Znanje, 1997. *Category:* Croatia.

1526 1998. *Grandpapa Car. Original Title:* Dedecek automobil. Adolf Branald. *Illustrator:* Kamil Lhoták. Albatros, 1996. *Category:* Czech Republic.

1527 1998. *The Tale of the Beans. Original Title:* Pupos pasaka. Pauliaus Augiaus. *Illustrator:* Pauliaus Augiaus. Lietus, 1996. *Category:* Lithuania.

1528 1998. *Illustrated Polish History. Original Title:* Ilustrowane dzieje polski. Dariusz Banaszak. Tomasz Biber. *Illustrator:* Lech Siejkowski. Podsiedlik Raniowski, 1997. *Category:* Poland.

1529 1998. *Fuffy and Max. Original Title:* Fuffy und Max. Gerd Fuchs. Nagel & Kimche, 1997. *Category:* Switzerland.

1530 1998. *My Dog Loves Jazz. Original Title:* Moja sobaka ljubit dzaz. Marina L. Moskvina. *Illustrator:* Vladimir Burkin. Olimpionik, 1997. *Category:* Russia.

1531 1998. *The Story of My Canary. Original Title:* Kanaryamin öyküsü. Ayla Çinaroglu. *Illustrator:* Yaprak Berkkan. Uçanbalik Yayinlari, 1996. *Category:* Turkey.

1532 1998. *Symphonie in the Bathroom. Original Title:* Samfuni-i hammam. Farhad Hasan-zadah. Kitabha-i Banafša, 1995. *Category:* Iran (Persian).

1533 1998. *Vacation in the Village. Original Title:* Vacances au village. Pierre Yves Njeng. *Illustrator:* Pierre Yves Njeng. Akoma Mba, 1996. *Category:* Cameroon.

1534 1998. *This is the House Near the Bent Tree. Original Title:* Dit is het huis bij de kromme boom. Imme Dros. *Illustrator:* Harrie Geelen. Querido, 1997. *Category:* The Netherlands (Dutch).

1535 1998. *Bitter Sweetness. Original Title:* Doçura amarga. Ana Saldanha. *Illustrator:* José Pedro Costa. Edinter, 1997. *Category:* Portugal.

1536 1998. *The Round Square Forest. Original Title:* A Négyszögletü Kerek Erdõ. Ervin Lázár. *Illustrator:* László Réber. Osiris K., 1997. *Category:* Hungary.

1537 1998. *Green Dishes for Young Cooks. Original Title:* Gröna rätter för unga kockar. Lotta Brinck. *Illustrator:* Andréa Räder. Rabén & Sjögren, 1996. *Category:* Sweden.

1538 1998. *The Pirate with Different Eyes. Original Title:* Ho peirates me ta alliotika matia. Tonia Chatzedake. *Illustrator:* Nikolas Andrikopulos. Hellenika Grammata, 1997. *Category:* Greece.

1539 1998. *Enchanted Journeys.* Robert Dunbar (ed.). O'Brien, 1997. *Category:* Ireland.

1540 1998. *The Ghost of Trastevere and Other Tales. Original Title:* Il fantasma di Trastevere e altri racconti. Marcello Argilli. *Illustrator:* Giovanni Manna. Fatatrac, 1997. *Category:* Italy.

1541 1998. *The Hidden Child. Original Title:* L'enfant caché. Berthe Burko-Falcman. Éditions du Seuil, 1997. *Category:* France.

1542 1998. *Hevi's ABC. Original Title:* Heviho ABC. Daniel Hevier. *Illustrator:* Daniel Hevier. Hevi, 1996. *Category:* Slovakia.

1543 1998. *The Cases of Detective Karel Loot. Original Title:* Primeri detektiva Karla Loota. Jelena Sitar. *Illustrator:* Igor Cvetko. DZS, 1996. *Category:* Slovenia.

1544 1998. *Original Title:* Marieke, Marieke. Jaak Dreesen. *Illustrator:* Annemie Heymans. Altiora, 1997. *Category:* Belgium (Dutch).

1545 1998. *Give Me Your Hand, Arthur. Original Title:* Donne-moi la main, Arthur. Corine Jamar. *Illustrator:* Laurence DeKemmeter. Casterman, 1997. *Category:* Belgium (French).

1546 1998. *The Wolves' Banquet. Original Title:* Ospatul lupilor. Diana Irimescu. Ed. Prahova, 1996. *Category:* Romania.

1547 1998. *Jakey.* Lesley Beake. Tafelberg, 1997. *Category:* South Africa.

1548 1998. *I Am a Fiery Dragon! Original Title:* Wo biancheng yi zhi pen huo long le! Ma Lai. *Illustrator:* Ma Lai. Guoyu Ribao, 1996. *Category:* China.

1549 1998. *Once Upon a Time There Will Be. Original Title:* Seráse una vez. Consuelo Armijo. *Illustrator:* Fernando Gómez. Espasa Calpe, 1997. *Category:* Spain.

1550 1998. *The White Lady. Original Title:* La Dama Blanca. Rosa Maria Colom. *Illustrator:* Mercè Canals. Edicions de la Magrana, 1997. *Category:* Spain (Catalan).

1551 1998. *Marriage Forbidden, Papa! Original Title:* ¡Prohibido casar, papá! Fina Casalderrey. *Illustrator:* Marta Rivera Ferner. Galaxia, 1996. *Category:* Spain (Galician).

1552 1998. *Original Title:* Hector. Henry Thiel. *Illustrator:* Bertola. La Joie de Lire, 1997. *Category:* Switzerland (French).

1553 1998. *Free as the Desert Wind.* Elsa Marston. *Illustrator:* Abdel Aziz El Guindi. Hoopoe Books, 1996. *Category:* Egypt.

1554 1998. *Janjo and Shika.* Dan Fulani. *Illustrator:* Patrick Kirby. Jacaranda Designs, 1995. *Category:* Kenya.

1555 1998. *The Autumn of Flamingoes Has Begun. Original Title:* Flamingohøsten har begynt. Heidi Bonde. J. W. Cappelen, 1997. *Category:* Norway.

1556 1998. *You Can Kiss Me If You Want To. Original Title:* Pode me beijar se quiser. Ivan Angelo. *Illustrator:* Ricardo Azevedo. Ed. Ática, 1997. *Category:* Brazil.

1557 1998. *Neptune's Children.* David Whitton. Macmillan Boleswa, 1997. *Category:* Swaziland.

1558 1998. *Marita Goes to School.* Stephen Alumenda. Baobab, 1997. *Category:* Zimbabwe.

1559 1998. *Original Title:* Leo Z. Jukka Lemmetty. *Illustrator:* Jukka Lemmetty. Otava, 1996. *Category:* Finland.

1560 1998. *Evening Hour with Papa. Original Title:* Kvöldstund með pabba. Guðjón Sveinsson. *Illustrator:* Erlu Sigurðardóttur. Mánabergsútgáfan, 1997. *Category:* Iceland.

1561 1998. *Original Title:* Stefano. María Teresa Andruetto. Ed. Sudamericana, 1997. *Category:* Argentina.

1562 1998. *Baba.* Ruth Brown. Andersen, 1997. *Category:* Great Britain.

1563 1998. *Legends Below the Southern Cross. Original Title:* Leyendas bajo la Cruz del Sur. Alicia Morel. *Illustrator:* Tomás Gerber. Ed. Andrés Bello, 1996. *Category:* Chile.

1564 1998. *Endless Fleeing. Original Title:* Evig flugt. Fahmy Almajid. *Illustrator:* Inni Karine Melbye. Høst & Søn, 1996. *Category:* Denmark.

1565 1998. *If You Could Wear My Sneakers.* Sheree Fitch. *Illustrator:* Darcia Labrosse. Doubleday, 1997. *Category:* Canada.

1566 1998. *Dare Truth or Promise.* Paula Boock. Longacre Press, 1997. *Category:* New Zealand.

1567 1998. *The Toy Horse.* Deepa Agarwal. *Illustrator:* Ajanta Guhathakurta. Children's Book Trust, 1997. *Category:* India.

1568 1998. *Leaves for Mr. Walter.* Janeen Brian. *Illustrator:* David Cox. Margaret Hamilton, 1997. *Category:* Australia.

1569 1998. *The Wonderous Snowman. Original Title:* Fushigina yukidaruma. Kumiko Fujimaki. *Illustrator:* Yoshiharu Tsuchida. Kin no hoshisha, 1996. *Category:* Japan.

1570 1998. *Trucas. Original Title:* Trucas. *Illustrator:* Juan Gedovius. Fondo de Cultura Económica, 1997. *Category:* Mexico.

1571 1999. *The Ten Friends in the Countryside. Original Title:* Os dez amigos no campo. *Illustrator:* Anna Göbel. Formato, 1998. *Category:* Brazil.

1572 1999. *Don't Wake Me. Original Title:* Mos më zgjoni. Besiana Avdyli. Kuvendi, 1997. *Category:* Albania.

1573 1999. *The Survivor. Original Title:* El sobreviviente. Ruth Mehl. Ed. Sudamericana, 1998. *Category:* Argentina.

1574 1999. *Bumface.* Morris Gleitzman. Puffin/Penguin, 1998. *Category:* Australia.

1575 1999. *The Game of Kings. Original Title:* Das Königsspiel. Maria Blazejovsky. *Illustrator:* Maria Blazejovsky. Jungbrunnen, 1998. *Category:* Austria.

1576 1999. *Fox and Hare. Original Title:* Vos en Haas. Sylvia van den Heede. *Illustrator:* Tjong-Khing Thé. Lannoo, 1998. *Category:* Belgium (Dutch).

1577 1999. *We Are Going to Mopti. Original Title:* On ira à Mopti. Eva Gelber. *Illustrator:* Serge Dehaes. Editions Labor, 1998. *Category:* Belgium (French).

1578 1999. *The Postdog. Original Title:* Pas pismonoša. Alija Hasagic Dubocanin. *Illustrator:* Mirza Ibrahimpašic. Sarajevo-Publishing, 1998. *Category:* Bosnia-Herzegovina.

1579 1999. *An Alphabet of Cyprus. Original Title:* Alphabetari tes Kypru. Alexa Apostolake, Helene Stampogle. Kaleidoskopio, 1997. *Category:* Greece.

1580 1999. *Hunting for Letters. Original Title:* Lov slov. Jozef Pavlovic. *Illustrator:* Martin Kellenberger. Vydavatelstvo Matice slovenskej, 1997. *Category:* Slovakia.

1581 1999. *The Princess and the Pea. Original Title:* Die Erbsenprinzessin. Martin Auer. *Illustrator:* Daniela Kulot-Frisch. Thienemann, 1998. *Category:* Germany.

1582 1999. *How to Climb a Cake. Original Title:* Cómo escalar un pastel. Ana Gabriela Bautista. *Illustrator:* Claudine Coupry. Ed. Petra, 1997. *Category:* Mexico.

1583 1999. *Liselotje Goes Camping. Original Title:* Liselotje gaat kamperen. Marianne Busser. *Illustrator:* Ron Schröder. Van Holkema & Warendorf, 1998. *Category:* The Netherlands (Dutch).

1584 1999. *On Clapping Hands and Pat-A-Cake. Original Title:* Fan hantsjeklap en sukerbak. Jant van der Weg. *Illustrator:* Karin Poiesz. Afuk, 1998. *Category:* The Netherlands (Frisian).

1585 1999. *I Am Not Esther.* Fleur Beale. Longacre, 1998. *Category:* New Zealand.

1586 1999. *Uncle Rin-Tin-Tin's Legacy. Original Title:* Arven etter Onkel Rin-Tin-Tei. Ingvar Ambjørnsen. *Illustrator:* Per Dybvig. J. W. Cappelens Forlag, 1998. *Category:* Norway.

1587 1999. *The Mats*. Francisco Arcellana. *Illustrator:* Hermès Alègrè. Tahanan, 1998. *Category:* Philippines.

1588 1999. *The August That I Have Never Forgotten. Original Title:* O agosto que nunca esquecei. António Mota. *Illustrator:* Lúcia Ana. Edinter, 1998. *Category:* Portugal.

1589 1999. *Roma ABC. Original Title:* Romani chib ubeca. Leksa Manuš. *Illustrator:* Karlis Rudevics. Spriditis, 1997. *Category:* Latvia.

1590 1999. *Christmas. Original Title:* Rozdestvo. Natal'ja Budur (ed.). *Illustrator:* Ol'ga Ionajtis. Kontrakt, 1997. *Category:* Russia.

1591 1999. *My Neighbors Are Witches. Original Title:* Otonari wa majo. Junko Akahane. *Illustrator:* Shun Sekiguchi. Bunken shuppan, 1998. *Category:* Japan.

1592 1999. *Catkins. Whacky Poems. Original Title:* Majnice. Fulaste pesmi. Tone Pavcek. *Illustrator:* Kostja Gatnik. Zalozba Mladika, 1997. *Category:* Slovenia.

1593 1999. *Hippo's River Café*. Lindsay Camp. *Illustrator:* Peta Coplans. Tafelberg, 1998. *Category:* South Africa.

1594 1999. *The Wonderful Tale of the Sixth Ocean. Original Title:* Inciértico o La rica historia del Sexto Océano. Marta Echegaray. *Illustrator:* Jorge Castillo. Ed. Siruela, 1998. *Category:* Spain.

1595 1999. *I Come from Everywhere. Original Title:* Jo vinc de tot arreu. Carme Garriga, Anna Giménez. *Illustrator:* Anna Giménez. Galera, 1998. *Category:* Spain (Catalan).

1596 1999. *We Have Our Dreams.* A.K. Johnson. Macmillan Boleswa, 1997. *Category:* Swaziland.

1597 1999. *The Steel Castle. Original Title:* Stålborgen. Erik Eriksson. Eriksson & Lindgren, 1998. *Category:* Sweden.

1598 1999. *Original Title:* Zoë und Rea. Maja Gerber-Hess. Rex-Verl, 1998. *Category:* Switzerland.

1599 1999. *The River. Original Title:* La rivière. Claude Martingay. *Illustrator:* Xavier Cardinaux. Joie de Lire, 1998. *Category:* Switzerland.

1600 1999. *Minnie and Moo Go to the Moon.* Denys Cazets. *Illustrator:* Denys Cazets. DKInk, 1998. *Category:* U.S.A.

1601 1999. *Don't Shoot-Smile! Original Title:* Nu trageti în ... zîmbete! Vlad Popescu. *Illustrator:* Vlad Popescu. Lumina Lex, 1996. *Category:* Romania.

1602 1999. *Riddles from Chad. Original Title:* Hije gusar. *Illustrator:* Abdel Kader Badaoui. Sépia, 1996. *Category:* France.

1603 1999. *The Ruse. Original Title:* La ruse. Idrissou Njoya. *Illustrator:* Idrissou Njoya. Éd. Akomba Mba, 1996. *Category:* Cameroon (French).

1604 1999. *Zack.* William Bell. Doubleday Canada, 1998. *Category:* Canada.

1605 1999. *Little Weenie. Original Title:* Petit zizi. Thierry Lenain. *Illustrator:* Stéphane Poulin. Les 400 Coups, 1997. *Category:* Canada (French).

1606 1999. *The Sea of Marvels. Original Title:* El Mar de las Maravillas. Jacqueline Balcells. *Illustrator:* Andrés Jullian. Bello, 1997. *Category:* Chile.

1607 1999. *The Biography of King Gelong'er. Original Title:* Gerlong'er wang zhuanji. Qunying He. Shibao Wenhua, 1995. *Category:* China.

1608 1999. *The Kingdom of the Five Moons. Original Title:* El imperio de las cinco lunas. Celso Román. *Illustrator:* Alekos. Ed. Norma, 1998. *Category:* Colombia.

1609 1999. *Damjan's Lake. Original Title:* Damjanovo jezero. Anto Gardaš. *Illustrator:* Zeljko Prstec. Znaje, 1998. *Category:* Croatia.

1610 1999. *The World of Animals. Original Title:* Svet zvírat. Karel štatstný. Vladimír Bejcek. *Illustrator:* Petr Hloušek. Albatros, 1998. *Category:* Czech Republic.

1611 1999. *Diyenkoroba or As Old as the World. Original Title:* Diyenkoroba ou Vieux-comme-le-monde. Baabilen Kulubali. *Illustrator:* Fatinia Aaron. Donniya, 1997. *Category:* Mali.

1612 1999. *Original Title:* Aapelus. Kaarina Helakisa. *Illustrator:* Taru Castren. Kolibri, 1998. *Category:* Finland.

1613 1999. *Vampires — Centaurs — Dragons. Original Title:* Vampiri — Gunduraci — Zmej. Krasimir Mircev. *Illustrator:* Viktor Paunov. Panorama, 1998. *Category:* Bulgaria.

1614 1999. *Dream On!* Steve Barlow. *Illustrator:* Steve Skidmore. Picadilly, 1998. *Category:* Great Britain.

1615 1999. *The Tall, Thin Boy from Outer Space. Original Title:* Ip bacakli uzayli çocuk. Aytül Akal. *Illustrator:* Ayla Delibas Yetkin. Uçanbalik, 1997. *Category:* Turkey.

1616 1999. *Frakk, the Cat's Terror. Original Title:* Frakk, a macskák réme. Ágnes Bálint. *Illustrator:* György Várnai. Morá, 1998. *Category:* Hungary.

1617 1999. *The Old Woman Wants Payment for Her Spinning Whorl. Original Title:* Kerling vill hafa nokkuð fyrir snúð sinn. Guðrún Hannesdóttir. *Illustrator:* Guðrún Hannesdóttir, Forlagið 1998. *Category:* Iceland.

1618 1999. *There's Another Way!* Deepa Agarwal (ed.). *Illustrator:* Tapas Guha. Madhuban Educational, 1998. *Category:* India.

1619 1999. *Original Title:* Papar. Muhammad Mirkiyani. *Illustrator:* Ayta Huraminazad. Kanun-i Parwari_-i Fikri-i, 1997. *Category:* Iran.

1620 1999. *It's a Jungle Out There.* Ed Milano. *Illustrator:* Ed Milano. Wolfhound, 1997. *Category:* Ireland.

1621 1999. *The Story of Francis, the Saint Who Knew How to Laugh. Original Title:* Storia di Francesco il santo che sepava ridere. Teresa Buongiorno, Chiara Frugoni. *Illustrator:* Chiara Carrer. Laterza, 1998. *Category:* Italy.

1622 1999. *Sinabani, the Nest Egg. Original Title:* Sinabani, la petite dernière. Fatou Keïta. *Illustrator:* Claire Mobio. Ivoiriennes, 1997. *Category:* Ivory Coast.

1623 1999. *Burned Earth. Original Title:* Brændt jord. Anne-Grethe Dahms. Høst & Søn, 1998. *Category:* Denmark.

1624 1999. *Bernardo and Canelo. Original Title:* Bernardo y Canelo. Fernando Krahn. *Illustrator:* Fernando Krahn. Ed. Ekaré, 1998. *Category:* Venezuela.

1625 2000. *Run, Lilly, Run! Original Title:* Lauf, Lilly, lauf! Helga Hegewisch. Atrium-Verl, 1999. *Category:* Switzerland (German).

1626 2000. *The Trouble Party. Original Title:* Le trouble-fête. Roselyne Bertin. Rageot, 1999. *Category:* France.

1627 2000. *My Mother Wears Me Out. Original Title:* Ma mère m'épuise. Hubert BenKemoun. Hachette Jeunesse, 1999. *Category:* France.

1628 2000. *At the Foot of My Tree. Original Title:* Au pied de mon arbre. Éric Battut. *Illustrator:* Éric Battut. Milan, 1999. *Category:* France.

1629 2000. *Haiti, the Naked Pearl. Original Title:* Haïti, la perle nue. Gérard Barthélémy, Mimi Barthélémy. Vents d'ailleurs, 1999. *Category:* France.

1630 2000. *The Poet and Ill-Humor. Original Title:* Le poète et la méchante humeur. Jean-Marie Barnaud. *Illustrator:* Martine Mellinette. Cheyne, 1999. *Category:* France.

1631 2000. *Mommy! Original Title:* Maman! Mario Ramos. *Illustrator:* Mario Ramos. École des Loisirs, 1999. *Category:* Belgium (French).

1632 2000. *The Cross of El Dorado. Original Title:* La cruz de El Dorado. César Mallorquí. *Illustrator:* Jordi Vila Declòs. Edebé, 1999. *Category:* Spain.

1633 2000. *The Piano Elf. Original Title:* Der Klavierling. Lotte Kinskofer. *Illustrator:* Verena Ballhaus. Palazzo-Verl, 1999. *Category:* Switzerland (German).

1634 2000. *A Flash of Sun. Original Title:* Coup de soleil. Michèle Daufresne. *Illustrator:* Michèle Daufresne. Bilboquet, 1999. *Category:* France.

1635 2000. *The Miracle of Jasina. A Christmas Story. Original Title:* Das Wunder von Jasina. Petr Chudozilov. *Illustrator:* Jindra Capek. Sauerländer, 1999. *Category:* Switzerland (German).

1636 2000. *Moon and Morning Star. A Tale from Africa. Original Title:* Mond und Morgenstern. Eine Geschichte aus Afrika. Wolfram Frommlet. *Illustrator:* Henning Wagenbreth. Hammer, 1999. *Category:* Germany.

1637 2000. *In the Night. Original Title:* Nachts. Wolf Erlbruch. *Illustrator:* Wolf Erlbruch. Hammer, 1999. *Category:* Germany.

1638 2000. *The Wolf Is Dead. Original Title:* Der Wolf ist tot. Dörte Damm. Tabuphil, 1999. *Category:* Germany.

1639 2000. *Not Chicago. Not Here. Original Title:* Nicht Chicago. Nicht hier. Kirsten Boie. Oetinger, 1999. *Category:* Germany.

1640 2000. *Why Hares Have Long Ears. Original Title:* Warum der Hase lange Ohren hat. Martin Auer. *Illustrator:* Linda Wolfsgruber. Gabriel, 1999. *Category:* Austria.

1641 2000. *The Crocodile Who Thought it Was a Flower.... Original Title:* Le crocodile qui se prenait pour une fleur.... Bénédicte Guettier. *Illustrator:* Bénédicte Guettier. Casterman, 1999. *Category:* Belgium (French).

1642 2000. *The Night of the Wolves. Original Title:* La notte dei lupi. Pinin Carpi. *Illustrator:* Pinin Carpi. Einaudi Ragazzi, 1999. *Category:* Italy.

1643 2000. *A Son Among Daughters.* Jasper Onuekwusi. Heinemann, 1998. *Category:* Nigeria.

1644 2000. *Legends from Dobrudja. Original Title:* Legenede din tinuturi dobrogene. Eugenia Doina Gemala. *Illustrator:* Lucia Ruffu Manea. Carminis, 1998. *Category:* Romania.

1645 2000. *A Spiral of Smoke at the End of the Sea. Original Title:* Um fio de fumo nos confins do mar. Alice Vieira. Caminho, 1999. *Category:* Portugal.

1646 2000. *Riding on a Broom. Original Title:* A cavallo della scopa. Bianca Pitzorno. *Illustrator:* Antongionata Ferrari. Mondadori, 1999. *Category:* Italy.

1647 2000. *Original Title:* Maria Moll Cappero. Paola Pallottino. *Illustrator:* Nicoletta Ceccoli. Fatatrac, 1999. *Category:* Italy.

1648 2000. *The Moon Man. Original Title:* L'uomo della luna. Beatrice Masini. *Illustrator:* Nicoletta Ceccoli. Ed. Arka, 1999. *Category:* Italy.

1649 2000. *The Water's Memory. Original Title:* La memoria dell'acqua. Silvana Gandolfi. *Illustrator:* Giulia Orecchia. Salani, 1999. *Category:* Italy.

1650 2000. *Mama, Why Do You Love Me? Original Title:* Maman, pourquoi tu m'aimes? Stephanie Blake. *Illustrator:* Stephanie Blake. Albin Michel Jeunesse, 1999. *Category:* France.

1651 2000. *Pea Pods and Butterflies ... Who's Cuter—Boys or Girls? Original Title:* Piselli e farfalline ... son piú belli i maschi o le bambine? Vittoria Facchini. *Illustrator:* Vittoria Facchini. Fatatrac, 1999. *Category:* Italy.

1652 2000. *Original Title:* Alboum. Christian Bruel. *Illustrator:* Nicole Claveloux. Être, 1999. *Category:* France.

1653 2000. *The Route of the Warrior. Original Title:* La strada del guerriero. Pierdomenico Baccalario. Piemme Junior, 1999. *Category:* Italy.

1654 2000. *The Promise. Original Title:* La promesse. Yaël Hassan. Castor Poche Flammarion, 1999. *Category:* France.

1655 2000. *The Words Have Faces. Original Title:* Les mots ont des visages. Joël Guenoun. Autrement Jeunesse, 1999. *Category:* France.

1656 2000. *To Life, To Death. Original Title:* À la vie, à la mort. Paule DuBouchet. Gallimard, 1999. *Category:* France.

1657 2000. *The Son of the Witch and the Wolf. Original Title:* Le fils de la sorcière et du loup. Chris Donner. *Illustrator:* Emmanuelle Houdart. Grasset-Jeunesse, 1999. *Category:* France.

1658 2000. *Proper Gentlemen. Original Title:* Messieurs Propres. Christine Destours. *Illustrator:* Christine Destours. Éd. du Rouergue, 1999. *Category:* France.

1659 2000. *The Ugly Duckling*. Hans Christian Andersen. *Illustrator:* Jerry Pinkney. Morrow, 1999. *Category:* U.S.A.

1660 2000. *Lidia and the Turks. Original Title:* Lidia e i turchi. Giuseppe Ferrandino. Mondadori, 1999. *Category:* Italy.

1661 2000. *Hello Baby*. Jenni Overend. *Illustrator:* Julie Vivas. ABC Books, 1999. *Category:* Australia.

1662 2000. *When Zachary Beaver Came to Town*. Kimberly Willis Holt. Holt, 1999. *Category:* U.S.A.

1663 2000. *Jamela's Dress*. Niki Daly. *Illustrator:* Niki Daly. Lincoln, 1999. *Category:* Great Britain.

1664 2000. *Tell Me No Lies*. Malorie Blackman. Macmillan, 1999. *Category:* Great Britain.

1665 2000. *Little Soldier*. Bernard Ashley. Orchard, 1999. *Category:* Great Britain.

1666 2000. *The Video Shop Sparrow*. Joy Cowley. *Illustrator:* Gavin Bishop. Mallinson Rendel, 1999. *Category:* New Zealand.

1667 2000. *Lester*. Bernard Beckett. Longacre Press, 1999. *Category:* New Zealand.

1668 2000. *Cheerful Spirits*. Gita Iyengar. *Illustrator:* Pulak Biswas. National Book Trust, 1998. *Category:* India.

1669 2000. *Well, a Crocodile Can!* Malachy Doyle. *Illustrator:* Britta Teckentrup. Lincoln, 1999. *Category:* Great Britain.

1670 2000. *Yumba Days*. Herb Wharton. *Illustrator:* Ron Hurley. University of Queensland Press, 1999. *Category:* Australia.

1671 2000. *My Brother Sammy*. Becky Edwards. *Illustrator:* David Armitage. Bloomsbury, 1999. *Category:* Great Britain.

1672 2000. *Stony Heart Country*. David Metzenthen. Penguin, 1999. *Category:* Australia.

1673 2000. *Once Upon a Place*. Robert Ingpen. *Illustrator:* Robert Ingpen. Lothian, 1999. *Category:* Australia.

1674 2000. *Angels Passing By*. Judith Clarke. Puffin/Penguin, 1999. *Category:* Australia.

1675 2000. *Sink or Swim*. Ron Bunney. Fremantle Arts Centre Press, 1999. *Category:* Australia.

1676 2000. *The Worst Band in the Universe*. Graeme Base. *Illustrator:* Graeme Base. Viking/Penguin, 1999. *Category:* Australia.

1677 2000. *The Talking Walking Stick*. Tendai Makura. *Illustrator:* Thomas Pasirayi. Zimbabwe Publishing House, 1999. *Category:* Zimbabwe.

1678 2000. *The Mealie-cob Doll*. Marianna Brandt. *Illustrator:* Samantha van Riet. Tafelberg, 1998. *Category:* South Africa.

1679 2000. *Chikka. Original Title:* Chikka. Hira Nirodi Chandran. *Illustrator:* Shankar Gaidhane. Gul Mohar/Orient Longman, 1998. *Category:* India.

1680 2000. *The Clay Ladies.* Michael Bedard. *Illustrator:* Les Tait. Tundra Books, 1999. *Category:* Canada (English).

1681 2000. *The Word Shop. Original Title:* La tienda de palabras. Jesús Marchamalo. Ed. Siruela, 1999. *Category:* Spain.

1682 2000. *Share the Sky.* Ting-xing Ye. *Illustrator:* Suzane Langlois. Annick, 1999. *Category:* Canada (English).

1683 2000. *Earthlings Inside and Out.* Valerie Wyatt. *Illustrator:* Dušan Petrièiæ. Kids Can Press, 1999. *Category:* Canada (English).

1684 2000. *The Inuksuk Book.* Mary Wallace. *Illustrator:* Mary Wallace. Greey de Pencier, 1999. *Category:* Canada (English).

1685 2000. *Flags.* Maxine Trottier. *Illustrator:* Paul Morin. Stoddart Kids, 1999. *Category:* Canada (English).

1686 2000. *We Share Everything.* Robert Munsch. *Illustrator:* Michael Martchenko. Scholastic, 1999. *Category:* Canada (English).

1687 2000. *Kou-Skelowh = We Are the People. Illustrator:* Barbara Marchand. Theytus Books, 1999. *Category:* Canada (English).

1688 2000. *The Gruffalo.* Julia Donaldson. *Illustrator:* Axel Scheffler. Macmillan, 1999. *Category:* Great Britain.

1689 2000. *Muslim Child.* Rukhsana Khan. *Illustrator:* Patty Gallinger. Napoleon Publ., 1999. *Category:* Canada (English).

1690 2000. *Unbroken.* Jessie Haas. Greenwillow Books, 1999. *Category:* U.S.A.

1691 2000. *Is Anybody Listening?* Larry O'Loughlin. Wolfhound Press, 1999. *Category:* Ireland (English).

1692 2000. *Benny and Omar.* Eoin Colfer. O'Brien Press, 1999. *Category:* Ireland (English).

1693 2000. *A Leaf in Time.* David Walker. *Illustrator:* Mic Rolph. Portland Press, 1999. *Category:* Great Britain.

1694 2000. *Wonders Never Cease*! James Pope. Piccadilly Press, 1998. *Category:* Great Britain.

1695 2000. *Landlocked.* Catherine Johnson. Pont Books/Gomer Press, 1999. *Category:* Great Britain.

1696 2000. *Hangman.* Julia Jarman. Andersen Press, 1999. *Category:* Great Britain.

1697 2000. *Wake Up, World!* Beatrice Hollyer. Lincoln, 1999. *Category:* Great Britain.

1698 2000. *The Bone Talker.* Shelley A. Leedahl. *Illustrator:* Bill Slavin. Red Deer Press, 1999. *Category:* Canada (English).

1699 2000. *My First Year in Parliament. Original Title:* Mitt första år i riksdagen. Kent Härstedt. *Illustrator:* Erja Lempinen. LL-Förl, 1999. *Category:* Sweden.

1700 2000. *I Will. Original Title:* Tahdon. Kari Levola. Tammi, 1999. *Category:* Finland.

1701 2000. *Suvi Kinos and the Directives of Life. Original Title:* Suvi Kinos ja elämän eväät. Jukka Parkkinen. Söderström, 1999. *Category:* Finland.

1702 2000. *Nuka's Summer. Original Title:* Nukas sommer. Pia Rosing Heilmann. *Illustrator:* Nina Spore Kreutzmann. Atuakkiorfik, 1998. *Category:* Greenland.

1703 2000. *Twenty-four Per Second. Original Title:* 24 i sekundet. Bjørn Sortland. *Illustrator:* Lars Elling. Norske Samlaget, 1999. *Category:* Norway.

1704 2000. *Very Blue. Original Title:* Veldig blå. Ingvild Røstbø Kausland. *Illustrator:* Jens Kristensen. Norske Samlaget, 1999. *Category:* Norway.

1705 2000. *The Gospel of the Elephant. Original Title:* Elefantevangeliet. Hans Sande. *Illustrator:* Akin Düzakin. Gyldendal Tiden, 1999. *Category:* Norway.

1706 2000. *The End of the World. Original Title:* Finis mundi. Laura Gallego García. Ed. SM, 1999. *Category:* Spain.

1707 2000. *Original Title:* Freddrik. Walter Vik. *Illustrator:* Silje Granhaug. Cappelen, 1999. *Category:* Norway.

1708 2000. *The Girl Who Shrunk. Original Title:* Pigen der krøb. Kim Fupz Aakeson. *Illustrator:* Cato Thau-Jensen. Carlsen, 1998. *Category:* Denmark.

1709 2000. *The Winter of Wild Animals. Original Title:* Vildvinter. Anna-Karin Palm. *Illustrator:* Anna Bengtsson. Natur och Kultur, 1999. *Category:* Sweden.

1710 2000. *One Cannot Tell Everything. Original Title:* Man kan inte säga allt. Peter Pohl. Rabén & Sjögren, 1999. *Category:* Sweden.

1711 2000. *The Book of Death. Original Title:* Dödenboken. Pernilla Stalfelt. *Illustrator:* Pernilla Stalfelt. Eriksson & Lindgren, 1999. *Category:* Sweden.

1712 2000. *Read a Book. Original Title:* Läsa bok. Anna-Clara Tidholm. *Illustrator:* Anna-Clara Tidholm. Alfabeta, 1999. *Category:* Sweden.

1713 2000. *The People of Birka. The Age of the Vikings. Original Title:* Folket i Birka. På Vikingarnas tid. Mats Wahl, Björn Ambrosiani. *Illustrator:* Sven Nordqvist. BonnierCarlsen, 1999. *Category:* Sweden.

1714 2000. *Short Skirt. Original Title:* Kort kjol. Christina Nord Wahldén. Tiden, 1999. *Category:* Sweden.

1715 2000. *Devil, Dragon, Fatal Sisters, Magicians, Evil Fairies, Vampires. Original Title:* Djavol, zmej, orisnici, mag'osnici, samovili, vampiri. Lilija Stareva. Lista, 1998. *Category:* Bulgaria.

1716 2000. *Heartache. Original Title:* Hjerte-smerte. Marianne Viermyr. *Illustrator:* Anders Kaardahl. Damm, 1999. *Category:* Norway.

1717 2000. *The Seer. Original Title:* El adivino. Cuento popular. *Illustrator:* Rosana Faría. Playco Ed, 1998. *Category:* Venezuela (Spanish).

1718 2000. *The Great Thunderer. Original Title:* O Grande Tronante. Gloria Sánchez, Domínguez López. *Illustrator:* Domínguez López. Ed. Xerais, 1999. *Category:* Spain (Galician).

1719 2000. *Martha and the Bicycle. Original Title:* Marta et la bicyclette. Germano Zullo. *Illustrator:* Albertine. Joie de Lire, 1999. *Category:* Switzerland (French).

1720 2000. *The Story of Shooting Arrows and the Cloud. Original Title:* Historia de Flechazo y la nube. Ricardo Mariño. *Illustrator:* Marcelo Elizalde. Alfaguara, 1999. *Category:* Argentina (Spanish).

1721 2000. *Fox Tales. Original Title:* Cuentos del zorro. Gustavo Roldán. *Illustrator:* Carlos Nine. Ed. Sudamericana, 1999. *Category:* Argentina (Spanish).

1722 2000. *Who Does What? Original Title:* Quem faz o quê? Ricardo Aleixo. *Illustrator:* Regina Miranda. Formato, 1999. *Category:* Brazil.

1723 2000. *The Cow's Revenge. Original Title:* La venganza de la vaca. Sergio Aguirre. Grupo Ed. Norma, 1998. *Category:* Colombia.

1724 2000. *No! It Wasn't Me! Original Title:* ¡No, no fui yo! Ivar da Coll. *Illustrator:* Ivar da Coll. Panamericana Ed, 1999. *Category:* Colombia.

1725 2000. *The Princess's Wings. Original Title:* Prinsessan siivet. Kaarina Helakisa. *Illustrator:* Heli Hieta. Otava, 1999. *Category:* Finland.

1726 2000. *The Toad Who Didn't Want to Eat. Original Title:* El sapo que no quería comer. Martha Sastrías. *Illustrator:* Francisco Nava Bouchaín. Fondo de Cultura Económica, 1998. *Category:* Mexico.

1727 2000. *Edda's Summer-House. Original Title:* Eddas lysthus. Jacob Clausen. *Illustrator:* Lilian Brøgger. Forum, 1999. *Category:* Denmark.

1728 2000. *Kaarai the Alcaraván Bird. A Wayuu Tale. Original Title:* Kaarai el alcaraván. Literatura wayuu. Romer Urdaneta. *Illustrator:* Javier Rondón. Ed. Tinta, 1999. *Category:* Venezuela (Spanish).

1729 2000. *DO for Dolores. Original Title:* DO pour Dolorès. Carole Fréchette. Courte Échelle, 1999. *Category:* Canada (French).

1730 2000. *The Other Life of Noël Bouchard. Original Title:* L'autre vie de Noël Bouchard. Hélène Gagnier. *Illustrator:* Christiane Gaudette. Tisseyre, 1998. *Category:* Canada (French).

1731 2000. *Charlotte and the Island of Fate. A Story. Original Title:* Charlotte et l'île du Destin. Une histoire. Olivier Lasser. *Illustrator:* Stéphane Jorisch. Les 400 Coups, 1998. *Category:* Canada (French).

1732 2000. *The Collector of Stories. A Story. Original Title:* Le cueilleur d'histoires. Un conte. Sonia Sarfati. *Illustrator:* Alfred Pellan. Musée du Québec, 1999. *Category:* Canada (French).

1733 2000. *Alex, the Little Hockey Player. Original Title:* Alex, le petit joueur de hockey. Gilles Tibo. *Illustrator:* Philippe Germain. Dominique et Compagnie, 1999. *Category:* Canada (French).

1734 2000. *The Concordant Gambusians. Original Title:* Svorni gambusini a jine pribehy. Jaroslav Foglar. *Illustrator:* Bohumir Cermak. Olympia, 1999. *Category:* Czech Republic.

1735 2000. *Four Friends for Eternity. Original Title:* Los cuatro amigos de siempre. Gilberto Rendón Ortiz. *Illustrator:* Rossana Bohórquez. Ed. SM, 1999. *Category:* Mexico.

1736 2000. *The Turtle Who Wanted to Fly. Original Title:* Uçmak isteyen kaplumbaga. Ismail Kaya. *Illustrator:* Ismail Kaya. Kök Yayincilik, 1997. *Category:* Turkey.

1737 2000. *Tales From Ancient Thracia. Original Title:* Prikazki ot drevna Trakija. Anatol Vesel. *Illustrator:* Venelin Valkanov. AB Veliko Tarnovo, 1997. *Category:* Bulgaria.

1738 2000. *Let the Verse Take You by the Hand. Original Title:* Aph'ste ton sticho na sas pareap'to cheri. Kostas Montes. Montis, 1999. *Category:* Cyprus (Greek).

1739 2000. *A. Diamantes. The Journey of the Little Gnarled Branch. Original Title:* A. Diamantes. To taxidi tes mikres rozus. Theodora Oronte-Siantu. *Illustrator:* Theodora Oronte-Siantu. Oronte-Siantu, 1996. *Category:* Cyprus (Greek).

1740 2000. *Legendary Fortresses. Original Title:* Legendás Váraink. Csaba Csorba. Magyar Könyvklub, 1999. *Category:* Hungary.

1741 2000. *Mirr Murr Takes a Ramble Through Budapest. Original Title:* Mirr Murr nyomoz Budapesten. István Csukás. *Illustrator:* Ferenc Cakó. Városháza, 1999. *Category:* Hungary.

1742 2000. *The Fantasy of Turnip and Reason. Original Title:* Fantasi-i šalgam wa ʿaql. Muhammad Muhammadi. Kitab-i Maryam, 1998. *Category:* Iran.

1743 2000. *The Girl with the Half-moon on Her Forehead. Original Title:* Mahpišani. Nasir Yusufi. *Illustrator:* Mihran Zamani. Našr-i Ufuq, 1997. *Category:* Iran.

1744 2000. *Now You See What Happened .... Original Title:* Dat komt er nou van .... Ingrid Schubert. *Illustrator:* Dieter Schubert. Lemniscaat, 1999. *Category:* The Netherlands (Dutch).

1745 2000. *Travel in the Year, 2150. Original Title:* 2150 yilina yolculuk. Zeliha Akçagüner. *Illustrator:* Gözde Bozkurt. Bu Yayinevi 1999. *Category:* Turkey.

1746 2000. *Do Not Enter! Original Title:* Verboden toegang. Beatrijs Nolet. *Illustrator:* Yvonne Jagtenberg. Van Holkema & Warendorf, 1999. *Category:* The Netherlands (Dutch).

1747 2000. *Mother's Light. Original Title:* Nur Ana. Nuran Turan. *Illustrator:* Serdar Demircan. Türkiye I° Bankasi, 1998. *Category:* Turkey.

1748 2000. *The Lost Tales. Original Title:* Les histories perdudes. Jordi Sierra i Fabra. *Illustrator:* Victòria Tubau. Ed. Cruïlla, 1999. *Category:* Spain (Catalan).

1749 2000. *Cosme and the Monster Wordmuncher. Original Title:* En Cosme i el monstre Menjamots. Núria Carol. *Illustrator:* Isidro Ferrer. Publ. de l'Abadia de Montserrat, 1999. *Category:* Spain (Catalan).

1750 2000. *Ioshi and the Rain. Original Title:* Ioshi i la pluja. Montserrat Canela. *Illustrator:* Max. LaGalera, 1999. *Category:* Spain (Catalan).

1751 2000. *I Have No Words. Original Title:* No tinc paraules. *Illustrator:* Arnal Ballester. Media Vaca, 1999. *Category:* Spain (Catalan).

1752 2000. *Photos of Sara. Original Title:* Las fotos de Sara. Gabriela Rubio. *Illustrator:* Gabriela Rubio. Ed. Destino, 1999. *Category:* Spain.

1753 2000. *Three Kings' Days. Original Title:* Días de Reyes Magos. Emilio Pascual. *Illustrator:* Javier Serrano. Anaya, 1999. *Category:* Spain.

1754 2000. *The Man-Eater.* Tagrid Arif an Naggar. *Illustrator:* Lamya Abd-as-Sahib. as-Salwa, 1998. *Category:* Jordon.

1755 2000. *A Saving Decision. Original Title:* Spasonosna odluka. Gordana Maletic-Vrhovac. *Illustrator:* Dragan Bosni. Knjigoteka, 1999. *Category:* Federal Republic of Yugoslavia.

1756 2000. *Spinners.* Donna Jo Napoli. *Illustrator:* Richard Tchen. Dutton, 1999. *Category:* U.S.A.

1757 2000. *Checkered Ideals. Original Title:* Kostkovaný ideály aneb breviár pro teenagery. Amulet, 1999. *Category:* Czech Republic.

1758 2000. *We Are Musicians, We Know Nothing. Original Title:* My nic, my muzikanti. Vera Stiborová. *Illustrator:* Václav Kabát. Albatros, 1999. *Category:* Czech Republic.

1759 2000. *Apple Tales. Original Title:* Obuoliu pasakos. Vytautas V. Landsbergis. *Illustrator:* Rimvydas Kepezinskas. Vaga, 1999. *Category:* Lithuanua.

1760 2000. *The Fairy. Original Title:* Feja Skazka. Izbrannye skazki dlja detej i vzroslych. Valerija F. Dauwalder. *Illustrator:* Valerija F. Dauwalder. Izdat. Arnika, 1998. *Category:* Russia.

1761 2000. *The Life of Famous Animals. Original Title:* Zizn' zamecatel'nych zverej. Michail D. Jasnov. *Illustrator:* V. Ju. Cernoglazov. Obrazovanie-Kul'tura, 1999. *Category:* Russia.

1762 2000. *Sweeteatology. Original Title:* Konfetoedenie. Grigorij B. Oster. *Illustrator:* Denis Burusov. Rosmen, 1999. *Category:* Russia.

1763 2000. *Once There Was an Angel. Original Title:* Henas angelos mia phora. Mania Duka. *Illustrator:* Andreas Malekos. Adam, 1999. *Category:* Cyprus (Greek).

1764 2000. *The Under-the-Bed Kobold. Original Title:* Podposteljni škrat. Saša Bogataj Ambrozic. *Illustrator:* Saša Bogataj Ambrozic. DZS, 1999. *Category:* Slovenia.

1765 2000. *When the Great Were Boys. Original Title:* Kdyz velci byli kluci. Hana Doskocilová. *Illustrator:* Gabriel Filcik. Amulet, 1999. *Category:* Czech Republic.

1766 2000. *The Wicked Fairy. Original Title:* Heksenfee. Brigitte Minne. *Illustrator:* Carll Cneut. Uitg. de Eenhoorn, 1999. *Category:* Belgium (Dutch).

1767 2000. *The Snowman Who Didn't Want to Melt. Original Title:* Van de sneeuwman die niet smelten wou. Henri VanDaele. *Illustrator:* Klaas Verplancke. Uitg. Altiora, 1999. *Category:* Belgium (Dutch).

1768 2000. *When Mouse Went for a Walk. Original Title:* Muis ging eens op wandel. Guido VanGenechten. *Illustrator:* Guido VanGenechten. Clavis, 1999. *Category:* Belgium (Dutch).

1769 2000. *Mart and Maki. Original Title:* Mart en de liefde. Arend van Dam. Uitg. Piramide, 1999. *Category:* The Netherlands (Dutch).

1770 2000. *Nanseli, Where are You Running To? Original Title:* Nanseli, waar ren je heen? Thea Dubelaar. *Illustrator:* Gitte Spee. Ploegsma, 1999. *Category:* The Netherlands (Dutch).

1771 2000. *What Is Written There? Original Title:* Wat staat daar? Rindert Kromhout. *Illustrator:* Annemarie van Haeringen. Leopold, 1999. *Category:* The Netherlands (Dutch).

1772 2000. *The Red-White Striped Sock. Original Title:* Een sok met streepjes. Leren lezen met plaatjes. Joke van Leeuwen. *Illustrator:* Joke van Leeuwen. Zwijsen, 1999. *Category:* The Netherlands (Dutch).

1773 2000. *The Life of Famous Children. Original Title:* Zizn' zamecatel'nych detej. Valerij M. Voskobojnikov. *Illustrator:* A. G. Starostin. Obrazovanie-Kul'tura, 1997. *Category:* Russia.

1774 2000. *Pontaro, the Bouncing Rubber-headed Boy. Original Title:* Pontaro, den. Shinta Cho. *Illustrator:* Shinta Cho. Doshinsha, 1998. *Category:* Japan.

1775 2000. *The Boy Who Became a Frog*. Ruth L. Makotsi. East African Educational Publishers, 1999. *Category:* Kenya.

1776 2000. *Zorro. In the Year of the Horse. Original Title:* Zorro. Im Jahr des Pferdes. Katja Behrens. Beltz & Gelberg, 1999. *Category:* Germany.

1777 2000. *Animal Companions. Original Title:* Animais de compañía. M. Lourenzo González. *Illustrator:* Enjamio. Kalandraka, 1998. *Category:* Spain (Galician).

1778 2000. *Original Title:* Batter; 2. Atsuko Asano. *Illustrator:* Makiko Sato. Kyoiku Gageki, 1998. *Category:* Japan.

1779 2000. *The Calf in Springtime. Original Title:* Koushi no haru. Taro Gomi. *Illustrator:* Taro Gomi. Kaiseisha, 1999. *Category:* Japan.

1780 2000. *Our Mr. Marshmallow. Original Title:* Bokutachi no Konnyaku sensei. Hiroko Hoshikawa. *Illustrator:* Hiroko Hoshikawa. Shogakukan, 1998. *Category:* Japan.

1781 2000. *No End of Hard Tests. Original Title:* Nigiyaka na okeiko. Hiroshi Ito. *Illustrator:* Hiroshi Ito. Tokuma Shoten, 1998. *Category:* Japan.

1782 2000. *What a Lovely Meeting! Original Title:* Yatto aeta. Eiko Konishi. *Illustrator:* Eiko Konishi. Shikosha, 1998. *Category:* Japan.

1783 2000. *The Moon Ship. Original Title:* Tsuki no fune. Eto Mori. Kodansha, 1998. *Category:* Japan.

1784 2000. *The Sunken Ship of the Wizard. Original Title:* Wushi-de-chenchuan. Ma Ban. 21-Shiji-Chubanshe, 1998. *Category:* China.

1785 2000. *The Girl Who Can and Other Stories.* Ama Ata Aidoo. Sub-Saharan Publishers, 1997. *Category:* Ghana.

1786 2000. *The Caterpillar's Dream. Original Title:* Xiaoqingchong-de-meng. Bo Bing. *Illustrator:* Xiang Zhou. Hunan-Shaonian-Ertong-Chubanshe, 1997. *Category:* China.

1787 2000. *The Scarecrow. Original Title:* Daocaoren. Shengtao Ye. *Illustrator:* Dungu Xu. Huashan-Wenyi-Chubanshe, 1997. *Category:* China.

1788 2000. *Red Fox. Original Title:* Honghuli. Shixi Shen. *Illustrator:* Aozi Xiao. Jiangsu-Shaonian-Ertong-Chubanshe, 1998. *Category:* China.

1789 2000. *A Bridge to the Other World. Original Title:* Oni no hashi. Yu Ito. *Illustrator:* Daihachi Æta. Fukuinkan Shoten, 1998. *Category:* Japan.

GREAT BRITAIN

1790 Aventis Prize for Science Books (formerly Rhone-Poulenc Prize for Science Books)

SPONSOR: Aventis. CONTACT: COPUS (Committee on the Public Understanding of Science). ADDRESS: The Royal Society, 6 Carlton Terrace, London, United

Kingdom SW1Y 5AG. PHONE: 020 7839 5561. ESTABLISHED: 2000. AWARD: £10, 000. The annual award is given to a popular non-fiction science and technology book.

1791 2000. *The Dorling Kindersley Guide to Space.* Peter Bond. Dorling Kindersley.

1792 Blue Peter Book Awards

SPONSOR: BBC Children's Programme. CONTACT: Scottish Book Trust. ADDRESS: Scottish Book Centre, 137 Dundee Street, Edinburgh, Scotland EH11 IBG. PHONE: 0131 229 3663. ESTABLISHED: 2000. Children aged 15 years and under across the U.K. vote for their favorite book in three categories: Book I Couldn't Put Down, Best Book To Read Aloud, Special Book to Keep Forever.

1793 2000. *The Shadow of the Minotaur.* Alan Gibbons. Orion, 1999. *Category:* Book I Couldn't Put Down.

1794 2000. *Pilgrim's Progress.* Geraldine McCaughrean (retold). Hodder, 1999. *Category:* Special Book To Keep Forever.

1795 2000. *The Gruffalo.* Julia Donaldson. Macmillan, 1999. *Category:* Best Book to Read Aloud.

1796 Branford Boase Award

SPONSOR: Founding Friends Scheme. CONTACT: Lois Beeson. ADDRESS: 18 Grosvenor Road, Portswood, Southampton, United Kingdom SO17 1RT. PHONE: 023 8055 5057. ESTABLISHED: 1999. AWARD: £1,000. The annual award is given for an outstanding first-time novel for children.

1797 2000. *Song Quest.* Katherine Roberts. Element Children's Books, 1999.

1798 Carnegie Medal

SPONSOR: The Library Association. CONTACT: Carl Clayton. ADDRESS: 7 Ridgmount Street, London, United Kingdom WC1E 7AE. PHONE: (071) 636 7543. ESTABLISHED: 1936. AWARD: A medal. The medal is awarded annually for "an outstanding book for children and young people."

1799 1990. *Wolf.* Gillian Cross. 1990.

1800 1991. *Dear Nobody.* Berlie Doherty. 1991.

1801 1992. *Flour Babies.* Anne Fine. 1992.

1802 1993. *Stone Cold.* Robert Swindells. 1993.

1803 1994. *Whispers in the Graveyard.* Theresa Breslin. 1994.

1804 1995. *Northern Lights.* Philip Pullman. 1995.

1805 1996. *Junk.* Melvin Burgess. Andersen Press, 1996.

1806 1997. *River Boy.* Tim Bowler. Oxford, 1997.

1807 1998. *Skellig.* David Almond. Hodder, 1998.

1808 1999. *Postcards from No Man's Land.* Aidan Chambers. Bodley Head, 1999.

1809 Children's Book Award

SPONSOR: Federation of Children's Book Groups. CONTACT: Marianne Adey. ADDRESS: The Old Malt House Aldbourne, Marlborough, Wiltshire, United Kingdom SN8 2DW. PHONE: 01672 540629. ESTABLISHED: 1980. AWARD: A sculpture by Graham Stewart of a silver tree symbolising growth and knowledge. The award is given annually for the best work of fiction published in the year preceding the year of the award. There are three category winners: picture book; shorter novel; and longer novel.

1810 1990. *Threadbear.* Mick Inkpen. Hodder & Stoughton, 1990.

1811 1991. *Kiss the Dust.* Elizabeth Laird. Heinemann, 1991.

1812 1993. *The Suitcase Kid.* Jacqueline Wilson. Heinemann, 1993.

1813 1994. *The Boy in the Bubble.* Ian Strachan. Methuen, 1994. *Category:* longer novel.

1814 1994. *The Finders.* Nigel Hinton. Viking, 1994. *Category:* shorter novel.

1815 1994. *Amazing Anthony Ant.* Lorna Philpot. *Illustrator:* Graham Philpot. Orion, 1994. *Category:* picture book.

1816 1995. *Walk Two Moons.* Sharon Creech. Pan Macmillan, 1995. *Category:* longer novel.

1817 1995. *Harriet's Hare.* Dick King-Smith. Doubleday, 1995. *Category:* shorter novel.

1818 1995. *Paul the Rascally Cake.* Jeanne Willis. *Illustrator:* Jeanne Willis. Andersen Press, 1995. *Category:* picture book.

1819 1996. *The Wreck of the Zanzibar.* Michael Morpurgo. Heinemann, 1996. *Category:* longer novel.

1820 1996. *Double Act.* Jacqueline Wilson. Doubleday, 1996. *Category:* shorter novel.

1821 1996. *Solo.* Paul Geraghty. *Illustrator:* Paul Geraghty. Hutchinson, 1996. *Category:* picture book.

1822 1997. *The Hundred-Mile-An-Hour Dog.* Jeremy Strong. *Illustrator:* Nick Sharratt. Viking, 1997. *Category:* shorter novel.

1823 1997. *Which Way Is Home?* Ian Strachan. Mammoth, 1997. *Category:* longer novel.

1824 1997. *Mr. Bear to the Rescue.* Debi Glori. *Illustrator:* Debi Glori. Orchard, 1997. *Category:* picture book.

1825 1998. *Harry Potter and the Philosopher's Stone.* J.K. Rowling. Bloomsbury, 1998. *Category:* longer novel.

1826 1998. *Nightmare Stairs.* Robert Swindells. Doubleday, 1998. *Category:* shorter novel.

1827 1998. *The Lion Who Wanted to Love.* Giles Andreae. *Illustrator:* David Wojtowycz. Orchard, 1998. *Category:* picture book.

1828 1999. *What!* Kate Lum. *Illustrator:* Adrian Johnson. Bloomsbury, 1999. *Category:* picture books.

1829 1999. *Harry Potter and the Chamber of Secrets.* J.K. Rowling. Bloomsbury, 1999. *Category:* longer novel.

1830 1999. *Little Dad.* Pat Moon. *Illustrator:* Nick Sharratt. Mammoth, 1999. *Category:* shorter novel.

1831 2000. *Harry Potter and the Prisoner of Azkaban.* J.K. Rowling. Bloomsbury, 2000. *Category:* longer novel.

1832 2000. *Kensuke's Kingdom.* Michael Morpurgo. *Illustrator:* Michael Foreman. Mammoth, 2000. *Category:* shorter novels.

1833 2000. *Demon Teddy.* Nicholas Allan. *Illustrator:* Nicholas Allan. Hutchinson, 2000. *Category:* picture book.

1834 Earthworm Award

Discontinued. ESTABLISHED: 1987. The aim of the award was to promote environmental awareness and sensitivity in literature for children of all ages. Books must have been written in English, and either published or distributed in the United Kingdom. The books must have been published during the preceding year.

1835 1990. *The Young Green Consumer Guide.* John Elkington, Julia Hailes. *Illustrator:* Tony Ross. Gollancz, 1990.

1836 1991. No award given.
1992. No award given.

1837 1993. *Strange Orbit.* Margaret Simpson. State University of New York Press, 1997.

1838 1994. *Project Kite.* Sian Lewis. Arrow Books Ltd, 1994.

1839 Eleanor Farjeon Award

SPONSOR: The Children's Book Circle. CONTACT: Susan Barry. ADDRESS: 96 Leonard Street, London, United Kingdom EC2A 4RH. PHONE: 020 7739 2929. ESTABLISHED: 1965. AWARD: A certificate and £500. The award is made to an individual in recognition of their distinguished contribution to the world of children's books.

1840 1990. Jill Bennett.

1841 1991. Patricia Crampton.

1842 1992. Stephanie Nettell.

1843 1993. Susan Belgrave.

1844 1994. Eileen Colwell.

1845 1995. Helen Paiba.

1846 1996. Books for Keeps.
1847 1997. Michael Rosen.
1848 1998. Gina Pollinger.
1849 1999. Klaus Flugge.
1850 2000. Julia Eccleshare.

1851 Fidler Award (formerly Kathleen Fidler Award)

SPONSOR: Hodder Children's Books and Scottish Book Trust. ADDRESS: The Scottish Book Centre, 137 Dundee Street, Edinburgh, Scotland EH11 IBG. PHONE: 0131 229 3663. ESTABLISHED: 1996. AWARD: An advance of £1000, plus a royalty package, and a rosewood and silver trophy. The annual award is given to the author and illustrator of a children's book which combines excellence in both text and illustration.

1852 1997. *Slate Mountain.* Mark Leyland. Hodder Children's Books, 1998.
1853 1998. *The Falcon's Quest.* John Smirthwaite. Hodder Children's Books, 1998.
1854 1999. *The Memory Prisoner.* Thomas Bloor. Hodder Children's Books, 1999.
1855 2000. *The Ivy Crown.* Gill Vickery. Hodder Children's Books, 2001.

1856 Guardian Children's Fiction Award

SPONSOR: The Guardian. CONTACT: Stephanie Nettell — Children's Book Editor. ADDRESS: 119 Farringdon Road, London, United Kingdom EC1R 3ER. PHONE: (01) 278 2332. ESTABLISHED: 1967. AWARD: £500. The award is given annually for a work of fiction published in Britain by a British or Commonwealth author in the previous year. Picture books and books by previous winners are excluded.

1857 1990. *Goggle-Eyes.* Anne Fine. Hamish Hamilton, 1989.
1858 1991. *The Kingdom by the Sea.* Robert Westall. 1990.
1859 1992. *Paper Faces.* Rachel Andersen. 1991.
1860 1992. *The Exiles.* Hilary McKay. 1991.
1861 1993. *Low Tide.* William Mayne. 1992.
1862 1994. *The Mennyms.* Sylvia Waugh. 1993.
1863 1995. *Maphead.* Lesley Howarth. 1994.
1864 1996. *Northern Lights.* Philip Pullman. 1995.
1865 1997. *Junk.* Melvin Burgess. Andersen Press, 1996.
1866 1998. *Fire, Bed and Bone.* Henrietta Brandford. Walker, 1997.
1867 1999. *The Sterkarm Handshake.* Susan Price. Scholastic, 1998.
1868 2000. *The Illustrated Mum.* Jacqueline Wilson. Transworld, 1999.

1869 Harvey Darton Award

SPONSOR: Children's Books History Society. ADDRESS: 25 Field Way, Hoddesdon Hertfordshire, United Kingdom EN11 0QN. The biennial award is given for a distinguished contribution to the history of British children's literature.

1870 1994. *From the Beast to the Blonde.* Marina Warner. Chatto and Windus.

1871 1996. *G. A. Henty 1832-1902.* Peter Newbolt. Scolar Press.

1872 1996. *The Natural History of Make-Believe.* John Goldthwaite. Oxford.

1873 Kate Greenaway Medal

SPONSOR: The Library Association. CONTACT: Carl Clayton. ADDRESS: 7 Ridgmount Street, London, United Kingdom WC1E 7AE. PHONE: (071) 636 7543. ESTABLISHED: 1955. AWARD: A medal. The award is given annually to the artist who has produced (in the opinion of The Library Association) the best illustration for children's books. The book must be published in the preceding year in the United Kingdom. Medals can be awarded to the same illustrator more than once.

1874 1991. *The Jolly Christmas Postman.* Allan Ahlberg, Janet Ahlberg. *Illustrator:* Allan Ahlberg, Janet Ahlberg. Heinemann, 1990.

1875 1992. *Zoo.* Anthony Browne. *Illustrator:* Anthony Browne. 1991.

1876 1993. *Black Ships Before Troy.* Rosemary Sutcliff. *Illustrator:* Alan Lee. 1992.

1877 1994. *The Way Home.* Libby Hathorn. *Illustrator:* Gregory Rogers. 1993.

1878 1995. *The Christmas Miracle of Jonathan Toomey.* Susan Wojciechowski. *Illustrator:* P.J. Lynch. 1994.

1879 1996. *The Baby Wouldn't Go to Bed.* Helen Cooper. *Illustrator:* Helen Cooper. Picture Corgi, 1995.

1880 1997. *When Jessie Came Across the Sea.* Amy Hest. *Illustrator:* P.J. Lynch. Walker, 1996.

1881 1998. *Pumpkin Soup.* Helen Cooper. *Illustrator:* Helen Cooper. Doubleday, 1997.

1882 1999. *Alice's Adventures in Wonderland.* Lewis Carroll. *Illustrator:* Helen Oxenbury. Walker Books, 1998.

1883 Kathleen Fidler Award

Discontinued. ESTABLISHED: 1980. The award was given for a children's novel in the 8–12 age group. It must have been the author's first novel for this age group.

1884 1990. *Magic with Everything.* Roger Burt. Blackie, 1990.

1885 1993. *48 Hours with Franklin.* Mij Kelly.

1886 Kurt Maschler Award

SPONSOR: Book Trust. CONTACT: Sandra Vince. ADDRESS: Book House, 45 East Hill, London, United Kingdom SW18 2QZ. PHONE: (020) 8516 2972. ESTABLISHED: 1982. AWARD: An "Emil" a bronze figure of Erich Kastner's character and £1000. The award is made to the author and illustrator of a children's book which combines excellence in both text and illustration. Entries for the award must have been published during the preceding year.

1887 1990. *All Join In.* Quentin Blake. *Illustrator:* Quentin Blake. Cape, 1990.

1888 1991. *Have You Seen Who's Moved in Next Door to Us?* Colin McNaughton. *Illustrator:* Colin McNaughton. Walker, 1991.

1889 1992. *The Man.* Raymond Briggs. *Illustrator:* Raymond Briggs. Julia McRae, 1992.

1890 1993. *Think of an Eel.* Karen Wallace. *Illustrator:* Mike Bostock. Walker, 1993.

1891 1994. *So Much.* Trisha Cooke. *Illustrator:* Helen Oxenbury. Walker Books, 1994.

1892 1995. *The Little Boat.* Kathy Hendersen. *Illustrator:* Patrick Benson. Walker, 1995.

1893 1996. *Drop Dead.* Babette Cole. *Illustrator:* Babette Cole. Cape, 1996.

1894 1997. *Lady Muck.* William Mayne. *Illustrator:* Jonathan Heale. Heinemann, 1997.

1895 1998. *Voices in the Park.* Anthony Browne. *Illustrator:* Anthony Browne. Doubleday, 1998.

1896 1999. *Alice's Adventures in Wonderland.* Lewis Carroll. *Illustrator:* Helen Oxenbury. Walker, 1999.

1897 Lancashire County Library Children's Book of the Year Award

SPONSOR: Lancashire County Council. ADDRESS: PO Box 61, County Hall, Preston, United Kingdom PR1 8RJ. PHONE: 01772 264008. ESTABLISHED: 1986. AWARD: £500 and an engraved decanter. The award is presented annually to the best work of fiction aimed at 11 to 14 year-olds written by an author from the U.K. and first published between 1 September and 31 August of the previous year.

1898 1990. *Plague 99.* Jean Ure. Methuen, 1988.

1899 1991. *Mattimeo.* Brian Jacques. Hutchinson, 1989.

1900 1992. *The Whitby Witches.* Robin Jarvis. Simon & Schuster, 1990.

1901 1993. *Gulf.* Robert Westall. Methuen, 1991.

1902 1993. *Salamandastron.* Brian Jacques. Hutchinson, 1992.

1903 1994. *The Boy in the Bubble.* Ian Strachan. Methuen, 1993.

1904 1995. *The Electric Kid.* Garry Kilworth. Transworld, 1994.

1905 1996. *Chandra.* Frances Mary Hendry. Oxford University Press, 1995.

1906 1997. *Sea of Peril.* Elizabeth Hawkins. Orchard Books, 1996.
1907 1998. *Jay.* Elizabeth Laird. Mammoth, 1997.
1908 1999. *Out of the Darkness.* Nigel Hinton. Puffin Books, 1998.
1909 2000. *Shadows.* Tim Bowler. Oxford University Press, 1999.

1910 Mary Vaughan Jones Award

SPONSOR: Welsh Book Council. CONTACT: Gwerfyl Pierce Jones. ADDRESS: Castell Brychan, Aberystwyth, Ceredigion, Wales SY23 2JB. PHONE: (01970) 62 4151. ESTABLISHED: 1985. AWARD: A silver trophy depicting characters from Mary Vaughan Jones's books. The prize is awarded every three years to a person who has made an outstanding contribution to literature in the Welsh language over a considerable period of time.

1911 1991. T. Llew Jones.
1912 1994. W.J. Jones.
1913 1997. Roger Boore.
1914 2000. J. Selwyn Lloyd.

1915 Macmillan Prize

Discontinued. ESTABLISHED: 1986. The award was given for a work by an illustrator which the jury considered to be an original contribution to the field.

1916 1990. Peter Lubach. *Category:* second prize.
1917 1990. Patrick Yee. *Category:* third prize.
1990. No award given. *Category:* first prize.
1918 1990. Alice Dumas. *Category:* third prize.
1995. No award given.
1996. No award given.
1919 1997. Angela Simpkin.
1920 1998. Katherine Redfern.
1921 1999. Candice Whatmore.

1922 Mother Goose Award

Discontinued. ESTABLISHED: 1979. Awarded to the most exciting newcomer to British children's book illustration. The award's aim was to encourage illustrators at the beginning of their careers, by drawing serious critical attention to their work, and to encourage children's book publishers to continue to foster new talent in the field of illustration.

1923 1990. *Strat and Chatto.* David Hughes. Walker, 1989.
1924 1991. *A Close Call.* Amanda Harvey. *Illustrator:* Amanda Harvey. 1990.
1925 1992. *Inside the Whale and Other Animals.* Steve Parker. *Illustrator:* Ted Dewan. 1991.

1926 1993. *The Seashell Song.* Susie Jenkin-Pearce. *Illustrator:* Claire Fletcher. 1992.

1927 1994. *Where the Great Bear Watches.* James Sage. *Illustrator:* Lisa Flather. 1993.

1928 1995. *I Love Animals.* Flora McDonnell. *Illustrator:* Flora McDonnell. 1994.

1929 1996. *When Martha's Away.* Bruce Ingman. *Illustrator:* Bruce Ingman. 1995.

1930 1997. *Catherine and the Lion.* Clare Jarrett. *Illustrator:* Clare Jarrett. HarperCollins, 1996.

1931 1998. *Motley the Cat.* Mary Fedden. *Illustrator:* Mary Fedden. Viking, 1997.

1932 1999. *The Gigantic Turnip and Tales of Wisdom and Wonder.* Niamh Sharkey. *Illustrator:* Niamh Sharkey. Barefoot Books, 1998.

1933 NASEN Special Needs Book Awards

SPONSOR: National Association for Special Educational Needs and the Educational Publishers Council. CONTACT: The Publishers Association. ADDRESS: 1 Kingsway, London, United Kingdom WC2B 6XF. PHONE: 020 7565 7474. ESTABLISHED: 1994. This award is given to the book of any genre that most successfully provides a positive image of children or young people with special needs.

1934 1994. *See Ya, Simon.* David Hill. Penguin.

1935 1995. *The Golden Bird.* Berlie Doherty. Heinemann.

1936 1996. *How to Write Really Badly.* Anne Fine. Methuen.

1937 1997. *Charlie's Eye.* Dorothy Horgan. Hamish Hamilton.

1938 1998. *The Crowstarver.* Dick King-Smith. Doubleday.

1939 1999. *Sweet Clarinet.* James Riordan. Oxford.

1940 2000. *Susan Laughs.* Jeanne Willis. Andersen Press.

1941 National Art Library Illustration Awards (formerly W.H. Smith Illustration Award)

SPONSOR: The Enid Linder Foundation. ADDRESS: 35 Tranquil Vale, Blackheath, London, United Kingdom. PHONE: 020 8297 9884. ESTABLISHED: 1995. AWARD: The overall winner receives £2,500; the two second prize winners receive £1,000. The annual award is given for illustration in books and magazines.

1942 1995. *Celebration Song.* James Berry. *Illustrator:* Louise Brierley. Hamish Hamilton, 1994. *Category:* second prize.

1943 1995. *Button.* Sara Fanelli. *Illustrator:* Sara Fanelli. ABC, 1994. *Category:* overall winner.

1944 1996. *When Martha's Away.* Bruce Ingman. *Illustrator:* Bruce Ingman. Methuen, 1995. *Category:* overall winner.

1945 1996. *Clown.* Quentin Blake. *Illustrator:* Quentin Blake. Jonathan Cape, 1995. *Category:* second prize.

1946 1997. *The It-Doesn't Matter Suit.* Sylvia Plath. *Illustrator:* Rotraut Susanne Berner. Faber & Faber, 1996. *Category:* second prize.

1947 1997. *The Complete Entertainments.* Geoff Grandfield. *Illustrator:* Geoff Grandfield. The Folio Society, 1996. *Category:* overall winner.

1948 1998. *The Scarlet Pimpernel.* Emmuska Orczy. *Illustrator:* Lucy Weller. The Folio Society, 1997. *Category:* second prize.

1949 1998. *Cautionary Tales and Other Verses. Illustrator:* Posy Simmonds. The Folio Society, 1997. *Category:* overall winner.

1950 1999. *The Hare and Tortoise.* Helen Ward. *Illustrator:* Helen Ward. Templar Publishing, 1998. *Category:* second prize.

1951 1999. *The Ring of Words.* Roger McGough (editor). *Illustrator:* Satoshi Kitamura. Faber & Faber, 1998. *Category:* overall winner.

1952 2000. *The Boy Who Lost His Bellybutton.* Jeanne Willis. *Illustrator:* Tony Ross. Andersen Press, 1999. *Category:* second prize.

1953 2000. *The Sea-Thing Child.* Russell Hoban. *Illustrator:* Patrick Benson. Walker Books, 1999. *Category:* overall winner.

1954 Nestle Smarties Book Prize

SPONSOR: Book Trust. CONTACT: Book House. ADDRESS: 45 East Hill, London, United Kingdom SW18 2QZ. PHONE: (081) 870 9055. ESTABLISHED: 1985. AWARD: Three categories: 5 years and under, 6–8 years, and 9–11 years. Each receive £1000. The award is given for excellence in writing for children and to stimulate interest in children's books.

1955 1990. *Esio Trot.* Roald Dahl. *Illustrator:* Quentin Blake. Cape, 1990. *Category:* 6–8 years.

1956 1990. *Midnight Blue.* Pauline Fisk. Lion, 1990. *Category:* grand prize.

1957 1990. *Six Dinner Sid.* Inga Moore. *Illustrator:* Inga Moore. Simon & Schuster, 1990. *Category:* under 5 years.

1958 1991. *Krindledrax.* Philip Ridley. Cape, 1991. *Category:* 9–11 years.

1959 1991. *Farmer Duck.* Martin Waddell. *Illustrator:* Helen Oxenbury. Walker Books, 1991. *Category:* under 5 years (grand prize).

1960 1991. *Jose Smith and Eileen.* Magdalen Nabb. Collins, 1991. *Category:* 6–8 years.

1961 1992. *The Story of Creation.* Jane Ray. Orchard Books, 1992. *Category:* 6–8 years.

1962 1992. *Nice Work, Little Wolf.* Hilda Offen. *Illustrator:* Hilda Offen. Hamish Hamilton, 1992. *Category:* under 5 years.

1963 1992. *The Great Elephant Chase.* Gillian Grosse. Oxford, 1992. *Category:* 9–11 years (grand prize).

1964 1993. *Hue Boy.* Rita Phillips Mitchell. *Illustrator:* Rita Phillips Mitchell. Gollancz, 1993. *Category:* under 5 years.

1965 1993. *Listen to the Dark.* Maeve Henry. Heinemann, 1993. *Category:* 9–11.

1966 1993. *War Game.* Michael Foreman. Pavilion, 1993. *Category:* 6–8 years (grand prize).

1967 1994. *Dimanche Diller.* Henrietta Brandford. *Illustrator:* Lesley Harker. Young Lions, 1994. *Category:* 6–8 years.

1968 1994. *So Much.* Trisha Cooke. *Illustrator:* Helen Oxenbury. Walker Books, 1994. *Category:* under 5 years.

1969 1994. *The Exiles at Home.* Hilary McKay. Gollancz, 1994. *Category:* 9–11 years (grand prize).

1970 1995. *Double Act.* Jacqueline Wilson. Doubleday, 1995. *Category:* 9–11 years (grand prize).

1971 1995. *The Last Noo-Noo.* Jill Murphy. *Illustrator:* Jill Murphy. Walker Books, 1995. *Category:* under 5 years.

1972 1995. *Thomas and the Tonners.* Jill Paton Walsh. Macdonald Young Books, 1995. *Category:* 6–8 years.

1973 1996. *Oops!* Colin McNaughton. *Illustrator:* Colin McNaughton. Andersen Books, 1996. *Category:* under 5 years (grand prize).

1974 1996. *The Beautiful Lion.* Michael Morpurgo. *Illustrator:* Christian Birmingham. Collins, 1996. *Category:* 6–8 years (grand prize).

1975 1996. *The Firework-Maker's Daughter.* Philip Pullman. *Illustrator:* Nick Harris. Corgi Yearling, 1996. *Category:* 9–11 years (grand prize).

1976 1997. *Ginger.* Charlotte Voake. *Illustrator:* Charlotte Voake. Walker Books, 1997. *Category:* under 5 years (grand prize).

1977 1997. *Harry Potter and the Philosopher's Stone.* J.K. Rowling. Bloomsbury, 1997. *Category:* 9–11 years (grand prize).

1978 1997. *The Owl Tree.* Jenny Nimmo. *Illustrator:* Anthony Lewis. Walker Books, 1997. *Category:* 6–8 years (grand prize).

1979 1998. *Last of the Gold Diggers.* Harry Horse. Puffin Books, 1998. *Category:* 6–8 years (grand prize).

1980 1998. *Cowboy Baby.* Sue Heap. *Illustrator:* Sue Heap. Walker Books, 1998. *Category:* under 5 years (grand prize).

1981 1998. *Harry Potter and the Chamber of Secrets.* J.K. Rowling. Bloomsbury, 1998. *Category:* 9–11 years (grand prize).

1982 1999. *The Gruffalo.* Julia Donaldson. *Illustrator:* Axel Scheffler. Macmillan. *Category:* 0–5.

1983 1999. *Harry Potter and the Prisoner of Azkaban.* J.K. Rowling. Bloomsbury, 1999. *Category:* 9–11.

1984 1999. *Snow White and the Seven Aliens.* Laurence Anholt. *Illustrator:* Arthur Robins. Orchard Books. *Category:* 6–8.

1985 2000. *Max.* Bob Graham. Walker Books. *Category:* 0–5.

1986 2000. *Lizzie Zipmouth.* Jacqueline Wilson. Young Corgi. *Category:* 6–8.

1987 2000. *The Wind Singer.* William Nicholson. Mammoth. *Category:* 9–11.

1988 North East Book Award

SPONSOR: Northumberland School Library Service. CONTACT: Eileen Armstrong. ADDRESS: Cramlington Community High School, Cramlington, Northumberland, United Kingdom NE23 6BN. PHONE: 01670 712 311. ESTABLISHED: 1999. The prize is awarded to a book first published in paperback in the previous year and written by an author resident in the United Kingdom.

1989 1999. *Harry Potter and the Chamber of Secrets.* J.K. Rowling. Bloomsbury, 1998.

1990 Rhone-Poulenc Prize (formerly Science Book Prizes)

Discontinued. ESTABLISHED: 1991. The award was given to the best popular science book in the under 14 years category. The books must have been written in English and published in the United Kingdom in the previous calendar year.

1991 1991. *Cell Wars.* Fran Balkwill, Mic Rolph. Collins, 1990.

1992 1991. *Cells Are Us.* Fran Balkwill, Mic Rolph. Collins, 1990.

1993 1992. *The Amazing Voyage of the Cucumber Sandwich.* Peter Rowan. Dorling Kindersley, 1991.

1994 1992. *How Nature Works.* David Burnie. Dorling Kindersley, 1991.

1995 1993. *Mighty Microbes.* Thompson Yardley. Cassell, 1992.

1996 1994. *The Ultimate Dinosaur Book.* David Lambert. Dorling Kindersley, 1993.

1997 1994. *Science with Weather.* Rebecca Heddle, Paul Shipton. Usborne, 1993.

1998 1994. *Eyewitness Guide: Evolution.* Linda Gamlin. Dorling Kindersley, 1993.

1999 1995. *The Most Amazing Pop-Up Science Book.* Jay Young. Watts, 1994.

2000 1996. *The World of Weather.* Chris Maynard. Kingfisher, 1995.

2001 1997. *Horrible Science: Ugly Bugs.* Nick Arnold, Tony De Saulles. Scholastic, 1996.

2002 1997. *Horrible Science: Blood, Bones and Body Bits.* Nick Arnold, Tony De Saulles. Weidenfeld & Nicolson, 1996.

2003 1998. *The Kingfisher Book of Oceans.* David Lambert. Kingfisher, 1997.

2004 1999. *The Usborne Complete Book of the Microscope.* Kirsteen Rogers. Usborne, 1998.

2005 Sainsbury's Baby Book Award

SPONSOR: Book Trust. CONTACT: Tarryn McKay. ADDRESS: 45 East Hill, London, United Kingdom SW18 2QZ. PHONE: 020 8516 2972. ESTABLISHED: 1999. AWARD: £2,000 and a trophy to the author. The annual award is for best book for a baby.

2006 1999. *Tickle, Tickle.* Helen Oxenbury. *Illustrator:* Helen Oxenbury. Walker, 1998.

2007 2000. *Boo Barney.* Alex Ayliffe. *Illustrator:* Alex Ayliffe. Orchard Books, 1999.

2008 Sheffield Children's Book Award

CONTACT: Jennifer Wilson (Book Award Coordinator). ADDRESS: c/o Schools Library Service, Sheffield, United Kingdom. PHONE: 0114 250 6843. ESTABLISHED: 1989. AWARD: A trophy. The award is presented annually.

2009 1990. *The Promise. Category:* 12+.

2010 1992. *Gulf. Category:* 12+.

2011 1993. *The Dog That Dug.* Jonathan Long. *Illustrator:* Korky Paul. Bodley Head.

2012 1994. *A Time of Fire.*

2013 1998. *Mucky Pup.* Ken Brown. *Category:* picture book.

2014 1998. *Pirate Pandemonium.* Jeremy Strong. *Illustrator:* Judy Brown. *Category:* shorter novel.

2015 1998. *Harry Potter and the Philosopher's Stone.* J.K. Rowling. *Category:* longer novel.

2016 1999. *The Time It Took Tom.* Nick Sharratt, Stephen Tucker. Scholastic. *Category:* picture book.

2017 1999. *Buried Alive.* Jacqueline Wilson. *Illustrator:* Nick Sharratt. Yearling. *Category:* shorter novel.

2018 1999. *Abomination.* Robert Swindells. *Category:* longer novel.

2019 2000. *Cry Wolf.* Susan Gates. Scholastic. *Category:* shorter novel.

2020 2000. *Harry and the Bucketful of Dinosaurs.* Ian Whybrow. *Illustrator:* Adrain Reynolds. David & Charles Children's Books. *Category:* picture book.

2021 2000. *Harry Potter and the Prisoner of Azkaban.* J.K. Rowling. Bloomsbury. *Category:* longer novel.

2022 Signal Poetry Award

SPONSOR: Thimble Press. CONTACT: Nancy Chambers. ADDRESS: Lockwood, Station Road, Woodchester Stroud, Gloucester, United Kingdom GL5 5EQ. PHONE: (01453) 873716. ESTABLISHED: 1979. AWARD: A certificate designed by Michael Harvey and £100. The award is given for a published work in the following categories: single-poet collections, anthologies, the body of work of a contemporary poet, and critical or educational activity promoting poetry for children.

2023 1990. *Heard It in the Playground.* Allan Ahlberg. Viking Kestrel, 1989.
2024 1991. *This Poem Doesn't Rhyme.* Gerard Benson (editor). Viking, 1990.
2025 1992. *Shades of Green.* Anne Harvey (editor). Julia McRae, 1991.
2026 1993. *Two's Company.* Jackie Kay. Blackie, 1992.
2027 1994. *The All-Nite Cafe.* Philip Gross. Faber, 1993.
2028 1995. *Secrets.* Helen Dunmore. Bodley Head, 1994.
2029 1996. *Buns for the Elephant.* Mike Harding. Viking, 1995.
2030 1997. *Stopping for Death.* Carol Ann Duffy (editor). Viking, 1996.
2031 1998. *Bad, Bad Cats.* Roger McGough. Viking, 1996.
2032 1999. *The Frog Who Dreamed She Was an Opera Singer.* Jackie Kay. Bloomsbury, 1997.
2033 2000. *All Sorts.* Christopher Reid. *Illustrator:* Sara Fanelli. Ondt & Gracehoper, 1998.

2034 Times Educational Supplement Information Book Awards

SPONSOR: The Times Educational Supplement. CONTACT: The Co-ordinator. ADDRESS: 66–68 East Smithfield, London, United Kingdom E1W 1BX. PHONE: (020) 7782 3269. ESTABLISHED: 1972. AWARD: £500 to authors with a possible £250 to illustrators. The award is given for the best information book published in the U.K. or the Commonwealth.

2035 1990. *The New Oxford School Atlas.* Patrick Wiegand (ed.). Oxford, 1990. *Category:* senior.
2036 1990. *The Tree.* Judy Hindley. *Illustrator:* Alison Wisenfeld. ABC, 1990. *Category:* junior.
2037 1991. *An Egyptian Pyramid.* Jacqueline Morley, Mark Bergin. Simon & Schuster, 1990. *Category:* senior.
2038 1991. *Ian and Fred's Big Green Book.* Fred Pearce, Ian Winton. Kingfisher/Bennett Books, 1990. *Category:* junior.
2039 1992. *Black and British.* David Bygott. Oxford University Press, 1991. *Category:* senior.
2040 1992. *My First Book of Time.* Claire Llewellynn. Dorling Kindersley, 1991. *Category:* junior.
2041 1993. *Think of an Eel.* Karen Wallace. Walker, 1992. *Category:* junior.
2042 1993. *Getting Physical.* Aric Sigman. BBC, 1992. *Category:* senior.
1994. No award given.
1995. No award given.
2043 1996. *Children Just Like Me.* Barnabas Kindersley, Anabel Kindersley. Dorling Kindersley, 1995. *Category:* junior.
2044 1996. *Keeping Clean: A Very Peculiar History.* Daisy Kerr. Watts Books, 1995. *Category:* senior.

2045 1996. *Young Citizen's Passport.* The Citizen Foundation. Hodder & Stoughton, 1995. *Category:* senior.

2046 1997. *The World of Shakespeare.* Rebecca Treays. Usborne, 1996. *Category:* senior.

2047 1997. *What's Under the Bed?* Mick Manning. Watts, 1996. *Category:* junior.

2048 1998. *Time and the Universe.* Mary Gribbon, John Gribbon. Hodder, 1995. *Category:* junior.

2049 1998. *Big Bang.* Heather Couper, Nigel Henbest. Dorling Kindersley, 1997. *Category:* senior.

2050 1999. *Letters to Henrietta.* Neil Marshall. Cambridge University Press, 1998. *Category:* junior.

2051 1999. *Witnesses to War.* Michael Leapman. Viking, 1998. *Category:* senior.

2052 2000. *A Visitor's Guide to Ancient Rome.* Lesley Sims. *Illustrator:* Christyan Fox. Usborne, 1999. *Category:* senior.

2053 2000. *The Emperor's Egg.* Martin Jenkins. Walker Books, 1999. *Category:* junior.

2054 Tir Na n-Og Awards

SPONSOR: Welsh Book Council. CONTACT: Gwerfyl Pierce Jones—Director. ADDRESS: Castell Brychan, Aberystwyth, Dyfed, Wales SY23 2JB. PHONE: (0970) 624151. ESTABLISHED: 1976. AWARD: £350. The aim of the award is to acknowledge the work of the authors and illustrators of children's books, to raise the standard of writing for children and young adults, and to bring these books to the attention of readers. The award is given for the best original book published in the year prior to the announcement. There are three categories: best original Welsh fiction, best original Welsh non-fiction, and English book with an authentic Welsh background.

2055 1990. *Lleuad yn Olau.* T. Llew Jones. *Illustrator:* Jac Jones. Gwasg Gomer, 1989. *Category:* Welsh (best book of the year).

1990. No award given. *Category:* Anglo-Welsh.

2056 1990. *Llygedyn o Heulwen.* Mair Wynn Hughes. Gwasg Gomer, 1989. *Category:* Welsh (fiction).

1991. No award given. *Category:* English language.

2057 1991. *Original Title:* Cymru Ddoe a Heddiw. Geraint H. Jenkins. Gwasg Prifysgol Rhydychen/CBAC, 1990. *Category:* Welsh-language non-fiction.

2058 1991. *Original Title:* O Ddawns i Ddawns. Gareth F. Williams. Y Lolfa, 1990. *Category:* Welsh-language fiction.

2059 1992. *Who Stole a Bloater?* Frances Thomas. Seren Books, 1992. *Category:* English language.

2060 1992. *Original Title:* Yn y Dechreuad. Robert M. Morris. *Illustrator:*

Catrin Stephens. Gwasg Prifysgol Rhydychen/CBAC, 1991. *Category:* Welsh-language non-fiction.

2061 1992. *Original Title:* Broc Môr. Gwen Redvers Jones. Gwasg Gomer, 1991. *Category:* Welsh-language fiction.

2062 1992. *Original Title:* Wmffra. Emily Huws. Gwasg Gomer, 1991. *Category:* Welsh-language fiction.

2063 1993. *Original Title:* 'Tisio Tshipsan? Emily Huws. Gwasg Gomer, 1992. *Category:* Welsh-language fiction.

2064 1993. *Original Title:* Chwedl Taliesin. Gwyn Thomas. *Illustrator:* Margaret Jones. Gwasg Prifysgol Cymru, 1992. *Category:* Welsh-language non-fiction.

1993. No award given. *Category:* English language.

2065 1994. *Denny and the Magic Pool.* Pamela Purnell. Pont/Gomer Press, 1993. *Category:* English language.

2066 1994. *Original Title:* Cristion Ydw I. Huw John Hughes. *Illustrator:* Rheinallt Thomas. Canolfan Genedlaethol Addysg Grefyddol, 1993. *Category:* Welsh-language non-fiction.

2067 1994. *Original Title:* Sothach a Sglyfath. Angharad Tomos. Y Lolfa, 1993. *Category:* Welsh-language fiction.

2068 1995. *The Candle Man.* Catherine Fisher. Bodley Head, 1994. *Category:* English language.

2069 1995. *Original Title:* Geiriadur Gomer i'r Ifanc. D. Geraint Lewis. Gwasg Gomer, 1994. *Category:* Welsh-language non-fiction.

2070 1995. *Original Title:* Pam fi, Duw, Pam Fi? John Owen. Y Lolfa, 1994. *Category:* Welsh-language fiction.

2071 1996. *Who's Afraid of the Bwgan-wood?,* Anne Lewis. Honno, 1995. *Category:* English language.

2072 1996. *Original Title:* Sbectol Inc. Eleri Ellis Jones. *Illustrator:* Marian Delyth. Y Lolfa, 1995. *Category:* Welsh-language non-fiction.

2073 1996. *Original Title:* Coch yw Lliw Hunllef. Mair Wynn Hughes. Gomer, 1995. *Category:* Welsh-language fiction.

2074 1997. *Original Title:* Ydy Fe! John Owen. Iaith Cyf. 1996. *Category:* Welsh-language fiction.

2075 1997. *Cities in the Sea.* Sian Lewis. *Illustrator:* Jackie Morris. Pont/Gomer Press, 1996. *Category:* English language.

2076 1997. *Original Title:* Dirgelwch Loch Ness. Gareth F. Williams. Y Lolfa, 1996. *Category:* Welsh-language non-fiction.

2077 1998. *Alwna's Garden.* Mary Oldham. Pont Books, 1997. *Category:* Anglo-Welsh.

2078 1998. *Original Title:* Dyddiau Cŏn. Gwen Redbers Jones. Gomer, 1997. *Category:* Welsh (best fiction).

2079 1998. *Original Title:* Stori Branwen. Tegwyn Jones, Jac Jones. Gomer, 1997. *Category:* Welsh (best non-fiction).

2080 1999. *Rhian's Song.* Gillian Drake. Pont, 1998. *Category:* English language.

2081 1999. *Original Title:* Byw a Bod yn y Bath. Lis Jones. Gwasg Carreg Gwalch, 1998. *Category:* Welsh-language non-fiction.

2082 1999. *Original Title:* Pam Fi Eto, Duw? John Owen. Y Lolfa, 1998. *Category:* Welsh-language fiction.

2083 2000. *Original Title:* Chwedlau o 'r Gwledydd Celtaidd. Rhiannon Ifans. *Illustrator:* Margaret Jones. Y Lolfa, 1999. *Category:* Welsh-language non-fiction.

2084 2000. *Original Title:* Ta-Ta Tryweryn. Gwenno Hughes. Gomer, 1999. *Category:* Welsh-language fiction.

2085 2000. *Artworks On ... Interiors.* Jo Dahn. *Illustrator:* Justine Baldwin. FBA Publications, 1999. *Category:* English Language.

2086 W.H. Smith Illustration Award (formerly Francis Williams Illustration Award)

Discontinued. ESTABLISHED: 1972. The award was given for the best illustration of a book published in the United Kingdom. The award was discontinued in 1994.

2087 1990. *Aesop's Fables. Illustrator:* John Vernon Lord. Cape. *Category:* overall winner.

2088 1990. *War Boy. Illustrator:* Michael Foreman. Pavilion/Michael Joseph. *Category:* second prize.

2089 1991. *The Hidden House. Illustrator:* Christopher Wormell. 1990. *Category:* second prize.

2090 1991. *An Alphabet of Animals. Illustrator:* Angel Barrett. Walker Books. *Category:* overall winner.

2091 1992. *Fruit. Illustrator:* Charlotte Knox. Mitchell Beazley. *Category:* overall winner.

2092 1992. *Snow-White. Illustrator:* Angel Barrett. Hutchinson. *Category:* second prize.

2093 1993. *Key to the Kingdom. Illustrator:* Tony Meeuwissen. Pavilion. *Category:* overall winner.

2094 1993. *Songs from Shakespeare. Illustrator:* Louise Brierley. Walker Books. *Category:* second prize.

2095 1994. *Harvey Slumfenburger's Christmas Present. Illustrator:* John Burningham. Walker Books. *Category:* overall winner.

2096 1994. *Crackling Brat. Illustrator:* Tomek Bogacki. Methuen. *Category:* overall winner.

2097 Whitbread Children's Book of the Year Awards

SPONSOR: Whitbread PCC. CONTACT: Karen Earl Ltd. ADDRESS: 2-3 Ledbury Mews, London, United Kingdom W11 2AE. PHONE: 020 7243 0064. ESTABLISHED: 1972. AWARD: £50,000. The award is given for a book written by an author from the United Kingdom that promotes the best of contemporary British writing.

2098 1990. *AK.* Peter Dickinson. Gollancz, 1990.

2099 1991. *Harvey Angell.* Diana Hendry. Julia MacRae, 1991.

2100 1992. *The Great Elephant Chase.* Gillian Grosse. Oxford, 1992.

2101 1993. *Flour Babies.* Anne Fine. Hamish Hamilton, 1992.

2102 1994. *Gold Dust.* Geraldine McCaughrean. Oxford, 1990.

2103 1995. *The Wreck of the Zanzibar.* Michael Morpurgo. Heinemann/Mammoth, 1995.

2104 1996. *The Tulip Touch.* Anne Fine. Hamish Hamilton, 1996.

2105 1997. *Aquila.* Andrew Norris. Hamish Hamilton, 1997.

2106 1998. *Skellig.* David Almond. Hodder, 1998.

2107 1999. *Harry Potter and the Prisoner of Azkaban.* J.K. Rowling. Bloomsbury, 1998.

2108 2000. *Coram Boy.* Jamila Gavin. Mammoth, 1999.

GREECE

2109 Circle of the Greece Children's Book Prizes

SPONSOR: IBBY. CONTACT: Loty Petrovits. ADDRESS: Bouboulinas 28, GR-10682 Athens, Greece. PHONE: 301 8222296. ESTABLISHED: 1974. AWARD: Varying sum of money, a diploma, and also (since 1999) a medal. The annual prizes are given to Greek authors and illustrators for published and unpublished works for children. In 1988 three new prizes for distinguished books for children were given — two for children's authors and one for illustration. The books must be published in the previous year. The Circle of Greek Children's Books continues to hold the annual competition for manuscripts anonymously entered.

2110 1990. *Big Trouble. Original Title:* O megalos belas. Filisa Hatjihanna. *Category:* younger children.

2111 1990. *My Dear Noah. Original Title:* Agapimene mou Noe. Petros Gaetanos. *Illustrator:* Dimitris Giannopoulos, Niki Papastathopoulou. *Category:* illustration.

2112 1990. *The Star in Love. Original Title:* To erotevmeno asteri. Maria Veleta-Vasiliadou. Sychroni Epohi, 1988. *Category:* younger children.

2113 1991. *The Trip That Kills. Original Title:* To taxidi pou skotoni. Manos Kondoleon. *Category:* older children and young adults.

2114 1991. *Ilias. Original Title:* Iliada. Kalliope Sfaellou. *Illustrator:* Anna Mendrinou. *Category:* illustration.

2115 1991. *A Thousand and One Nights in the Balkans. Original Title:* Hilies kai mia nyhtes ton Valkanion. Katerina Karizoni. *Category:* younger children.

2116 1993. *A Tree Looks for a Yard. Original Title:* Ena dentro zitai avli. Litsa Panayiotopoulou. *Category:* younger children.

2117 1993. *Have You Ever Seen the Invisible? Original Title:* Mipos idate ton Aorato? Maro Loizou. *Category:* younger children.

2118 1993. *The Cat's Passing. Original Title:* To perasma tis gatas. Iro Papamoschou. *Category:* intermediate readers.

2119 1993. *Yaloussa. Original Title:* I yaloussa. Irini Marra. *Category:* older children and young adults.

2120 1994. *The Forgotten Drawer. Original Title:* To xehasmeno syrtari. Katerina Mouriki. *Category:* intermediate readers.

2121 1994. *A Song for Three. Original Title:* Tragoudi yia tris. Loty Petrovits. *Category:* older children and young adults.

2122 1994. *Ninette. Original Title:* Ninette. George Sari. *Category:* older children and young adults.

2123 1995. *Persephone's Tears. Original Title:* Ta dakrya tis Persephonis. Litsa Psarafti. *Category:* intermediate readers.

2124 1995. *Our Mommy Russia. Original Title:* I miteroula mas i Rossia. Maro Loizou. *Category:* older children and young adults.

2125 1995. *Mandolois. Original Title:* O Mandolois. Fotini Stefanidi. *Illustrator:* Fotini Stefanidi. *Category:* illustration.

2126 1995. *The Adventures of Cat-Baron Niar-niaouzen. Original Title:* I peripeties tou gatonou Niar-niaouzen. Maria Veleta-Vasiliadou. *Category:* younger children.

2127 1996. *Bridge to the East. Original Title:* To gefyri tis Anatolis. Iro Papamoschou. *Category:* older children and young adults.

2128 1996. *Friends, Friends, Dear Friends. Original Title:* Fili, fili, kardiofili. Sofia Zarambouka. *Category:* intermediate readers.

2129 1996. *Four Giants and a Fifth. Original Title:* Tesseris gigantes ki enas pemptos. Mania Kaplanoglou. *Category:* intermediate readers.

2130 1996. *The Jealous Stars. Original Title:* Ta asteria pou zilevan. Melina Karakosta. *Category:* younger children.

2131 1996. *Hekate's Smile. Original Title:* To hamogelo tis Ekatis. Litsa Psarafti. *Category:* older children and young adults.

2132 1997. *Once There Was a Hunter. Original Title:* Kapote o kynigos. Eleni Sarantiti. *Category:* older children and young adults.

2133 1997. *Lukullus Eats Glow-Worms. Original Title:* O Loukoullos troei pygolambides. Eugene Trivizas. *Category:* younger children.

2134 1997. *A Ticket, Please! Original Title:* Ena isitirio, parakalo! Poly Miliori. *Category:* older children and young adults.

2135 1997. *A Bag of Hair. Original Title:* Ena saki malia. Pantelis Kaliotsos. *Category:* intermediate readers.

2136 1998. *The Water of Immortality. Original Title:* To athanato nero. Maro Loizou. *Category:* older children and young adults.

2137 1999. *The Small Shoes Tell Stories. Original Title:* Ta papoutsakia pou lene istories. Angeliki Varella. *Category:* younger children.

2138 1999. *The Rolled Stone. Original Title:* Petra kilisameni. Yannis Stefanidis. *Illustrator:* Yannis Stefanidis. *Category:* illustration.

2139 1999. *The Lazy-Bone's Christmas. Original Title:* Ta Hristougenna tou tembeli. Alexandros Papadiamandis. *Illustrator:* Nicholas Andrikooulos. *Category:* illustration.

2140 1999. *The Dance of Life. Original Title:* O horos tis zois. George Sari. *Category:* older children and young adults.

2141 2000. *The Statue That Felt Cold. Original Title:* To agalma pou kryone. Hristos Boulotis. *Category:* older children and young adults.

2142 2000. *The Snow-Man Took Mommy Away. Original Title:* O hionanthropos pire ti mama. Voula Mastori. *Category:* younger children.

2143 2000. *Signals Through Mirrors. Original Title:* Siniala me kathreftes. Elsa Hiou. *Category:* older children and young adults.

2144 2000. *The Adventure of a Goldfinch. Original Title:* I peripetia mias karderinas. Georgia Anezini-Leraki. *Illustrator:* Eva Mela. *Category:* illustration.

2145 Gynekia Logotehniki Syntrofia (Women's Literary Society Prizes)

CONTACT: Angeliki Varella, President. ADDRESS: Androu 17, GR-14562 Kifissia, Athens, Greece. ESTABLISHED: 1958. The awards are given for unpublished manuscripts entered anonymously in the competition. Categories include: historical novel, poetry, fiction, fairy tales and nonfiction.

2146 1990. *Three Collections in One.* Nikos Kanakis. *Category:* poetry.

2147 1990. *Personal.* Antonis Delonis. *Category:* poetry.

2148 1991. *Hear Me, My Son.* Elsa Hiou. *Category:* novel.

2149 1991. *Songs and Wings.* Markos Pappas. *Category:* poetry.

2150 1991. *When the Persians.* Angeliki Nikolopoulou. *Category:* novel.

2151 1991. *The Stolen Sunray.* Hrisi Kanaki-Yianitsiou. *Category:* novel.

2152 1991. *The Ghosts of the Plain.* Elsa Hiou. *Category:* short story.
2153 1991. *For the Love of a Fairy Tale.* Olvia Papailiou. *Category:* short story.
2154 1991. *The Star That Was Afraid of the Dark.* Eleni Tsialta. *Category:* short story.
2155 1991. *The Beautiful Years.* Yannis Santarmis. *Category:* poetry.
2156 1991. *Written on the Waves.* Nitsa Tsortsoglou. *Category:* novel.
2157 1991. *The Waves of the Aegean Sea.* Nitsa Kaissou. *Category:* novel.
2158 1996. *The River That Comes from the North.* Loulia Zannaki-Lialiou. *Category:* novel.
2159 1996. *My Grandmother Maritsa.* Lili Mavrokefalou. *Category:* novel.
2160 1997. *The Song of the Blackbird.* Avtzis Merkouris. *Category:* fairy tale.
2161 1998. *With the Gaze Turned Towards.* Ninnina Sakka-Niklopoulou. *Category:* novel.
2162 1998. *A Godmother for Denada.* Nitsa Kaissou. *Category:* novel.
2163 1998. *Poems for Children.* Sofia Filntisi. *Category:* poetry.
2164 1998. *Little Fireflies.* Sofia Parasshou-Hatzidimitrou. *Category:* poetry.
2165 1999. *Longtime Waiting.* Vangelis Iliopoulos. *Category:* novel.
2166 1999. *How Was It in Volos, Koataki?* Yannis Remoundos. *Category:* novel.
2167 2000. *Ioannis Kapodistrias and His Age.* Kiriakos Lerakis. *Category:* novel.
2168 2000. *The Years of Rebellion.* Aliki Melissiddou-Siaveli. *Category:* novel.
2169 2000. *From the Cherry Tree to the Internet.* Theodora Georgoudi. *Category:* novel.

2170 Penelope Delta Award

SPONSOR: Circle of the Greek Children's Book. CONTACT: Loty Petrovits. ADDRESS: Bouboulinas 28, GR-10682 Athens, Greece. PHONE: 301 8222296. ESTABLISHED: 1988. AWARD: A diploma. The annual award is given to persons who have made a lasting contribution to Greek literature for children.

2171 1990. Alexandra Plakotari.
2172 1990. Takis Lappas.
2173 1991. Rena Karthaios.
2174 1992. Eleni Valavani.
2175 1993. Alki Goulimi.
2176 1994. Alexandra Stavropulos.
2177 1995. Avgi Papakou-Lagou.
2178 1995. Penelope Maximou.
2179 1996. Vito Angelopoulou.
2180 1997. I.D. Ioannides.
2181 1997. Theti Hortiati.
2182 1998. Nitsa Georgeoglou.

2183 1999. Dina Hatzinikolaou.
2184 1999. Dimitris Manthopoulos.
2185 2000. Pepi Daraki.
2186 2000. Yolanda Pateraki.

2187 State Prize for Children's Literature

SPONSOR: Ministry of Culture. CONTACT: Mr. C. Koroulis, Director. ADDRESS: Rethymnou 1, GR-10682 Athens, Greece. ESTABLISHED: 1989. AWARD: A diploma and a sum of money. The annual award is given for a novel written for children by a Greek author. From 1989 to 1997 there was only one annual award to a children's book of fiction. Since 1998, two more prizes are distributed, one to a non-fiction children's book and one to a children's book for its illustrations — a total of three prizes.

1990. No award given.
2188 1991. *The Identity of a Sun-ray. Original Title:* I taftotita mias iliahtidas. Giorges Krokos. Athens, 1990. *Category:* fiction.
2189 1992. *The Red of the East. Original Title:* To kokkino tis anatolis. Anna Gertsou-Sari. *Category:* fiction.
2190 1993. *Keramidotrahalos. Original Title:* O keramidotrahalos. Alki Zei. Category: fiction.
2191 1994. *Ninette. Original Title:* Ninette. George Sari. *Category:* Fiction.
2192 1995. *Our Mommy Russia. Original Title:* I miteroula mas i Rossia. Maro Loizou. *Category:* fiction.
2193 1996. *Hekate's Smile. Original Title:* To hamogelo tis Ekatis. Litsa Psarafti. *Category:* fiction.
2194 1997. *Once There Was a Hunter. Original Title:* Kapote o kynigos.... Eleni Sarantiti. *Category:* fiction.
2195 1998. *Mask on the Moon. Original Title:* Maska sto fengari. Manos Kondoleon. *Category:* fiction.
2196 1998. *Corinth. Original Title:* Korinthos. Angeliki Varella. *Category:* non-fiction.
2197 1998. *The Night Visitor. Original Title:* O episkeptis tis nyhtas. Melina Karakosta. *Illustrator:* Vasso Psaraki. *Category:* illustration.
2198 1999. *The Lighted Windows Tell Stories. Original Title:* Ta fotismena parathyra diigounte istories. Eleni Kallia. *Category:* non-fiction.
2199 1999. *The Pirates of the Lake Country. Original Title:* I pirates tis limnohoras. Nicholas Andrikopoulos. *Illustrator:* Nicholas Andrikopoulos. *Category:* illustration.
2200 1999. *The Family of the Sun. Original Title:* I ecogenia tou Iliou. Loty Petrovits. *Category:* fiction.

2201 2000. *The Statue That Felt Cold. Original Title:* To agalma pou kryone. Hristos Boulotis. *Category:* fiction.

2201/a 2000. *With Paper and Inkpot. Original Title:* Me harti kai kalamari. Thanos Markopoulos. *Category:* non-fiction.

2201/b 2000. *The Adventure of a Goldfinch. Original Title:* I peripetia mias karderinas. Georgia Anezini-Leraki. *Illustrator:* Eva Mela. *Category:* illustration.

ICELAND

2202 Islandsafdelings Anerkendelse (Icelandic IBBY Award)

SPONSOR: Börn og bækur, Islandsdeild IBBY. CONTACT: Ms. Idunn Steinsdóttir. ADDRESS: P.O. Box 7191, IS-127 Reykjavík, Iceland. PHONE: 354 553 28 04. The award is given annually for contribution to children's literature and culture.

2203 1997. *Wandering Spirits. Original Title:* Her a reiki. Gunnhildir Hrolfsdottir.

1998. No award given.

2204 1999. Complete works. Gudrun Helgadottir.

2205 Reykjaviks Undervisningsradspris (Reykjavik Board of Education Prize)

SPONSOR: The Reykjavik Board of Education. ADDRESS: Fríkirkjuvegur 1, 101 Reykjavík, Iceland. PHONE: 354 535 5000. ESTABLISHED: 1973. The prize is given for an original manuscript published in the previous year.

2206 1997. *The Silver Cross. Original Title:* Silfurkrossinn. Illugi Jokulsson.

2207 1998. *Comet. Original Title:* Halastjarna. Thorarinn Eldjarn. *Illustrator:* Sigrun Eldjarn.

2208 1999. *My Name Is Blidfinnur, But You Can Call Me Bobo. Original Title:* Eg heiti Blidfinnur en pu matt kalla mig Bobo. Thorrvaldur Thorsteinsson.

2209 Verdlaunasjodur Islensku Barnabóka (Icelandic Children's Book Prize)

SPONSOR: Vaka-Helgafell, Börn og baekur. CONTACT: Bjarni Thorsteinsson. ADDRESS: Noatun 17, 105 Reykjavik, Iceland. PHONE: (+354) 511 5700. ESTABLISHED: 1985.

AWARD: A diploma and ISK 300.000. The prize is given to authors of Icelandic books of high quality for children.

2210 1990. *Up in His Sleeve. Original Title:* I pokahorninu. Karl Helgason.

2211 1991. *Through the Thorn. Original Title:* Gegnum thyrnigerdid. Idunn Steinsdottir.

2212 1992. *Bejamin Dove. Original Title:* Benjamin dufa. Fridrik Erlingsson.

2213 1993. *Deep in the Glacier. Original Title:* Brak og brestir. Elias Snæland Jonsson.

2214 1994. *Striped Whimbrels. Original Title:* Röndottir spoar. Gudrun H. Eiriksdottir.

2215 1995. *Applescraps. Original Title:* Eplasneplar. Thorey Friðbjörnsdottir.

2216 1995. *The Feast in the Pram. Original Title:* Veislan í barnavagninum. Herdis Egilsdottir. *Illustrator:* Erlu Sigurdardóttur. *Category:* Illustrated.

2217 1996. *Grilled Bananas. Original Title:* Grilladir bananar. Ingibjörg Möller. *Illustrator:* Frida Sigurdardottir.

2218 1996. *The Thievish Giant. Original Title:* Risinn þjofotti og skyrfjallid. Guðrun Hannesdóttir. *Illustrator:* Sigrun Helgadottir. *Category:* Illustrated.

2219 1997. *Fear in the Dark. Original Title:* Margt by í myrkrinu. Thorgrimur Thrainsson.

2220 1998. *The Yodeller. Original Title:* Heljarstökk afturabak. Gudmundur Olafsson.

2221 2000. *A Winning Chance. Original Title:* Leikur a bordi. Ragnheidur Gestdottir.

IRAN

2222 Institute for the Intellectual Development of Children and Young Adults Award

SPONSOR: Institute of Intellectual Development of Children and Young Adults.
ADDRESS: Kanoone Parvareshe Feki, no. 24 Khaled, Eslamboli, Teheran, Iran.

PHONE: 98218715547-47. ESTABLISHED: 1988. Little information was available at the time of publication.

2223 Ministry of Ershad Award

SPONSOR: Ministry of Ershad. ADDRESS: Vezarate Farhang va Ershade Eslami, Baharestan, Teheran, Iran. ESTABLISHED: 1986. AWARD: 200 Rials. Little information was available at the time of publication.

2224 Prize of the Iranian Children's Book Council

SPONSOR: The Children's Book Council of Iran. CONTACT: Noushine Ansari. ADDRESS: P.O. Box 13145-133, 69 Abou Reyhan Ave., Teheran, Iran. PHONE: 9821 6408074. ESTABLISHED: 1963. AWARD: A bronze plaque with the CBCI logo, and the name of the work and the year of the award. The annual award is given for writers and illustrators of children's literature. Each year the number of books awarded varies according to the standard of excellence set out by the council.

2225 Soroush Publishing Award

SPONSOR: Soroush Publishing Company. ADDRESS: Jame Jam Building, adj. to Shahid Mofateh St., Teheran, Iran. PHONE: 9821 6404255. ESTABLISHED: 1988. Little information was available at the time of publication.

IRELAND

2226 Children's Books Ireland/Bisto Awards

SPONSOR: Irish Children's Book Trust. CONTACT: Gillian Perdue (Chairperson). ADDRESS: 19 Parnell Square, Dublin 1, Ireland. PHONE: 01 872 5854. ESTABLISHED: 1990. AWARD: IR1,000 and a perpetual bronze trophy by Joseph Sloane. The award is given to an author or illustrator born or currently living in Ireland. Books must be in either the Irish or English language, and published in the previous calendar year.

2227 1991. *Grandma's Bill.* Martin Waddell. *Category:* young readers.

2228 1991. *Brian Boru.* Morgan Llywelyn. O'Brien Press. *Category:* best emerging author.

2229 1991. *The Island of Ghosts.* Eilis Dillon.
2230 1992. *The Secret of the Ruby Ring.* Yvonne MacGrory.
2231 1992. *Wildflower Girl.* Marita Conlon McKenna. O'Brien Press. *Category:* historical fiction.
2232 1992. *The Summer of Lily and Esme.* John Quinn.
2233 1993. *Put a Saddle on the Pig.* Sam McBratney. *Category:* teenage fiction.
2234 1993. *The Blue Horse.* Marita Conlon McKenna. O'Brien Press.
2235 1993. *Strongbow.* Morgan Llywellyn. O'Brien Press, 1992. *Category:* historical fiction.
2236 1994. *When Stars Stop Spinning.* Jane Mitchell.
2237 1995. *Blaeberry Sunday.* Elizabeth O'Hara. Poolbeg Press, 1994.
2238 1996. *The Christmas Miracle of Jonathan Twoomey. Illustrator:* P.J. Lynch.
2239 1997. *The Guns of Easter.* Gerard Whelan. O'Brien Press. *Category:* historical fiction.
2240 1997. *Sisters....No Way!* Siobhan Parkinson. O'Brien Press.
2241 1998. *Dream Invader.* Gerard Whelan. O'Brien Press.
2242 2000. *Faraway Home.* Marilyn Taylor. O'Brien Press.

2243 Eilis Dillion Memorial Award

SPONSOR: Irish Children's Book Trust. CONTACT: Gillian Perdue (Chairperson). ADDRESS: 19 Parnell Square, Dublin 1, Ireland. PHONE: 01 872 5854. ESTABLISHED: 1994. AWARD: IR500. The award is given to the author of an outstanding first children's book.

2244 1995. *Melody for Nora.* Mark O'Sullivan. Wolfhound Press, 1994.
2245 1996. *Lockie and Dadge.* Frank Murphy. O'Brien Press, 1995.
2246 1997. *The Guns of Easter.* Gerard Whelan. O'Brien Press, 1996.
2247 1998. *It's a Jungle Out There.* Ed Miliano. Wolfhound Press, 1997.
2248 2000. *Fierce Milly.* Marilyn McLaughlin. *Illustrator:* Leonie Shearing. Mammoth, 1998.

2249 RAI (Reading Association of Ireland)

CONTACT: Wesley College. ADDRESS: Ballinteer, Dublin 16, Ireland. This award is given for an outstanding book of prose for children published in the preceding year in Ireland.

2250 1991. *Under the Hawthorn Tree.* Marita Conlon McKenna. O'Brien Press, 1992.
2251 1993. *Strongbow.* Morgan Llywelyn. O'Brien Press, 1992.
2252 1999. *Angels Without Wings.* Mark O'Sullivan. Wolfhound Press, 1993.

ISRAEL

2253 Ben-Yitzkak Award

SPONSOR: Israel Museum. ADDRESS: Ruth Young Wing, Israel Museum, Box 71117, Jerusalem 91710, Israel. PHONE: 009722 6708036. ESTABLISHED: 1978. AWARD: A certificate and $1000. The biennial award is given for the best illustration of a children's book in Israel. Books must be published in the two years previous to the award.

2254 1990. *What I See from My Window. Original Title:* Ma Nishkaf Behaloni. Leah Goldberg. *Illustrator:* Ruth Zarfati. Sifriat Hapo'alim.

1992. No award given.

2255 1994. *Original Title:* Five Witches Went for a Walk. Ora Eyal Israel.

2256 1996. *Original Title:* Sun is Falling Night is Calling. Ora Eitan.

2257 1998. *Original Title:* Who Stole the Show? Avner Katz.

2258 2000. *Original Title:* Where? Rutu Modan.

ITALY

2259 Fiera di Bologna per l'Infanzia e la Gioventù (Bologna Children and Youth Book Prizes)

SPONSOR: Ente Autonomo per le Fiere di Bologna. CONTACT: Francesca Ferrari. ADDRESS: Piazza Costituzione 6, 40128 Bologna, Italy. PHONE: (051) 282.111. ESTABLISHED: 1966. The awards are given for fiction and non-fiction. A complete list of winners was unavailable at the time of publication.

2260 1990. *My Hero. Original Title:* Mijn Held. Katrien Holland. *Illustrator:* Katrien Holland. Querido (The Netherlands) 1989. *Category:* children.

2261 1990. *The Story of the Goosling Who Wasn't Fast Enough. Original Title:* Die Geschichte von der kleinen Gans, die nicht schnell genug war. Hanna Johansen. *Illustrator:* Käthi Bhend. Nagel & Kimche (Switzerland) 1989. *Category:* youth.

2262 1994. *The Rainbabies.* Laura Krauss Melmed. *Illustrator:* Jim La Marche. Lothrop. *Category:* children's.

2263 1994. *Original Title:* Les grande peus sous les étoiles. Jo Hoestlandt. *Illustrator:* Johanna Kang. Editions Ayros. *Category:* young adult.

2264 Premio Critici in Erba (Critici in Erba Prize)

SPONSOR: Ente Autonomo per le Fiere di Bologna. CONTACT: Francesca Ferrari. ADDRESS: Piazza Costituzione 6, 40128 Bologna, Italy. PHONE: (051) 282.111. ESTABLISHED: 1966. The annual prize is given to the best international book selected by a panel of children between the ages of 6 to 9 years. A current list of winners was unavailable at the time of publication.

2265 1990. *A Frog Prince.* Henry Holt. *Category:* U.S.A.

JAPAN

2266 Mimizuku-sho (Owl Prize)

Discontinued. The annual award was given to an illustrator of a picture book for children.

2267 1990. *George and Matilda Mouse ... and the Floating School. Illustrator:* Heather S. Buchanan. Methuen (Great Britain).

2268 Noma Concours for Children's Picture Book Illustrations

SPONSOR: Asian/Pacific Cultural Center for UNESCO. ADDRESS: 6, Fukuromachi, Shinjuku-ku, Tokyo 162-8484, Japan. PHONE: 81-3-3269-4435. ESTABLISHED: 1978. AWARD: Grand Prize is a medal and US $3,000; Second Prize is a medal and US $1,000; runners-up a medal and US$300. The award aims to encourage illustrators (either professional or non-professional) in Asia and the Pacific (excl. Japan), Latin America, the Caribbean, Africa, and the Arab States to show their works more widely. Entrants should be nationals of UNESCO Member States in Asia and the Pacific, Latin America, and the Caribbean, Africa, and the Arab States.

2269 1990. *Animals Have Many Faces. Illustrator:* Enrique Martinez Blanco.
2270 1992. *The Ugly Duckling. Illustrator:* Park Sung-Woan.
2271 1994. *How Animals Chose Their Colours. Illustrator:* Sief Edeen L'owta.
2272 1996. *The Real Elephant. Illustrator:* Mohd. Yusof bin Ismail.
2273 1998. *Majed and His Friends. Illustrator:* Hussein Gamaan.

LITHUANIA

2274 Lithuanian Children's Book Award

SPONSOR: IBBY Lithuanian and Sarunas Marciulionis. CONTACT: Kestutis Urba. ADDRESS: Children's Literature Center, Gedimino ave. 51, 2600 Vilnius, Lithuania. PHONE: (370 2) 611454. ESTABLISHED: 1993. AWARD: The work is included in the Honour Book of IBBY Lithuanian, and the book is published in Lithuania. The award is given for the most outstanding, original, distinguished children's book of the year written by a Lithuanian author for a fiction book, published in the current year.

2275 1993. *Ice-Rink Music.* Bite Vilimaite. Vyturys.

2276 1994. *Lullaby of the Little Perch.* Ramute Skucaite. Vyturys.

2277 1995. *Stories of Little Rednose.* Vytautas V. Landsbergis. Kaunas: Gabija.

2278 1996. *Grandma from Paris or Nightingale in Zarasai.* Juozas Erlickas. Alma Littera.

2279 1997. *A Slipper.* Vytautas Racickas. Lietuvos rašytoju sajunos leidykla.

2280 1997. *Tiputape.* Vytaute Zilinskaite. Lietus.

2281 1998. *Junda's Fate.* Renata Šerelyte. Tverme.

2282 1999. *A Letter to Sunday.* Ramute Skucaite. Vaga.

2283 2000. *Witchcraft of Bony Hag.* Martynas Vainilaitis. Meralas.

MEXICO

2284 Premio Nacional de Literatura Infantil y Juvenil (National Award for Children's and Juvenile Literature)

SPONSOR: Ediciones Castillo S.A. de C.V. Convoca AL. CONTACT: Patricia Laborde. ADDRESS: Privada Francisco L. Rocha No 7, Col. San Jeronico, 64630 Monterrey, N.L., Mexico. PHONE: (8) 333 24 98. ESTABLISHED: 2000. AWARD: 500,000 pesos in prizes. The awards are given to Mexican authors in four categories: 5 years, 7 years, 9 years, and 12 years.

2285 2000. *The Useful Life of Pillo Polilla. Original Title:* La vida útil de Pillo Polilla. Vivian Mansour Manzur. *Illustrator:* Lupina Flores. Ediciones Castillo S.A.

2286 2000. *Treehouse Stories. Original Title:* Los cuentos de la casa del árbol. Norma Muñoz Ledo Carrasco. *Illustrator:* John Alexander Olsen. Ediciones Castillo S.A.

2287 2000. *It Counts, It Counts. Original Title:* Cuenta, Cuenta. Héctor Anaya. *Illustrator:* Sergio Moreno. Ediciones Castillo S.A.

2288 2000. *Maraca. Original Title:* Maraca. Alfonso Suarez Romero. *Illustrator:* Luis Gabriel Pacheco, Dalia Alvarado. Ediciones Castillo S.A.

2289 2000. *The World Inside September. Original Title:* El mundo, septiembre adentro. Guadalupe Alemán Lascurian. *Illustrator:* Leovigildo Martínez Torres. Ediciones Castillo S.A.

2290 2000. *Fernanda's Order. Original Title:* El encargo de Fernanda. Gabriela Riveros Elizondo. *Illustrator:* Jesús Castillo. Ediciones Castillo S.A.

2291 2000. *The Blue Egg. Original Title:* El huevo azul. Silvia Jaeger Cordero. Ediciones Castillo S.A.

2292 2000. *Felica and Odicia. Original Title:* Felica y Odicia. María Eugenia Blanco. *Illustrator:* Alma Rosa Pacheco. Ediciones Castillo S.A.

2293 2000. *Friends on the Other Side. Original Title:* Amigos del Otro Lado. Ana Luisa Anza Costabile. *Illustrator:* Eddie Martínez Gómez. Ediciones Castillo S.A.

2294 2000. *The Last Life of a Cat and Other Stories. Original Title:* La última vida de un gato y otrosa cuentos. Fidencio Gonzalez Montes. *Illustrator:* Leonardo Arenas Beltran. Ediciones Castillo S.A.

2295 2000. *The Last Frontier. Original Title:* En la última frontera. Gilberto Rendón Ortiz. *Illustrator:* Fabricio Vanden Broeck. Ediciones Castillo S.A.

2296 2000. *The Mirror in the Water. Original Title:* El espejo en al agua. E. Gabriela Aguileta Estrada. *Illustrator:* Guillermo de Gante. Ediciones Castillo S.A.

NETHERLANDS

2297 Glazen Globe (Glass Globe)

SPONSOR: Royal Dutch Geographical Society. ADDRESS: Postbus 80123, 3508 TC Utrecht, Netherlands. PHONE: 030 253 40 56. ESTABLISHED: 1987. AWARD: A globe of glass. The award is given to authors for literature for young adults which contributes to their knowledge of their world and the cultural diversity within it.

2298 1990. *Original Title:* Moenli en de moeder van de wolven. Klaus Kordon. Van Holkema & Warendorf.

2299 1992. *Original Title:* Wij zijn Koerdistan. Elizabeth Laird. Hans Elzenga.

2300 1994. *Original Title:* Een mondvol aarde. Stephanie Zweig. Piramide.

2301 1996. *Original Title:* Engelen van het asfalt. Ineke Holtwijk. Lemniscaat.

2302 1998. *Original Title:* Stiefland. Karlijn Stoffels. Querido.

2303 Gouden Griffel and Zilveren Griffel (Golden Plaque and Silver Plaque)

SPONSOR: Foundation for the Collective Promotion for the Dutch Book. ADDRESS: Postbus 10576, 1001 EN Amsterdam, Netherlands. PHONE: 20 626 49 71. ESTABLISHED: 1971. The annual award is given for the best children's book for ages 6 to 9 years and for the best juvenile book.

2304 1990. *Original Title:* De eikelvreters. Els Pelgrom. *Category:* gold.

2305 1990. *Original Title:* Roosje kreeg een ballon. Imme Dros.

2306 1990. *Original Title:* Het moment. Midas Dekker.

2307 1990. *Original Title:* Kikker is verliefd. Max Velthuijs.

2308 1990. *Original Title:* De Tunnel. Anthony Brown.

2309 1990. *Original Title:* Moenli en de moeder van de wolven. Klaus Kordon.

2310 1990. *Original Title:* Ik was de zee. Ienne Bieman.

2311 1990. *Original Title:* Langzaam, zo snel als zij maar konden. Toon Tellegen.

2312 1990. *The Way Things Work. Original Title:* Over de werking van de kurketrekker en andere machines. David Macaulay.

2313 1991. *Original Title:* Kleine Bever en de echo. Andy Macdonald.

2314 1991. *Original Title:* Mijn botjes zijn bekleed met deftig vel. Ted van Lieshout.

2315 1991. *Original Title:* Gevangen in de Andes. Lyll Becerra de Jenkins.

2316 1991. *Original Title:* Peppino. Rindert Kromhout.

2317 1991. *Original Title:* De o van opa. Imme Dros.

2318 1991. *Original Title:* Tinus-in-de-war. Jacques Vriens.

2319 1991. *Original Title:* Toen er nog bizons waren. Käthe Recheis.

2320 1991. *Original Title:* Als je goed om je heen kijkt zie je dat alles gekleurd is. Tine van Buul, Bianca Stigter. *Category:* gold.

2321 1992. *Original Title:* Rooie. Willem van Toorn.

2322 1992. *Original Title:* Het gouden oog. Hans Hagen.

2323 1992. *Original Title:* Het is nacht, we gaan op jacht. Hans Hagen.

2324 1992. *Original Title:* Kikker en het vogeltje. Max Velthuijs. *Category:* gold.

2325 1992. *Original Title:* De storm. Gaye Hicyilmaz.

2326 1992. *Original Title:* De prinses van de moestuin. Annemie Heyman, Margriet Heyman.

2327 1992. *Original Title:* Ik wil die! Imme Dros.

2328 1993. *Original Title:* Nachtverhaal. Paul Biegel. *Category:* gold.

2329 1993. *Original Title:* Lieve engerd, de groetjes. Inez van Eijk, Marijn Backer.

2330 1993. *Original Title:* Kikker in de kou. Max Velthuijs.

2331 1993. *Original Title:* Toen onze daniel dood ging. Janni Howker.

2332 1993. *Original Title:* Niet wiet, wel nel. Joke van Leeuwen.

2333 1993. *Original Title:* Marie Pouceline of de nicht van de generaal. Simone Schell.

2334 1993. *Original Title:* Allemaal bedrog. Gerard Brands.

2335 1993. *Original Title:* Elfenmiddag. Janet Taylor Lisle.

2336 1993. *Original Title:* Eilandheimwee. Selma Noort.

2337 1993. *Original Title:* Met je rug tegen de muur. Klaus Kordon.

2338 1994. *Original Title:* De blauwe stoel, de ruziestoel. Imme Dros.

2339 1994. *Original Title:* Bijna iedereen kon omvallen. Toon Tellegen. *Category:* gold.

2340 1994. *Original Title:* Een mond vol dons. Lydia Rood.

2341 1994. *Original Title:* Motu-Iti, het meeuweneiland. Roberto Piumini.

2342 1994. *Original Title:* De tolbrug. Aidan Chambers.

2343 1994. *Original Title:* Het wilhelmus. Willem Wilmink.

2344 1994. *Original Title:* Robin en god. Sjoerd Kuijper.

2345 1994. *Original Title:* Jannes. Toon Tellege.

2346 1994. *Original Title:* Aan de verkeerde kant van de aarde. Jean Fritz.

2347 1994. *Original Title:* Herman het kind en de dingen. Harrie Geelen.

2348 1995. *Original Title:* Veren. Veronica Hazelhoff. Querido.

2349 1995. *Original Title:* Een zeer geheime reiskist. Simone Schell.

2350 1995. *Original Title:* Odysseus, een man van verhalen. Imme Dros. Querido.

2351 1995. *Original Title:* Raad een hoeveel ik van je hou. Sam McBratney. Lemniscaat.

2352 1995. *Original Title:* Het eiland klaasje. Sjoerd Kuyper. Leopold.

2353 1995. *Original Title:* 's nachts op dak. K. Schippers. Querido.

2354 1995. *Original Title:* Klik, ik heb je. Marije van der Hoeven. Sjaloom.

2355 1995. *Original Title:* Begin een torentje van niks. Ted van Lieshout. *Category:* gold.

2356 1995. *Original Title:* Vallen. Anna Provoost. Houtekiet/Fontein.
2357 1996. *Original Title:* Klein verhaal over liefde. Marit Törnqvist. Querido.
2358 1996. *Original Title:* Ik maak nooit iets mee en andere avonturen. Guus Middag. *Category:* gold.
2359 1996. *Original Title:* Ik ben ik. Joke van Leeuwen. Zwijsen.
2360 1996. *Original Title:* Het zout der aarde en het domme schaap. Sheila Och. Houtekiet/Fon-tein.
2361 1996. *Original Title:* Blote handen. Bart Moeyaert. Querido.
2362 1996. *Original Title:* Ik maak nooit iets mee en andere avonturen. Imme Dros. Querido.
2363 1996. *Original Title:* De eerste lente. Klaus Kordon. Van Holkema & Warendorf.
2364 1996. *Original Title:* Vreemd land. Rita Verschuur. Van Goor.
2365 1996. *Original Title:* De plant van Jan. Harrie Geelen. Van Goor.
2366 1997. *Original Title:* Toen de wereld nog jong was. Jürg Schubiger. Ludion.
2367 1997. *Original Title:* Iep. Joke van Leeuwen. Querido.
2368 1997. *Original Title:* Lieve oma pluis. Dick Bruna. Mercis Publishing.
2369 1997. *Original Title:* Teunis. Toon Tellegen. Querido.
2370 1997. *Original Title:* Mijn tuin, mijn tuin. Ted van Lieshout. Querido.
2371 1997. *Original Title:* Robin en God. Sjoerd Kuijper. *Category:* gold.
2372 1997. *Original Title:* Wat vliegt daar? Wat kruipt daar? Wat prikt daar? Ditte Merle. Van Reemst.
2373 1998. *Original Title:* De kat en de adelaar. Hans Hagen. Van Goor.
2374 1998. *Original Title:* Zwart als inkt. Wim Hofman. *Category:* gold.
2375 1998. *Original Title:* De vrolijke keuken. Philip Mechanicus. Leopold.
2376 1998. *Original Title:* Zwarte rugzak. Abbing Cleeff, Van Cleeff. Leopold.
2377 1998. *Original Title:* Dit is het huis bij de kromme boom. Imme Dros. Querido.
2378 1998. *Original Title:* Mario Loves Olimpia. Babett van Ogtrop, Liesbet Ruben. KIT.
2379 1998. *Original Title:* Mariken. Peter van Gestel. Fontei.
2380 1999. *Original Title:* Sok of sprei. K. Schipper. Querido.
2381 1999. *Original Title:* Leonard. Wolf Erlbruch. Querido.
2382 1999. *Original Title:* Kukel. Joke van Leeuwen. Querido.
2383 1999. *Original Title:* Hee meneer eland. Eva Gerlach. Querido.
2384 1999. *Original Title:* Helden op sokken. Annie Keuper-Makkink. *Category:* gold.
2385 1999. *Original Title:* De verjaardag van alle anderen. Toon Tellegen. Querido.

2386 2000. *Original Title:* Voor altijd samen, amen. Guus Kuijer. *Category:* gold.

2387 2000. *Original Title:* De schaduw van skellig. David Almond. Querido.

2388 2000. *Original Title:* De voek van cornelia. Martha Heesen. Querido.

2389 2000. *Original Title:* Dierenpraat. Amando. Leopold.

2390 2000. *Original Title:* Rembrandt doe-boek voor kinderen. Ceciel de Bie, Martijn Leenen. V+K Publishing.

2391 Gouden Penseel and Zilveren Penseel (Golden Brush and Silver Brush)

SPONSOR: Foundation for the Collective Promotion for the Dutch Book. ADDRESS: Postbus 10576, 1001 EN Amsterdam, Netherlands. PHONE: 20 626 49 71. ESTABLISHED: 1973. The annual award is given for the best illustration of a children's book.

2392 1990. *The Way Things Work. Original Title:* Over de werking van de kurketrekker en andere machines. David Macauley. *Illustrator:* David Macauley. *Category:* silver.

2393 1990. *Original Title:* Teus Langneus. James Krüss. *Illustrator:* Stasys Eidrigevicius. *Category:* silver.

2394 1990. *Original Title:* Boris Beer. Dick Bruna. *Illustrator:* Dick Bruna. *Category:* gold.

2395 1991. *Original Title:* Shrek. William Steig. *Illustrator:* William Steig. *Category:* silver.

2396 1991. *Original Title:* Lieve kinderen hoor mijn lied. Rudy Kousbroek. *Illustrator:* Peter Vos. *Category:* gold.

2397 1991. *Original Title:* Het bad van de zandloper. Rindert Kromhout. *Illustrator:* Sylia Weve. *Category:* silver.

2398 1992. *Original Title:* Juffrouw kachel. Toon Tellegen. *Illustrator:* Harrie Geelen. *Category:* silver.

2399 1992. *Original Title:* Max en het vogeltje. Max Velthuijs. *Illustrator:* Max Velthuijs. *Category:* silver.

2400 1992. *Original Title:* Waarom niet. Sylvia Hofsepian. *Illustrator:* Friso Henstra. *Category:* gold.

2401 1993. *Original Title:* Kikker in de kou. Max Velthuijs. *Illustrator:* Max Velthuijs. *Category:* gold.

2402 1993. *Original Title:* De kleine koning. Hans Gartner. *Illustrator:* Kvéta Pacovská. *Category:* silver.

2403 1993. *Stop. Original Title:* Stop. Andrew Kuhlman. *Illustrator:* Andrew Kuhlman. *Category:* silver.

2404 1994. *Original Title:* Kun je fluiten johanna. Ulf Stark. *Illustrator:* Anna Hoglund. *Category:* silver.

2405 1994. *Original Title:* Benno en het berekind. Rascal. *Illustrator:* Mario Ramos. *Category:* silver.

2406 1994. *Original Title:* Lui Lei Enzo. Rindert Kromhout. *Illustrator:* Jan Jutte. *Category:* gold.

2407 1995. *Original Title:* Muis en haar vriendjes. Lucy Cousins. *Illustrator:* Lucy Cousins. *Category:* silver.

2408 1995. *Original Title:* Het beertje Pippeloentje. Annie Schmidt. *Illustrator:* Harrie Geelen. *Category:* gold.

2409 1995. *Original Title:* Zij is altijd de eerste. Hiawyn Oram. *Illustrator:* Tony Ross. *Category:* silver.

2410 1996. *Original Title:* Afrika achter het hek. Bart Moeyaert. *Illustrator:* Anna Hoglund. *Category:* silver.

2411 1996. *Original Title:* De verjaardag van de eekhoorn. Toon Tellegen. *Illustrator:* Ten Bosch Geerten. *Category:* gold.

2412 1996. *Original Title:* Nijntje in de tent. *Illustrator:* Dick Bruna. *Category:* silver.

2413 1997. *Original Title:* Het avontuur. *Illustrator:* Rotraut Susanne Berner. *Category:* silver.

2414 1997. *Original Title:* Kikker is kikker. Max Velthuijs. *Illustrator:* Max Velthuijs. *Category:* gold.

2415 1997. *Original Title:* Mijn oom gilbert. *Illustrator:* Benoit. *Category:* silver.

2416 1998. *Original Title:* Hoe papa zijn oude tante vermoordde. *Illustrator:* Helene Riff. *Category:* silver.

2417 1998. *Original Title:* De wezen van Woesteland. Margriet Heymans. *Illustrator:* Margriet Heymans. *Category:* gold.

2418 1998. *Original Title:* Mevrouw Meijer, de merel. *Illustrator:* Wolf Elbruch. *Category:* silver.

2419 1999. *Original Title:* Malmok. Annemarie van Haeringen. *Illustrator:* Annemarie van Haeringen. *Category:* gold.

2420 1999. *Original Title:* Afdankertjes. Frederique Bertrand. *Illustrator:* Frederique Bertrand. *Category:* silver.

2421 1999. *Original Title:* 22 wezen. Tjibbe Veldkamp. *Illustrator:* Tjibbe Veldkamp. *Category:* silver.

2422 2000. *Original Title:* De prinses met de lange haren. Annemarie van Haeringen. *Illustrator:* Annemarie van Haeringen. *Category:* gold.

2423 2000. *Alice in Wonderland.* Lewis Carroll. *Illustrator:* Lisbeth Zwerger. *Category:* silver.

2424 2000. *The Prince in Love. Original Title:* De verliefde prins. Ron Langenus. *Illustrator:* Gerda Dendooven. *Category:* silver.

2425 Jenny Smelik-Kiggenprijs (Jenny Smelik Kiggen Prize)

SPONSOR: Dutch IBBY. ADDRESS: P.O. Box 226, NL 3720 AE, Bilthoven, Netherlands. PHONE: (3732) 22 95 09. The annual award is given to an author or illustrator for a work of children's fiction which contributes to a better understanding of ethnic minorities.

2426 1993. *A Pelican in the Street. Original Title:* Een pelikann op straat. Anton van der Kolk. *Illustrator:* Camila Fialkowski. van Goor, 1992.

2427 1996. *Original Title:* De weg naar het noorden. Naima El Bezaz. Contact, 1995.

2428 1998. *Original Title:* FeestVerHalen. Jos van Hest, Saskia van der Valk. Gottmer, 1998.

2429 Nienke van Hichtumprijs (Nienke van Hichtum Prize)

CONTACT: Jan Campertstichting. ADDRESS: Burg de Monchyplein 9, The Hague, Netherlands. AWARD: 5000 guilders. The award is given to a Dutch author of young adult literature.

2430 1991. *Original Title:* Vrienden van de maan. Mensje van Keulen.

2431 1993. *Original Title:* De prinses van de moestuin. Annemie Heymans Margriet Heymans.

2432 1995. *Original Title:* Veren. Veronica Hazelhoff.

2433 1997. *Original Title:* Vreemd land. Rita Verschuur.

2434 1999. *Original Title:* Hee meneer Eland. Eva Gerlach.

2435 Theo Thijssen-prijs voor Kinder- en Jeugdliteratuur (Theo Thijssen Prize for Children's and Youth Literature — formerly the State Prize for Children's and Youth Literature)

SPONSOR: Stichting P. C. Hooft-prijs voor Letterkunde. CONTACT: A.J.M. Meinderts. ADDRESS: Postbus 90515, 2509 LM The Hague, Netherlands. PHONE: 070 47 11 14. ESTABLISHED: 1964. AWARD: A sculpture by Hans Bayens and 25.000 Dutch guilders. The award is given once every three years to a Dutch author.

2436 1991. Wim Hofman.

2437 1994. Els Pelgrom.

2438 1997. Toon Tellegen.

2439 2000. Joke van Leeuwen.

NEW ZEALAND

2440 Esther Glen Award

SPONSOR: Library and Information Association of New Zealand. ADDRESS: P.O. Box 12-212, Wellington, New Zealand. PHONE: (04)47 35 834. ESTABLISHED: 1945. AWARD: A medal and $50.00. The annual award is given to the New Zealand author for a book which is considered to be the most distinguished contribution to literature for children.

2441 1990. *Alex in Winter.* Tessa Duder. Oxford, 1989.
2442 1991. *Agnes in the Sheep.* William Taylor. Ashton Scholastic, 1990.
2443 1992. *Alessandra: Alex in Rome.* Tessa Duder. Oxford, 1991.
2444 1993. *Underrunners.* Margaret Mahy. Hamish Hamilton, 1992.
2445 1994. *Sasscat to Win.* Paula Boock. McIndoe, 1993.
2446 1995. *The Fat Man.* Maurice Gee. Viking, 1994.
2447 1996. *Crossroads.* Janice Marriott. Reed, 1995.
2448 1997. *Sanctuary.* Kate de Goldi. Penguin, 1996.
2449 1998. *Fat, Four-Eyed and Useless.* David Hill. Scholastic, 1997.
1999. No award given.
2000. No award given.

2450 Gaelyn Gordon Award

ADDRESS: PO Box 96 094, Balmoral, Auckland, New Zealand. PHONE: 09 620 8440. ESTABLISHED: 1998. The annual award is given for a book by a New Zealand author that has proved itself a long-standing favorite with New Zealand children. It is for a book by a living author; it must still be in print and have been in print for at least five years.

2451 1999. *The Runaway Settlers.* Elsie Locke. *Illustrator:* Gary Hebley. Hazard Press, 1993.
2452 2000. *Grandpa's Slippers.* Joy Watson. *Illustrator:* Wendy Hodder. Scholastic, 1989.

2453 Margaret Mahy Lecture Award

SPONSOR: New Zealand Children's Book Foundation. ADDRESS: PO Box 96 094, Balmoral, Auckland, New Zealand. PHONE: 09 620 8440. ESTABLISHED: 1991. The annual award is given in recognition of excellence in children's literature, publishing and literacy in New Zealand.

2454 1991. Margaret Mahy.
2455 1992. Joy Cowley.

2456 1993. Dorothy Butler.
2457 1994. Betty Gilderdale.
2458 1995. Elsie Locke.
2459 1996. Tessa Duder.
2460 1997. Ann Mallinson.
2461 1998. William Taylor.
2462 1999. Lynley Dodd.
2463 2000. Gavin Bishop.

2464 New Zealand Library Association Young People's Nonfiction Award

SPONSOR: Library and Information Association of New Zealand. ADDRESS: P.O. Box 12-212, Wellington, New Zealand. PHONE: (04)47 35 834. ESTABLISHED: 1987. AWARD: A medal and a monetary prize. The annual award is given to the New Zealand author for a book which is the most distinguished contribution to non-fiction for young people.

2465 1990. *The Web.* Deborah Furley. Collins, 1989.
2466 1991. *Model Boats That Really Go.* John Reid. Random Century, 1990.
2467 1992. *The Damselfly.* Peter Garland. Nelson Price Milburn, 1990.
2468 1993. *Albatross Adventure.* Kim Westerskov. *Illustrator:* Kim Westerskov. Nelson Price Milburn, 1992.
2469 1994. *Paikea.* Robyn Kakukiwa. *Illustrator:* Robyn Kakukiwa. Viking, 1993.
2470 1995. *Shadows on the Wall.* Barbara Cairns, Helen Martin. Longman Paul, 1994.
2471 1996. *Laura's Poems.* Laura Ranger. Godwit, 1995.
2472 1997. *The Field (I Spy Wildlife).* Diana Noonan. *Illustrator:* Nic Bishop (photographs). Heinemann Education, 1996.
2473 1998. *The Life-Size Guide to Native Trees and Other Common Plants of New Zealand's Native Forest.* Andrew Crowe. Viking, 1997.
1999. No award given.
2000. No award given.

2474 New Zealand Post Children's Book Awards (formerly AIM Children's Book Awards)

SPONSOR: Booksellers New Zealand. CONTACT: Sara Tricker. ADDRESS: P.O. Box 11-377, Wellington, New Zealand. PHONE: (04) 47 28 678. ESTABLISHED: 1997. AWARD: Winners in each category receive $5,000: Best First Book receives $1,000, Bronze sculpture for Children's Choice. The annual award is given to New Zealand writers and illustrators for the best in New Zealand children's books.

2475 1997. *The Battle of Pook Island.* Jack Lasenby. Longacre, 1996. *Category:* first prize. *Level:* junior fiction.

2476 1997. *Mechanical Harry.* Bob Kerr. Mallinson Rendel, 1996. *Level:* children's choice.

2477 1997. *Picture Book Magic.* Chris Gaskin. *Illustrator:* Denis Page. Reed, 1996. *Category:* first prize. *Level:* non-fiction.

2478 1997. *Reliable Friendly Girls.* Jane Westaway. Longacre, 1996. *Level:* best first book.

2479 1997. *Santuary.* Kate de Goldi. Penguin, 1996. *Category:* first prize. *Level:* senior fiction.

2480 1997. *The Bantam and the Soldier.* Jennifer Beck. *Illustrator:* Robyn Belton. Scholastic, 1996. *Category:* first prize. *Level:* picture book.

2481 1998. *Dare Truth or Promise.* Paula Boock. Longacre, 1997. *Category:* first prize. *Level:* senior fiction.

2482 1998. *The Know, Sow and Grow Kids' Book of Plants.* Diana Noonan. *Illustrator:* Keith Olsen. Bridge Hill, 1997. *Category:* first prize. *Level:* non-fiction.

2483 1998. *Ticket to the Sky Dance.* Joy Cowley. Viking, 1997. *Category:* first prize. *Level:* junior fiction.

2484 1998. *Trapped.* Judy Knox. Scholastic, 1997. *Level:* best first book.

2485 1998. *Alphabet Apartments.* Lesley Moyes. *Illustrator:* Lesley Moyes. Mallinson Rendel, 1997. *Level:* children's choice.

2486 1999. *Starbright and the Dream Eater.* Joy Cowley. Viking, 1998. *Category:* first prize. *Level:* junior fiction.

2487 1999. *Taur.* Jack Lasenby. Longacre, 1998. *Category:* first prize. *Level:* senior fiction.

2488 1999. *The Natural World of New Zealand.* Gerald Hutching. Viking, 1998. *Category:* first prize. *Level:* non-fiction.

2489 1999. *A Summery Saturday Morning.* Margaret Mahy. *Illustrator:* Selina Young. Viking, 1998. *Category:* first prize. *Level:* picture book.

2490 1999. *The Life-Sized Inflatable Whale.* Gaelyn Gordon. *Illustrator:* John Tarlton. Scholastic, 1998. *Level:* children's choice.

2491 1999. *Footsteps of the Gods.* Hana Hiriana Erlbeck. *Illustrator:* Manawa-Ote-Rangi Waipara. Reed, 1998. *Level:* best first book.

2492 2000. *The House That Jack Built.* Gavin Bishop. *Illustrator:* Gavin Bishop. Scholastic, 1999. *Category:* picture book.

2493 2000. *Hairy Maclary and Zachary.* Lynley Dodd. Mallinson Rendel, 1999. *Category:* children's choice.

2494 2000. *The House That Jack Built.* Gavin Bishop. Scholastic, 1998. *Category:* children's book of the year.

2495 2000. *The Tiggie Tompson Show.* Tessa Duder. Penguin, 1999. *Category:* senior fiction.

2496 2000. *Te Wao Nui A Tane.* Hirini Melbourne. *Illustrator:* Te Maari Gardiner. Huia Publishers, 1999. *Category:* non-fiction.

2497 2000. *2MUCH4U.* Vince Ford. Scholastic, 1999. *Category:* junior fiction.

2498 Russell Clark Award

SPONSOR: Library and Information Association of New Zealand. ADDRESS: P.O. Box 12-212, Wellington, New Zealand. PHONE: (04)47 35 834. ESTABLISHED: 1978. AWARD: An inscribed medal and $250.00. The annual award is given to a New Zealand illustrator for the most distinguished illustrations in a children's or young adult's book.

2499 1990. *A Walk to the Beach.* Chris Gaskin. *Illustrator:* Chris Gaskin. Heinemann Reed, 1989.

2500 1991. *Arthur and the Dragon.* Pauline Cartwright. *Illustrator:* David Elliot. Nelson Price MHodder & Stoughton, 1990.

2501 1992. *One Lonely Kakapo.* Sandra Morris. *Illustrator:* Sandra Morris. Hodder & Stoughton, 1991.

2502 1993. *Lily and the Present.* Christine Ross. *Illustrator:* Christine Ross. Methuen, 1992.

2503 1994. *The Trolley.* Patricia Grace. *Illustrator:* Kerry Gemmill. Viking, 1993.

2504 1995. *Kotuku: The Flight of the White Heron.* Philip Temple. *Illustrator:* Chris Gaskin. Hodder & Stoughton, 1994.

2505 1996. *The Cheese Trap.* Joy Cowley. *Illustrator:* Linda McClelland. Scholastic, 1995.

2506 1997. *George's Monster.* Amanda Jackson. *Illustrator:* Murray Grimsdale. Learning Media, 1996.

2507 1998. *Emily's Wonderful Pie.* Jane Cornish. *Illustrator:* Sue Hitchcock-Pratt. Scholastic, 1997.

1999. No award given.

2000. No award given.

2508 Te Kura Pounamu (Maori Book Award)

SPONSOR: Library and Information Association of New Zealand. ADDRESS: P.O. Box 12-212, Wellington, New Zealand. PHONE: (04) 47 35 834. ESTABLISHED: 1996. The annual award is given for the most outstanding publication exhibiting overall excellence and making a distinguished contribution to literature written in Te Reo Maori for children and young people. The author must be a citizen or resident of Aotearoa New Zealand.

2509 1996. *Cry-baby Moon. Original Title:* Marama Tangiweto. Katerina Mataira, Terewai Kemp. Ahura Press, 1992.

2510 1997. *My Kuia Is a Special Kuia. Original Title:* He tino Kuia taku Kuia. Katerina Mataira. *Illustrator:* Te Maari Gardiner. Learning Media, 1996.

2511 1998. *Whirikoki and His Seal. Original Title:* Whirikoki me tana Kekeno. Mere Clarke. *Illustrator:* Manu Smith. Huia Publishers, 1997.

1999. No award given.

2000. No award given.

2512 Tom Fitzgibbon Award

SPONSOR: Scholastic New Zealand Ltd. ADDRESS: PO Box 96 094, Balmoral, Auckland, New Zealand. PHONE: 09 620 8440. ESTABLISHED: 1996. The annual award is given for a previously unpublished writer for a work of fiction for children aged 7 to 13 years. The author must be a New Zealand citizen or reside in New Zealand.

2513 1996. *Summer of Shadows.* Iona McNaughton. Scholastic, 1997.

2514 1997. *Dark Horses.* Heather Cato. Scholastic, 1997.

2515 1998. *2Much4U.* Vince Ford. Scholastic, 1999.

2516 1999. *The Stolen.* Shirley Corlett. Scholastic, 2000.

2517 2000. *Knocked for Six.* Alison Robertson. Scholastic, 2001.

NORWAY

2518 Askeladd Prisen (Askeladd Award)

SPONSOR: Norwegian IBBY. CONTACT: Cathrine Senje. ADDRESS: Norsk barnebokforum, Østmarkveien 19 D, N-0687 Oslo, Norway. PHONE: 47 22 26 22 71. ESTABLISHED: 1981. AWARD: A picture. The award is given every other year to a person or organization who promotes children's books.

2519 1991. Inger Margrethe Gaarder.

2520 1993. Norsk barnebokinstitutt.

2521 1995. Barneradioen — NRK.

2522 1997. Rogaland fylkesbibliotek.

2523 Brageprisen (Norwegian Literature Prize)

SPONSOR: Den norske Forleggerforening. ADDRESS: DNF Øvre Vollgt. 15, 0158 Oslo, Norway. PHONE: 22 00 75 80. ESTABLISHED: 1992. AWARD: A statue and 50.000 NOR. The award is selected by a jury established by the Norwegian Publishers Association.

2524 1992. *Original Title:* Ein motorsykkel i natta. Ragnar Hovland.

2525 1993. *Original Title:* Skjulte ærend. Torill Eide.

2526 1994. *Original Title:* Markus og Diana. Klaus Hagerup.

2527 1995. *Original Title:* Tvillingsøster. Liv Marie Austrem. *Illustrator:* Akin Düzakin. Samlaget.

2528 1996. *The Quest for Truth. Original Title:* Jakten på sannheten. Eirik Newth. Tiden.

2529 1997. *Inside Out. Original Title:* Vreng. Harald Rosenløw Eeg. Aschehoug.

2530 1998. *Egg. Original Title:* Eggg. Stein Erik Lunde. Gyldendal Tiden.

2531 1999. *The Salamander Rider. Original Title:* Salamanderryttaren. Erna Osland. Samlaget.

2532 2000. *Original Title:* Ein naken gut. Rune Belsvik.

2533 Kulturdepartementets Pris (Award from the Ministry of Culture)

SPONSOR: Ministry of Education. ADDRESS: Kronprinsensgate 9, Postadresse 8145 Dep, 0033 Oslo, Norway. PHONE: 47 21 02 17 00. ESTABLISHED: 1948. The prize is given to Norwegian authors and illustrators of children's books. Books must be published 12 months preceding the prize presentations.

2534 1990. *Original Title:* Kabalmysteriet. Jostein Gaarder. Aschehoug, 1989. *Category:* novel.

2535 1990. *Original Title:* Lille Pille og lille Fille i den dype skogs teater. Cecilie Løveid. *Illustrator:* Hilde Kramer. Gyldendal, 1989. *Category:* picture book.

2536 1990. *Original Title:* Maurits og den store barnålkrigen. Geirr Lystrup. *Illustrator:* Malgorzata Piotrowska. Ex Libris, 1989. *Category:* illustration.

2537 1991. *Original Title:* Gurin med reverompa. Kjell Aukrust. Helge Erichsens forlag, 1990. *Category:* picture book.

2538 1991. *Original Title:* Kysset som fikk snøen til å smelte. Tor Fretheim. Damm forlag, 1990. *Category:* novel.

2539 1991. *Original Title:* Tankenes reise. Sossen Krohg, Guy Krohg. Gyldendal, 1990. *Category:* non-fiction.

2540 1992. *Original Title:* I går var i dag i morgen. Klaus Hagerup. Aschehoug, 1991. *Category:* novel.

2541 1992. *Original Title:* Kattens skrekk. Fam Ekman. Cappelen, 1991. *Category:* picture book.

2542 1992. *Original Title:* Tenk om…! Arild Nyquist. *Illustrator:* Finn Graff. Eide forlag, 1991. *Category:* illustration.

2543 1993. *Original Title:* Tiden bor ingensteder. Gerhard Stoltz. Eide forlag, 1992. *Category:* picture book.

2544 1993. *Original Title:* Ved kilden. Kirsti Birkeland. *Illustrator:* Ingrid Jangaard Ousland. Cappelen, 1992. *Category:* illustration.

2545 1993. *Original Title:* Månefeen. Kjersti Scheen. Gyldendal Norsk Forlag, 1992. *Category:* novel.

2546 1993. *Original Title:* Potetboka. Olav Norheim. *Illustrator:* Mikael Holmberg. Det Norske Samlaget, 1992. *Category:* non-fiction.

2547 1994. *Original Title:* Dustefjerten og den store marsipanfesten. Rune Belsvik. J.W. Cappelens Forlag, 1993. *Category:* novel.

2548 1994. *Original Title:* Katten på sjørøverøya. Karin Bang. *Illustrator:* Per Dybvig. Bonnier Carlsen, 1993. *Category:* picture book.

2549 1994. *Original Title:* Eg greier meg. Rønnaug Kleiva. *Illustrator:* Lars Elling. Det Norske Samlaget, 1993. *Category:* illustration.

2550 1994. *Original Title:* Sola—vår egen stjerne. Eirik Newth. Bonnier Carlsen, 1993. *Category:* non-fiction.

2551 1995. *Original Title:* Rått parti. Per Knutsen. Cappelens, 1994. *Category:* novel.

2552 1995. *Original Title:* Tvillingbrødrene. Håvard Rem. *Illustrator:* Harald Nordberg. Aschehoug, 1994. *Category:* picture book.

2553 1995. *Original Title:* Vår gamle gudelære. Tor Åge Bringsværd. Gyldendal Norsk, 1994. *Category:* non-fiction.

2554 1995. *Original Title:* Morovers. André Bjerke. *Illustrator:* Fam Ekman. Aschehoug, 1994. *Category:* illustration.

2555 1996. *Original Title:* Den store røde hunden. Erlend Loe. *Illustrator:* Kim Hiorthøy. Cappelens, 1995. *Category:* picture book.

2556 1996. *Love Light.* Bjørn Sortland. Det Norske Samlaget, 1995. *Category:* novel.

2557 1996. *Original Title:* Jakten på sannheten. Eirik Newth. Gyldendal Tiden, 1995. *Category:* non-fiction.

2558 1996. *Original Title:* Eventyret om Mozar. Minken Fossheim. *Illustrator:* Marek Woloszyn. Bonnier Carlsen, 1995. *Category:* illustration.

2559 1997. *Original Title:* Ikke gløym å klappe katten. Rønnaug Kleiva. *Illustrator:* Inger Lise Belsvik. Det Norske Samlaget, 1996. *Category:* illustration.

2560 1997. *Original Title:* Noa. Tor Åge Bringsværd. *Illustrator:* Akin Düzakin. Gyldendal Tiden, 1996. *Category:* non-fiction.

2561 1997. *Original Title:* Ikkje gløym å klappe katten. Rønnaug Kleiva. *Illustrator:* Inger Lise Belsvik. Samlaget, 1996. *Category:* novel.

2562 1997. *Original Title:* To og to. Lars Elling. Cappelens, 1996. *Category:* picture book.

2563 1998. *Original Title:* Pappa! Svein Nyhus. Gyldendal, 1997. *Category:* picture book.

2564 1998. *Original Title:* Den store faktaboka om språk. Helene Uri. Damm NW & Søn, 1997. *Category:* non-fiction.

2565 1998. *Egg. Original Title:* Eggg. Svein Erik Lunde. *Illustrator:* Kim Hiorthøy. Gyldendal, 1997. *Category:* novel.

2566 1998. *Egg. Original Title:* Eggg. Svein Erik Lunde. *Illustrator:* Kim Hiorthøy. Gyldendal, 1997. *Category:* illustration.

2567 1999. *Original Title:* Sola er en feit gud. Jon Ewo. Omnipax, 1998. *Category:* novel.

2568 1999. *Original Title:* Pode. Tor Arve Røssland. *Illustrator:* Øyvind Torseter. Norske Samlaget, 1998. *Category:* illustration.

2569 1999. *Original Title:* Fremtiden. Hva skjer etter år 2000? Eirik Newth. Gyldendal Tiden, 1998. *Category:* non-fiction.

2570 1999. *Original Title:* Over fjell over hav. Arne Ruset. *Illustrator:* Anne Kristin Hagesæther. Norske Samlaget, 1998. *Category:* picture book.

2571 Norsk Litteraturkritikerlags (Norwegian Critic's Award)

SPONSOR: Norsk litteraturkritikerlag. ADDRESS: Boks 352 Sentrum, N-0101 Oslo 1, Norway. PHONE: 02 41 94 09. ESTABLISHED: 1978. The award is given annually.

2571/a 1990. *Original Title:* Kabalmysteriet. Jostein Gaarder. Aschehoug, 1990.

2572 1991. *Original Title:* Finn Inga. Helga Gunerius Eriksen. Samlaget 1991.

2573 1992. *Original Title:* Stillemann- historien om et drap. Arne Berggren 1992.

2574 1993. *Original Title:* Å plukke en smørblomst. Laila Stien. 1993.

2575 1994. *Original Title:* Sugemerket. Unni Lindell. 1994.

2576 1995. *Original Title:* Det mørke lyset. Mette Newth. 1995.

2577 1996. *Original Title:* Dustefjerten og den store vårdagen. Run Belsvik. Cappelen, 1996.

2578 1997. *Original Title:* Ikkje gløym å klappe katten. Rønnaug Kleiva. *Illustrator:* Inger Lise Belsvik. Samlaget, 1996.

2579 1998. *Original Title:* Kurt — Quo vadis. Erlend Loe. Cappelen, 1998.

2580 1999. *Original Title:* Salamanderryttaren. Erna Osland. Samlaget, 1999.

2581 2000. *Original Title:* Raketter. Henning Mortensen.

2582 Riksmålsprisen — Barne- og Ungdomsbøker (Riksmalsforenings Children's Book Award)

SPONSOR: Oslo Riksmalsforening. ADDRESS: Inkognitogaten 24, 0256 Oslo, Norway. PHONE: 22 56 29 50. ESTABLISHED: 1977. The award is given annually to honor authors of Norwegian children's books.

2583 1990. Torstein Bugge Høverstad.
2584 1991. Eyvind Skeie.
2585 1992. Nicole Macé.
2586 1993. Paul Leer Salvesen.
2587 1994. Gunnar Staalesen.
2588 1995. Atla Lund.
2589 1996. Minken Fosheim.
2590 1997. Elisabeth Bjørnson.
2591 1998. Else Færden.
2592 1999. Tor Åge Bringsværd.
2593 2000. Henning Hagerup.
2594 2000. Elin Brodin.

2595 Skolebibliotekarforeningens Litteraturpris (Norwegian School Librarian Association's Award)

SPONSOR: Skolebibliotekarforeningen i Norge. ADDRESS: v/Synnove Folstad, Rosslyngvn. 27, N-7087 Gimse, Norway. ESTABLISHED: 1982. Given annually to the person for a single work or a body of work for children's or young adult's literature.

2596 1990. Stig Holmas.
2597 1991. Ole Røsholdt.
2598 1992. Erna Osland.
2599 1993. Jostein Gaarder.
2600 1994. Kjersti Scheen.
2601 1995. Torun Lian.
2602 1996. Paul Leer Salvesen.
2603 1997. Tormod Haugen.
2604 1998. Egil Hyldmo.
2605 1999. Bjørn Sortland.
2606 2000. Svein Nyhus.

POLAND

2607 International Janusz Korczak Prize

SPONSOR: IBBY Poland. ADDRESS: Ul. Slupecka 9, 02 309 Warsaw, Poland. PHONE: 4822 22823. ESTABLISHED: 1979. AWARD: A medal and 50,000 zlotys. The prize is given every two years to international authors for children and books about children.

2608 1990. *Island on Bird Street.* Uri Orlev.

2609 1992. *Year of the Dragon. Original Title:* Rok smoka. Joanna Rudnianska.

2610 1994. *Invisible Walls.* Ofra Gelbert-Avni.

2611 1996. *Jocker's Forecast. Original Title:* Kabalmysteriet. Jostein Gaarder.

2612 1998. *Out Time or the Lion of Kauba. Original Title:* Auszeit oder der Lowe von Kauba. Reinhardt Jung.

2613 1998. *Sun on the Ceiling. Original Title:* Solnce na patolkie. Oleg F. Kurguzow.

2614 2000. *An Island on the Sea. Original Title:* En øy i havet. Annika Thor.

RUSSIA

2615 Maxim Gorky International Award for Literature for Children and Youth

SPONSOR: IBBY Russia. ADDRESS: 5 Strastnoi bulvar K-6, 101409 Moscow, Russia. The biennial award is given to honor outstanding works of fiction. A current list of winners was unavailable at the time of publication.

SLOVAK REPUBLIC

2616 Bienále Ilustrácií Bratislava (Biennale of Illustrations)

SPONSOR: IBBY Slovakia. CONTACT: Secretariat BIB. ADDRESS: Panská 41, 815 39 Bratislava, Slovak Republic. PHONE: 421 0754434986. ESTABLISHED: 1967. The biennial award is given for outstanding illustration of children's books. The Golden Apple is given for an international book which has won awards. The grand prize is the highest award given.

2617 1991. *Original Title:* Der gestiefekte Kater. Charles Perrault. *Illustrator:* Stasys Eidrigevicius. Nord-Sud Verlag, 1990. *Category:* Poland. *Level:* grand prize.

2618 1991. *Original Title:* Hélico et l'Iceburg. André Dahan. *Illustrator:* André Dahan. Gallimard, 1989. *Category:* France. *Level:* golden apple.

2619 1991. *Original Title:* Wieso das Känguruh so lange beine hat. Rudyard Kipling. *Illustrator:* John Rowe. Neugebauer, 1990. *Category:* Great Britain. *Level:* golden apple.

2620 1991. *Original Title:* A Christmas Carol. Charles Dickens. *Illustrator:* Robert Innocenti. Creative Education, 1990. *Category:* Italy. *Level:* golden apple.

2621 1991. *Original Title:* Jeder nach seiner Art. Hoffman von Fallersleben. *Illustrator:* Klaus Ensikat. Betz und Gelberg, 1991. *Category:* Germany. *Level:* golden apple.

2622 1991. *Original Title:* The Big Pets. Lane Smith. *Illustrator:* Lane Smith. Viking, 1990. *Category:* U.S.A. *Level:* golden apple.

2623 1993. *Original Title:* Le sourire du loup. Anne Brouillard. *Illustrator:* Anne Brouillard. Dessain, 1991. *Category:* Belgium. *Level:* golden apple.

2624 1993. *Original Title:* Der zwerg Base. Lizbeth Zwerger. *Illustrator:* Lizbeth Zwerger. Neugebauer, 1992. *Category:* Austria. *Level:* golden apple.

2625 1993. *A Fox Spirit in a Desolate Garden.* Z. Yuan. *Illustrator:* Gao Cai. Zhe Jiang, 1991. *Category:* China. *Level:* golden apple.

2626 1993. *Original Title:* Zwischen Lenen, Jazz und Harry Lime. Marcus Herrenberger. *Illustrator:* Marcus Herrenberger. Verlag an der Este, 1992. *Category:* Germany. *Level:* plaque.

2627 1993. *Follow That Hat!* Pierre Pratt. *Illustrator:* Pierre Pratt. Annick, 1992. *Category:* Canada. *Level:* golden apple.

2628 1993. *Original Title:* Eugenio. Marianne Cockenpot. *Illustrator:* Lorenzo Mattotti. Seuil Jeunesse, 1993. *Category:* Italy. *Level:* grand prize.

2629 1995. *Chinese Fables.* Lin Hal-yin. *Illustrator:* Shi-Ming Chang. Grimm Press, 1995. *Category:* Taiwan. *Level:* golden apple.

2630 1995. *Original Title:* Eva ou le pays des fleurs. Rascal. *Illustrator:* Louis Joos. Ecole des Loisirs, 1995. *Category:* Belgium. *Level:* golden apple.

2631 1995. *Adam and Eva. Original Title:* Adam a Eva. Ondrej Sliacky. *Illustrator:* Jana Kiselova-Sitekova. Mlade Leta, 1994. *Category:* Solvakia. *Level:* golden apple.

2632 1995. *Original Title:* Die entstehung der Gurteltiere. Rudyard Kipling.

Illustrator: John Rowe. Neugebauer, 1994. *Category:* Great Britain. *Level:* grand prize.

2633 1995. *Original Title:* Vive la musique. Les Chates Peles. *Illustrator:* Les Chates Peles. Seuil Jeunesse, 1995. *Category:* France. *Level:* golden apple.

2634 1997. *Original Title:* Seisho Monogatari. Yoshihiko Funazaki. *Illustrator:* Kakashi Kitami. Holp Shuppan, 1997. *Category:* Japan. *Level:* golden apple.

2635 1997. *Original Title:* Warabe-Uta. Nobuko Kondo. *Illustrator:* Toshio Kajiyama. Fukuinkan-Shoten, 1997. *Category:* Japan. *Level:* golden apple.

2636 1997. *Original Title:* Die Wette, wer zuerst wütend wird. Italo Calvino. *Illustrator:* Susanne Janssen. Carl Hanser, 1994. *Category:* Germany. *Level:* golden apple.

2637 1997. *Original Title:* Die Prinzessin mit dem Dicken po. Armando. *Illustrator:* Susanne Janssen. Carl Hanser, 1997. *Category:* Germany. *Level:* golden apple.

2638 1997. *Original Title:* Les chocottes. Oliver Douzou. *Illustrator:* Isabelle Chatellard. Editions du Rouergue, 1996. *Category:* France. *Level:* golden apple.

2639 1997. *Original Title:* Le colosse machinal. Michel Chaillou. *Illustrator:* Martin Jarrie. Nathan, 1996. *Category:* France. *Level:* grand prize.

2640 1997. *Original Title:* Toc! Toc! Monsieur Cric-Crac! Alain Serres. *Illustrator:* Martin Jarrie. Nathan, 1995. *Category:* France. *Level:* grand prize.

2641 1997. *Original Title:* Wolf oder Schaf böse oder brav? Linda Wolfsgruber. *Illustrator:* Linda Wolfsgruber. Kerle Verlag, 1996. *Category:* Austria. *Level:* golden apple.

2642 1999. *Original Title:* Old Hikoichi in Wilderness of Okhotsk. Y. A. Togawa. *Illustrator:* Toshitaka Sekiya. Poplar Publishing, 1996. *Category:* Japan. *Level:* golden apple.

2643 1999. *In the Night Kindergarten.* Shuntaro Tanikawa. *Illustrator:* Etsuko Nakatsuji. Fukuinkan-Shoten, 1998. *Category:* Japan. *Level:* grand prize.

2644 1999. *Original Title:* Gulliverove Cesty I. Jonathan Swift. *Illustrator:* Peter Uchnár. Spolok slovenskych spisovatelov, 1998. *Category:* Slovakia. *Level:* golden apple.

2645 1999. *Original Title:* WC- Papier in den wind laten wapperen. Janneke Derwig. *Illustrator:* Janneke Derwig. van Halkema, 1995. *Category:* Netherlands. *Level:* golden apple.

2646 1999. *Original Title:* Apo-Stroph. Adelheid Dahimene. *Illustrator:*

Heide Stoellinger. Verlag Grosser, 1997. *Category:* Austria. *Level:* golden apple.

2647 1999. *Original Title:* Marta et la bicyclette. Germano Zullo. *Illustrator:* Albertine Zullo. La Yoie de Lire, 1999. *Category:* Switzerland. *Level:* golden apple.

2648 1999. *Original Title:* Josefine. Silvia Bauman. *Illustrator:* Heide Stoellinger. Verlag Grosser, 1998. *Category:* Austria. *Level:* golden apple.

SLOVENIA

2649 Levstikova Nagrada (Fran Levstik Prize)

SPONSOR: Mladinska knjiga. CONTACT: Andrej Ilc. ADDRESS: Slovenska 29, 1000 Ljubljana, Slovenia. PHONE: 386 01 241 3258. ESTABLISHED: 1949. AWARD: A plaque and monetary award. The biennial award is given to the best authors and illustrators in the field of children and young adult fiction and non-fiction.

2650 1990. *Nicky and the Wigglers. Original Title:* Nejc in drobnozivke. Aleksander Konjajev. Mladinska knjig, 1990. *Category:* non-fiction.

2651 1990. *Chronicle of Love Happenings. Original Title:* Kronika wypodków mylosnych. Dušan Muc. *Illustrator:* Tadeusz Konwicki. Mladinska knjig, 1990. *Category:* non-fiction.

2652 1990. *There Comes the Lion. Original Title:* Prišel je lev. Lojze Krakar. Mladinska knjig, 1990. *Category:* fiction.

2653 1993. *Energy. Original Title:* Energij. Samo Kušcer. Mladinska knjiga, 1993. *Category:* non-fiction.

2654 1993. *Evening Sonata. Original Title:* Vecerna sonata. Vida Jeraj Hribar. Mladinska knjig, 1993. *Category:* fiction.

2655 1993. *The Brocade Portrait, Tales of the Chinese Minorities. Original Title:* Brokatna podoba, Pravljice kitajskih manjšin. *Illustrator:* Wang Huiquin. Mladinska knjig, 1993. *Category:* illustration.

2656 1995. *Chasing the Stars. Original Title:* Lov na zvezde. Neli Kodric. Mladinska knjiga, 1995. *Category:* fiction.

2657 1997. *Pooey Louie and Farty Smarty. Original Title:* Zbirka povesti o Drekcu Pekcu in Pukcu Smukcu. Dim Zupan. Mladinska knjig, 1997. *Category:* fiction.

2658 1997. *Flying Cats. Original Title:* Leteci mecki. Dim Zupan. *Illustrator:* Dim Zupan. Mladinska knjiga, 1997. *Category:* children's fiction.

2659 1997. *The Pearl Shell. Original Title:* Biscernica. Jelka Godec Schmidt. *Illustrator:* Jelka Godec Schmidt. Mladinska knjig, 1996. *Category:* illustration.

2660 1997. *Playing with Letters. Original Title:* Stavnica. Viljenka Jalovec. *Illustrator:* Igor Ribic. Mladinska knjig, 1996. *Category:* non-fiction.

2661 1999. *Wormy Poems.* Andrej Rozman Roza. Mladinska knjig, 1999. *Category:* poetry.

2662 1999. *Original Title:* Enci benci na kamenci vol. 2. *Illustrator:* Zvonko Coh. Mladinska knjig, 1999. *Category:* illustration.

2663 Moja Najljibsa Knijiga (My Favorite Book Award)

SPONSOR: Knjiznica Otona Zupancica. ADDRESS: Komenskega 9, 1000 Ljubljana, Slovenia. PHONE: 386 1 434 36 31. ESTABLISHED: 1998. AWARD: A diploma. The award is given for a favorite book written by a Slovenian author. Each year a book is chosen by the young readers in the schools and public libraries all over Slovenia.

2664 1998. *Matilda. Original Title:* Matilda. Roald Dahl. *Illustrator:* Quentin Blake. *Translator:* Bogdan Gradišnik. Mladinska knjiga, 1998.

2665 1998. *Nina's Poets Two. Original Title:* Ninina pesnika dva. Bogdan Novak. Novak, 1995.

2666 1999. *Basketball It Is! Original Title:* Košarkar naj bo! Primoz Suhodlocan. *Illustrator:* Uroš Horvat. Karantanija, 1999.

2667 1999. *Lying Suzy. Original Title:* Lazniva Suzi. Desa Muck. Mladinska knjiga, 1997.

2668 1999. *Matilda. Original Title:* Matilda. Roald Dahl. *Illustrator:* Quentin Blake. *Translator:* Bogdan Gradišnik. Mladinska knjiga, 1998.

2669 2000. *Matilda. Original Title:* Matilda. Roald Dahl. *Illustrator:* Quentin Blake. *Translator:* Bogdan Gradišnik. Mladinska knjiga, 1998.

2670 2000. *Sylvia. Original Title:* Silvija. Nejka Omahen. DZS, 1999.

2671 2000. *Basketball it is! Original Title:* Košarkar naj bo! Primoz Suhodlocan. *Illustrator:* Uroš Horvat. Karantanija, 1999.

SOUTH AFRICA

2672 Alba Bouwer Prize

SPONSOR: South African Academy of Science and Arts. CONTACT: Dr. D.J.C. Geldenhuys. ADDRESS: S.A. Akademie vir Wetenskap en Kuns, P.O. Box 538, Pretoria 0001, South Africa. PHONE: (012) 28-5082. ESTABLISHED: 1989. AWARD: A monetary prize and charter from the S.A. Akademie vir Wetenskap en Kuns. The award is given in recognition of Afrikaans literature for children ages 7 to 12 years. The prize can be awarded to the same author more than once. The work must be original. The prize is given every three years.

2673 1992. *Dream Chariot. Original Title:* Droomwa. Barrie Hough.
2674 1992. *Brahm and the Angel. Original Title:* Braam en die engel. Marietjie de Jong.
2675 1995. *The White Butterfly; The Magic Bag and Other Stories. Original Title:* Die wit vlinder; Die towersak en ander stories. Corlia Fourie.
2676 1998. *Do Not Tickle a Mealie. Original Title:* Moenie 'n mielie kielie nie. Philip de Vos.

2677 ATKV Children's Book Prize

SPONSOR: Afrikaanse Taal- en Kultuurorganisasie (Afrikaans Language and Cultural Organization). ADDRESS: Surreylaan 348, Posbus 4586, Randburg 2125, South Africa. PHONE: 011 886-4888. ESTABLISHED: 1991. The award is given to authors and illustrators in five age categories: 3–5 years; 6–7 years; 8–9 years; 10–12 years and 13–15 years.

2678 1991. *Tortoise and Dove. Original Title:* Skilpad en duif. Wilna Panagos. *Category:* 3–5 years.
2679 1991. *Snater. Original Title:* Snater. Brenda Schroder. *Category:* 6–7 years.
2680 1991. *A Story About a Musical Insect. Original Title:* Vincent van Gogga. Philip de Vos. *Category:* 8–9 years.
2681 1991. *Hockey Centre Forward. Original Title:* Middelvoor. Carl Steyn. *Category:* 10–12 years.
2682 1992. *The House with Green Eyes. Original Title:* Die huis met groen oë. Mari Grobler. *Category:* 8–9 years.
2683 1992. *Jorsie. Original Title:* Jorsie. Sophie Muller. *Category:* 3–5 years.
2684 1992. *The Loner. Original Title:* Eenkantkind. Marita van der Vyver. *Category:* 13–15 years.

2685 1992. *An Elephant Will Always Be an Elephant. Original Title:* Olifant bly olifant. Mart Meij. *Category:* 6–7 years.

2686 1992. *Each for the Other. Original Title:* Elk vir mekander. Nel Swart. *Category:* 10–12 years.

2687 1993. *Ora. Original Title:* Ora. Tess Koller. *Category:* 3–5 years.

2688 1993. *In Full Flight. Original Title:* Vlerkdans. Barrie Hough. *Category:* 13–15 years.

2689 1993. *Original Title:* Grys Gomgommer. Anita Potgieter. *Category:* 6–7 years.

2690 1993. *The Fairy Garden. Original Title:* Die feetjietuin. Mariki Wessels. *Category:* 10–12 years.

2691 1993. *Leandie and the Magic Yoyo. Original Title:* Leandie en die wonderklimtol. Erna Muller. *Category:* 8–9 years.

2692 1994. *Smaartie is Squint-eyed. Original Title:* Smaartie is skeel. Maretha Maartens. *Category:* 10–12 years.

2693 1994. *The Eleventh Hurdle. Original Title:* Die elfde hekkie. P.H. Nortjé. *Category:* 13–15 years.

2694 1994. *The Adventures of Ster and Polka. Original Title:* Die avonture van Ster en Polka. Wilna Panagos. *Category:* 3–5 years.

2695 1994. *Mrs. O'Malley's Dog. Original Title:* Mev. Molle se hond. Peitjie Olivier. *Category:* 6–7 years.

2696 1994. *Granny Hester with the Blue Hair Who Can Do Clever Spells. Original Title:* Ouma Hester met die blou hare wat so slim kan toor. Marelize Goldie. *Category:* 8–9 years.

2697 1996. *There's a Ghost in My Cupboard. Original Title:* Daar's 'n spook in my kas. Martie Preller. *Category:* 6–7 years.

2698 1996. *You and Toetenkat. Original Title:* Jy en Toetenkat. Martie Preller. *Category:* 8–9 years.

2699 1996. *Sterling. Original Title:* Sterling. Marlene le Roux. *Category:* 13–15 years.

2700 1996. *Rebel. Original Title:* Rebel. Tertia Botha. *Category:* 10–12 years.

2701 1997. *First Year Blues. Original Title:* Reënboogrant- studente: Eerstejaar blues. Heila Fourie. *Category:* 13–15 years.

2702 1997. *The Secret of Groukatlaagte. Original Title:* Die geheim van Groukatlaagte. Louise Prinsloo. *Category:* 10–12 years.

2703 1997. *Monstermoon: What Is Bubbling in the Pot? Original Title:* Monstermaan: Wat borrel in die pot? Louise van Niekerk. *Category:* 8–9 years.

2704 1997. *An Anthology of Stories. Original Title:* Stippe stappe stories. Elsabe Steenberg (compiler) *Category:* 3–5 years.

2705 1997. *Moon Eggs. Original Title:* Maaneiers. Nanette van Rooyen. *Category:* 6–7 years.

2706 1998. *The Adventures of Rodger, the Rhinoceros. Original Title:* Die avonture van Rodger, die renoster. Ernst Mare. *Category:* 6–7 years.

2707 1998. *The Angel in the Attic. Original Title:* Die engeltjie op die solder. Carl Steyn. *Category:* 10–12 years.

2708 1998. *That's It, Dawid! Original Title:* Ditsem Dawid! Hans du Plessis. *Category:* 13–15 years.

2709 1999. *The Waterthing. Original Title:* Die waterding. Francois Bloemhof. *Category:* 10-12 years.

2710 1999. *Teddie's Secret. Original Title:* Teddie se geheim. Loraine Hattingh. *Category:* 8–9 years.

2711 1999. *Dreams at Dune Bay. Original Title:* Drome op Duinebaai. Janie Oosthuysen. *Category:* 13–15 years.

2712 2000. *Tamara. Original Title:* Tamara. Helen Brain. *Category:* 13–15 years.

2713 2000. *Room 13. Original Title:* Kamer 13. Francois Bloemhof. *Category:* 10–12 years.

2714 2000. *Boots to Wonderland. Original Title:* Steweltjies na Wonderland. Alida Bothma Heester Hesse. *Category:* 6–7 years.

2715 2000. *Stories for Young Ears. Original Title:* Stories vir jong ore. Ewald van Rensburg. *Category:* 3–5 years.

2716 2000. *The Mealie-cob Doll. Original Title:* Die mieliestronkpop. Marianna Brandt. *Category:* 8–9 years.

2717 C P Hoogenhout Award

SPONSOR: Stigting vir Afrikaans (Foundation for Afrikaans). CONTACT: Thomas van der Walt. ADDRESS: Arcadiastraat 1064, Hatfield 0083, South Africa. PHONE: (0)12- 342 2646. ESTABLISHED: 1960. AWARD: A medal. The award is given to an author of Afrikaans children's books published during the two preceding years. The book must be suitable for children ages 7 to 12 years. After 1982, the award was given biennially.

2718 1992. *Dream Chariot. Original Title:* Droomwa. Barrie Hough.

2719 1996. *The Land on the Other Side. Original Title:* Anderkantland. Martie Preller.

2720 2000. *Ms Buggbuster and the Brainwashers; Grandma Duckitt and the Dreadnought Mark II. Original Title:* Die breinwassers; Ouma Hester en die Dreadnought Merk II. Juffrou Luisenbosch. *Translator:* Janie Oosthuysen.

2721 Katrine Harries Award

SPONSOR: South African Library Association. ADDRESS: address unknown, South Africa. ESTABLISHED: 1974. AWARD: A medal gold. The award is given to the South African illustrator for a book published in the preceding two years. The illustrator must be a permanent South African resident. After 1983, the award was given biennially.

2722 1990. *Dancing Elephants. Illustrator:* Joan Rankin.

2723 1990. *Ask Frederika. Original Title:* Vra vir Frederika. Rene Deetlefs. *Illustrator:* Joan Rankin.

2724 1991. *The Twelve Days of Christmas. Illustrator:* Joan Rankin.

2725 1993. *Armien's Fishing Trip.* Catherine Stock. *Illustrator:* Catherine Stock. David Philip Publishers.

2726 1994. *Kalinzu and the Oxpeckers. Illustrator:* Jeremy Grimsdell.

2727 1996. *The Gift of the Sun.* Dianne Stewart. *Illustrator:* Jude Daly.

2728 M E R Prize

SPONSOR: Tafelberg Publishers. ADDRESS: PO Box 879, Cape Town, 8000, South Africa. PHONE: (021) 424-1320. ESTABLISHED: 1984. AWARD: R 10000 and a framed certificate. The annual award is given for books published in the preceding year.

2729 1990. *Down Street.* Lawrence Bransby. Tafelberg, 1989.

2730 1991. *The Girl Who Sang Like a Magic Bird. Original Title:* Die meisie wat soos 'n bottervoël sing. Corlia Fourie. *Illustrator:* Alida Bothma. Tafelberg, 1990.

2731 1992. *For Each Other. Original Title:* Elk vir mekander. Nel Swart, 1991.

2732 1993. *The Delmonico Two o Five.* Allan Jermieson, 1992.

2733 1994. *Kaljander from the Karoo. Original Title:* Kaljander van die Karoo. Elizabeth van der Merwe, 1993.

2734 1995. *The Magic Bag and Other Stories. Original Title:* Die towersak en ander stories. Corlia Fourie, 1994.

2735 1996. *Do Not Tickle a Mealie. Original Title:* Moenie 'n mielie kielie nie. Philip de Vos, 1995.

2736 1997. *One Magic Moment.* Jenny Robson, 1996.

2737 1998. *The Pro. Original Title:* Die pro. Leon de Villers, 1997.

2738 1999. *Russian Dolls That Fit into One Another. Original Title:* Skilpoppe. Barrie Hough, 1998.

2739 2000. *Similar or Different. Original Title:* Eenders of anders. Freda Linde, 1999.

2740 Percy Fitzpatrick Award

SPONSOR: English Academy of Southern Africa. ADDRESS: PO Box 124, Wits 2052, South Africa. PHONE: (011) 717-9339. ESTABLISHED: 1974. AWARD: A certificate and a cheque. The award is given to the author of an English book living in South Africa. The book must be published in South Africa. After 1982, the award was given biennially.

2741 1990. *A Cageful of Butterflies.* Lesley Beake. Maskew Miller Longman, 1989.

2742 1992. *92 Queens Road.* Dianne Case. Maskew Miller Longman, 1991.

2743 1994. *Stories South of the Sun.* C. Bodenstein, L. Rode. Tafelberg Publishers, 1993.

2744 1996. *The Boy Who Counted to a Million.* Lawrence Bransby. Human & Rosseau, 1994.

2745 2000. *The Slayer of Shadows.* Elana Bregin. Gecko Press, 1996.

2746 Sanlam Prize

SPONSOR: The Nasionale Boekhandel. CONTACT: Louise Steyn. ADDRESS: PO Box 879, Cape Town, 8000, South Africa. PHONE: 021-4241320. ESTABLISHED: 1984. AWARD: A gold award and monetary prize of R 8,000. The awards were given to authors of English and Afrikaans children's books.

2747 1990. *Place of the Dolphins. Original Title:* Plek van dolfyne. Maretha Maartens. *Category:* gold.

2748 1990. *Dream Chariot. Original Title:* Droomwa. Barrie Hough. *Category:* silver.

2749 1990. *Whose Heart Can Take It? Original Title:* Wie se hart kan dit dan hou? Kowie Rossouw. *Category:* bronze.

2750 1992. *In Full Flight. Original Title:* Vlerkdans. Barrie Hough. *Category:* gold.

2751 1992. *Leave Me Alone Palookas! Original Title:* Los my uit, paloekas! George Weideman. *Category:* silver.

2752 1992. *Spider Summer. Original Title:* Spinnekopsomer. Maretha Maartens. *Category:* bronze.

2753 1994. *Rebel. Original Title:* Rebel. Tertia Botha. *Category:* bronze.

2754 1994. *The Land on the Other Side. Original Title:* Anderkantland. Martie Preller. *Category:* silver.

2755 1994. *The Parade of the Unfortunates. Original Title:* Die optog van die aftjoppers. George Weideman. *Category:* gold.

2756 1996. *In the Time of Evil. Original Title:* In die tyd van Esob. Martie Preller. *Category:* gold.

2757 1996. *Gamkab. Original Title:* Gamkab. Betsie van Niekerk. *Category:* silver.

2758 1996. *Lurch-Lurch. Original Title:* Slinger-slinger. Francois Bloemhof. *Category:* bronze.

2759 1996. *The Pro. Original Title:* Die pro. Leon de Villers. *Category:* special prize.

2760 1998. *The Sign of Cross. Original Title:* Die teken van die crux. Elsa Meiring Hamersa. *Category:* gold.

2761 1998. *Russian Dolls That Fit into One Another. Original Title:* Skilpoppe. Barrie Hough. *Category:* silver.

2762 1998. *Dana's Fantastic Year. Original Title:* Dana se jaar duisend. George Weideman. *Category:* bronze.

2763 1998. *Right, Commander. Original Title:* Reg, kommandant. Anna Schultz. *Category:* special prize.

2764 2000. *The Summer Holiday That Was Too Long. Original Title:* Die somervakansie wat te lank was. Rena Schuller. *Category:* silver.

2765 2000. *Skeletons Don't Wear Clothes. Original Title:* Geraamtes dra nie klere nie. Jan Vermeulen. *Category:* gold.

2766 Scheepers Prize for Youth Literature

SPONSOR: South African Academy of Science and Arts. CONTACT: Dr. D.J.C. Geldenhuys. ADDRESS: S.A. Akademie vir Wetenskap en Kuns, P.O. Box 538, Pretoria 0001, South Africa. PHONE: (012) 28-5082. ESTABLISHED: 1956. AWARD: A monetary prize and charter from the S.A. Akademie vir Wetenskap en Kuns. The award is given to provide recognition for the advancement of Afrikaans literature for young people. The prize is given every three years.

2767 1992. *There Are Footprints on the Moon. Original Title:* Daar is spore op die maan. Eleanor Baker.

2768 1995. *The Parade of the Unfortunates. Original Title:* Die optog van die aftjoppers. George Weideman.

2769 1998. *The Pro. Original Title:* Die pro. Leon de Villers.

2770 Tienie Holloway Medal for Nursery School Literature

SPONSOR: South African Academy of Science and Arts. CONTACT: Dr. D.J.C. Geldenhuys. ADDRESS: S.A. Akademie vir Wetenskap en Kuns, P.O. Box 538, Pretoria 0001, South Africa. PHONE: (012) 28-5082. ESTABLISHED: 1969. AWARD: A gold medal and a monetary sum. The award is given in recognition of authors who have written the best books for children under 8 years. It is given every three years for original work in Afrikaans.

2771 1991. *The Girl That Sings Like a Magic Bird. Original Title:* Die meisie wat soos 'n bottervoël sing. Corlia Fourie. *Illustrator:* Alida Bothma. Tafelberg.

2772 1994. *Kaljander from the Karoo. Original Title:* Kaljander van die Karoo. Elizabeth van der Merwe.

2773 1997. *Elenoceros on the Roof. Original Title:* Olinosters op die dak. Marita van der Vyver. *Illustrator:* Piet Grobler.

2774 2000. *Dear Witch and the Computer. Original Title:* Liewe Heksie en die rekenaar. Verna Vels.

2775 Vivian Wilkes Award

SPONSOR: South African Children's Book Forum. CONTACT: Mr Jay Heale. ADDRESS: PO Box 847, Howard Place, 7450, South Africa. PHONE: (21) 532. 0555. ESTABLISHED: 1996. AWARD: R3000 and a certificate. The award is given for an outstanding illustrated South African children's book. The book may be fact or fiction, and the text in any language of South Africa. Books produced as part of a reading scheme or literacy programme are eligible, provided that the book had a South African edition published and that the illustrator is normally resident within South Africa.

2776 1996. *The King's Magic Drum.* Thomas Nevin (retold). *Illustrator:* Ian Lusted. Garamond.

2777 1997. *The Red Dress. Illustrator:* Anneliese Voigt. Garamond.

2778 1998. *Mufaro's Magic Blanket. Illustrator:* Elisabeth Pulles. Tafelberg.

2779 1999. *Jamela's Dress.* Niki Daly. *Illustrator:* Niki Daly. Tafelberg.

SPAIN

2780 Premio Apel-les Mestres (Apel-les Mestres Prize)

SPONSOR: Ediciones Destino. ADDRESS: Provença, 260, 4ª planta, 08008 Barcelona, Espanya. PHONE: 34 93 496 70 01. ESTABLISHED: 1981. AWARD: 750.000 pesetas. The prize is given for text and illustration of a children's book in any Spanish dialect.

2781 1990. *Original Title:* Carn i ungla. Gustavo Ariel. *Illustrator:* Ricardo Alcàntara. Destino, 1989.

2782 1991. *Original Title:* El asunto de mis papás. Mabel Poveda Pierola. Destino, 1990.

2783 1992. *Original Title:* En Zip i el xai de la son. Montse Ganges. *Illustrator:* Imma Pla. Destino, 1991.

2784 1993. *Mic's Family. Original Title:* La familia de Mic. Ana López Escrivá. *Illustrator:* Miguel Àngel Pacheclo. Destino, 1992.

2785 1994. *Original Title:* No us podeu imaginar. Chiara Carrer. *Illustrator:* Elisabeth Duckett. Destino, 1993.

2786 1995. *Original Title:* Berta la Modista. Marcella Mola. *Illustrator:* Biagio Bagini. Destino, 1994.

2787 1996. *Original Title:* Històries de sols. Davi. Destino, 1995.

2788 1997. *Original Title:* El viatge d'Alexandre. Gisela Mehrem. *Illustrator:* Gisela Mehrem. Destino, 1996.

2789 1998. *Tim and the Moon. Original Title:* Tim a la Lluna. Sophie Fatus. *Illustrator:* Sophie Fatus. Destino, 1997.

2790 Premio C.C.E.I. de Ilustración Infantil (C.C.E.I. Prize for Children's Book Illustration)

SPONSOR: La Comisión Católica Española de la Infancia. CONTACT: Doris Maria Alvarez. ADDRESS: Alfonso XI 4, 4º, 28014 Madrid, España. PHONE: (91) 531 06 90. ESTABLISHED: 1996. AWARD: A medal. The prize is given annually for the best book illustrated in the previous year by a Spanish illustrator.

2791 1996. *Matthew and the Magos Kings. Original Title:* Mateo y los Reyes Magos. Fernando Alonso. *Illustrator:* Alberto Urdiales. Altea, 1995.

2792 1997. *Original Title:* Barquichuelo de papel. María Puncel. *Illustrator:* Nivio López. Bruño, 1996.

2793 1998. *The Bible Counts All the People. Original Title:* La Biblia contada a todas las gentes. *Illustrator:* José Ramón Sánchez. Anaya, 1997.

2794 1999. *Ratona and Elefante. Original Title:* Ratona y Elefante. *Illustrator:* Ana López Escrivá. Bruño, 1998.

2795 2000. *Columbeta, the Island Book. Original Title:* Columbeta, la isla libro. *Illustrator:* Miguel Calatayud. Anaya, 1999.

2796 Premio C.C.E.I. para Libros Infantiles y Juveniles (C.C.E.I. Prize for Children's and Young Adult Literature)

SPONSOR: La Comisión Católica Española de la Infancia. CONTACT: Doris Maria Alvarez. ADDRESS: Alfonso XI 4, 4º, 28014 Madrid, España. PHONE: (91) 531 06 90. ESTABLISHED: 1962. AWARD: A medal. The prize is given annually for the best book published in the previous year by a Spanish author.

2796/a 1990. *Memories of a Coward. Original Title:* Memorias de una gallina Concha López Narváez. *Illustrator:* José Ramón Alonso. Anaya, 1989.

2797 1991. *The Painted House. Original Title:* La casa pintada. Montserra del Amo. *Illustrator:* Francisco Solé. SM, 1990.

2798 1992. *The Last Set. Original Title:* El última Set. Jordi Serra i Fabra. SM, 1991.

2799 1993. *The House of the Devils. Original Title:* La casa de los diablos. Lucía Baquedano. Labor, 1992.

2800 1994. *The Sword and the Rose. Original Title:* La espada y la rosa. A. Martínez Menchén. Alfaguara, 1993.

2801 1995. *Tell Me of the Sun. Original Title:* Háblame del sol. Angel Esteban. Bruño, 1994.

2802 1996. *Original Title:* Guárdate de los idus. Lola González. SM, 1995.

2803 1997. *The Man from Cero. Original Title:* El señor del Cero. María Isabel Molina. *Illustrator:* Francisco Solé. Alfaguara, 1996.

2804 1998. *The Long Hours. Original Title:* Las horas largas. Concha López Narváez. *Illustrator:* José Ramón Alonso. Anaya, 1997.

2805 1999. *Where Is My Heart. Original Title:* Donde esté mi corazón. Jordi Serra i Fabra. Edebe, 1998.

2806 2000. *My Sister Aixa. Original Title:* Mi hermana Aixa. Meri Torras. *Illustrator:* M. Valverde. La Galera, 1999.

2807 Premio el Barco de Vapor (Steamboat Prize)

SPONSOR: La Fundación Santa María. ADDRESS: calle Doctor Esquerdo, 125, 28007 Madrid, España. PHONE: 34 91 573 0299. ESTABLISHED: 1979. AWARD: 4.000.000 pesetas. The awards are given annually to promote reading for children up to 13 years. The provinces of Castilia, Cataluna, Galicia and Euskadi give prizes in their languages.

2808 1990. *Original Title:* O deus desaparecido. Carballude, Andrés García Vilariño. SM, 1991. *Category:* Gallego.

2809 1990. *Original Title:* El misterio de la mujer autónoma. José Manuel Gisbert. SM, 1991. *Category:* Castellan.

2810 1990. *Original Title:* Un llibre monstruós. Jordi Sierra i Fabra. SM, 1990. *Category:* Catalan.

2811 1991. *Original Title:* O conto dos sete medos. Antón Cortizas. SM, 1992. *Category:* Gallego.

2812 1991. *Original Title:* Silvia y la Máquina Qué. Fernando Lalana. *Illustrator:* José María Almarcegui. SM, 1992. *Category:* Castellan.

2813 1991. *Original Title:* S'ha de ser animal! Mercè Canela Garayoa. SM, 1991. *Category:* Catalan.

2814 1991. *Original Title:* Begigorritarren erlojua. Yolanda Arrieta Malaxetsebarria. SM, 1992. *Category:* Euskcera.

2815 1992. *Original Title:* Os naufragos de Malakadula. Alberto Aveñdano. SM, 1993. *Category:* Gallego.

1992. No award given.

2816 1992. *Original Title:* La medalla. Andreu Sotorra. SM, 1992. *Category:* Catalan.

2817 1993. *Original Title:* O castron de ouro. Darío Xohan Cabana. SM, 1994. *Category:* Gallego.

2818 1993. *Gangster, Treasonous, You Will Die! Original Title:* Canalla, traidor, morirás! José Antonio del Cañizo. SM, 1994. *Category:* Castellan.

2819 1993. *Original Title:* 1948ko uda. Patxi Zubizarreta. SM, 1994. *Category:* Euskcera.

1993. No award given. *Category:* Castellan.

1994. No award given. *Category:* Euskcera.

2820 1994. *Original Title:* O misterio dos fillos da Lua. Fina Casalderrey Fraga. SM, 1995. *Category:* Gallego.

2821 1994. *The Wings of the Panther. Original Title:* Las alas de la pantera. Carlos Puerto. SM, 1995. *Category:* Castellan.

2822 1994. *Original Title:* L'Albert i la menjabrossa. Daniel Nel lo Colom. SM, 1995. *Category:* Catalan.

2823 1995. *Original Title:* Vull jugar. María Jesús Bolta. SM, 1996. *Category:* Catalan.

2824 1995. *Original Title:* Os gritos das illas lobeiras. Antón Cortizas. SM, 1996. *Category:* Gallego.

2825 1995. *Original Title:* Lili sin disfraz, libertad con disfraz. Gonzalo Moure. SM, 1996. *Category:* Castellan.

1995. No award given. *Category:* Euskcera.

2826 1996. *Original Title:* A pirata penamoura. Daniel Buján. SM, 1997. *Category:* Gallego.

1996. No award given. *Category:* Castellan.

2827 1996. *Original Title:* Gau, gau, gau (Oi zein ituna). Juan Kruz Igerabide, Karlos Linazasoro. SM, 1997. *Category:* Euskcera.

2828 1996. *Original Title:* La noia del temps. Eva Piquer. SM, 1997. *Category:* Catalan.

2829 1997. *Original Title:* Hola, Pep! Jaume Cela. SM, 1998. *Category:* Catalan.

2830 1997. *Original Title:* Valldemuller. Xosé Antón Neira Cruz. SM, 1998. *Category:* Gallego.

1997. No award given. *Category:* Euskcera.

2831 1997. *King Arturi Rides Again, More or Less. Original Title:* El rey Arturi cabalga de nuevo, más o menos. Miguel Angel Moleón Viana. SM, 1998. *Category:* Castellan.

2832 1998. *Original Title:* Les histoires perdues. Jordi Sierra i Fabra. SM, 1999. *Category:* Catalan.

2833 1998. *Original Title:* A lenda do capitan Miñoca. María Dolores Ruiz Gestoso. SM, 1999. *Category:* Gallego.

2834 1998. *Original Title:* Printzesa Puzkertia. Arrate Egaña Jimenéz. SM, 1999. *Category:* Euskcera.

2835 1998. *Original Title:* Finis Mundi. Laura Gallego García. SM, 1999. *Category:* Castellan.

2836 Premio Gran Angular (Gran Angular Prize)

SPONSOR: La Fundación Santa María. ADDRESS: calle Doctor Esquerdo, 125, 28007 Madrid, España. PHONE: 34 91 573 0299. ESTABLISHED: 1979. AWARD: 1.000.000 pesetas. The prize is given to foster the creation of literature for adolescents. The winning manuscript is published.

2837 1990. *Original Title:* El último set. Jordi Serra i Fabra. Ediciones SM.

2838 1990. *Original Title:* L'Estret del Temps. Pere Pons i Clar. Ediciones SM.

2839 1991. *Original Title:* Que farem, que direm? Pep Coll. Ediciones SM.

2840 1991. *Original Title:* Scratch. Fernando Lalana. Ediciones SM.

2841 1992. *Original Title:* El pes de la carrega. Francesc Sales.

2842 1993. *Dark Brown of October. Original Title:* Brunas de octubre. Dolores González Lorenzo. Ediciones SM.

2843 1993. *Original Title:* Doble joc. Antoni Dalmases. Ediciones SM.

2844 1994. *Original Title:* El misterio del eunuco. José Luis Velasco. Ediciones SM.

2845 1994. *Original Title:* Els arbres passaven ran de finestra. Enric Larreula.

2846 1995. *Original Title:* Les joies de la princesa berber. Montserrat Beltrán. Ediciones SM.

2847 1996. *Garden of the Robots. Original Title:* Jardín de los Autómatas. Armando Boix Milian. Ediciones SM.

2848 1996. *The Good Times. Original Title:* El temps felic. Daniel Palomeras. Ediciones SM.

2849 1997. *Original Title:* Jordi d'Urtx. Octavi Egea. Ediciones SM.

2850 1997. *Southern Magician. Original Title:* Mágico Sur. Manuel Peña Muñoz. Ediciones SM.

2851 1998. *It's Not So Easy to Skip an Examination. Original Title:* No es tan fácil saltarse un examen. Luchi Núñez. Ediciones SM.

2852 1998. *Original Title:* Els gegants adormits. Jaume Cela. *Illustrator:* Jordi Magallon. Ediciones SM.

2853 Premio Internacional de Ilustración (International Illustration Prize)

SPONSOR: La Fundación Santa María. ADDRESS: calle Doctor Esquerdo, 125, 28007 Madrid, España. PHONE: 34 91 573 0299. ESTABLISHED: 1990. AWARD: 1.000.000 pesetas. The prize promotes artists whose work is aimed at children. All illustrations must be unpublished.

2854 1990. *The Rock. Original Title:* La Roca. Carme Solé Vendrell. Ediciones SM.

2855 1991. *By Air. Original Title:* Por los aires. Asun Balzola. Ediciones SM.

2856 1992. *The Anxious Tree. Original Title:* El árbol inquieto. Miguel Calatayud. Ediciones SM.

2857 1993. *The Man, the Tree and the Way. Original Title:* El hombre, el árbol y el camino. Juan Farias. *Illustrator:* Juan Ramon Alonso. Ediciones SM.

2858 1994. *Original Title:* El capirote de Onofre. Jesus Gabán. Ediciones SM.

2859 1995. *Friends. Original Title:* Amigos. Los Durán. *Illustrator:* Perico Pastor. Ediciones SM.

2860 1996. *One Night of Colors. Original Title:* Una noche de colores. Pablo Echevarría. Ediciones SM.

2861 1997. *I Don't Know! Original Title:* No sé! Mabel Piérola. Ediciones SM.

2862 1998. *The Flight of Mr. Popol. Original Title:* El vuelo del señor Popol. Judith Morales. *Illustrator:* Adria Godia. Ediciones SM.

2863 Premio Joaquím Ruyra (Joaquím Ruyra Prize)

SPONSOR: Editorial Laia S.A. ADDRESS: Diputació 250, 08007 Barcelona, Espanya. PHONE: 93 412 0030. ESTABLISHED: 1963. AWARD: 1.000.000 pesetas. The prize is given to an author for a book written in Catalan. The winning writer's work is published in a collection each year.

1990. No award given.

1991. No award given.

1992. No award given.

2864 1993. *Original Title:* El mar i el desig. Maria Àngels Gardella. Laia, 1994.

2865 1994. *Original Title:* Somnies, estimada? Montserrat Galicia. Laia, 1995.

2866 1995. *Original Title:* El galió de les illes Cies. Josep Lorman i Roig. Laia, 1996.

2867 1996. *Original Title:* Concert en sol major. Jordi Sierra i Fabra. Laia, 1997.

2868 1997. *Original Title:* El malefici dels Da. Josep Lorman i Roig. Laia, 1998.

2869 1998. *Original Title:* Espasa de constel lació. Antoni Garcia Llorca. Laia, 1999.

2870 1999. *Original Title:* Les muntanyes de foc. Miquel Rayó i Ferrer. Laia, 2000.

2871 2000. *Original Title:* Remant cap al sol. Joan Pons. Laia, 2001.

2872 Premio Josep Maria Folch i Torres (Josep Maria Folch i Torres Prize)

SPONSOR: La Galera, S.A. Editorial. ADDRESS: Diputació, 250, 08007 Barcelona, Espanya. PHONE: 93 412 0030. ESTABLISHED: 1963. AWARD: 2.000.000 pesetas. The prize is given annually to stimulate the production of children's books in the Catalan language. The prize winners are published in Catalan and Castilian.

1990. No award given.

2873 1991. *Original Title:* Tereseta la bruixeta. Josep Gregori. La Galera, 1991.

2874 1992. *Original Title:* Quin patarrabum! Enric Bayé. La Galera, 1992.

2875 1993. *Original Title:* El Mar dels Naufragis. Salvador Comelles. La Galera, 1993.

1994. No award given.

2876 1995. *Original Title:* Ull d'ocell. Antoni Garcia Llorca. La Galera, 1995.

2877 1996. *Original Title:* Contes a una cama trencada. Dolors Garcia. La Galera, 1996.

2878 1997. *Original Title:* Quin parell! Jaume Cela i Ollé. La Galera, 1997.

2879 1998. *Original Title:* Es busca portera. Xavier Bertran Alcalde. La Galera, 1998.

2880 1999. *Original Title:* Ulldevellut. Joan Francesc Delgado, Hermínia Mas. La Galera, 1999.

2881 Premio Lazarillo (Guide Prize)

SPONSOR: Organización Española para el Libro Infantil y Juvenil. CONTACT: Secretariat. ADDRESS: Santiago Rusiñol 8, 28040 Madrid, España. PHONE: 3491 553 08 21. ESTABLISHED: 1958. AWARD: 1.000.000 pesetas for illustration, 1.000.000 pesetas for literature. The award is given to the best young adult works written in any of the languages of Spain and targeting particularly readers above 12 years old. The award for illustration is given for the best new illustrations of a children's book.

2882 1990. *Original Title:* Quina nit de reis. *Illustrator:* Marta Balaguer. SM. *Category:* illustration.

2883 1990. *Original Title:* Contos por palabras. Agustin Fernández Paz. *Category:* text.

2884 1991. *Original Title:* Devuelve el anillo, pelo cepillo. Enrique Páez. *Category:* text.

2885 1991. *Little Wu-lli. Original Title:* La pequeña Wu-lli. *Illustrator:* Gusti. *Category:* illustration.

2886 1992. *Poetic Anthology of Vicente Huidobro. Original Title:* Antología poética de Vicente Huidobro. *Illustrator:* José Mª Carmona. *Category:* illustration.

2887 1992. *Between the Game and the Fire. Original Title:* Entre el juego y el fuego. *Illustrator:* José Mª Carmona. *Category:* illustration.

2888 1992. *The Secret of the 211 Doors. Original Title:* El secreto de las 211 puertas. Francisco A. Díaz Guerra. *Category:* text.

2889 1993. *Bzzz.... Original Title:* Bzzz.... *Illustrator:* Gabriela Rubio. *Category:* illustration.

1993. No award given. *Category:* text.

2890 1994. *Original Title:* Chumplufated... *Illustrator:* Samuel Velasco. *Category:* illustration.

2891 1994. *Original Title:* T'he agafat caputxeta. Carles Cano Peiró. *Category:* text.

2892 1995. *Original Title:* Una casa com un cabàs. *Illustrator:* Lluis Farré Estrada. *Category:* illustration.

2893 1995. *Three Stories of Sergio. Original Title:* Tres historias de Sergio. José Zafra Castro. *Category:* text.

2894 1996. *A Summer with Friends. Original Title:* El verano y sus amigos. *Illustrator:* Isidro Ferrer. *Category:* illustration.

2895 1996. *Original Title:* Los zapatos de murano. M. Angel Pacheco. *Category:* text.

2896 1997. *The Boy and the Fish. Original Title:* El niño que dejó de ser pez. *Illustrator:* Manuel Barbero Richart. *Category:* illustration.

2897 1997. *The Mystery of Velázquez. Original Title:* El misterio Velázquez. Eliacer Cansino. *Category:* text.

2898 1998. *Day of Kings Magos. Original Title:* Día de Reyes Magos. Emilio Pascual. *Category:* text.

2899 1998. *Original Title:* No eres más que una pequeña hormiguita. *Illustrator:* Judit Morales Villanueva. *Category:* illustration.

2900 1999. *Not All Cows Are Equal. Original Title:* No todas las vacas son iguales. *Illustrator:* Pablo Amargo. *Category:* illustration.

2901 1999. *Original Title:* A banda sen futuro. Marilar Aleixandre. Edicións Xerais, 1999. *Category:* text.

2902 Premio Lola Anglada (Lola Anglada Prize)

SPONSOR: Caixa d'Estalvis de Terrassa S.A. CONTACT: Rafael Claret. ADDRESS: Portal Nou, 3708221 Terrassa, Barcelona, Espanya. PHONE: 93 739 77 00. ESTABLISHED: 1982. AWARD: Monetary prize. The prize winner must exhibit in their works humanistic and civic virtues, which distinguished the works of Lola Anglada i Sarriera.

2903 1990. *Original Title:* Si les persones parlessin.... Xavier Bertran. caixaterrassa, 1991.

2904 1991. *Original Title:* Contes per a un món millor. Enric Larreula. caixaterrassa, 1992.

2905 1992. *Original Title:* Nyatiti: la Filla del Clan. Andreu Sotorra. caixaterrassa, 1993.

2906 1993. *Original Title:* Qui vol un conte? Joles Sennell. caixaterrassa, 1994.

1994. No award given.

2907 1995. *Original Title:* Els contes del llop. Ramón Montón i Lara. caixaterrassa, 1996.

2908 1996. *Original Title:* La Dama Blanca i altres rondalles. Rosa María Colom i Bernat. caixaterrassa, 1997.

2909 1997. *Original Title:* El tresor de la Nit de Nadal. Pep Coll. caixaterrassa, 1998.

2910 1998. *Original Title:* Sopa de nit. Dolors Garcia i Cornella. caixaterrassa, 1999.

2911 1999. *Original Title:* Joaquim, aixo no es fa! Joan Armangué i Herrero. caixaterrassa, 2000.

2912 Premio Merlín (Merlin Prize)

SPONSOR: Ediciones Xerais de Galicia S.A. ADDRESS: Doutor Marañón, 12, 36211 Vigo, España. PHONE: 34 986 214888. ESTABLISHED: 1986. AWARD: 1.000.000 pesetas. The prize is given annually to an author of any nationality for an unpublished, original text written in Gallega.

2913 1990. *Original Title:* Fafarraios. Gloria Sánchez. Edicións Xerais, 1991.

2914 1991. *Original Title:* Dúas bágoas por Máquina. Fina Casalderrey. Edicións Xerais, 1992.

2915 1992. *Original Title:* Os Mornias. Dolores González. Edicións Xerais, 1993.

2916 1993. *Original Title:* O gaiteiro e o Rato Pérez. Bernardino Graña. Edicións Xerais, 1994.

2917 1994. *Original Title:* A expedición do Pacífico. Marilar Aleixandre. Edicións Xerais, 1995.

2918 1995. *Original Title:* Perigo vexetal. Ramón Caride. Edicións Xerais, 1996.

2919 1996. *Original Title:* Na Fogueira dos versos. Antonio G. Teijeiro. Edicións Xerais, 1997.

2920 1997. *Original Title:* ¡Sireno, Sireno! An Alfaya. Edicións Xerais, 1998.

2921 1998. *Original Title:* Memorias dun raposo. Antonio Reigosa. Edicións Xerais, 1999.

2922 1999. *Original Title:* A noite das cabras do aire. Bieito Iglesias. Edicións Xerais, 2000.

2923 2000. *Original Title:* As cousas claras. Xosé Antón Neira Cruz. Edicións Xerais, 2001.

2924 Premio Nacional de Literatura Infantil y Juvenil (Creación) (National Prize for Children's and Young Adult Literature)

SPONSOR: Dirección General del Libro y Bibliotecas, Ministerio de Cultura. CONTACT: Fernando Cendán. ADDRESS: Santiage Rusiñol, 8, 28040 Madrid, España. PHONE: 91536 88 00. ESTABLISHED: 1978. AWARD: 2,500,000 pesetas. The prize is given to help in the creation, production and distribution of literature for children and youth.

2925 1990. *Original Title:* La rosa de Sant Jordi. Joles Sennell.

2926 1991. *Original Title:* Morirás en Chafarinas. Fernando Lalana.

2927 1992. *Original Title:* Un monstruo en el armario. Carmen Vázquez Vigo.

2928 1993. *Original Title:* No soy un libro. José María Merino.

2929 1994. *Original Title:* Han cremat el mar. Gabriel Janer Manila.

2930 1995. *Original Title:* Cando petan na porta pola noite. Xabier Puente Docampo.

2931 1996. *Original Title:* O misterio dos fillos de Lúa. Fina Casalderrey.

2932 1997. *Original Title:* L'amiga mès amiga de la formiga Piga. Emili Teixidor.

2933 1998. *Original Title:* Los trapos sucios. Elvira Lindo.

2934 1999. *Original Title:* Oscar y el León de Correos. Vicente Muñoz Puelles.

SWEDEN

2935 Astrid Lindgren Priset (Astrid Lindgren Prize)

SPONSOR: Rabén & Sjögren. ADDRESS: Box 2052, S-104 30 Stockholm, Sweden. ESTABLISHED: 1967. AWARD: 25,000 kronor. The annual award is given to honor achievements in writing for children.

2936 1990. Maj Bylock.

2937 1991. Max Lundgren.

2938 1992. Sven Christer Swahn.
2939 1993. Ulf Stark.
2940 1994. Eva Wikander.
2941 1995. Peter Pohl.
2942 1996. Henning Mankell.
2943 1997. Anna-Clara Tidholm, Thomas Tidholm.
2944 1998. Bo R. Holmberg.
2945 1999. Per Nilsson.
2946 2000. Annika Thor.

2947 Augustpriset (August Prize)

SPONSOR: Svenska Förläggareföreningen. ADDRESS: Drottninggatan 97, 2 tr, 113 12 Stockholm, Sweden. PHONE: 08-736 19 40. ESTABLISHED: 1989. AWARD: 100.000 kronor and a bronze statuette by Mikael Fare. The award is given for the year's best book by a Swedish writer for a children's and young adult book.

2948 1992. *Original Title:* Jag saknar dig, jag saknar dig! Peter Pohl. *Illustrator:* Kinna Gieth.
2949 1993. *Original Title:* Vinterviken. Mats Wahl.
2950 1994. *Original Title:* Mästaren och de fyra skrivarna. Ulf Nilsson.
2951 1995. *Original Title:* Flickan som inte ville kyssas. Rose Lagercrantz.
2952 1996. *Original Title:* Min syster är en ängel. Ulf Stark. *Illustrator:* Anna Höglund.
2953 1997. *Original Title:* Sanning eller konsekvens. Annika Thor.
2954 1998. *Original Title:* Resan till världens ände. Henning Mankell.
2955 1999. *Original Title:* Spelar död. Stefan Casta.
2956 2000. *Original Title:* Gittan och gråvargarna. Pija Linderbaum.

2957 Bokjuryn (Book Jury)

SPONSOR: The Swedish Library Association. CONTACT: Stina Sjölund. ADDRESS: Box 2175, 103 14 Stockholm, Sweden. PHONE: 08–545 222 44. ESTABLISHED: 1997. Children throughout Sweden vote for their favorite books. There are four categories: ages 0–6, 7–9, 10–12 and 13–19.

2958 1997. *Original Title:* Lägerhästarnas natt. Erik Eriksson. *Category:* 13–19.
2959 1997. *Original Title:* Flyg, sa Alfons Åberg! Gunilla Bergström. *Category:* 0–6.
2960 1997. *Original Title:* Sanning eller konsekvens. Annika Thor. *Category:* 10–12.
2961 1997. *Original Title:* Bara Tsatsiki. Moni Nilsson-Brännström. *Category:* 7–9.

2962 1998. *Original Title:* Eva & Adam: fusk och farligheter. Måns Gahrton. *Illustrator:* Johan Unenge. *Category:* 10–12.

2963 1998. *Original Title:* Castor målar. Lars Klinting. *Category:* 0–6.

2964 1998. *Original Title:* Havets djup. Annika Thor. *Category:* 13–19.

2965 1998. *Original Title:* Matilda tänker bara på fotboll. Kirsten Boie. *Category:* 7–9.

2966 1999. *Original Title:* Frippe lagar allt. Lars Klinting. *Category:* 0–6.

2967 1999. *Original Title:* Berts bokslut. Sören Olsson. *Illustrator:* Anders Jacobsson. *Category:* 13–19.

2968 1999. *Original Title:* Tsatsiki och kärleken. Moni Nilsson-Bränns. *Category:* 7–9.

2969 1999. *Original Title:* Eva & Adam: jul, jul pinsamma jul. Måns Gahrton. *Illustrator:* Johan Unenge. *Category:* 10–12.

2970 Carl von Linné-plaketten (Carl von Linné Plaque)

SPONSOR: Svensk Biblioteksfornening. ADDRESS: Saltmatargatan 3 A Box 3127, 103 62 Stockholm, Sweden. PHONE: 08-545 132 30. ESTABLISHED: 1998. The award is given annually.

2971 1999. *Original Title:* Se huset. Kerstin Nilsson. *Illustrator:* Ulf Lundkvist.

2972 2000. *Original Title:* Nyfiken på naturvetenskap. Hans Persson. *Illustrator:* Lotta Glave, Anders Nyberg.

2973 Elsa Beskow Plaketten (Elsa Beskow Plaque)

SPONSOR: Svensk Biblioteksforening. ADDRESS: Biblioteksforeningen Saltmatargatan 3 A Box 3127, 103 62 Stockholm, Sweden. PHONE: 08-545-132 30. ESTABLISHED: 1981. The award is given annually to the illustrator of the best Swedish picture book published in the preceding year.

2974 1990. *Collected works as book illustrator. Illustrator:* Gunna Gräs.

2975 1991. *The Children from Tibet. Original Title:* Barnen från Tibet. *Illustrator:* Bodil Hagbrink. AWE/ Gebers 1990.

2976 1992. *Original Title:* Nisse hos frisören. *Illustrator:* Olof Landström.

2977 1993. *Original Title:* Bra Börje. *Illustrator:* Pija Lindenbaum.

2978 1994. *Original Title:* Banvaktsbarn, Fredrik Matsson blir kär. *Illustrator:* Anna Bengtsson.

2979 1995. *Original Title:* Gunnar i granskogen. *Illustrator:* Eva Lindström.

2980 1996. *Original Title:* Dockvandringen. *Illustrator:* Lisa Örtengren.

2981 1997. *Original Title:* Hårboken. *Illustrator:* Pernilla Stalfelt.

2982 1998. *Original Title:* ABCD-boken. *Illustrator:* Mati Lepp.

2983 1999. *Original Title:* Var är Sailor och Pekka. *Illustrator:* Jockum Nordström.

2984 2000. *Original Title:* Rut och Knut ställer ut; Rut och Knut börjar träna. *Illustrator:* Stina Wirsén.

2985 Expressens Heffaklump (Heffaklumpen Prize)

SPONSOR: Kvallstidningen Expressen. ADDRESS: Gjorwellsg 30, S-105 16 Stockholm, Sweden. PHONE: 08 738 3000. ESTABLISHED: 1966. AWARD: A sculpture by Swedish artist, K.G. Bejemark. The annual award is given to the author of the best Swedish children's book.

2986 1990. *Original Title:* Else-Marie och småpapporna. Pija Lindenbaum.
2987 1991. *Original Title:* Majken och skyddsängeln. Margareta Strömstedt.
2988 1992. *Original Title:* En barkbåt till Eddie. Viveca Lärn Sundvall.
2989 1993. *Original Title:* Mamma Mu gungar, Lillebror och Billan, Gunga lite grann. Jujja Wieslander, Tomas Wieslander.
2990 1994. *Original Title:* Otto och Stures hemliga liv. Lena Klefelt.
2991 1995. *Original Title:* Storebrorsan. Ulf Stark.
2992 1996. *Original Title:* Pojken som sov med snö i sin säng. Henning Mankell.
2993 1997. *Collected Works of the Author.* Anna Höglund.
2994 1998. *Original Title:* Sailor och Pekka. Jockum Nordström.
2995 1999. *Original Title:* Esperanza. Jakob Wegelius.
2996 2000. *Original Title:* Kotten. Lena Anderson.

2997 Gulliver Award

SPONSOR: IBBY Sweden. CONTACT: Ms. Catrine Grimlund. ADDRESS: Odengatan 61, S-113 22 Stockholm, Sweden. PHONE: 4633 16 40 77. ESTABLISHED: 1969. The award is given annually to the person who through critical, theoretical or practical work, is considered to have made an essential contribution to an increased understanding of books for children and young adults in Sweden.

2998 1991. Birgitta Fransson.
2999 1992. Sonja Svensson.
3000 1993. Jan Nilsson.
3001 1994. Gunilla Lundgren.
3002 1995. Ulla Lundqvist.
3003 1996. Birgitta Lundborg.
3004 1997. Kersti Westin.
3005 1998. Lena Kåreland.
3006 1999. Britt Isaksson.
3007 2000. Kjell Andersson.

3008 Nils Holgersson Plaketten (Nils Holgersson Plaque)

SPONSOR: Svensk Biblioteksforening. ADDRESS: Biblioteksforeningen Saltmatargatan 3 A Box 3127, 103 62 Stockholm, Sweden. PHONE: 08-545-132 30. ESTABLISHED: 1950. The award is given annually to the author of the best Swedish children's book published in the preceding year.

3009 1990. *Original Title:* Amada! Amanda. Annika Holm.

3010 1991. *The Dog That Ran Towards a Star. Original Title:* Hunden som sprang mot en stjärna. Henning Mankell. Rabén & Sjögren, 1990.

3011 1992. *Eddie and Maxon Jaxon. Original Title:* Eddie och Maxon Jaxon. Viveca Lärn Sundvall.

3012 1993. *Original Title:* Barnens svenska historia. Sonja Hulth.

3013 1994. *Original Title:* Förr i tiden i skogen. Thomas Tidholm.

3014 1995. *Original Title:* Gravitation. Inger Edelfeldt.

3015 1996. *Original Title:* Jag Julia, Min läsebok. Helena Dahlbäck.

3016 1997. *Original Title:* Anarkai. Per Nilsson.

3017 1998. *Original Title:* Bara Tsatsiki. Moni Nilsson-Brännström.

3018 1999. *Original Title:* Havets djup. Annika Thor.

3019 2000. *Original Title:* Spelar död. Stefan Casta.

3020 Peter Pan Award

SPONSOR: IBBY Sweden. CONTACT: Ms. Gunilla Borén. ADDRESS: Odengatan 61, S-113 22 Stockholm, Sweden. PHONE: 4633 16 40 77. ESTABLISHED: 2000. AWARD: A diploma created by illustrator Eva Eriksson. The award is given for a book from any country, language or culture for children or youth. The Peter Pan Award is the first Swedish one for translated books.

3021 2000. *Holes.* Louis Sachar. *Translator:* Peter Lindforss. Bonnier Carlsen, 1999. *Category:* adolescents. *Level:* Silver Star.

3022 2000. *Original Title:* Eine Woche voller Samstage. Paul Maar. *Translator:* Gunilla Borén. Opal, 1999. *Category:* children´s book. *Level:* Silver Star.

3023 2000. *Katie´s War.* Aubrey Flegg. *Translator:* Gunilla Borén. Berghs, 1999.

3024 2000. *Jamela´s Dress. Translator:* Britt Isaksson. Forlaget Hjulet, 1999. *Category:* picture book. *Level:* Silver Starz.

SWITZERLAND

3025 Blaue Brillenschlange (Blue Cobra)

SPONSOR: terre des hommes schweiz and Berne Declaration. CONTACT: Helene Schär. ADDRESS: Kinderbuchfonds Baobab, Laufenstrasse 16, CH-4018 Basel, Switzerland. PHONE: 41 61 333 27 27. ESTABLISHED: 1985. AWARD: A work of art by artist Burkina Faso. The award is given to one, two or three best books for children and young people published in the past year in the entire German-speaking community. It is given for books about third-world topics and racism. The award intends to encourage authors and publishers to publish well-written books about these topics without prejudice, discrimination and xenophobia.

1990. No award given.

3025 1991. *Phyllisia. Original Title:* Phyllisia. Rosa Guy. Alibaba, 1990.

3026 1992. *No Tigers in Africa. Original Title:* Keine Tiger in Afrika. Norman Silver. Beltz & Gelberg, 1992.

3027 1993. *Zorro Means Fox. Original Title:* Zorro heisst Fuchs. *Translator:* Margreth Wannenmacher. Lamuv, 1992.

3028 1993. *Life! Life! Life! Original Title:* Leben! Leben! Leben! Feng Jacai. *Translator:* Karin Hasselblatt. Sauerlander, 1993.

3029 1993. *Tough Boy and Sister. Original Title:* Starker Sohn und Schwester. Kirkpatrick Hill. *Translator:* Susanne Koppe. Beltz & Gelberg, 1993.

3030 1994. *One Morning the Komreh Was Empty. Original Title:* Eines Morgens war die Chomreh leer. Hushang Moradi Kermani. *Translator:* Mehrafagh Gallenbacher. Jungbrunnen, 1993.

3031 1994. *A Foreign Land. Original Title:* Ein fremdes Land. Fran Leeper Buss. *Translator:* Heike Brandt. Beltz & Gelberg, 1994.

3032 1995. *Lelee, the Girl. Original Title:* Lelee, das Hirtenmädchen. Abdoua Kanta. *Translator:* A. Burckhardt. Nagel & Kimche, 1994.

3033 1995. *The Life and Passion of Pandonar, the Cruel One. Original Title:* Leben und Leidenschaft von Pandonar dem Grausamen. João Ubaldo Ribeiro. *Translator:* Ray-Güde Mertin. Hanser, 1994.

3034 1995. *Childhood Hunger. Original Title:* Kindheitshunger. Axel Gauvin. *Translator:* Heinrich Raatschen. P. Hammer, 1995.

3035 1996. *Original Title:* Da musst du durch, Lurch. Jenny Robson. *Translator:* Marion Schweizer. Elefanten Press, 1996.

3036 1997. *Children in the Dark. Original Title:* Kinder im Dunkeln. Júlio Emílio Braz. *Translator:* Bettina Neumann. Nagel & Kimche, 1996.

3037 1997. *Panther in the Cellar. Original Title:* Panther im Keller. Amos Oz. *Translator:* Vera Loos and Naomi Nir-Bleimling. Carl Hanser, 1997.

3038 1998. *At Night Over the Mountains. Original Title:* In der Nacht über die Berge. Mahmut Baksi. *Illustrator::* Elin Clason. *Translator:* Christine Holliger. Nagel & Kimche, 1997.

3039 1998. T*he Secrets of the Yingzi. Original Title:* Die Geheimnisse der Yingzi. Haiyin Lin. *Translator:* Susanne Hornfeck. Carl Hanser 1997.

3040 1999. *Azouz, the Boy on the Outskirts of Town. Original Title:* Azouz, der Junge vom Stadtrand. Eine Algerische Kindheit in Lyon. Azouz Begag. *Translator:* Regina Keil. Nagel & Kimche, 1998.

3041 Hans Christian Andersen Awards

SPONSOR: IBBY Secretariat. ADDRESS: Nonnenweg 12, Postfach, CH-4003 Basel, Switzerland. PHONE: 4161 272 29 17. ESTABLISHED: 1956. AWARD: A gold medal and a diploma. The medal is given to an author and an illustrator every two years who on the basis of their complete works are considered by the Board to have made an enduring contribution to children's and young adult literature.

3042 1990. Lisbeth Zwerger. *Category:* Austria. *Illustration.*
3043 1990. Tormod Haugen. *Category:* Norway.
3044 1992. Virginia Hamilton. *Category:* U.S.A.
3045 1992. Kveta Pacovska. *Category:* Czechoslovakia. *Illustration.*
3046 1994. Michio Mado. *Category:* Japan.
3047 1994. Jorg Muller. *Category:* Switzerland. *Illustration.*
3048 1996. Klaus Ensikat. *Category:* Germany. *Illustration.*
3049 1996. Uri Orlev. *Category:* Israel.
3050 1998. Tomi Ungerer. *Category:* France. *Illustration.*
3051 1998. Katherine Paterson. *Category:* U.S.A.
3052 2000. Ana Maria Machada. *Category:* Brazil.
3053 2000. Anthony Browne. *Category:* U.K. *Illustration.*

3054 Prix Enfantaisie (Children's Prize)

SPONSOR: La Joie de Lire. CONTACT: Mme. Francine Bouchet. ADDRESS: rue St-Léger 2bis, 1205 Genève, Switzerland. PHONE: (4122) 807 3399. ESTABLISHED: 1988. AWARD: 5000 francs. The award is given to a recent work of quality intended for children ages 7 to 14 years. Children vote for the best book.

3055 1990. *The Blue Dog. Original Title:* Le chien bleu. Nadjy. Ecole des loisirs, 1989.

3056 1991. *The Song of Hannah. Original Title:* La Chanson de Hannah. Jean-Paul Nozière. Nathan, 1990.

3057 1992. *Cinderella, A Tale of Christmas and White Rose. Original Title:* Cendrillon, Un conte de Noël et rose blanche. Roberto Innocenti. Gallimard, 1991.

3058 1993. *Rebelle the Wolf. Original Title:* Rebelle le loup. Jacqueline Delaunay. Syros, 1992.

3059 1994. *The Gentleman from the Street Next to Ours. Original Title:* Le monsieur de la rue d'à côté. Alice Dumas. *Illustrator:* Marine Laffon. Syros, 1993.

3060 1995. *One Night, One Cat. Original Title:* Un nuit, un chat. Yvan Pommaux. Ecole des loisirs, 1994.

3061 1996. *The Zinzin Store. Original Title:* Magasin zinzin. Frédéric Clément. Ipomée-Albin Michel, 1995.

3062 1997. *The Fifth Season. Original Title:* La cinquième saison. Hortense Dufour. Éd. du Seuil, 1996.

3063 1998. *The Phantom Train. Original Title:* Le train fantôme. Paul Yee. *Illustrator:* Harvey Chan. Circonflexe, 1997.

3064 1999. *The Collector of Moments. Original Title:* Le collectionneur d'instants. Quint Buchholz. Milan, 1998.

3065 2000. *The Prohibited Dance. Original Title:* La danse interdite. Rachel Hausfater-Douieb. Thierry Magnier, 1999.

3066 Schweizer Jugendbuchpreis (Switzerland Children's Literature Prize)

SPONSOR: Swiss Teachers Association. ADDRESS: Ringstrasse 54, Postfach 189, 8057 Zürich, Switzerland. PHONE: (01) 315 54 54. ESTABLISHED: 1943. AWARD: 1000 Swiss Francs. The annual award is given to a Swiss author of juvenile literature.

3067 1990. *Animal Stories. Original Title:* Tiergeschichten. Hanna Johansen, Käthi Bhend.

3068 1991. Complete works. Hans Manz.

3069 1992. Complete works. Helene Schär.

3070 1993. Complete works. Brigitte Schär.

3071 1993. Complete works. Jürg Obrist.

3072 1993. Complete works. Emil Zopfi.

3073 1993. Complete works. Max Huwyler.

3074 1994. *The Giant. Original Title:* Der Riese und die Erdbeerkonfitüre. Franz Hohler.

3075 1995. *Long Nose. Original Title:* So eine lange Nase. Lukas Hartmann.

3076 1996. *When the World Was New. Original Title:* Als die Welt noch jung war. Jürg Schubiger. Annick Press, 1996.

1997. No award was given.

3077 1998. *Bevel Types. Original Title:* Schräge Typen. Christian Urech.

3078 1999. Complete works. Zapp Zappina.

3079 2000. *Tita and Leo. Original Title:* Tita und Leo. Angelika Waldis. Haffmans, 1999.

3080 Vache Qui Lit (Reading Cow)

SPONSOR: Kinderbuchladen Zurich. ADDRESS: Oberdorfstrasse 32, CH-8001 Zürich, Switzerland. PHONE: (01) 261 53 50. ESTABLISHED: 1977. AWARD: A wooden statue of a Swiss cow and 3000 Swiss Francs. The prize alternates yearly between a children's book and a youth book. The author must be German-speaking and the book must have been published in the preceding year.

3081 1990. *Small Head. Original Title:* Der Zwerg im Kopf. Christine Nöstlinger. Beltz & Gelberg, 1989.

3082 1991. *Back to the Wall. Original Title:* Mit dem Rücken zur Wand. Klaus Kordon. Beltz & Gelberg, 1990.

3083 1992. *Lena and the Wolf Den. Original Title:* Lena vom Wolfsgraben. Tilde Michels. Nagel & Kimche, 1991.

3084 1993. *Journey in August. Original Title:* Reise im August. Gudrun Pausewang. Ravenburger, 1992.

3085 1994. *Mustafa. Original Title:* Mustafa mit dem Bauchladen. Ghazi Abel-Qadir. Nagel & Kimche, 1993.

3086 1995. *When Luck Comes. Original Title:* Wenn das Glück kommt, muss man ihm einen Stuhl hinstellen. Mirjam Pressler. Beltz & Gelberg, 1994.

3087 1996. *Bonizaz and the Robber. Original Title:* Bonizaz und der Räuber Knapp. Josef Holub. Beltz & Gelberg, 1995.

3088 1997. *Lausige Times. Original Title:* Lausige Zeiten. Josef Holub. Beltz & Gelberg, 1996.

3089 1998. *A Sea Full of Stars. Original Title:* Ein Meer voller Sterne. Sigrid Zeevart. Dressler, 1997.

3090 1999. *Ask the New World, Mr. Ober. Original Title:* Bitte eine neue Welt, Herr Ober. Sheila Och. Sauerländer, 1998.

3091 2000. *Gentleman Thieves. Original Title:* Herr der Diebe. Cornelia Funke. Dressler, 1999.

UNITED STATES

3092 Aesop Prize

SPONSOR: American Folklore Society. ADDRESS: 4350 N. Fairfax Dr., Suite 640, Arlington, Virginia 22203. PHONE: (703) 528-1902. ESTABLISHED: 1992. The award is given to the outstanding book or books incorporating folklore and published in English for children or young adults.

3093 1992. *Days of Awe: Stories for Rosh Hashanah and Yom Kippur.* Eric A. Kimmel. *Illustrator:* Erika Weihs. Viking, 1992.

3094 1992. *Aesop and Company with Scenes from His Legendary Life.* Barbara Bader. *Illustrator:* Arthur Geisert. Houghton Mifflin, 1992.

3095 1993. *Love Flute.* Paul Goble. *Illustrator:* Paul Goble. Bradbury, 1993.

3096 1993. *Cut from the Same Cloth: American Women in Myth, Legend, and Tall Tale.* Robert San Souci. *Illustrator:* Brian Pinkney. Philomel, 1993.

3097 1994. *John Henry.* Julius Lester. *Illustrator:* Jerry Pinkney. Dial, 1994.

3098 1995. *Fair Is Fair: World Folktales of Justice.* Sharon Creeden. August House, 1994.

3099 1996. *Next Year in Jerusalem.* Howard Schwartz. *Illustrator:* Neil Waldman. Viking, 1996.

3100 1996. *Nursery Tales Around the World.* Judy Sierra. *Illustrator:* Stefano Vitale. Clarion, 1996.

3101 1997. *Earth Tales from Around the World.* Michael J. Caduto. *Illustrator:* Adelaide Murphy Tyrol. Fulcrum, 1997.

3102 1997. *The Hired Hand: An African-American Folktale.* Robert San Souci. *Illustrator:* Jerry Pinkney. Dial, 1997.

3103 1998. *Echoes of the Elders: The Stories and Paintings of Chief Lelooska.* Chief Lelooska. *Illustrator:* Chief Lelooska. DK Publishing, Inc., 1997.

3104 1999. *Trickster and the Fainting Birds.* Howard Norman. *Illustrator:* Tom Pohrt. Harcourt Brace, 1999.

3105 1999. *King Solomon and His Magic Ring.* Elie Wiesel. *Illustrator:* Mark Podwal. Greenwillow, 1999.

3106 2000. *The Day the Rabbi Disappeared: Jewish Holiday Tales of Magic.* Howard Schwartz. *Illustrator:* Monique Passicot. Viking, 2000.

3107 ALAN Award

SPONSOR: Assembly on Literature for Adolescents of the National Council of Teachers of English. ADDRESS: 1111 Kenyon Road, Urbana, Illinois, 61801. ESTABLISHED: 1974. AWARD: A plaque. The award is given to honour the professional for his or her outstanding achievements in writing or for distinguished service in the field of adolescent literature.

3108 1990. Richard Peck.

3109 1991. Gary Paulsen.

3110 1992. Don Gallo.

3111 1993. Chris Crutcher.

3112 1994. Walter Dean Myers.

3113 1995. Robert Small.
3114 1996. Bill Morris.
3115 1997. Mildred Taylor.
3116 1998. S.E. Hinton.
3117 1999. Phyllis Reynolds Naylor.

3118 American Booksellers Book of the Year (ABBY) Award

SPONSOR: American Booksellers Association. ADDRESS: 828 South Broadway, Tarrytown, New York, 10591. PHONE: 1-800-637-0037. ESTABLISHED: 1991. AWARD: $5,000 and an engraved Tiffany glass prism. The award is given to honor the "hidden treasures" that ABA bookstore members most enjoyed recommending to their customers during the previous year. The children's award was added in, 1993. Four ABBY Honor Books were also designated in each category.

3119 1991. *The Education of Little Tree.* Forrest Carter. University of New Mexico Press, 1990.
3120 1992. *Brother Eagle, Sister Sky.* Susan Jeffers. *Illustrator:* Susan Jeffers. Dial Books for Young Readers, 1991.
3121 1993. *Old Turtle.* Douglas Wood. *Illustrator:* Cheng-Khee Chee. Pfeifer-Hamilton Publishing, 1992.
3122 1994. *Stellaluna.* Janell Cannon. Harcourt Brace, 1993.
3123 1995. *The Rainbow Fish.* Marcus Pfister. North-South Books, 1992.
3124 1996. *Guess How Much I Love You.* Sam McBratney. *Illustrator:* Anita Jeram. Candlewick Press, 1995.
3125 1997. *Lilly's Purple Plastic Purse.* Kevin Henkes. Greenwillow Books, 1996.
3126 1998. *The Hat.* Jan Brett. *Illustrator:* Jan Brett. Putnam Publishing, 1997.
3127 1999. *Harry Potter and the Sorcerer's Stone.* J.K. Rowling. *Illustrator:* Mary Grandpré. Scholastic 1998.

3128 Américas Award

SPONSOR: Consortium of Latin American Studies Programs (CLASP) University of Wisconsin-Milwaukee. ADDRESS: 2513 E. Hartland Avenue, Pearse Hall 168, Milwaukee, Wisconsin, 53201. PHONE: (414) 229-4401. The award is given in recognition of U.S. works of fiction, poetry, folklore, or selected non-fiction (from picture books to works for young adults) published in the previous year in English or Spanish that authentically and engagingly portray Latin America, the Caribbean, or Latinos in the United States.

3129 1993. *Original Title:* Vejigante Masquerader. Lulu Delacre. Scholastic, 1992.

3130 1994. *The Mermaid's Twin Sister.* Lynn Joseph. Clarion, 1993.

3131 1995. *Tonight, by Sea.* Frances Temple. Orchard, 1994.

3132 1996. *In My Family. Original Title:* En mi familia. Carmen Lomas Garza. *Illustrator:* Carmen Lomas Garza. Children's Book Press, 1994.

3133 1997. *Parrot in the Oven: Mi Vida.* Victor Martínez. HarperCollins, 1995.

3134 1997. *The Circuit.* Francisco Jiménez. University of New Mexico Press, 1996.

3135 1997. *The Face at the Window.* Regina Hanson. *Illustrator:* Linda Saport. Clarion, 1996.

3136 1998. *Barrio: José's Neighborhood.* George Ancona. Harcourt Brace, 1997.

3137 1998. *Mama and Papa Have a Store.* Amelia Lau Carling. Dial, 1997.

3138 1999. *Crashboomlove.* Juan Felipe Herrera. University of New Mexico Press 1998.

3139 Anne Spencer Lindbergh Prize in Children's Literature

SPONSOR: Charles A. and Anne Morrow Lindbergh Foundation. ADDRESS: 2150 Third Avenue North, Suite 310, Anoka, Minnesota, 55303-2200. AWARD: $5000. The award is given to the author whose children's fantasy novel is judged to be the best published in the English language over a two-year period.

3140 1996. *Cold Shoulder Road.* Joan Aiken. Delacorte Press, 1996.

3141 1998. *Harry Potter and the Sorcerer's Stone.* J.K. Rowling. *Illustrator:* Mary Grandpré. Scholastic 1998.

3142 Arizona Young Readers Award

SPONSOR: Arizona State Library Association. ADDRESS: 3839 N. Drinkwater Blvd., Scottsdale, Arizona, 85251-4452. PHONE: (480) 312-7323. ESTABLISHED: 1977. AWARD: A plaque. The award is given annually for outstanding literature written for young adults. The children vote to select the winning author.

3143 1991. *Meanwhile Back at the Ranch.* Trina Hakes Noble. *Illustrator:* Tony Ross. Puffin, 1987.

3144 1991. *The Jolly Postman.* Allan Ahlberg, Janet Ahlberg. *Illustrator:* Allan Ahlberg, Janet Ahlberg. Heinemann, 1986.

3145 1991. *There's a Boy in the Girl's Bathroom.* Louis Sachar. Knopf, 1987.

3146 1991. *Thomas' Snowsuit.* Robert Munsch. *Illustrator:* Michael Martchenko. Annick, 1985.

3147 1991. *Where's Waldo.* Martin Handford. *Illustrator:* Martin Handford. Candlewick, 1990.

3148 1993. *The Very Quiet Cricket.* Eric Carle. *Illustrator:* Eric Carle. Philomel, 1990. *Category:* picture book.

3149 1993. *Wayside School Is Falling Down.* Louis Sachar. *Illustrator:* Joel Schick. Lothrop, Lee & Shepard, 1989. *Category:* intermediate.

3150 1994. *Nothing but the Truth.* Avi. Jackson/Orchard, 1991. *Category:* middle school.

3151 1994. *Shiloh.* Phyllis Reynolds Naylor. Atheneum, 1991. *Category:* intermediate.

3152 1994. *The Three Little Javelinas.* Susan Lowell. *Illustrator:* Jim Harris. Rising Moon, 1992. *Category:* picture book.

3153 1995. *The Three Little Wolves and the Big Bad Pig.* Eugene Trivizas. *Illustrator:* Helen Oxenbury. Margaret McElderry, 1993. *Category:* picture book.

3154 1995. *Totally Disgusting.* Bill Wallace. *Illustrator:* Leslie Morrill. Holiday House, 1991. *Category:* intermediate.

3155 1995. *The Giver.* Lois Lowry. Houghton Mifflin, 1993. *Category:* middle school.

3156 1996. *Freak the Mighty.* Rodman Philbrick. Scholastic, 1993. *Category:* middle school.

3157 1996. *Soft Child: How Rattle Snake Got Its Fangs.* Joe Hayes. *Illustrator:* Kay Sather. Roberts Rinehard Publishing, 1993. *Category:* picture book.

3158 1996. *Aliens Ate My Homework.* Bruce Coville. *Illustrator:* Katherine Coville. Minstral, 1993. *Category:* intermediate.

3159 1997. *Mick Harte Was Here.* Barbara Park. Knopf, 1995. *Category:* intermediate.

3160 1997. *The Name of the Game Was Murder.* Joan Lowery Nixon. Delacorte, 1993. *Category:* middle school.

3161 1997. *The Toll Bridge Troll.* Patricia Rae Wolff. *Illustrator:* Kimberly Bulken Root. Browndeer Press, 1995. *Category:* picture book.

3162 1998. *Harvey Potter's Balloon Farm.* Jerdine Harold Nolen. *Illustrator:* Mark Buehner. Lothrop, Lee & Shepard, 1995. *Category:* picture book.

3163 1998. *Phoenix Rising.* Karen Hesse. Henry Holt, 1994. *Category:* middle school.

3164 1998. *Running Out of Time.* Margaret Peterson Haddix. Simon & Schuster, 1995. *Category:* intermediate.

3165 1999. *Stephanie's Ponytail.* Robert Munsch. *Illustrator:* Michael Martchenko. Annick, 1996. *Category:* picture book.

3166 1999. *Drive-By.* Lynne Ewing. HarperCollins, 1996. *Category:* intermediate.

3167 1999. *Ella Enchanted.* Gail Carson Levine. HarperCollins, 1998. *Category:* middle school.

3168 2000. *Harry Potter and the Sorcerer's Stone.* J.K. Rowling. *Illustrator:* Mary Grandpré. Scholastic, 1998. *Category:* middle school.

3169 2000. *Riding Freedom.* Pam Munoz Ryan. *Illustrator:* Brian Selznick. Scholastic, 1998. *Category:* intermediate.

3170 2000. *Chocolatina.* Erik Kraft. *Illustrator:* Denise Brunkus. BridgeWater, 1999. *Category:* picture book.

3171 Arkansas Diamond Primary Book Award

SPONSOR: Arkansas Elementary School Council. CONTACT: Cathy Howser. ADDRESS: Arkansas State Library, Extension Services, One Capitol Mall, Little Rock, Arkansas 72201. ESTABLISHED: 1998. The award is selected by students in K–3 who vote for their favorite book.

3172 1999. *Roses Are Pink, Your Feet Really Stink.* Dianne DeGroat. *Illustrator:* Dianne DeGroat. Morrow, 1996.

3173 2000. *The Three Little Pigs.* Steven Kellogg (retold). *Illustrator:* Steven Kellogg. Morrow 1997.

3174 Bill Martin, Jr., Picture Book Award

SPONSOR: Kansas Reading Association. ADDRESS: 6625 S.W. 26th Ct., Topeka, Kansas 66614. PHONE: 785-862-1150. ESTABLISHED: 1996. This award is given to an outstanding author or illustrator.

3175 1997. *Tops and Bottoms.* Janet Stevens. *Illustrator:* Janet Stevens. Harcourt Brace, 1995.

3176 1998. *Piggie Pie.* Margie Palatini. *Illustrator:* Howard Fine. Clarion Books, 1995.

3177 1999. *The Hat.* Jan Brett. *Illustrator:* Jan Brett. Putnam Publishing, 1997.

3178 2000. *Stella Louella's Runaway Book.* Lisa Campbell Ernst. *Illustrator:* Lisa Campbell Ernst. HarperCollins.

3179 Black-Eyed Susan Book Award

SPONSOR: Maryland Education Media Organization. ADDRESS: P. O. Box 21127, Baltimore, Maryland 21228. ESTABLISHED: 1992. AWARD: An engraved pewter plate. The annual award is given for outstanding books written in the last 3 years.

3180 1992. *Matilda.* Roald Dahl. *Illustrator:* Quentin Blake. Viking, 1988.

3181 1992. *The True Story of the Three Little Pigs by A. Wolf.* Jon Scieszka. *Illustrator:* Lane Smith. Viking. *Category:* picture book.

3182 1993. *The Silver Kiss.* Annette Curtis Klause. Delacorte, 1990. *Category:* grade 6–9.

3183 1993. *Fudge-a-mania.* Judy Blume. Dutton, 1990. *Category:* grade 4–6.

3184 1993. *The Araboolies of Liberty Street.* Sam Swope. Random, 1989. *Category:* picture book.

3185 1994. *Stepping on the Cracks.* Mary Downing Hahn. Clarion, 1991. *Category:* grade 6–9.

3186 1994. *Trouble with Trolls.* Jan Brett. *Illustrator:* Jan Brett. G.P. Putnam's Sons, 1992. *Category:* picture book.

3187 1994. *Jeremy Thatcher, Dragon Hatcher.* Bruce Coville. *Illustrator:* Gary A. Lippincott. Minstrel Books, 1992. *Category:* grade 4–6.

3188 1995. *The Giver.* Lois Lowry. Houghton Mifflin, 1993. *Category:* grade 6–9.

3189 1995. *Go Away, Big Green Monster.* Ed Emberley. Little, Brown & Co., 1993. *Category:* picture book.

3190 1995. *Fourth Grade Rats.* Jerry Spinelli. Apple, 1996. *Category:* grade 4–6.

3191 1996. *Harvey Potter's Balloon Farm.* Jerdine Harold Nolen. *Illustrator:* Mark Buehner. Lothrop, Lee & Shepard, 1995. *Category:* picture book.

3192 1996. *Ghosts Don't Get Goosebumps.* Elvira Woodruff. Holiday, 1993. *Category:* grade 4–6.

3193 1996. *Night Terrors.* Jim Murphy. Scholastic, 1993. *Category:* grade 6–9.

3194 1997. *Time for Andrew: A Ghost Story.* Mary Downing Hahn. Clarion, 1994. *Category:* grade 4–6.

3195 1997. *Soap! Soap! Don't Forget the Soap!* Tom Birdseye. *Illustrator:* Andrew Glass. Holiday House, 1993. *Category:* picture book.

3196 1997. *The Name of the Game Was Murder.* Joan Lowery Nixon. Delacorte, 1993. *Category:* grade 6–9.

3197 1998. *Running Out of Time.* Margaret Peterson Haddix. Simon & Schuster, 1995. *Category:* grade 6–9.

3198 1998. *Piggy Pie!* Margie Palatini. *Illustrator:* Howard Fine. Clarion Books, 1995. *Category:* picture book.

3199 1998. *The 13th Floor: A Ghost Story.* Sid Fleischman. Greenwillow, 1995. *Category:* grade 4–6.

3200 1999. *Just Another Ordinary Day.* Rod Clement. HarperCollins, 1995. *Category:* picture book.

3201 1999. *Frindle.* Andrew Clements. *Illustrator:* Brian Selznick. Simon & Schuster, 1996. *Category:* grade 4–6.

3202 1999. *Don't You Dare Read This, Mrs. Dunphrey.* Margaret Peterson Haddix. Simon & Schuster, 1996. *Category:* grade 6–9.

3203 2000. *Ella Enchanted.* Gail Carson Levine. HarperCollins, 1997. *Category:* grade 6-9.

3204 2000. *Danger Zone.* David Klass. Scholastic, 1996. *Category:* high school.

3205 2000. *101 Ways to Bug Your Parents.* Lee Wardlaw. Dial, 1996. *Category:* grade 4–6.

3206 2000. *A Bad Case of Stripes.* David Shannon. *Illustrator:* David Shannon. Blue Sky Press, 1998. *Category:* picture book.

3207 Blue Hen Book Award

SPONSOR: Children's Services Division of the Delaware Library Association. ADDRESS: P.O. Box 816, Dover, Delaware 19903. ESTABLISHED: 1996. Each year children vote for their favorite picture books published in the previous year. The book that receives the most votes wins the award.

3208 1996. *Harvey Potter's Balloon Farm.* Jerdine Harold Nolen. *Illustrator:* Mark Buehner. Lothrop, Lee & Shepard, 1995.

3209 1997. *Miss Bindergarten Gets Ready for Kindergarten.* Joseph Slate. *Illustrator:* Ashley Wolff. Dutton Bo, 1996.

1998. No award given.

3210 1999. *Grandpa's Teeth.* Rod Clement. *Illustrator:* Rod Clement. HarperCollins, 1998.

3211 2000. *A Bad Case of Stripes.* David Shannon. *Illustrator:* David Shannon. Blue Sky Press, 1998.

3212 Blue Spruce Award

SPONSOR: Colorado Library Association and others. ADDRESS: 4350 Wadsworth Blvd. #340, Wheat Ridge, Colorado 80033. PHONE: (303) 463-6400. ESTABLISHED: 1985. The award is given to a contemporary American author whose books are written for the young adult audience. The books must be fiction or non-fiction, currently in print, and published within the last five years.

3213 1990. *The Cradle Will Fall.* Mary Higgins Clark. Lightyear, 1995.

3214 1991. *Pet Sematary.* Stephen King. Econo-Clad Books, 1999.

3215 1992. *Changes in Latitude.* Will Hobbs. Flare, 1994.

3216 1993. *Jurassic Park.* Michael Crichton. Knopf, 1990.

3217 1994. *It.* Stephen King. New American Library, 1999.

3218 1995. *The Client.* John Grisham. Doubleday, 1993.

3219 1996. *The Face on the Milk Carton.* Caroline Cooney. Bantam, 1990.

3220 1997. *Downriver.* Will Hobbs. Atheneum, 1991.

3221 1998. *Downriver.* Will Hobbs. Atheneum, 1991.

3222 1999. *Chicken Soup for the Teenage Soul.* Jack Canfield. Health Communications, 1997.

3223 2000. *Holes.* Louis Sachar. Farrar Straus Giroux, 1998.

3224 Book Publishers of Texas Children's/Young People's Award

SPONSOR: Texas Institute of Letters. CONTACT: Mark Busby. ADDRESS: Dept. of English, University of Texas, El Paso, Texas 79968. ESTABLISHED: 1983. AWARD:

$250.00 U.S. The award is given irregularly to a Texas author, or to an author who writes about Texas. Only books published for the first time in the year preceding the award are eligible.

3225 1990. *The Last Innocent Summer.* Zinita Fowler. Texas A&M University Press, 1990.

3226 1991. *The Trail North.* Charlotte Baker. Panda Books, 1991.

3227 1992. *Song of the Buffalo.* Sherry Garland. Harcourt Brace, 1992.

3228 1993. *The Astonishing Armadillo.* Dee Stuart. Carolrhoda Books, 1993.

3229 1994. *Breathing Room.* Barbara Elmore. Royal Fireworks, 1994.

3230 1995. *Liza's Blue Moon.* Diane Stevens. Greenwillow, 1995.

3231 1996. *Uncle Comanche.* J.A. Benner. Texas Christian University, 1996.

3232 1997. *Habibi.* Naomi Shihab Nye. Simon & Schuster, 1997.

3233 1998. *This Big Sky.* Pat Mora. *Illustrator:* Steve Jenkins. Scholastic, 1998.

3234 1999. *Grandma Fina and Her Wonderful Umbrellas. Original Title:* La Abuelita Fina y Sus Sombrillas Maravillosas. Benjamin Alire Saenz. *Illustrator:* Pilar Herrera. *Translator:* Benjamin Alire Sáenz. Cinco Puntos, 1999.

3235 Book Sense Book of the Year Award (formerly the ABBY Awards)

SPONSOR: American Booksellers Association. ADDRESS: 828 South Broadway, Tarrytown, New York 10591. PHONE: 1-800-637-0037. ESTABLISHED: 2000. AWARD: $5,000 cash prize and an engraved Steuben crystal prism. Book Sense independent booksellers from across the country nominate the books that they most enjoyed handselling to their customers throughout the year.

3236 2000. *The Quiltmaker's Gift.* Jeff Brumbeau. *Illustrator:* Gail de Marcken. Pfeiffer-Hamilton, 1999.

3237 Boston Globe Horn Book Awards

SPONSOR: The Boston Globe and The Horn Book Magazine. CONTACT: Karen Walsh. ADDRESS: The Horn Book, Inc., 56 Roland St., Suite 200, Boston, Massachusetts 02129. PHONE: 617-628-0225. ESTABLISHED: 1967. AWARD: $500.00 U.S. and an engraved silver bowl. Presented in three categories: fiction or poetry, picturebook, and non-fiction, publishers may submit up to ten books in the categories. Authors and illustrators from any country can also submit their books, however, the book must be published in the United States in the previous year.

3238 1990. *Insect Metamorphosis: From Egg to Adult.* Ron Goor, Nancy Goor. Atheneum, 1989. *Category:* non-fiction honor.

3239 1990. *Lon Po Po: A Red Riding Hood Story from China.* Ed Young (translated). *Illustrator:* Ed Young. Philomel, 1989. *Category:* picture book.

3240 1990. *Maniac Magee.* Jerry Spinelli. Little, Brown & Co., 1989. *Category:* fiction.

3241 1990. *Saturnalia.* Paul Fleischman. Harper, 1989. *Category:* fiction honor.

3242 1990. *Shadows and Reflections.* Tana Hoban. *Illustrator:* Tana Hoban. Greenwillow, 1989. *Category:* non-fiction honor.

3243 1990. *Stonewords.* Pam Conrad. Harper, 1989. *Category:* fiction honor.

3244 1990. *The Great Little Madison.* Jean Fritz. Putnam, 1989. *Category:* non-fiction.

3245 1990. *Valentine & Orsen.* Nancy Ekholm Burkert. *Illustrator:* Nancy Ekholm Burkert. Farrar, 1989. *Category:* creative excellence.

3246 1990. *We're Going on a Bear Hunt.* Michael Rosen (retold). *Illustrator:* Helen Oxenbury. McElderry Books, 1989. *Category:* picture book honor.

3247 1990. *Chicka Chicka Boom Boom.* Bill Martin, Jr., John Archambault. *Illustrator:* Lois Ehlert. Simon & Schuster, 1989. *Category:* picture book honor.

3248 1991. *Appalachia: The Voices of Sleeping Birds.* Cynthia Rylant. *Illustrator:* Barry Moser. Harcourt, 1990. *Category:* non-fiction.

3249 1991. *The True Confessions of Charlotte Doyle.* Avi. Jackson/Orchard, 1990. *Category:* fiction.

3250 1991. *The Tale of the Mandarin Ducks.* Katherine Paterson. *Illustrator:* Leo Dillon. Diane Dillon. Lodestar, 1990. *Category:* picture book.

3251 1992. *Missing May.* Cynthia Rylant. Jackson/Orchard, 1991. *Category:* fiction.

3252 1992. *Seven Blind Mice.* Ed Young. *Illustrator:* Ed Young. Philomel, 1991. *Category:* picture book.

3253 1992. *Talking with Artists.* Pat Cummings (editor). Bradbury, 1991. *Category:* non-fiction.

3254 1993. *Sojourner Truth: Ain't I a Woman?* Patricia McKissack, Fredrick McKissack. Scholastic, 1992. *Category:* non-fiction.

3255 1993. *The Fortune Tellers.* Lloyd Alexander. *Illustrator:* Trina Schart Hyman. Dutton, 1992. *Category:* picture book.

3256 1993. *Ajeemah and His Son.* James Berry. Harper, 1992. *Category:* fiction.

3257 1994. *Eleanor Roosevelt: A Life of Discovery.* Russell Freedman. Clarion, 1993. *Category:* non-fiction.

3258 1994. *Grandfather's Journey.* Allen Say. *Illustrator:* Allen Say. Houghton Mifflin, 1993. *Category:* picture book.

3259 1994. *Scooter.* Vera B. Williams. Greenwillow, 1993. *Category:* fiction.

3260 1995. *Abigail Adams: Witness to a Revolution.* Natalie S. Bober. Atheneum, 1994. *Category:* non-fiction.

3261 1995. *Some of the Kinder Planets.* Tim Wynne-Jones. Kroupa/Orchard, 1994. *Category:* fiction.

3262 1995. *John Henry.* Julius Lester (retold). *Illustrator:* Jerry Pinkney. Dial, 1994. *Category:* picture book.

3263 1996. *In the Rain with Baby Duck.* Amy Hest. *Illustrator:* Jill Barton. Candlewick, 1995. *Category:* picture book.

3264 1996. *Orphan Train Rider: One Boy's True Story.* Andrea Warren. Houghton, 1995. *Category:* non-fiction.

3265 1996. *Poppy.* Avi. *Illustrator:* Brian Floca. Jackson/Orchard, 1995. *Category:* fiction.

3266 1997. *The Adventures of Sparrowboy.* Brian Pinkney. *Illustrator:* Brian Pinkney. Simon, 1996. *Category:* picture book.

3267 1997. *The Friends.* Kazumi Yumoto. *Translator:* Cathy Hirano. Farrar, 1996. *Category:* fiction and poetry.

3268 1997. *A Drop of Water: A Book of Science and Wonder.* Walter Wick. *Illustrator:* Walter Wick. Scholastic, 1996. *Category:* non-fiction.

3269 1998. *The Circuit: Stories from the Life of a Migrant Child.* Francisco Jiménez. University of New Mexico Press, 1997. *Category:* fiction and poetry.

3270 1998. *And If the Moon Could Talk.* Kate Banks. *Illustrator:* Georg Hallensleben. Foster/Farrar, 1997. *Category:* picture book.

3271 1998. *Leon's Story.* Leon Walter Tillage. *Illustrator:* Susan L. Roth. Farrar, 1997. *Category:* non-fiction.

3272 1999. *Holes.* Louis Sachar. Farrar Straus Giroux, 1998. *Category:* fiction.

3273 1999. *The Top of the World: Climbing Mount Everest.* Steve Jenkins. *Illustrator:* Steve Jenkins. Houghton, 1998. *Category:* non-fiction.

3274 1999. *Red-Eyed Tree Frog.* Joy Cowley. *Illustrator:* Nic Bishop. Scholastic Press, 1998. *Category:* picture book.

3275 2000. *The Folk Keeper.* Franny Billingsley. Atheneum, 1999. *Category:* fiction.

3276 2000. *Sir Walter Ralegh and the Quest for El Dorado.* Marc Aronson. Clarion, 1999. *Category:* non-fiction.

3277 2000. *Henry Hikes to Fitchburg.* D. B. Johnson. *Illustrator:* D. B. Johnson. Houghton, 1999. *Category:* picture book.

3278 Buckeye Children's Book Award

SPONSOR: The State Library of Ohio. CONTACT: Children's Services Consultant. ADDRESS: 65 South Front Street, Columbus, Ohio 43215-4163. PHONE: (614) 644-7064. ESTABLISHED: 1982. AWARD: A plaque and certificate. The award is given biennially to "promote teacher and librarian involvement in children's literature programs and to commend authors of such literature," Ohio children nominate and select the award recipient. Until 1985, the award was given annually.

3279 1991. *Hatchet.* Gary Paulsen. *Level:* Grades 6–8. Bradbury, 1987.

3280 1991. *The Polar Express.* Chris van Allsburg. *Illustrator:* Chris van Allsburg. Houghton Mifflin, 1985. *Level:* Grades K–2.

3281 1991. *There's a Boy in the Girl's Bathroom.* Louis Sachar. Knopf, 1987. *Level:* Grades 3–5.

3282 1993. *Scary Stories 3: More Tales to Chill Your Bones.* Alvin Schwartz. HarperCollins, 1991. *Level:* Grades 3–5.

3283 1993. *The Very Quiet Cricket.* Eric Carle. *Illustrator:* Eric Carle. Philomel, 1990. *Level:* Grades K–2.

3284 1993. *Maniac Magee.* Jerry Spinelli. Little, Brown & Co., 1989. *Level:* Grades 6–8.

3285 1995. *Say Cheese and Die.* R.L. Stine. Scholastic. *Level:* Grades 6–8.

3286 1995. *Shiloh.* Phyllis Reynolds Naylor. Atheneum, 1991. *Level:* Grades 3–5.

3287 1995. *The Stinky Cheese Man and Other Fairly Stupid Tales.* Jon Scieszka. *Illustrator:* Lane Smith. Viking, 1992. *Level:* Grades K–2.

3288 1997. *Dogzilla.* Dav Pilkey. *Illustrator:* Dav Pikley. Harcourt Brace, 1993. *Level:* Grades K–2.

3289 1997. *The Haunted Mask II.* R.L. Stine. Scholastic, 1995. *Level:* Grades 3–5.

3290 1997. *The Giver.* Lois Lowry. Houghton Mifflin, 1993. *Level:* Grades 6–8.

3291 1999. *Wayside School Gets a Little Stranger.* Louis Sachar. Morrow, 1995. *Level:* Grades 3–5.

3292 1999. *Verdi.* Janell Cannon. Harcourt Brace, 1997. *Level:* Grades K–2.

3293 1999. *Seedfolks.* Paul Fleischman. HarperCollins, 1997. *Level:* Grades 6–8.

3294 California Book Awards

SPONSOR: Commonwealth Club of California. CONTACT: Jim Wilson, Book Awards Coordinator. ADDRESS: 595 Market Street, San Francisco, California 94105. PHONE: (415) 597-6722. ESTABLISHED: 1931. AWARD: Gold medal winners receive $2,000, silver medal winners receive $300 U.S. The award is given to honor the California writer of fiction and non-fiction of juvenile literature.

1990. No award given.

3295 1991. *Babushka's Doll.* Patricia Polacco. *Illustrator:* Patricia Polacco. Simon & Schuster, 1994. *Category:* 10 & under.

3296 1991. *The Fabulous Fifty.* Morton Grosser. Atheneum, 1990. *Category:* 11–16.

3297 1992. *Fly Away Home.* Eve Bunting. *Illustrator:* Ronald Himler. Clarion Books, 1991. *Category:* 10 & under.

3298 1992. *Jayhawker.* Patricia Beatty. Beech Tree Books, 1995. *Category:* 11–16.

3299 1993. *Earthquake at Dawn.* Kristiana Gregory. Gulliver/ Harcourt Brace, 1994. *Category:* juvenile.

3300 1993. *A Bowl of Mischief.* Ellen Kindt McKenzie. Henry Holt & Company, 1992. *Category:* juvenile.

3301 1993. *Chicken Sunday.* Patricia Polacco. *Illustrator:* Patricia Polacco. Philomel, 1992. *Category:* juvenile.

3302 1994. *Grandfather's Journey.* Allen Say. *Illustrator:* Allen Say. Houghton Mifflin, 1993. *Category:* juvenile.

3303 1994. *Bull Run.* Paul Fleischman. *Illustrator:* David Frampton. HarperCollins, 1993. *Category:* juvenile.

3304 1994. *Dragon's Gate.* Laurence Yep. HarperCollins, 1993. *Category:* juvenile.

3305 1995. *Smoky Night.* Eve Bunting. *Illustrator:* David Diaz. Harcourt Brace, 1994. *Category:* 10 & under.

3306 1995. *Catherine, Called Birdy.* Karen Cushman. Clarion, 1994. *Category:* 11–16.

3307 1996. *Canto Familiar.* Gary Soto. *Illustrator:* Annika Nelson. Harcourt Brace, 1995. *Category:* 11–16.

3308 1996. *A Time for Dancing.* Davida Wills Hurwin. Little, Brown & Co., 1995. *Category:* juvenile.

3309 1996. *The Faithful Friend.* Robert San Souci. *Illustrator:* Brian Pinkney. Simon and Schuster, 1995. *Category:* 10 & under.

3310 1997. *The Hired Hand.* Robert San Souci. *Illustrator:* Jerry Pinkney. Dial, 1997. *Category:* 10 & under.

3311 1998. *I Rode a Horse of Milk White Jade.* Diane Lee Wilson. Orchard Books, 1998. *Category:* 11–16.

3312 1998. *Sitting Ducks.* Michael Bedard. *Illustrator:* Michael Bedard. Putnam Pub., 1998. *Category:* 10 & under.

3313 1999. *Crooked.* Laura McNeal, Tom McNeal. Knopf 1999. *Category:* 11–16.

3314 1999. *Little Bo.* Julie Andrews Edwards. *Illustrator:* Henry Cole. Hyperion Press, 1999. *Category:* 10 & under.

3315 California Young Reader Medal

SPONSOR: California Library Association. ADDRESS: 717 K Street, Suite 300, Sacramento, California 95814-3477. PHONE: (916) 447-8541. ESTABLISHED: 1974. AWARD: A bronze medal and a plaque. The awards are given in four categories:

primary, intermediate, junior high and young adult to honor favorite authors and illustrators. Winners are determined by number of votes received from young readers. The books must be written by a living author and have been published in the last five years.

3316 1990. *Eyes of the Dragon.* Margaret Leaf. *Illustrator:* Ed Young. Lothrop, 1987. *Level:* primary.

3317 1990. *Izzy, Willy Nilly.* Cynthia Voigt. Atheneum, 1986. *Level:* young adult.

3318 1990. *The Other Side of Dark.* Joan Lowery Nixon. Delacorte, 1986. *Level:* junior high.

3319 1990. *The War With Grandpa.* Robert Kimmel Smith. *Illustrator:* Richard Lauter. Delacorte, 1984. *Level:* intermediate.

3320 1991. *December Stillness.* Mary Downing Hahn. Clarion, 1988. *Category:* middle school/junior high.

3321 1991. *Harry's Mad.* Dick King-Smith. Crown, 1987. *Category:* intermediate.

3322 1991. *Tacky the Penguin.* Helen Lester. *Illustrator:* Lynn Munsinger. Houghton Mifflin, 1988. *Category:* primary.

3323 1991. *Night Kites.* M.E. Kerr. Harper & Row, 1986. *Category:* young adult.

3324 1992. *Never Spit on Your Shoes.* Denys Cazet. Clarion, 1986. *Category:* primary.

3325 1992. *All About Sam.* Lois Lowry. *Illustrator:* Diane DeGroat. Houghton Mifflin, 1988. *Category:* intermediate.

3326 1992. *Sniper.* Theodore Taylor. Harcourt Brace Jovanovich, 1989. *Category:* middle school/junior high.

3327 1992. *A Sudden Silence.* Eve Bunting. Harcourt Brace Jovanovich, 1989. *Category:* young adult.

3328 1993. *Julius, the Baby of the World.* Kevin Henkes. Greenwillow, 1990. *Category:* primary.

3329 1993. *Something Upstairs.* Avi. Orchard, 1988. *Category:* middle school/junior high.

3330 1993. *The Silver Kiss.* Annette Curtis Klause. Delacorte, 1990. *Category:* young adult.

3331 1993. *Fudge-a-Mania.* Judy Blume. Dutton, 1990. *Category:* intermediate.

3332 1994. *High-Wire Henry.* Mary Calhoun. *Illustrator:* Erick Ingraham. Morrow, 1991. *Category:* primary.

3333 1994. *Scared Stiff.* Willo Davis Roberts. Atheneum, 1991. *Category:* intermediate.

3334 1994. *There's a Girl in My Hammerlock.* Jerry Spinelli. Simon & Schuster, 1991. *Category:* middle school/junior high.

3335 1994. *We All Fall Down.* Robert Cormier. Delacorte, 1991. *Category:* young adult.

3336 1995. *Stonewords.* Pam Conrad. HarperCollins, 1990. *Category:* intermediate.

3337 1995. *Rescue Josh McGuire.* Ben Mikaelsen. Hyperion, 1991. *Category:* middle school/junior high.

3338 1995. *Downriver.* Will Hobbs. Atheneum, 1991. *Category:* young adult.

3339 1995. *Martha Speaks.* Susan Meddaugh. Houghton, 1992. *Category:* primary.

3340 1996. *Shadow of the Dragon.* Sherry Garland. Harcourt Brace, 1994. *Category:* young adult.

3341 1996. *Stellaluna.* Janell Cannon. Harcourt Brace, 1994. *Category:* primary.

3342 1996. *Time for Andrew: A Ghost Story.* Mary Downing Hahn. Clarion, 1994. *Category:* intermediate.

3343 1996. *Freak the Mighty.* Rodman Philbrick. Scholastic, 1993. *Category:* middle school/junior high.

3344 1997. *Staying Fat for Sarah Byrnes.* Chris Crutcher. Greenwillow, 1993. *Category:* young adult.

3345 1997. *Sparrow Hawk Red.* Ben Mikaelsen. Hyperion, 1993. *Category:* middle school/junior high.

3346 1997. *Don't Fidget A Feather!* Erica Silverman. *Illustrator:* S.D. Schindler. Macmillan, 1994. *Category:* primary.

3347 1997. *Jennifer Murdley's Toad.* Bruce Coville. Harcourt, 1992. *Category:* intermediate.

3348 1998. *Ironman.* Chris Crutcher. Greenwillow, 1995. *Category:* young adult.

3349 1998. *Dog Breath: The Horrible Terrible Trouble with Hally Tosis.* Dav Pilkey. Blue Sky Press, 1994. *Category:* primary.

3350 1998. *The Junkyard Dog.* Erika Tamar. Knopf, 1995. *Category:* intermediate.

3351 1998. *The Watsons Go to Birmingham.* Christopher Paul Curtis. Delacorte, 1995. *Category:* middle school/junior high.

3352 1999. *The Only Alien on the Planet.* Kristen Randle. Scholastic, 1995. *Category:* young adult.

3353 1999. *Under the Blood-Red Sun.* Graham Salisbury. Delacorte, 1994. *Category:* middle school/junior high.

3354 1999. *Livingstone Mouse.* Pam Edwards. *Illustrator:* Henry Cole. HarperCollins, 1996. *Category:* primary.

3355 1999. *The 13th Floor: A Ghost Story.* Sid Fleischman. *Illustrator:* Peter Sis. Greenwillow, 1995. *Category:* intermediate.

3356 2000. *Breaking Boxes.* A. M. Jenkins. Bantam Doubleday Dell, 1998. *Category:* young adult.

3357 2000. *Lost.* Paul Brett Johnson. *Illustrator:* Paul Brett Johnson. Orchard, 1996. *Category:* primary.

3358 2000. *Riding Freedom.* Pam Munoz Ryan. *Illustrator:* Brian Selznick. Scholastic, 1999. *Category:* intermediate.

3359 2000. *Ella Enchanted.* Gail Carson Levine. HarperCollins, 1997. *Category:* middle school/junior high.

3360 Carolyn W. Field Award

SPONSOR: Pennsylvania Library Association. ADDRESS: 3107 North Front Street, Harrisburg, Pennsylvania 17110. PHONE: (717) 233-3313. ESTABLISHED: 1984. AWARD: Engraved medallion. The award is given annually to an author or illustrator of a fiction or non-fiction book. The author or must have a primary residence in the commonwealth of Pennsylvania at the time of the book's publication. The book must be published in the year preceding the award year.

3361 1990. *Box Turtle at Long Pond.* William George. *Illustrator:* Lindsay George. Greenwillow, 1989.

3362 1991. *Maniac Magee.* Jerry Spinelli. Little, Brown & Co., 1990.

3363 1992. *I Am Regina.* Sally Keehn. Philomel Books, 1991.

3364 1993. *The Great Pumpkin Switch.* Megan McDonald. *Illustrator:* Ted Lewin. Orchard Books, 1992.

3365 1994. *Dreamplace.* George Ella Lyon. *Illustrator:* Peter Catalanotto. Orchard Books, 1993.

3366 1995. *How to Make an Apple Pie and See the World.* Marjorie Priceman. Knopf, 1994. *Category:* storybook.

3367 1996. *The Christmas Miracle of Jonathan Toomey.* Susan Wojciechowski. *Illustrator:* P.J. Lynch. Candlewick Press, 1995.

3368 1997. *Growing Up in Coal Country.* Susan Campbell Bartoletti. Houghton Mifflin, 1996.

3369 1998. *Wringer.* Jerry Spinelli. HarperCollins, 1997.

3370 1999. *I Am Mordred.* Nancy Springer. Philomel Books 1998.

3371 Carter G. Woodson Book Award

SPONSOR: National Council for the Social Studies. ADDRESS: 3501 Newark Street, North West, Washington, District of Columbia 20016-3167. PHONE: (202) 966-7840. ESTABLISHED: 1973. AWARD: A plaque. The annual award is given for a non-fiction book with an American setting. The book should include experiences of one or more racial/ethnic minority groups in the United States and accurately reflect the perspectives, cultures and values of the group. The book must have been published in the year preceding the award.

3372 1990. *In Two Worlds: A Yup'ik Eskimo Family.* Aylette Jenness, Alice Rivers. Houghton Mifflin, 1989. *Category:* elementary.

3373 1990. *Paul Robertson.* Rebecca Larsen. Franklin Watts, 1989. *Category:* secondary.

3374 1991. *Sorrow's Kitchen: The Life and Folklore of Zora Neal Hurston.* Mary E. Lyons. Scribners. *Category:* secondary.

3375 1991. *Shirley Chisholm.* Catherine Scheader. Enslow. *Category:* elementary.

3376 1992. *The Last Princess: The Story of Princess Ka'Iolani of Hawai'i.* Fay Stanley. Macmillan. *Category:* elementary.

3377 1992. *Native American Doctor: The Story of Susan LaFlesche Picotte.* Jeri Ferris. Carolrhoda, 1991. *Category:* secondary.

3378 1993. *Mississippi Challenge.* Mildred Pitts Walter. Bradbury, 1992. *Category:* secondary.

3379 1993. *Madame C. J. Walker.* Patricia McKissack, Fredrick McKissack. Enslow. *Category:* elementary.

3380 1994. *The March on Washington.* Jim Haskins. HarperCollins. *Category:* secondary.

3381 1994. *Starting Home: The Story of Horace Pippin, Painter.* Mary E. Lyons. Scribners. *Category:* elementary.

3382 1995. *What I Had Was Singing: The Story of Marian Anderson.* Jeri Ferris. Carolrhoda. *Category:* elementary.

3383 1995. *Till Victory Is Won: Black Soldiers in the Civil War.* Zak Mettger. Lodestar. *Category:* secondary.

3384 1996. *Songs from the Loom: A Navajo Girl Learns to Weave.* Monty Roessel. Lerner. *Category:* elementary.

3385 1996. *A Fence Away from Freedom: Japanese Americans and World War II.* Ellen Levine. Putnam. *Category:* secondary.

3386 1997. *The Harlem Renaissance.* Jim Haskins. Millbrook. *Category:* secondary.

3387 1997. *Ramadan.* Shahib Hamid Ghazi. *Illustrator:* Omar Rayyan. Holiday House. *Category:* elementary.

3388 1998. *Langston Hughes.* Milton Meltzer. *Illustrator:* Stephen Alsorn. Millbrook. *Category:* secondary.

3389 1998. *Leon's Story.* Leon Walter Tillage. *Illustrator:* Susan Roth. Farrar, Straus, Giroux. *Category:* elementary.

3390 1999. *Story Painter: The Life of Jacob Lawrence.* John Duggleby. *Illustrator:* Jacob Lawrence. Chronicle Books. *Category:* elementary.

3391 1999. *Edmonia Lewis: Wildfire in Marble.* Rinna Evelyn Wolfe. Dillon Press. *Category:* secondary.

3392 2000. *Through My Eyes.* Ruby Bridges. Scholastic. *Category:* elementary.

3393 2000. *Princess Ka'iulani: Hope of a Nation, Heart of a People.* Sharon Linnéa. William B. Eerdmans. *Category:* secondary.

3394 Charlie May Simon Children's Book Award

SPONSOR: Arkansas Elementary School Council. CONTACT: Cathy Howser. ADDRESS: Arkansas State Library, Extension Services, One Capitol Mall, Little Rock, Arkansas 72201. ESTABLISHED: 1970. AWARD: A medallion. The award is given to the author who receives the most votes from the children of Arkansas in grades 4 to 6. The books must be published 2 years preceding the award year.

3395 1990. *There's a Boy in the Girl's Bathroom.* Louis Sachar. Knopf, 1987.

3396 1991. *All About Sam.* Lois Lowry. *Illustrator:* Diane DeGroat. Houghton Mifflin, 1988.

3397 1992. *Number the Stars.* Lois Lowry. Houghton Mifflin, 1989.

3398 1993. *The Ghost Inside the Monitor.* Margaret J. Anderson. Knopf, 1990.

3399 1994. *Shiloh.* Phyllis Reynolds Naylor. Atheneum, 1991.

3400 1995. *Attaboy, Sam!* Lois Lowry. *Illustrator:* Diane DeGroat. Houghton Mifflin, 1992.

3401 1996. *The Secret Funeral of Slim Jim the Snake.* Elvira Woodruff. Holiday House, 1993.

3402 1997. *The Best School Year Ever.* Barbara Robinson. HarperCollins, 1994.

3403 1998. *The 13th Floor: A Ghost Story.* Sid Fleischman. Greenwillow, 1995.

3404 1999. *Frindle.* Andrew Clements. *Illustrator:* Brian Selznick. Simon & Schuster, 1996.

3405 2000. *Saving Shiloh.* Phyllis Reynolds Naylor. Atheneum, 1997.

3406 Charlotte Book Award

SPONSOR: New York State Reading Association. CONTACT: Rita Silverman. ADDRESS: Department of Education, Skidmore College, Saratoga Springs, New York 12866. ESTABLISHED: 1990. The award honors books in primary, intermediate, and young adult categories. New York state students vote for their favorites. The awards are given to authors and illustrators.

3407 1990. *The Way Things Work.* David Macauley. *Illustrator:* Neil Ardley. Houghton, 1988.

3408 1990. *The Magic School Bus at the Waterworks.* Joanna Cole. *Illustrator:* Bruce Degen. Scholastic, 1989.

3409 1990. *Piggins.* Jane Yolen. *Illustrator:* Jane Dyer. Harcourt, 1987.

3410 1992. *The Great Kapok Tree: A Tale of the Amazon Rain Forest.* Lynne Cherry. Harcourt Brace, 1990. *Category:* K–3.

3411 1992. *Number the Stars.* Lois Lowry. Houghton Mifflin, 1989. *Category:* 6–8.

3412 1992. *Maniac Magee.* Jerry Spinelli. Little, Brown & Co., 1990. *Category:* 6–8.

3413 1992. *Fallen Angels.* Walter Dean Myers. Scholastic, 1988. *Category:* 9–12.

3414 1994. *There's a Girl in My Hammerlock.* Jerry Spinelli. Simon & Schuster, 1991. *Category:* 6–8.

3415 1994. *Nothing But the Truth.* Orchard, 1991. *Category:* 9–12.

3416 1994. *Martha Speaks.* Susan Meddaugh. Houghton, 1992. *Category:* K–3.

3417 1994. *The Rag Coat.* Lauren Mills. Little, Brown & Co., 1991. *Category:* 6–8.

3418 1996. *Owl Babies.* Martin Waddell. *Illustrator:* Patrick Benson. Candlewick, 1996. *Category:* K–3.

3419 1996. *First Apple.* Ching Yeung Russell. *Illustrator:* Christopher Zhong-Yuan Zhang. Boyds Mills, 1994. *Category:* 3–5.

3420 1996. *Tell Them We Remember: The Story of the Holocaust.* Susan Bachrach. Little, Brown & Co., 1994. *Category:* 6–8.

3421 1996. *Phoenix Rising.* Karen Hesse. Henry Holt, 1994. *Category:* 9–12.

3422 1998. *When I Was Five.* Arthur Howard. *Illustrator:* Arthur Howard. Harcourt Brace, 1996. *Category:* primary.

3423 1998. *Freak the Mighty.* Rodman Philbrick. Scholastic, 1993. *Category:* young adult.

3424 2000. *I Was a Third Grade Science Project.* Mary Jane Auch. *Illustrator:* Herm Auch. Holiday House, 1998. *Category:* intermediate.

3425 2000. *Rotten Teeth.* Laura Simms. *Illustrator:* David Catrow. Houghton Mifflin, 1998. *Category:* primary.

3426 2000. *Harry Potter and the Sorcerer's Stone.* J.K. Rowling. *Illustrator:* Mary Grandpré. Scholastic, 1998. *Category:* young adult.

3427 Charlotte Zolotow Award

SPONSOR: Cooperative Children's Book Center, School of Education, University of Wisconsin-Madison. ADDRESS: 4290 Helen C. White Hall, 600 North Park Street, Madison, Wisconsin 53706. PHONE: 608-263-3720. ESTABLISHED: 1998. AWARD: $1000 and a bronze medallion are formally presented to the winning author. The award is given annually to the author of the best picture book text published in the United States in the preceding year. Any picture book for young children (birth through age seven), first published in the United States, written by a U.S. citizen or resident, is eligible for consideration for the award.

3428 1998. *Lucky Song.* Vera B. Williams. *Illustrator:* Vera B. Williams.Greenwillow, 1997. *Level:* Winner.

3429 1998. *Don't Laugh, Joe!* Keiko Kasza. *Illustrator:* Keiko Kasza. G.P. Putnam's Sons, 1997. *Level:* Honor.

3430 1999. *Snow.* Uri Shulevitz *Illustrator:* Uri Shulevitz. Farrar, Straus and Grioux, 1998. *Level:* Winner.

3431 1999. *John Willy and Freddy McGee.* Holly Meade. *Illustrator:* Holly Meade. Marshall Cavendish, 1998. *Level:* Honor.

3432 1999. *Pete's a Pizza.* William Steig. *Illustrator:* William Steig.HarperCollins, 1998. *Level:* Honor.

3433 2000. *Three Cheers for Catherine the Great.* Cari Best. *Illustrator:* Giselle Potter. Melanie Kroupa / DK Ink, 1999. *Level:* Honor.

3434 2000. *Bark, George.* Jules Feiffer. *Illustrator:* Jules Feiffer. Michael di Capua / HarperCollins, 1999. *Level:* Honor.

3435 2000. *When Sophie Gets Angry—Really, Really Angry.* Molly Bang. *Illustrator:* Molly Bang. Blue Sky / Scholastic, 1999. *Level:* Winner.

3436 Child Study Children's Book Award

SPONSOR: Children Study Children's Book Committee at Bank Street College of Education. ADDRESS: 610 West 112th Street, New York, New York 10025. PHONE: (212) 222-6700. ESTABLISHED: 1943. AWARD: A framed scroll and monetary prize. The award is given in honor of a children's or young adult book that shows a realistic and honest portrayal of problems which are universal: war, poverty, emotional stress, minority situations, family stress. The book must be published in the preceding calendar year.

3437 1990. *Secret City, USA.* Felice Holman. Scribner's, 1990.

3438 1991. *Shadow Boy.* Susan E. Kirby. Orchard, 1991.

3439 1992. *Blue Skin of the Sea.* Graham Salisbury. Delacorte, 1992.

3440 1993. *Make Lemonade.* Virginia Euwer Wolff. Henry Holt & Co. 1993.

3441 1994. *Earthshine.* Theresa Nelson. Orchard, 1994.

3442 1995. *The Watsons Go to Birmingham.* Christopher Paul Curtis. Delacorte, 1995.

3443 1996. *Music from a Place Called Half Moon.* Jerrie Oughton. Houghton Mifflin, 1995.

3444 1997. *The Cuckoo's Child.* Suzanne Freeman. Greenwillow, 1996.

3445 1994. *Wringer.* Jerry Spinelli. HarperCollins, 1997.

3446 Christopher Awards

SPONSOR: The Christophers. CONTACT: Peggy Flanagan. ADDRESS: 12 East 48th Street, New York, New York, 10017. PHONE: (212) 759-4050. ESTABLISHED: 1970. AWARD: An engraved bronze medal. The award is given annually to honor authors and illustrators whose work meets the critieria "affirmation of the highest values of the human spirit, artistic and technical proficiency and significant degree of public acceptance." Awards are given for picture books, fiction and non-fiction. Books must have been published during the preceding calendar year.

3447 1990. *William and Grandpa.* Alice Schertle. *Illustrator:* Lydia Dabcovich. Lothrop, 1989. *Level:* Ages 8-11.

3448 1990. *Can the Whales Be Saved?* Philip Whitfield. Viking, 1989. *Level:* ages 10–12.

3449 1990. *So Much to Tell You....* John Marsden. Little, Brown & Co., 1989. *Level:* young adult.

3450 1990. *Keeping a Christmas Secret.* Phyllis Reynolds Naylor. *Illustrator:* Lena Shiffman. Atheneum, 1989. *Level:* ages 4–7.

3451 1991. *Mississippi Bridge.* Mildred D. Taylor. *Illustrator:* Max Ginsburg. Dial, 1990. *Level:* ages 9–12.

3452 1991. *Paul Revere's Ride.* Henry Wadsworth Longfellow. *Illustrator:* Ted Rand. Dutton, 1990. *Level:* All ages.

3453 1992. *Somebody Loves You, Mr. Hatch.* Eileen Spinelli. *Illustrator:* Paul Yalowitz. Bradbury, 1991. *Level:* ages 4–6.

3454 1992. *Stephen's Feast.* Jean Richardson *Illustrator:* Alice Englander. Little, Brown & Co., 1991. *Level:* ages 6–8.

3455 1992. *The Star Fisher.* Laurence Yep. Morrow, 1991. *Level:* ages 10 and up.

3456 1992. *Where Does God Live? Questions and Answers for Parents and Children.* Marc Gellman, Thomas Hartman. *Illustrator:* William Zdinak. Triumph Books, 1991. *Level:* All ages.

3457 1992. *The Gold Coin.* Alma Flor Ada. *Illustrator:* Neil Waldman. *Translator:* Bernice Randall. Atheneum, 1991. *Level:* ages 8–10.

3458 1993. *Mississippi Challenge.* Mildred Pitts Walter. Bradbury, 1992. *Level:* ages 12 and up.

3459 1993. *Letters from Rifka.* Karen Hesse. Henry Holt, 1992. *Level:* ages 8–12.

3460 1993. *Rosie & the Yellow Ribbon.* Paula DePaolo. *Illustrator:* Janet Wolf. Little, Brown & Co., 1992. *Level:* ages 6–8.

3461 1993. *The Rainbow Fish.* Marcus Pfister. *Translator:* J. Alison James. North-South Books, 1992. *Level:* ages 5–8.

3462 1994. *Anne Frank: Beyond the Diary.* Ruud van der Rol, Rian Verhoeven. *Translator:* Tony Langham. Viking, 1993. *Level:* young adult.

3463 1994. *The Crystal Ball.* Gerda Marie Scheidl. *Illustrator:* Nathalie Duroussy. *Translator:* Rosemary Lanning. North-South Books, 1993. *Level:* ages 5–8.

3464 1994. *It's Our World, Too! Stories of Young People Who Are Making a Difference.* Phillip Hoose. Joy Street/Little, Brown & Co., 1993. *Level:* Ages 10 and up.

3465 1995. *I'll See You When the Moon Is Full.* Susi Gregg Fowler. *Illustrator:* Jim Fowler. Greenwillow, 1994. *Level:* Ages 4–6.

3466 1995. *Taking Hold: My Journey into Blindness.* Sally Hobart Alexander. Macmillan, 1994. *Level:* Ages 12 and up.

3467 1995. *Prize in the Snow.* Bill Easterling. *Illustrator:* Mary Beth Owens. Little, Brown & Co., 1994. *Level:* Ages 6–8.

3468 1995. *The Ledgerbook of Thomas Blue Eagle.* Jewel H. Grutman, Gay Matthaei. *Illustrator:* Adam Cvijanovic. Thomasson-Grant, 1994. *Level:* Ages 8–12.

3469 1996. *Been to Yesterdays: Poems of a Life.* Lee Bennett Hopkins. *Illustrator:* Charlene Rendeiro. Wordsong/Boyds Mills Press, 1995. *Level:* Ages 10–12.

3470 1996. *Mother Jones: One Woman's Fight for Labor.* Betsy Harvey Kraft. Clarion Books, 1995. *Level:* Ages 12–14.

3471 1996. *Parallel Journeys.* Eleanor Ayer, Helen Waterford. Atheneum, 1995. *Level:* young adult.

3472 1996. *The Christmas Miracle of Jonathan Toomey.* Susan Wojciechowski. *Illustrator:* P.J. Lynch. Candlewick Press, 1995. *Level:* Ages 6–9.

3473 1997. *The Log Cabin Quilt.* Ellen Howard. *Illustrator:* Ronald Himler. Holiday House, 1996. *Level:* Ages 4–6.

3474 1997. *Irrepressible Spirit: Conversations with Human Rights Activists.* Susan Kuklin. Putnam, 1996. *Level:* young adult.

3475 1997. *Frindle.* Andrew Clements. *Illustrator:* Brian Selznick. Simon & Schuster, 1996. *Level:* Ages 10–12.

3476 1997. *Minty: A Story of Young Harriet Tubman.* Alan Schroeder. *Illustrator:* Jerry Pinkney. Dial, 1996. *Level:* Ages 6–9.

3477 1997. *Glennis, Before and After.* Patricia Calvert. Atheneum, 1996. *Level:* Ages 12 and up.

3478 1998. *The Gardener.* Sarah Stewart. *Illustrator:* David Small. Farrar Straus Giroux, 1998. *Level:* Ages 5–8.

3479 1998. *When Jessie Came Across the Sea.* Amy Hest. *Illustrator:* P.J. Lynch. Candlewick Press, 1998. *Level:* Ages 8–10.

3480 1998. *The Silver Balloon.* Susan Bonners. *Illustrator:* Susan Bonners. Farrar Straus Giroux, 1998. *Level:* Ages 10–12.

3481 1998. *I Have Lived a Thousand Years: Growing Up in the Holocaust.* Livia Bitton-Jackson. Simon & Schuster, 1998. *Level:* young adult.

3482 1998. *Milo and the Magical Stones.* Marcus Pfister. *Illustrator:* Marcus Pfister. North-South Books, 1998. *Level:* picture book.

3483 1999. *Mary on Horseback: Three Mountain Stories.* Rosemary Wells. *Illustrator:* Peter McCarty. Dial, 1997. *Level:* Ages 10–12.

3484 1999. *Raising Dragons.* Jerdine Nolen. *Illustrator:* Elise Primavera. Harcourt Brace/Silver Whistle, 1997. *Level:* Ages 6–8.

3485 1999. *The Summer My Father Was Ten.* Pat Brisson. *Illustrator:* Andrea Shine. Boyds Mills Press, 1997. *Level:* Ages 8–10.

3486 1999. *Shipwreck Season.* Donna Hill. Clarion Books, 1997. *Level:* Ages 12 and up.

3487 2000. *Good Luck, Mrs. K.!* Louise Borden. *Illustrator:* Adam Gustavson. Simon & Schuster, 1999. *Level:* K–3.

3488 2000. *Grandad's Prayers for the Earth.* Douglas Wood. *Illustrator:* P.J. Lynch. Candlewick Press, 1999. *Level:* K–3.

3489 2000. *I Love You, Blue Kangaroo.* Emma Chichester Clark. *Illustrator:* Emma Chichester Clark. Bantam Doubleday, 1999. *Level:* preschool.

3490 2000. *Symphony of Whales.* Steve Schuch. *Illustrator:* Peter Sylvada. Harcourt, 1999. *Level:* K–3.

3491 Claudia Lewis Award

SPONSOR: Children's Book Committee at Bank Street College of Education. ADDRESS: 610 W. 112th Street, New York, New York 10025. PHONE: (212)-875-4540. ESTABLISHED: 1998. The award is given for the best poetry book of the year.

3492 1997. *The Invisible Ladder: An Anthology of Contemporary American Poems for Young Readers.* Liz Rosenberg (editor) Henry Holt & Co, 1997.

3493 1998. *I, Too, Sing America.* Catherine Clinton. Houghton Mifflin, 1998.

3494 1999. *Stop Pretending.* Sonya Sones. HarperCollins, 1999.

3495 Colorado Children's Book Award

SPONSOR: Colorado Council of the International Reading Association. CONTACT: Joan Rosenberger. ADDRESS: P.O. Box 101047, Littleton Colorado 80123. ESTABLISHED: 1976. AWARD: A certificate and an inscribed pewter figure. The awards are presented annually to the American author whose book has been selected as the favorite by Colorado children. There are two awards — picture book and junior novel.

3496 1990. *Tacky the Penguin.* Helen Lester. *Illustrator:* Lynn Munsinger. Houghton Mifflin, 1990.

3497 1991. *The Talking Eggs: A Folktale from the American South.* Robert San Souci. *Illustrator:* Jerry Pinkney. E P Dutton, 1989.

3498 1992. *Hershel and the Hanukkah Goblins.* Eric A. Kimmel. *Illustrator:* Trina Schart Hyman. Holiday House, 1994. *Category:* picture book.

3499 1992. *Wayside School Is Falling Down.* Louis Sachar. *Illustrator:* Joel Schick. Lothrop, Lee & Shepard, 1989. *Category:* junior novel.

3500 1993. *The Dog Who Had Kittens.* Polly Robertus. *Illustrator:* Janet Stevens. Holiday House, 1992. *Category:* picture book.

3501 1993. *Scary Stories 3: More Tales to Chill Your Bones.* Alvin Schwartz. *Illustrator:* Stephen Gammell. HarperCollins, 1991. *Category:* junior novel.

3502 1994. *Dinotopia.* James Gurney. *Illustrator:* James Gurney. HarperCollins, 1998. *Category:* junior novel.

3503 1994. *The Stinky Cheese Man and Other Fairly Stupid Tales.* Jon Scieszka. *Illustrator:* Lane Smith. Viking, 1992. *Category:* picture book.

3504 1995. *Jeremy Thatcher, Dragon Hatcher.* Bruce Coville. *Illustrator:* Gary A. Lippincott. Minstrel Books, 1992. *Category:* junior novel.

3505 1995. *Coyote Steals the Blanket.* Janet Stevens. *Illustrator:* Janet Stevens. Holiday House, 1994. *Category:* picture book.

3506 1996. *Arthur's Chicken Pox.* Marc Tolon Brown. *Illustrator:* Marc Tolon Brown. Little, Brown & Co., 1994. *Category:* picture book.

3507 1996. *Best School Year Ever.* Barbara Robinson. *Illustrator:* Michael Deas. HarperCollins, 1994. *Category:* junior novel.

3508 1997. *Wayside School Gets A Little Stranger.* Louis Sachar. Morrow, 1995. *Category:* junior novel.

3509 1997. *Piggie Pie.* Margie Palatini. *Illustrator:* Howard Fine. Accord Publishing, 1997. *Category:* picture book.

3510 1998. *Ten Little Dinosaurs.* Pattie L. Schnetzler. *Illustrator:* Jim Harris. Accord Publishing, 1996. *Category:* picture book.

3511 1998. *Shiloh Season.* Phyllis Reynolds Naylor. Atheneum, 1996. *Category:* junior novel.

3512 1999. *The Adventures of Captain Underpants.* Dav Pilkey. Scholastic, 1997. *Category:* junior novel.

3513 1999. *Parts.* Tedd Arnold. Dial, 1997. *Category:* picture book.

3514 2000. *Saving Shiloh.* Phyllis Reynolds Naylor. Atheneum, 1997. *Category:* junior novel.

3515 2000. *Psssst.It's Me the Bogeyman.* Barbara Park. *Illustrator:* Stephen Kroninger. Atheneum, 1998. *Category:* picture book.

3516 Coretta Scott King Award

SPONSOR: American Library Association. CONTACT: Social Responsibilities Round Table. ADDRESS: 50 East Huron Street, Chicago, Illinois 60611. PHONE: 1-800-545-2433. ESTABLISHED: 1969. AWARD: A plaque, an honorarium, and a set of Encyclopedia Britannica or World Book Encyclopedia. The annual award is given to African American authors and illustrators who have distinguished books which promote an understanding and appreciation of the culture and contribution of all people for the American dream. The books can be either fiction or non-fiction and be published in the calendar year preceding the year of the award.

3517 1990. *Nathaniel Talking.* Eloise Greenfield. *Illustrator:* Jan Spivey Gilchrist. Black Butterfly Children's Press, 1989. *Category:* illustration.

3518 1990. *A Long Hard Journey: The Story of the Pullman Porter.* Patricia McKissack, Frederick McKissack. Walker, 1989. *Category:* literature.

3519 1991. *Aida.* Price Leontyne. *Illustrator:* Leo Dillon, Diane Dillon. Harcourt, 1990. *Category:* illustration.

3520 1991. *The Road to Memphis.* Mildred D. Taylor. Dial, 1990. *Category:* literature.

3521 1992. *Now Is Your Time.* Walter Dean Myers. HarperCollins, 1991. *Category:* literature.

3522 1992. *Tar Beach.* Faith Ringgold. *Illustrator:* Faith Ringgold. Crown, 1991. *Category:* illustration.

3523 1993. *The Origin of Life on Earth.* David A. Anderson (retold). *Illustrator:* Kathleen Atkins. SANKOFA, 1992. *Category:* illustration.

3524 1993. *The Dark-Thirty: Southern Tales of the Supernatural.* Patricia McKissack. Knopf, 1992. *Category:* literature.

3525 1994. *Soul Looks Back in Wonder.* Phyllis Fogelman (editor). *Illustrator:* Tom Feelings. Dial, 1993. *Category:* illustration.

3526 1994. *Toning the Sweep.* Angela Johnson. Orchard, 1993. *Category:* literature.

3527 1995. *Christmas in the Big House, Christmas in the Quarters.* Patricia McKissack, Frederick McKissack. *Illustrator:* Patricia McKissack. Scholastic, 1994. *Category:* literature.

3528 1995. *The Creation.* James Weldon Johnson. *Illustrator:* James Ransome. Holiday House, 1984. *Category:* illustration.

3529 1996. *Her Stories.* Virginia Hamilton. Scholastic, 1995. *Category:* literature.

3530 1996. *The Middle Passage: White Ships Black Cargo.* Tom Feelings. *Illustrator:* Tom Feelings. Dial, 1995. *Category:* illustration.

3531 1997. *Minty: A Story of Young Harriet Tubman.* Alan Schroeder. *Illustrator:* Jerry Pinkney. Dial, 1996. *Category:* illustration.

3532 1997. *Slam!* Walter Dean Myers. Scholastic, 1996. *Category:* literature.

3533 1998. *Forged by Fire.* Sharon Draper. Atheneum, 1997. *Category:* literature.

3534 1998. *In Daddy's Arms I Am Tall.* Alan Schroeder. *Illustrator:* Javaka Steptoe. Lee & Low, 1997. *Category:* illustration.

3535 1999. *I See the Rhythm.* Toyomi Igus. *Illustrator:* Michele Wood. Children's Book Press, 1998. *Category:* illustration.

3536 1999. *Heaven.* Angela Johnson. Simon & Schuster, 1998. *Category:* literature.

3537 2000. *In the Time of the Drums.* Kim L. Siegelson. *Illustrator:* Brian Pinkney. Jump at the Sun/Hyperion, 1999. *Category:* illustration.

3538 2000. *Bud, Not Buddy.* Christopher Paul Curtis. Delacorte, 1999. *Category:* literature.

3539 David McCord Award

SPONSOR: Framingham State College and Nobscot Council. ADDRESS: P.O. Box 2134, Framingham Massachusetts 01703-2134. ESTABLISHED: 1986. AWARD: A framed citation, $500.00 U.S. and an engraved Jefferson cup. The annual award is given to the author or illustrator for "significant contribution to excellence in books for children."

3540 1990. Barbara Cooney.
3541 1991. Rosemary Wells.
3542 1992. Jerry Pinkney.
3543 1993. Jan Brett.
3544 1994. Joanna Cole.
3545 1995. Eric Carle.
3546 1996. Patricia Polacco.
3547 1997. Donald Crews, Ann Jonas.
3548 1998. Joseph Bruchac.
3549 1999. Kevin Henkes.

3550 Dorothy Canfield Fisher Children's Book Award

SPONSOR: Vermont Department of Education. CONTACT: Leda Schubert. ADDRESS: 120 State Street, Montpelier, Vermont 05602. PHONE: (802) 828-3402. ESTABLISHED: 1957. AWARD: A certificate illustrated by a Vermont artist. The award is given to the American author who receives the most votes from the children of Vermont in grades 4 to 8. The book must have been published in the previous year.

3551 1990. *Where It Stops, Nobody Knows.* Amy Ehrlich. Puffin, 1990.
3552 1991. *Number the Stars.* Lois Lowry. Houghton Mifflin, 1989.
3553 1992. *Maniac Magee.* Jerry Spinelli. Little, Brown & Co., 1990.
3554 1993. *Shiloh.* Phyllis Reynolds Naylor. Atheneum, 1991.
3555 1994. *Jennifer Murdley's Toad.* Bruce Coville. Harcourt, 1992.
3556 1995. *The Boggart.* Susan Cooper. Margaret McElderry, 1993.
3557 1996. *Time for Andrew: A Ghost Story.* Mary Downing Hahn. Clarion, 1994.

3558 1997. *Mick Harte Was Here.* Barbara Park. Knopf, 1995.

3559 1998. *Small Steps: The Year I Got Polio.* Peg Kehret. Albert Whitman, 1996.

3560 1999. *Ella Enchanted.* Gail Carson Levine. HarperCollins, 1997.

3561 2000. *Holes.* Louis Sachar. Farrar Straus & Giroux, 1998.

3562 Drexel Citation

SPONSOR: College of Information Studies, Drexel University and The Free Library of Philadelphia. ADDRESS: College of Information Studies, Drexel University, Philadelphia, Pennsylvania 19104. PHONE: (215) 895-2447. ESTABLISHED: 1963. AWARD: A hand-lettered citation. The award is given irregularly to honor Philadelphia and area authors, illustrators and others who have made a significant contribution to literature for children.

3563 1990. Carolyn Croll.

3564 1991. Aliki.

3565 1992. Jerry Pinkney.

3566 1993. Trina Schart Hyman.

3567 1994. Bernard Waber.

3568 1995. Susan Hirschman.

3569 1996. Jerry Spinelli.

3570 1997. Helen Mae Mullen.

3571 1998. Donna Jo Napoli.

3572 1999. E.B. Lewis.

3573 Edgar Allan Poe Award

SPONSOR: Mystery Writers of America Inc. ADDRESS: 17 E. 47th St., 6th floor, New York, New York 10017. PHONE: (212) 888-8171. ESTABLISHED: 1945. AWARD: A ceramic bust of Poe. The award is given annually for the best mystery fiction published in the United States appropriate for grades 5 to 7. Books are judged for writing and excellence in design. The titles must fit the specific subject category for the given year.

3574 1990. *Show Me the Evidence.* Alan Ferguson. Bradbury, 1989.

3575 1991. *Mote.* Chap Reaver. Delacorte. *Category:* young adult.

3576 1991. *Stonewords.* Pam Conrad. Harper & Row, 1990. *Category:* juvenile.

3577 1992. *The Weirdo.* Theodore Taylor. Harcourt Brace Jovanovich, 1991. *Category:* young adult.

3578 1992. *Wanted...Mud Blossom.* Betsy Byars. Delacorte, 1991. *Category:* juvenile.

3579 1993. *A Little Bit Dead.* Chap Reaver. Delacorte, 1992. *Category:* young adult.

3580 1993. *Coffin on a Case!* Eve Bunting. HarperCollins, 1992. *Category:* juvenile.

3581 1994. *The Name of the Game was Murder.* Joan Lowery Nixon. Delacorte, 1993. *Category:* young adult.

3582 1994. *The Twin in the Tavern.* Barbara Brooks Wallace. Atheneum, 1993. *Category:* juvenile.

3583 1995. *Toughing It.* Nancy Springer. Harcourt Brace, 1994. *Category:* young adult.

3584 1995. *The Absolutely True Story. How I Visited Yellowstone Park with the Terrible Rupes.* Willo Davis Roberts. Atheneum, 1994. *Category:* juvenile.

3585 1996. *Prophecy Rock.* Rob MacGregor. Simon & Schuster, 1995. *Category:* young adult.

3586 1996. *Looking for Jamie Bridger.* Nancy Springer. Dial, 1995. *Category:* juvenile.

3587 1997. *The Clearing.* Dorothy Reynolds Miller. *Illustrator:* John Dawson. Atheneum, 1996. *Category:* Juvenile.

3588 1997. *Twisted Summer.* Willo Davis Roberts. Atheneum, 1996. *Category:* young adult.

3589 1998. *Ghost Canoe.* Will Hobbs. Morrow Junior Books, 1997. *Category:* young adult.

3590 1998. *Sparrows in the Scullery.* Barbara Brooks Wallace. Atheneum, 1997. *Category:* juvenile.

3591 1999. *The Killer's Cousin.* Nancy Werlin. Delacorte Press, 1998. *Category:* young adult.

3592 1999. *Sammy Keyes and the Hotel Thief.* Wendelin Van Draanen. Knopf, 1998. *Category:* juvenile.

3593 2000. *Never Trust a Dead Man.* Vivian Van de Velde. HarperCollins, 1999. *Category:* young adult.

3594 2000. *The Night Flyers.* Elizabeth McDavid Jones. Pleasant Company Publications, 1999. *Category:* juvenile.

3595 Elizabeth Burr Award

SPONSOR: Wisconsin Library Association, Children's Book Award Committee. ADDRESS: 5250 E. Terrace Dr, Suite A1, Madison, Wisconsin 53718. ESTABLISHED: 1992. The annual award is given to a Wisconsin author or illustrator for a single publication and must be published in the calendar year preceding the presentation of the award. The work must be notable and contribute to the world of children's literature. Only original works written or illustrated for children or young adults will be considered. Books that are traditional in origin will be eligible if they are the result of original research and if the retelling or interpretation is that of the author or illustrator.

3596 1992. *Red Leaf, Yellow Leaf.* Lois Ehlert. Harcourt Brace Jovanovich 1991.
3597 1993. *Words of Stone.* Kevin Henkes. Greenwillow, 1992.
3598 1994. *Shizuko's Daughter.* Kyoko Mori. Henry Holt, 1993.
3599 1995. *Cranberries: Fruit of the Bogs.* Diane Burns. *Illustrator:* Cheryl Walsh Bellville. Carolrhoda, 1994.
3600 1996. *Protecting Marie.* Kevin Henkes. Greenwillow, 1995.
3601 1997. *Echoes for the Eye: Poems to Celebrate Patterns of Nature.* Barbara Juster Esbensen. HarperCollins, 1996.
3602 1998. *Sun & Spoon.* Kevin Henkes. Greenwillow, 1997.
3603 1999. *Freedom Train North: Stories of the Underground Railroad in Wisconsin.* Julia Pferdehirt. *Illustrator:* Jerry Butler. Living History Press, 1998.
3604 2000. *Sector 7.* David Wiesner. Houghton Mifflin, 2000.

3605 Empire State Award of Excellence in Literature for Young People

SPONSOR: Youth Services Section of the New York Library Association. ADDRESS: 252 Hudson Ave., Albany, New York 12210. PHONE: (518) 432-6952. ESTABLISHED: 1990. AWARD: Engraved medallion. The annual award is given to a living author or illustrator currently residing in New York State for excellence in children's or young adult literature and a body of work that has made a significant contribution to literature for young people.

3606 1990. Maurice Sendak.
3607 1991. Madeleine L'Engle.
3608 1992. Leo Dillon, Diane Dillon.
3609 1993. Russell Freedman.
3610 1994. Paula Fox.
3611 1995. Ed Young.
3612 1996. Nancy Willard.
3613 1997. Richard Peck.
3614 1998. Jean Craighead George.
3615 1999. Vera B. Williams.
3615/a 2000. Peter Spier.

3616 Eva L. Gordon Award for Children's Science Literature

SPONSOR: American Nature Study Society. ADDRESS: RR 2, Box 1010, Dingmans Ferry, Pennsylvania 18328. PHONE: (507) 828-9692. ESTABLISHED: 1964. AWARD: A certificate. The award is presented to an author of science books for children, whose work is of the highest standards in readability, accuracy, joyousness, understanding of interrelationships while encouraging children to make their own scientific observations.

3617 1990. Joanna Cole.
3618 1991. Jim Arnosky.
3619 1992. Byrd Baylor.
3620 1993. Augusta Goldin.
3621 1994. Eric Carle.
3622 1995. Joanne Ryder.
3623 1996. David Macaulay.
3624 1997. Gail Gibbons.
3625 1998. Margery Flackham.
3626 1999. Bruce Hiscock.
3627 2000. Laurence Pringle.

3628 Evelyn Sibley Lampman Award

SPONSOR: Oregon Library Association, Children's Section. ADDRESS: P.O. Box 2042, Salem, Oregon 97308. PHONE: (503) 370-7019. ESTABLISHED: 1982. AWARD: A plaque. The annual award is given to an Oregon author, librarian or educator who has made a significant contribution over a period of years to the children of Oregon and the Pacific Northwest in the field of literature and or library services.

3629 1990. B.J. Quinlan.
3630 1991. Eric Kimmel.
3631 1992. Walter Minkel.
3632 1993. Patricia Blair.
3633 1994. Rebecca Cohen, Rick Steber.
3634 1995. Sandi Olmstead.
3635 1996. Aletha Cox.
3636 1997. Jim Scheppke.
3637 1998. Barbara McKillip.
3638 1999. Tom Birdseye.
3639 2000. Nancy Spaulding.

3640 Ezra Jack Keats New Writer Award

SPONSOR: Ezra Jack Keats Foundation. CONTACT: ECRIC Branch, New York Public Library. ADDRESS: 66 LeRoy Street, New York, New York 10014. ESTABLISHED: 1983. AWARD: The Ezra Jack Keats silver medallion and a $1,000 U.S. The award is given annually to an outstanding new writer of picture books for children age 9 and under.

3641 1991. *Tell Me a Story Mama.* Angela Johnson. *Illustrator:* David Soman. Orchard, 1989.

3642 1993. *Tar Beach.* Faith Ringgold. *Illustrator:* Faith Ringgold. Crown, 1991.

3643 1995. *Taxi! Taxi!* Cari Best. *Illustrator:* Dale Gottlieb. Little, Brown & Co.

3644 1997. *Calling the Doves.* Juan Felipe Herrera. *Illustrator:* Elly Simmons. Children's Book Press, 1995.

3645 1999. *Elizabeti's Doll.* Stephanie Stuve-Bodeen. *Illustrator:* Christy Hale. Lee and Low Books.

3646 Flicker Tale Children's Book Award

SPONSOR: North Dakota Library Association. CONTACT: Donna Maston. ADDRESS: 515 North Fifth Street, Bismarck, North Dakota 58501. PHONE: (701) 222-6410. ESTABLISHED: 1978. AWARD: An inscribed plaque. The first children's book award given by the North Dakota Library Association was in 1978 under the name Children's Choice Award. This award was presented each year at the annual conference through, 1985. The award was not given in 1986. In September, 1986, the name was changed to the current name: Flicker Tale Children's Book Award.

3647 1990. *Hatchet.* Gary Paulsen. Bradbury, 1987. *Level:* older.

3648 1990. *Meanwhile Back at the Ranch.* Trina Hakes Noble. *Illustrator:* Tony Ross. Puffin, 1987. *Level:* younger.

3649 1991. *No Jumping on the Bed.* Tedd Arnold. *Illustrator:* Tedd Arnold. Dial, 1987. *Level:* younger.

3650 1991. *How to Fight A Girl.* Thomas Rockwell. Franklin Watts, 1987. *Level:* older.

3651 1992. *Scared Silly: A Halloween Treat.* James Howe. *Illustrator:* Leslie Morrill. William Morrow & Co., 1989. *Level:* younger.

3652 1992. *Maniac Magee.* Jerry Spinelli. Little, Brown & Co., 1990. *Level:* older.

3653 1993. *The Signmaker's Assistant.* Tedd Arnold. *Illustrator:* Tedd Arnold. Dial, 1992. *Level:* younger.

3654 1993. *Fudge-A-Mania.* Judy Blume. Dutton, 1990. *Level:* older.

3655 1994. *Shiloh.* Phyllis Reynolds Naylor. Atheneum, 1991. *Level:* older.

3656 1994. *The Stinky Cheese Man and Other Fairly Stupid Tales.* Jon Scieszka. *Illustrator:* Lane Smith. Viking, 1992. *Level:* younger.

3657 1995. *The River.* Gary Paulsen. Delacorte, 1991. *Level:* older.

3658 1995. *Easter Egg Farm.* Mary Jane Auch. Holiday House, 1992. *Level:* younger.

3659 1996. *Best School Year Ever.* Barbara Robinson. *Illustrator:* Michael Deas. HarperCollins, 1994. *Level:* younger.

3660 1996. *My Rotten Red-Headed Older Brother.* Patricia Polacco. *Illustrator:* Patricia Polacco. Simon & Schuster, 1994. *Level:* older.

3661 1997. *The Library Dragon.* Carmen Agra Deedy. *Illustrator:* Michael P. White. Peachtree Publishers, 1994. *Level:* older.

3662 1997. *Mick Harte Was Here.* Barbara Park. Knopf, 1995. *Level:* younger.

3663 1998. *Casey in the Bath.* Cynthia DeFelice. *Illustrator:* Chris Demarest. Farrar Straus & Giroux, 1996. *Level:* older.

3664 1998. *Rescue Josh McGuire.* Ben Mikaelsen. Hyperion, 1991. *Level:* younger.

3665 1999. *Grandpa's Teeth.* Rod Clement. *Illustrator:* Rod Clement. HarperCollins, 1998. *Level:* older.

3666 1999. *Shiloh Season.* Phyllis Reynolds Naylor. Atheneum, 1996. *Level:* younger.

3667 2000. *No, David.* David Shannon. Scholastic, 1998. *Level:* older.

3668 2000. *Holes.* Louis Sachar. Farrar Straus Giroux, 1998. *Level:* younger.

3669 Flora Stieglitz Straus Award

SPONSOR: Children's Book Committee at Bank Street College of Education. ADDRESS: 610 W. 112th Street, New York, New York 10025. PHONE: (212)-875-4540. ESTABLISHED: 1993. The award is given for the best non-fiction book of the year.

3670 1993. *Eleanor Roosevelt: A Life of Discovery.* Russell Freedman. Clarion Books, 1993.

1994. No award given.

3671 1995. *Parallel Journeys.* Eleanor Ayer. Atheneum, 1995.

1996. No award given.

3672 1997. *Oh, Freedom! Kids Talk About the Civil Rights Movement with the People Who Made It Happen.* Casey King, Linda Barrett Osborne. Knopf, 1997.

3673 1998. *Iqbal Masih and the Crusaders Against Child Slavery.* Susan Kuklin. Henry Holt & Co., 1998.

3674 1999. *Through My Eyes.* Rudy Bridges. Scholastic, 1999.

3675 FOCAL (Friends of Children and Literature Award)

SPONSOR: Children's Services Los Angeles Public Library. ADDRESS: 630 West Fifth Street. Los Angeles, California 90071. PHONE: (213) 228-7252. ESTABLISHED: 1980. AWARD: A handcrafted puppet representing a character in the book. The award is presented annually to the author or illustrator of a fiction or non-fiction work that enriches a child's knowledge and appreciation for California.

3676 1992. *Child of the Owl.* Laurence Yep. Harper, 1977.

3677 1993. *Children of the Dust Bowl.* Jerry Stanley. Crown, 1992.

3678 1994. *Frida Maria.* Deborah Nourse Lattimore. Browndeer Press, 1994.

3679 1995. *Earthshine.* Theresa Nelson. Orchard Books, 1994.

3680 1996. *California Blue.* David Klass. Point, 1996.

3681 1997. *Calling the Doves. Original Title:* El Canto de las Palomas. Juan Felipe Herrera. *Illustrator:* Elly Simmons. Children's Book Press, 1995.

3682 1998. *The Ballad of Lucy Whipple.* Karen Cushman. Clarion, 1996.

3683 1999. *So Far from the Sea.* Eve Bunting. *Illustrator:* Chris K. Soentpiet Clarion Books, 1998.

3684 Garden State Children's Book Award

SPONSOR: New Jersey Library Association. CONTACT: Children's Services Section. ADDRESS: Box 1534, Trenton New Jersey 08607. PHONE: (609) 394-8032. ESTABLISHED: 1977. AWARD: A framed certificate. The award is given to both author and illustrator in three categories: easy-to-read, younger fiction, and younger non-fiction. The books must be published three years earlier than the award year.

3685 1990. *Henry and Mudge in Puddle Trouble.* Cynthia Rylant. *Illustrator:* Sucie Stevenson. Simon & Schuster, 1996. *Category:* easy to read.

3686 1990. *Koko's Story.* Francine Patterson. Scholastic. *Category:* younger non-fiction.

3687 1990. *Nighty-Nightmare.* James Howe. *Illustrator:* Leslie Morrill. Atheneum, 1987. *Category:* younger fiction.

3688 1991. *Fox on the Job.* James Marshal. Dial, 1998. *Category:* easy to read.

3689 1991. *Teacher's Pet.* Johanna Hurwitz. *Illustrator:* Sheila Hamanka. Morrow, 1988. *Category:* younger fiction.

3690 1991. *The Burning Questions of Bingo Brown.* Betsy Byars. *Illustrator:* Cathy Bobak. Puffin, 1990. *Category:* younger fiction.

3691 1991. *Volcanoes.* Seymour Simon. Mulberry Books, 1995. *Category:* younger non-fiction.

3692 1992. *Henry and Mudge Get the Cold Shivers.* Cynthia Rylant. *Illustrator:* Sucie Stevenson. Aladdin, 1996. *Category:* easy to read.

3693 1992. *The Magic School Bus: Inside the Human Body.* Joanne Cole. *Illustrator:* Bruce Degen. Scholastic. *Category:* younger non-fiction.

3694 1992. *Wayside School Is Falling Down.* Louis Sachar. *Illustrator:* Joel Schick. Lothrop, Lee & Shepard, 1989. *Category:* younger fiction.

3695 1993. *Henry and Mudge and the Happy Cat.* Cynthia Rylant. *Illustrator:* Sucie Stevenson. Simon & Schuster, 1997. *Category:* easy to read.

3696 1993. *Muggie Maggie.* Beverly Cleary. *Illustrator:* Kay Life. William Morrow, 1990. *Category:* younger fiction.

3697 1993. *The Magic School Bus: Lost in the Solar System.* Joanne Cole. *Illustrator:* Bruce Degen. Scholastic, 1993. *Category:* younger non-fiction.

3698 1994. *Big Cats.* Seymour Simon. Harper. Trophy, 1994. *Category:* younger non-fiction.

3699 1994. *Henry and Mudge and the Bedtime Thumps*. Cynthia Rylant. *Illustrator:* Sucie Stevenson. Simon & Schuster, 1993. *Category:* easy to read.

3700 1994. *School's Out*. Johanna Hurwitz, *Illustrator:* Sheila Hamanka. Apple, 1995. *Category:* younger fiction.

3701 1995. *Attaboy, Sam!* Lois Lowry. *Illustrator:* Diane DeGroat. Houghton Mifflin, 1992. *Category:* younger fiction.

3702 1995. *Henry and the Long Weekend*. Cynthia Rylant. *Illustrator:* Sucie Stevenson. Simon & Schuster, 1994. *Category:* easy to read.

3703 1995. *The Magic School Bus on the Ocean Floor*. Joanne Cole. *Illustrator:* Bruce Degen. Scholastic, 1992. *Category:* younger non-fiction.

3704 1996. *Nibble, Nibble, Jerry Archer*. Ellen Conford. *Illustrator:* Diane Palmisciano. Little, Brown & Co., 1993. *Category:* younger fiction.

3705 1996. *Henry and Mudge and the Wild Wind*. Cynthia Rylant. *Illustrator:* Sucie Stevenson. Simon & Schuster, 1995. *Category:* easy to read.

3706 1996. *My Visit to the Aquarium*. Aliki. *Illustrator:* Aliki. HarperCollins, 1993. *Category:* younger non-fiction.

3707 1997. *The Big Bug Book*. Margery Facklam. *Illustrator:* Paul Facklam. Little, Brown & Co., 1994. *Category:* younger non-fiction.

3708 1997. *Amber Brown Is Not a Crayon*. Paula Danziger. *Illustrator:* Tony Ross. Putnam Pub., 1994. *Category:* younger fiction.

3709 1997. *Henry and Mudge and the Careful Cousin*. Cynthia Rylant. *Illustrator:* Sucie Stevenson. Simon & Schuster, 1996. *Category:* easy to read.

3710 1998. *Henry and Mudge and the Best Day of All*. Cynthia Rylant. *Illustrator:* Sucie Stevenson. Simon & Schuster, 1996. *Category:* easy to read.

3711 1998. *The Magic School Bus Inside a Hurricane*. Joanne Cole. *Illustrator:* Bruce Degen. Scholastic, 1996. *Category:* younger non-fiction.

3712 1998. *Wayside School Gets a Little Stranger*. Louis Sachar. Morrow, 1995. *Category:* younger fiction.

3713 1999. *Arthur's Reading Race*. Marc Tolon Brown. Random, 1996. *Category:* easy to read.

3714 1999. *Forever Amber Brown*. Paula Danziger. *Illustrator:* Tony Ross. Putnam Pub., 1996. *Category:* younger fiction.

3715 1999. *The Magic School Bus Inside a Beehive*. Joanne Cole. *Illustrator:* Bruce Degen. Scholastic, 1996. *Category:* younger non-fiction.

3716 2000. *Henry and Mudge in the Family Trees*. Cynthia Rylant. *Illustrator:* Sucie Stevenson. Simon and Schuster, 1997. *Category:* easy-to-read.

3717 2000. *The Adventures of Captain Underpants*. Dav Pilkey. Scholastic, 1997. *Category:* fiction.

3718 2000. *Lou Gehrig: The Luckiest Man.* David Adler. *Illustrator:* Terry Widener. Gulliver Books, 1997. *Category:* non-fiction.

3719 Garden State Teen Book Awards

SPONSOR: New Jersey Library Association. CONTACT: Adult/Young Adult Section. ADDRESS: Box 1534, Trenton, New Jersey 08607. PHONE: (609) 394-8032. ESTABLISHED: 1995. The award is given to the author in three categories: Grades 6–8 fiction, Grades 9–12 fiction, and non-fiction. It is based on teen appeal and quality of writing from the previous year's "Best Books" list.

3720 1995. *Nothing but the Truth.* Avi. Jackson/Orchard, 1991. *Category:* fiction (grades 6–8).

3721 1995. *Into the Mummy's Tomb.* Nicholas Reeves, Nan Froman. Time Quest Book. *Category:* non-fiction.

3722 1995. *Children of the Night.* Dan Simmons. Warner Books, 1993. *Category:* fiction (grades 9–12).

3723 1996. *The Giver.* Lois Lowry. Houghton Mifflin, 1993. *Category:* fiction (grades 6–8).

3724 1996. *Thor.* Wayne Smith. Ballantine Books, 1994. *Category:* fiction (grades 9–12).

3725 1996. *Anne Frank: Beyond the Diary.* Ruud van der Rol, Rian Verhoeven. *Translator:* Tony Langham. Viking, 1993. *Category:* non-fiction.

3726 1997. *Kids at Work: Lewis Hine and the Crusade Against Child Labor.* Russell Freedman. Clarion, 1994. *Category:* non-fiction.

3727 1997. *Driver's Ed.* Caroline Cooney. Delacorte, 1994. *Category:* fiction (grades 9–12).

3728 1997. *Loch.* Paul Zindel. Hyperion, 1995. *Category:* fiction (grades 6–8).

3729 1998. *The Hot Zone.* Richard Preston. Anchor, 1995. *Category:* non-fiction.

3730 1998. *Slot Machine.* Chris Lynch. Harper. Trophy, 1996. *Category:* fiction (grades 6–8).

3731 1998. *Relic.* Douglas Preston, Lincoln Child. Forge 1996. *Category:* fiction (grades 9–12).

3732 1999. *Into the Wild.* Jon Krakauer. Anchor, 1997. *Category:* non-fiction.

3733 1999. *Brian's Winter.* Gary Paulsen. Delacorte, 1996. *Category:* fiction (grades 6–8).

3734 1999. *Mount Dragon.* Douglas Preston, Lincoln Child. Forge, 1997. *Category:* fiction (grades 9–12).

3735 2000. *Tangerine.* Edward Bloor. Harcourt, 1997. *Category:* fiction (grades 6–8).

3736 2000. *Into Thin Air.* Jon Krakauer. *Illustrator:* Randy Rackliff. Random, 1998. *Category:* non-fiction.

3737 2000. *Blood and Chocolate.* Annette Curtis Klause. Bantam Books, 1997. *Category:* fiction (grades 9–12).

3738 Georgia Children's Book Award

SPONSOR: College of Education, University of Georgia. CONTACT: Dr. Linda DeGroff. ADDRESS: Athens, Georgia 30602. PHONE: (404) 542-4510. ESTABLISHED: 1969. AWARD: An engraved plaque. The award is given to encourage the use of trade books in grades 4 to 8. School children vote for their favorite fiction book. The title which receives the most votes is the winner. The book must be published in the United States and be written within the last five years. Newbery Award winners are excluded. The winning author of the award is excluded from competition the following year.

3739 1990. *There's a Boy in the Girl's Bathroom.* Louis Sachar. Knopf, 1987.

3740 1991. *Hatchet.* Gary Paulsen. Bradbury, 1987.

3741 1992. *All About Sam.* Lois Lowry. *Illustrator:* Diane DeGroat. Houghton Mifflin, 1988.

3742 1993. *The Doll in the Garden: A Ghost Story.* Mary Downing Hahn. Clarion, 1989.

3743 1994. *Jennifer Murdley's Toad.* Bruce Coville. Harcourt, 1992.

3744 1955. *Mayfield Crossing.* Vaunda Micheaux Nelson. *Illustrator:* Leonard Jenkins. Camelot, 1993.

3745 1996. *Time for Andrew: A Ghost Story.* Mary Downing Hahn. Clarion, 1994.

3746 1997. *Mick Harte Was Here.* Barbara Park. Knopf, 1995.

3747 1998. *The Best School Year Ever.* Barbara Robinson. HarperCollins, 1994.

3748 1999. *Frindle.* Andrew Clements. *Illustrator:* Brian Selznick. Simon & Schuster, 1996.

3749 2000. *The Imp that Ate My Homework.* Laurence Yep. HarperCollins, 1998.

3750 Georgia Children's Picture Storybook Award

SPONSOR: College of Education, University of Georgia. CONTACT: Dr. Linda DeGroff. ADDRESS: Athens, Georgia 30602. PHONE: (404) 542-4510. ESTABLISHED: 1976. AWARD: An engraved plaque. The award is given to encourage the use of trade books in kindergarten to grade 3. School children vote for their favorite fiction book. The title which receives the most votes is the winner. The book must be published in the United States and written in the last five years. Caldecott Award winners are excluded. The winning author/illustrator is excluded from competition the following year.

3751 1990. *No Jumping on the Bed.* Tedd Arnold. *Illustrator:* Tedd Arnold. Dial, 1987.

3752 1991. *We're Back! A Dinosaur's Story.* Hudson Talbott. *Illustrator:* Tedd Talbott. Crown, 1987.

3753 1992. *Two Bad Ants.* Chris van Allsburg. *Illustrator:* Chris van Allsburg. Houghton Mifflin, 1988.

3754 1993. *The Talking Eggs.* Robert San Souci. *Illustrator:* Jerry Pinkney. Dial, 1989.

3755 1994. *The Rough Face Girl.* Rafe Martin. *Illustrator:* David Shannon. Philomel, 1992.

3756 1995. *Hurricane City.* Sarah Weeks. *Illustrator:* James Warhola. HarperCollins, 1993.

3757 1996. *Martha Speaks.* Susan Meddaugh. Houghton, 1992.

3758 1997. *The Stinky Cheese Man and Other Fairly Stupid Tales.* Jon Scieszka. *Illustrator:* Lane Smith. Viking, 1992.

3759 1998. *Dog Breath! The Horrible Trouble with Hally Tosis.* Dav Pilkey. Blue Sky Press, 1994.

3760 1999. *Leo the Magnificat.* Ann M. Martin. *Illustrator:* Emily Arnold McCully. Scholastic, 1996.

3761 2000. *No, David.* David Shannon. Scholastic, 1998.

3762 Giverny Book Award

SPONSOR: 15 Degree Laboratory's Award Selection Committee. ADDRESS: Baton Rouge, Louisiana 70803. ESTABLISHED: 1998. AWARD: A gold seal, plaque. The award is given to an author and illustrator of a science picture book written in English and published within five years of the award date. The book must contain an important scientific principle, or encourage the reader toward specific science-related pursuits or inquiry.

3763 1998. *Common Ground: The Water, Earth and Air We Share.* Molly Bang. *Illustrator:* Molly Bang. The Blue Sky Press, 1997.

3764 1999. *Sam Plants a Sunflower.* Kate Petty. *Illustrator:* Axel Scheffler. Macmillan Children's Books, 1997.

3765 2000. *A Log's Life.* Wendy Pfeffer. *Illustrator:* Robin Brickman. Simon & Schuster, 1997.

3766 Gold Medallion Book Award

SPONSOR: Evangelical Christian Publishers Association. ADDRESS: 1969 East Broadway, Suite Two, Tempe, Arizona 85282. PHONE: (480) 966-3998. ESTABLISHED: 1978. AWARD: A Gold Medallion plaque. The annual awards are given to highlight religious books for children. Three categories include: preschool — books for children up to age 6, elementary children — books for children ages

7 to 12, and youth — book for junior high and senior high. The books must be in English and have been originally published in the United States. Only books published in the preceding calendar year are eligible, with the exception of Bibles or classics.

3767 1990. *Do You See Me, God?* Elspeth Campbell Murphy. David C. Cook Publishing.

3768 1990. *Destination: Moon.* James Irwin. Multnomah Press.

3769 1990. *Lifelines Introductory Series (Booklets 1–4).* Fran Sciacca, Jill Sciacca. World Wide Publications, 1987.

3770 1991. *The Kidderminster Kingdom Series — King Leonard's Celebration.* Christopher Lane. Victor Books.

3771 1991. *Treasure in an Oatmeal Box.* Ken Gire. NavPress.

3772 1991. *I Don't Remember Dropping the Skunk, but I Do Remember Trying to Breathe.* Ken Davis. Zondervan.

3773 1992. *If You Really Trust Me, Why Can't I Stay Out Later?* Lorraine Peterson. Bethany House.

3774 1992. *What Would Jesus Do?* Mack Thomas. Questar Publishers.

3775 1992. *The Beginner's Devotional.* Stephen Barclift. Questar Publishers.

3776 1993. *Don't Check Your Brains at the Door.* Josh McDowell, Bob Hostetler. Word, Inc.

3777 1993. *The Treasure Tree.* Gary Smalley, Norma Smalley. Word, Inc.

3778 1993. *Just In Case You Ever Wonder.* Max Lucado. Word, Inc.

3779 1994. *The Hosanna Bible.* Ken Abraham, Angela Abraham. Word, Inc.

3780 1994. *The One-Minute Bible for Kids.* Joyce K. Ellis (editor). *Illustrator:* Steve Bjorkman. Garborg's.

3781 1994. *Trying to Get the Toothpaste Back into the Tube.* Lorraine Peterson. Bethany House.

3782 1995. *Stories Jesus Told.* Questar Publishers.

3783 1995. *The Adventures in Odyssey Bible.* Word.

3784 1995. *Jumper Fables.* Ken Davis, Dave Lambert. Zondervan.

3785 1996. *Mouse in King Solomon's House.* Mack Thomas. Questar Publishers.

3786 1996. *Paw Paw Chuck's Big Ideas in the Bible.* Charles R. Swindoll. Word.

3787 1996. *I'm Outta Here! Facing the Tough Choices After High School.* Len Woods. Baker Books.

3788 1997. *Praise and Worship.* Ken Abraham, Angela Abraham. Thomas Nelson, Inc.

3789 1997. *The Children's Daily Devotional Bible.* Robert J. Morgan (editor). Thomas Nelson, Inc.

3790 1997. *Pure Excitement.* Joe White. Focus on the Family.

3791 1998. *The Parable Series.* Liz Curtis Higgs. Thomas Nelson, Inc.

3792 1998. *The Jubilee Family Illustrated Bible.* Claude-Bernard Costecalde (editor). Jubilee Publishing.

3793 1998. *It's Time to Be Bold.* Michael W. Smith. Word.

3794 1999. *WWJD Today?* Brian Shipman. Broadman & Holman Publishers.

3795 1999. *The Very First Christmas.* Paul L. Maier. Concordia Publishing.

3796 1999. *King of the Stable.* Melody Carlson. Crossway Books.

3797 2000. *The Rhyme Bible for Toddlers.* Linda Sattgast. Zondervan.

3798 2000. *Because I Love You.* Max Lucado. Crossway Books.

3799 2000. *What's the Big Deal About Sex?* Jim Burgen. Standard Publishing.

3800 Golden Archer Award (now WEMA Golden Archer Award)

Discontinued. ESTABLISHED: 1973. The Golden Archer Award and the Little Archer Award were given for books in two levels (K through 8), from 1974 to 1992.

3801 1990. *Number the Stars.* Lois Lowry. Houghton Mifflin, 1989.

3802 1991. *Maniac Magee.* Jerry Spinelli. Little, Brown & Co., 1990.

3803 1992. *Shiloh.* Phyllis Reynolds Naylor. Atheneum, 1991.

3804 Golden Kite Awards

SPONSOR: Society of Children's Book Writers. ADDRESS: 8271 Beverly Blvd., Los Angeles, California 90048. PHONE: (323)-782-1010. ESTABLISHED: 1973. AWARD: Golden Kite Statuette. Four awards: fiction, non-fiction, picture book text and picture illustration are given annually to the most outstanding children's book published during the year. The books are written by members of the Society for Children's Book writers and are chosen for their excellence in writing, illustration and appeal to the interests of children.

3805 1990. *Dinosaur Dream.* Dennis Nolan. *Illustrator:* Dennis Nolan. Macmillan, 1990. *Category:* illustration honor.

3806 1990. *Home Place.* Jerry Pinkney. *Illustrator:* Jerry Pinkney. Macmillan, 1990. *Category:* illustration.

3807 1990. *The Boy's War.* Jim Murphy. Clarion, 1990. *Category:* non-fiction.

3808 1990. *The True Confessions of Charlotte Doyle.* Avi. Jackson/Orchard, 1990. *Category:* fiction.

3809 1990. *Everywhere.* Bruce Brooks. HarperCollins, 1990. *Category:* fiction honor.

3810 1990. *Franklin Delano Roosevelt.* Russell Freedman. Clarion, 1990. *Category:* non-fiction honor.

3811 1991. *Where Does the Trail Lead?* Brian Pinkney. *Illustrator:* Brian Pinkney. Simon & Schuster, 1991. *Category:* illustration honor.

3812 1991. *The Wright Brothers.* Russell Freedman. Holiday House, 1991. *Category:* non-fiction.

3813 1991. *The Borning Room.* Paul Fleischman. HarperCollins, 1991. *Category:* fiction honor.

3814 1991. *Now Is Your Time!* Walter Dean Myers. HarperCollins, 1991. *Category:* non-fiction honor.

3815 1991. *Mama, Do You Love Me?* Barbara Lavallee. *Illustrator:* Barbara Lavalee. Chronicle, 1991. *Category:* illustration.

3816 1991. *The Raincatchers.* Jean Thesman. Houghton Mifflin, 1991. *Category:* fiction.

3817 1992. *Steal Away.* Jennifer Armstrong. Orchard, 1992. *Category:* fiction-honor.

3818 1992. *An Indian Winter.* Russell Freedman. Holiday House, 1992. *Category:* non-fiction honor.

3819 1992. *Chicken Sunday.* Patrica Polacco. *Illustrator:* Patricia Polacco. Philomel, 1992. *Category:* illustration.

3820 1992. *Letters from a Slave Girl.* Mary E. Lyons. Scribners, 1992. *Category:* fiction.

3821 1992. *The Fortune Tellers.* Trina Schart Hyman. *Illustrator:* Trina Schart Hyman. Dutton, 1992. *Category:* illustration honor.

3822 1992. *The Long Road to Gettysburg.* Jim Murphy. Clarion, 1992. *Category:* non-fiction.

3823 1993. *Lives of the Musicians.* Kathleen Krull. Harcourt, 1993. *Category:* non-fiction honor.

3824 1993. *Eleanor Roosevelt.* Russell Freedman. Clarion, 1993. *Category:* non-fiction.

3825 1993. *By the Light of the Halloween Moon.* Kevin Hawkes. *Illustrator:* Kevin Hawkes. Lothrop, 1993. *Category:* illustration.

3826 1993. *Owl in Love.* Patrice Kindl. Houghton Mifflin, 1993. *Category:* fiction honor.

3827 1993. *Santa Calls.* William Joyce. *Illustrator:* William Joyce. HarperCollins, 1993. *Category:* illustration honor.

3828 1993. *Make Lemonade.* Virginia Euwer Wolff. Holt, 1993. *Category:* fiction.

3829 1994. *The Ear, the Eye and the Arm.* Nancy Farmer. Orchard, 1994. *Category:* fiction honor.

3830 1994. *Big Fat Hen.* Keith Baker. *Illustrator:* Keith Baker. Harcourt Brace, 1994. *Category:* illustration.

3831 1994. *Catherine, Called Birdy.* Karen Cushman. Clarion, 1994. *Category:* fiction.

3832 1994. *Kids at Work: Lewis Hine and the Crusade Against Child Labor.* Russell Freedman. Clarion, 1994. *Category:* non-fiction.

3833 1994. *Shadow Catcher: The Life and Work of Edward S. Curtis.* Laurie Lawlor. Walker, 1994. *Category:* non-fiction honor.

3834 1994. *The Christmas Alphabet.* Robert Sabuda. *Illustrator:* Robert Sabuda. Orchard, 1994. *Category:* illustration honor.

3835 1995. *The Watsons Go to Birmingham: 1963.* Christopher Paul Curtis. Delacorte, 1995. *Category:* fiction.

3836 1995. *Been to Yesterdays.* Lee Bennett Hopkins. Bods Mills Press, 1995. *Category:* fiction honor.

3837 1995. *Fairy Wings.* Dennis Nolan, Lauren Mills. *Illustrator:* Dennis Nolan, Lauren Mills. Little, Brown & Co., 1995. *Category:* illustration.

3838 1995. *One More River to Cross.* Walter Dean Myers. Harcourt Brace, 1995. *Category:* non-fiction honor.

3839 1995. *The Loyal Cat.* Aki Sogabe. *Illustrator:* Aki Sogabe. Browndeer Press, 1995. *Category:* illustration honor.

3840 1995. *Abigal Adams.* Natalie S. Bober. Atheneum, 1995. *Category:* non-fiction.

3841 1996. *Leah's Pony.* Elizabeth Friedrich. *Illustrator:* Elizabeth Friedrich. Boyds Mills Press, 1996. *Category:* picture book honor.

3842 1996. *Minty: A Story of Young Harriet Tubman.* Alan Schroeder. *Illustrator:* Jerry Pinkney. Dial, 1996. *Category:* illustration honor.

3843 1996. *Saving Sweetness.* Diane Stanley. *Illustrator:* Diane Stanley. Putnam, 1996. *Category:* picture book.

3844 1996. *The Moorchild.* Eloise Jarvis McGraw. Margaret McElderry, 1996. *Category:* fiction.

3845 1996. *The Music of the Dolphins.* Karen Hesse. Scholastic, 1996. *Category:* fiction honor.

3846 1996. *Market Day.* Holly Berry. *Illustrator:* Holly Berry. HarperCollins, 1996. *Category:* illustration.

3847 1997. *To Market, to Market.* Janet Stevens. *Illustrator:* Janet Stevens. Harcourt Brace, 1997. *Category:* illustraton honor.

3848 1997. *The Paper Dragon.* Marguerite W. Davol. *Illustrator:* Robert Sabuda. Atheneum, 1997. *Category:* illustration.

3849 1997. *The Paper Dragon.* Marguerite W. Davol. *Illustrator:* Robert Sabuda. Atheneum, 1997. *Category:* picture book.

3850 1997. *Stones in Water.* Donna Jo Napoli. Dutton, 1997. *Category:* fiction.

3851 1997. *Seedfolks.* Paul Fleischman. HarperCollins, 1997. *Category:* fiction honor.

3852 1997. *December.* Eve Bunting. *Illustrator:* Eve Bunting. Harcourt Brace, 1997. *Category:* picture book honor.

3853 1998. *Zelda and Ivy.* Laura McGee Kvasnosky. *Illustrator:* Laura McGee Kvasnosky. Candlewick, 1998. *Category:* illustration honor.

3854 1998. *Zelda and Ivy.* Laura McGee Kvasnosky. *Illustrator:* Laura McGee Kvasnosky. Candlewick, 1998. *Category:* picture book honor.

3855 1998. *Whirligig.* Paul Fleischman. Henry Holt & Co., 1998. *Category:* fiction honor.

3856 1998. *Snow.* Uri Shulevitz. *Illustrator:* Uri Shulevitz. Farrar, Straus & Giroux, 1998. *Category:* illustraton.

3857 1998. *Rules of the Road.* Joan Bauer. Putnam, 1998. *Category:* fiction.

3858 1998. *Restless Spirit: The Life and Work of Dorothea Lange.* Elizabeth Partridge. Viking, 1998. *Category:* non-fiction honor.

3859 1998. *Martha Graham: A Dancer's Life.* Russell Freedman. Clarion, 1998. *Category:* non-fiction.

3860 1998. *Old Elm Speaks: Tree Poems.* Kristine O'Connell George. *Illustrator:* Kristine O'Connell George. Clarion, 1998. *Category:* picture book.

3861 1999. *A Band of Angels.* Deborah Hopkinson. *Illustrator:* Raul Colón. Atheneum, 1999. *Category:* picture.

3862 1999. *The Little Red Hen (Makes a Pizza).* Philomel Sturges. *Illustrator:* Amy Walrod. Dutton, 1999. *Category:* illustration.

3863 1999. *Speak.* Laurie Halse Anderson. Farrar, Straus & Giroux, Inc., 1999. *Category:* fiction.

3864 1999. *Space Station Science: Life in Free Fall.* Marianne J. Dyson. Scholastic Inc., 1999. *Category:* non-fiction.

3865 Great Stone Face Award

SPONSOR: CHILIS New Hampshire Library Association. CONTACT: Corrie Chiknas, Chair. ADDRESS: P.O. Box 2332, Concord, New Hampshire 03302. ESTABLISHED: 1980. AWARD: A hand-cut crystal etched with the Great Stone Face. The award is given annually to an author whose book receives the most votes from students in grades 4 through 6 throughout the state.

3866 1990. *Matilda.* Roald Dahl. *Illustrator:* Quentin Blake. Viking, 1988.

3867 1991. *The Secret of the Indian.* Lynne Reid Banks. Doubleday, 1989.

3868 1992. *Number the Stars.* Lois Lowry. Houghton Mifflin, 1989.

3869 1993. *Jeremy Thatcher, Dragon Hatcher.* Bruce Coville. *Illustrator:* Gary A. Lippincott. Minstrel Books, 1992.

3870 1994. *Shiloh.* Phyllis Reynolds Naylor. Atheneum, 1991.

3871 1995. *Junie B. Jones and the Stupid Smelly Bus.* Barbara Park. Random House, 1992.

3872 1996. *The Giver.* Lois Lowry. Houghton Mifflin, 1993.

3873 1997. *Math Curse.* Jon Scieszka. *Illustrator:* Lane Smith. Viking, 1995.

3874 1998. *Frindle.* Andrew Clements. *Illustrator:* Brian Selznick. Simon & Schuster, 1996.

3875 1999. *101 Ways to Bug Your Parents.* Lee Wardlaw. Dial, 1996.
3876 2000. *Harry Potter and the Sorcerer's Stone.* J.K. Rowling. *Illustrator:* Mary Grandpré. Scholastic, 1998.

3877 Helen Keating Ott Award for Outstanding Contribution to Children's Literature

SPONSOR: Church and Synagogue Library Association. ADDRESS: Box 19357, Portland, Oregon 97280. PHONE: (503) 244–6919. ESTABLISHED: 1980. AWARD: A citation. The award is given for a significant contribution in promoting high moral and ethical values through children's literature.

3878 1990. Elizabeth A. Van Steenwyk.
3879 1991. Miriam Johnson.
3880 1992. Boone City Board of Education.
3881 1993. Tomie de Paola.
3882 1994. David A. Adler.
3883 1995. National Family.
3884 1996. Marjorie Ainsborough Decker.
3885 1997. Eve Bunting.
3886 1998. Joan C. Hawxhurst.
1999. No award given.
3887 2000. Walter Wangerin, Jr.

3888 Hope S. Dean Award

SPONSOR: Foundation for Children's Books. ADDRESS: P.O. Box 284, Boston, Massachusetts 02132. PHONE: (617) 469-7222. ESTABLISHED: 1990. AWARD: A bronze sculpture. The annual award is given to individuals and groups who make a lasting contribution to the knowledge and appreciation of children's literature.

3889 1991. Ashley Bryan.
3890 1991. John Langstaff.
3891 1991. Margaret McElderry.
3892 1992. Walter Dean Meyers.
3893 1992. Ethel Heins, Paul Heins.
3894 1993. Joseph Bruchac.
3895 1993. Barbara Clark Elam.
3896 1994. Bernard Waber.
3897 1995. Eleanor Cameron.
3898 1995. Susan Hirschman.
3899 1996. Seymour Simon.

3900 1996. Barbara Elleman.
3901 1997. Jerry Pinkney.
3902 1997. Ginny Moore Kruse.
3903 1998. Barbara Harrison.
3904 1998. Eloise Greenfield.
3905 1999. Natalie Babbitt.
3906 1999. Mary Burns.
3907 1999. Ann Flowers.
3908 2000. Virginia Hamilton.
3909 2000. Betty Levin.

3910 Indian Paintbrush Book Award

SPONSOR: Wyoming Library Association. ADDRESS: Box 1387, Cheyenne, Wyoming 82003-1387. ESTABLISHED: 1986. AWARD: A plaque. The award winner is chosen by the Wyoming children in grades 4–6. Books must be fiction and have been published within the last 5 years.

3911 1990. *There's a Boy in the Girl's Bathroom.* Louis Sachar. Knopf, 1987.
3912 1991. *Matilda.* Roald Dahl. *Illustrator:* Quentin Blake. Viking, 1988.
3913 1992. *Maniac Magee.* Jerry Spinelli. Little, Brown & Co., 1990.
3914 1993. *Pathki Nana: Kootenai Girl Solves a Mystery.* Kenneth Thomasma. *Illustrator:* Jack Brouwer. Baker Book House, 1992.
3915 1994. *Shiloh.* Phyllis Reynolds Naylor. Atheneum, 1991.
3916 1995. *Rescue Josh McGuire.* Ben Mikaelsen. Hyperion, 1991.
3917 1996. *Moho Wat: A Sheepeater Boy Attempts a Rescue.* Kenneth Thomasma. *Illustrator:* Jack Brouwer. Baker Book House, 1994.
3918 1997. *Watchdog and Coyotes.* Bill Wallace. *Illustrator:* David Slonim. Minstrel Books, 1995.
3919 1998. *Crash!* Jerry Spinelli. Knopf, 1996.
3920 1999. *Saving Shiloh.* Phyllis Reynolds Naylor. Atheneum, 1997.
3921 2000. *Harry Potter and the Sorcerer's Stone.* J.K. Rowling. *Illustrator:* Mary Grandpré. Scholastic, 1998.

3922 International Brant Point Literary Prize

SPONSOR: What's Inside Press. ADDRESS: P.O. Box 16965, Beverly Hills, California 90209. ESTABLISHED: 1999. AWARD: $2,500.00 U.S. The annual award is given for an unpublished children's (ages 2–8) and young adult (ages 12–17) manuscript which powerfully shows a specific theme. The theme changes yearly.

3923 2000. *The Tree in the Field of Mathingamy Thame.* Walter Caldwell. *Illustrator:* Christiaan Rendle. What's Inside Press.

3924 International Reading Association Children's Book Award

SPONSOR: International Reading Association. ADDRESS: PO Box 8139, Newark, Delaware 19714-8139. PHONE: (302) 731-1600. ESTABLISHED: 1975. AWARD: $500.00 U.S. each. Four awards are given for fiction or non-fiction in two age categories: younger reader (ages 4–10) and older readers (ages 10–17). The awards are given for the author's first and second books. Books can be written in any language or be published in any country during the preceding calendar year.

3925 1990. *Children of the River.* Linda Crew. Delacorte, 1989. *Category:* older reader.

3926 1990. *No Star Nights.* Anna Egan Smucker. *Illustrator:* Steve Johnson. Knopf, 1989. *Category:* younger reader.

3927 1991. *Is This a House for Hermit Crabs?* Megan McDonald. Orchard, 1990. *Category:* younger reader.

3928 1991. *Under the Hawthorne Tree.* Marita Conlon-McKenna. Holiday House, 1990. *Category:* older reader.

3929 1992. *Rescue Josh McGuire.* Ben Mikaelsen. Hyperion, 1991. *Category:* older readers.

3930 1992. *Ten Little Rabbits.* Virginia Grossman. *Illustrator:* Sylvia Long. Chronicle Books, 1991. *Category:* younger reader.

3931 1993. *Old Turtle.* Douglas Wood, Cheng-Khee Chee. Pfeifer-Hamilton, 1992. *Category:* younger reader.

3932 1993. *Letters from Rifka.* Karen Hesse. Henry Holt, 1992. *Category:* older reader.

3933 1994. *Sweet Clara and the Freedom Quilt.* Deborah Hopkinson. Random House, 1993. *Category:* younger reader.

3934 1994. *Behind the Secret Window.* Nelly S. Toll. Dutton, 1993. *Category:* older reader.

3935 1995. *Stranded at Plimoth Plantation, 1626.* Gary Bowen. HarperCollins, 1994. *Category:* informational readers.

3936 1995. *Spite Fences.* Trudy Krisher. Bantam Books, 1994. *Category:* older readers.

3937 1995. *The Ledgerbook of Thomas Blue Eagle.* Gay Matthaei, Jewel Grutman. Thomasson-Grant, Inc., 1994. *Category:* younger readers.

3938 1996. *The Case of the Mummified Pigs and Other Mysteries of Nature.* Susan E. Quinlan. Boyds Mills Press, 1995. *Category:* informational readers.

3939 1996. *The King's Shadow.* Elizabeth Alder. Farrar, Straus & Giroux, 1995. *Category:* older readers.

3940 1996. *More About Anything Else.* Marie Bradby, Chris K. Soentpiet. Orchard Books, 1995. *Category:* younger readers.

3941 1997. *Don't You Dare Read This, Mrs. Dunphrey.* Margaret Peterson Haddix. Simon & Schuster, 1996. *Category:* older readers.

3942 1997. *The Famous Flying Fandinis.* Ingrid Slyder. Cobblehill, 1996. *Category:* younger readers.

3943 1997. *The Brooklyn Bridge.* Elizabeth Mann. Mikaya Press, 1996. *Category:* informational readers.

3944 1998. *Moving Mama to Town.* Ronder Thomas Young. Orchard, 1997. *Category:* older readers.

3945 1998. *Nim and the War Effort.* Milly Lee, Yangsook Choi. Farrar, Straus & Giroux, 1997. *Category:* younger readers.

3946 1998. *Just What the Doctor Ordered: The History of American Medicine.* Brandon Marie Miller. Lerner, 1997. *Category:* informational readers.

3947 1999. *First in the Field: Baseball Hero Jackie Robinson.* Derek T. Dingle. Hyperion, 1998. *Category:* informational readers.

3948 1999. *Choosing Up Sides.* John H. Ritter. Philomel, 1998. *Category:* older readers.

3949 1999. *My Freedom Trip: A Child's Escape from North Korea.* Frances Park, Ginger Park. Boyds Mills Press, 1998. *Category:* younger readers.

3950 2000. *Eleanor's Story: An American Girl in Hitler's Germany.* Eleanor Ramrath Garner. Peachtree, 1999. *Category:* informational readers.

3951 2000. *Bud, Not Buddy.* Christopher Paul Curtis. Delacorte, 1999. *Category:* older readers.

3952 2000. *Molly Bannaky.* Alice McGill. Houghton Mifflin, 1999. *Category:* younger readers.

3953 2000. *The Snake Scientist.* Sy Montgomery. Houghton Mifflin, 1999. *Category:* younger readers.

3954 Iowa Children's Choice Award

SPONSOR: Iowa Educational Media Association. ADDRESS: 2306 Sixth, Harlan, Iowa 51537. ESTABLISHED: 1980. AWARD: An engraved bell. The winning author is chosen by the children of Iowa in grades 3 to 6. The work of fiction must be original, written in English, and of high literary quality. Newbery Award winners are excluded.

3955 1990. *Wait Till Helen Comes.* Mary Downing Hahn. Clarion, 1986.

3956 1991. *There's a Boy in the Girl's Bathroom.* Louis Sachar. Knopf, 1987.

3957 1992. *Fudge.* Charlotte Towner Graeber. *Illustrator:* Cheryl Harness. Lothrop, 1987.

3958 1993. *Fudge-a-Mania.* Judy Blume. Dutton, 1990.

3959 1994. *Nightmare Mountain.* Peg Kehret. Dutton, 1989.

3960 1995. *Attaboy, Sam!* Lois Lowry. *Illustrator:* Diane DeGroat. Houghton Mifflin, 1992.

3961 1996. *Terror at the Zoo.* Peg Kehret. Cobblehill, 1992.

3962 1997. *The Best School Year Ever.* Barbara Robinson. HarperCollins, 1994.

3963 1998. *Mick Harte Was Here.* Barbara Park. Knopf, 1995.

3964 1999. *Shiloh Season.* Phyllis Reynolds Naylor. Atheneum, 1996.

3965 2000. *Saving Shiloh.* Phyllis Reynolds Naylor. Atheneum, 1997.

3966 Iowa Teen Award

SPONSOR: Iowa Educational Media Association. ADDRESS: 2306 Sixth, Harlan, Iowa 51537. ESTABLISHED: 1985. AWARD: A brass apple. The annual award winner is chosen by the teens of Iowa in grades 6 to 9. The books can be either fiction or non-fiction and must have been published within the last 6 years.

3967 1990. *Hatchet.* Gary Paulsen. Bradbury, 1987.

3968 1991. *Silver.* Norma Fox Mazer. Avon, 1995.

3969 1992. *Don't Look Behind You.* Lois Duncan. Delacorte, 1989.

3970 1993. *The Face on the Milk Carton.* Caroline Cooney. Bantam, 1990.

3971 1994. *Ryan White: My Own Story.* Ryan White. Dial, 1991.

3972 1995. *Jurassic Park.* Michael Crichton. Knopf, 1990.

3973 1996. *What Ever Happened to Janie.* Caroline Cooney. Delacorte, 1993.

3974 1997. *Harris and Me.* Gary Paulsen. Harcourt Brace, 1993.

3975 1998. *Brian's Winter.* Gary Paulsen. Delacorte, 1996.

3976 1999. *Crash!* Jerry Spinelli. Knopf, 1996.

3977 2000. *Ella Enchanted.* Gail Carson Levine. HarperCollins, 1997.

3978 Irma S. and James H. Black Award

SPONSOR: Bank Street College of Education. ADDRESS: 610 West 112th Street, New York, New York 10025. PHONE: (212) 875-4540. ESTABLISHED: 1972. AWARD: A scroll and a gold seal designed by Maurice Sendak. The award is given annually for excellence both in text and illustration in a book for young children, published in the previous year.

3979 1990. *Charlie Anderson.* Barbara Abercrombie. *Illustrator:* Mark Graham. McElderry, 1990.

3980 1991. *The Enchanted Wood.* Ruth Sanderson. Little, Brown & Co., 1990.

3981 1992. *The King's Equal.* Katherine Paterson. *Illustrator:* Vladimir Vagin. HarperCollins, 1991.

3982 1993. *Three Sacks of Truth.* Eric A. Kimmel. *Illustrator:* Robert Rayevsky. Holiday, 1992.

3983 1994. *Pink and Say.* Patricia Polacco. Philomel, 1994.

3984 1995. *Wicked Jack.* Connie Nordhielm Wooldridge (adapted). *Illustrator:* Will Hillenbrand. Holiday, 1994.

3985 1996. *Jojofu.* Michael P. Waite. *Illustrator:* Yoriko Ito. Lothrop, Lee & Shepard, 1995.

3986 1997. *Akiak: A Tale from the Iditarod.* Robert J. Blake. *Illustrator:* Robert J. Blake. Philomel Books, 1997.

3987 1998. *Raising Dragons.* Jerdine Nolen. *Illustrator:* Elise Primavera. Silver-Whistle, 1997.

3988 1998. *Zak's Lunch.* Margie Palatini. *Illustrator:* Howard Fine. Clarion, 1997.

3989 1999. *Tasty Baby Belly Buttons.* Judy Sierra. *Illustrator:* Meilo So. Knopf/Random House, 1998.

3990 1999. *A Dog Like Jack.* DyAnne DiSalvo-Ryan. Holiday House, 1998.

3991 Jane Addams Children's Book Award

SPONSOR: Jane Addams Peace Association. CONTACT: Jean Gore. ADDRESS: 777 United Nations Plaza, New York, New York 10017. PHONE: (303) 447-8668. ESTABLISHED: 1953. AWARD: A hand-illustrated scroll and silver seals affixed to the book jackets by the publisher. The award is presented annually for a book that most effectively promotes the cause of peace, social justice, world community, and the equality of the sexes and all races. The book must be published in the previous year and may be translated or published in English in other countries. Beginning in 1993, a Picture Book category was added to the award.

3992 1990. *Long Hard Journey.* Patricia McKissack, Frederick McKissack. *Illustrator:* photographs. Walker, 1990. *Level:* Gr. 7–9.

3993 1991. *The Big Book for Peace.* Ann Durell (editor), Marilyn Sachs, Dutton, 1990.

3994 1992. *Journey of the Sparrows.* Fran Leeper Buss, Daisy Cubias. Lodestar, 1991.

3995 1993. *A Taste of Salt: A Story of Modern Haiti.* Frances Temple. Orchard, 1992. *Category:* longer book.

3996 1993. *Aunt Harriet's Underground Railroad in the Sky.* Faith Ringgold. *Illustrator:* Faith Ringgold. Crown, 1992. *Category:* picture book.

3997 1994. *Freedom's Children: Young Civil Rights Activists Tell Their Stories.* Ellen Levine. G.P. Putnam's, 1993. *Category:* longer book.

3998 1994. *This Land Is My Land.* George Littlechild. *Illustrator:* George Littlechild. Children's Book Press, 1993. *Category:* picture book.

3999 1995. *Kids at Work: Lewis Hine and the Crusade Against Child Labor.* Russell Freedman. Clarion, 1994. *Category:* longer book.

4000 1995. *Sitti's Secrets.* Naomi Shihab Nye. *Illustrator:* Nancy Carpenter. Four Winds Press, 1994. *Category:* picture book.

1996. No award given. *Category:* picture book.

4001 1996. *The Well: David's Story.* Mildred D. Taylor. Dial Books for Young Readers, 1995. *Category:* longer book.

4002 1997. *Growing Up in Coal County.* Susan Campbell Bartoletti. Houghton Mifflin, 1996. *Category:* longer book.

4003 1997. *Wilma Unlimited.* Kathleen Krull. *Illustrator:* David Diaz. Harcourt Brace, 1996. *Category:* picture book.

4004 1998. *Habibi.* Naomi Shihab Nye. Simon & Schuster, 1997. *Category:* longer book.

4005 1998. *Seven Brave Women.* Betsy Hearne. *Illustrator:* Bethanne Andersen. Greenwillow, 1997. *Category:* picture book.

4006 1999. *Bat 6.* Virginia Euwer Wolff. Scholastic Press, 1998. *Category:* longer book.

4007 1999. *Painted Words/Spoken Memories: Marianthe's Story.* Aliki. *Illustrator:* Aliki. Greenwillow, 1998. *Category:* picture book.

4008 2000. *Through My Eyes.* Ruby Bridges. Scholastic Press, 1999. *Category:* longer book.

4009 2000. *Molly Bannaky.* Alice McGill. *Illustrator:* Chris K. Soentpiet. Houghton Mifflin, 1999. *Category:* picture book.

4010 Jefferson Cup Award

SPONSOR: Virginia Library Association. CONTACT: Ilze B. Long. ADDRESS: 80 South Early Street, Alexandria, Virginia 22304. ESTABLISHED: 1983. AWARD: An engraved silver cup and $100.00 U.S. The award honors the writer of the best book for children or young adults in the field of American history, historical fiction or American biographies. The book must be an original publication about an American person set between 1492 and the present. The author must reside in the United States.

4011 1990. *Shades of Gray.* Carolyn Reeder. Macmillan, 1989.

4012 1991. *Franklin Delano Roosevelt.* Russell Freedman. Clarion, 1990.

4013 1992. *The Wright Brothers.* Russell Freedman. Holiday House, 1991.

4014 1993. *Children of the Dust Bowl.* Jerry Stanley. Crown, 1992.

4015 1994. *Across America in an Emigrant Train.* Jim Murphy. Clarion, 1993.

4016 1995. *Pink and Say.* Patricia Polacco. Philomel, 1994.

4017 1996. *The Great Fire.* Jim Murphy. Scholastic, 1995.

4018 1997. *The Ornament Tree.* Jean Thesman. Houghton Mifflin, 1996.

4019 1998. *Leon's Story.* Leon Walter Tillage. Farrar, 1997.

4020 1999. *Soldier's Heart.* Gary Paulsen. Delacorte, 1998.

4021 2000. *Preacher's Boy.* Katherine Paterson. Houghton Mifflin, 1999.

4022 Jeremiah Ludington Memorial Award

SPONSOR: Educational Paperback Association. CONTACT: Marilyn Abel. ADDRESS: P.O. Box 1399, East Hampton, New York 11937. PHONE: 92120 879-6850. ESTABLISHED: 1978. AWARD: A framed certificate and $1,000.00 U.S. The award is presented annually to an individual who has made a significant contribution to the paperback book business.

4023 1990. Patricia Reilly Giff.
4024 1991. Norman Bridwell.
4025 1992. Bernice Culliman.
4026 1993. Walter Dean Myers.
4027 1994. Gary Paulsen.
4028 1995. Katherine Paterson.
4029 1996. Barbara Elleman.
4030 1997. Doris Bass.
4031 1998. Lois Lowry.

4032 Jo Osborne Award for Humor in Children's Literature

SPONSOR: Ohio Library Foundation. ADDRESS: 35 East Gay Street, Suite 305, Columbus, Ohio 43215. ESTABLISHED: 1995. The award recognizes authors and illustrators who have caused us to laugh or smile while reading. A jury of librarians, teachers, authors, illustrators, and academics select a winner. The award may honor just one book or a body of work.

4033 1995. Patricia Polacco.
4034 1996. Sid Fleischman.
4035 1997. Steven Kellogg.
4036 1998. Steven Kellogg.
4037 1999. Jon Scieszka.
4038 2000. William Steig.

4039 John and Patricia Beatty Award

SPONSOR: California Library Association. ADDRESS: 717 K Street, Suite 300, Sacramento, California 95814-3477. PHONE: (916) 447-8541. ESTABLISHED: 1988. AWARD: An engraved plaque and $500.00 U.S. The award is given "to encourage the writing of quality children's books highlighting California, its culture, heritage and/or future." Any children's book set in California and published in the United States during the preceding calendar year are eligible.

4040 1990. *The Great American Goldrush.* Rhoda Blumberg. Bradbury, 1989.
4041 1991. *Baseball in April: And Other Stories.* Gary Soto. Harcourt Brace Jovanovich, 1990.
4042 1992. *Sierra.* Diane Siebert. *Illustrator:* Wendell Minor. HarperCollins, 1991.
4043 1993. *Children of the Dust Bowl.* Jerry Stanley. Crown, 1992.
4044 1994. *Dragon's Gate.* Laurence Yep. HarperCollins, 1993.
4045 1995. *Cat Running.* Zilpha Keatley Snyder. Delacorte, 1994.

4046 1996. *Summer on Wheels.* Gary Soto. Scholastic, 1995.

4047 1997. *The Ballad of Lucy Whipple.* Karen Cushman. Clarion, 1996.

4048 1998. *The Circuit: Stories from the Life of a Migrant Child.* Francisco Jiménez. University of New Mexico Press, 1997.

4049 1999. *Bandit's Moon.* Sid Fleischman. Greenwillow Books, 1998.

4050 2000. *The Perilous Journey of the Donner Party.* Marian Calabro. Clarion Books, 1999.

4051 John Newbery Award

SPONSOR: American Library Association. ADDRESS: 50 East Huron Street, Chicago, Illinois 60611. PHONE: 1-800-545-2433. ESTABLISHED: 1922. AWARD: A gold medal and certificate. The award is given annually to the author who has made the most distinguished contribution to American literature for children.

4052 1990. *Shabanu Daughter of the Wind.* Suzanne Fisher Staples. *Illustrator:* Stephen T. Johnson. Knopf, 1989. *Category:* honor.

4053 1990. *Number the Stars.* Lois Lowry. Houghton Mifflin, 1989.

4054 1990. *The Winter Room.* Gary Paulsen. *Illustrator:* John Ward. Orchard, 1989. *Category:* honor.

4055 1990. *Afternoon of the Elves.* Janet Taylor Lisle. *Illustrator:* Ponder Goembel. Orchard, 1989. *Category:* honor.

4056 1991. *Maniac Magee.* Jerry Spinelli. Little, Brown & Co., 1990.

4057 1991. *The True Confessions of Charlotte Doyle.* Avi. Jackson/Orchard, 1990. *Category:* honor.

4058 1992. *Shiloh.* Phyllis Reynolds Naylor. Atheneum, 1991.

4059 1992. *Nothing but the Truth: A Documentary Novel.* Avi. Jackson/Orchard, 1991. *Category:* honor.

4060 1992. *The Wright Brothers.* Russell Freedman. Holiday House, 1991. *Category:* honor.

4061 1993. *What Hearts.* Bruce Brooks. HarperCollins, 1992. *Category:* honor.

4062 1993. *Missing May.* Cynthia Rylant. Jackson/Orchard, 1992.

4063 1993. *The Dark-Thirty: Southern Tales of the Supernatural.* Patricia McKissack. Knopf, 1992. *Category:* honor.

4064 1993. *Somewhere in the Darkness.* Walter Dean Myers. Scholastic, 1992. *Category:* honor.

4065 1994. *Eleanor Roosevelt: A Life of Discovery.* Russell Freedman. Clarion Books, 1993. *Category:* honor.

4066 1994. *Dragon's Gate.* Laurence Yep. HarperCollins, 1993. *Category:* honor.

4067 1994. *Crazy Lady.* Jane Leslie Conly. HarperCollins, 1993. *Category:* honor.
4068 1994. *The Giver.* Lois Lowry. Houghton Mifflin, 1993.
4069 1995. *The Ear, the Eye and the Arm.* Nancy Farmer. Jackson/Orchard, 1994. *Category:* honor.
4070 1995. *Catherine, Called Birdy.* Karen Cushman. Clarion, 1994. *Category:* honor.
4071 1995. *Walk Two Moons.* Sharon Creech. HarperCollins, 1994.
4072 1996. *What Jamie Saw.* Carolyn Coman. Front Street, 1995. *Category:* honor.
4073 1996. *The Great Fire.* Jim Murphy. Scholastic, 1995. *Category:* honor.
4074 1996. *The Watsons Go to Birmingham: 1963.* Christopher Paul Curtis. Delacorte, 1995. *Category:* honor.
4075 1996. *The Midwife's Apprentice.* Karen Cushman. Clarion, 1995.
4076 1996. *Yolonda's Genius.* Carol Fenner. Margaret McElderry, 1995. *Category:* honor.
4077 1997. *The Moorchild.* Eloise McGraw. Margaret McElderry, 1996. *Category:* honor.
4078 1997. *The Thief.* Megan Whalen Turner. Greenwillow, 1996. *Category:* honor.
4079 1997. *A Girl Named Disaster.* Nancy Farmer. Jackson/Orchard, 1996. *Category:* honor.
4080 1997. *The View from Saturday.* E.L. Konigsburg. Jean Karl. Atheneum, 1996.
4081 1997. *Belle Prater's Boy.* Ruth White. Farrar Straus Giroux, 1996. *Category:* honor.
4082 1998. *Out of the Dust.* Karen Hesse. Scholastic, 1997.
4083 1998. *Wringer.* Jerry Spinelli. HarperCollins, 1997. *Category:* honor.
4084 1998. *Ella Enchanted.* Gail Carson Levine. HarperCollins, 1997. *Category:* honor.
4085 1998. *Lily's Crossing.* Patricia Reilly Giff. Delacorte, 1997. *Category:* honor.
4086 1999. *A Long Way from Chicago.* Richard Peck. Dial, 1998. *Category:* honor.
4087 1999. *Holes.* Louis Sachar. Farrar Straus Giroux, 1998.
4088 2000. *Bud, Not Buddy.* Christopher Paul Curtis. Delacorte, 1999.
4089 2000. *Getting Near to Baby.* Audrey Couloumbis. Putnam, 1999. *Category:* honor.
4090 2000. *Our Only May Amelia.* Jennifer L. Holm. HarperCollins, 1999. *Category:* honor.
4091 2000. *26 Fairmount Avenue.* Tomie de Paola. Putnam, 1999. *Category:* honor.

4092 Josette Frank Award (formerly the Children's Book Award)

SPONSOR: Children's Book Committee at Bank Street College of Education. ADDRESS: 610 W. 112th Street, New York, New York 10025. PHONE: (212)-875-4540. ESTABLISHED: 1997. The award is given annually for fiction of outstanding literary merit in which children and young adults deal in a positive and realistic way with difficulties in their world and grow emotionaly and morally.

4093 1997. *No Turning Back: A Novel of South Africa.* Beverley Naidoo. HarperCollins, 1997.
4094 1998. *My Louisiana Sky.* Kimberly Willis Holt. Henry Holt & Co., 1998.
4095 1999. *Figuring Out Frances.* Gina Willner-Pardo. Clarion Books, 1999.

4096 Judy Lopez Memorial Award for Children's Literature

SPONSOR: Women's National Book Association/LA. CONTACT: Margaret Flanders, Chair. ADDRESS: 1225 Selby Ave., Los Angeles, California 90024. PHONE: (310) 474-9917. The award honors the best American book for 9–12 year olds.

4097 1991. *The True Confessions of Charlotte Doyle.* Avi. Orchard, 1990.
4098 1992. *Blue Skin of the Sea.* Graham Salibury. Bantam/Doubleday/Dell.
4099 1993. *The Boggart.* Susan Cooper. McElderry.
4100 1997. *Habibi.* Naomi Shihab Nye. Simon and Schuster, 1997.
4101 1997. *Red Scarf Girl: A Memoir of the Cultural Revolution.* Ji-li Jiang. HarperCollins, 1997.

4102 Keene (New Hampshire) State College Children's Literature Festival Award

SPONSOR: Keene State College. CONTACT: David White. ADDRESS: Keene State College, 229 Main St., Keene, New Hampshire 03435-2611. ESTABLISHED: 1986. AWARD: An engraved pewter Revere bowl and a cash award. The award is given to an author and/or illustrator who has made outstanding contributions over a period of at least ten years, is currently writing or illustrating, and whose body of work shows variety and diversity while maintaining the highest standards in literature for children.

4103 1990. Betsy Byars.
4104 1991. Trina Schart Hyman.
4105 1992. Eric Carle.
4106 1993. Natalie Babbitt.
4107 1994. Patricia McKissack.
4108 1995. Jane Yolen.
4109 1996. Jerry Pinkney.
4110 1997. Jean Fritz.

4111 1998. Tomie de Paola.

4112 1999. Lois Lowry.

4113 Kentucky Bluegrass Award

SPONSOR: Northern Kentucky University Learning Resource Center. CONTACT: Jennifer Smith. ADDRESS: W. Frank Steely Library, Highland Heights, Kentucky 41099. PHONE: (859) 572-6620. ESTABLISHED: 1982. The annual award is presented to encourage Kentucky children to read a wide variety of books for their enjoyment. It is divided into two categories: K–3, 4–8. Children vote on their favorite books.

4114 1990. *The Lady with the Alligator Purse.* Nadine Wescott. *Illustrator:* Nadine Wescott. Little, Brown & Co., 1988. *Level:* K–3.

4115 1990. *The Stranger.* Chris van Allsburg. *Illustrator:* Chris van Allsberg. Houghton Mifflin, 1988. *Level:* 4–8.

4116 1991. *Chicka Chicka Boom Boom.* Bill Martin, Jr. John Archambault. *Illustrator:* Lois Ehlert. Simon & Schuster, 1989. *Level:* K–3.

4117 1991. *The Butterfly Jar.* Jeff Moss. *Illustrator:* Chris Demarest. Bantam, 1989. *Level:* 4–8.

4118 1992. *Something Big Has Been Here.* Jack Prelutsky. *Illustrator:* James Stevenson. Greenwillow, 1990. *Level:* 4–8.

4119 1992. *Basket.* George Ella Lyon. *Illustrator:* Mary Szaligyi. Orchard, 1990. *Level:* K–3.

4120 1993. *Brother Eagle, Sister Sky.* Susan Jeffers. *Illustrator:* Susan Jeffers. Dial, 1991. *Level:* 4–8.

4121 1993. *Tuesday.* David Wiesner. Clarion, 1991. *Level:* K–3.

4122 1994. *Pigs Aplenty, Pigs Galore!* David McPhail. *Illustrator:* David McPhail. Puffin, 1992. *Level:* K–3.

4123 1994. *Bob and Jack: A Boy and His Yak.* Jeff Moss. *Illustrator:* Chris Demarest. Bantam, 1992. *Level:* 4-8.

4124 1995. *The Hero of Bremen.* Margaret Hodges (retold). *Illustrator:* Charles Mikolaycak. Holiday House, 1993. *Level:* 4-8.

4125 1995. *The Cow Who Wouldn't Come Down.* Paul B. Johnson. Orchard, 1993. *Level:* K–3.

4126 1996. *The Christmas of the Reddle Moon.* J. Patrick Lewis. *Illustrator:* Gary Kelley. Dial, 1994. *Level:* 4–8.

4127 1996. *Harvey Potter's Balloon Farm.* Jerdine Harold Nolan. *Illustrator:* Mark Buehner. Mulberry, 1994. *Level:* K–3.

4128 1997. *Officer Buckle and Gloria.* Peggy Rathmann. Putnam, 1995. *Level:* K–3.

4129 1997. *Piggie Pie!* Margie Palatini. *Illustrator:* Howard Fine. Clarion, 1995. *Level:* 4–8.

4130 1998. *Lilly's Purple Plastic Purse.* Kevin Henkes. Greenwillow, 1996. *Level:* K–3.

4131 1998. *Minty: A Story of Young Harriet Tubman.* Alan Schroeder. *Illustrator:* Jerry Pinkney. Dial, 1996. *Level:* 4–8.

4132 1999. *A Perfect Pork Stew.* Paul B. Johnson. Orchard, 1997. *Level:* K–3.

4133 1999. *Christopher Changes His Name.* Itah Sadu. *Illustrator:* Roy Condy. Firefly, 1997. *Level:* 4–8.

4134 2000. *Smoky Mountain Rose.* Alan Schroeder. *Illustrator:* Brad Sneed. Dial, 1998. *Level:* 4–8.

4135 2000. *Hooway for Wodney Wat.* Helen Lester. *Illustrator:* Lynn Munsinger. Houghton Mifflin, 1998. *Level:* K–3.

4136 Kerlan Award

SPONSOR: Children's Literature Research Collections. ADDRESS: University of Minnesota, 113 Andersen, Lib., 221 21st Ave. Minneapolis, Minnesota 55455. PHONE: (612) 624-4576. ESTABLISHED: 1975. AWARD: A plaque. The award is presented annually "in recognition of singular attainments in the creation of children's literature and in appreciation for generous donation of unique resources to the Kerlan Collection for the study of children's literature."

4137 1990. Madeleine L'Engle.

4138 1991. Leonard Everett Fisher.

4139 1992. Barbara Cooney.

4140 1993. Mary Stolz.

4141 1994. Myra Cohn Livingston.

4142 1995. Phyllis Reynolds Naylor.

4143 1995. Margot Tomes.

4144 1996. Marion Dane Bauer.

4145 1996. Paul Galdone.

4146 1997. Theodore Taylor.

4147 1998. Dahlov Ipcar.

4148 1999. Norine Odland.

4149 1999. Edward B Stanford.

4150 1999. Lois Lenski.

4151 1999. Eve Bunting.

4152 2000. Irvin Kerlan.

4153 2000. Patricia Lauber.

4154 Knickerbocker Award for Juvenile Literature

SPONSOR: School Library Media Section of the New York Library. CONTACT: Jacalyn Groves, Edward R. Andrews Elementary School. ADDRESS: Box 990, Morrisville, New York 13408. ESTABLISHED: 1991. AWARD: A crystal award. The award recognizes a New York State author who has demonstrated, through a body of work, a consistently superior quality which supports the curriculum and the educational goals of New York State schools. It is presented annually to a living author/illustrator currently residing in New York State.

4155 1991. Jean Craighead George.
4156 1992. Jean Fritz.
4157 1993. Russell Freedman.
4158 1994. Seymour Simon.
4159 1995. Robert Kimmel Smith.
4160 1996. Joseph Bruchac.
4161 1997. Bruce Coville.
4162 1998. Cynthia DeFelice.
4163 1999. M.E. Kerr.
4164 2000. Mary Jane Auch.

4165 Land of Enchantment Book Award

SPONSOR: New Mexico Library Association. CONTACT: Peggy Twyeffort. ADDRESS: 220 W. 5th St., Truth or Consequences, New Mexico 87901. PHONE: (505) 894-2257. ESTABLISHED: 1981. AWARD: A Nambé plate with the award logo etched in the center. The award is given annually for a book of literary merit with appeal for children in grades 3 to 9. The book must have been published within the last 5 years and currently be in print. The winning author must be living in the United States at the time of nomination and is excluded from competition the following year.

4166 1990. *There's a Boy in the Girl's Bathroom.* Louis Sachar. Knopf, 1987.
4167 1991. *Pecos Bill: A Tall Tale.* Steven Kellogg. William Morrow, 1986.
4168 1992. *Wayside School Is Falling Down.* Louis Sachar. *Illustrator:* Joel Schick. Lothrop, Lee & Shepard, 1989.
4169 1993. *Maniac Magee.* Jerry Spinelli. Little, Brown & Co., 1989.
4170 1994. *Shiloh.* Phyllis Reynolds Naylor. Atheneum, 1991.
4171 1995. *Terror at the Zoo.* Peg Kehert. Cobblehill, 1992.
4172 1996. *Knights of the Kitchen Table.* Jon Scieszka. *Illustrator:* Lane Smith. Viking, 1991.
4173 1997. *The Giver.* Lois Lowry. Houghton Mifflin, 1993.
4174 1998. *The Best School Year Ever.* Barbara Robinson. HarperCollins, 1994.
4175 1999. *Poppy.* Avi. *Illustrator:* Brian Floca. Orchard, 1995.
4176 2000. *Library Lil.* Suzanne Williams. *Illustrator:* Steven Kellogg. Dial, 1997. *Category:* Children's Division.
4177 2000. *The Watsons Go to Birmingham: 1963.* Christopher Paul Curtis. Delacorte, 1995. *Category:* young adult Division.

4178 Laura Ingalls Wilder Award

SPONSOR: American Library Association. ADDRESS: 50 East Huron Street, Chicago, Illinois 60611. PHONE: 1-800-545-2433. ESTABLISHED: 1954. AWARD: A medal designed by Garth Williams. The award is presented to an author or illustrator whose books have made a substantial and lasting contribution to literature for children for a period of years. The books must be published in the United States. Until 1980, the award was given every five years, and now it is given every three years.

4179 1992. Marcia Brown.
4180 1995. Virginia Hamilton.
4181 1998. Russell Freedman.

4182 Lee Bennett Hopkins Promising Poet Award

SPONSOR: International Reading Association. ADDRESS: PO Box 8139, Newark, Delaware 19714-8139. PHONE: (302) 731-1600. ESTABLISHED: 1995. AWARD: $500.00. The award is given every three years to a promising new author of children's poetry (for children and young adults up to Grade 12) who has published no more than two books of children's poetry. A book-length single poem may be submitted. "Children's Poetry" is defined as poetry, rather than light verse. The award is for published works only.

4183 1995. Deborah Chandra.
4184 1998. Kristine O'Connell.

4185 Little Archer Award (now WEMA Golden Archer Award)

Discontinued. ESTABLISHED: 1976. The Golden Archer Award and the Little Archer Award were given for books in two levels (K through 8), from 1974 to, 1992.

4186 1990. *Tub People.* Pam Conrad. Harper & Row, 1989.
4187 1991. *Borrequita and the Coyote.* Verna Aardema. Knopf/Random House, 1991.
4188 1992. *Easter Egg Farm.* Mary Jane Auch. Holiday House, 1992.

4189 Louisiana Young Readers' Choice Award

SPONSOR: State Library of Louisiana. CONTACT: Youth Services Consultant. ADDRESS: PO Box 131, Baton Rouge, Louisiana 70821. PHONE: (225) 342-3547. ESTABLISHED: 2000. The award is given for literary excellence in a children's book. Children vote for their favorite book.

4190 2000. *Verdi.* Janell Cannon. *Illustrator:* Janell Cannon. Harcourt Brace, 1997.

4191 Lupine Award

SPONSOR: Maine Library Association. ADDRESS: Community Drive, Augusta, Maine 04330. ESTABLISHED: 1989. The annual award is given to recognize an outstanding contribution to children's literature of Maine. It honors a living author or illustrator who is a resident of Maine, or who has created a work whose focus is Maine, as shown through the work's characterization, plot or setting. An author or artist will be considered a resident if he or she was born in this state, or is currently residing in Maine for all or part of the year.

4192 1990. *Hattie and the Wild Waves.* Barbara Cooney. *Illustrator:* Barbara Cooney. Viking, 1990.

4193 1991. *Rosebud and Red Flannel.* Ethel Pochocki. *Illustrator:* Mary Beth Owens. Holt, 1990.

4194 1992. *Sing to the Sun.* Ashley Bryan. *Illustrator:* Ashley Bryan. Harper Trophy, 1996.

4195 1993. *Wild Fox.* Cherie Mason. *Illustrator:* Jo Ellen MacAllister Stammen. Down East Books, 1993.

4196 1994. *Prize in the Snow.* Bill Easterling. *Illustrator:* Mary Beth Owens. Little, Brown & Co., 1994.

4197 1995. *A Year on Monhegan Island.* Julia Dean. Ticknor & Fields, 1995.

4198 1996. *Grandmother Bryant's Pocket.* Jacqueline Briggs Martin. *Illustrator:* Petra Mathers. Houghton Mifflin, 1996.

4199 1997. *Marven of the Great North Woods.* Kathryn Lasky. *Illustrator:* Kevin Hawkes. Harcourt Brace, 1997.

4200 1998. *Snowflake Bentley.* Jacqueline Briggs Martin. *Illustrator:* Mary Azarian. Houghton Mifflin, 1998.

4201 1999. *Seal Island School.* Susan Bartlett. *Illustrator:* Tricia Tusa. Viking, 1999.

4202 Maine Student Book Award

SPONSOR: Maine Library Association. ADDRESS: Windham Public Library 217 Windham, Center Road, Windham, Maine 04062. PHONE: (207)-892-1908. ESTABLISHED: 1990. The annual award is given for the most popular title published for young readers in the preceeding year. It is chosen by the readers from an annotated list of outstanding fiction and non-fiction for grades 4-8 throughout the state of Maine.

4203 1991. *Number the Stars.* Lois Lowry. Houghton Mifflin, 1989.

4204 1992. *Fudge-a-Mania.* Judy Blume. Dutton, 1990.

4205 1993. *Shiloh.* Phyllis Reynolds Naylor. Atheneum, 1991.

4206 1994. *The Stinky Cheese Man and Other Fairly Stupid Tales.* Jon Scieszka. *Illustrator:* Lane Smith. Viking, 1992.

4207 1995. *The Giver.* Lois Lowry. Houghton Mifflin, 1993.

4208 1996. *Pink and Say.* Patricia Polacco. Philomel, 1994.
4209 1997. *Math Curse.* Jon Scieszka. *Illustrator:* Lane Smith. Viking, 1995.
4210 1998. *Falling Up.* Shel Silverstein. HarperCollins, 1996.
4211 1999. *Ella Enchanted.* Gail Carson Levine. HarperCollins, 1997.
4212 2000. *Holes.* Louis Sachar. Farrar Straus Giroux, 1998.

4213 Margaret A. Edwards Award (YASD/School Library Journal Young Adult Author Award)

SPONSOR: American Library Association, Young Adult Services Division. ADDRESS: 50 East Huron Street, Chicago, Illinois 60611. PHONE: (312) 280-4390. ESTABLISHED: 1988. AWARD: A citation and $2,000.00 U.S. The annual award honors an author's lifetime achievement for writing books that have been popular with teenagers. The books must be published in the United States no less than five years prior to nominations.

4214 1990. Richard Peck.
4215 1991. Robert Cormier.
4216 1992. Lois Duncan.
4217 1993. M.E. Kerr.
4218 1994. Walter Dean Myers.
4219 1995. Cynthia Voigt.
4220 1996. Judy Blume.
4221 1997. Gary Paulsen.
4222 1998. Madeleine L'Engle.
4223 1999. Anne McCaffrey.
4224 2000. Chris Crutcher.

4225 Mark Twain Award

SPONSOR: Missouri Association of School Librarians. ADDRESS: 1552 Rue Riviera, Bonne Terre, Missouri 63628-9349. ESTABLISHED: 1972. AWARD: A bronze bust of Mark Twain. The award is given annually to the author who receives the most votes from the children of Missouri. Books must be written by an author living in the United States. Fiction and non-fiction titles are eligible.

4226 1990. *There's a Boy in the Girl's Bathroom.* Louis Sachar. Knopf, 1987.
4227 1991. *All About Sam.* Lois Lowry. *Illustrator:* Diane DeGroat. Houghton Mifflin, 1988.
4228 1992. *The Doll in the Garden: A Ghost Story.* Mary Downing Hahn. Clarion, 1989.
4229 1993. *Maniac Magee.* Jerry Spinelli. Little, Brown & Co., 1990.
4230 1994. *Shiloh.* Phyllis Reynolds Naylor. Atheneum, 1991.
4231 1995. *The Man Who Loved Clowns.* June Rae Wood. Putnam, 1992.

4232 1996. *The Ghosts of Mercy Manor.* Betty Ren Wright. Scholastic, 1993.

4233 1997. *Time for Andrew: A Ghost Story.* Mary Downing Hahn. Clarion, 1994.

4234 1998. *Titanic Crossing.* Barbara Williams. Dial Books for Young Readers, 1995.

4235 1999. *Small Steps: The Year I Got Polio.* Peg Kehret. Albert Whitman & Co, 1996.

4236 2000. *Saving Shiloh.* Phyllis Reynolds Naylor. Atheneum, 1997.

4237 Maryland Children's Book Award

SPONSOR: Maryland International Reading Association Council. CONTACT: Gerri Frazier. ADDRESS: 43898 Barnegate Way, Leonardtown, Maryland, 20650. PHONE: (301) 863-4095. ESTABLISHED: 1988. The award winners are chosen by the Maryland children in three categories: primary, middle school and intermediate. The award winning author must be living in the U.S.A. and the nominated titles must currently be in print.

4238 1990. *The Haunting of Cabin 13.* Kristi Holl. Royal Fireworks, 1997.

4239 1991. *The Doll in the Garden: A Ghost Story.* Mary Downing Hahn. Clarion, 1989. *Category:* intermediate.

4240 1992. *My Teacher Is an Alien.* Bruce Coville. *Illustrator:* Mike Wimmer. Minstrel Books, 1990. *Category:* intermediate.

4241 1993. *Grasshopper Summer.* Ann Turner. Troll, 1991. *Category:* intermediate.

4242 1993. *Two Bad Ants.* Chris van Allsburg. *Illustrator:* Chris van Allsburg. Houghton Mifflin, 1988. *Category:* primary.

4243 1994. *High Wire Henry.* Mary Calhoun. *Illustrator:* Erick Ingraham. William Morrow, 1991. *Category:* primary.

4244 1994. *Danger in Quicksand Swamp.* Bill Wallace. Holiday House, 1989. *Category:* intermediate.

4245 1994. *Sniper.* Theodore Taylor. Harcourt Brace, 1989. *Category:* middle school.

4246 1995. *Flight #116 Is Down.* Caroline Cooney. Scholastic, 1992. *Category:* middle school.

4247 1995. *Hurricane City.* Sarah Weeks. *Illustrator:* James Warhola. HarperCollins, 1993. *Category:* primary.

4248 1995. *The Boys Start the War.* Phyllis Reynolds Naylor. Delacorte, 1993. *Category:* intermediate.

4249 1996. *Randall's Wall.* Carol Fenner. Margaret McElderry, 1991. *Category:* middle school.

4250 1996. *Dogs Don't Wear Sneakers.* Laura Joffe Numeroff. *Illustrator:* Joe Mathieu. Simon & Schuster, 1993. *Category:* primary.

4251 1996. *Time for Andrew: A Ghost Story.* Mary Downing Hahn. Clarion, 1994. *Category:* intermediate.

4252 1997. *Poison Ivy and Eyebrow Wigs.* Bonnie Pryor. *Illustrator:* Gail Owens. William Morrow, 1993. *Category:* intermediate.

4253 1997. *Cadillac.* Charles Temple. *Illustrator:* Lynne N. Lockhart. Putnam, 1995. *Category:* primary.

4254 1997. *Freak the Mighty.* Rodman Philbrick. Scholastic, 1993. *Category:* middle school.

4255 1998. *Poppy.* Avi. *Illustrator:* Brian Floca. Orchard, 1995. *Category:* intermediate.

4256 1998. *Stranded.* Ben Mikaelsen. Hyperion, 1995. *Category:* middle school.

4257 1998. *Tops and Bottoms.* Janet Stevens. *Illustrator:* Janet Stevens. Harcourt Brace, 1995. *Category:* primary.

4258 1999. *Verdi.* Janell Cannon. Harcourt Brace, 1997. *Category:* primary.

4259 1999. *Crash!* Jerry Spinelli. Knopf, 1996. *Category:* middle school.

4260 1999. *Santa Paws.* Nicholas Edwards. Scholastic, 1996. *Category:* intermediate.

4261 2000. *The Polar Bear Son.* Lydia Dabcovich. *Illustrator:* Lydia Dabcovich. Clarion Books, 1997. *Category:* primary.

4262 2000. *Tangerine.* Edward Bloor. Harcourt Brace, 1997. *Category:* middle school.

4263 2000. *My Life as a Fifth-Grade Comedian.* Elizabeth Levy. HarperCollins, 1997. *Category:* intermediate.

4264 Massachusetts Children's Book Award

SPONSOR: Division of Graduate and Continuing Education, Salem State College. CONTACT: Dr. Diane E. Bushner. ADDRESS: Salem State College, 352 Lafayette Street, Salem, Massachusetts 01970-5353. PHONE: (978) 542-7042. ESTABLISHED: 1976. AWARD: A Paul Revere bowl. The award is given annually for primary fiction, paperback books appropriate for readers at grades 4 to 6.

1990. No award given.

4265 1991. *There's a Boy in the Girl's Bathroom.* Louis Sachar. Knopf, 1987.

4266 1992. *Matilda.* Roald Dahl. *Illustrator:* Quentin Blake. Viking, 1988.

4267 1993. *Maniac Magee.* Jerry Spinelli. Little, Brown & Co., 1990.

4268 1994. *Shiloh.* Phyllis Reynolds Naylor. Atheneum, 1991.

4269 1995. *Hatchet.* Gary Paulsen. Bradbury, 1987.

4270 1996. *The True Confessions of Charlotte Doyle.* Avi. Jackson/Orchard, 1990.

4271 1997. *Wayside School Gets a Little Stranger.* Louis Sachar. Morrow, 1995.

4272 1998. *Crash!* Jerry Spinelli. Knopf, 1996.

4273 1999. *Frindle.* Andrew Clements. *Illustrator:* Brian Selznick. Simon & Schuster, 1996.

4274 2000. *Harry Potter and the Sorcerer's Stone.* J.K. Rowling. *Illustrator:* Mary Grandpré. Scholastic, 1998.

4275 Maud Hart Lovelace Book Award

SPONSOR: Friends of the Minnesota Valley Regional Library. CONTACT: Phyllis Deer. ADDRESS: 10380 250th St. E., Lakeville, Minnesota 55044. ESTABLISHED: 1982. AWARD: A plaque. The annual award is given to the author who receives the most votes from the children of Minnesota in grades 3 to 8.

4276 1990. *Wait Til Helen Comes.* Mary Downing Hahn. Clarion, 1986.

4277 1991. *Hatchet.* Gary Paulsen. Bradbury, 1987.

4278 1992. *This Island Isn't Big Enough for the Four of Us.* Gary Greer, Bob Ruddick. Harper. Trophy, 1989.

4279 1993. *The Dead Man in Indian Creek.* Mary Downing Hahn. Clarion, 1990.

4280 1994. *38 Weeks Til Summer Vacation.* Mona Kerby. Econo-Clad Books, 1999.

4281 1995. *Nightmare Mountain.* Peg Kehret. Dutton, 1989.

4282 1996. *Cages.* Peg Kehret. Minstrel Books, 1993.

4283 1997. *The Summer I Shrank My Grandmother.* Elvira Woodruff. *Illustrator:* Katherine Coville. Yearling, 1992. *Category:* division I.

4284 1997. *The Devil's Arithmetic.* Jane Yolen. Viking, 1988. *Category:* division II.

4285 1998. *Mick Harte Was Here.* Barbara Park. Knopf, 1995. *Category:* division I and ll.

4286 1999. *Frindle.* Andrew Clements. *Illustrator:* Brian Selznick. Simon & Schuster, 1996. *Category:* division I.

4287 1999. *Crash!* Jerry Spinelli. Knopf, 1996. *Category:* division II.

4288 2000. *Danger in the Desert.* Terri Fields. Rising Moon, 1997. *Category:* division I.

4289 2000. *Tangerine.* Edward Bloor. Harcourt, 1997. *Category:* division II.

4290 Michael L. Printz Award

SPONSOR: American Library Association. ADDRESS: 50 E. Huron, Chicago, Illinois 60611. PHONE: 1-800-545-2433. ESTABLISHED: 2000. AWARD: citation. The award is given for a book that exemplifies literary excellence in young adult literature. The award-winning book can be fiction, non-fiction, poetry or an anthology, and can be a work of joint authorship or editorship. The books must be published between January 1 and December 31 of the preceding year and be designated by its publisher as being either a young adult book or one published for the age range that YALSA defines as young adult, e.g. ages 12 through 18.

4291 2000. *Monster.* Walter Dean Myers. HarperCollins, 1999.

4292 Mildred L. Batchelder Award

SPONSOR: American Library Association. CONTACT: Association for Library Services to Children. ADDRESS: 50 East Huron Street, Chicago, Illinois 60611. PHONE: 1-800-545-2433. ESTABLISHED: 1968. AWARD: A citation. The award is given annually to an American publisher for the most outstanding children's book, originally published in a foreign language in a foreign country.

4293 1990. *Buster's World.* Bjarne Reuter. *Illustrator:* Paul O. Zelinsky. *Translator:* Anthea Bell. Dutton, 1989.

4294 1991. *A Hand Full of Stars.* Rafik Schami. *Translator:* Rika Lesser. Dutton, 1990.

4295 1992. *The Man from the Other Side.* Uri Orlev. *Translator:* Hillel Halkin. Houghton Mifflin, 1991.

1993. No award given.

4296 1994. *The Apprentice.* Pilar Molina Llorente. *Translator:* Robin Longshaw. Farrar, Straus & Giroux, 1993.

4297 1995. *The Boys from St. Petri.* Bjarne Reuter. *Translator:* Guner Ener. Dutton, 1994.

4298 1996. *The Lady with the Hat.* Uri Orlev. *Translator:* Hillel Halkin. Houghton Mifflin, 1995.

4299 1997. *The Friends.* Kazumi Yumoto. *Translator:* Cathy Hirano. Farrar, Straus & Giroux, 1996.

4300 1998. *The Robber and Me.* Josef Holub. *Translator:* Elizabeth D. Crawford. Henry Holt, 1997.

4301 1999. *Thanks to My Mother.* Schoschana Rabinovici. *Translator:* James Skofield. Dial, 1998.

4302 2000. *The Baboon King.* Anton Quintana. Walker and Company, 2000.

4303 Missouri Building Block Picture Book Award

SPONSOR: Missouri Library Association. ADDRESS: 1306 Business 63 South, Suite B, Columbia, Missouri 65201. PHONE: (573) 449-4627. ESTABLISHED: 1996. The award is given annually to the author and illustrator of the picture book voted most popular by preschool children in Missouri's public libraries.

4304 1996. *Splash, Splash.* Jeff Sheppard. *Illustrator:* Dennis Panek. Macmillan, 1994.

4305 1997. *Hi, Pizza Man!* Virginia Walters. *Illustrator:* Ponder Goembel. Orchard Books, 1995.

4306 1998. *Cock-a-Doodle-Moo.* Bernard Most. *Illustrator:* Bernard Most. Harcourt Brace, 1996.

4307 1999. *No, David!* David Shannon. *Illustrator:* David Shannon. Blue Sky Press, 1998.

4308 Mythopoeic Fantasy Award

SPONSOR: Mythopoeic Society. CONTACT: Awards Administrator. ADDRESS: P.O. Box 320486, San Francisco, California 94132-0486. The award is given to the author of a fantasy book for younger readers (from young adults to picture books) published during the previous year.

4309 1992. *Haroun and the Sea of Stories.* Salman Rushdie. Viking Penguin, 1991.

4310 1993. *Knight's Wyrd.* Debra Doyle, James D. Macdonald. Harcourt Brace, 1992.

4311 1994. *The Kingdom of Kevin Malone.* Suzy McKee Charnas. Harcourt Brace, 1993.

4312 1995. *Owl in Love.* Patrice Kindl. Penguin, 1994.

4313 1996. *The Crown of Dalemark.* Diana Wynne Jones. HarperCollins, 1995.

4314 1997. *The Wood Wife.* Terri Windling. Tor Books, 1997.

4315 1998. *The Young Merlin Trilogy: Passager, Hobby and Merlin.* Jane Yolen. Harcourt Brace & Company, 1996.

4316 1999. *Dark Lord of Derkholm.* Diana Wynne Jones. HarperCollins, 1998.

4317 2000. *The Folk Keeper.* Franny Billingsley. Atheneum, 1999.

4318 National Book Award for Young People's Literature

SPONSOR: National Book Foundation. ADDRESS: 260 Fifth Avenue-9th Floor, New York, New York 10001. PHONE: (212) 685-0261. ESTABLISHED: 1996. AWARD: $10,000 and a crystal sculpture. The award committee will consider books of all genres written for children and young adults by U.S. writers with an emphasis on literary merit.

4319 1996. *Parrot in the Oven: Mi Vida.* Victor Martinez. Harcourt Brace, 1996.

4320 1997. *Dancing on the Edge.* Han Nolan. Harcourt Brace, 1997.

4321 1998. *Holes.* Louis Sachar. Farrar Straus Giroux, 1998.

4322 National Council of Teachers of English Award for Excellence in Poetry for Children

SPONSOR: National Council of Teachers of English. ADDRESS: 1111 Kenyon Road, Urbana, Illinois 61801. PHONE: (800) 369-6283. ESTABLISHED: 1977. AWARD: A plaque and a seal for the jacket covers of the books. The award is presented every three years to a living American poet for his or her body-of-work. All members of the NCTE can provide nominations. Until 1982, the award was given annually.

4323 1991. Valerie Worth.
4324 1994. Barbara Juster Esbensen.
4325 1997. Eloise Greenfield.
4326 2000. X.J. Kennedy.

4327 Nebraska Golden Sower Award

SPONSOR: Nebraska Library Association. ADDRESS: 118 Henzlik Hall, University of Nebraska, Lincoln, Nebraska 68588-0355. PHONE: (402) 472-3390. ESTABLISHED: 1981. AWARD: A plaque. Three awards: fiction appropriate for grades 4 to 6, picture books appropriate for children in kindergarten to grade 3, and young adult are presented annually. Titles must be in print and published in a three year period preceding the current year to be eligible. Authors and illustrators must be living in the United States at the time of nominations. Only one title of an author or illustrator can be included in any given year. The winning author/ illustrator is excluded from competition the following year.

4328 1990. *The Magic School Bus at the Waterworks.* Joanna Cole. *Illustrator:* Bruce Degen. Scholastic, 1989. *Level:* K–3.
4329 1990. *Wait Till Helen Comes.* Mary Downing Hahn. Clarion, 1986. *Level:* 4–6.
4330 1991. *Tacky the Penguin.* Helen Lester. *Illustrator:* Lynn Munsinger. Houghton Mifflin, 1990. *Category:* K–3.
4331 1991. *There's a Boy in the Girl's Bathroom.* Louis Sachar. Knopf, 1987. *Category:* 4–6.
4332 1992. *Is Anybody There?* Eve Bunting. Harper Trophy, 1990. *Category:* 4–6.
4333 1992. *The Talking Eggs.* Robert San Souci. *Illustrator:* Jerry Pinkey. Dial, 1989. *Category:* K–3.
4334 1993. *Whispers from the Dead.* Joan Lowery Nixon. Laurel Leaf, 1991. *Category:* young adult.
4335 1993. *Nightmare Mountain.* Peg Kehret. Dutton, 1989. *Category:* 4–6.
4336 1993. *Riptide!...* Francis Ward Weller. *Illustrator:* Robert J. Blake. Philomel, 1990. *Category:* K–3.
4337 1994. *The Rough-Face Girl.* Rafe Martin. *Illustrator:* David Shannon. Philomel, 1992. *Category:* K–3.
4338 1994. *Flight #116 Is Down.* Caroline Cooney. Scholastic, 1992. *Category:* young adult.

4339 1994. *Stepping on the Cracks.* Mary Downing Hahn. Clarion, 1991. *Category:* 4–6.

4340 1995. *The Giver.* Lois Lowry. Houghton Mifflin, 1993. *Category:* young adult.

4341 1995. *Martha Speaks.* Susan Meddaugh. Houghton, 1992. *Category:* K–3.

4342 1995. *Rescue Josh McGuire.* Ben Mikaelsen. Hyperion, 1991. *Category:* 4–6.

4343 1996. *The Grand Escape.* Phyllis Reynolds Naylor. Atheneum, 1993. *Category:* 4–6.

4344 1996. *Soap! Soap! Don't Forget the Soap!* Tom Birdseye. *Illustrator:* Andrew Glass. Holiday House, 1993. *Category:* K–3.

4345 1996. *Heart of a Champion.* Carl Deuker. Avon, 1993. *Category:* young adult.

4346 1997. *Freak the Mighty.* Rodman Philbrick. Scholastic, 1993. *Category:* young adult.

4347 1997. *John Henry.* Julius Lester. *Illustrator:* Jerry Pinkney. Dial, 1994. *Category:* K–3.

4348 1997. *Best School Year Ever.* Barbara Robinson. *Illustrator:* Michael Deas. HarperCollins, 1994. *Category:* Grades 4–6.

4349 1998. *The Toll-Bridge Troll.* Patricia Rae Wolf. *Illustrator:* Kimberly Bulken Root. Browndeer Press, 1995. *Category:* K–3.

4350 1998. *Titanic Crossing.* Barbara Williams. Dial Books for Young Readers, 1995. *Category:* 4–6.

4351 1998. *Danger Zone.* David Klass. Scholastic, 1996. *Category:* young adult.

4352 1999. *The True Colors of Caitlynne Jackson.* Carol Lynch Williams. Delacorte, 1997. *Category:* young adult.

4353 1999. *Rugby and Rosie.* Nan Parson Rossiter. *Illustrator:* Nan Parson Rossiter. Dutton, 1997. *Category:* K–3.

4354 1999. *Shiloh Season.* Phyllis Reynolds Naylor. Atheneum, 1996. *Category:* 4–6.

4355 2000. *Don't You Dare Read This, Mrs. Dunphrey.* Margaret Peterson Haddix. Simon & Schuster, 1996. *Category:* young adult.

4356 2000. *Jaguar.* Roland Smith. Hyperion Books, 1997. *Category:* 4–6.

4357 2000. *No Such Thing.* Jackie French Koller. *Illustrator:* Betsy Lewin. Boyds Mills Press, 1997. *Category:* K–3.

4358 Nene Award

SPONSOR: Hawaii Library Association. ADDRESS: Children's Section, 478 South King Street, Honolulu, Hawaii 96813. PHONE: (808) 586-3510. ESTABLISHED: 1964. AWARD: A carved koa wood platter. The aim of the award is to acquaint

Hawaiian children with the best contemporary children's writers, and to develop an awareness of qualities that make good literature. The winning work of fiction must be suitable for grades 4 to 6 and have been published within the last 6 years.

4359 1990. *Fudge.* Charlotte Towner Graeber. *Illustrator:* Cheryl Harness. Lothrop, 1987.

4360 1991. *There's a Boy in the Girl's Bathroom.* Louis Sachar. Knopf, 1987.

4361 1992. *The Whipping Boy.* Sid Fleischman. Greenwillow, 1986.

4362 1993. *Fudge-a-Mania.* Judy Blume. Dutton, 1990.

4363 1994. *Shiloh.* Phyllis Reynolds Naylor. Atheneum, 1991.

4364 1995. *My Teacher Is an Alien.* Bruce Coville. *Illustrator:* Mike Wimmer. Minstrel Books, 1990.

4365 1996. *Maniac Magee.* Jerry Spinelli. Little, Brown & Co., 1989.

4366 1997. *Ghosts of Fourth Grade.* Graham Hiser. *Illustrator:* Cat Bowman Smith. Holiday House, 1991.

4367 1998. *Under the Red-Blood Sky.* Graham Salisbury. Delacorte, 1994.

4368 1999. *Best School Year Ever.* Barbara Robinson. *Illustrator:* Michael Deas. HarperCollins, 1994.

4369 2000. *Harry Potter and the Sorcerer's Stone.* J.K. Rowling. *Illustrator:* Mary Grandpré. Scholastic, 1999.

4370 Nevada Young Readers Award

SPONSOR: Nevada Library Association. CONTACT: Betsy Johnson, Children's Librarian. ADDRESS: Henderson Public Libraries, Malcolm, Branch 80 N. Pecos Rd., Henderson, Nevada 89014. ESTABLISHED: 1987. AWARD: A plaque. The award is presented to honor outstanding works of children's literature. It is presented in four categories: picture book, young readers, intermediate, and young adult. Young readers in Nevada vote for their favorite books.

4371 1990. *There's a Boy in the Girl's Bathroom.* Louis Sachar. Knopf, 1987. *Category:* intermediate.

4372 1990. *Experiment in Terror.* Bernal C. Payne, Jr. Houghton Mifflin, 1987. *Category:* young adult.

4373 1990. *Heckedy Peg.* Audrey Wood. *Illustrator:* Don Wood. Harcourt, 1987. *Category:* primary.

4374 1991. *We're Back: A Dinosaur's Story.* Hudson Talbott. *Illustrator:* Tedd Talbott. Crown, 1987. *Category:* picture book.

4375 1991. *Princess Ashley.* Richard Peck. Doubleday, 1987. *Category:* young adult.

4376 1991. *My Teacher Is An Alien.* Bruce Coville. *Illustrator:* Mike Wimmer. Minstrel Books, 1990. *Category:* intermediate.

4377 1992. *Call of the Wolves.* Jim Murphy. *Illustrator:* Jim Murphy. Scholastic, 1994. *Category:* picture book.

4378 1992. *Matilda.* Roald Dahl. *Illustrator:* Quentin Blake. Viking, 1988. *Category:* intermediate.

4379 1992. *Whispers from the Dead.* Joan Lowery Nixon. Laurel Leaf, 1991. *Category:* young adult.

4380 1993. *Fudge-A-Mania.* Judy Blume. Dutton, 1990. *Category:* younger reader.

4381 1993. *The Dog Who Had Kittens.* Polly Robertus. *Illustrator:* Janet Stevens. Holiday House, 1992. *Category:* picture book.

4382 1993. *Jurassic Park.* Michael Crichton. Knopf, 1990. *Category:* young adult.

4383 1993. *Maniac McGee.* Jerry Spinelli. Little, Brown & Co., 1990. *Category:* intermediate.

4384 1994. *Jeremy Thatcher, Dragon Hatcher.* Bruce Coville. *Illustrator:* Gary A. Lippincott. Minstrel Books, 1992. *Category:* younger reader.

4385 1994. *Look Out, Patrick.* Paul Geraghty. Atheneum, 1990. *Category:* picture book.

4386 1994. *Shiloh.* Phyllis Reynolds Naylor. Atheneum, 1991. *Category:* intermediate.

4387 1994. *Plague Year.* Stephanie Tolan. Fawcett, 1991. *Category:* young adult.

4388 1995. *Moe the Dog in Tropical Paradise.* Diane Stanley. *Illustrator:* Elise Primavera. Paper Star, 1999. *Category:* picture book.

4389 1995. *Flight #116 Is Down.* Caroline Cooney. Scholastic, 1992. *Category:* intermediate.

4390 1995. *The Giver.* Lois Lowry. Houghton Mifflin, 1993. *Category:* young adult.

4391 1995. *The Boys Start the War.* Phyllis Reynolds Naylor. Delacorte, 1993. *Category:* younger reader.

4392 1996. *The Name of the Game Was Murder.* Joan Lowery Nixon. Delacorte, 1993. *Category:* intermediate.

4393 1996. *Junie B. Jones and Her Big Fat Mouth.* Barbara Park. Random House, 1993. *Category:* younger reader.

4394 1996. *Coyote Steals the Blanket: A Ute Tale.* Janet Stevens. Holiday, 1993. *Category:* primary.

4395 1996. *Winners and Losers.* Stephen Hoffius. Simon & Schuster, 1993. *Category:* young adult.

4396 1997. *Shadow.* Joyce Sweeney. Delacorte, 1994. *Category:* young adult.

4397 1997. *Loch.* Paul Zindel. Hyperion, 1995. *Category:* intermediate.

4398 1997. *Harvey Potter's Balloon Farm.* Jerdine Nolan. *Illustrator:* Mark Buehner. Lothrop, Lee & Shepard, 1995. *Category:* primary.

4399 1997. *Shape-Changer.* Bill Brittain. Harper Trophy, 1995. *Category:* younger reader.

4400 1998. *The Secret Shortcut.* Mark Teague. Scholastic, 1996. *Category:* primary.

4401 1998. *Tarot Says Beware.* Betsy Byars. Viking, 1995. *Category:* younger reader.

4402 1998. *Crash!* Jerry Spinelli. Knopf, 1996. *Category:* intermediate.

4403 1998. *Companions of the Night.* Vivian van de Velde. Harcourt Brace, 1995. *Category:* young adult.

4404 1999. *Tangerine.* Edward Bloor. Harcourt, 1997. *Category:* young adult.

4405 1999. *Just Another Ordinary Day.* Rod Clement. HarperCollins, 1995. *Category:* primary.

4406 1999. *The Doom Stone.* Paul Zindel. HarperCollins, 1995. *Category:* intermediate.

4407 1999. *Frindle.* Andrew Clements. *Illustrator:* Brian Selznick. Simon & Schuster, 1996. *Category:* younger reader.

4408 2000. *Gallows Hill.* Lois Duncan. Delacorte, 1997. *Category:* young adult.

4409 2000. *John Willy and Freddy McGee.* Holly Meade. *Illustrator:* Holly Meade. Marshall Cavendish, 1998. *Category:* picture books.

4410 2000. *Virtually Perfect.* Dan Gutman. Hyperion, 1998. *Category:* intermediate.

4411 2000. *Harry Potter and the Sorcerer's Stone.* J.K. Rowling. *Illustrator:* Mary Grandpré. Scholastic, 1998. *Category:* young reader.

4412 New England Book Award

SPONSOR: New England Booksellers Association. ADDRESS: 847 Massachusetts Avenue, Cambridge, Massachusetts 02139. PHONE: 1-800-466–8711. ESTABLISHED: 1990. The award is given to New England authors and publishers who have produced a body of work that stands as a significant contribution to New England's culture.

4413 1990. Jan Brett.

4414 1991. Barbara Cooney.

4415 1992. Katherine Paterson.

4416 1993. William Steig.

4417 1994. Ashley Bryan.

4418 1995. Natalie Babbitt.

4419 1996. Steven Kellogg.

4420 1997. Natalie Kinsey-Warnock.

4421 1998. Susan Meddaugh.

4422 1999. Karen Hesse.

4423 2000. Marcia Sewall.

4424 North Carolina Children's Book Award

SPONSOR: North Carolina Association of School Librarians and the Children's Services Section of the North Carolina Library Association. ADDRESS: 1057 Greenly Drive, Pfafftown, North Carolina 27040. PHONE: (336) 945-9637. The annual award is given in two categories: picture book and junior book.

4425 1992. *In a Dark, Dark Room and Others Scary Stories.* Alvin Schwartz. *Illustrator:* Dirk Zimmer. Harper, 1985. *Category:* picture book.

4426 1993. *The Seven Chinese Brothers.* Margaret Mahy. *Illustrator:* Jean Teng. Mou-Sien Tseng. Scholastic, 1994. *Category:* picture book.

4427 1994. *The Stinky Cheese Man and Other Fairly Stupid Tales.* Jon Scieszka. *Illustrator:* Lane Smith. Viking, 1992. *Category:* picture book.

4428 1995. *The Boys Start the War.* Phyllis Reynolds Naylor. Delacorte, 1993. *Category:* junior book.

4429 1995. *The Rainbow Fish.* Marcus Pfister. North-South Books, 1992. *Category:* picture book.

4430 1996. *The Man Who Tricked a Ghost.* Laurence Yep. *Illustrator:* Isadore Seltzer. Bridgewater Books, 1993. *Category:* picture book.

4431 1996. *My Teacher Fried My Brains.* Bruce Coville. Minstrel Books, 1991. *Category:* junior book.

4432 1997. *Officer Buckle and Gloria.* Peggy Rathmann. Putnam, 1995. *Category:* picture book.

4433 1997. *Wicked Jack.* Connie Nordhielm Wooldridge (adapted). *Illustrator:* Will Hillenbrand. Holiday. *Category:* junior book.

4434 1998. *Roses Are Pink, Your Feet Really Stink.* Dianne DeGroat. *Illustrator:* Dianne DeGroat. Morrow. *Category:* picture book.

4435 1998. *Shiloh Season.* Phyllis Reynolds Naylor. Atheneum, 1996. *Category:* junior book.

4436 1999. *Verdi.* Janell Cannon. *Illustrator:* Janell Cannon. Harcourt Brace, 1997. *Category:* picture book.

4437 1999. *Frindle.* Andrew Clements. *Illustrator:* Brian Selznick. Simon & Schuster, 1996. *Category:* junior book.

4438 2000. *Crash!* Jerry Spinelli. Knopf, 1996. *Category:* junior book.

4439 2000. *Ghost of Sifty Sifty Sam.* Angela Shelf Medearis. *Illustrator:* Jacqueline Rogers. Scholastic, 1997. *Category:* picture book.

4440 Nutmeg Children's Book Award

SPONSOR: Connecticut Library Association (CLA). CONTACT: Ann Marie Lund. ADDRESS: West Hartford Public Library, 20 South, Main Street, West Hartford,

Connecticut 06107. PHONE: (860) 523-3280. ESTABLISHED: 1993. The award is given for a work of fiction for readers in grades 4–6, written by an author who is currently a resident in the United States. The book must be published in the United States no more than five years from the date of the award.

4441 1993. *My Teacher Is an Alien.* Bruce Coville. *Illustrator:* Mike Wimmer. Minstrel Books, 1990.

4442 1994. *Shiloh!* Phyllis Reynolds Naylor. Atheneum, 1991.

4443 1995. *The Biggest Klutz in the Fifth Grade.* Bill Wallace. Holiday House, 1992.

4444 1996. *The Grand Escape.* Phyllis Reynolds Naylor. Atheneum, 1993.

4445 1997. *Shape-Changer.* Bill Brittain. Harper. Trophy, 1995.

4446 1998. *The Private Notebook of Katie Roberts, Age 11.* Amy Hest. *Illustrator:* Sonja Lamut. Candlewick, 1995.

4447 1999. *Mick Harte Was Here.* Barbara Park. Knopf, 1995.

4448 2000. *Million Dollar Shot.* Dan Gutman. Hyperion, 1997.

4449 Ohioana Book Awards

SPONSOR: Ohioana Library Association. ADDRESS: 65 S. Front Street, Suite 1105, Columbus, Ohio 43266-0334. PHONE: (614) 466-3831. ESTABLISHED: 1943. AWARD: A medallion and certificate. The award is given for the best book by an Ohio author or the best book about Ohio. The author must be from Ohio or have lived in Ohio for five years. The book must be published within the previous two calendar years.

4450 1990. *But I'll Be Back Again.* Cynthia Rylant. Orchard Books, 1989.

4451 1991. *With a Name Like Lulu, Who Needs More Trouble?* Tricia Springstubb. *Illustrator:* Jill Kastner. Delacorte, 1989.

4452 1992. *Appalachia: The Voices of Sleeping Birds.* Cynthia Rylant. *Illustrator:* Barry Moser. Harcourt Brace, 1991.

4453 1993. *The Falcon's Wing.* Dawna Lisa Buchanan. Orchard Books, 1992.

4454 1994. *In the Small, Small Pond.* Denise Fleming. *Illustrator:* Denise Fleming. Henry Holt & Company, 1993.

4455 1995. *Jericho.* Janet Hickman. Greenwillow, 1994.

4456 1996. *The King's Shadow.* Elizabeth Alder. Bantam Books, 1997.

4457 1997. *Her Stories: African American Folktales, Fairy Tales and True Tales.* Virginia Hamilton. *Illustrator:* Leo Dillon, Diane Dillon. Scholastic, 1995.

4458 1998. *The Heart Is Big Enough.* Michael Rosen. *Illustrator:* Matthew Valiquette. Harcourt, 1997.

4459 1999. *Goosebumps.* R.L. Stine. Apple, 1999.

4460 1999. *Fear Street.* R.L. Stine. Econo-Clad Books, 1999.

4461 2000. *The Mouse of Amherst.* Elizabeth Spires. *Illustrator:* Claire A. Nivola. Frances Foster Books, 1999.

4462 Oklahoma Book Award

SPONSOR: The Oklahoma Center for the Book. ADDRESS: Oklahoma Dept. of Libraries 200 NE 18th St., Oklahoma City, Oklahoma 73105-3298. PHONE: (405) 521-2502. ESTABLISHED: 1990. The award is given for the best book for children and young adults written by an Oklahoma author.

4463 1990. *Tyrannosaurus Rex and His Kin.* Helen Roney Sattler. Lothrop Lee & Shepard, 1989.
4464 1991. *Capitol for the Nation.* Stan Hoig. Cobblehill, 1990.
4465 1992. *Hillback to Boggy.* Bonnie Speer. Reliance Press, 1991.
4466 1993. *Red Dirt Jessie.* Anna Myers. Puffin, 1992.
4467 1994. *Cherokee Summer.* Diane Hoyt-Goldsmith. Holiday House, 1993.
4468 1995. *The Choctaw Code.* Russell G. Davis, Brent Ashabranner. Linnet Books, 1994.
4469 1996. *Graveyard Girl.* Anna Myers. Walker & Co, 1995.
4470 1997. *Stone Water.* Barbara Snow Gilbert. Front Street, 1996.
4471 1998. *Hero.* S.L. Rottman. Peachtree, 1997.
4472 1999. *Broken Chords.* Barbara Snow Gilbert. Front Street, 1998.
4473 2000. *Brief Garland.* Harold Keith. Eakin Press, 1999.

4474 Orbis Pictus Award

SPONSOR: National Council of Teachers of English. ADDRESS: 1111 Kenyon Road, Urbana, Illinois 61801-1096. PHONE: 1-800-369-6283. ESTABLISHED: 1990. AWARD: A plaque. The award is given for outstanding non-fiction for children.

4475 1990. *The Great Little Madison.* Jean Fritz. Putnam.
4476 1991. *Franklin Delano Roosevelt.* Russell Freedman. Clarion, 1990.
4477 1992. *Flight: The Journey of Charles Lindbergh.* Robert Burleigh. Philomel, 1991.
4478 1993. *Children of the Dust Bowl.* Jerry Stanley. Crown, 1992.
4479 1994. *Across America in an Emigrant Train.* Jim Murphy. Clarion, 1993.
4480 1995. *Safari Beneath the Sea.* Diane Swanson. Sierra, 1994.
4481 1996. *The Great Fire.* Jim Murphy. Scholastic, 1995.
4482 1997. *Leonardo da Vinci.* Diane Stanley. Morrow, 1996.
4483 1998. *An Extraordinary Life: The Story of a Monarch Butterfly.* Laurence Pringle. *Illustrator:* Bob Marstall. Orchard Books, 1997.
4484 1999. *Shipwreck at the Bottom of the World: The Extraordinary True Story of Schackleton and the Endurance.* Jennifer Armstrong. Crown, 1998.
4485 2000. *Through My Eyes.* Ruby Bridges. *Illustrator:* Margo Lundell. Scholastic Press, 1999.

4486 Outstanding Pennsylvania Author

SPONSOR: Pennsylvania School Librarians Association. ADDRESS: 49 Dogwood Court, Lancaster Pennsylvania 17603. ESTABLISHED: 1975. AWARD: A certificate. The award is given to a native Pennsylvania author, either living in the state or writing about the state, who has made a significant contribution to literature for children or young adults.

4487 1991. Aliki.
4488 1993. Paula Danzinger.
4489 1997. Nancy Springer.
4490 1999. Judith Gorog.

4491 Pacific Northwest Young Reader's Choice Award

SPONSOR: Pacific Northwestern Library Association. CONTACT: Betty Holbrook, Marshall Public Library. ADDRESS: 113 S. Garfield, Pocatello, Idaho 83204. PHONE: (208) 232-9266. ESTABLISHED: 1940. AWARD: A medal. The award is given annually to an author of a book appropriate for grades 4 to 12. Students from Alaska, Alberta, British Columbia, Idaho, Montana, Oregon, and Washington are eligible to vote. The book must have been published three years earlier.

4492 1990. *There's a Boy in the Girl's Bathroom.* Louis Sachar. Knopf, 1987.
4493 1991. *Ten Kids, No Pets.* Ann Martin. Holiday, 1988. *Category:* youth.
4494 1991. *Sex Education.* Jenny Davis. Orchard House, 1989. *Category:* senior.
4495 1992. *Eva.* Peter Dickinson. Delacorte, 1990. *Category:* senior.
4496 1992. *Danger in Quicksand Swamp.* Bill Wallace. Holiday, 1991. *Category:* youth.
4497 1993. *The Face on the Milk Carton.* Caroline Cooney. Bantam, 1990. *Category:* senior.
4498 1993. *Maniac Magee.* Jerry Spinelli. Little, Brown & Co., 1990. *Category:* youth.
4499 1994. *Shiloh.* Phyllis Reynolds Naylor. Atheneum, 1991. *Category:* youth.
4500 1994. *Wolf by the Ears.* Ann Rinaldi. Scholastic, 1993. *Category:* senior.
4501 1995. *Who Killed My Daughter? The True Story of a Mother's Search for Her Daughter's Murderer.* Lois Duncan. Delacorte, 1992. *Category:* senior.
4502 1995. *Terror at the Zoo.* Peg Kehret. Dutton, 1992. *Category:* youth.
4503 1996. *The Boys Start the War.* Phyllis Reynolds Naylor. Delacorte, 1993. *Category:* youth.
4504 1996. *The Giver.* Lois Lowry. Houghton Mifflin, 1993. *Category:* senior.
4505 1997. *Nasty Stinky Sneakers.* Eve Bunting. HarperCollins, 1994. *Category:* youth.

4506 1997. *Driver's Ed.* Caroline Cooney. Delacorte, 1994. *Category:* senior.
4507 1998. *The Midwife's Apprentice.* Karen Cushman. Clarion, 1995. *Category:* senior.
4508 1998. *Wayside School Gets a Little Stranger.* Louis Sachar. Morrow, 1995. *Category:* youth.
4509 1999. *SOS Titanic.* Eve Bunting. Harcourt Brace, 1996. *Category:* senior.
4510 1999. *Frindle.* Andrew Clements. *Illustrator:* Brian Selznick. Simon & Schuster, 1996. *Category:* youth.
4511 2000. *A Mouse Called Wolf.* Dick King-Smith. Crown, 1997. *Category:* youth.
4512 2000. *The Taking of Room 114.* Mel Glenn. Lodestar, 1997. *Category:* senior.

4513 Parents' Choice Award

SPONSOR: Parents' Choice Foundation. ADDRESS: Box 185, Waban, Massachusetts 02168. ESTABLISHED: 1980. AWARD: A ribbon. The award is given to honor outstanding illustration in children's books. Parents nominate books they and their children enjoy together. A complete list was unavailable at the time of publication.

4514 1990. *Hey! Get Off Our Train.* John Burningham. *Illustrator:* John Burningham. Crown, 1990. *Category:* picture book.
4515 1990. *Bingo Brown, Gypsy Lover.* Betsy Byars. Viking, 1990. *Category:* literature.
4516 1990. *Box and Cox.* Grace Chetwin. *Illustrator:* David Small. Bradbury, 1990. *Category:* picture book.
4517 1990. *Crow and Weasel.* Barry Lopez. *Illustrator:* Tom Pohrt. North Point, 1990. *Category:* picture book.
4518 1990. *Ducks Fly.* Lydia Dabcovich. *Illustrator:* Lydia Dabcovich. Dutton, 1990. *Category:* picture book.
4519 1990. *Shadows and Reflections.* Tana Hoban. *Illustrator:* Tana Hoban. Greenwillow, 1990. *Category:* picture book.
4520 1990. *Uncle Wizzmo's New Used Car.* Rodney A. Greenblat. *Illustrator:* Rodney A. Greenblat. Harper, 1990. *Category:* picture book.
4521 1990. *The Wheels on the Bus.* Paul O. Zelinsky (adapted). *Illustrator:* Paul O. Zelinsky. Dutton, 1990. *Category:* picture book.
4522 1990. *The Squeaky Wheel.* Robert Kimmel Smith. Delacorte, 1990. *Category:* literature.
4523 1990. *The Mouse Rap.* Walter Dean Myers. Harper, 1990. *Category:* literature.
4524 1990. *The Midnight Horse.* Sid Fleischman. *Illustrator:* Peter Sis. Greenwillow, 1990. *Category:* literature.

4525 1990. *The Boy Who Owned the School.* Gary Paulsen. Orchard, 1990. *Category:* literature.

4526 1990. *The Adventures of Taxi Dog.* Debra Barracca, Sal Barracca. *Illustrator:* Mark Buehner. Dial, 1990. *Category:* picture book.

4527 1990. *Elizabeth and Larry.* Marilyn Sadler. *Illustrator:* Roger Bollen. Simon & Schuster, 1990. *Category:* literature.

4528 1990. *Shrek.* William Steig. *Illustrator:* William Steig. Farrar, 1990. *Category:* picture book.

4529 1990. *Further Tales of Uncle Remus.* Julius Lester. *Illustrator:* Jerry Pinkney. Dial, 1990. *Category:* literature.

4530 1990. *Rice Without Rain.* Minfong Ho. Lothrop, 1990. *Category:* literature.

4531 1990. *Puss in Boots.* Charles Perrault. *Illustrator:* Fred Marcellino. Farrar, 1990. *Category:* picture book.

4532 1990. *Possum Come A-Knockin'.* Nancy van Laan. *Illustrator:* George Booth. Knopf, 1990. *Category:* picture book.

4533 1990. *Nessa's Fish.* Nancy Luenn. *Illustrator:* Neil Waldman. Atheneum, 1990. *Category:* literature.

4534 1990. *My Daddy Was a Soldier.* Deborah Kogan Ray. Holiday, 1990. *Category:* literature.

4535 1990. *More Bugs in Boxes.* David A. Carter. *Illustrator:* David A. Carter. Simon & Schuster, 1990. *Category:* picture book.

4536 1990. *Maxie, Rosie, and Earl—Partners in Grime.* Barbara Park. Knopf, 1990. *Category:* literature.

4537 1990. *Laura Charlotte.* Katherine Galbraith. *Illustrator:* Floyd Cooper. Philomel, 1990. *Category:* literature.

4538 1990. *Stonewords.* Pam Conrad. Harper, 1990. *Category:* literature.

4539 1990. *I Hate English!* Ellen Levine. *Illustrator:* Steve Bjorkman. Scholastic, 1990. *Category:* literature.

4540 1991. *The Alphabet Parade.* Seymour Chwast. Harcourt.

4541 1991. *Rats on the Roof and Other Stories.* James Marshall. Dial.

4542 1991. *Rosie Swanson.* Barbara Park. Knopf.

4543 1991. *Diego.* Jonah Winter. Knopf.

4544 1991. *Wolf.* Gillian Cross. Holiday.

4545 1991. *Aunt Flossie's Hats and Crab Cakes Later.* Elizabeth Fitzgerald Howard. Clarion.

4546 1995. *Poppa's New Pans.* Angela Shelf Medearis. Holiday, 1994. *Category:* storybook.

4547 1995. *The 13th Floor: A Ghost Story.* Sid Fleischman. Greenwillow, 1994. *Category:* storybook.

4548 1995. *Add It, Dip It, Fix It: A Book of Verbs.* R.M. Schneider. *Illustrator:* R.M. Schneider. Houghton Mifflin, 1994. *Category:* picture book.

4549 1995. *Shortcut.* David Macaulay. *Illustrator:* David Macaulay. Houghton Mifflin, 1994. *Category:* picture book.

4550 1995. *The Do-It-Yourself House That Jack Built.* John Yeoman. *Illustrator:* Quentin Blake. Atheneum, 1994. *Category:* picture book.

4551 1995. *Yang the Third and Her Impossible Family.* Lensey Namioka. Little, 1994. *Category:* storybook.

4552 1998. *Buoy: Home at Sea.* Bruce Balan. *Illustrator:* Raul Colón. Delacorte Press. *Category:* picture book. *Level:* all ages.

4553 1998. *A Handful of Beans.* Jeanne Steig. *Illustrator:* William Steig. HarperCollins. *Category:* picture book. *Level:* 5–10 yrs.

4554 1998. *Old Mother Hubbard: A Nursery Rhyme. Illustrator:* David A. Johnson. Margaret K. McElderry Books. *Category:* picture book. *Level:* 3–7 yrs.

4555 1998. *P.S. Longer Letter Later.* Paula Danziger. Ann M. Martin. Scholastic, Inc. *Category:* storybook. *Level:* 10 & up.

4556 1998. *Red Scarf Girl: A Memoir of the Cultural Revolution.* Ji-Li Jiang. HarperCollins. *Category:* storybook. *Level:* 12 & up.

4557 1998. *Leon's Story.* Leon Walter Tillage. Farrar, Straus & Giroux, 1997. *Category:* storybook. *Level:* 10 & up.

4558 1998. *Thank You, Mr. Falker.* Patricia Polacco. Philomel, 1998. *Category:* storybook. *Level:* 6–10 yrs.

4559 1998. *Passage to Freedom: The Sugihara Story.* Ken Mochizuki. *Illustrator:* Dom Lee. Lee & Low Books, 1997. *Category:* storybook. *Level:* 6–10 yrs.

4560 1998. *The Long March.* Marie-Louise Fitzpatrick. Beyond Words Publishing, 1998. *Category:* storybook. *Level:* all ages.

4561 1998. *Shape Up: Fun with Triangles.* David Adler. *Illustrator:* Nancy Tobin. Holiday House. *Category:* picture book. *Level:* 4–8 yrs.

4562 1998. *The Secret Life of Amanda K. Woods.* Ann Cameron. Farrar, Straus & Giroux. *Category:* storybook. *Level:* 8–12 yrs.

4563 1998. *Measuring Penny.* Loreen Leedy. Henry Holt. *Category:* picture book. *Level:* 6–10 yrs.

4564 1999. *The Blunder of the Rogues.* Tim Egan. *Illustrator:* Tim Egan. Houghton Mifflin. *Category:* picture book. *Level:* 4–8 yrs.

4565 1999. *One Giant Leap: The Story of Neil Armstrong.* Don Brown. Houghton Mifflin. *Category:* picture book. *Level:* 4–8 yrs.

4566 1999. *Tough Cookie.* David Wisniewski. Lothrop, Lee & Shepard Books. *Category:* picture book. *Level:* 4–8 yrs.

4567 1999. *Hooway for Wodney Wat.* Helen Lester. *Illustrator:* Lynn Munsinger. Walter Lorraine Books. *Category:* picture book. *Level:* 4–8 yrs.

4568 1999. *The Little Match Girl.* Hans Christian Andersen. *Illustrator:* Jerry Pinkney. Phyllis Fogelman. *Category:* picture book. *Level:* 4–8 yrs.

4569 1999. *Aneesa Lee and the Weaver's Gift.* Nikki Grimes. *Illustrator:* Ashley Bryan. Lothrop, Lee & Shepard Books. *Category:* picture book. *Level:* 4–8 yrs.

4570 1999. *This Train.* Paul Collicutt. *Illustrator:* Paul Collicutt. Farrar, Straus & Giroux. *Category:* picture book. *Level:* Infant–3 yrs.

4571 1999. *Kevin and His Dad.* Irene Smalls. *Illustrator:* Michael Hayes. Little, Brown & Co.. *Category:* picture book. *Level:* Infant–3 yrs.

4572 1999. *Here Comes Mother Goose.* Iona Opie. *Illustrator:* Rosemary Wells. Candlewick Press. *Category:* picture book. *Level:* Infant–3 yrs.

4573 1999. *Beep! Beep!* Anne Miranda. *Illustrator:* David Murphy. Turtle. *Category:* picture book. *Level:* Infant–3 yrs.

4574 1999. *Lyle at Christmas.* Bernard Waber. Walter Lorraine Books. *Category:* picture book. *Level:* 4–8 yrs.

4575 1999. *Bird Boy.* Elizabeth Starr Hill. Farrar, Straus & Giroux. *Category:* storybook. *Level:* 8–12 yrs.

4576 1999. *Unbroken.* Jessie Haas. Greenwillow Books. *Category:* storybook. *Level:* 10 & up.

4577 1999. *The Baboon King.* Anton Quintana. Walker, 2000. *Category:* storybook. *Level:* 10 & up.

4578 1999. *Preacher's Boy.* Katherine Paterson. Houghton Mifflin, 1999. *Category:* storybook. *Level:* 10 & up.

4579 1999. *Gypsy Rizka.* Lloyd Alexander. Dutton. *Category:* storybook. *Level:* 10 & up.

4580 1999. *The Birchbark House.* Louise Erdrich. Hyperion, 1999. *Category:* storybook. *Level:* 8–12 yrs.

4581 1999. *Wind Child.* Shirley Rousseau Murphy. *Illustrator:* Leo Dillon, Diane Dillon. HarperCollins. *Category:* picture book. *Level:* 4–8 yrs.

4582 1999. *Beyond Mayfield.* Vaunda Micheaux Nelson. Putnam. *Category:* storybook. *Level:* 8–12 yrs.

4583 1999. *The Day Gogo Went to Vote.* Elinor Batezat Sisulu. *Illustrator:* Sharon Wilson. Little, Brown & Co. *Category:* storybook. *Level:* 4–8 yrs.

4584 1999. *Bud, Not Buddy.* Christopher Paul Curtis. Delacorte, 1999. *Category:* storybook. *Level:* 10 & up.

4585 1999. *Night Golf.* William Miller. *Illustrator:* Cedric Lucas. Lee & Low Books. *Category:* storybook. *Level:* 4–8 yrs.

4586 2000. *Buttons.* Brock Cole. *Illustrator:* Brock Cole. Farrar, Straus & Giroux. *Category:* storybook. *Level:* 4–8 yrs.

4587 2000. *Yang the Eldest and His Odd Jobs.* Lensey Namioka. *Illustrator:* Kees de Kiefte. Little, Brown & Co. *Category:* storybook. *Level:* 8–12 yrs.

4588 2000. *The Yellow Star.* Carmen Agra Deedy. *Illustrator:* Henri Sorensen. Peachtree Publishers. *Category:* picture book. *Level:* 8–12 yrs.
4589 2000. *The Saturday Kid.* Edward Sorel. *Illustrator:* Cheryl Carlesimo. Simon & Schuster. *Category:* picture book. *Level:* 5–9 yrs.
4590 2000. *A Day, A Dog.* Gabrielle Vincent. *Illustrator:* Gabrielle Vincent. Front Street. *Category:* picture book. *Level:* All ages.
4591 2000. *The Hunter.* Mary Casanova. *Illustrator:* Ed Young. Simon & Schuster. *Category:* picture book. *Level:* 5–8 yrs.
4592 2000. *The Silver Swan.* Michael Morpurgo. *Illustrator:* Christian Birmingham. Penguin Putnam. *Category:* picture book. *Level:* 4–8 yrs.
4593 2000. *Tales from Old Ireland.* Malachy Doyle. *Illustrator:* Niamh Sharkey. Barefoot Books. *Category:* picture book. *Level:* 10 & up.
4594 2000. *Is It Far to Zanzibar?* Nikki Grimes. *Illustrator:* Betsy Lewin. Lothrop, Lee & Shepard Books. *Category:* storybook. *Level:* 4–8 yrs.
4595 2000. *Mountain Town.* Bonnie Geisert. *Illustrator:* Arthur Geisert. Houghton Mifflin. *Category:* picture book. *Level:* 4–8 yrs.
4596 2000. *Alice's Adventures in Wonderland.* Lewis Carroll. *Illustrator:* Helen Oxenbury. Candlewick Press. *Category:* storybook. *Level:* 8 & up.
4597 2000. *Shiva's Fire.* Suzanne Fisher Staples. Farrar, Straus & Giroux. *Category:* storybook. *Level:* 12 & up.
4598 2000. *The Blues of Flats Brown.* Walter Myers. *Illustrator:* Nina Laden. Holiday House. *Category:* storybook. *Level:* 4–8 yrs.
4599 2000. *Olivia.* Ian Falconer. *Illustrator:* Ian Falconer. Simon & Schuster. *Category:* picture book. *Level:* 3–7 yrs.

4600 Paul A. Witty Short Story Award

SPONSOR: International Reading Association. ADDRESS: Box 8139, Newark, Delaware 19714-8139. PHONE: (302) 731-1600. ESTABLISHED: 1986. AWARD: $1,000.00 U.S. The award is given to the author of a short story published for the first time in a periodical for children in the preceding year.

4601 1990. Eric Kimmel.
4602 1991. Anthony Holcroft.
4603 1992. Pnina Kass.
4604 1993. Shizuko Obo Koster.
4605 1994. Elsa Marston.
4606 1995. Joan Lowery Nixon.
4607 1996. Nicole Ball.
4608 1997. Teresa Bateman.
1998. Award not given.
4609 1999. William J. Buchanan.
4610 2000. Bill Pronzini.

4611 PEN/Norma Klein Award

SPONSOR: PEN American Center. ADDRESS: 568 Broadway, New York New York 10012. ESTABLISHED: 1990. AWARD: $3,000. The award is given to new authors whose books (for elementary school to young adult readers) demonstrate the adventuresome and innovative spirit that characterizes the best children's literature.

4612 1991. Cynthia D. Grant.
4613 1993. Graham Salisbury.
4614 1995. Angela Johnson.
4615 1997. Rita Williams-Garcia.
4616 1999. Valerie Hobbs.

4617 Pennsylvania Young Reader's Choice Award

SPONSOR: Pennsylvania School Librarians Association. ADDRESS: 49 Dogwood Court, Lancaster, Pennsylvania 17603. ESTABLISHED: 1991. The award is given to authors whose work has been recognized by the children of Pennsylvania. There are three categories K–3, 3-6, and 6–8.

4618 1992. *My Teacher Is an Alien.* Bruce Coville. *Illustrator:* Mike Wimmer. Minstrel Books, 1990. *Category:* grades 3-5.
4619 1992. *Maniac Magee.* Jerry Spinelli. Little, Brown & Co., 1990. *Category:* grades 6–8.
4620 1993. *Fudge-A-Mania.* Judy Blume. Dutton, 1990. *Category:* grades 3-5.
4621 1993. *Shiloh.* Phyllis Reynolds Naylor. Atheneum, 1991. *Category:* grades 6–8.
4622 1994. *The Stinky Cheese Man and Other Fairly Stupid Tales.* Jon Scieszka. *Illustrator:* Lane Smith. Viking, 1992. *Category:* grades 3-8.
4623 1995. *The Giver.* Lois Lowry. Houghton Mifflin, 1993. *Category:* grades 3-8.
4624 1995. *Martha Speaks.* Susan Meddaugh. Houghton, 1992. *Category:* K–3.
4625 1996. *The Three Little Wolves and the Big Bad Pig.* Eugene Trivizas. Margaret McElderry, 1993. *Category:* K–3.
4626 1996. *The Sweetest Fig.* Chris van Allsburg. *Illustrator:* Chris van Allsburg. Houghton Mifflin, 1993. *Category:* grades 3-8.
4627 1997. *Heart of a Champion.* Carl Deuker. Joy Street, 1993. *Category:* grades 6–8.
4628 1997. *Swamp Angel.* Anne Isaacs. Dutton, 1994. *Category:* grades 3-6.
4629 1997. *Officer Buckle and Gloria.* Peggy Rathmann. Putnam, 1995. *Category:* K–3.

4630 1998. *Buz.* Richard Egielski. HarperCollins, 1995. *Category:* K–3.
4631 1998. *Spying on Miss Muller.* Eve Bunting. *Illustrator:* Ellen Thompson. Clarion Books, 1995. *Category:* grades 6–8.
4632 1998. *The Best School Year Ever.* Barbara Robinson. HarperCollins, 1994. *Category:* grades 3-6.
4633 1999. *Shiloh Season.* Phyllis Reynolds Naylor. Atheneum, 1996. *Category:* grades 3-6.
4634 1999. *No More Water in the Tub.* Tedd Arnold. Dial, 1995. *Category:* K–3.
4635 1999. *Crash!* Jerry Spinelli. Knopf, 1996. *Category:* grades 6–8.
4636 2000. *Holes.* Louis Sachar. Farrar Straus Giroux, 1998. *Category:* grades 6–8.
4637 2000. *Frindle.* Andrew Clements. *Illustrator:* Brian Selznick. Simon & Schuster, 1996. *Category:* grades 3-6.
4638 2000. *The Adventures of Captain Underpants.* Dav Pilkey. Scholastic, 1997. *Category:* K–3.

4639 Phoenix Award

SPONSOR: Children's Literature Association. ADDRESS: P.O. Box 138, Battle Creek, Michigan 49016-0138. PHONE: (616) 965-8180. ESTABLISHED: 1985. AWARD: A brass statue. The annual award is given to an author whose writing in English for children has been published 20 years earlier. At the time of publication, the book must not have won any major awards.

4640 1990. *Enchantress from the Stars.* Sylvia Louise Engdahl. *Illustrator:* Rodney Shackell. Atheneum, 1970.
4641 1991. *A Long Way from Verona.* Jane Gardam. H. Hamilton, 1971.
4642 1992. *A Sound of Chariots.* Mollie Hunter. H. Hamilton, 1972.
4643 1993. *Carrie's War.* Nina Bawden. Gollancz, 1973.
4644 1994. *Of Nightingales That Weep.* Katherine Paterson. Crowell, 1974.
4645 1995. *Dragonwings.* Laurence Yep. HarperCollins, 1975.
4646 1996. *The Stone Book.* Alan Garner. Collins, 1976.
4647 1997. *I Am the Cheese.* Robert Cormier. *Illustrator:* Robert Vickery. Pantheon, 1977.
4648 1998. *A Chance Child.* Jill Paton Walsh. Macmillan, 1978.
4649 1999. *Throwing Shadows.* E.L. Konigsburg. Atheneum, 1979.
4650 2000. *The Keeper of the Isis Light.* Monica Hughes. Atheneum, 1979.

4651 Please Touch Book Award

SPONSOR: Please Touch Museum for Children. ADDRESS: 210 North 21st Street, Philadelphia, Pennsylvania 19103. PHONE: (215) 963-0667. ESTABLISHED: 1985.

AWARD: A medal. The award is given annually to a picture book which effectively explores concepts including: colors, shapes, sizes, senses, and feelings, for children ages three years or younger. The book must be published in the United States in the previous year.

4652 1990. *What's Inside?* Duanne Daughty. *Illustrator:* Duanne Daughty. Knopf, 1984.

4653 1991. *Prize in the Snow.* Bill Easterling. *Illustrator:* Mary Beth Owens. Little, Brown & Co., 1994.

4654 1992. *Maisy Goes to Bed.* Lucy Cousins. *Illustrator:* Lucy Cousins. Little, Brown & Co., 1990.

4655 1993. *Is It Larger? Is It Smaller?* Tana Hoban. *Illustrator:* Tana Hoban. Harcourt.

4656 1994. *Hippity Hop, Frog on Top.* Natasha Wing. *Illustrator:* Deloss McGraw. Simon & Schuster, 1994.

4657 1995. *Fiddle-I-Fee : A Farmyard Song for the Very Young.* Melissa Sweet. *Illustrator:* Jakki Wood. Little, Brown & Co., 1994.

4658 1996. *Dinosaurs, Dinosaurs.* Byron Barton. *Illustrator:* Byron Barton. Harper. Trophy, 1993.

4659 1997. *Claude and Sun.* Matt Novak. Atheneum, 1987.

4660 1998. *Arnold Always Answers.* Deborah Kotter. *Illustrator:* Jane Conteh-Morgan. Doubleday, 1993.

4661 Prairie Pasque Award

SPONSOR: South Dakota Library Association. ADDRESS: 501 E. St. Joseph St., Rapid City, South Dakota 57701. PHONE: (605) 394-1258. ESTABLISHED: 1987. The award is determined by fourth, fifth, and sixth grade students throughout the state. They read and vote for their favorite book of the year. The book with the most votes wins the award.

4662 1990. *This Island Isn't Big Enough for the Four of Us.* Gery Greer, Bob Ruddick. Harper. Trophy 1989.

4663 1991. *All About Sam.* Lois Lowry. *Illustrator:* Diane DeGroat. Houghton Mifflin, 1988.

4664 1992. *The Doll in the Garden: A Ghost Story.* Mary Downing Hahn. Clarion, 1989.

4665 1993. *Hugh Glass, Mountain Man.* Robert McClung. William Morrow, 1990.

4666 1994. *Shiloh.* Phyllis Reynolds Naylor. Atheneum, 1991.

4667 1995. *Devil's Bridge.* Cynthia de Felice. Farrar Straus & Giroux, 1995.

4668 1996. *Someone Was Watching.* David Patneaude. *Illustrator:* Paul Micich. Albert Whitman, 1993.

4669 1997. *The Best School Year Ever.* Barbara Robinson. HarperCollins, 1994.

4670 1998. *Titanic Crossing.* Barbara Williams. Dial Books for Young Readers, 1995.

4671 1999. *Frindle.* Andrew Clements. *Illustrator:* Brian Selznick. Simon & Schuster, 1996.

4672 2000. *The Adventures of Captain Underpants.* Dav Pilkey. Scholastic 1997.

4673 Pura Belpré Award

SPONSOR: Association for Library Service to Children (ALSC) and National Association to Promote Library Services to the Spanish Speaking. ADDRESS: 50 E. Huron St., Chicago, Illinois 60611. PHONE: 1-800-545-2433. ESTABLISHED: 1996. The award is given to a Latino/Latina writer and illustrator whose work best portrays, affirms, and celebrates the Latino cultural experience in an outstanding work of literature for children and youth. The awards are given biennially.

4674 1996. *An Island Like You: Stories of the Barrio*. Judih Ortiz Cofer. Orchard Books, 1995. *Category:* fiction.

4675 1996. *Chato's Kitchen.* Gary Soto. *Illustrator:* Susan Guevara. Putnam, 1995. *Category:* illustration.

4676 1998. *Parrot in the Oven: Mi Vida.* Victor Martinez. HarperCollins, 1996. *Category:* fiction.

4677 1998. *Snapshots from the Wedding.* Gary Soto. *Illustrator:* Stephanie Garcia. Putnam, 1997. *Category:* illustration.

4678 2000. *Magic Windows.* Carmen Lomas Garza. *Illustrator:* Carmen Lomas Garza. Children's Book Press, 1999. *Category:* illustration.

4679 2000. *Under the Royal Palms: A Childhood in Cuba*. Alma Flor Ada. Atheneum Books, 1998. *Category:* narrative.

4680 Randolph Caldecott Award

SPONSOR: American Library Association. CONTACT: Association for Library Services for Children. ADDRESS: 50 East Huron Street, Chicago Illinois 60611. PHONE: 1-800-545-2433. ESTABLISHED: 1938. AWARD: A gold medal and certificate. The annual award is given to the artist of the most distinguished picture book for children. The award is restricted to artists who are citizens or residents of the United States.

4681 1990. *The Talking Eggs.* Robert San Souci. *Illustrator:* Jerry Pinkney. Dial, 1989. *Category:* honor.

4682 1990. *Color Zoo.* Lois Ehlert. *Illustrator:* Lois Ehlert. Lippincott, 1989. *Category:* honor.

4683 1990. *Hershel and the Hanukkah Goblins.* Eric A. Kimmel. *Illustrator:* Trina Schart Hyman. Holiday, 1989. *Category:* honor.

4684 1990. *Lon Po Po: A Red Riding Hood Story from China.* Ed Young. *Illustrator:* Ed Young. Philomel, 1989.

4685 1990. *Bill Peet.* Bill Peet. *Illustrator:* Bill Peet. Houghton Mifflin, 1989. *Category:* honor.

4686 1991. *Puss in Boots.* Charles Perrault. *Illustrator:* Fred Marcellino. *Translator:* Malcolm Arthur. Farrar, Straus & Giroux, 1990. *Category:* honor.

4687 1991. *More More More Said the Baby.* Vera B. Williams. *Illustrator:* Vera B. Williams. William Morrow, 1990. *Category:* honor.

4688 1991. *Black & White.* David Macaulay. *Illustrator:* David Macaulay. Houghton Mifflin, 1990.

4689 1992. *Tuesday.* David Wiesner. *Illustrator:* David Wiesner. Clarion, 1991.

4690 1992. *Tar Beach.* Faith Ringgold. *Illustrator:* Faith Ringgold. Crown, 1991. *Category:* honor.

4691 1993. *The Stinky Cheese Man and Other Fairly Stupid Tales.* Jon Scieszka. *Illustrator:* Lane Smith. Viking, 1992. *Category:* honor.

4692 1993. *Seven Blind Mice.* Ed Young. *Illustrator:* Ed Young. Philomel, 1982. *Category:* honor.

4693 1993. *Working Cotton.* Anne Williams. *Illustrator:* Carole Byard. Harcourt Brace, 1992. *Category:* honor.

4694 1993. *Mirette on the High Wire.* Emily McCully. *Illustrator:* Emily McCully. Putnam, 1992.

4695 1994. *Grandfather's Journey.* Allen Say. *Illustrator:* Allen Say. Houghton Mifflin, 1993.

4696 1994. *In a Small, Small Pond.* Denise Fleming. *Illustrator:* Denise Fleming. Henry Holt & Co., 1993. *Category:* honor.

4697 1994. *Owen.* Kevin Henkes. *Illustrator:* Kevin Henkes. Greenwillow, 1993. *Category:* honor.

4698 1994. *Peppe the Lamplighter.* Elisa Bartone. *Illustrator:* Ted Lewin. Lothrop, Lee & Shepard, 1993. *Category:* honor.

4699 1994. *Raven.* Gerald McDermott. *Illustrator:* Gerald McDermott. Harcourt Brace, 1993. *Category:* honor.

4700 1994. *Yo! Yes?* Chris Raschka. *Illustrator:* Chris Raschka. Orchard, 1993. *Category:* honor.

4701 1995. *John Henry.* Julius Lester. *Illustrator:* Jerry Pinkney. Dial, 1994. *Category:* honor.

4702 1995. *Smoky Night.* Eve Bunting. *Illustrator:* David Diaz. Harcourt Brace, 1994.

4703 1995. *Swamp Angel.* Anne Isaacs. *Illustrator:* Paul O. Zelinsky. Dutton, 1994. *Category:* honor.

4704 1995. *Time Flies.* Eric Rohmann. *Illustrator:* Eric Rohmann. Crown, 1994. *Category:* honor.

4705 1996. *Tops and Bottoms.* Janet Stevens. *Illustrator:* Janet Stevens. Harcourt Brace, 1995. *Category:* honor.

4706 1996. *Officer Buckle and Gloria.* Peggy Rathmann. *Illustrator:* Peggy Rathmann. Putnam, 1995.

4707 1996. *Zin! Zin! Zin! A Violin.* Lloyd Moss. *Illustrator:* Majorie Priceman. Simon & Schuster, 1995. *Category:* honor.

4708 1996. *Alphabet City.* Stephen T. Johnson. *Illustrator:* Stephen T. Johnson. Viking, 1995. *Category:* honor.

4709 1996. *The Faithful Friend.* Robert San Souci. *Illustrator:* Brian Pinkney. Simon and Schuster, 1995. *Category:* honor.

4710 1997. *Golem.* David Wisniewski. *Illustrator:* David Wisniewski. Clarion, 1996.

4711 1997. *Hush! A Thai Lullaby.* Minfong Ho. *Illustrator:* Holly Meade. Orchard, 1996. *Category:* honor.

4712 1997. *Starry Messenger.* Peter Sis. *Illustrator:* Peter Sis. Farrar, Straus & Giroux, 1996. *Category:* honor.

4713 1997. *The Graphic Alphabet.* David Pelletier. *Illustrator:* David Pelletier. Orchard, 1996. *Category:* honor.

4714 1997. *The Paperboy.* Dav Pilkey. *Illustrator:* Dav Pilkey. Orchard, 1996. *Category:* honor.

4715 1998. *The Gardener.* Sarah Stewart. *Illustrator:* David Small. Farrar, Straus & Giroux, 1997. *Category:* honor.

4716 1998. *Rapunzel.* Paul O. Zelinsky. *Illustrator:* Paul O. Zelinsky. Dutton, 1997.

4717 1998. *There Was an Old Lady Who Swallowed a Fly.* Simms Taback. *Illustrator:* Simms Taback. Viking, 1997. *Category:* honor.

4718 1998. *Harlem: A Poem.* Walter Dean Myers. *Illustrator:* Christ Myers. Scholastic, 1997. *Category:* honor.

4719 1999. *Snowflake Bentley.* Mary Azarian. *Illustrator:* Mary Azarian. Houghton Mifflin, 1998.

4720 1999. *Duke Ellington: The Piano Prince and His Orchestra.* Andrea Davis Pinkney. *Illustrator:* Brian Pinkney. Disney, 1998. *Category:* honor.

4721 1999. *No, David!* David Shannon. *Illustrator:* David Shannon. Scholastic, 1998. *Category:* honor.

4722 1999. *Snow.* Uri Shulevitz. *Illustrator:* Uri Shulevitz. Farrar, Straus & Giroux, 1998. *Category:* honor.

4723 1999. *Tibet Through the Red Box.* Peter Sis. *Illustrator:* Peter Sis. Farrar, Straus & Giroux, 1998. *Category:* honor.

4724 2000. *Joseph Had a Little Overcoat.* Simms Taback. *Illustrator:* Simms Taback. Viking, 1999.

4725 2000. *The Ugly Duckling.* Hans Christian Andersen. *Illustrator:* Jerry Pinkney. Morrow, 1999. *Category:* honor.

4726 2000. *When Sophie Gets Angry—Really, Really Angry.* Molly Bang. *Illustrator:* Molly Bang. Scholastic, 1999. *Category:* honor.

4727 2000. *Sector 7.* David Wiesner. *Illustrator:* David Wiesner. Clarion Books, 1999. *Category:* honor.

4728 2000. *A Child's Calendar.* John Updike. *Illustrator:* Trina Schart Hyman. Holiday House, 1999. *Category:* honor.

4729 Rebecca Caudill Young Readers' Book Award

SPONSOR: Illinois State Library, a Division of the Office of Secretary of State. ADDRESS: Office of the Secretary of State, State Library, Springfield Illinois 62756. PHONE: (217) 782-2522. ESTABLISHED: 1988. AWARD: A plaque. The annual award is presented to the author of a book voted to be the most outstanding by children of Illinois in grades 4 to 8. The book must have been published in the last five years.

4730 1990. *Wait Till Helen Comes.* Mary Downing Hahn. Clarion, 1986.

4731 1991. *Matilda.* Roald Dahl. *Illustrator:* Quentin Blake. Viking, 1988.

4732 1992. *Number the Stars.* Lois Lowry. Houghton Mifflin, 1989.

4733 1993. *Maniac Magee.* Jerry Spinelli. Little, Brown & Co., 1989.

4734 1994. *Shiloh.* Phyllis Reynolds Naylor. Atheneum, 1991.

4735 1995. *Flight #116 Is Down.* Caroline Cooney. Scholastic, 1992.

4736 1996. *The Giver.* Lois Lowry. Houghton Mifflin, 1993.

4737 1997. *Best School Year Ever.* Barbara Robinson. *Illustrator:* Michael Deas. HarperCollins, 1994.

4738 1998. *Mick Harte Was Here.* Barbara Park. Knopf, 1995.

4739 1999. *Frindle.* Andrew Clements. *Illustrator:* Brian Selznick. Simon & Schuster, 1996.

4740 2000. *Ella Enchanted.* Gail Carson Levine. HarperCollins, 1997.

4741 Red Clover Children's Choice Picture Book Award

SPONSOR: Vermont Center for the Book, Windham County Reads, the Vermont Department of Education and the Vermont Department of Libraries. CONTACT: Wendy Martin. ADDRESS: Vermont Center for the Book, 256 Haywood Rd., Chester, Vermont 05143. PHONE: (802) 875-2751. ESTABLISHED: 1995. AWARD: A whimsical clay statue created by Alan Pascall. The award is designed to foster awareness, understanding and appreciation of the picture book.

4742 1997. *Piggie Pie!* Margie Palatini. *Illustrator:* Howard Fine. Clarion Books, 1995.

4743 1998. *Art Dog.* Thacher Hurd. *Illustrator:* Thacher Hurd. HarperCollins, 1996.

4744 1999. *Akiak : A Tale from the Iditarod.* Robert J. Blake. *Illustrator:* Robert J. Blake. Philomel Books, 1997.

4745 2000. *Ten Minutes Till Bedtime.* Peggy Rathmann. *Illustrator:* Peggy Rathmann. Putnam, 1998.

4746 Regina Medal

SPONSOR: The Catholic Library Association. ADDRESS: 100 North Street, Suite 224, Pittsfield, Massachusetts 01201-5109. PHONE: (413) 443-2252. ESTABLISHED: 1959. AWARD: An oval shaped silver medal. The award may be given to an author, illustrator, editor or publisher to honor sustained excellence in the writing of literature for children in English.

4747 1990. Virginia Hamilton.

4748 1991. Leonard Everett Fisher.

4749 1992. Jane Yolen.

4750 1993. Chris van Allsburg.

4751 1994. Lois Lowry.

4752 1995. Gary Paulsen.

4753 1996. Russell Freedman.

4754 1997. Eve Bunting.

4755 1998. Patricia McKissack, Fredrick McKissack.

4756 1999. Eric Carle.

4757 2000. Milton Meltzer.

4758 2001. E.L. Konigsburg.

4759 Rhode Island Children's Book Award

SPONSOR: Rhode Island Office of Library and Information Services (OLIS). CONTACT: Joy Helmold. ADDRESS: 1 Capitol Hill, Providence, Rhode Island 02908. ESTABLISHED: 1990. AWARD: A decorative pen holder. The annual award is given to an author living in the United States at the time of nomination for a book appropriate for grades 3–6 and was published in the last 3 years.

4760 1991. *Something Upstairs.* Avi. Orchard, 1988.

4761 1992. *Maniac Magee.* Jerry Spinelli. Little, Brown & Co., 1990.

4762 1993. *The Houdini Box.* Brian Selznick. Knopf, 1991.

4763 1994. *The Stinky Cheese Man and Other Fairly Stupid Tales.* Jon Scieszka. *Illustrator:* Lane Smith. Viking, 1992.

4764 1995. *The Sweetest Fig.* Chris van Allsburg. *Illustrator:* Chris van Allsburg. Houghton Mifflin, 1993.

4765 1996. *Jacob and the Stranger.* Sally Derby. *Illustrator:* Leonid Gore. Ticknor & Fields; 1994.

4766 1997. *Mick Harte Was Here.* Barbara Park. Knopf, 1995.

4767 1998. *Frindle.* Andrew Clements. *Illustrator:* Brian Selznick. Simon & Schuster, 1996.

4768 1999. *The Adventures of Captain Underpants.* Dav Pilkey. Scholastic, 1997.

4769 2000. *Thank You, Mr. Falker.* Patricia Polacco. Philomel, 1998.

4770 Sasquatch Book Award

SPONSOR: Washington Library Media Association. CONTACT: Joanne Hjort. ADDRESS: P.O. Box 25026, Seattle Washington 98125-1926. ESTABLISHED: 1999. The award is given to an author for a fiction or non-fiction book for the intermediate reader.

4771 1999. *Frindle.* Andrew Clements. *Illustrator:* Brian Selznick. Simon & Schuster, 1996.

4772 2000. *Harry Potter and the Sorcerer's Stone.* J.K. Rowling. *Illustrator:* Mary Grandpré. Scholastic, 1998.

4773 Science-Writing Award in Physics and Astronomy for Articles or Books Intended for Children

SPONSOR: American Institute of Physics. ADDRESS: One Physics Ellipse College Park, College Park, Maryland 20740-3843. PHONE: (301)209-3090. ESTABLISHED: 1988. AWARD: $3,000, a Windsor Chair, and a certificate. The award is given for an article, booklet, or book written in English or translated into English for children from preschool ages to 15 years dealing primarily with physics and astronomy.

4774 1990. *The Way Things Work.* David Macaulay. *Illustrator:* Neil Ardley. Houghton Mifflin, 1989.

4775 1991. *Airborne.* Richard Maurer. Simon & Schuster, 1990.

4776 1992. *Almost the Real Thing.* Gloria Skurzynski. Bradbury Press, 1991.

4777 1993. *Stargazers.* Gail Gibbons. Holiday House, 1992.

4778 1994. *Make It Work!* Wendy Baker, Andrew Haslam. Macmillan, 1993.

4779 1995. *The Third Planet: Exploring the Earth from Space.* Sally Ride, Tam O'Shaughnessy. Crown, 1994.

4780 1996. *Bouncing and Bending Light.* Steve Tomecek. W.H. Freeman, 1995.

4781 1997. *Extinction Is Forever.* Donald Silver. Silver Burdett, 1996.

4782 1998. *Earth Explained.* Barbara Taylor. Henry Holt, 1997.

4783 1999. *Close Encounters.* Elaine Scott. Hyperion, 1998.

4784 2000. *Science Play!* Jill Frankel Hauser. Williamson Publishing, 1999.

4785 2000. *Gizmos & Gadgets.* Jill Frankel Hauser. Williamson Publishing, 1999.

4786 Scott O'Dell Historical Fiction Award

SPONSOR: Scott O'Dell Foundation. ADDRESS: Bulletin of the Center of Children's Books, 1100 E. 57th St., Chicago, Illinois 60637. PHONE: (312) 702-8284. ESTABLISHED: 1981. AWARD: $5,000.00 U.S. The award is given annually to the author of a distinguished work of historical fiction set in the New World. The book must be published in English for children or young adults by a United States publisher and written by an American.

4787 1990. *Shades of Gray.* Carolyn Reeder. Macmillan, 1989.
4788 1991. *A Time of Troubles.* Pieter van Raven. Atheneum, 1990.
4789 1992. *Stepping on the Cracks.* Mary Downing Hahn. Clarion, 1991.
4790 1993. *Morning Girl.* Michael Dorris. Hyperion Books, 1992.
4791 1994. *Bull Run.* Paul Fleischman. *Illustrator:* David Frampton. HarperCollins, 1993.
4792 1995. *Under the Blood Red Sun.* Graham Salisbury. Delacorte, 1994.
4793 1996. *The Bomb.* Theodore Taylor. Harcourt Brace, 1995.
4794 1997. *Jip: His Story.* Katherine Paterson. Lodestar Books, 1996.
4795 1998. *Out of the Dust.* Karen Hesse. Scholastic, 1997.
4796 1999. *Forty Acres and Maybe a Mule.* Harriette Gillem Robinet. Atheneum, 1998.

4797 Sequoyah Children's Book Award

SPONSOR: Oklahoma Library Association. CONTACT: Lana Voss. ADDRESS: 300 Hardy Drive, Edmond, Oklahoma 73013. PHONE: (405) 348-0506. ESTABLISHED: 1959. AWARD: A plaque. The award winner is chosen annually by children in grades 2 to 6. The author must be an American currently living in the United States whose work has been published no more than three years preceding the award year.

4798 1990. *Fudge.* Charlotte Towner Graeber. *Illustrator:* Cheryl Harness. Lothrop, 1987.
4799 1991. *Beauty.* Bill Wallace. Holiday House, 1988.
4800 1992. *The Doll in the Garden.* Dorothy Hahn. Clarion Books, 1989.
4801 1993. *Weasel.* Cynthia DeFelice. Macmillan, 1990.
4802 1994. *Shiloh.* Phyllis Reynolds Naylor. Atheneum, 1991.
4803 1995. *Horror at the Haunted House.* Peg Kehret. Cobblehill Books, 1992.
4804 1996. *The Ghosts of Mercy Manor.* Betty Ren Wright. Scholastic, 1993.
4805 1997. *Nasty, Stinky Sneakers.* Eve Bunting. HarperCollins, 1994.

4806 1998. *Titanic Crossing.* Barbara Williams. Dial Books for Young Readers, 1995.

4807 1999. *101 Ways to Bug Your Parents.* Lee Wardlaw. Dial, 1996.

4808 2000. *The Million Dollar Shot.* Dan Gutman. *Illustrator:* Mark Buehner. Hyperion, 1997.

4809 Sequoyah Young Adult Book Award

SPONSOR: Oklahoma Library Association. CONTACT: Sally Epp. ADDRESS: 300 Hardy Drive, Edmond, Oklahoma 73013. PHONE: (405) 348-0506. ESTABLISHED: 1988. AWARD: A plaque. The award winner is chosen annually by children in grades 7 to 9. The author must be an American currently living in the United States, whose works have been published no more than two years preceding the award year.

4810 1990. *Hatchet.* Gary Paulsen. Bradbury, 1987.

4811 1991. *A Sudden Silence.* Eve Bunting. Harcourt, 1988.

4812 1992. *Appointment with a Stranger.* Jean Thesman. Houghton Mifflin, 1989.

4813 1993. *The Silver Kiss.* Annette Curtis Klause. Delacorte, 1990.

4814 1994. *What Daddy Did.* Neal Shusterman. HarperCollins, 1991.

4815 1995. *Flight #116 Is Down.* Caroline Cooney. Scholastic, 1992.

4816 1996. *The Giver.* Lois Lowry. Houghton Mifflin, 1993.

4817 1997. *Walk Two Moons.* Sharon Creech. HarperCollins, 1994.

4818 1998. *Running Out of Time.* Margaret Peterson Haddix. Simon & Schuster, 1995.

4819 1999. *Danger Zone.* David Klass. Scholastic, 1996.

4820 2000. *I Have Lived a Thousand Years.* Livia Bitton-Jackson. Simon and Schuster, 1997.

4821 Show Me Readers Award

SPONSOR: Missouri Association of School Librarians. ADDRESS: 1552 Rue Riviera, Bonne Terre, Missouri 63628-9349. ESTABLISHED: 1995. The annual award honours literature, literacy, and reading in Missouri elementary schools for grades one through three, and promotes recognition of authors and illustrators of books that are favorites of Missouri children in these grades.

4822 1995. *Sukey and the Mermaid.* Robert San Souci. *Illustrator:* Brian Pinkney. Simon & Schuster, 1992.

4823 1996. *Soap! Soap! Don't Forget the Soap!* Tom Birdseye. *Illustrator:* Andrew Glass. Holiday House, 1993.

4824 1997. *My Rotten Red-Headed Older Brother.* Patricia Polacco. *Illustrator:* Patricia Polacco. Simon & Schuster, 1994.

4825 1998. *Heart of a Tiger.* Marsha Diane Arnold. *Illustrator:* Jamichael Henterly. Dial, 1995.

4826 1999. *Duke, the Dairy Delight Dog.* Lisa Campbell. Ernst, 1996.

4827 Soaring Eagle — Wyoming Young Adult Book Award

SPONSOR: Wyoming Council of the International Reading Association and Wyoming Educational Media Association. CONTACT: Carla Howard. ADDRESS: Library Services, N.C.S.D. #1, 970 North Glen Road, Casper, Wyoming 82601. PHONE: (307) 577-6767. ESTABLISHED: 1989. The award is given to an author for his or her body-of-work in one of two categories: grades 7-9 and grades 10-12.

4828 1990. *Of Love and Shadows.* Isabel Allende. Econo-Clad Books, 1988. *Category:* 10–12.

4829 1990. *Someone Is Hiding on Alcatraz Island.* Eve Bunting. Berkley Pub Group, 1986. *Category:* 7–9.

4830 1991. *Princess Ashley.* Richard Peck. Doubleday, 1987. *Category:* 10–12.

4831 1991. *Trapped in Death Cave.* Bill Wallace. Holiday, 1984. *Category:* 7–9.

4832 1992. *Dances with Wolves.* Michael Blake. Fawcett Books, 1990.

4833 1993. *Hugh Glass, Mountain Man.* Robert McClung. William Morrow, 1990.

4834 1994. *Desperate Pursuit.* Gloria Milowitz. 1992.

4835 1995. *Jurassic Park.* Michael Crichton. Knopf, 1990.

4836 1996. *Whispers from the Dead.* Joan Lowery Nixon. Laurel Leaf, 1991.

4837 1997. *Hatchet.* Gary Paulsen. Bradbury, 1987.

4838 1998. *Freak the Mighty.* Rodman Philbrick. Scholastic, 1993.

4839 1999. *Chicken Soup for the Teenage Soul.* Jack Canfield. Health Communications, 1997.

4840 Society of Midland Authors Award

SPONSOR: Society for Midland Authors. ADDRESS: PO Box 10419, Chicago, Illinois 60611. ESTABLISHED: 1980. AWARD: A plaque and $500.00 U.S. The award honors outstanding works of fiction and non-fiction, written by an author who is currently living in Illinois, Indiana, Iowa, Kansas, Michigan, Minnesota, Missouri, Nebraska, North Dakota, Ohio, South Dakota, or Wisconsin. The book must be published in the previous year.

1990. No awards given.

4841 1991. *Robodad.* Alden R. Carter. Putnam Publishers, 1990. *Category:* non-fiction.

4842 1991. *Woodsong.* Gary Paulsen. Bradbury Press, 1990. *Category:* fiction.

4843 1992. *A Place to Claim as Home.* Patricia Willis. Clarion, 1991. *Category:* fiction.

4844 1992. *The Heroine of the Titanic.* Joan Blos. Morrow, 1991. *Category:* non-fiction.

4845 1993. *Rosa Parks: My Story.* Rosa Parks, Jim Haskins. Penguin, 1992. *Category:* non-fiction.

4846 1993. *The Original Freddie Ackerman.* Hadley Irwin. McElderry Books, 1992. *Category:* fiction.

4847 1994. *Night of the Full Moon.* Gloria Whelan. Knopf, 1993. *Category:* fiction.

4848 1994. *Many Thousand Gone: African Americans from Slavery to Freedom.* Virginia Hamilton. Random House, 1993. *Category:* non-fiction.

4849 1995. *Jericho.* Janet Hickman. Greenwillow Books, 1994. *Category:* fiction.

4850 1995. *Hearing Us Out.* Roger Sutton. Little, Brown & Co., 1994. *Category:* non-fiction.

4851 1996. *Out of the Storm.* Patricia Willis. Clarion Books, 1995. *Category:* fiction.

4852 1996. *Our Endangered Planet: Atmosphere.* Mary Hoff. *Illustrator:* Mary M. Rodgers. Lerner Publications, 1995. *Category:* non-fiction.

4853 1997. *Orphan Train Rider: One Boy's True Story.* Andrea Warren. Houghton Mifflin, 1996. *Category:* non-fiction.

4854 1997. *Would My Fortune Cookie Lie?* Stella Pevsner. Clarion Books, 1996. *Category:* fiction.

4855 1998. *The Twins: The Pirates and the Battle of New Orleans.* Harriette Gillem Robinet. Atheneum, 1997. *Category:* fiction.

4856 1998. *Just What the Doctor Ordered.* Brandon Marie Miller. Lemer, 1997. *Category:* non-fiction.

4857 1999. *Pioneer Girl: Growing Up on the Prairie.* Andrea Warren. Morrow, 1998. *Category:* non-fiction.

4858 1999. *Susannah.* Janet Hickman. Greenwillow Press, 1998. *Category:* fiction.

4859 2000. *Black Hands, White Sails: The Story of African-American Whalers.* Patricia McKissack. *Illustrator:* Fredrick L. McKissack. Scholastic, 1999. *Category:* non-fiction.

4860 2000. *Trapped Between the Lash and the Gun.* Arvella Whitmore. Penguin Putnam, 1999. *Category:* fiction.

4861 South Carolina Children's Book Award

SPONSOR: South Carolina Association of School Librarians. CONTACT: David Cobb, SCASL Executive Secretary. ADDRESS: Box 2442, Columbia, South Carolina 29202. PHONE: (803) 796–8427. ESTABLISHED: 1975. AWARD: A medal. South Carolina children in grades 4 to 8 vote for their favorite book. It can be either fiction or non-fiction, excluding Newbery winners. The book must be published in the last three years and must currently appear in Books In Print.

4862 1990. *Class Clown.* Johanna Hurwitz. *Illustrator:* Sheila Hamanka. Morrow, 1987.

4863 1991. *Is Anybody There?* Eve Bunting. Harper. Trophy, 1990.

4864 1992. *Snot Stew.* Bill Wallace. *Illustrator:* Lisa McCue. Holiday House 1989.

4865 1993. *Weasel.* Cynthia DeFelice. Macmillan, 1990.

4866 1994. *Fourth Grade Rats.* Jerry Spinelli. Apple, 1996.

4867 1995. *Sukey and the Mermaid.* Robert San Souci. *Illustrator:* Brian Pinkney. Simon & Schuster, 1992.

4868 1996. *The Boys Start the War.* Phyllis Reynolds Naylor. Delacorte, 1993.

4869 1997. *Best School Year Ever.* Barbara Robinson. *Illustrator:* Michael Deas. HarperCollins, 1994.

4870 1998. *The Story of Ruby Bridges.* Robert Coles. *Illustrator:* George Ford. Scholastic, 1995.

4871 1999. *Tornado.* Betsy Byars. HarperCollins, 1996.

4872 2000. *Rumpelstiltskin's Daughter.* Diane Stanley. *Illustrator:* Diane Stanley. William Morrow & Company, 1997.

4873 South Carolina Junior Book Award

SPONSOR: South Carolina Association of School Librarians. CONTACT: David Cobb, SCASL Executive Secretary. ADDRESS: Box 2442, Columbia, South Carolina 29202. PHONE: (803) 796–8427. ESTABLISHED: 1992. AWARD: A medal. The award will encourage middle/junior high school students to vote for their favorite authors.

4874 1993. *The Dead Man in Indian Creek.* Mary Downing Hahn. Clarion, 1990.

4875 1994. *Stepping on the Cracks.* Mary Downing Hahn. Clarion, 1991.

4876 1995. *A Ghost in the House.* Betty Ren Wright. Econo-Clad Books, 1999.

4877 1996. *Baby.* Patricia MacLachlan. Delacorte, 1993.

4878 1997. *Phoenix Rising.* Karen Hesse. Henry Holt, 1994.

4879 1998. *Mick Harte Was Here.* Barbara Park. Knopf, 1995.

4880 1999. *Crash!* Jerry Spinelli. Knopf, 1996.

4881 2000. *The True Colors of Caitlynne Jackson.* Carol Lynch Williams. Delacorte, 1997.

4882 South Carolina Young Adult Book Award

SPONSOR: South Carolina Association of School Librarians. CONTACT: David Cobb, SCASL Executive Secretary. ADDRESS: Box 2442, Columbia, South Carolina

29202. PHONE: (803) 796–8427. ESTABLISHED: 1980. AWARD: A medal. South Carolina children in grades 9 to 12 vote for their favorite fiction or non-fiction book. Newbery award winners are excluded. The book must be published in the last three years and currently appear in Books in Print.

4883 1990. *The Year Without Michael.* Susan Beth Pfeffer. Delacorte, 1986.

4884 1991. *Fallen Angels.* Walter Dean Myers. Scholastic, 1988.

4885 1992. *On the Devil's Court.* Carl Deuker. Avon, 1991.

4886 1993. *The Silver Kiss.* Annette Curtis Klause. Delacorte, 1990.

4887 1994. *Jurassic Park.* Michael Crichton. Knopf, 1990.

4888 1995. *What You Don't Know Can Kill You.* Fran Arrick. Bantam Doubleday, 1992.

4889 1996. *Detour for Emmy.* Marilyn Reynolds. Morning Glory, 1993.

4890 1997. *Harris and Me.* Gary Paulsen. Harcourt Brace, 1993.

4891 1998. *A Time for Dancing.* Davida Wills Hurwin. Little, Brown & Co., 1995.

4892 1999. *Slam!* Walter Dean Myers. Scholastic, 1996.

4893 2000. *Blood and Chocolate.* Annette Curtis Klause. Bantam Books, 1997.

4894 Southern California Council on Literature for Children and Young People Annual Children's Literature Awards

SPONSOR: SCCLCYP, Orange Public Library. ADDRESS: P.O. Box 5249, North Hollywood, California 91616. ESTABLISHED: 1961. AWARD: A plaque. The awards are given in a variety of areas each year to authors and illustrators who live in Southern California. The winning books must be published within the previous year.

4895 1990. *Once Upon a Horse.* Suzanne Jurmain. Lodestar, 1989. *Category:* non-fiction.

4896 1990. *Wrestling with Honor.* David Klass. Lodestar, 1989. *Category:* fiction.

4897 1990. *An Autobiography by Bill Peet.* Bill Peet. *Illustrator:* Bill Peet. Houghton Mifflin, 1989.

4898 1990. *The Wednesday Surprise.* Eve Bunting. *Illustrator:* Donald Carrick. Clarion, 1989. *Category:* fiction.

4899 1991. *The Wall.* Eve Bunting. Clarion, 1990. *Category:* fiction.

4900 1991. *Dixie Storms.* Barbara Hall. Harcourt, 1990. *Category:* fiction.

4901 1991. *The Dragon's Robe.* Deborah Nourse Lattimore. HarperCollins, 1990. *Category:* picture book.

4902 1991. *Christopher Columbus: Voyager to the Unknown.* Nancy Smiler Levinson. Lodestar, 1990. *Category:* non-fiction.

4903 1992. *Native American Doctor: The Story of Susan La Fleshe Piconte.* Jeri Ferris. Carolrhoda, 1991. *Category:* biography.

4904 1992. *Piggies.* Aubrey Wood. *Illustrator:* Don Wood. Harcourt, Brace, 1991. *Category:* picture book.

4905 1992. *Blue Skye.* Lael Littke. Scholastic, 1991. *Category:* fiction.

4906 1992. *What Daddy Did.* Neal Shusterman. Little, 1991. *Category:* young adults.

4907 1993. *Snowshoe Thompson.* Nancy Smiler Levinson. Harper & Row, 1992. *Category:* non-fiction.

4908 1993. *Hummingbirds: Jewels in the Sky.* Esther Tyrrell. *Illustrator:* Robert Tyrrell. Crown, 1992. *Category:* non-fiction.

4909 1993. *Going to Sleep on the Farm.* Juan Wijngaard. *Illustrator:* Juan Wijngaard. Dial, 1992. *Category:* picture book.

4910 1994. *Extra Innings: Baseball Poems.* Lee Bennett Hopkins. *Illustrator:* Scott Medlock. Harcourt Brace, 1993. *Category:* illustration.

4911 1994. *Lives of the Musicians.* Kathleen Krull. Harcourt Brace, 1993. *Category:* non-fiction.

4912 1994. *Stellaluna.* Janell Cannon. *Illustrator:* Janell Cannon. Harcourt Brace, 1993. *Category:* picture book.

4913 1995. *Earthshine.* Theresa Nelson. Orchard, 1994. *Category:* fiction.

4914 1995. *The Tale of Rabbit and Coyote.* Tony Johnston. *Illustrator:* Tomie de Paola. Putnam, 1994. *Category:* folklore.

4915 1995. *Smoky Night.* Eve Bunting. *Illustrator:* David Diaz. Harcourt Brace, 1994. *Category:* picture book.

4916 1996. *Advice for a Frog.* Alice Schertle. Lothrop, 1995.

4917 1996. *V Is for Victory.* Kathleen Krull. Knopf, 1995. *Category:* non-fiction.

4918 1996. *The Bomb.* Theodore Taylor. Harcourt Brace, 1995. *Category:* fiction.

4919 1996. *Down the Road.* Alice Schertle. Harcourt Brace, 1995.

4920 1997. *The Language of Doves.* Gred Shed. *Illustrator:* Gred Shed. Dial, 1996. *Category:* illustration.

4921 1997. *The Abracadabra Kid: A Writer's Life.* Sid Fleischman. Greenwillow, 1996.

4922 1997. *Danger Zone.* David Klass. Scholastic, 1996. *Category:* young adult fiction.

4923 1998. *For Your Eyes Only.* Joanne Rocklin. Scholastic, 1997. *Category:* fiction.

4924 1998. *Seven Silly Eaters.* Marla Frazee. *Illustrator:* Marla Frazee. Browndeer Press/Harcourt Brace, 1997. *Category:* illustration.

4925 1998. *The Dark Side of Nowhere.* Neal Shusterman. Little, Brown & Co., 1997. *Category:* young adult fiction.

4926 1998. *Burnt Toast on Davenport Street.* Tim Egan. Houghton Mifflin, 1997. *Category:* picture book.

4927 1999. *Frontier Merchants.* Jerry Stanley. Crown, 1998. *Category:* non-fiction.

4928 1999. *No, David.* David Shannon. Blue Sky Press, 1998. *Category:* picture book.

4929 1999. *Old Elm Speaks: Tree Poems.* Kristine O'Connell George. Clarion Books, 1998. *Category:* poetry.

4930 1999. *Riding Freedom.* Pam Munoz Ryan. Scholastic, 1998. *Category:* first novel.

4931 Spur Award

SPONSOR: Western Writers of America Inc. ADDRESS: 60 Sandpiper, Conway, Arizona 72032. PHONE: (501) 450-0086. ESTABLISHED: 1954. AWARD: A plaque with a mounted golden spur. The award is given to fiction and non-fiction books for children.

4932 1990. *Woodsong.* Gary Paulsen. Delacorte, 1990. *Category:* non-fiction.

4933 1990. *Honey Girl.* Madge Harrah. Harper & Row, 1990. *Category:* fiction.

4934 1991. *Rescue Josh McGuire.* Ben Mikaelsen. Hyperion, 1991.

4935 1992. *Children of the Dust Bowl.* Jerry Stanley. Crown Publishers, 1992. *Category:* non-fiction.

4936 1992. *The Haymeadow.* Gary Paulsen. Delacorte, 1992. *Category:* fiction.

4937 1993. *Cowboys, Indians and Gunfighters.* Albert Martin. Atheneum, 1993. *Category:* non-fiction.

4938 1993. *Leaving Eldorado.* Joann Mazzio. Houghton Mifflin, 1993. *Category:* fiction.

4939 1994. *A Trail of Tears.* David Fremon. Silver Burdett, 1994.

4940 1995. *Indio.* Sherry Garland. Harcourt Brace, 1995. *Category:* fiction.

4941 1995. *Camels for Uncle Sam.* Diane Yancey. Hendrick-Long, 1995. *Category:* non-fiction.

4942 1996. *Far North.* Will Hobbs. William Morrow, 1996. *Category:* fiction.

4943 1996. *The Life and Death of Crazy Horse.* Russell Freedman. Holiday House, 1996. *Category:* non-fiction.

1997. No award given.

4944 1998. *Danger Along the Ohio.* Patricia Willis. Clarion, 1997. *Category:* fiction.

4945 1998. *Rattlesnake Dance.* Jennifer Owings Dewey. Boyds Mills, 1997. *Category:* non-fiction.

4946 1999. *Cowboy with a Camera: Erwin E. Smith, Cowboy Photographer.* Don Worcester. Amon Carter Museum, 1998. *Category:* non-fiction.

4947 1999. *Petey.* Ben Mikaelson. Hyperion, 1998. *Category:* fiction.

4948 2000. *Wrango.* Brian Burks. Harcourt Brace, 1999. *Category:* fiction.
4949 2000. *The Wild Colorado.* Richard Maurer. Crown Publishers, 1999. *Category:* non-fiction.

4950 Sunshine State Young Reader's Award

SPONSOR: School Library Media Services, Florida Department of Education. ADDRESS: 325 W. Gaines Street Suite 532, Tallahassee, Florida 32399. PHONE: (850) 488-8184. ESTABLISHED: 1984. AWARD: Glass etched bookends. The annual awards are presented to authors of books voted as most outstanding by participating Florida students. Two categories grades 3 to 5 and grades 6 to 8 each vote for their favorite author.

4951 1990. *Teacher's Pet.* Johanna Hurwitz. *Illustrator:* Sheila Hamanka. Morrow, 1988. *Level:* grades 3–5.
4952 1990. *Trapped in Death Cave.* Bill Wallace. Holiday, 1984. *Level:* grades 6–8.
4953 1991. *There's a Boy in the Girls' Bathroom.* Louis Sachar. Knopf, 1987.
4954 1992. *Fudge.* Charlotte Towner Graeber. *Illustrator:* Cheryl Harness. Lothrop, 1987. *Category:* grades 3–5.
4955 1992. *Something Upstairs.* Avi. Orchard, 1988. *Category:* grades 6–8.
4956 1993. *Nightmare.* Willo Davis Roberts. Aladdin, 1992. *Category:* grades 6–8.
4957 1993. *Fudge-A-Mania.* Judy Blume. Dutton, 1990. *Category:* grades 3–5.
4958 1994. *The True Confessions of Charlotte Doyle.* Avi. Jackson/Orchard, 1990. *Category:* grades 6–8.
4959 1994. *The Summer I Shrank My Grandmother.* Elvira Woodruff. *Illustrator:* Katherine Coville. Yearling, 1992. *Category:* grades 3–5.
4960 1995. *Devil's Bridge.* Cynthia de Felice. Farrar Straus & Giroux, 1995. *Category:* grades 6–8.
4961 1995. *Knights of the Kitchen Table.* Jon Scieszka. *Illustrator:* Lane Smith. Viking, 1991. *Category:* grades 3–5.
4962 1996. *Black Water Swamp.* Bill Wallace. Holiday House, 1994. *Category:* grades 3–5.
4963 1996. *Seventh-Grade Weirdo.* Lee Wardlaw. Apple, 1994. *Category:* grades 6–8.
4964 1997. *Nasty, Stinky Sneakers.* Eve Bunting. HarperCollins, 1994. *Category:* grades 3–5.
4965 1997. *Nasty, Stinky Sneakers.* Eve Bunting. HarperCollins, 1994. *Category:* grades 6–8.
4966 1998. *Tornado.* Betsy Byars. HarperCollins, 1996. *Category:* grades 3–5.
4967 1998. *Ghosts Don't Get Goose Bumps.* Elvira Woodruff. Holiday, 1993. *Category:* grades 6–8.

4968 1999. *101 Ways to Bug Your Parents.* Lee Wardlaw. Dial, 1996. *Category:* grades 6–8.

4969 1999. *101 Ways to Bug Your Parents.* Lee Wardlaw. Dial, 1996. *Category:* grades 3–5.

4970 2000. *Jaguar.* Roland Smith. Hyperion Books, 1997. *Category:* grades 6–8.

4971 2000. *The Volcano Disaster.* Peg Kehret. Minstrel Books, 1998. *Category:* grades 3–5.

4972 Sydney Taylor Body-of-Work Award

SPONSOR: Association of Jewish Libraries. CONTACT: Linda Silver. ADDRESS: 15 East 26th Street Room 1034, New York, New York 10010. PHONE: (212) 725-5359. ESTABLISHED: 1979. AWARD: A plaque, $1,000.00 U.S. and a gold seal to attach to the book. The award is given to the author whose entire works have held up over time and given a lasting positive message to their readers.

1990. No award given.
1991. No award given.
1992. No award given.
1993. No award given.
1994. No award given.
1995. No award given.
1996. No award given.
4973 1997. Barbara Diamond Goldin.
1998. No award given.
1999. No award given.
2000. No award given.

4974 Sydney Taylor Book Award

SPONSOR: Association of Jewish Libraries. CONTACT: Linda Silver. ADDRESS: 15 East 26th Street Room 1034, New York NY 10010. PHONE: (212) 725-5359. ESTABLISHED: 1968. AWARD: A plaque, $1,000.00 U.S. and a gold seal to attach to the book. The award is presented annually for the book or books considered to have made the most outstanding contribution to the field of Jewish literature for children published during the previous year.

4975 1990. *My Grandmother's Stories.* Adèle Geras. *Illustrator:* Jael Jordan. Alfred A. Knopf, 1990. *Category:* older children.

4976 1990. *The Chanukkah Guest.* Eric A. Kimmel. *Illustrator:* Giora Carmi. Holiday House, 1990. *Category:* picture book.

4977 1991. *Daddy's Chair.* Sandy Lanton. *Illustrator:* Shelly O. Haas. Kar-Ben, 1991. *Category:* picture book.

4978 1991. *Cakes and Miracles: A Purim Tale.* Barbara Diamond Goldin. *Illustrator:* Erika Weihs. Viking, 1991. *Category:* older children.

4979 1991. *The Diamond Tree: Jewish Tales from Around the World.* Howard Schwartz, Barbara Rush. *Illustrator:* Uri Shulevitz. HarperCollins, 1991. *Category:* older children.

4980 1992. *Something from Nothing.* Phoebe Gilman. *Illustrator:* Phoebe Gilman. North Winds Press, 1992. *Category:* picture book.

4981 1992. *Letters from Rifka.* Karen Hesse. Henry Holt, 1992. *Category:* older children.

4982 1993. *The Uninvited Guest.* Nina Jaffe. *Illustrator:* Elivia Savadier. Scholastic, 1993. *Category:* picture book.

4983 1993. *Sworn Enemies.* Carol Matas. Bantam Doubleday Dell, 1993. *Category:* older children.

4984 1994. *The Shadow Children.* Steven Schnur. *Illustrator:* Herbert Tauss. Morrow Junior Books, 1994. *Category:* older children.

4985 1994. *The Always Prayer Shawl.* Sheldon Oberman. *Illustrator:* Ted Lewin. Boyds Mill Press, 1994. *Category:* picture book.

4986 1995. *Star of Fear, Star of Hope.* Jo Hoestlandt. *Illustrator:* Johanna Kang. Walker and Company, 1995. *Category:* picture book.

4987 1995. *Dancing on the Bridge of Avignon.* Ida Vos. Houghton Mifflin, 1995. *Category:* older children.

4988 1996. *When I Left My Village.* Maxine Rose Schur. *Illustrator:* Brian Pinkney. Dial Books, 1996. *Category:* picture book.

4989 1996. *Shalom, Haver: Goodbye, Friend.* Barbara Sofer. Kar-Ben, 1996. *Category:* older children.

4990 1997. *When Zaydeh Danced on Eldridge Street.* Elsa Okon Rael. *Illustrator:* Marjorie Priceman. Simon & Schuster, 1997. *Category:* picture book.

4991 1997. *The Mysterious Visitor: Stories of the Prophet Elijah.* Nina Jaffe. *Illustrator:* Elivia Savadier. Scholastic, 1997. *Category:* older children.

4992 1998. *Nine Spoons.* Marci Stillerman. *Illustrator:* Pesach Gerber. HaChai Publishers, 1998. *Category:* picture book.

4993 1998. *Stones in Water.* Donna Jo Napoli. Dutton, 1998. *Category:* older children.

4994 1999. *Speed of Light.* Sybil Rosen. Atheneum, 2000. *Category:* older children.

4995 1999. *The Peddler's Gift.* Maxine Rose Schur. *Illustrator:* Kimberly Bulcken. Dial Books for Young Readers, 2000. *Category:* picture book.

4996 Teddy Book Award

SPONSOR: Austin Writers' League. ADDRESS: 1501 W. Fifth St., Suite E-2, Austin, Texas 78703. PHONE: (512) 499-8914. ESTABLISHED: 1995. AWARD: $1,000 cash and a trophy. The award is given to an outstanding children's book—fiction or non-fiction, picture books to young adult—published in the previous year. A complete list of winners was not available at the time of publication.

4997 1999. *Louisiana Sky.* Kimberly Willis Holt.

4998 Texas Bluebonnet Award

SPONSOR: Texas Library Association. ADDRESS: 3355 Bee Cave Road No. 401, Austin, Texas 78746-6763. PHONE: (512) 328-1518. ESTABLISHED: 1979. AWARD: A medallion encased in lucite. Student's in grades 3 to 6 vote for their favorite fiction or non-fiction book. The authors must be American, living in the United States, and have had the book published three years prior to the award.

4999 1990. *There's a Boy in the Girl's Bathroom.* Louis Sachar. Knopf, 1987.

5000 1991. *Aliens for Breakfast.* Jonathan Etra. Random House, 1988.

5001 1992. *Snot Stew.* Bill Wallace. *Illustrator:* Lisa McCue. Holiday House, 1989.

5002 1993. *The Houdini Box.* Brian Selznick. Knopf, 1991.

5003 1994. *Shiloh.* Phyllis Reynolds Naylor. Atheneum, 1991.

5004 1995. *The Stinky Cheese Man and Other Fairly Stupid Tales.* Jon Scieszka. *Illustrator:* Lane Smith. Viking, 1992.

5005 1996. *Time for Andrew: A Ghost Story.* Mary Downing Hahn. Clarion, 1994.

5006 1997. *Math Curse.* Jon Scieszka. *Illustrator:* Lane Smith. Viking, 1995.

5007 1998. *Tornado.* Betsy Byars. HarperCollins, 1996.

5008 1999. *Verdi.* Janell Cannon. Harcourt Brace, 1997.

5009 2000. *The Ghost of Fossil Glen.* Cynthia DeFelice. Farrar, Straus & Giroux 1998.

5010 Tomás Rivera Mexican American Children's Book Award

SPONSOR: SWT School of Education. ADDRESS: 2001 Education Building 601 University, San Marcos, Texas 78666. ESTABLISHED: 1995. AWARD: A certificate and $3,000.00 U.S. This award is given annually to the author/illustrator of the most distinguished book for children and young adults that authentically reflects the lives and experiences of Mexican Americans in the Southwestern region of the United States.

5011 1995. *The Farolitos of Christmas.* Rudolfo Anaya. *Illustrator:* Edward Gonzales. Hyperion, 1995.

5012 1995. *Chato's Kitchen.* Gary Soto. *Illustrator:* Susan Guevara. Putnam, 1995.

5013 1996. *In My Family. Original Title:* En mi familia. Carmen Lomas Garza. *Illustrator:* Carmen Lomas Garza. Children's Book Press, 1994.

5014 1997. *Tomás and the Library Lady.* Pat Mora. *Illustrator:* Raul Colón. Knopf, 1997.

5015 1998. *The Three Pigs. Original Title:* Los Tres Cerdos. Bobbi Salinas. *Illustrator:* Bobbi Salinas. Pinata Pubns, 1998.

5016 1999. *My Land Sings: Stories from the Rio Grande.* Rudolfo Anaya. *Illustrator:* Amy Cordova. Morrow, 1999.

5017 Treasure State Award

SPONSOR: Missoula County Schools and Missoula Public Library. ADDRESS: 301 East Main, Missoula, Montana 59802-4799. PHONE: (406) 721-2665. ESTABLISHED: 1994. Children vote for their favorite picture book.

5018 1994. *Trouble with Trolls.* Jan Brett. *Illustrator:* Jan Brett. G.P. Putnam's Sons, 1992.

5019 1995. *Coyote Steals the Blanket: A Ute Tale.* Janet Stevens. Holiday House, 1993.

5020 1996. *Zomo the Rabbit: A Trickster Tale from West Africa.* Gerald McDermott. *Illustrator:* Gerald McDermott. Harcourt Brace, 1992.

5021 1997. *Three Cheers for Tacky.* Helen Lester. Houghton Mifflin, 1994.

5022 1998. *The Girl Who Wanted to Hunt.* Emery Bernhard. *Illustrator:* Druga Bernhard. Holiday House, 1994.

5023 1999. *A Bad Case of Stripes.* David Shannon. Blue Sky Press, 1998.

5024 2000. *Punia and the King of Sharks: A Hawaiian Folktale.* Lee Wardlaw. *Illustrator:* Felipe Davalos. Dial, 1997.

5025 UNICEF–Ezra Jack Keats International Award for Excellence in Children's Book Illustration

SPONSOR: Ezra Jack Keats Foundation. ADDRESS: 331 East 38th Street, 8th floor. New York, New York 10016. PHONE: (212) 503-0340. ESTABLISHED: 1986. AWARD: $5,000.00 U.S. and a silver medal. The award is given biennially to any illustrator of children's books throughout the world who has published at least one, but not more than five, children's picture books in the five years preceding the presentation of the award. An organization, publisher, friend of the illustrator, or even the illustrator may purpose an individual. The illustrator's book should reflect the goals of the United Nations and UNICEF by showing at least one of the following topics: the family, peace, nature, celebration, youth, cultural unity and diversity.

5026 1990. Jan Thornhill.

5027 1992. Arone Raymond Meeks.

5028 1994. Vera B. Williams.

5029 1998. Barbara Reid.

5030 University of Southern Mississippi Medallion

SPONSOR: University of Southern Mississippi. ADDRESS: Southern Station, Box 5148, Hattiesburg, Mississippi 39406. PHONE: (601) 266-4349. ESTABLISHED: 1969. AWARD: A silver medallion. The award is given to an author and/or illustrator for outstanding contributions in the field of children's literature.

5031 1990. Charlotte Zolotow.
5032 1991. Richard Peck.
5033 1992. James Marshall.
5034 1993. Quentin Blake.
5035 1994. Ashley Bryan.
5036 1995. Tomie de Paola.
5037 1996. Patricia MacLachlan.
5038 1997. Eric Carle.
5039 1998. E.L. Konigsburg.
5040 1999. Russell Freedman.
5041 2000. David Macaulay.

5042 Utah Children's Book Award

SPONSOR: Children's Literature Association of Utah. ADDRESS: 4351 South 3200 East, West Valley City, Utah 84119. ESTABLISHED: 1980. The annual award is given to the author who receives the most votes from the children of Utah. There are four categories: Utah Children's Picture Book Award; Utah Children's Book Award; Utah Children's Informational Book Award; and Utah Young Adults' Book Award.

5043 1990. *How to Make Pop-Ups.* Joan Irvine. *Illustrator:* Barbara Reid. William Morrow & Co., 1988. *Category:* informational.

5044 1990. *This Island Isn't Big Enough for the Four of Us.* Gary Greer, Bob Ruddick. Harper. Trophy, 1989. *Category:* children's book.

5045 1991. *Matilda.* Roald Dahl. *Illustrator:* Quentin Blake. Viking, 1988. *Category:* children's book.

5046 1991. *Bill Peet: An Autobiography.* Bill Peet. *Illustrator:* Bill Peet. Houghton Mifflin, 1989. *Category:* informational.

5047 1991. *The Other Side of Dark.* Joan Lowery Nixon. Delacorte, 1986. *Category:* young adult.

5048 1992. *Ant Colony.* H. Fischner-Nagel. Carolrhoda Books, 1990. *Category:* informational.

5049 1992. *Don't Look Back.* Lois Duncan. Delacorte, 1989. *Category:* young adult.

5050 1992. *There's a Boy in the Girls' Bathroom.* Louis Sachar. Knopf, 1987. *Category:* children's book.

5051 1993. *The Dead Man in Indian Creek.* Mary Downing Hahn. Clarion, 1990. *Category:* children's book.

5052 1993. *Dolphin Adventure.* Wayne Grover. *Illustrator:* Jim Fowler. Avon, 1993. *Category:* informational.

5053 1993. *Sniper.* Theodore Taylor. Harcourt Brace, 1989. *Category:* young adult.

5054 1994. *The True Confessions of Charlotte Doyle.* Avi. Jackson/Orchard, 1990. *Category:* young adult.

5055 1994. *Stephen Biesty's Incredible Cross Sections.* Richard Platt. *Illustrator:* Stephen Biesty. Knopf, 1992. *Category:* informational.

5056 1994. *Jeremy Thatcher, Dragon Hatcher.* Bruce Coville. *Illustrator:* Gary A. Lippincott. Minstrel Books, 1992. *Category:* children's book.

5057 1995. *Amazing Gracie.* A.E. Cannon. Laureleaf, 1996. *Category:* young adult.

5058 1995. *The Ghosts of Mercy Manor.* Betty Ren Wright. Scholastic, 1993. *Category:* children's book.

5059 1995. *Sadako.* Eleanor Coerr. *Illustrator:* Ed Young. Putnam Pub., 1993. *Category:* informational.

5060 1996. *Nothing to Fear.* Jackie French Koller. Harcourt Brace, 1993. *Category:* young adult.

5061 1996. *Time for Andrew: A Ghost Story.* Mary Downing Hahn. Clarion, 1994. *Category:* children's book.

5062 1996. *Two of Everything: A Chinese Folktale.* Judith Mathews (editor). *Illustrator:* Lily Toy Hong. Albert Whitman & Co., 1993. *Category:* picture book.

5063 1996. *Mummies and Their Mysteries.* Charlotte Wilcox. Carolrhoda Books, 1993. *Category:* informational.

5064 1997. *A Job for Wittilda.* Caralyn Buehner. *Illustrator:* Mark Buehner. Dial, 1993. *Category:* picture book.

5065 1997. *Never Take a Pig to Lunch and Other Poems About the Fun of Eating.* Nadine Bernard Westcott (editor). *Illustrator:* Nadine Bernard Westcott. Orchard Books, 1994. *Category:* informational.

5066 1997. *In My Father's House.* Ann Rinaldi. Point, 1996. *Category:* young adult.

5067 1997. *Watchdog and the Coyotes.* Bill Wallace. *Illustrator:* David Slonim. Minstrel Books, 1995. *Category:* children's book.

5068 1998. *It's a Spoon, Not a Shovel.* Caralyn Buehner. *Illustrator:* Mark Buehner. Puffin, 1995. *Category:* informational.

5069 1998. *Anansi and the Talking Melon.* Eric Kimmel. *Illustrator:* Janet Stevens. Holiday House, 1994. *Category:* picture book.

5070 1998. *Someone Was Watching.* David Patneaude. *Illustrator:* Paul Micich. Albert Whitman & Co, 1993. *Category:* children's book.

5071 1998. *Merlin Effect.* T.A. Barron. Philomel, 1994. *Category:* young adult.

5072 1999. *Passage to Freedom: The Sugihara Story*. Ken Mochizuki. *Illustrator:* Dom Lee. Lee & Low Books, 1997. *Category:* informational.

5073 1999. *Earthquake Terror*. Peg Kehret. Cobblehill, 1996. *Category:* children's book.

5074 1999. *Watch Out! Big Bro's Coming!* Jez Alborough. *Illustrator:* Jez Alborough. Candlewick, 1998. *Category:* picture book.

5075 1999. *SOS Titanic*. Eve Bunting. Harcourt Brace, 1996. *Category:* young adult.

5076 2000. *A Drop of Water: A Book of Science and Wonder*. Walter Wick. *Illustrator:* Walter Wick. Scholastic, 1997. *Category:* informational.

5077 2000. *Frindle*. Andrew Clements. *Illustrator:* Brian Selznick. Simon & Schuster, 1996. *Category:* children's book.

5078 2000. *A Bad Case of Stripes*. David Shannon. *Illustrator:* David Shannon. Blue Sky Press, 1998. *Category:* picture book.

5079 2000. *Little Sister*. Kara Dalkey. Harcourt Brace, 1996. *Category:* young adult.

5080 Virginia Young Reader's Award

SPONSOR: Virginia State Reading Association. CONTACT: Al Buchanan. ADDRESS: 2922 Tamarack Trail, Roanoke, Virginia 24018. PHONE: (703) 890-4796. ESTABLISHED: 1981. AWARD: Pewter Jeffersen Cup engraved with the Young Readers logo. Four awards are given to the popular book at the primary, elementary, middle and high school levels. The book must be published within the previous ten years.

5081 1990. *The Magic School Bus Inside the Earth*. Joanna Cole. *Illustrator:* Bruce Degen. Scholastic, 1989. *Category:* primary.

5082 1990. *Hatchet*. Gary Paulsen. Bradbury, 1987. *Category:* middle.

5083 1990. *Wolf Rider: A Tale of Terror*. Avi. Simon & Schuster, 1986. *Category:* high school.

5084 1990. *Christina's Ghost*. Betty Ren Wright. Holiday, 1985. *Category:* elementary.

5085 1991. *Two Bad Ants*. Chris van Allsburg. *Illustrator:* Chris van Allsburg. Houghton Mifflin, 1988. *Category:* primary.

5086 1991. *Matilda*. Roald Dahl. *Illustrator:* Quentin Blake. Viking, 1988. *Category:* elementary.

5087 1991. *Good Night, Mr. Tom*. Michelle Magorian. HarperCollins, 1982. *Category:* middle school.

5088 1991. *Say Goodnight, Gracie*. Julie Rice Deaver. Harper, 1988. *Category:* high school.

5089 1992. *Don't Look Behind You*. Lois Duncan. Delacorte, 1989. *Category:* high school.

5090 1992. *A Family Apart.* Joan Lowery Nixon. Laureleaf, 1996. *Category:* middle school.

5091 1992. *The Great White Man-Eating Shark.* Margaret Mahy. *Illustrator:* Jonathan Allen. Puffin, 1996. *Category:* primary.

5092 1992. *The Doll in the Garden: A Ghost Story.* Mary Downing Hahn. Clarion, 1989. *Category:* elementary.

5093 1993. *Plague Year.* Stephanie Tolan. Fawcett, 1991. *Category:* high school.

5094 1993. *Maniac Magee.* Jerry Spinelli. Little, Brown & Co., 1990. *Category:* middle school.

5095 1993. *Exploring the Titanic.* Robert D. Ballard. Scholastic, 1993. *Category:* elementary.

5096 1993. *Talking Eggs.* Robert San Souci. *Illustrator:* Jerry Pinkney. E P Dutton, 1989. *Category:* primary.

5097 1994. *Ten Kids, No Pets.* Ann Martin. Holiday, 1988. *Category:* elementary.

5098 1994. *The Dead Man in Indian Creek.* Mary Downing Hahn. Clarion, 1990. *Category:* middle school.

5099 1994. *How Could You Do It Diane*? Stella Pevsner. Clarion. *Category:* high school.

5100 1994. *Beware of Boys.* Tony Blundell. Greenwillow, 1990. *Category:* primary.

5101 1995. *Jumping the Nail.* Eve Bunting. Harcourt Brace, 1991. *Category:* high school.

5102 1995. *The Rough-Faced Girl.* Rafe Martin. *Illustrator:* David Shannon. Philomel, 1992. *Category:* primary.

5103 1995. *Flight #116 Is Down.* Caroline Cooney. Scholastic, 1992. *Category:* middle school.

5104 1995. *Ghost Cadet.* Elaine Alphin. Apple, 1992. *Category:* elementary.

5105 1996. *Just Like Martin.* Ossie Davis. Simon, 1993. *Category:* high school.

5106 1996. *The Giver.* Lois Lowry. Houghton Mifflin, 1993. *Category:* middle school.

5107 1996. *A Haunting in Williamsburg.* Lou Kassem. Avon, 1993. *Category:* elementary.

5108 1996. *Dogzilla.* Dav Pilkey. Harcourt Brace, 1993. *Category:* primary.

5109 1997. *Copycat.* Ruth Brown. *Illustrator:* Ruth Brown. Dutton Books, 1994. *Category:* primary.

5110 1997. *Time for Andrew: A Ghost Story.* Mary Downing Hahn. Clarion, 1994. *Category:* elementary.

5111 1997. *Tears of a Tiger.* Sharon Draper. Simon & Schuster, 1994. *Category:* high school.

5112 1997. *Walk Two Moons.* Sharon Creech. HarperCollins, 1994. *Category:* middle school.

5113 1998. *Daughter of the Stars.* Phyllis A Whitney. Fawcett Books, 1995. *Category:* high school.

5114 1998. *The Ear, the Eye, and the Arm.* Nancy Farmer. Jackson/Orchard, 1994. *Category:* middle school.

5115 1998. *Fig Pudding.* Ralph Fletcher. *Illustrator:* Arthur Howard. Clarion Books, 1995. *Category:* elementary.

5116 1998. *Suddenly!* Colin McNaughton. Harcourt Brace, 1995. *Category:* primary.

5117 1999. *Earthquake Terror.* Peg Kehret. Cobblehill, 1996. *Category:* elementary.

5118 1999. *Crash!* Jerry Spinelli. Knopf, 1996. *Category:* middle school.

5119 1999. *My Little Sister Ate One Hare.* Bill Grossman. *Illustrator:* Kevin Hawkes. Crown, 1996. *Category:* primary.

5120 1999. *The China Garden.* Liz Berry. Farrar Straus & Giroux, 1996. *Category:* high school.

5121 2000. *The Red Racer.* Audrey Wood. *Illustrator:* Audrey Wood. Simon & Schuster, 1996. *Category:* primary.

5122 2000. *The Junkyard Dog.* Erika Tamar. Knopf, 1995. *Category:* elementary.

5123 2000. *Spirit Seeker.* Jean Lowery Nixon. Laurel Leaf, 1997. *Category:* middle school.

5124 2000. *Chicken Soup for the Teenage Soul.* Jack Canfield. Health Communications, 1997. *Category:* high school.

5125 Volunteer State Book Award

SPONSOR: Tennessee Library Association. CONTACT: Kathy Patten. ADDRESS: Middle Tennessee State University, Box 91, Murfreesboro, Tennessee 37132. PHONE: (615) 898-2804. ESTABLISHED: 1979. AWARD: A plaque. The annual awards are given in four categories: primary, intermediate, middle/junior high and senior. Authors must be American and have had the book published within five years prior to the year of the award.

5126 1990. *Putting on an Act.* Christi Killien. Houghton Mifflin, 1986. *Level:* 7–9.

5127 1990. *Locked in Time.* Lois Duncan. Little, Brown & Co., 1985. *Level:* 10–12.

5128 1990. *Abiyoyo.* Pete Seeger. *Illustrator:* Michael Hays. Macmillan, 1986. *Level:* K–3.

5129 1990. *Christina's Ghost.* Betty Ren Wright. Holiday, 1985. *Level:* 4–6.

5130 1991. *Say Goodnight, Gracie.* Julie Rice Deaver. Harper, 1988. *Category:* 10–12.

5131 1991. *Beetles, Lightly Toasted.* Phyllis Reynolds Naylor. Atheneum, 1986. *Category:* 4–6.

5132 1991. *The Magic School Bus at the Waterworks.* Joanna Cole. Scholastic, 1986. *Category:* K–3.
5133 1991. *The Shadow Club.* Neal Shusterman. Little, 1988. *Category:* 7–9.
5134 1992. *No Jumping on the Bed!* Tedd Arnold. *Illustrator:* Tedd Arnold. Dial, 1987. *Category:* K–3.
5135 1992. *There's a Boy in the Girls' Bathroom.* Louis Sachar. Knopf, 1987. *Category:* 4–6.
5136 1992. *A Sudden Silence.* Eve Bunting. Harcourt, 1988. *Category:* 7–9.
5137 1992. *Don't Look Behind You.* Lois Duncan. Delacorte, 1989. *Category:* 10–12.
5138 1993. *The Killing Freeze.* Lynn Hall. Morrow, 1988. *Category:* young adult.
5139 1993. *Wayside School Is Falling Down.* Louis Sachar. *Illustrator:* Joel Schick. Camelot, 1990. *Category:* 4–6.
5140 1993. *The Very Quiet Cricket.* Eric Carle. Philomel, 1990. *Category:* K–3.
5141 1994. *Don't Look Behind You.* Lois Duncan. Delacorte, 1989. *Category:* young adult.
5142 1994. *Our Sixth Grade Sugar Babies.* Eve Bunting. Lippincott, 1990. *Category:* 4–6.
5143 1994. *Taily Po.* Jan Wahl. Holt, 1991. *Category:* K–3.
5144 1995. *Land of Gray Wolf.* Thomas Locker. Dial, 1991. *Category:* K–3.
5145 1995. *The Face on the Milk Carton.* Caroline Cooney. Bantam, 1990. *Category:* young adult.
5146 1995. *Fudge-a-Mania.* Judy Blume. Dutton, 1990. *Category:* 4–6.
5147 1996. *Heart of a Champion.* Carl Deuker. Joy Street, 1993. *Category:* young adult.
5148 1996. *The Ghosts of Mercy Manor.* Betty Ren Wright. Scholastic, 1993. *Category:* 4–6.
5149 1996. *The Three Little Wolves and the Big Bad Pig.* Eugene Trivizas. Margaret McElderry, 1993. *Category:* K–3.
5150 1997. *The Best School Year Ever.* Barbara Robinson. HarperCollins, 1994. *Category:* 4–6.
5151 1997. *Dogzilla.* Dav Pilkey. Harcourt Brace, 1993. *Category:* K–3.
5152 1997. *Deadly Deception.* Betsy Haynes. Delacorte, 1994. *Category:* young adult.
5153 1998. *Hallo-Weiner.* Dav Pilkey. Scholastic, 1995. *Category:* K–3.
5154 1998. *Help! I'm Trapped in My Teacher's Body.* Todd Strasser. Scholastic, 1994. *Category:* 4–6.
5155 1998. *Driver's Ed.* Caroline Cooney. Delacorte, 1994. *Category:* young adult.
5156 1999. *Shiloh Season.* Phyllis Reynolds Naylor. Atheneum, 1996. *Category:* 4–6.

5157 1999. *Tears of a Tiger.* Sharon Draper. Simon & Schuster, 1994. *Category:* young adult.

5158 1999. *Martha Calling.* Susan Meddaugh. Houghton Mifflin, 1994. *Category:* K–3.

5159 2000. *Parts.* Tedd Arnold. Dial, 1997. *Category:* K–3.

5160 2000. *Brian's Winter.* Gary Paulsen. Delacorte, 1996. *Category:* young adult.

5161 2000. *Million Dollar Shot.* Dan Gutman. Hyperion, 1997. *Category:* 4–6.

5162 Washington Children's Choice Picture Book Award

SPONSOR: Washington Library Media Association. ADDRESS: Box 1413, Bothell, Washington 98041. ESTABLISHED: 1982. AWARD: A plate with the book award logo. The annual award is given to the author who receives the most votes from the children of Washington state. Books must be of picture book format not limited to fiction. Books must be published or distributed in the United States 3 or 4 years before the award year.

5163 1990. *Amos the Story of an Old Dog and His Couch.* Susan Seligson. *Illustrator:* Susan Seligson. Little, Brown & Co.

5164 1991. *Two Bad Ants.* Chris van Allsburg. *Illustrator:* Chris van Allsburg. Houghton Mifflin, 1988.

5165 1992. *Hershel and the Hanukkah Goblins.* Eric A. Kimmel. *Illustrator:* Trina Schart Hyman. Holiday, 1989.

5166 1993. *The Great White Man-Eating Shark.* Margaret Mahy. *Illustrator:* Jonathan Allen. Puffin, 1996.

5167 1994. *The Dog Who Had Kittens.* Polly Robertus. *Illustrator:* Janet Stevens. Holiday House, 1992.

5168 1995. *Tiger.* Judy Allen. Demco, 1994.

5169 1996. *Soap! Soap! Don't Forget the Soap!* Tom Birdseye. *Illustrator:* Andrew Glass. Holiday House, 1993.

5170 1997. *Harvey Potter's Balloon Farm.* Jerdine Harold Nolen. *Illustrator:* Mark Buehner. Lothrop, Lee & Shepard, 1995.

5171 1998. *Heart of a Tiger.* Marsha Diane Arnold. *Illustrator:* Jamichael Henterly. Dial, 1995.

5172 1999. *The Secret Shortcut.* Mark Teague. Scholastic, 1996.

5173 2000. *Akiak: A Tale from the Iditarod.* Robert J. Blake. *Illustrator:* Robert J. Blake. Philomel Books 1997.

5174 Washington Irving Children's Book Choice Award

SPONSOR: Westchester Library Association. ADDRESS: 410 Saw Mill River Road, Ardsley, New York 10502. PHONE: (914) 592-8214. ESTABLISHED: 1982. AWARD:

A medal. The award is given every two years to honor Westchester authors of children's books. The author must be a resident of Westchester County at the time the book is published. Children in Kindergarten through grade 8 vote for their favorite author.

5175 1990. *Bring Back the Deer.* Jeffery Prusski. *Illustrator:* Neil Waldman. Harcourt Brace, 1988. *Category:* illustration.

5176 1990. *Dinosaur Cousins?* Bernard Most. Harcourt Brace, 1990. *Category:* younger fiction.

5177 1990. *One Day in the Woods.* Jean Craighead George. *Illustrator:* Gary Allen. HarperCollins, 1988. *Category:* non-fiction.

5178 1990. *Too Much Magic.* Betsy Sterman. Harper Trophy, 1994. *Category:* older fiction.

5179 1992. *The Highwayman.* Alfred Noyes. *Illustrator:* Neil Waldman. Harcourt Brace. *Category:* illustration.

5180 1992. *Max's Chocolate Chicken.* Rosemary Wells. Dial, 1986. *Category:* younger fiction.

5181 1992. *On the Far Side of the Mountain.* Jean Craighead George. Dutton. *Category:* older fiction.

5182 1992. *For Your Own Protection: Stories Science Photos Tell.* Vicki Cobb. Lothrop, Lee & Shepard. *Category:* non-fiction.

5183 1994. *Brother Eagle, Sister Sky.* Susan Jeffers. *Illustrator:* Susan Jeffers. Dial, 1991. *Category:* older fiction.

5184 1994. *Back Home.* Gloria Pinkney. *Illustrator:* Jerry Pinkney. Dial, 1992. *Category:* middle grades.

5185 1994. *A Visit to Oma.* Marisabina Russo. Greenwillow, 1991. *Category:* younger fiction.

5186 1996. *Little Painter of Sabana Grande.* Patricia Maloney Markun. *Illustrator:* Robert Casilla. Simon & Schuster, 1993. *Category:* illustration.

5187 1996. *Kangaroos on Location.* Kathy Darling. *Illustrator:* Tara Darling. Lothrop Lee & Shepard, 1993. *Category:* non-fiction.

5188 1996. *Emma Bean.* Jean van Leeuwen. *Illustrator:* Juan Wijngaard. Dial, 1993. *Category:* younger fiction.

5189 1996. *The Shadow Children.* Steven Schnur. *Illustrator:* Herbert Tauss. Morrow Junior Books, 1994. *Category:* older fiction.

5190 1998. *Sam and the Tigers.* Julius Lester. *Illustrator:* Jerry Pinkney. Dial, 1996. *Category:* illustration.

5191 1998. *Abe Linclon for Class President.* Todd Strasser. Apple, 1997. *Category:* older fiction.

5192 1998. *A Dog Named Sam.* Janice Boland. *Illustrator:* G. Brian Karas. Dial, 1996. *Category:* younger fiction.

5193 1998. *The Tie Man's Miracle.* Steven Schnur. *Illustrator:* Stephen T. Johnson. William Morrow & Co., 1995. *Category:* middle grades.

5194 2000. *Yoko.* Rosemary Wells. *Illustrator:* Rosemary Wells. Hyperion. *Category:* younger fiction.

5195 2000. *Black Cowboys, Wild Horses: A True Story.* Julius Lester. *Illustrator:* Jerry Pinkney. Dial. *Category:* illustration.

5196 2000. *Saratoga Secret.* Betsy Sterman. Dial. *Category:* older fiction.

5197 2000. *Nothing Ever Happens on 90th Street.* Roni Schotter. *Illustrator:* Kyrsten Booker. Orchard. *Category:* middle grades.

5198 Washington Post/Children's Books Guild Nonfiction Award

SPONSOR: Children's Book Guild of Washington D.C. ADDRESS: 4405 'W' Street, N.W., Washington D.C. 20007. PHONE: (202) 965-0403. ESTABLISHED: 1977. AWARD: A Baccarat crystal cube engraved with the author's name, award name and date, and $1,000.00 U.S. The annual award honors an author or author-illustrator whose body of work has significantly contributed to the quality of non-fiction for children.

5199 1990. Brent Ashabranner.

5200 1991. Joanna Cole.

5201 1992. Russell Freedman.

5202 1993. Seymour Simon.

5203 1994. Jim Haskins.

5204 1995. Albert Marrin.

5205 1996. James Cross Giblin.

5206 1997. Rhoda Blumberg.

5207 1998. Jean Craighead George.

5208 1999. Laurence Pringle.

5209 2000. Diane Stanley.

5210 WEMA Golden Archer Award

SPONSOR: Wisconsin Educational Media Association. CONTACT: Mary Ann Blahnik. ADDRESS: 1230 Michigan Street, Sturgeon Bay, Wisconsin 54901. ESTABLISHED: 1996. AWARD: Hand crafted medal and certificate. Wisconsin school children, in grades 4 to 8, annually vote for their favorite fiction or non-fiction book. The books must be written by a living American author and published during the past five years.

5211 1996. *Jumanji.* Chris van Allsburg. *Illustrator:* Chris van Allsburg. Houghton Mifflin, 1981. *Category:* primary.

5212 1996. *Where the Sidewalk Ends.* Shel Silverstein. *Illustrator:* Shel Silverstein. HarperCollins, 1974. *Category:* intermediate.

5213 1996. *The Giver.* Lois Lowry. Houghton Mifflin, 1993. *Category:* middle/junior high.

5214 1997. *Harris and Me.* Gary Paulsen. Harcourt Brace, 1993. *Category:* middle/junior.

5215 1997. *The Stinky Cheese Man and Other Fairly Stupid Tales.* Jon Scieszka. *Illustrator:* Lane Smith. Viking, 1992. *Category:* intermediate.

5216 1997. *Officer Buckle and Gloria.* Peggy Rathmann. Putnam, 1995. *Category:* primary.

5217 1998. *Number the Stars.* Lois Lowry. Houghton Mifflin, 1989. *Category:* middle/junior.

5218 1998. *Falling Up.* Shel Silverstein. HarperCollins, 1996. *Category:* intermediate.

5219 1998. *Junie B. Jones and the Stupid Smelly Bus.* Barbara Parks. *Illustrator:* Denise Brunkus. Random House, 1992. *Category:* primary.

5220 1999. *The Hallo-Weiner.* Dav Pilkey. Blue Sky, 1995. *Category:* primary.

5221 1999. *Wayside School Gets a Little Stranger.* Louis Sachar. *Illustrator:* Joel Schick. Morrow, 1995. *Category:* intermediate.

5222 1999. *Brian's Winter.* Gary Paulsen. Delacorte, 1996. *Category:* junior high.

5223 2000. *Harry Potter and the Sorcerer's Stone.* J.K. Rowling. A.A. Levine Books, 1998. *Category:* junior high.

5224 2000. *Crash.* Jerry Spinelli. Knopf, 1996. *Category:* intermediate.

5225 2000. *A Bad Case of the Stripes.* David Shannon. Blue Sky Press, 1998. *Category:* primary.

5226 William Allen White Children's Book Award

SPONSOR: Emporia State University and the Trusler Foundation. ADDRESS: 1200 Commercial, Box 4051, Emporia, Kansas 66801-5038. PHONE: (316) 341-5038. ESTABLISHED: 1952. AWARD: A bronze medal. The award is given to the author who receives the most votes from the children of Kansas in grade 4 to 8. The book must be published in English in the United States, Canada or Mexico within the calendar year preceding the award selection. Fiction poetry and nonfiction are eligible.

5227 1990. *Hatchet.* Gary Paulsen. Bradbury, 1987.

5228 1991. *Beauty.* Bill Wallace. Holiday House, 1988.

5229 1992. *The Doll in the Garden: A Ghost Story.* Mary Downing Hahn. Clarion, 1989.

5230 1993. *Maniac Magee.* Jerry Spinelli. Little, Brown & Co., 1989.

5231 1994. *Shiloh.* Phyllis Reynolds Naylor. Atheneum, 1991.

5232 1995. *The Man Who Loved Clowns.* June Rae Wood. Putnam, 1992.

5233 1997. *Time for Andrew: A Ghost Story.* Mary Downing Hahn. Clarion, 1994.

5234 1997. *The Giver.* Lois Lowry. Houghton Mifflin, 1993.
5235 1998. *Mick Harte Was Here.* Barbara Park. Knopf, 1995.
5236 1999. *Frindle.* Andrew Clements. *Illustrator:* Brian Selznick. Simon & Schuster, 1996.
5237 2000. *White Water.* P.J. Petersen. Simon & Schuster, 1997.

5238 Young Hoosier Book Award

SPONSOR: Association for Indiana Media Educators. ADDRESS: 6408 Carrollton Avenue, Indianapolis, Indiana 46220. PHONE: (317) 257-2040. ESTABLISHED: 1975. AWARD: A plaque bearing an engraved seal of the Young Hoosier Book Award. The awards are given to authors who receive the most votes from Indiana children in grades 4 to 6 and 6 to 8. The authors must currently reside in the United States and have had their work of fiction published within the last 5 years.

5239 1990. *The Dark and Deadly Pool.* Lois Lowery Nixon. Laureleaf, 1993. *Category:* 6–8.
5240 1990. *Fudge.* Charlotte Towner Graeber. *Illustrator:* Cheryl Harness. Lothrop, 1987. *Category:* 4–6.
5241 1991. *Hatchet.* Gary Paulsen. Bradbury, 1987. *Category:* 6–8.
5242 1991. *Ten Kids, No Pets.* Ann Martin. Holiday, 1988. *Category:* 4–6.
5243 1992. *Don't Look Behind You.* Lois Duncan. Delacorte, 1989. *Category:* 6–8.
5244 1992. *Heckedy Peg.* Audrey Wood. *Illustrator:* Don Wood. Harcourt, 1987. *Category:* K–3.
5245 1992. *Nightmare Mountain.* Peg Kehret. Dutton, 1989. *Category:* 4–6.
5246 1993. *Tuesday.* David Wiesner. *Illustrator:* David Wiesner. Clarion, 1991. *Category:* K–3.
5247 1993. *The Dead Man in Indian Creek.* Mary Downing Hahn. Clarion, 1990. *Category:* 4–6.
5248 1993. *The Face on the Milk Carton.* Caroline Cooney. Bantam, 1990. *Category:* 6–8.
5249 1994. *Strider.* Beverly Cleary. *Illustrator:* Paul O. Zelinsky. William Morrow and Co., 1992. *Category:* 6–8.
5250 1994. *The Dog Who Had Kittens.* Polly Robertus. *Illustrator:* Janet Stevens. Holiday House, 1992. *Category:* K–3.
5251 1994. *Shiloh.* Phyllis Reynolds Naylor. Atheneum, 1991. *Category:* 4–6.
5252 1995. *Whispers from the Dead.* Joan Lowery Nixon. Laurel Leaf, 1991. *Category:* 6–8.
5253 1995. *Enchanted Wood.* Ruth Sanderson. Little, Brown & Co., 1991. *Category:* K–3.

5254 1995. *Horror at the Haunted House.* Peg Kehret. Cobblehill Book, 1992. *Category:* 4–6.

5255 1996. *Harris and Me.* Gary Paulsen. Harcourt Brace, 1993. *Category:* 6–8.

5256 1996. *Zomo the Rabbit: A Trickster Tale from West Africa.* Gerald McDermott. *Illustrator:* Gerald McDermott. Harcourt Brace, 1992. *Category:* K–3.

5257 1996. *A Ghost in the House.* Betty Ren Wright. Scholastic, 1993. *Category:* 4–6.

5258 1997. *Nightjohn.* Gary Paulsen. *Illustrator:* Jerry Pinkney. Delacorte, 1993. *Category:* 6–8.

5259 1997. *Wayside School Gets a Little Stranger.* Louis Sachar. Morrow, 1995. *Category:* 4–6.

5260 1997. *Harvey Potter's Balloon Farm.* Jerdine Harold Nolen. *Illustrator:* Mark Buehner. Lothrop, Lee & Shepard, 1995. *Category:* K–3.

5261 1998. *Heart of a Tiger.* Marsha Diane Arnold. *Illustrator:* Jamichael Henterly. Dial, 1995. *Category:* K–3.

5262 1998. *Mick Harte Was Here.* Barbara Park. Knopf, 1995. *Category:* 4–6.

5263 1998. *The Doom Stone.* Paul Zindel. *Illustrator:* Wayne McLaughlin. HarperCollins, 1995. *Category:* 6–8.

5264 1999. *My Little Sister Ate One Hare.* Bill Grossman. *Illustrator:* Kevin Hawkes. Crown, 1996. *Category:* K–3.

5265 1999. *Frindle.* Andrew Clements. *Illustrator:* Brian Selznick. Simon & Schuster, 1996. *Category:* 4–6.

5266 1999. *Twisted Summer.* Willo Davis Roberts. Atheneum, 1996. *Category:* 6–8.

5267 2000. *Double Trouble in Walla Walla.* Andrew Clements. *Illustrator:* Sal Murdocca. Millbrook, 1997. *Category:* K–3.

5268 2000. *Saving Shiloh.* Phyllis Reynolds Naylor. Atheneum, 1997. *Category:* 4–6.

5269 2000. *Ella Enchanted.* Gail Carson Levine. HarperCollins, 1997. *Category:* 6–8.

Author Index

Aakeson, Kim Fupz 1121, 1141, 1177, 1178, 1708
Aardema, Verna 4187
Aaron, Moses 300
Aas, Erlend 440
Abdallah, Mohammed ben 1458
Abdulla, Ian 265
Abel-Qadir, Ghazi 3085
Abercrombie, Barbara 3979
Abraham, Angela 3779, 3788
Abraham, Ken 3779, 3788
Abraham, Peter 1486
Ada, Alma Flor 3457, 4679
Adams, Jeannie 55
Adler, David 3882
Agarwal, Deepa 1567, 1618
Agertoft, Ejnar 1153
Aguileta Estrada, E. Gabriela 2296
Aguirre, Sergio 1723
Ahlberg, Allan 2023, 3144
Ahlberg, Janet 3144
Aidoo, Ama Ata 1785
Aiken, Joan 3140
Ainsborough Decker, Marjorie 3884
Akahane, Junko 1591
Akal, Aytül 1615
Akalestu, Rula 1493
Akçagüner, Zeliha 1745
Aker, Don 640
Albaut, Corinne 1467
Alberti, Rafael 1077
Alborough, Jez 5074
Alcántara, Ricardo 1517
Alder, Elizabeth 3939, 4456
Alderman, Belle 163
Aldridge, James 277
Aleixandre, Marilar 2901, 2917
Aleixo, Ricardo 1722
Alemán Lascurian, Guadalupe 2289
Alexander, Lloyd 1522, 3255
Alexander, Sally Hobart 3466
Alfaya, An 2920
Aliki (Brandenberg, Liacouras) 3564, 3706, 4007, 4487
Alire Saenz, Benjamin 3234
Allan, Nicholas 1833
Allen, Judy 5168
Allen, Pamela 152
Allende, Isabel 4828
Almajid, Fahmy 1564
Almond, David 1807, 2106, 2387
Alonso, Dora 1040, 1056, 1110, 1114
Alphin, Elaine 5104
Als, Roald 1438
Alshuler, Ernesto 1070
Altschuler, Sally 1134, 1148
Alumenda, Stephen 1515, 1558
Ambjørnsen, Ingvar 1586
Ambrosiani, Björn 1713
Amelin, Michel 1496
Amo, Montserrat del 2797
Anagnostopulos, Basiles 1461
Anaya, Héctor 2287
Anaya, Rudolfo 5011, 5016
Ancona, George 3136
Andersen, Hans Christian 1464, 1659
Andersen, Jens 1161
Andersen, Rachel 1859
Andersen, Vita 1126
Anderson, David A. 3523
Anderson, Laurie Halse 3863
Anderson, Lena 1475, 2996
Anderson, Margaret J. 3398
Andersson, Kjell 3007
Andreae, Giles 1827
Andrews, Jan 1478
Andrews, Virginia 30
Andrikopoulos, Nicholas 2199
Andruetto, María Teresa 1561
Anezini-Leraki, Georgia 2144, 2201
Anfousse, Ginette 804
Angelo, Ivan 1556
Angelopoulou, Vito 2179
Anholt, Laurence 1984
Antoni, Birgit 380
Anza Costabile, Ana Luisa 2293
Apostolake, Alexa 1579
Arcellana, Francisco 1587
Ardley, Bridget 1477
Argilli, Marcello 1497, 1540
Arias, Máinor 1008
Ariel, Gustavo 2781
Armangué I Herrero, Joan 2911
Armijo, Consuelo 1549
Armstrong, Jennifer 3817, 4484
Armstrong, Patricia G. 985
Arnold, Marsha Diane 4825, 5171, 5261
Arnold, Nick 2001, 2002
Arnold, Tedd 3513, 3649, 3653, 3751, 4634, 5134, 5159
Arnosky, Jim 3618
Aroneanu, Pierre 1292
Aronson, Marc 3276
Arrick, Fran 4888
Arrigan, Mary 1476
Artiles, Emma 1034, 1039, 1093
Arvaarluk Kusugak, Michael 937
Asano, Atsuko 1778
Asbjørnsen, Peter Christen 1424
Ashabranner, Brent 4468, 5199
Ashby, Ruth (editor) 1451
Ashley, Bernard 1665
Asquith, Ros 443
Atkinson, Kathie 183
Auch, Mary Jane 3424, 3658, 4164, 4188
Auer, Martin 386, 394, 429, 449, 463, 466, 1472, 1524, 1581, 1640

Augiaus, Pauliaus 1527
Aukrust, Kjell 2537
Aura, Alejandro 1453
Austrem, Liv Marie 1470, 2527
Avdyli, Besiana 1572
Aveñdano, Alberto 2815
Ayer, Eleanor 3471, 3671
Ayliffe, Alex 2007
Azevedo, Ricardo 611, 612, 1442

Babbitt, Natalie 3905, 4106, 4418
Baccalario, Pierdomenico 1653
Bachrach, Susan 3420
Backer, Marijn 2329
Bader, Barbara 3094
Bailey, Linda 648, 651
Baillie, Alan 7, 257
Baker, Charlotte 3226
Baker, Eleanor 2767
Baker, Jeannie 62, 100, 178, 188, 221, 329
Baker, Keith 3830
Baker, Wendy 4778
Baksi, Mahmut 453, 3038
Balcells, Jacqueline 1606
Bálint, Ágnes 1616
Balkwill, Fran 1991, 1992
Ball, Duncan 233, 236, 242, 285, 299
Ball, Nicole 4607
Ballard, Robert D. 5095
Ban, Ma 1784
Banaszak, Dariusz 1528
Bang, Karin 2548
Bang, Molly 3435, 3763
Banks, Kate 3270
Banks, Lynne Reid 3867
Bansch, Helga 390
Baquedano, Lucía 2799
Barclift, Stephen 3775
Barkhouse, Joyce 635
Barlett, Joan 13
Barlow, Steve 1614
Barnaud, Jean-Marie 1630
Barrio, Juana 1058
Barron, T.A. 5071
Barthélémy, Gérard 1629
Bartlett, Susan 4201
Bartoletti, Susan Campbell 3368, 4002
Barton, Byron 4658
Base, Graeme 102, 135, 165, 332, 1676
Bass, Doris 4030
Bateman, Teresa 4608
Bates, Di 240
Battut, Éric 1628
Bauer, Joan 3857
Bauer, Marion Dane 4144
Baum, L. Frank 444
Bautista, Ana Gabriela 1582
Bawden, Nina 4643
Bayé, Enric 2874
Baylor, Byrd 3619
Beake, Lesley 1547, 2741
Beale, Fleur 1585
Beatty, Patricia 3298
Becerra de Jenkins, Lyll 2315
Beck, Jennifer 2480
Beckett, Bernard 1667
Bedard, Michael 654, 701, 763, 771, 1680, 3312
Begag, Azouz 3040
Behrens, Katja 1776
Bejcek, Vladimír 1610
Belgrave, Susan 1843
Belisle, Jean 883
Bell, Helen 314
Bell, William 786, 834, 837, 933, 1604
Belsvik, Rune 2532, 2547, 2577
Beltrán, Montserrat 2846
Benameur, J. 1272
BenKemoun, Hubert 1627
Benner, J.A. 3231
Bennett, Jill 1840
Benson, Gerard 2024
Bentele, Günther 1368
Berebrouckx, Annemie 519
Berger, Holler 388
Berggren, Arne 2573
Bergin, Mark 2037
Bergström, Gunilla 2959
Bernauw, Patrick 572
Bernbaum, Israel 1332
Bernhard, Emery 5022
Berreby, Élie-Georges 874
Berry, Holly 3846
Berry, James 3256
Berry, Liz 5120
Bertin, Roselyne 1626
Bertran, Xavier 2879, 2903
Bertrand-Paradis, Claudine 897
Best, Cari 3433, 3643
Bhend, Käthi 3067
Bianchi, Page 1285
Biegel, Paul 2328
Bieman, Ienne 2310
Bille, S. Corinna 1504
Billingsley, Franny 3275, 4317
Binet, Laurence 1315
Bing, Bo 1786
Birdseye, Tom 3195, 3638, 4344, 4823, 5169
Birkeland, Kirsti 2544
Birmajer, Marcelo 1505
Bishop, Gavin 2463, 2492, 2494
Bitton-Jackson, Livia 3481, 4820
Bjerke, André 2554
Bjørnson, Elisabeth 2590
Blackman, Malorie 1664
Blaimert, Richard 891
Blain, Christophe 603
Blain, David 1317
Blair, Patricia 3632
Blake, Michael 4832
Blake, Quentin 1887, 5034
Blake, Robert J. 3986, 4744, 5173
Blake, Stephanie 1650
Blanc, Jean-Noël 1297
Blanco, María Eugenia 2292
Blay, Charlotte 1150, 1168
Blazejovsky, Maria 382, 1523, 1575
Bloch, Muriel 604
Bloemhof, Francois 2709, 2713, 2758
Bloor, Edward 3735, 4262, 4289, 4404
Bloor, Thomas 1854
Blos, Joan 4844
Bluitgen, Kåre 1144, 1166
Blumberg, Rhoda 4040, 5206
Blume, Judy 21, 3183, 3331, 3654, 3958, 4204, 4220, 4362, 4380, 4620, 4957, 5146
Blundell, Tony 5100
Bly, David 917
Bober, Natalie S. 3260, 3840
Bodenstein, C. 2743
Bødker, Cecil 1133
Bogart, Jo Ellen 944
Bogataj Ambrozic, Saša 1764
Boie, Kirsten 1639, 2965
Boisset, E 1276
Boix Milian, Armando 2847
Boland, Janice 5192
Bolta, María Jesús 2823
Bolton, Reg 318
Bond, Peter 1791
Bondar, Barbara 746
Bondar, Roberta 746
Bonde, Heidi 1555
Bonilla, Alejandra Castro 1015, 1016
Bonners, Susan 3480
Boock, Paula 1450, 1566, 2445, 2481
Book, Rick 992
Boonen, Heide 1492
Boore, Roger 1913
Boraks-Nemetz, Lillian 956
Borden, Louise 3487

Borges Triana, Joaquín 1042
Borkovcová, Hana 1473
Botha, Tertia 2753
Bothma, Alida 2714
Bouchard, Dave 929
Boucher-Mativat, Marie-Andrée 903
Boulet, Tania 869
Boulotis, Hristos 2141, 2201
Bourgeat, Lene og Pierre 1132
Bourre, Martine 604
Bowen, Gary 3935
Bowers, Vivien 753
Bowler, Tim 500, 1806, 1909
Bradby, Marie 3940
Bradford, Karleen 668
Brain, Helen 2712
Branald, Adolf 1526
Brandes, Sophie 442
Brandford, Henrietta 1866, 1967
Brandis, Marianne 690, 694
Brands, Gerard 2334
Brandt, Marianna 1678, 2716
Bransby, Lawrence 1456, 2722, 2744
Braz, Júlio Emílio 445, 3036
Bredsdorff, Bodil 1185, 1471
Bregin, Elana 2745
Brenes, Annie 1007
Breslin, Theresa 1803
Brett, Jan 3126, 3177, 3186, 3543, 4413
Brewster, Hugh 927, 968
Brian, Janeen 1568
Bridges, Ruby 3392, 4008, 4485
Bridges, Rudy 3674
Bridwell, Norman 4024
Briggs, Raymond 1889
Brinck, Lotta 1537
Bringsværd, Tor Åge 2553, 2560, 2592
Brisson, Pat 3485
Brittain, Bill 4399, 4445
Brodin, Elin 2594
Broeckhoven, Diane 491
Brooks, Bruce 3809, 4061
Brooks, Martha 673, 800, 843, 945
Broome, Errol 310
Brouillard, Anne 1495
Brousseau, Linda 899, 1439
Brown, Anthony 2308
Brown, Ken 2013
Brown, Marc Tolon 3506, 3713
Brown, Marcia 4179
Brown, Ruth 1562, 5109
Browne, Anthony 1895, 3053
Bruchac, Joseph 3548, 3894, 4160
Bruel, Christian 1652
Brumbeau, Jeff 3236
Bruna, Dick 2368
Bryan, Ashley 3889, 4194, 4417, 5035
Buchanan, Dawna Lisa 4453
Buchanan, William J. 4609
Buchholz, Quint 3064
Budde, Nadia 1362
Budur, Natal'ja 1590
Buehner, Caralyn 5064, 5068
Buffie, Margaret 795, 979
Buján, Daniel 2826
Bunney, Ron 1675
Bunting, Eve 3297, 3305, 3327, 3580, 3683, 3852, 3885, 4151, 4505, 4509, 4631, 4754, 4805, 4811, 4829, 4863, 4898, 4899, 4915, 4964, 4965, 5075, 5101, 5136, 5142
Buongiorno, Teresa 1465, 1621
Burgen, Jim 3799
Burger, Reinhard 1379
Burgess, Melvin 1805, 1865
Burkert, Nancy Ekholm 3245
Burko-Falcman, Berthe 1541
Burks, Brian 4948
Burleigh, Robert 4477
Burnie, David 1994
Burns, Diane 3599
Burns, Mary 3906
Burt, Roger 1884
Buss, Fran Leeper 3031, 3994
Busser, Marianne 1583
Butler, Dorothy 2456
Butler, Geoff 941
Butler, Mark 1446
Buttkus, Thomas 405
Buul, Tine van 2320
Byars, Betsy 3578, 3690, 4103, 4401, 4871, 4966, 5007
Bygott, David 2039
Bylock, Maj 2936

Cabrera Delgado, Luis 1101
Caduto, Michael J. 3101
Cairns, Barbara 2470
Caissés Sánchez, Luis 1046
Çakiroglu, Atila 1489
Calabro, Marian 4050
Calcines, Carlo 1047
Caldwell, Walter 3923
Calhoun, Mary 3332, 4243
Calvert, Patricia 3477
Calzadilla, Julia 1107
Cameron, Eleanor 3897
Camp, Lindsay 1593
Campbell, Lisa 3178, 4826
Canault, Nina 1298
Canela Garayoa, Mercè 2813
Canela, Montserrat 1750
Canetti, Yanitzia 1049
Canfield, Jack 3222, 4839, 5124
Cannon, A.E. 5057
Cannon, Janell 3122, 3292, 3341, 4190, 4258, 4436, 4912, 5008
Cano Peiró, Carles 2891
Cansino, Eliacer 2897
Cardenas Angulo, Teresa 1104
Caride, Ramón 2918
Carle, Eric 3148, 3283, 3545, 3621, 4105, 4756, 5038, 5140
Carling, Amelia Lau 3137
Carlson, Melody 3796
Carmody, Isabelle 68, 90
Carol, Núria 1749
Carpi, Pinin 1642
Carrer, Chiara 2785
Carrier, Roch 704
Carroll, Jessica 109, 232, 343
Carroll, Lewis 1896
Carter, Alden R. 4841
Carter, Anne 991
Carter, Forrest 3119
Carvalho, Carlos 1512
Casalderrey Fraga, Fina 1551, 2820, 2914, 2931
Case, Dianne 2742
Cashford, Jules 1469
Cassabois, Jacques 1296
Casta, Stefan 2955, 3019
Castanha, Mar 617
Castro, José Zafra 2893
Caswell, Brian 92, 267
Cato, Heather 2514
Cazarré, Lourenço 607
Cazets, Denys 1600, 3324
Cela i Ollé, Jaume 2878
Cela, Jaume 2829, 2852
Ceng, Yangqing 1459
Chabas, J.F. 603
Chacón Nardi, Rafaela 1103
Chambers, Aidan 1808, 2342
Chamlian, Regina 1514
Chandra, Deborah 4183
Chandran, Hira Nirodi 1679
Chappaz, Maurice 1504
Chatzedake, Tonia 1538
Chee, Cheng-Khee 3121, 3931
Cheng, Christopher 193
Cherry, Lynne 3410
Chichester Clark, Emma 3489
Chidolue, Dagmar 1423
Child, Lincoln 3731, 3734
Cho, Shinta 1774

Choi, Yangsook 3945
Choyce, Lesley 638
Chudozilov, Petr 1635
Çinaroglu, Ayla 1531
Cincurová, Emília 1482
Clark Elam, Barbara 3895
Clark, Joan 693, 821, 982
Clark, Mary Higgins 3213
Clarke, Judith 282, 1674
Clarke, Mere 2511
Clausen, Jacob 1171, 1727
Claverie, Jean 1293
Cleary, Beverly 3696, 5249
Cleeff, Abbing 2376
Cleeff, Van 2376
Clément, Frédéric 3061
Clement, Gary 736
Clement, Jesper 1172
Clement, Rod 50, 110, 113, 147, 171, 239, 325, 3200, 3210, 3665, 4405
Clements, Andrew 3201, 3404, 3475, 3748, 3874, 4273, 4286, 4407, 4437, 4510, 4637, 4671, 4739, 4767, 4771, 5077, 5236, 5265, 5267
Clinton, Catherine 3493
Clyne, Densey 187, 189
Cobb, Vicki 5182
Coelho, Raquel 613, 620
Coerr, Eleanor 5059
Cofer, Judih Ortiz 4674
Cohen, Rebecca 3633
Colasanti, Marina 998
Cole, B. 583
Cole, Babette 1893
Cole, Joanna 3408, 3544, 3617, 3693, 3697, 3703, 3711, 3715, 4328, 5081, 5132, 5200
Coles, Robert 4870
Coles, William E. 1474
Colfer, Eoin 1692
Coll, Ivar da 1724
Coll, Pep 2839, 2909
Collins, Lilyjane 1483
Colom I Bernat, Rosa María 1550, 2908
Colwell, Eileen 1844
Coman, Carolyn 4072
Comelles, Salvador 2875
Conford, Ellen 3704
Conlon McKenna, Marita 2231, 2234, 2250, 3928
Conly, Jane Leslie 4067
Conrad, Pam 723, 3243, 3336, 3576, 4186
Cooke, Trisha 1891, 1968
Cooney, Barbara 3540, 4139, 4192
Cooney, Caroline 3219, 3727, 3970, 3973, 4246, 4338, 4389, 4414, 4497, 4815, 5103, 5145, 5155, 5248
Cooper, Susan 3556, 4099
Coran, Pierre 565
Cordero, Silvia Jaeger 2291
Corlett, Shirley 2516
Cormier, Robert 1375, 3335, 4215, 4647
Cortizas, Antón 2811, 2824
Costecalde, Claude-Bernard 3792
Côté, Denis 859, 871
Couloumbis, Audrey 4089
Couper, Heather 2049
Couprie, Katy 1284
Courtenay, Bryce 227, 296
Cousins, Lucy 4654
Coville, Bruce 3158, 3187, 3347, 3504, 3555, 3743, 3869, 4161, 4240, 4364, 4376, 4384, 4431, 4441, 4618, 5056
Cowley, Joy 1666, 2455, 2483, 2486, 3274
Cox, Aletha 3635
Crampton, Patricia 1841
Creech, Sharon 360, 1816, 3098, 4071, 4817, 5112
Crew, Gary 3, 34, 59, 66, 69, 70, 271
Crew, Linda 3925
Crews, Donald 3547
Crichton, Michael 40, 3216, 3972, 4382, 4835, 4887
Croll, Carolyn 3563
Cross, Gillian 1799
Crowe, Andrew 2473
Crump, Barry 1485
Crutcher, Chris 3111, 3344, 3348, 4224
Csorba, Csaba 1740
Csukás, István 1741
Cubias, Daisy 3994
Culliman, Bernice 4025
Cummings, Pat 3253
Curtis, Christopher Paul 3351, 3442, 3538, 3835, 3951, 4074, 4088, 4177
Cushman, Karen 3306, 3682, 3831, 4047, 4070, 4075, 4507

Dabcovich, Lydia 4261
Dadson, Nana 1510
Dahimène, Adelheid 451
Dahl, Roald 19, 23, 24, 27, 28, 31, 43, 136, 137, 141, 144, 585, 594, 1955, 2664, 2668, 2669, 3180, 3866, 3912, 4266, 4378, 4731, 5045, 5086
Dahlbäck, Helena 3015
Dahms, Anne-Grethe 1623
Dahn, Jo 2085
Dalkey, Kara 5079
Dalmases, Antoni 2843
Daly, Niki 1663
Dam, Arend van 1769
Damm, Dörte 1638
Danek, Adolf 1433
Daniëls, Guy 557
Danyan, Neun 438
Danzinger, Paula 3708, 3714, 4488
Daraki, Pepi 2185
Darling, Kathy 5187
Daufresne, Michèle 1634
Daughty, Duanne 4652
Dauwalder, Valerija F. 1760
Davey, Thyrza 10
David, Patricia 566
Davidts, Jean-Pierre 830, 900
Davies, Hunter 290
Davis, Jenny 4494
Davis, Ken 3772, 3784
Davis, Ossie 5105
Davis, Russell G. 4468
Davol, Marguerite W. 3848, 3849
Day, Brenda 211
Dean, Julia 4197
Deaver, Julie Rice 5088, 5130
de Bel, Marc 558
de Bie, Ceciel 2390
de Blanck, Olga 1090
Deedy, Carmen Agra 3661
DeFelice, Cynthia 3663, 4162, 4667, 4801, 4865, 4960, 5009
de Goldi, Kate 2448, 2479
DeGroat, Dianne 3172, 4434
de Jong, Marietjie 2674
Dekkers, Midas 1425, 2306
de Kockere, Geert 553
de Koster, Bea 479
Delacre, Lulu 3129
Delaunay, Jacqueline 3058
Delaunois, Angèle 731
del Cañizo, José Antonio 2818
Delgado, Johnny Mora 1011
Delonis, Antonis 2147
de Maeyer, Gregie 492, 577
Demers, Barbara 923
Demers, Dominique 855, 856, 858, 863, 907
de Mesa de Inchauste, Isabel 996
Denning, Ken 1140
Denton, Terry 48, 345, 350, 352

de Paola, Tomie 3881, 4091, 4111, 5036
DePaolo, Paula 3460
Derby, Sally 4765
de Saulles, Tony 2001, 2002
Desplat-Duc, Anne-Marie 598
Desrosiers, Sylvie 865, 876, 1484
de Sterck, Marita 494, 567
Destours, Christine 1658
Deuker, Carl 4345, 4627, 4885, 5147
Deutsch, Xavier 1316
de Villers, Leon 2737, 2759, 2769
de Vos, Philip 2676, 2735
Diago, Ariel Ribeaux 1018, 1024, 1067, 1108
Díaz Guerra, Francisco A. 2888
Díaz, Pérez 1025, 1035
Dickinson, Peter 1373, 2098, 4495
Didelez, Guy 572
Diebold, Ute 1488
Dietl, Erhard 421
Dillon, Diane 3608
Dillon, Eilis 2229
Dillon, Leo 3608
Dingle, Derek T. 3947
DiSalvo-Ryan, DyAnne 3990
Dische, Irene 1356
Disher, Garry 64
Docampo, Xabier Puente 1508, 2930
Dodd, Lynley 2462, 2493
Doherty, Berlie 1800, 1935
Donaldson, Julia 1688, 1795, 1982
Donner, Chris 602, 1657
Dörfler, Robert 406
Dorris, Michael 4790
Doskocilová, Hana 1765
Douzou, Oliver 1311
Dovjak-Matkovic, Blanka 1434
Dowd, John 645
Doyle, Brian 660, 756, 809, 826, 974
Doyle, Debra 4310
Doyle, Malachy 1669
Drake, Gillian 2080
Draper, Sharon 3533, 5111, 5157
Dreesen, Jaak 485, 550, 1426, 1544
Dros, Imme 1534, 2305, 2317, 2327, 2338, 2350, 2362, 2377
Dubé, Jasmine 886
Dubelaar, Thea 1770
Dubocanin, Alija Hasagic 1578
Dubosarsky, Ursula 6, 274
du Bouchet, Paule 1281
DuBouchet, Paule 1656
Duchesne, Christiane 700, 707, 888, 908
Duder, Tessa 2441, 2443, 2459, 2495
Dufour, Hortense 3062
Duggleby, John 3390
Duka, Mania 1763
Dumas, Alice 1918, 3059
Dunbar, Robert 1539
Duncan, Lois 3969, 4216, 4408, 4501, 5049, 5089, 5127, 5137, 5141, 5243
Dunmore, Helen 2028
du Plessis, Hans 2708
Durán, Esther Suárez 1083, 1087
Durán, Teresa 1513
Durell, Ann 3993
Dyson, Marianne J. 3864

Earls, Nick 87
Easterling, Bill 3467, 4196, 4653
Eccleshare, Julia 1850
Echegaray, Marta 1594
Edelfeldt, Inger 3014
Edwards, Becky 1671
Edwards, Julie Andrews 3314
Edwards, Nicholas 4260
Edwards, Pam 3354
Eg, Harald Rosenløw 2529
Egan, Tim 4926
Egea, Octavi 2849
Egielski, Richard 4630
Egilsdottir, Herdis 2216
Ehlert, Lois 3596
Ehrlich, Amy 3551
Eide, Torill 414, 2525
Eilstrup, Lena 358, 1173
Eiriksdottir, Gudrun H. 2214
Eken, Cecilie 1187
Ekker, Ernst A. 436
Ekman, Fam 2541
El Bezaz, Naima 2427
Eldjarn, Thorarinn 2207
Elias, Bettie 484, 501, 511, 564
Elizondo, Gabriela Riveros 2290
Elkington, John 1835
Elleman, Barbara 3900, 4029
Elling, Lars 2562
Ellis, Joyce K. 3780
Ellis, Sarah 706, 778, 819, 958, 978
Elmore, Barbara 3229
Emberley, Ed 3189
Emmett, John (editor) 17
Ende, Torill 408
Engdahl, Sylvia Louise 4640
Enríquez, Lázaro 1105
Ensikat, Klaus 3048
Eriksen, Helga Gunerius 2572
Eriksson, Erik 1597, 2958
Erlbeck, Hana Hiriana 2491
Erlbruch, Wolf 1339, 1637, 2381
Erlickas, Juozas 1430, 2278
Erlingsson, Fridrik 2212
Esbensen, Barbara Juster 3601, 4324
Escobar, Froilán 1043
Espino, José Manuel 1063, 1066, 1076, 1089
Espinosa, Norge 1061
Esteban, Angel 2801
Esterl, Arnica 407
Etra, Jonathan 5000
Ewing, Lynne 3166
Ewo, Jon 2567

Facchini, Vittoria 1651
Facklam, Margery 3707
Færden, Else 2591
Farcy, Claudine 880
Farmer, Nancy 3829, 4069, 4079, 5114
Fatus, Sophie 2789
Faurby, Bent 1203
Fedden, Mary 1931
Feelings, Tom 3530
Feiffer, Jules 3434
Feijoo, Samuel 1097
Felipe, Nersys 1091
Fenner, Carol 4076, 4249
Ferdjoukh, Malika 1290
Ferguson, Alan 3574
Fernández Paz, Agustin 2883
Fernandez Retamar, Roberto 1059
Fernández, Nieves 1113
Ferrandino, Giuseppe 1660
Ferris, Jeri 3377, 3382, 4903
Fields, Terri 4288
Fienberg, Anna 5, 61
Filntisi, Sofia 2163
Findon, Joanne 766
Fine, Anne 1801, 1857, 1936, 2101, 2104
Fischner-Nagel, H. 5048
Fisher, Catherine 2068
Fisher, Leonard Everett 4138, 4748
Fisk, Pauline 1956
Fitch, Sheree 639, 740, 810, 983, 1565

Flackham, Margery 3625
Flegg, Aubrey 3023
Fleischman, Paul 3293, 3303, 3813, 3851, 3855, 4791
Fleischman, Sid 605, 3199, 3241, 3355, 3403, 4049, 4361, 4921
Fleming, Denise 4454
Fletcher, Ralph 5115
Flugge, Klaus 1849
Fogelman, Phyllis 3525
Foglar, Jaroslav 1734
Ford, Vince 2497, 2515
Foreman, Michael 1966
Forrestal, Elaine 80
Fossheim, Minken 2558, 2589
Fourie, Corlia 2675, 2730, 2734, 2771
Fourie, Heila 2701
Fowler, Susi Gregg 3465
Fowler, Zinita 3225
Fox, Mem 103, 157, 177
Fox, Paula 3610
Francesc Delgado, Joan 2880
Franck, Ed 474, 515, 576
Frankel Hauser, Jill 4784, 4785
Fransson, Birgitta 2998
Frazee, Marla 4924
Fréchette, Carole 1729
Freedman, Russell 3609, 3670, 3810, 3812, 3818, 3824, 3832, 3859, 3999, 4012, 4013, 4060, 4065, 4157, 4181, 4476, 4753, 4943, 5040, 5201
Freeman, Suzanne 3444
Fremon, David 4939
French, Jackie 85
French, Simon 215
Fretheim, Tor 422, 2538
Friðbjörnsdottir, Thorey 2215
Fried, Amelie 1357
Friedrich, Elizabeth 3841
Friesen, Bernice 989
Friesen, Gayle 674, 782, 848
Frischmuth, Barbara 434, 450, 1444
Fritz, Jean 2346, 3244, 4110, 4156, 4475
Froissart, Benedicte 699
Fromberg, Karen Margrethe 1162
Frommlet, Wolfram 1636
Frugoni, Chiara 1621
Fuchs, Gerd 1529
Fujimaki, Kumiko 1569
Fulani, Dan 1554
Funazaki, Yoshihiko 1519
Funke, Cornelia 356, 3091
Furley, Deborah 2465
Gaarder, Inger Margrethe 2519
Gaarder, Jostein 359, 1342, 2534, 2571, 2599, 2611
Gabe, Dora 1445
Gaetanos, Petros 2111
Gagnier, Hélène 1730
Gahrton, Måns 2962, 2969
Galdone, Paul 4145
Galicia, Montserrat 2865
Gallego Alfonso, Emilia 1115
Gallego García, Laura 1706, 2835
Gallo, Don 3110
Gamlin, Linda 1998
Gandolfi, Silvana 1649
Ganges, Montse 2783
Gansemans, Walter 477, 570
Garcia I Cornella, Dolors 2877, 2910
Garcia Llorca, Antoni 2869, 2876
García Vilariño, Andrés 2808
Gardam, Jane 4641
Gardaš, Anto 1609
Gardella, Maria Àngels 2864
Garland, Peter 2467
Garland, Sherry 3227, 3340, 4940
Garner, Alan 4646
Garner, Eleanor Ramrath 3950
Gärtner, Hans 417
Garza, Carmen Lomas 3132, 4678, 5013
Gaskin, Chris 2477
Gates, Susan 2019
Gauvin, Axel 3034
Gavin, Jamila 2108
Gay, Marie-Louise 841, 948
Gee, Maurice 2446
Geelen, Harrie 2347, 2365
Gelber, Eva 1577
Gelbert-Avni, Ofra 2610
Gellman, Marc 3456
Gemala, Eugenia Doina 1644
George, Jean Craighead 3614, 4155, 5177, 5181, 5207
George, Kristine O'Connell 3860, 4929
George, William 3361
Georgeoglou, Nitsa 2182
Georgoudi, Theodora 2169
Geraghty, Paul 1821, 4385
Geras, Adèle 4975
Gerber-Hess, Maja 1598
Gerlach, Eva 2383, 2434
Gertsou-Sari, Anna 2189
Gestdottir, Ragnheidur 2221
Ghazi, Shahib Hamid 3387
Gibbons, Alan 1793
Gibbons, Gail 3624, 4777
Giblin, James Cross 5205
Giff, Patricia Reilly 4023, 4085
Gilderdale, Betty 2457
Gillmor, Don 825
Gilman, Phoebe 935, 976, 4980
Gilmore, Rachna 735
Giménez, Anna 1595
Gingras, Charlotte 737
Gire, Ken 3771
Gisbert, José Manuel 2809
Gleeson, Libby 78, 89, 258
Gleitzman, Morris 29, 47, 108, 112, 115, 138, 146, 148, 174, 180, 214, 234, 331, 347, 348, 353, 1574
Glenn, Mel 4512
Glistrup, Eva 1157
Glori, Debi 1824
Goble, Paul 3095
Godfrey, Martyn 787
Godkin, Celia 742
Goldberg, Leah 2254
Goldie, Marelize 2696
Goldin, Augusta 3620
Goldin, Barbara Diamond 4973, 4978
Goldthwaite, John 1872
Gomi, Taro 1779
Gonzalez Montes, Fidencio 2294
González, Alberto Domingo 1048
González, Dolores 2842, 2915
González, Lola 2802
González, M. Lourenzo 1777
González, Nelson Simón 1026, 1030
Goobie, Beth 918
Goodall, Jane 402
Goor, Nancy 3238
Goor, Ron 3238
Gordon, Gaelyn 2490
Gorog, Judith 4490
Goulimi, Alki 2175
Graeber, Charlotte Towner 3957, 4359, 4798, 4954, 5240
Graham, Bob 58, 63, 91, 153, 1985
Graña, Bernardino 2916
Granfield, Linda 747, 749, 767, 926
Grant, Cynthia D. 4612
Gravel Galouchko, Annouchka 722, 965
Gravel, Francoise 703, 806, 868, 882
Greene, Gracie 205, 273, 311

Greenfield, Eloise 3517, 3904, 4325
Greenwood, Barbara 748, 752, 817, 938
Greenwood, T. 335, 338
Greer, Gary 4278, 4662, 5044
Grégoire, Caroline 911
Grégoire, Hélène 892
Gregori, Josep 2873
Gregory, Kristiana 3299
Gregory, Nan 822, 957
Grenier, Michel 890
Gribbon, John 2048
Gribbon, Mary 2048
Griffiths, Andy 52, 154, 238, 241, 349, 351
Grisham, John 3218
Grobler, Mari 2682
Grosmaire, Jean-Louis 896
Gross, Philip 2027
Grosse, Gillian 1963, 2100
Grosser, Morton 3296
Grossman, Bill 5119, 5264
Grossman, Virginia 3930
Grover, Wayne 5052
Grutman, Jewel H. 3468, 3937
Gryski, Camilla 743
Gschwendtner, Ruth 459
Gu, Jun 1503
Guan, Jiaqi 1507
Guenoun, Joël 1655
Guettier, Bénédicte 1641
Guggenmos, Josef 470
Guido, Van Genechten 547
Guillet, Jean-Pierre 757, 760
Gurney, James 3502
Gutierrez, José Antonio 1072, 1099
Gutman, Claude 871, 1294
Gutman, Dan 4410, 4448, 4808, 5161
Guy, Rosa 3025
Gwynne, Phillip 84, 133

Haas, Jessie 1690
Habinger, Renate 387, 465
Hacks, Peter 1320
Haddix, Margaret Peterson 3164, 3197, 3202, 3941, 4355, 4818
Hagen, Hans 2322, 2323, 2373
Hagerup, Henning 2593
Hagerup, Klaus 2526, 2540
Hahn, Dorothy 4800
Hahn, Mary Downing 3185, 3194, 3320, 3342, 3557, 3742, 3745, 3955, 4228, 4233, 4239, 4251, 4276, 4279, 4329, 4339, 4664, 4730, 4789, 4874, 4875, 5005, 5051, 5061, 5092, 5098, 5110, 5229, 5233, 5247
Hall, Barbara 4900
Hall, Lynn 5138
Hall, W. 580
Hamersa, Elsa Meiring 2760
Hamilton, Virginia 3044, 3529, 3908, 4180, 4457, 4747
Handford, Martin 25, 3147
Handke, Peter 464
Hannesdóttir, Guðrún 1617, 2218
Hansen, Hans Chr. 1167, 1204
Hansen, Michael 11, 39
Hanson, Regina 3135
Harada, Takehide 1448
Harding, Mike 2029
Harrah, Madge 4933
Harranth, Wolf 395, 430
Harrison, Barbara 3903
Härstedt, Kent 1699
Hartman, Thomas 3456
Hartmann, Lukas 3075
Hartmann, Nils 1145
Hartnett, Sonia 280
Harvey, Anne 2025
Harvey, Amanda 1924
Hasan-zadah, Farhad 1532
Haskins, Jim 3380, 3386, 4845, 5203
Haslam, Andrew 4778
Hassan, Yaël 1277, 1654
Hastrup, Hanne 1127
Hatjihanna, Filisa 2110
Hattingh, Loraine 2710
Hatzinikolaou, Dina 2183
Haugen, Tormod 2603, 3043
Hausfater-Douieb, Rachel 3065
Hawkes, Kevin 3825
Hawkins, Elizabeth 1906
Hawxhurst, Joan C. 3886
Hayes, Joe 3157
Haynes, Betsy 5152
Hazelhoff, Veronica 2348, 2432
He, Qunying 1607
Heap, Sue 1980
Hearn, Shirley 16
Hearne, Betsy 4005
Hébert, Marie-Francine 853
Heddle, Rebecca 1997
Heesen, Martha 2388
Hegewisch, Helga 1625
Heilmann, Pia Rosing 1702
Heinämaa, Anna 1264
Heins, Ethel 3893
Heins, Paul 3893
Helakisa, Kaarina 1612, 1725
Helgadottir, Gudrun 2204
Helgason, Karl 2210
Helmer, Marilyn 770, 832, 835
Hendersen, Kathy 1892
Hendry, Diana 2099
Hendry, Frances Mary 1905
Heneghan, James 646, 959
Henkes, Kevin 3125, 3328, 3549, 3597, 3600, 3602, 4130
Henry, Maeve 1965
Hermans, Ronni 489
Herrera, Ana Cecilia Brenes 1006
Herrera, Juan Felipe 3138, 3644, 3681
Hesse, Karen 3163, 3421, 3459, 3845, 3932, 4082, 4422, 4795, 4878, 4981
Hest, Amy 3263, 3479, 4446
Heuck, Sigrid 403, 486
Heurté, Yves 872
Hevier, Daniel 1542
Heymans, Annemie 2326, 2431
Heymans, Margriet 2326, 2431
Hickman, Janet 4455, 4849, 4858
Hicyilmaz, Gaye 2325
Hietala, Mirjami 1261
Higgs, Liz Curtis 3791
Hill, Anthony 15
Hill, David 1934, 2449
Hill, Donna 3486
Hill, Kirkpatrick 3029
Hindley, Judy 2036
Hinton, Nigel 1814, 1908
Hinton, S.E. 22, 3116
Hiou, Elsa 2143, 2148, 2152
Hirschman, Susan 3568, 3898
Hiscock, Bruce 3626
Hiser, Graham 4366
Hoban, Tana 3242, 4655
Hobbs, Valerie 4616
Hobbs, Will 3215, 3220, 3221, 3338, 3589, 4942
Hochgatterer, Paulus 363, 462
Hodges, Margaret 4124
Hoestlandt, Jo 2263, 4986
Hoet, Lieve 499
Hofbauer, Friedl 471
Hoff, Mary 4852
Hoffius, Stephen 4395
Hoffmann, E.T.A. 1479
Hofman, Wim 2374, 2436
Höglund, Anna 1348, 2993
Hohler, Franz 3074

Hoig, Stan 4464
Holcroft, Anthony 4602
Holl, Kristi 4238
Holland, Katrien 2260
Hollyer, Beatrice 1697
Holm, Annika 3009
Holm, Jennifer L. 4090
Holman, Felice 3437
Holmas, Stig 2596
Holmberg, Bo R 2944
Holt, Kimberly Willis 4094, 4997
Holten, Knud 1170
Holtwijk, Ineke 2301
Holub, Josef 1380, 3087, 3088, 4300
Holubitsky, Katherine 675, 783
Homes, A.M. 1338
Honaker, Miche 590, 1300
Honey, Elizabeth 342
Hoose, Phillip 3464
Hopkins, Lee Bennett 3469, 3836, 4910
Hopkinson, Deborah 3861, 3933
Horgan, Dorothy 1937
Hornung, Helmut 1337
Horowitz, Anthony 495
Horrocks, Anita 849, 922
Horse, Harry 362, 1979
Hortiati, Theti 2181
Hoshikawa, Hiroko 1780
Hostetler, Bob 3776
Hotakainen, Kari 1259
Hough, Barrie 2673, 2688, 2718, 2738, 2748, 2750, 2761
Høverstad, Torstein Bugge 2583
Hovland, Ragnar 2524
Howard, Arthur 3422
Howard, Ellen 3473
Howarth, Lesley 1863
Howe, James 600, 3651, 3687
Howes, Jim 195
Howker, Janni 2331
Hoyt-Goldsmith, Diane 4467
Hribar, Vida Jeraj 2654
Hrolfsdottir, Gunnhildir 2203
Huda-gu, Furuzanda 1498
Hudec, Ivan 1428
Hudson, Jan 914
Hughes, David 1343, 1923
Hughes, Gwenno 2084
Hughes, Huw John 2066
Hughes, Mair Wynn 2056, 2073
Hughes, Monica 916, 4650
Hulth, Sonja 3012
Hundal, Nancy 952
Hunt, Nan 278
Hunter, Bernice Thurman 925, 973
Hunter, Mollie 4642
Huovi, Hannele 1207, 1218
Hurd, Thacher 4743
Hurwin, Davida Wills 3308, 4891
Hurwitz, Johanna 3689, 3700, 4862, 4951
Hutching, Gerald 2488
Hutchins, Hazel 915, 921
Hüttner, Hannes 1321
Huws, Emily 2062, 2063
Huwyler, Max 3073
Hyldmo, Egil 2604
Hyman, Trina Schart 3566, 3821, 4104

Ifans, Rhiannon 2083
Iglesias, Bieito 2922
Igus, Toyomi 3535
Iliopoulos, Vangelis 2165
Ilse, Heylen 548
Ingman, Bruce 1929
Ingoglio, Gina 36, 107
Ingpen, Robert 1673
Inkpen, Mick 1810
Innocenti, Roberto 3057
Inuk, Lotte 1182, 1183
Ioannides, I.D. 2180
Ipcar, Dahlov 4147
Irimescu, Diana 1546
Irvine, Joan 5043
Irwin, Hadley 4846
Irwin, James 3768
Isaacs, Anne 4628
Isaksson, Britt 3006
Isau, Ralf 1325
Itkonen, Jukka 1221
Ito, Hiroshi 1781
Ito, Yu 1789
Iyengar, Gita 1668

Jacai, Feng 3028
Jacobsen, Søren Kragh 1160
Jacques, Brian 284, 286, 287, 288, 298, 1899, 1902
Jafa, Manorama 1460
Jaffe, Nina 4982, 4991
Jalonen, Riitta 1249
Jalovec, Viljenka 2660
Jam, Teddy 705
Jamar, Corine 1545
Janer Manila, Gabriel 2929
Janisch, Heinz 375, 379, 384, 397, 458, 460
Jarlskov, Flemming 1143
Jarman, Julia 1696
Jarrett, Clare 1930
Järvi, Annukka 1215
Jarvis, Robin 1900
Jasnov, Michail D. 1761
Jatzek, Gerald 373
Jeffers, Susan 3120, 4120, 5183
Jenkin-Pearce, Susie 1926
Jenkins, A.M. 3356
Jenkins, Geraint H. 2057
Jenkins, Martin 2053
Jenkins, Steve 3273
Jenness, Aylette 3372
Jennings, Paul 26, 32, 94, 97, 98, 105, 140, 142, 148, 168, 169, 172, 176, 185, 220, 223, 224, 226, 228, 230, 231, 245, 246, 247, 248, 250, 251, 252, 253, 254, 289, 293, 295, 321, 326, 327, 328, 330, 333, 335, 336, 338, 339, 347
Jennings, Sharon 712
Jensen, Jørn 1202
Jensen, Louis 1139
Jermieson, Allan 2732
Jiang, Ji-Li 4101
Jimenéz, Arrate Egaña 2834
Jiménez, Francisco 3134, 3269, 4048
Jiménez, Juan Ramón 1071
Jinks, Catherine 74, 79, 281
Johansen, Anders 1184
Johansen, Hanna 423, 1466, 2261, 3067
Johnson, A.K. 1596
Johnson, Angela 3526, 3536, 3641, 4614
Johnson, Catherine 1695
Johnson, D.B. 3277
Johnson, James Weldon 3528
Johnson, Julie 670, 939
Johnson, Miriam 3879
Johnson, Paul Brett 3357, 4125, 4132
Johnston, Julie 709, 716, 776
Johnston, Tony 4914
Jokulsson, Illugi 2206
Jolin, Dominique 852, 860
Jonas, Ann 3547
Jones, Eleri Ellis 2072
Jones, Elizabeth McDavid 3594
Jones, Gwen Redbers 2061, 2078
Jones, Jac 2079
Jones, Lis 2081
Jones, T. Llew 1911, 2055
Jones, Tegwyn 2079
Jones, W.J. 1912
Jonsson, Elias Snæland 2213
Jooß, Erich 437
Jordan, Sherryl 517
Jørgensen, Majken 1159

Jorisch, Stéphane 711, 734
Joseph, Lynn 3130
Joyce, William 3827
Jung, Reinhardt 432, 446, 2612
Jurmain, Suzanne 4895
Juvonen, Riikka 1243

Kähkönen, Sirpa 1265
Kaiser, Reinhard 1351
Kaissou, Nitsa 2157, 2162
Kakukiwa, Robyn 2469
Kaliotsos, Pantelis 2135
Kallia, Eleni 2198
Kallioniemi, Tuula 1208, 1229
Kanaki-Yianitsiou, Hrisi 2151
Kanakis, Nikos 2146
Kanta, Abdoua 3032
Kaplanoglou, Mania 2129
Kaps-Gabler, Heide 416
Karakosta, Melina 2130, 2197
Kåreland, Lena 3005
Karizoni, Katerina 2115
Karrebæk, Dorte 1137, 1151, 1186
Karthaios, Rena 2173
Kass, Pnina 4603
Kassem, Lou 5107
Kasza, Keiko 3429
Katz, Welwyn Wilton 940, 977
Kay, Jackie 2026, 2032
Kaya, Ismail 1736
Keehn, Sally 3363
Kehret, Peg 3559, 3959, 3961, 4171, 4235, 4281, 4282, 4335, 4502, 4803, 4971, 5073, 5117, 5245, 5254
Keïta, Fatou 1622
Keith, Harold 4473
Kelleher, Victor 99, 222, 291
Kellogg, Steven 3173, 4035, 4036, 4167, 4419
Kelly, Mij 1885
Kennedy, X.J. 4326
Ker Wilson, Barbara 166
Kerby, Mona 4280
Kérisel, François 1307
Kerlan, Irvin 4152
Kerloc'h, J.P. 1270
Kerner, Charlotte 1364
Kerr, Bob 2476
Kerr, Daisy 2044
Kerr, M.E. 3323, 4163, 4217
Keuper-Makkink, Annie 2384
Khan, Rukhsana 1689
Kidd, Diane 2, 260
Killien, Christi 5126
Kilworth, Garry 1904
Kimmel, Eric A. 3093, 3498, 3630, 3982, 4601, 4976, 5069, 5165
Kindersley, Anabel 2043
Kindersley, Barnabas 2043
Kindl, Patrice 3826, 4312
King, Bridget 1506
King, Casey 3672
King, Edna 982
King, Stephen 3214, 3217
King-Smith, Dick 143, 297, 596, 1817, 1938, 3321, 4511
Kinsey-Warnock, Natalie 4420
Kinskofer, Lotte 1633
Kirby, Susan E. 3438
Kirschner, David 35
Klass, David 3204, 3680, 4351, 4819, 4896, 4922
Klause, Annette Curtis 3182, 3330, 3737, 4813, 4886, 4893
Klefelt, Lena 2990
Klein, Robin 54, 95, 96, 158, 272
Kleiva, Rønnaug 2549, 2559, 2561, 2578
Klinting, Lars 2963, 2966
Knox, Judy 2484
Knudsen, Lisbeth 1158
Knutsen, Per 2551
Kodric, Neli 2656
Koller, Jackie French 4357, 5060
Koller, Tess 2687
Kondoleon, Manos 2113, 2195
Koné Doh Fandanh, Joël 1491
Konigsburg, E.L. 4080, 4649, 4758, 5039
Konishi, Eiko 1782
Konjajev, Aleksander 2650
Kontio, Tomi 1227
Kordon, Klaus 1322, 1345, 2298, 2309, 2337, 2363, 3082
Korkos, Alain 876
Korman, Gordon 785
Korschunow, Irina 581
Koster, Shizuko Obo 4604
Kotter, Deborah 4660
Kouros, Alexis 1224
Kraft, Betsy Harvey 3470
Kraft, Erik 3170
Krahn, Fernando 1624
Krakar, Lojze 2652
Krakauer, Jon 3732, 3736
Krausnick, Michail 1336
Krauss Melmed, Laura 2262
Krauß, Irma 1383
Krisher, Trudy 3936
Kristensen, Jane 1175
Krog, Kirsten Mejlhede 1165, 1205
Krohg, Guy 2539
Krohg, Sossen 2539
Krohn, Leena 1251
Krokos, Giorges 2188
Kromhout, Rindert 1771, 2316
Krotov, Viktor G. 1490
Kruger, Louis 435
Krull, Kathleen 3823, 4003, 4911, 4917
Kruz Igerabide, Juan 2827
Kuhonta, Ma. Michelle 1449
Kuijer, Guus 2386
Kuijper, Sjoerd 2344, 2371
Kuiper, Nannie 1502
Kuklin, Susan 3474, 3673
Kulubali, Baabilen 1611
Kunna, Kirsi 1250
Kunnas, Mauri 1232
Kurguzow, Oleg F. 2613
Kušcer, Samo 2653
Kustermans, Paul 503
Kuyper, Sjoerd 2352

L'Engle, Madeleine 3607, 4137, 4222
La Fontaine, Jean de 1499
Lacasse, Marie-Ève 895
Lagercrantz, Rose 1436, 2951
Lago, Ângela 615
Lagrou, Patrick 560, 562
Lai, Ma 1548
Laird, Elizabeth 1811, 1907, 2299
Lake, Denise 9
Lalana, Fernando 2812, 2840, 2926
Lambert, David 1996, 2003, 2784
Landsbergis, Vytautas V. 1759, 2277
Lane, Christopher 3770
Langenus, Ron 483
Langstaff, John 3890
Lanton, Sandy 4977
Lappas, Takis 2172
Lardone, Lilia 1002
Larmola, Maija 1263
Larreula, Enric 2845, 2904
Larsen, Jens Peder 1181
Larsen, Rebecca 3373
Lasenby, Jack 2475, 2487
Lasky, Kathryn 4199
Lasser, Olivier 1731
Lattimore, Deborah Nourse 3678, 4901
Laube, Sigrid 447
Lauber, Patricia 4153
Laubi, Werner 419

Laulajainen, Leena 1214, 1225, 1245
Lavallee, Barbara 3815
Lawlor, Laurie 3833
Lawrence, Iain 697
Lawson, Julie 955
Lázár, Ervin 1536
Lazure, Jacques 877, 885, 906
Le Gall, Frank 1301
le Roux, Marlene 2699
Leaf, Margaret 3316
Leapman, Michael 2051
Lebeaultl, Fabrice 1305
Leblanc, Louise 851, 910
Lee, Milly 3945
Leedahl, Shelley A. 1698
Leenen, Martijn 2390
Lefoy, Mike 312
Leggat, Gillian 1455
Legge, David 41, 116, 145, 341
Lehtinen, Tuija 1256
Leja, Gunta 1431
Lelooska, Chief 3103
Lembcke, Marjaleena 456
Lemieux, Jean 854, 875
Lemmens, Riske 546
Lemmetty, Jukka 1559
Lenain, Thierry 1306, 1605
Lenski, Lois 4150
Leontyne, Price 3519
Lerakis, Kiriakos 2167
Leslie, Donna 123
Lester, Julius 3262
Lester, Alison 302
Lester, Helen 3322, 3496, 4135, 4330, 5021
Lester, Julius 3097, 4347, 5190, 5195
Letén, Mats 1147, 1174
Leth, Wivi 1188
Levin, Betty 3909
Levine, Ellen 3385, 3997
Levine, Gail Carson 3167, 3203, 3359, 3560, 3977, 4211, 4740, 5269
Levinson, Nancy Smiler 4902, 4907
Levola, Kari 1216, 1226, 1700
Levy, Elizabeth 4263
Lewis, Anne 2071
Lewis, D. Geraint 2069
Lewis, E.B. 3572
Lewis, J. Patrick 4126
Lewis, Naomi 266
Lewis, Sian 1838, 2075
Leyland, Mark 1852
Lian, Torun 2601
Lightburn, Sandra 960
Lin, Haiyin 3039
Linazasoro, Karlos 2827
Linde, Freda 2739
Lindell, Unni 2575
Lindenbaum, Pija 2956, 2986
Lindo, Elvira 2933
Linnéa, Sharon 3393
Lisle, Janet Taylor 4055
Lisson, Deborah 309, 315, 316
Littke, Lael 4905
Little, Jean 779
Littlechild, George 3998
Livingston, Myra Cohn 4141
Llanes, Julio M. 1060
Llewellynn, Claire 2040
Llorach, Esteban 1109
Llorente, Pilar Molina 4296
Lloyd, J. Selwyn 1914
Llywellyn, Morgan 2228, 2235, 2251
Locke, Elsie 2451, 2458
Locker, Thomas 5144
Loe, Erlend 2555, 2579
Loizou, Maro 2117, 2124, 2136, 2192
Long, Jonathan 2011
Longfellow, Henry Wadsworth 3452
López Narváez, Concha 2796, 2804
Lorman i Roig, Josep 2866, 2868
Lottridge, Celia Barker 656, 691, 765, 781, 946
Louhi, Kristiina 1241
Løveid, Cecilie 2535
Lowe, Pat 317
Lowell, Susan 3152
Lowry, Lois 3155, 3188, 3290, 3325, 3396, 3397, 3400, 3411, 3552, 3701, 3723, 3741, 3801, 3868, 3872, 3960, 4031, 4053, 4068, 4112, 4173, 4203, 4207, 4340, 4390, 4504, 4623, 4663, 4732, 4736, 4751, 4816, 5106, 5213, 5217, 5234
Loynaz, Dulce Maria 1057
Lubach, Peter 1916
Lucado, Max 3778, 3798
Lucas, Berny 814
Lucht, Irmgard 1330
Luisenbosch, Juffrou 2720
Lum, Kate 1828
Lumme, Leena 1263
Lund, Atla 2588
Lundborg, Birgitta 3003
Lunde, Svein Erik 2530, 2565, 2566
Lundgren, Gunilla 3001
Lundgren, Max 2937
Lundqvist, Ulla 3002
Lunin, Viktor 1429
Lunn, Janet 733, 745, 758, 764, 811
Lynch, Chris 3730
Lyon, George Ella 3365, 4119
Lyons, Mary E. 3374, 3381, 3820
Lystrup, Geirr 2536

Maar, Paul 3022
Maartens, Maretha 1372, 2692, 2747, 2752
Macan, Darko 1525
Macaulay, David 2312, 3407, 3623, 4774, 5041
Macdonald, Andy 2313
MacDonald, Betty 589
Macdonald, James D. 4310
Macé, Nicole 2585
MacFarlane, Sheryl 710, 775
MacGregor, Rob 3585
MacGregor, Roy 792
MacGrory, Yvonne 2230
Machado, Ana Maria 618, 3052
MacIntyre, R.P. (editor) 672
MacLachlan, Patricia 4877, 5037
Madeleine-Perdrillat, Alain 1435
Mado, Michio 3046
Madsen, Svend Åge 1124
Magorian, Michelle 5087
Mahy, Margaret 2444, 2454, 2489, 4426, 5091, 5166
Maier, Paul L. 3795
Major, Kevin 636, 642, 655, 829, 975
Mäkelä, Hannu 1254
Makotsi, Ruth L. 1775
Makura, Tendai 1677
Malaxetsebarria, Yolanda Arrieta 2814
Maletic-Vrhovac, Gordana 1755
Malling, Hannah 1154
Mallinson, Ann 2460
Mallorquí, César 1632
Maloney Markun, Patricia 5186
Mankell, Henning 1340, 1376, 2942, 2954, 2992, 3010
Mann, Elizabeth 3943
Manning, Mick 2047
Mansour Manzur, Vivian 2285
Manthopoulos, Dimitris 2184
Manuš, Leksa 1589
Manz, Hans 468, 3068
Mappin, Alf 160
Marais, Anna Louise 1457
Marchamalo, Jesús 1681

Marchetta, Melina 37, 51, 65, 225, 262, 292
Marco, Jose R. 1044
Marcotte, Danielle 726, 831
Mare, Ernst 2706
Marineau, Michèle 714, 873, 881
Mariño, Ricardo 999, 1720
Markopoulos, Thanos 2201
Marra, Irini 2119
Marrin, Albert 5204
Marriott, Janice 2447
Marris, Sharee 198
Marsden, John 46, 83, 104, 111, 114, 117, 151, 155, 170, 173, 179, 229, 237, 249, 263, 294, 301, 303, 305, 331, 337, 357, 3449
Marshall, James 3688, 5033
Marshall, Neil 2050
Marston, Elsa 1553, 4605
Martel, Suzanne 715
Martí, José 1078
Martin, Bill, Jr. 3247, 4116
Martin, Albert 4937
Martin, Ann M. 3760, 4493, 5097, 5242
Martin, Helen 2470
Martin, Jacqueline Briggs 4198, 4200
Martin, Rafe 3755, 4337, 5102
Martínez Menchén, A. 2800
Martinez, Raul 1065
Martínez, Victor 3133, 4319, 4676
Martingay, Claude 1599
Martinheimo, Asko 1209
Martinigol, D. 1275
Marttinen, Tittamari 1222
Masini, Beatrice 1648
Mason, Cherie 4195
Mastori, Voula 2142
Mataira, Katerina 2509, 2510
Matas, Carol 790, 847, 962, 4983
Mathews, Judith 5062
Mathiassen, Jørn 1136
Mathieu, Valérie 877
Matthaei, Gay 3468, 3937
Mauffret, Yvon 1271
Maurer, Richard 4775, 4949
Mauri Sierra, Omar Felipe 1052, 1073, 1106
Mavrokefalou, Lili 2159
Maximou, Penelope 2178
Mayer, Jeri 789
Mayer-Skumanz, Lene 393, 404, 428
Mayne, William 1861, 1894
Mazer, Norma Fox 3968
Mazzio, Joann 4938
McBratney, Sam 2233, 2351, 3124
McCaffrey, Anne 4223
McCaughrean, Geraldine 1371, 1794, 2102
McClintock, Norah 647, 649, 650
McClung, Robert 4665, 4833
McDermott, Gerald 5020, 5256
McDonald, Megan 3364, 3927
McDonald, Meme 82
McDonnell, Flora 1928
McDowell, Josh 3776
McElderry, Margaret 3891
McGaw, Laurie 44
McGee Kvasnosky, Laura 3853, 3854
McGill, Alice 3952, 4009
McGough, Roger 2031
McGraw, Eloise Jarvis 3844, 4077
McGraw, Laurie 963
McGugan, Jim 717
McIntyre, Rod 987
McKay, Hilary 1860, 1969
McKee Charnas, Suzy 4311
McKenzie, Ellen Kindt 3300
McKillip, Barbara 3637
McKissack, Frederick 3518, 3527, 3992, 4755
McKissack, Patricia 3254, 3379, 3518, 3524, 3527, 3992, 4063, 4107, 4755, 4859
McLaughlin, Marilyn 2248
McNaughton, Colin 1888, 1973, 5116
McNaughton, Iona 2513
McNaughton, Janet 641, 643, 695, 780
McNeal, Tom 3313
McNicoll, Sylvia 791, 964
McPhail, David 4122
McVeity, Jen 202
Meade, Holly 3431, 4409
Mebs, Gudrun 588
Mechanicus, Philip 2375
Meddaugh, Susan 3339, 3416, 3757, 4341, 4421, 4624, 5158
Medearis, Angela Shelf 4439
Meeks, Arone Raymond 5027
Mehl, Ruth 1573
Mehrem, Gisela 2788
Meij, Mart 2685
Meikle, Marg 970
Melbourne, Hirini 2496
Melissiddou-Siaveli, Aliki 2168
Melling, O.R. 936
Mello, Roger 608
Meltzer, Milton 3388, 4757
Ménard, Jean-François 595
Merino, José María 2928
Merkouris, Avtzis 2160
Merle, Ditte 2372
Mettger, Zak 3383
Metzenthen, David 276, 1672
Michels, Tilde 3083
Middag, Guus 2358
Mikaelsen, Ben 3337, 3345, 3664, 3916, 3929, 4256, 4342, 4934, 4947
Milano, Ed 1620, 2247
Miliori, Poly 2134
Miller, Brandon Marie 3946, 4856
Miller, Dorothy Reynolds 3587
Mills, Lauren 3417, 3837
Milne, Chris 346
Milowitz, Gloria 4834
Mingarelli, Hubert 875
Minkel, Walter 3631
Minne, Brigitte 1766
Mircev, Krasimir 1613
Mirkiyani, Muhammad 1619
Mitchell, Jane 2236
Mitchell, Rita Phillips 1964
Mochizuki, Ken 5072
Moe, J. E. 1424
Moeyaert, Bart 480, 481, 490, 502, 504, 512, 522, 554, 578, 1354, 2361
Mola, Marcella 2786
Moleón Viana, Miguel Angel 2831
Molina, María Isabel 2803
Møllehave, Johannes 1122
Mollel, Tololwa Marti 702, 919
Möller, Ingibjörg 2217
Möller, Ingrid 1381
Moloney, James 75, 76, 216, 217, 268, 523
Montes, Graciela 1443
Montes, Kostas 1738
Montgomery, Sy 3953
Montiel, Edgar 1092
Montón I Lara, Ramón 2907
Moon, Pat 1830
Moore Kruse, Ginny 3902
Moore, Inga 1957
Mora, Pat 3233, 5014
Moradi Kermani, Hooshang 426, 3030
Morel, Alicia 1516, 1563
Morgan, Robert J. 3789
Morgenstern, Susie 509, 599, 1312
Mori, Eto 1783

Mori, Kyoko 3598
Morimoto, Junko 81
Morley, Jacqueline 2037
Mörö, Mari 1220
Morpurgo, Michael 1819, 1832, 1974, 2103
Morriña, Oscar 1098
Morris, Bill 3114
Morris, Jill 200
Morris, Robert M. 2060
Mortensen, Henning 2581
Morton, Alexandra 953
Moser, Erwin 1386
Moskvina, Marina L 1530
Moss, Jeff 4117, 4123
Most, Bernard 4306, 5176
Mota, António 1588
Moure, Gonzalo 2825
Mouriki, Katerina 2120
Mourlevat, J.C. 1289
Moyes, Lesley 2485
Muc, Dušan 2651
Muck, Desa 2667
Muhammadi, Muhammad 1742
Mullen, Helen Mae 3570
Muller, Erna 2691
Muller, Jorg 3047
Muller, Sophie 2683
Mullins, Patricia 184, 206
Muñoz Ledo Carrasco, Norma 2286
Muñoz Puelles, Vicente 2934
Munsch, Robert 867, 1686, 3146, 3165
Murail, Marie-Aude 587
Murphy, Elspeth Campbell 3767
Murphy, Frank 2245
Murphy, Jill 582, 3807
Murphy, Jim 1971, 3193, 3822, 4015, 4017, 4073, 4377, 4479, 4481
Musschoot, Dirk 473
Myers, Anna 4466, 4469
Myers, Walter Dean 3112, 3413, 3521, 3532, 3814, 3838, 3892, 4026, 4064, 4218, 4291, 4884, 4892

Nabb, Magdalen 1960
Nadaud, Claire 1283
Naggar, Tagrid Arif an 1754
Naidoo, Beverley 4093
Nan Zhang, Song 813
Napoli, Donna Jo 1756, 3571, 3850, 4993
Narelle, Oliver 73
Naylor, Phyllis Reynolds 3117, 3151, 3286, 3399, 3405, 3450, 3511, 3514, 3554, 3655, 3666, 3803, 3870, 3915, 3920, 3964, 3965, 4058, 4142, 4170, 4205, 4230, 4236, 4248, 4268, 4343, 4354, 4363, 4386, 4391, 4428, 4435, 4442, 4444, 4499, 4503, 4621, 4633, 4666, 4734, 4802, 4868, 5003, 5131, 5156, 5231, 5251, 5268
Neira Cruz, Xosé Antón 2830, 2923
Nel lo Colom, Daniel 2822
Nelson, Theresa 3441, 3679, 4913
Nelson, Vaunda Micheaux 3744
Nettell, Stephanie 1842
Neves, Luis Carlos 994
Newbolt, Peter 1871
Newth, Eirik 2528, 2550, 2557, 2569
Newth, Mette 2576
Nichol, Barbara 827
Nicholson, John 208, 210, 212
Nicholson, William 1987
Nielsen, Bent 1167
Nielsen, Unni 366
Nieuwenhuizen, Agnes 161
Nikolopoulou, Angeliki 2150
Nilsson, Eleanor 4, 60
Nilsson, Jan 3000
Nilsson, Kerstin 2971
Nilsson, Per 1352, 2945, 3016
Nilsson, Ulf 2950
Nilsson-Brännström, Moni 2961, 2968, 3017
Nimmo, Jenny 1978
Nixon, Jean Lowery 3160, 3196, 3318, 3581, 4334, 4379, 4392, 4606, 4836, 5047, 5090, 5123, 5239, 5252
Njeng, Pierre Yves 1533
Njoya, Idrissou 1603
Noble, Trina Hakes 3143, 3648
Noël, Michel 728, 887
Nolan, Dennis 3805, 3837
Nolan, Han 4320
Nolan, Jerdine Harold 3162, 3191, 3208, 3484, 3987, 4127, 4398, 5170, 5260
Nolet, Beatrijs 1746
Noonan, Diana 2472, 2482
Noort, Selma 2336
Nopola, Sinikka 1213
Nopola, Tiina 1213
Nordström, Jockum 2994
Norheim, Olav 2546
Norman, Howard 3104
Norris, Andrew 2105
North, Sterling 584
Nortjé, P.H. 2693
Nöstlinger, Christine 372, 374, 3081
Nousiainen, Inka 1252
Novak, Bogdan 2665
Novak, Boris A. 1427
Novak, Matt 4659
Noyes, Alfred 5179
Nozière, Jean-Paul 873, 3056
Numeroff, Laura Joffe 4250
Núñez, Luchi 2851
Nuotio, Eppu 1242
Nye, Naomi Shihab 3232, 4000, 4004, 4100
Nyhus, Svein 2563, 2606
Nyquist, Arild 2542
Nyström, Bente Olesen 1146

Oberman, Sheldon 797, 4985
Obrist, Jürg 3071
Och, Sheila 1353, 2360, 3090
O'Connell, Kristine 4184
Odland, Norine 4148
Offen, Hilda 1962
O'Hara, Elizabeth 2237
Olafsson, Gudmundur 2220
Oldham, Mary 2077
Oliva Alices, Felipe 1074
Oliver, Narelle 201
Olivier, Peitjie 2695
Olmstead, Sandi 3634
O'Loughlin, Larry 1691
Olsen, Ib Spang 1119
Olsson, Sören 2967
Omahen, Nejka 2670
Onana, Désiré 1480
Onichimowska, Anna 1487
Onuekwusi, Jasper 1643
Oosthuysen, Janie 2711
Oppel, Kenneth 661, 663, 739, 828, 838, 930, 949, 969
Orlando Rodríguez, Antonio 1020, 1022, 1075, 1079, 1080
Orlev, Uri 2608, 3049, 4295, 4298
Oronte-Siantu, Theodora 1739
Orr, Wendy 71
Osborne, Linda Barrett 3672
O'Shaughnessy, Tam 4779
Osland, Erna 2531, 2580, 2598
Osojnik, Mojca 454
Oster, Grigorij B. 1762
O'Sullivan, Mark 2244, 2252
Oughton, Jerrie 3443
Oulad-Chaâra, Malika 563
Overend, Jenni 266, 1661
Owen, John 2070, 2074, 2082
Owings Dewey, Jennifer 4945

Oxenbury, Helen 2006
Oz, Amos 3037

Pacheco, Gumersindo 1055
Pacheco, M. Angel 2784, 2895
Pacovska, Kveta 1335, 3045
Paes, José Paulo 614
Páez, Enrique 2884
Paiba, Helen 1845
Palatini, Margie 3176, 3198, 3509, 3988, 4129, 4742
Pallottino, Paola 1647
Palm, Anna-Karin 1709
Palomeras, Daniel 2848
Panagos, Wilna 2678, 2694
Panayiotopoulou, Litsa 2116
Papadiamandis, Alexandros 2139
Papailiou, Olvia 2153
Papakou-Lagou, Avgi 2177
Papamoschou, Iro 2118, 2127
Pappas, Markos 2149
Parasshou-Hatzidimitrou, Sofia 2164
Parent, Raymond 864
Park, Barbara 3159, 3515, 3558, 3662, 3746, 3871, 3963, 4285, 4393, 4447, 4738, 4766, 4879, 5235, 5262
Park, Frances 3949
Park, Ginger 3949
Park, Ruth 38, 101
Parker, Steve 1925
Parkinson, Siobhan 2240
Parkkinen, Jukka 1210, 1701
Parks, Barbara 5219
Parks, Rosa 4845
Parry, Glyn 313, 319
Partridge, Elizabeth 3858
Partsch, Susanna 1355
Parvel, Timo 1219
Pascual, Emilio 1753, 2898
Pateraki, Yolanda 2186
Paterson, Katherine 3051, 3250, 3981, 4021, 4028, 4415, 4644, 4794
Patneaude, David 4668, 5070
Patterson, Francine 3686
Paulsen, Gary 3109, 3279, 3647, 3657, 3733, 3740, 3967, 3974, 3975, 4020, 4027, 4054, 4221, 4269, 4277, 4752, 4810, 4837, 4842, 4890, 4932, 4936, 5082, 5160, 5214, 5222, 5227, 5241, 5255, 5258
Pausacker, Jenny 275
Pausewang, Gudrun 475, 3084
Pavcek, Tone 1592
Pavlovic, Jozef 1580
Payne, Bernal C., Jr. 4372
Pean, Stanley 839
Pearce, Fred 2038
Pearson, Kit 653, 689, 692, 727, 777, 788, 793, 803, 928, 942, 981
Peck, Richard 3108, 3613, 4086, 4214, 4375, 4830, 5032
Peet, Bill 4897, 5046
Peglez González, Pedro 1116
Pelgrom, Els 2304, 2437
Pelz, Monika 381, 385, 399, 457
Peña Muñoz, Manuel 2850
Pérez Díaz, Enríque 1062, 1081, 1082, 1100, 1117
Perez, Olga Marta 1037, 1102
Persson, Hans 2972
Peskine, Brigitte 597
Petersen, Martin 1189
Petersen, P.J. 5237
Peterson, Lorraine 3773, 3781
Peterson, Ol'ga Michajlovna 1481
Petri, Walther 1319
Petrick, Nina 1382
Petrovits, Loty 2121, 2200
Petty, Kate 3764
Pevsner, Stella 4854, 5099
Pfeffer, Susan Beth 4883
Pfeffer, Wendy 3765
Pferdehirt, Julia 3603
Pfister, Marcus 3123, 3461, 3482, 4429
Philbrick, Rodman 3156, 3343, 3423, 4254, 4346, 4838
Philpot, Lorna 1815
Pi Andreu, Andrés Manuel 1031
Piérola, Mabel 2782
Pilkey, Dav 3288, 3349, 3512, 3717, 3759, 4638, 4672, 4768, 5108, 5151, 5153, 5220
Pinkney, Brian 3266, 3811
Pinkney, Gloria 5184
Pinkney, Jerry 3542, 3565, 3806, 3901, 4109
Pio Urbach, Carlos 1058
Piquer, Eva 2828
Pistra, Riemkje 1437
Pitzorno, Bianca 1646
Piummini, Roberto 1391, 2341
Place, François 1299, 1390
Plakotari, Alexandra 2171
Plante, Raymond 874, 904
Platt, Richard 5055
Pludra, Benno 1323
Pochocki, Ethel 4193
Pohl, Peter 1331, 1710, 2941, 2948
Poitras, Anique 857, 862
Polacco, Patricia 3295, 3301, 3546, 3660, 3819, 3983, 4016, 4033, 4208, 4769, 4824
Pollinger, Gina 1848
Pommaux, Yvan 3060
Pond, Roy 12
Pons I Clar, Pere 2838
Pons, Joan 2871
Ponti, Claude 1309
Pope, James 1694
Popescu, Vlad 1601
Posadas, Carmen 1509
Potgieter, Anita 2689
Pottie, Marjolein 514
Pouttu, Riitta 1244
Poveda Pierola, Mabel 2782
Pratt, Pierre 1304
Preller, Martie 2697, 2698, 2719, 2754, 2756
Prelutsky, Jack 4118
Pressler, Mirjam 1346, 3086
Preston, Douglas 3731, 3734
Preston, Richard 3729
Price, Susan 1867
Priceman, Marjorie 3366
Prieto, Iliana 1033, 1045, 1085
Pringle, Laurence 3627, 4483, 5208
Prinsloo, Louise 2702
Pristawkin, Anatoli 1333
Procházková, Iva 420
Proctor, André 1454
Pronzini, Bill 4610
Proulx-Weaver, Ginette 755
Provoost, Anna 478, 496, 510, 539, 551, 552, 2356
Prusski, Jeffery 5175
Pryor, Bonnie 4252
Pryor, Boori 82
Psarafti, Litsa 2123, 2131, 2193
Puerto, Carlos 2821
Pullman, Philip 1804, 1864, 1975
Purnell, Pamela 2065
Pyers, Greg 199

Qadir, Ghazi Abdel 427
Quijano, Laura 1013
Quinlan, B.J. 3629
Quinlan, Susan E. 3938
Quinn, John 2232
Quintana, Anton 540, 4302
Quintero, Aramís 1023, 1028, 1029, 1041, 1084, 1088

Rabinovici, Schoschana 4301
Racickas, Vytautas 2279

Rael, Elsa Okon 4990
Ramos, Graciliano 621
Ramos, Juan Antonio 1000
Ramos, Mario 1631
Randle, Kristen 3352
Ranger, Laura 2471
Raschka, Chris 601
Rasmussen, Bent 1123, 1163
Rasmussen, Halfdan 1125
Rathmann, Peggy 4128, 4432, 4629, 4745, 5216
Raustela, Lasse 1248
Ray, Jane 1961
Rayó i Ferrer, Miquel 2870
Reaver, Chap 3575, 3579
Recheis, Käthe 418, 433, 2319
Redfern, Katherine 1920
Reeder, Carolyn 4011, 4787
Reeves, Nicholas 3721
Reid, Barbara 729, 5029
Reid, Christopher 2033
Reid, John 2466
Reigosa, Antonio 2921
Reilly, Pauline 186
Reit, S. 591
Rem, Håvard 2552
Remoundos, Yannis 2166
Rendón Ortiz, Gilberto 1735, 2295
Reuter, Bjarne 1129, 1131, 1363, 4293, 4297
Reyes, Yolanda 1518
Reynolds, Marilyn 4889
Reynolds, Sandra Lynn 667
Ribeiro, João Ubaldo 3033
Riber Christensen, Jørgen 1175
Richards, Tom 1447
Richardson, Jean 3454
Richler, Mordecai 823
Richter, Jutta 1392
Ride, Sally 4779
Ridley, Philip 1958
Riff, Hélène 1314
Rinaldi, Ann 4500, 5066
Rindel, Gerd 1120
Ringgold, Faith 3522, 3642, 3996
Riordan, James 1939
Rissanen, Veikko 1217
Ritter, John H. 3948
Rivas, Ivonne 1440
Rivers, Alice 3372
Roberts, Katherine 1797
Roberts, Willo Davis 3333, 3584, 3588, 4956, 5266
Robertson, Alison 2517
Robertus, Polly 3500, 4381, 5167, 5250
Robinet, Harriette Gillem 4796, 4855
Robinson, Barbara 3402, 3507, 3659, 3747, 3962, 4174, 4348, 4368, 4632, 4669, 4737, 4869, 5150
Robson, Jenny 2736, 3055
Rocklin, Joanne 4923
Rockwell, Thomas 3650
Rodda, Emily 57, 67, 118, 150, 175, 324, 334
Rode, L. 2743
Rodríguez, Eduardo García 1012
Rodríguez, Heriberto 1014
Roessel, Monty 3384
Rogers, Kirsteen 2004
Roldán, Gustavo 1721
Rolph, Mic 1991, 1992
Román, Celso 1001, 1608
Rood, Lydia 2340
Rosen, Michael 1847, 3246, 4458
Rosen, Sybil 4994
Rosenberg, Liz 3492
Rosero, Evelio José 1003
Røsholdt, Ole 2597
Rossell, Joel Franz 1054, 1064, 1068
Rossiter, Nan Parson 4353
Røssland, Tor Arve 2568
Rossouw, Kowie 2749
Røstbø Kausland, Ingvild 1704
Rottman, S.L. 4471
Rowan, Peter 1993
Rowe, Jennifer 162
Rowe, John A. 424
Rowe, John E. 431
Rowling, J.K. 304, 364, 1288, 1825, 1829, 1831, 1977, 1981, 1983, 1989, 2015, 2021, 2107, 3141, 3168, 3227, 3426, 3876, 4274, 4411, 4772, 5223
Roy, Dorothée 861
Rozman Roza, Andrej 2661
Ruben, Liesbet 2378
Rubinstein, Gillian 72, 243, 261, 322
Rubio, Carlos 1005
Rubio, Gabriela 1752
Ruddick, Bob 4278, 5044
Rudnianska, Joanna 2609
Ruiz Gestoso, María Dolores 2833
Ruo, Wen 1511
Ruset, Arne 2570
Rush, Barbara 4979
Rushdie, Salman 4309
Russell, Ching Yeung 3419
Russo, Marisabina 5185
Rutyne, Anne 561
Ryan, Pam Munoz 3169, 3358, 4930
Ryder, Joanne 3622
Rylant, Cynthia 3248, 3251, 3685, 3692, 3695, 3699, 3702, 3705, 3709, 3710, 3716, 4062, 4369, 4450, 4452

Sabuda, Robert 3834
Sachar, Louis 3021, 3145, 3149, 3223, 3272, 3281, 3291, 3395, 3499, 3508, 3561, 3668, 3694, 3712, 3739, 3911, 3956, 4087, 4166, 4168, 4212, 4226, 4265, 4271, 4321, 4331, 4360, 4371, 4492, 4508, 4636, 4953, 4999, 5050, 5135, 5139, 5221, 5259
Sachs, Marilyn 3993
Sadu, Itah 4133
Sage, James 1927
Sakka-Niklopoulou, Ninnina 2161
Saldaña, Excilia 1053
Saldanha, Ana 1535
Sales, Francesc 2841
Salibury, Graham 4098, 4367
Salinas, Bobbi 5015
Salisbury, Graham 3353, 3439, 4613, 4792
Salmine, Hellevi 1255
Salmon, Michael 323
Salvesen, Paul Leer 2586, 2602
San Souci, Robert 3096, 3102, 3309, 3310, 3497, 3754, 4333, 4822, 4867, 5096
Sánchez Ochea, Magaly 1112
Sánchez, Gloria 1718, 2913
Sánchez, Magaly 1051
Sande, Hans 1705
Sanders, Alex 602
Sanderson, Ruth 3980, 5253
Santarmis, Yannis 2155
Santos Moray, Mercedes 1086
Sarantiti, Eleni 2132, 2194
Sarfati, Sonia 721, 1732
Sari, George 2122, 2140, 2191
Sastrías, Martha 1726
Sattgast, Linda 3797
Sattler, Helen Roney 4463
Savulescu-Voudouris, Monic 1463
Say, Allen 3258, 3302
Schami, Rafik 1385, 4294
Schär, Brigitte 3070
Schär, Helene 3069
Scheader, Catherine 3375
Scheen, Kjersti 2545, 2600
Scheidl, Gerda Marie 3463
Schell, Simone 2333, 2349

Scheppke, Jim 3636
Schertle, Alice 3447, 4916, 4919
Schipper, K. 2353, 2380
Schmidt, Jelka Godec 2659
Schnetzler, Pattie L. 3510
Schnur, Steven 4984, 5189, 5193
Scholes, Katherine 270
Schotter, Roni 5197
Schreiber, Mark 355
Schroder, Brenda 2679
Schroeder, Alan 3476, 3531, 3534, 3842, 4131, 4134
Schubert, Ingrid 1744
Schubiger, Jürg 508, 1347, 2366, 3076
Schuch, Steve 3490
Schuller, Rena 2764
Schultz, Anna 2763
Schur, Maxine Rose 4988, 4995
Schuyesmans, Willy 559
Schwartz, Alvin 3282, 3501, 4425
Schwartz, Howard 3099, 3106, 4979
Sciacca, Fran 3769
Sciacca, Jill 3769
Scieszka, Jon 3181, 3287, 3503, 3656, 3758, 3873, 4037, 4172, 4206, 4209, 4427, 4622, 4763, 4961, 5004, 5006, 5215
Scott, Elaine 4783
Scrimger, Richard 833, 836
Seeberg, Peter 409
Seeger, Pete 5128
Seligson, Susan 5163
Selznick, Brian 4762, 5002
Sendak, Maurice 3606
Senger, G. 1273
Sennell, Joles 2906, 2925
Šerelyte, Renata 2281
Sernine, Daniel 872
Sewall, Marcia 4423
Sfaellou, Kalliope 2114
Shakely, Jamil 506
Shannon, David 3206, 3211, 3667, 3761, 4307, 4928, 5023, 5078, 5225
Sharkey, Niamh 1932
Sharpe, Elaine 256
Shaw-MacKinnon, Margaret 796
Shed, Gred 4920
Shen, Shixi 1788
Sheppard, Jeff 4304
Shipman, Brian 3794
Shipton, Paul 1997
Shulevitz, Uri 3430, 3856
Shusterman, Neal 4814, 4906, 4925, 5133
Siebert, Diane 4042
Siegelson, Kim L. 3537
Sierra, Judy 3100, 3989
Sierra i Fabra, Jordi 1748, 2798, 2805, 2810, 2832, 2837, 2867
Sigman, Aric 2042
Silk, Julie 209
Silver, Donald 4781
Silver, Norman 3026
Silverman, Erica 3346
Silverstein, Shel 4210, 5212, 5218
Simard, Eric 1279
Simard, Rémy 718, 730, 820
Simmons, Dan 3722
Simms, Laura 3425
Simoen, Jan 507
Simón, Nelson 1096
Simon, Seymour 3691, 3698, 3899, 4158, 5202
Simpkin, Angela 1919
Simpson, Margaret 1837
Sims, Lesley 2052
Sis, Peter 1361
Sitar, Jelena 1543
Skeie, Eyvind 2584
Skira, Rosabianca 1295
Skucaite, Ramute 2276, 2282
Skurzynski, Gloria 4776
Slate, Joseph 3209
Slater, Pat 203
Slupetzky, Stefan 376, 455
Slyder, Ingrid 3942
Small, Robert 3113
Smalley, Gary 3777
Smalley, Norma 3777
Smeyers, Katharina 521
Smirthwaite, John 1853
Smith, Craig 109
Smith, Michael W. 3793
Smith, Robert Kimmel 3319, 4159
Smith, Roland 4356, 4970
Smith, Wayne 3724
Smucker, Anna Egan 3926
Smucker, Barbara 774
Snow Gilbert, Barbara 4470, 4472
Snyder, Zilpha Keatley 4045
Soentpiet, Chris K. 3940
Sofer, Barbara 4989
Sogabe, Aki 3839
Sollie, André 513
Solotareff, Grégoire 1350
Sones, Sonya 3494
Sørensen, Anders 1135
Sortland, Bjørn 439, 1703, 2556, 2605
Soto, Gary 3307, 4041, 4046, 4675, 4677, 5012
Sotorra, Andreu 2816, 2905
Spaulding, Nancy 3639
Speer, Bonnie 4465
Spillner, Wolf 1334
Spinelli, Eileen 3453
Spinelli, Jerry 3190, 3240, 3284, 3334, 3362, 3369, 3412, 3414, 3445, 3553, 3652, 3802, 3913, 3919, 3976, 4056, 4083, 4169, 4229, 4259, 4267, 4272, 4287, 4365, 4383, 4402, 4438, 4498, 4619, 4635, 4733, 4761, 4866, 4880, 5094, 5118, 5224, 5230
Spires, Elizabeth 4461
Springer, Nancy 3370, 3583, 3586, 4489
Springstubb, Tricia 4451
Spudvilas, Anna 86
Ssarfati, Sonia 879
Staalesen, Gunnar 2587
Stalfelt, Pernilla 1711
Stampogle, Helene 1579
Stanford, Edward B. 4149
Stanley, Diane 3843, 4388, 4482, 4873, 5209
Stanley, Fay 3376
Stanley, Jerry 3677, 4014, 4043, 4478, 4927, 4935
Staples, Suzanne Fisher 4052
Stareva, Lilija 1715
Stark, Ulf 1341, 2939, 2952, 2991
Stavropulos, Alexandra 2176
Steber, Rick 3633
Steenberg, Elsabe 2704
Stefanidi, Fotini 2125
Stefanidis, Yannis 2138
Stefanovic, Mirjana 1432
Steig, William 3432, 4038, 4416
Steiner, Jörg 1329
Steinhöfel, Andreas 365, 1326
Steinsdottir, Idunn 2211
Stemm, Antje von 1365
Sterling, Shirley 954
Sterman, Betsy 5178, 5196
Stevens, Diane 3230
Stevens, Janet 3175, 3505, 3847, 4257, 4394, 5019
Stewart, Robin E. 207
Stewart, Sarah 3478
Stewart, Sean 669
Steyn, Carl 2681, 2707
Stiborová, Vera 1758
Stien, Laila 2574
Stigter, Bianca 2320
Stillerman, Marci 4992

Stine, R.L. 3285, 3289, 4459, 4460
Stoffels, Karlijn 2302
Stöllinger, Heide 452
Stoltz, Gerhard 2543
Stolz, Mary 4140
Stow, Randolph 33
Strachan, Ian 1813, 1823, 1903
Strahan, Ronald 194
Strasser, Todd 5154, 5191
Strömstedt, Margareta 2987
Strong, Jeremy 1822, 2014
Stuart, Dee 3228
Sturges, Philomel 3862
Stuve-Bodeen, Stephanie 3645
Suárez Crespo, Lorenzo 1050
Suarez Romero, Alfonso 2288
Suhodlocan, Primoz 2666, 2671
Sundvall, Viveca Lärn 2988, 3011
Sutton, Roger 4850
Sveinsson, Guðjón 1560
Svensson, Sonja 2999
Swahn, Sven Christer 2938
Swanson, Diane 4480
Swart, Nel 2686, 2731
Sweeney, Joyce 4396
Sweet, Melissa 4657
Swindells, Robert 1802, 1826, 2018
Swindoll, Charles R. 3786
Swope, Sam 3184
Sydor, Colleen 799
Sylloge Pruse, Kosta 1452
Szyszkowitz, Gerald 371

Talbott, Hudson 3752, 4374
Tamar, Erika 3350, 5122
Tanaka, Shelley 750, 751, 824, 966
Taylor, Barbara 4782
Taylor, Cora 658
Taylor, Marilyn 2242
Taylor, Mildred D. 3115, 3451, 3520, 4001
Taylor, Theodore 3326, 3577, 4146, 4245, 4793, 4918, 5053
Taylor, William 2442, 2461
Taylor Lisle, Janet 2335
Teague, Mark 4400, 5172
Teijeiro, Antonio G. 2919
Teisson, Janine 1287
Teixidor, Emili 2932
Tellegen, Toon 544, 2311, 2339, 2345, 2369, 2385, 2438
Temple, Charles 4253
Temple, Frances 3131, 3995
Thau-Jensen, Cato 1149
Thesman, Jean 3816, 4018, 4812
Thiel, Henry 1552
Thiele, Colin 14, 139, 164, 190
Thomas, Frances 2059
Thomas, Gwyn 2064
Thomas, Mack 3774, 3785
Thomasma, Kenneth 3914, 3917
Thomsen, Thorstein 1169
Thor, Annika 1360, 2614, 2946, 2953, 2960, 2964, 3018
Thornhill, Jan 744, 5026
Thorsteinsson, Thorrvaldur 2208
Thrainsson, Thorgrimur 2219
Tiainen, Marja-Leena 1258
Tibo, Gilles 708, 724, 840, 1733
Tidholm, Anna-Clara 1712, 2943
Tidholm, Thomas 2943, 3013
Tiitinen, Esko-Pekka 1230, 1266
Tikka, Eeva 1212, 1262
Tillage, Leon Walter 3271, 3389, 4019
Timm, Uwe 493, 1328
Timossi, Jorge 1069
Tjerkstra, Willem 1494
Toivola, Ritva 1231
Tolan, Stephanie 4387, 5093
Tolkin, J.R.R. 42
Toll, Nelly S. 3934
Tomecek, Steve 4780
Tomes, Margot 4143
Tomos, Angharad 2067
Törnqvist, Marit 2357
Torras, Meri 2806
Toupet, A. 1274
Townsend, Sue 20
Tramacci, Joe 205
Treays, Rebecca 2046
Treiber, Jutta 377, 441
Trembath, Don 920
Tremblay, Carole 866
Trivizas, Eugene 2133, 3153, 4625, 5149
Trondheim, Lewis 1310
Trottier, Maxine 659, 842, 1685
Tsialta, Eleni 2154
Tsortsoglou, Nitsa 2156
Turan, Nuran 1747
Turgeon, Élaine 893
Turnball, Andy 845
Turner, Ann 4241
Turner, Megan Whalen 4078
Tyrrell, Esther 4908
Ulitzka, Irene 425
Umansky, Kaye 487
Unger, Heinz Rudolf 401
Ungerer, Tomi 3050
Urdaneta, Romer 1728
Ure, Jean 1898
Urech, Christian 3077
Uri, Helene 2564
Utemorrah, Daisy 259
Utley, Jaspar 1500
Utton, Peter 411

Vachon, Hélène 884, 901
Vainilaitis, Martynas 2283
Vainio, Pirkko 1240
Valavani, Eleni 2174
Valgardson, W.D. 818, 990
Vallverdú, Josep 586
van Allsburg, Chris 3280, 3753, 4115, 4242, 4626, 4750, 4764, 5085, 5164, 5211
van Daele, Henri 497, 520, 1767
van de Velde, Vivian 3593, 4403
van den Heede, Sylvia 488, 498, 518, 555, 568, 1576
van der Hoeven, Marije 2354
van der Kolk, Anton 2426
van der Merwe, Elizabeth 2733, 2772
van der Rol, Ruud 1343, 3462, 3725
van der Valk, Saskia 2428
van der Vyver, Marita 2684, 2773
Vandewijer, Ina 574
van Doorselaer, Willy 505
van Draanen, Wendelin 3592
van Eijk, Inez 2329
van Erkel, Gerda 571
VanGenechten, Guido 1768
van Gestel, Peter 542, 2379
van Keulen, Mensje 2430
van Leeuwen, Jean 5188
van Leeuwen, Joke 541, 1772, 2332, 2359, 2367, 2382, 2439
van Lieshout, Ted 1358, 2314, 2355, 2370
van Niekerk, Betsie 2757
van Niekerk, Louise 2703
van Ogtrop, Babett 2378
van Raven, Pieter 4788
van Rensburg, Ewald 2715
van Rooyen, Nanette 2705
van Steenwyk, Elizabeth 593, 3878
van Toorn, Willem 2321
Varella, Angeliki 2137, 2196

Vargas, Demóstenes 609
Väyrynen, Tarmo 1257
Väyrynen, Taru 1257
Vázquez Vigo, Carmen 2927
Vebel, Susanne 1156
Vejlby, Gitte 1159
Velasco, José Luis 2844
Veleta-Vasiliadou, Maria 2112, 2126
Vels, Verna 2774
Velthuijs, Max 2307, 2324, 2330
Verhoeven, Rian 3462, 3725
Verleyen, Karel 516, 573
Vermeulen, Jan 2765
Veromme, H. 592
Verreydt, Detty 476
Verschuur, Rita 543, 2364, 2433
Vesel, Anatol 1737
Vian, Enid 1111
Vian, Ivette 1094
Vickery, Gill 1855
Vieira, Alice 1645
Viermyr, Marianne 1716
Vik, Walter 1707
Vilimaite, Bite 2275
Villeneuve, Anne 912
Vincent, Gabrielle 1302
Víquez, Alí 1010
Vivas, Julie 159
Voake, Charlotte 1976
Voigt, Cynthia 3317, 4219
von Holck, Anne 1172
von Meysenbug, Alfred 1387
von Reinhardt, Jung 461
Vos, Ida 1987
Voskobojnikov, Valerij M. 1773
Vriens, Jacques 2318
Vuori, Pekka 1246
Vuorio, Maria 1253

Waber, Bernard 3896
Waddell, Martin 415, 1959, 2227, 3418
Waechter, Friedrich K. 1359
Wagner, Friederike 383
Wahl, Jan 5143
Wahl, Mats 1349, 1713, 2949
Wahldén, Christina Nord 1714
Waite, Michael P. 3985
Waldis, Angelika 3079
Waldschütz, Barabara 378
Walker, David 1693
Wallace, Barbara Brooks 3582, 3590
Wallace, Bill 3154, 3918, 4244, 4443, 4799, 4831, 4952, 4962, 5001, 5067, 5228
Wallace, Ian 769
Wallace, Karen 1890, 2041
Wallace, Mary 1684
Walsh, Jill Paton 1972, 4648
Walter, Mildred Pitts 3378, 3458
Walters, Eric 947, 967, 971
Walters, Virginia 4305
Wangerin, Walter, Jr. 3887
Wardlaw, Lee 3205, 3875, 4807, 4963, 4968, 4969, 5024
Warner, Marina 1870
Warren, Andrea 3264, 4853, 4857
Wasserfall, Kurt 1367
Waterford, Helen 3471
Watson, Joy 2452
Watts, Irene N. 696
Waugh, Sylvia 367, 1862
Weeks, Sarah 3756, 4247
Weg, Jant van der 1584
Wegelius, Jakob 2995
Weideman, George 2751, 2755, 2762, 2768
Weigand, Roberto 610
Weinreich, Torben 1138
Weller, Francis Ward 4336
Wells, Rosemary 3483, 3541, 5180, 5194
Welsh, Renate 389, 392, 448
Werlin, Nancy 3591
Wescott, Nadine 4114
Wesely, Peter 413
Wessels, Mariki 2690
Westall, Robert 1858, 1901
Westaway, Jane 2478
Westcott, Nadine Bernard 5065
Westerskov, Kim 2468
Westin, Kersti 3004
Wharton, Herb 1670
Whatley, Bruce 49
Whatmore, Candice 1921
Wheeler, John 986
Whelan, Gerard 2239, 2241, 2246
Whelan, Gloria 4847
White, Joe 3790
White, Ruth 4081
White, Ryan 3971
Whitfield, Philip 3448
Whitmore, Arvella 4860
Whitney, Phyllis A. 5113
Whitton, David 1557
Whybrow, Ian 2020
Wick, Walter 3268, 5076
Wiegand, Patrick 2035
Wieler, Diana 665, 798, 816, 932
Wiesel, Elie 3105
Wieslander, Jujja 2989
Wieslander, Tomas 2989
Wiesner, David 3604, 4121, 5246
Wijngaard, Juan 4909
Wikander, Eva 2940
Wilcox, Charlotte 5063
Wild, Margaret 45, 56, 106, 235
Willard, Nancy 3612
Williams, Barbara 4234, 4350, 4670, 4806
Williams, Carol Lynch 4352, 4881
Williams, Gareth F. 2058, 2076
Williams, Suzanne 4176
Williams, Vera B. 3259, 3428, 3615, 5028
Williams-Garcia, Rita 4615
Willis, Jeanne 1818, 1940
Willis, Patricia 4843, 4851, 4944
Willis Holt, Kimberly 1662
Willner-Pardo, Gina 4095
Wilmink, Willem 2343
Wilson, Budge 637, 666
Wilson, Diane Lee 3311
Wilson, Jacqueline 1812, 1820, 1868, 1970, 1986, 2017
Winding, Thomas 1128, 1179, 1180
Windling, Terri 4314
Winer, Yvonne 191
Wing, Natasha 4656
Winnem, Christian 1155
Winton, Ian 2038
Winton, Tim 192, 218, 307, 308, 340, 344
Wippersberg, Walter 410
Wittkamp, Frantz 469
Witzmann, Reingard 412
Wojciechowski, Susan 3367, 3472
Wolfe, Rinna Evelyn 3391
Wolff, Patricia Rae 3161, 4349
Wolff, Virginia Euwer 3440, 3828, 4006
Wolfsgruber, Linda 398
Wood, Audrey 4373, 4904, 5121, 5244
Wood, Douglas 3488, 3931
Wood, June Rae 4231, 5232
Woodhouse, Jena 264
Woodruff, Elvira 3192, 3401, 4283, 4959, 4967
Woods, Len 3787
Wooldridge, Connie Nordhielm 3984, 4433
Worcester, Don 4946
Worth, Valerie 4323

Wright, Betty Ren 4232, 4804, 4876, 5058, 5084, 5129, 5148, 5257
Wyatt, Valerie 1683
Wynn, Gwyneth 1462
Wynne Jones, Diana 4313, 4316
Wynne-Jones, Tim 657, 662, 671, 713, 719, 759, 980, 988, 3261

Xohan Cabana, Darío 2817

Yancey, Diane 4941
Yanez, Alberto 1036
Yardley, Thompson 1995
Ye, Shengtao 1787
Ye, Ting-xing 1682
Yee, Patrick 1917
Yee, Paul 725, 773, 934, 943, 951, 3063
Yep, Laurence 3304, 3455, 3676, 3749, 4044, 4066, 4430, 4645
Yerxa, Leo 815
Yi, Chuan 1520
Yolen, Jane 3409, 4108, 4284, 4315, 4749
Young, Ed 3239, 3252, 3611
Young, Jay 1999
Young, Ronder Thomas 3944
Yumoto, Kazumi 3267, 4299
Yusufi, Nasir 1743
Zamora, León 995, 1441
Zannaki-Lialiou, Loulia 2158
Zappina, Zapp 3078
Zarambouka, Sofia 2128
Zeevart, Sigrid 3089
Zei, Alki 2190
Zeman, Ludmila 720
Zilinskaite, Vytaute 2280
Zindel, Paul 3728, 4397, 4406, 5263
Zitelman, Arnulf 482
Zolotow, Charlotte 5031
Zopfi, Emil 3072
Zubizarreta, Patxi 2819
Zullo, Germano 1719
Zupan, Dim 2657, 2658
Zweig, Stephanie 2300
Zwerger, Lizbeth 396, 1388, 1389, 3042

Awards and Sponsors Index

ACT Library Service 93
Aesop Prize 3092
Afrikaanse Taal-en Kulteurorganisasie 2677
ALAN Award 3107
Alan Marshall Prize for Children's Literature 1
Alba Bouwer Prize 2672
Alex-Wedding Preis (Alex Wedding Prize) 1318
Amelia Frances Howard-Gibbon Illustrators Award 622
American Booksellers Association 3118, 3235
American Booksellers Book of the Year (ABBY) Award 3118
American Folklore Society 3092
American Institute of Physics 4773
American Library Association 3516, 4051, 4178, 4213, 4290, 4292, 4680
American Nature Study Society 3616
Américas Award 3128
Ann-Connor Brimer Award 634
Anne Spencer Lindbergh Prize in Children's Literature. 3139
Anni Swanin Mitali (Anni Swan Medal) 1206
Arizona State Library Association 3142
Arizona Young Readers Award 3142
Arkansas Diamond Primary Book Award 3171
Arkansas Elementary School Council 3171, 3394
Arthur Ellis Award 644
Arvid Lydeckenin Palkinto (Arvid Lydecken Prize) 1211
Asian/Pacific Cultural Center for UNESCO 2268
Askeladd Prisen (Askeladd Award) 2518
Assembly on Literature for Adolescents of the National Council of Teachers of English 3107
Asociación de Escritores de la UNEAC 1017
Association des auteures et auteurs de l'Ontario français et de l'Outaouais québécois 894
Association des écrivains québécois pour la jeunesse 889
Association des Libraires Spécialisés Jeunesse 1286
Association du prix des incorruptibles 1267
Association for Indiana Media Educators 5238
Association for Library Service to Children (ALSC) 4673
Association of Finnish Writers for Children and Youth 1211, 1247
Association of Jewish Libraries 4972, 4974
ASTED Association pour l'avancement des sciences et des techniques de la documentation 878
Astrid Lindgren Priset (Astrid Lindgren Prize) 2935
ATKV Children's Book Prize 2677
Augustpriset (August Prize) 2947
Austin Writers' League 4996
Australian Christian Book of the Year 8
Australian Christian Literature Society 8
Aventis Prize for Science Books (formerly Rhone-Poulenc Prize for Science Books) 1790

Bank Street College of Education 3978
BBC Children's Programme 1792
Ben-Yitzkak Award 2253
Bienále Ilustrácií Bratislava (Biennale of Illustrations) 2616
BILBY (Books I Love Best Yearly) 18
Bilderbuchmuseum der Stadt Troisdorf 1393
Bill Martin Jr. Picture Book Award 3174
Black-Eyed Susan Book Award 3179
Blaue Brillenschlange (Blue Cobra) 3025
Blue Hen Book Award 3207
Blue Peter Book Awards 1792
Blue Spruce Award 3212
BMF's Bornebogspris (Danish Booksellers Association Prize) 1118
Boekenleeuw & Boekenwelpen (Booklion and Bookcubs) 472
Boekenpauw & Boekenpluimen (Bookpeacock and Bookfeathers) 524
Bokjuryn (The Book Jury) 2957
Book Publishers of Texas Children's/Young People's Award 3224
Book Sense Book of the Year Award (formerly the ABBY Awards) 3235
Book Trust 1886, 1954, 2005

Booksellers New Zealand 2474
Börn og bækur, Islandsdeild IBBY 2202
Boston Globe and The Horn Book Magazine 3237
Boston Globe Horn Book Awards 3237
Brageprisen (Norwegian Literature Prize) 2523
Branford Boase Award 1796
Buckeye Children's Book Award 3278
Bundeskanzleramt, Sektion für Kunstangelegenheiten 391, 400, 467
Buxtehuder Bulle (Buxtehuder Bull) 1324

C P Hoogenhout Award 2717
Caixa d'Estalvis de Terrassa S.A. 2902
California Book Awards 3294
California Library Association 3315, 4039
California Young Reader Medal 3315
Cámera Brasileira do Livro 606
Canada Council 698
Canadian Association of Children's Librarians 652
Canadian Authors Association 972, 984
Canadian Children's Book Centre 688, 844
Canadian Library Association Book of the Year for Children 652
Canadian Library Association Young Adult Book Award 664
Canadian Library Asssociation 622, 664
Carl von Linné-plaketten 2970
Carnegie Medal 1798
Carolyn W. Field Award 3360
Carter G. Woodson Book Award 3371
Catholic Library Association 4746
Charles A. and Anne Morrow Lindbergh Foundation 3139
Charlie May Simon Children's Book Award 3394
Charlotte Book Award 3406
Charlotte Zolotow Award 3427
Child Study Children's Book Award 3436
Children Study Children's Book Committee at Bank Street College of Education 3436, 3669
Children's Book Award 1809
Children's Book Circle 1839
Children's Book Committee at Bank Street College of Education 3491, 4092
Children's Book Council — Victorian Branch 119
Children's Book Council of Australia 53, 204
Children's Book Council of Australia (Queensland Branch) 18
Children's Book Council of Iran 2224
Children's Book Guild of Washington D.C. 5198
Children's Book of the Year Award 53
Children's Books History Society 1869
Children's Books Ireland/Bisto Awards 2226
Children's Literature Association 4639
Children's Literature Association of Utah 5042
Children's Literature Research Collections 4136
Children's Peace Literature Award 88
Children's Roundtables of Canada 741
Children's Services Division of the Delaware Library Association 3207
Children's Services Los Angeles Public Library 3675
CHILIS New Hampshire Library Association 3865
Christie, Brown and Company 801
Christopher Awards 3446
Church and Synagogue Library Association 3877
CIELJ (Centre International d'Etudes en Littérature de Jeunesse) 1282
Circle of the Greece Children's Book Prizes 2109, 2170
City of Hasselt 545
Claudia Lewis Award 3491
College of Education, University of Georgia 3738, 3750
College of Information Studies Drexel University and The Free Library of Philadelphia 3562
Colorado Children's Book Award 3495
Colorado Council of the International Reading Association 3495
Colorado Library Association 3212
Comisión Católica Española de la Infancia 2790, 2796
Commonwealth Club of California 3294
Communication-Jeunesse 850
Connecticut Library Association (CLA) 4440
Consortium of Latin American Studies Programs (CLASP) 3128
COOL (Canberra's Own Outstanding List) 93
Cooperative Children's Book Center, School of Education, University of Wisconsin-Madison 3427
Coretta Scott King Award 3516
Court Oldmeadow Children's Literature Foundation 156
Crichton Award for Illustration 119
Crime Writers of Canada 644
Cross Pen Prize for Young Adult Fiction (formerly Sheaffer Prize for Adult Young Fiction) 132
CROW (Children Reading Outstanding Writers) 134
CYBER Award (Children's Yearly Best Ever Reads) 149

Danish Association of School Librarians 1130, 1164
Danish Booksellers Assistants Association 1118
Danmarks Skolebibliotekarforenings bornebogpris (Danish Association of School Librarians) 1130
David McCord Award 3539
Davidsfonds/Infodok Publishing 569
Den norske Forleggerforening 2523
Deutscher Jugendliteraturpreis (German Youth Literature Prize) 1327
Dirección de Literatura, Instituto Cubano del Libro 1027, 1032
Dirección de Literatura del Instituto Cubano del Libro 1027, 1032
Dirección General del Libro y

Bibliotecas, Ministerio de Cultura 2924
Division of Graduate and Continuing Education, Salem State College 4264
Dorothy Canfield Fisher Children's Book Award 3550
Drexel Citation 3562
Dromkeen Medal 156
Dymocks Children's Choice Awards 167

Earthworm Award 1834
Edgar Allan Poe Award 3573
Ediciones Castillo S.A. de C.V. Convoca AL 2284
Ediciones Destino 2780
Ediciones Xerais de Galicia S.A. 2912
Editoral Costa Rica 1004, 1009
Editorial Laia S.A. 2863
Educational Paperback Association 4022
Eilis Dillion Memorial Award 2243
Eleanor Farjeon Award 1839
Elizabeth Burr Award 3595
Elizabeth Mrazik-Cleaver Canadian Picture Book Award 676
Elsa Beskow Plaketten (Elsa Beskow Plaque) 2973
Empire State Award of Excellence in Literature for Young People 3605
Emporia State University and the Trusler Foundation 5226
English Academy of Southern Africa 2740
Enid Linder Foundation 1941
Enka de Colombia S.A. 993
Ente Autonomo per le Fiere di Bologna 2259, 2264
Environmental Award for Children's Literature 182
Esther Glen Award 2440
Eva L. Gordon Award for Children's Science Literature 3616
Evangelical Christian Publishers Association 3766
Eve Pownall Award for Information Books 204
Evelyn Sibley Lampman Award 3628
Expressens Heffaklump (Heffaklumpen Prize) 2985
Ezra Jack Keats Foundation 3640, 5025
Ezra Jack Keats New Writer Award 3640
Family Award 213
Fédération des parents d'élèves de l'enseignement public (PEEP) 1268
Federation of Children's Book Groups 1809
Fidler Award 1851
Fiera di Bologna per l'infanzia e la gioventù (Bologna Children and Youth Book Prizes) 2259
15 Degree Laboratory's Award Selection Committee 3762
Finlandia Junior 1223
Flicker Tale Children's Book Award 3646
Flora Stieglitz Straus Award 3669
FOCAL (Friends of Children and Literature Award) 3675
Forlaget Gyldendals Boglegat for Bornebogsfattere og — Billedkundtnere (Gyldendal Publishers Prize) 1142
Fortis Bank 472, 524
Foundation for Children's Books 3888
Foundation for the Collective Promotion for the Dutch Book 2303, 2391
Founding Friends Scheme 1796
Framingham State College and Nobscot Council 3539
Friedrich-Gerstäcker-Preis (Friedrich Gerstäcker Prize) 1366
Friends of the Minnesota Valley Regional Library 4275
Fundação Biblioteca Nacional 619
Fundación para el Fomento de la Lectura, Fundalectura y por la Editorial Norma de Colombia 997
Fundación Santa María 2807, 2836, 2853

Gaelyn Gordon Award 2450
Galera, S.A. Editorial 2872
Garden State Children's Book Award 3684
Garden State Teen Book Awards 3719
Guardian 1856
Geoffrey Bilson Award for Historical Fiction for Young People 688
Georgia Children's Book Award 3738
Georgia Children's Picture Storybook Award 3750
Giverny Book Award 3762
Glazen Globe (Glass Globe) 2297
Gold Medallion Book Award 3766
Golden Archer Award (now WEMA Golden Archer Award) 3800
Golden Kite Awards 3804
Gouden Griffel and Zilveren Griffel (Golden Plaque and Silver Plaque) 2303
Gouden Penseel and Zilveren Penseel (Golden Brush and Silver Brush) 2391
Gouden Uil (Golden Owl) 538
Governor General's Literary Awards 698
Great Stone Face Award 3865
Guardian Children's Fiction Award 1856
Gulliver Award 2997
Gyldendal Publishers 1142
Gynekia Logotehniki Syntrofia (Women's Literary Society Prizes) 2145

Hackmatack Children's Choice Award 738
Hans Christian Andersen Awards 3041
Harvey Darton Award 1869
Hawaii Library Association 4358
Helen Keating Ott Award for Outstanding Contribution to Children's Literature 3877
Hodder Children's Books and Scottish Book Trust 1851
Hope S. Dean Award 3888

IBBY 1327, 2109
IBBY Canada 676
IBBY Cuba 1038
IBBY Denmark 1152
IBBY Finland 1206
IBBY Iceland 2202
IBBY Lithuanian and Sarunas Marciulionis 2274
IBBY Netherlands 2425
IBBY Norway 2518
IBBY Poland 2607
IBBY Secretariat 3041
IBBY Slovakia 2616
IBBY Sweden 2997, 3020

IBBY U.S.S.R. 2615
Illinois State Library, a Division of the Office of Secretary of State 4729
Illustratorenprijs van de Stad Hasselt (Illustration Award of the City of Hasselt) 545
Indian Paintbrush Book Award 3910
Information Book Award 741
Institute for the Intellectual Development of Children and Young Adults Award 2222
Institute of Intellectual Development of Children and Young Adults 2222
International Brant Point Literary Prize 3922
International Janusz Korczak Prize 2607
International Order of Daughters of the Empire 761, 772
International Reading Association 3924, 4182, 4600
International Reading Association Children's Book Award 754, 3924
Internationale Jugendbibliothek (International Youth Library) 1422
Interprovinciale Prijs (Interprovincial Award for Children's and Youth Books) 549
IODE Book Award — Toronto Chapter 761
IODE Violet Downey Book Award — National Chapter 772
Iowa Children's Choice Award 3954
Iowa Educational Media Association 3954, 3966
Iowa Teen Award 3966
Irish Children's Book Trust 2226, 2243
Irma S. and James. H. Black Award 3978
Islandsafdelings Anerkendelse (Icelandic IBBY Award) 2202
Israel Museum 2253

Jane Addams Children's Book Award 3991
Jane Addams Peace Association 3991
Jefferson Cup Award 4010
Jenny Smelik-Kiggenprijs (Jenny Smelik Kiggen Prize) 2425
Jeremiah Ludington Memorial Award 4022
Jo Osborne Award for Humor in Children's Literature 4032
John and Patricia Beatty Award 4039
John Newbery Award 4051
Joie de Lire 3054
Josette Frank Award (formerly the Children's Book Award) 4092
Judy Lopez Memorial Award for Children's Literature 4096
Jury der Jungen Leser 354

Kansas Reading Association 3174
Kate Greenaway Medal 1873
Kathleen Fidler Award 1883
Katholischer Kinder- und Jugendbuchpreis (Catholic Children's Book Prize) 1369
Katrine Harries Award 2721
Keene (New Hampshire) State College Children's Literature Festival Award 4102
Keene State College 4102
Kentucky Bluegrass Award 4113
Kerlan Award 4136
Kinder- en Jeugdjury Vlaanderen (Children and Youth Jury Flanders Award) 556
Kinder- und Jugendbuchpreisen der Stadt Wien (Children's Book Award of the City of Vienna) 370
Kinderbuchladen Zurich 3080
Klods Hans Prisen (Clumsy Hans Prize) 1152
Knickerbocker Award for Juvenile Literature 4154
Knjiznica Otona Zupancica 2663
KOALA Award (Kids' Own Australian Literature Award) 219
Kommunernes Skolebiblioteksforenings Forfatterpris (Danish School Library Association Prize) 1164
KROC Award (Kids Reading OZ Choice) 244
Kulturamt der Stadt Wien 370
Kulturdepartementets Pris (Awards from the Ministry of Culture) 2533
Kulturinstitut der Stadt Braunschweig 1366
Kulturministeriets Børnebogspris (Ministry of Culture Children's Book Prize) 1176
Kulturministeriets Illustratorpris (Ministry of Cultural Affairs Prize for Illustration) 1190
Kurt Maschler Award 1886
Kvallstidningen Expressen 2985

Lancashire County Council 1897
Lancashire County Library Children's Book of the Year Award 1897
Land of Enchantment Book Award 4165
Lasten Oman Kirjakerhon Kuvakirjapalkinto (Finnish Picture Book Prize) 1228
Laura Ingalls Wilder Award 4178
League of Families 579
Lee Bennett Hopkins Promising Poet Award 4182
Levstikova Nagrada (Fran Levstik Prize) 2649
Library and Information Association of New Zealand 2440, 2464, 2498, 2508
Library and Information Service of Western Australia 306
Literaturhaus 354
Lithuanian Children's Book Award 2274
Little Archer Award (now WEMA Golden Archer Award) 4185
Louisiana Young Readers' Choice Award 4189
Lupine Award 4191

M E R Prize 2728
Macmillan Prize 1915
Maine Library Association 4191, 4202
Maine Student Book Award 4202
Manitoba School Library Audio Visual Association 784
Manitoba Young Reader's Choice Award 784
Margaret A. Edwards Award (YASD/ School Library Journal Young Adult Author Award) 4213
Margaret Mahy Lecture Award 2453
Mark Twain Award 4225

Mary Vaughan Jones Award 1910
Maryland Children's Book Award 4237
Maryland Education Media Organization 3179
Maryland International Reading Association Council 4237
Massachusetts Children's Book Award 4264
Maud Hart Lovelace Book Award 4275
Maxim Gorky International Award for Literature for Children and Youth 2615
McNally Robinson Book for Young People Award 794
McNally Robinson Booksellers 794
Michael L. Printz Award 4290
Mildred L. Batchelder Award 4292
Mimizuku-sho (Owl Prize) 2266
Minister fur Kultur der Deutschen DDR 1318
Ministère des Affaires internationales, Direction générale de l'Europe 905
Ministerie van de Vlaamse Gemeenschap 575
Ministry of Ershad 2223
Ministry of Ershad Award 2223
Missoula County Schools and Missoula Public Library 5017
Missouri Association of School Librarians 4225, 4821
Missouri Building Block Picture Book Award 4303
Missouri Library Association 4303
Mr. Christie Book Awards 801
Mladinska knjiga 2649
Moja Najljibsa Knijiga (My Favorite Book Award) 26
Mother Goose Award 1922
MultiCultural Affairs Office of Australia 255
Multicultural Children's Literature Award 255
Mystery Writers of America Inc. 3573
Mythopoeic Fantasy Award 4308
Mythopoeic Society 4308

NASEN Special Needs Book Awards 1933
Nasionale Boekhandel 2746
National Art Library Illustration Awards 1941
National Association for Special Educational Needs and the Educational Publishers Council 1933
National Book Award for Young People's Literature 4318
National Book Foundation 4318
National Council for the Social Studies 3371
National Council of Teachers of English 4322, 4474
National Council of Teachers of English Award for Excellence in Poetry for Children 4322
Nebraska Golden Sower Award 4327
Nebraska Library Association 4327
Nene Award 4358
Nestle Smarties Book Prize 1954
Nevada Library Association 4370
Nevada Young Readers Award 4370
New England Book Award 4412
New England Booksellers Association 4412
New Jersey Library Association 3684, 3719
New Mexico Library Association 4165
New South Wales and Victorian Family Therapy Associations 213
New York State Reading Association 3406
New Zealand Children's Book Foundation 2453
New Zealand Library Association Young People's Nonfiction Award 2464
New Zealand Post Children's Book Awards (formerly AIM Children's Book Awards) 2474
Nienke van Hichtumprijs (Nienke van Hichtum Prize) 2429
Nils Holgersson Plaketten (Nils Holgersson Plaque) 3008
Noma Concours for Children's Picture Book Illustrations 2268
Norma Fleck Award 844
Norsk Litteraturkritikerlags (Norwegian Critic's Award) 2571
North Carolina Association of School Librarians 4424
North Carolina Children's Book Award 4424
North Dakota Library Association 3646
North East Book Award 1988
Northern Kentucky University Learning Resource Center 4113
Northern Territory Library Promotion Council 244
Northumberland School Library Service 1988
Nova Scotia Library Association 634
Nova Scotia Provincial Library 738
NSW Ministry for the Arts 269
NSW State Literary Award — Children's Book Award 269
Nutmeg Children's Book Award 4440

Ohio Library Foundation 4032
Ohioana Book Awards 4449
Ohioana Library Association 4449
Oklahoma Book Award 4462
Oklahoma Center for the Book 4462
Oklahoma Library Association 4797, 4809
Oldenburger Kinder- und Jugendbuchpreis 1377
Ontario Arts Council 931
Ontario Library Association 846, 961
Ontario Red Maple Award 846
Orbis Pictus Award 4474
Oregon Library Association, Children's Section 3628
Organización Española para el Libro Infantil y Juvenil 2881
Oslo Riksmalsforening 2582
Österreichischen Würdigungspreis für Kinder- und Jugendliteratur (Austrian Appreciation Prize for Children's and Young Adult Literature) 391
Österreichischer Kinder- und Jugendbuchpreis (Austrian National Children's and Juvenile Book Award) 400
Österreichischer Staatspreis für

Kinder- und Jugendliteratur (Austrian State Prize for Children's and Young Adult Literature) 467
Ottawa Valley Council of the International Reading Association 754
Outstanding Pennsylvania Author 4486

Pacific Northwest Young Reader's Choice Award 4491
Pacific Northwestern Library Association 4491
Palme Livromagie de l'Imprimerie Gagné 850
Parents' Choice Award 4513
Parents' Choice Foundation 4513
Paul A. Witty Short Story Award 4600
PEN American Center 4611
PEN/Norma Klein Award 4611
Penelope Delta Award 2170
Pennsylvania Library Association 3360
Pennsylvania School Librarians Association 4486, 4617
Pennsylvania Young Reader's Choice Award 4617
Percy Fitzpatrick Award 2740
Peter Pan Award 3020
Peter-Härtling-Preis für Kinder- und Jugendlitatur (Peter Härtling Prize for Children's Literature) 1378
Phoenix Award 4639
Please Touch Book Award 4651
Please Touch Museum for Children 4651
Prairie Pasque Award 4661
Premio Apel–les Mestres (Apel–les Mestres Prize) 2780
Premio C.C.E.I. de Ilustración Infantil (C.C.E.I. Prize for Children's Book Illustration) 2790
Premio C.C.E.I. para Libros Infantil y Juveniles (C.C.E.I. Prize for Children and Young Adult Literature) 2796
Premio Carmen Lyra (Carmen Lyra Prize) 1004
Premio Critici in Erba (Critici in Erba Prize) 2264
Premio David de Literatura Infantil (David Award) 1017
Premio El Barco de Vapor (Steamboat Prize) 2807
Premio ENKA (ENKA Prize) 993
Premio Gran Angular (Gran Angular Prize) 2836
Premio Internacional de Ilustracion (International Illustration Prize) 2853
Premio Ismaelillo (Ismaelillo Prize) 1019
Prêmio Jabuti (Jabuti Prize) 606
Premio Joaquím Ruyra (Joaquím Ruyra Prize) 2863
Premio Josep Maria Folch i Torres (Josep Maria Folch i Torres Prize) 2872
Premio Joven Creación (Young Creation Prize) 1009
Premio Latinoamericano de literatura infantil y juvenil Norma-Fundalectura (Latin American Prize for Children's and Juvenile Literature) 997
Premio Lazarillo (Guide Prize) 2881
Premio Lola Anglada (Lola Anglada Prize) 2902
Premio Merlín (Merlin Prize) 2912
Prêmio Monteiro Lobato (Monteiro Lobato Prize) 619
Premio Nacional de Literatura infantil y juvenil (Creación) (National Prize for Children's and Young Adult Literature) 2924
Premio Nacional de Literatura Infantil y Juvenil (National Award for Children's and Juvenile Literature) 2284
Premios Edad de Oro (Golden Age Awards) 1027
Premios Pinos Nuevos (New Pines Prizes) 1032
Prijs Knokke-Heist (Knokke-Heist Prize) 569
Prijs van de Vlaamse Gemeenschap (Belguim Government Prizes) 575
Prix 12/17 Brive 870
Prix Alvine Bélisle (Alvine Bélisle Prize) 878
Prix Bernard Versele (Bernard Versele Prize) 579
Prix Cécile-Gagnon (Cécile-Gagnon Prize) 889
Prix des Incorruptibles 1267
Prix des jeunes lecteurs PEEP (Young Readers Prize) 1268
Prix Enfantaisie (Children's Prize) 3054
Prix Lire au collège 1280
Prix Littéraire le Droit (Le Droit Literature Prize) 894
Prix Littéraires Desjardins — Littérature jeunesse (Desjardins Literature Prize) 898
Prix Monique Corriveau (Monique Corriveau Prize) 902
Prix Octogones (Octagon Prize) 1282
Prix Québec/Wallonie-Bruxelles du livre de la jeunesse (Quebec Prize) 905
Prix Sorcières (Witches Prize) 1286
Prix Totem (Totem Prize) 1291
Prize of the Iranian Children's Book Council 2224
Psychologists for the Prevention of War 88
Pura Belpré Award 4673

R. Ross Annett Award for Children's Literature 913
Rabén & Sjögren 2935
RAI (Reading Association of Ireland) 2249
Randolph Caldecott Award 4680
Rattenfänger-Literaturpreis (Pied Piper Prize) 1384
Rebecca Caudill Young Readers' Book Award 4729
Red Cedar Book Award 924
Red Clover Children's Choice Picture Book Award 4741
Regina Medal 4746
Reykjavik Board of Education 2205
Reykjaviks Undervisningsradspris (Reykjavik Board of Education Prize) 2205
Rhode Island Children's Book Award 4759
Rhode Island Office of Library and Information Services (OLIS) 4759
Rhone-Poulenc Prize (formerly Science Book Prizes) 1990
Riksmålsprisen — Barne- og Ungdomsbøker (Riksmals-forenings Children's Book Award) 2582
Rosa Blanca (White Rose Award) 1038

Royal Dutch Geographical Society 2297
Rudolf Koivun Palkinto (Rudolf Koivu Prize) 1233
Russell Clark Award 2498
Ruth Schwartz Children's Book Award 931

Sainsbury's Baby Book Award 2005
Salon du livre de Montréal 870
Salon du livre de Montreuil 1291
Salon du livre de Québec 898
Sanlam Prize 2746
Sasquatch Book Award 4770
SCCLCYP, Orange Public Library 4894
Scheepers Prize for Youth Literature 2766
Scholastic New Zealand Ltd 2512
School Libraries Section (WA Group) of ALIA 283
School Library Media Section of the New York Library 4154
School Library Media Services, Florida Department of Education 4950
Schweizer Jugendbuchpreis (Switzerland Children's Literature Prize) 3066
Science-Writing Award in Physics and Astronomy for Articles or Books Intended for Children 4773
Scott O'Dell Foundation 4786
Scott O'Dell Historical Fiction Award 4786
Sequoyah Children's Book Award 4797
Sequoyah Young Adult Book Award 4809
Sheaffer Prize for Adult Young Fiction (formerly Alan Marshall Prize for Children's Literature) 279
Sheffield Children's Book Award 2008
Sheila A. Egoff Children's Book Prize 950
Show Me Readers Award 4821
Signal Poetry Award 2022
Silver Birch Award 961
Skolebibliotekarforeningen i Norge 2595
Skolebibliotekarforeningens Litteraturpris (Norwegian School Librarian Association's Award) 2595
Skriverprisen (Skriver's Award) 1201
Soaring Eagle — Wyoming Young Adult Book Award 4827
Society of Children's Book Writers 3804
Society of Midland Authors 4840
Society of Midland Authors Award 4840
Soroush Publishing Award 2225
Soroush Publishing Company 2225
South African Academy of Science and Arts 2672, 2766, 2770
South African Children's Book Forum 2775
South African Library Association 2721
South Carolina Association of School Librarians 4861, 4873, 4882
South Carolina Children's Book Award 4861
South Carolina Junior Book Award 4873
South Carolina Young Adult Book Award 4882
South Dakota Library Association 4661
Southern California Council on Literature for Children 4894
Spur Award 4931
Stadt Buxtehude 1324
Stadt Hameln 1384
Stadtbibliothek Oldenburg 1377
Standaard Uitgeverij (Standard Publishers) 538
State Library of Louisiana 4189
State Library of Ohio 3278
State Prize for Children's Literature 2187
Stichting P. C. Hooft-prijs voor Letterkunde 2435
Stigting vir Afrikaans (Foundation for Afrikaans) 2717
Sunshine State Young Reader's Award 4950
Suomalainen kuvakirja-palkinto (formerly Lasten Oman Kirjakerhon Kuvakirjapalkinto) 1239
Suomen Kirjasäätiö (Finnish Book Foundation) 1223, 1233
Svensk Biblioteksforening 2970, 2973, 3008
Svenska Förläggareföreningen 2947
Swedish Library Association 2957
Swiss Teachers Association 3066
SWT School of Education 5010
Sydney Taylor Body-of-Work Award 4972
Sydney Taylor Book Award 4974

Tafelberg Publishers 2728
Te Kura Pounamu (Maori Book Award) 2508
Teddy Book Award 4996
Tennessee Library Association 5125
Texas Bluebonnet Award 4998
Texas Institute of Letters 3224
Texas Library Association 4998
Theo Thijssen-prijs voor Kinder- en Jeugdliteratuur (Theo Thijssen Prize for Children's and Youth Literature 2435
Thimble Press 2022
Tienie Holloway Medal for Nursery School Literature 2770
Times Educational Supplement 2034
Times Educational Supplement Information Book Awards 2034
Tir Na n-Og Awards 2054
Tom Fitzgibbon Award 2512
Tomás Rivera Mexican American Children's Book Award 5010
Topelius-palkinto (Topelius Prize) 1247
Treasure State Award 5017
Troisdorfer Bilderbuchpreis (Troisdorfer Picture Book Prize) 1393

Undervisningsministeriets 1201
UNICEF-Ezra Jack Keats International Award for Excellence in Children's Book Illustration 5025
Unión de Escritores y Artistas de Cuba 1019, 1038

University of Southern Mississippi 5030
University of Southern Mississippi Medallion 5030
Utah Children's Book Award 5042

Vache qui lit (Reading Cow) 3080
Vaka-Helgafell, Börn og baekur 2209
Valtion Kirjallisuuspalkinto (National Awards for Literature) 1260
Verdlaunasjodur Islensku Barnabóka (Icelandic Children's Book Prize) 2209
Verlag Beltz & Gelberg 1378
Vermont Center for the Book, Windham County Reads 4741
Vermont Department of Education 3550
Vicky Metcalfe Award 972
Vicky Metcalfe Short Story Award 984
Virginia Library Association 4010
Virginia State Reading Association 5080
Virginia Young Reader's Award 5080
Vivian Wilkes Award 2775
Vlaamse Interprovinciale Commissie voor Letterkunde (Flemish Interprovincial Board for Literature) 549
Volunteer State Book Award 5125

W.H. Smith Illustration Award 2086
Washington Children's Choice Picture Book Award 5162
Washington Irving Children's Book Choice Award 5174
Washington Library Media Association 4770, 5162
Washington Post/Children's Books Guild Nonfiction Award 5198
Weissen Raben (White Ravens) 1422
Welsh Book Council 1910, 2054
WEMA Golden Archer Award 5210
West Australian Young Readers' Book Award 283
West Coast Book Prize Society 950
Westchester Library Association 5174
Western Australian Premier's Book Award — Children's Section 306
Western Writers of America Inc. 4931
What's Inside Press 3922
Whitbread Children's Book of the Year Awards 2097
Wilderness Society 182
William Allen White Children's Book Award 5226
Wisconsin Educational Media Association 5210
Wisconsin Library Association, Children's Book Award Committee 3595
Women's National Book Association/LA 4096
Writers Guild of Alberta 913
Wyoming Council of the International Reading Association 4827
Wyoming Educational Media Association 4827
Wyoming Library Association 3910

Young Australian Best Book Award (YABBA) 320
Young Australian Best Book Award Council 320
Young Hoosier Book Award 5238
Young Reader's Choice Awards Society of British Columbia 924
Youth Services Section of the New York Library Association 3605

Zentralstelle Medien der Deutschen Bischofskonferenz 1369

Illustrator Index

Aaron, Fatinia 1611
Aertssen, Kristien 529
Æta, Daihachi 1789
af Enehielm, Cris 1234
Ahlberg, Allan 1874
Alborough, Jez 5074
Alcàntara, Ricardo 2781
Alègrè, Hermès 1587
Alexandrino, Helena 1514
Allan, Nicholas 1833
Allen, Jonathan 5091
Alonso, José Ramón 2796, 2804, 2857
Als, Roald 1438
Alsorn, Stephen 3388
Alumenda, Stephen 1515
Amargo, Pablo 2900
Ana, Lúcia 1588
Andersen, Bethanne 4005
Anderson, Lena 1475
Andrikopoulos, Nicholas 1538, 2139, 2199
Àngel Pacheclo, Miguel 2784
Antoni, Birgit 380
Ardley, Neil 1477, 3407
Arenas Beltran, Leonardo 2294
Armitage, David 1671
Arnold, Tedd 3649, 3653, 3751, 5134
Atkins, Kathleen 3523
Auch, Herm 3424
Audras, Agnès 1307
Augiaus, Pauliaus 1527
Ayliffe, Alex 2007
Azarian, Mary 4200, 4719
Azevedo, Ricardo 1442, 1556

Bacelar, Manuela 1464
Badaoui, Abdel Kader 1602
Baeten, Lieve 528
Bagini, Biagio 2786
Baker, Jeannie 62, 100, 188
Baker, Keith 3830
Balaguer, Marta 2882
Baldwin, Justine 2085
Ballester, Arnal 1751
Ballhaus, Verena 1633
Bang, Molly 3763, 4726
Bansch, Helga 390
Barbero Richart, Manuel 2896
Baro, Ariel 1037
Barrett, Angel 2090, 2092
Bartolic, Stjepan 1525
Barton, Byron 4658
Barton, Jill 3263
Base, Graeme 102, 135, 1676
Battut, Éric 1628
Bauer, Jutta 1413
Beddows, Eric 723
Béha, Philippa 802, 827, 855
Belisle, Jean 883
Bellville, Cheryl Walsh 3599
Belsvik, Inger Lise 2559, 2561
Belton, Robyn 2480
Bengtsson, Anna 1709, 2978
Benson, Patrick 594, 1892, 1953, 3418
Berkkan, Yaprak 1531
Bernbaum, Israel 1332
Berner, Rotraut Susanne 1418, 1946, 2413
Bernhard, Druga 5022
Berry, Holly 3846
Bertrand, Frederique 2420
Bestard Cruz, Luis 1110
Bhend, Käthi 1466, 2261
Biesty, Stephen 5055
Birmingham, Christian 1974, 4592
Bishop, Gavin 1666, 2492
Bishop, Nic 2472, 3274
Biswas, Pulak 1668
Bjorkman, Steve 3780, 4539
Blain, Christophe 1317
Blake, Quentin 136, 137, 141, 144, 1887, 1945, 3180, 4378, 4550
Blake, Robert J. 3986, 4336, 4744
Blake, Stephanie 1650
Blanc, Michel 755
Blazejovsky, Maria 1523, 1575
Bobak, Cathy 3690
Boddin, Heidrun 1402
Bogacki, Tomek 2096
Bogataj Ambrozic, Saša 1764
Bohórquez, Rossana 1735
Bollen, Roger 4527
Bonners, Susan 3480
Booker, Kyrsten 5197
Booth, George 4532
Boratynski, Antoni 437
Bornová, Erika 1433
Bosnic, Dragan 1755
Bostock, Mike 1890
Bothma, Alida 2730, 2771
Bozkurt, Gözde 1745
Brandes, Sophie 442, 1396
Brett, Jan 3126, 3177, 3186, 5018
Brickman, Robin 3765
Brierley, Louise 1942, 2094
Briggs, Raymond 1889
Brochard, Philippe 910
Broekstra, Lorette 131
Brøgger, Lilian 1727
Brouillard, Anne 1495, 2623
Brown, Judy 2014
Brown, Ruth 5109
Browne, Anthony 1875, 1895, 3053
Bruna, Dick 2394, 2412
Brunkus, Denise 5219
Bryan, Ashley 4194, 4569
Buchanan, Heather S. 2267
Buchholz, Quint 1394
Bucker, Jutta 466
Budde, Nadia 1421
Buehner, Mark 3191, 3208, 4127, 4398, 4526, 4808, 5064, 5068
Bulcken, Kimberly 4995
Burkert, Nancy Ekholm 3245
Burkin, Vladimir 1530

Burningham, John 2095, 4514
Burusov, Denis 1762
Butler, Geoff 941
Butler, Jerry 3603
Buttkus, Thomas 405
Byard, Carole 4693

Cai, Gao 2625
Cakó, Ferenc 1741
Calatayud, Miguel 2795
Calderón, Gloria 1521
Campbell Ernst, Lisa 3178
Campos Garcia, Alejandro 1034, 1039
Canals, Mercè 1550
Cannon, Janell 4190, 4436, 4912
Cáp, Vladimír 1482
Capek, Jindra 1635
Cardinaux, Xavier 1599
Carle, Eric 3283, 4105, 4756
Carlesimo, Cheryl 4589
Carmi, Giora 4976
Carmona, José Mª 2886, 2887
Carpenter, Nancy 4000
Carpi, Pinin 1642
Carrer, Chiara 1621
Carrick, Donald 4898
Carroll, Jessica 109
Carter, David A. 4535
Carvalho, Carlos 1512
Casilla, Robert 5186
Castillo, Jesús 2290
Castillo, Jorge 1594
Castillo, Raul 1036
Castren, Taru 1612
Catalanotto, Peter 3365
Catrow, David 3425
Cazets, Denys 1600
Ceballos, Ubaldo 1044
Ceccarelli, Serge 1467
Ceccoli, Nicoletta 1647, 1648
Cermak, Bohumir 1734
Cernoglazov, V. Ju. 1761
Chan, Harvey 630, 684, 725, 934, 943, 946, 3063
Chang, Shi-Ming 2629
Chatellard, Isabelle 2638
Chee, Cheng-Khee 3121
Chichester Clark, Emma 3489
Cho, Shinta 1774
Chong, Osvaldo 1040, 1061
Chrismann, Hierry 593
Chuyn, Oscar F. 1042
Cimatoribus, Alessandra 1497
Claveloux, Nicole 1652
Clement, Gary 736
Clements, Rod 110, 113, 171, 3210, 3665
Cneut, Carll 536, 1766
Coelho, Raquel 613, 620
Coh, Zvonko 2662
Cohen, Sheldon 704
Cole, Babette 1893
Cole, Brock 4586
Cole, Henry 3354
Coll, Ivar da 1724
Collicutt, Paul 4570
Collins, Heather 748, 752, 817, 938
Colón, Raul 3861, 4552, 5014
Condy, Roy 4133
Conteh-Morgan, Jane 4660
Cooney, Barbara 4192
Cooper, Floyd 4537
Cooper, Helen 1879, 1881
Coplans, Peta 1593
Cordova, Amy 5016
Costa, José Pedro 1535
Cotte, Carlos 1501
Coupry, Claudine 1582
Cousins, Lucy 2407, 4654
Cox, David 1568
Cristaudo, Noel 1483
Cvetko, Igor 1543
Cvijanovic, Adam 3468

Dabcovich, Lydia 3447, 4518
Dahan, André 2618
Daly, Jude 2727
Daly, Niki 1663, 2779
Daniel, Alan 745, 756, 764, 811
Darling, Tara 5187
Daufresne, Michèle 1634
Daughty, Duanne 4652
Dauwalder, Valerija F. 1760
Davalos, Felipe 5024
de Gante, Guillermo 2296
de Kiefte, Kees 4587
de la Rosa, Sandro 1018, 1067
de Marcken, Gail 3236
de Paola, Tomie 4111, 4914
Deas, Michael 3659, 4348, 4869
Degen, Bruce 3408, 3693, 3697, 4329
DeGroat, Dianne 3172, 3325, 3701, 4434
Dehaes, Serge 1577
Dehong, Cheng 1292
DeKemmeter, Laurence 1545
Delibas Yetkin, Ayla 1615
Delyth, Marian 2072
Demarest, Chris 3663, 4117, 4123
Demircan, Serdar 1747
Dendooven, Gerda 525, 530, 535, 1492, 2424
Denton, Kady MacDonald 623, 632, 686, 732, 807
Denton, Terry 261
Derwig, Janneke 2645
Destours, Christine 1658
Dewan, Ted 1925
Dewanckel, Goele 534
Diaz, David 4003, 4702, 4915
Díaz, Raquel 1049
Diebold, Ute 1488
Dietl, Erhard 421
Dillon, Leo 3250, 3519, 4581
Dobrajs, Karlis 1431
Dominguez, Nelson 1055
Dörfler, Robert 406
Duckett, Elisabeth 2785
Duroussy, Nathalie 3463
Düzakin, Akin 1470, 1705, 2527, 2560
Dybvig, Per 1586, 2548
Dye, Sharon 200
Dyer, Jane 3409

Egan, Tim 4564
Ehlert, Lois 3247, 4116, 4682
Eidrigevicius, Stasys 1398, 2393, 2617
Ekman, Fam 2554
El Guindi, Abdel Aziz 1553
Elbruch, Wolf 2418
Eldjarn, Sigrun 2207
Elizalde, Marcelo 1720
Elling, Lars 439, 1703, 2549
Elliot, David 2500
Englander, Alice 3454
Enríquez, Lázaro 1105
Ensikat, Klaus 1399, 2621, 3048
Erlbruch, Wolf 1339, 1420, 1637
Eskola, Tomás 1116
Eyolfson, Norman 823

Fabelo, Roberto 1059, 1094
Facchini, Vittoria 1651
Facklam, Paul 3707
Falconer, Ian 4599
Fanelli, Sara 1943
Faría, Rosana 1717
Farré Estrada, Lluis 2892
Fatus, Sophie 2789
Fedden, Mary 1931
Feelings, Tom 3525, 3530
Fernández, Laura 944
Ferrari, Antongionata 1646
Ferrer, Isidro 1749, 2894
Fialkowski, Camila 2426
Filcik, Gabriel 1765
Fine, Howard 3176, 3198, 3988, 4129, 4742
Fitzgerald, Joanne 705, 765
Flather, Lisa 1927
Fleming, Denise 4454, 4696

Fletcher, Claire 1926
Flores, Lupina 2285
Fontein, Elsbeth 557
Forcadell, María Gabriela 1505
Ford, George 4870
Foreman, Michael 1832
Fowler, Jim 3465, 5052
Fox, Christyan 2052
Frazee, Marla 4924
Frély, Gilles 1496
Friedrich, Elizabeth 3841
Futterer, Ralf 1417

Gaidhane, Shankar 1679
Gal, Laszlo 796
Gallinger, Patty 1689
Gamaan, Hussein 2273
Garcia, Stephanie 4677
Gardiner, Te Maari 2496, 2510
Garneau, Julie 854
Garza, Carmen Lomas 4678, 5013
Gaskin, Chris 2499, 2504
Gatnik, Kostja 1592
Gaudette, Christiane 1730
Gay, Marie-Louise 825, 841, 851, 948
Gedovius, Juan 1570
Geelen, Harrie 1534, 2398, 2408
Geerten, Ten Bosch 2410
Geisert, Arthur 3094, 4595
Gemmill, Kerry 2503
George, Imelda 642, 829
George, Lindsay 3361
Gepp, Gerhard 425
Geraghty, Paul 1821
Gerber, Mary Jane 781
Gerber, Pesach 4992
Gerber, Thomas 1516
Gerber, Tomás 1563
Germain, Philippe 1733
Giannopoulos, Dimitris 2111
Gieth, Kinna 2948
Gilchrist, Jan Spivey 3517
Gilman, Phoebe 4980
Giménez, Anna 1595
Ginsburg, Max 3451
Glass, Andrew 3195, 4344, 4823
Glave, Lotta 2972
Gleich, Jacky 1357
Glori, Debi 1824
Göbel, Anna 1571
Goble, Paul 3095
Godia, Adria 2862
Goembel, Ponder 4305
Gómez, Fernando 1549
Gomi, Taro 1779
Gonzales, Edward 5011
González Giménez, Miriam 1082, 1084, 1102, 1107, 1117
González Linares, Bladimir 1043, 1088, 1104
González Marinello, Perla 1074
Gordeev, Denis Dmitrievic 1481
Graff, Finn 2542
Graham, Bob 58, 63
Graham, Mark 3979
Grandfield, Geoff 1947
Grandpré, Mary 3127, 4411
Granhaug, Silje 1424, 1707
Gräs, Gunna 2974
Gravel Galouchka, Annouchka 722, 965
Greder, Armin 258
Greenblat, Rodney A. 4520
Grégoire, Caroline 911
Grimsdale, Murray 2506
Grimsdell, Jeremy 2726
Grobler, Piet 2773
Guettier, Bénédicte 1641
Guevara, Susan 4675, 5012
Guha, Tapas 1618
Guhathakurta, Ajanta 1567
Guido, Van Genechten 547
Gukova, Julia 1453
Gultiajeva, Nadezda 1430
Gustavson, Adam 3487
Gutierrez Varela, Rita 1028, 1041, 1090

Haas, Shelly O. 4977
Haeringen, Annemarie van 2422
Hagbrink, Bodil 2975
Hagesæther, Anne Kristin 2570
Hakkarainen, Anna-Liisa 1225, 1245
Hallensleben, Georg 3270
Hamanka, Sheila 3689, 3700, 4862
Hannesdóttir, Guðrún 1617
Harada, Takehide 1448
Harichandan, Deepak 1460
Harjes, Stefanie 1416
Harker, Lesley 1967
Harness, Cheryl 4798
Harris, Nick 1975
Harvey, Amanda 1924
Harvey, Roland 195
Hauff, Wilhelm 1389
Hawkes, Kevin 3825, 4199
Hayes, Michael 4571
Hays, Michael 5128
Heale, Jonathan 1894
Heap, Sue 1980
Hebley, Gary 2451
Heerden, Marjorie van 1455
Helgadottir, Sigrun 2218
Henkes, Kevin 4697
Henstra, Friso 2400
Henterly, Jamichael 4825
Herrenberger, Marcus 2626
Hevier, Daniel 1542
Heymans, Annemie 1544
Heymans, Margriet 2417
Hieta, Heli 1725
Hillenbrand, Will 3984, 4433
Himler, Ronald 3473
Hiorthøy, Kim 2555, 2565, 2566
Hitchcock-Pratt, Sue 2507
Hloušek, Petr 1610
Hoban, Tana 3242, 4519, 4655
Hobbs, Dan 753
Hodder, Wendy 2452
Höglund, Anna 1341, 2404, 2410
Holdcroft, Tina 970
Holland, Katrien 2260
Holmberg, Mikael 2546
Honey, Elizabeth 77
Hong, Lily Toy 5062
Hopman, Philip 1502
Hoshikawa, Hiroko 1780
Houdart, Emmanuelle 1657
Howard, Arthur 3422, 5115
Howe, J. 600
Hu, Shourong 1520
Huang, Zhong-Yang 633
Hughes, David 1343
Huiquin, Wang 2655
Huraminazad, Ayta 1619
Hurd, Thacher 4743
Hurley, Ron 1670
Hyman, Trina Schart 3255, 3566, 3821, 4104, 4683, 4728

Ibrahimpašic, Mirza 1578
Iglesias, Rubén 1066
Ingman, Bruce 1929, 1944
Ingpen, Robert 1673
Ingraham, Erick 3332
Innocenti, Robert 2620
Ionajtis, Ol'ga 1590
Ito, Hiroshi 1781
Ito, Yoriko 3985
Izawa, Yôji 1519

Jacobs, Una 1400
Jacobsson, Anders 2967
Jagtenberg, Yvonne 1746
Janssen, Susanne 2636, 2637
Janssen-Mechler, Susanne 1405
Jaraba, Fran 1508

Jarrett, Clare 1930
Jarrie, Martin 2639, 2640
Jeffers, Susan 4120
Jeram, Anita 3124
Johansen, Hanna 423
Johnson, Adrian 1828
Johnson, D.B. 3277
Johnson, David A. 4554
Johnson, Paul Brett 3357
Johnson, Stephen T. 4708
Jolin, Dominique 852, 861, 866
Jones, Jac 2055
Jones, Margaret 2064
Joos, Louis 909, 2630
Jordan, Jael 4975
Jorisch, Stéphane 711, 734, 1731
Joyce, William 3827
Jullian, Andrés 1606
Jutte, Jan 2406
Juvonen, Riikka 1229, 1243

Kaardahl, Anders 1716
Kabát, Václav 1758
Kaergel, Julia 1412
Kajiyama, Toshio 2635
Kakukiwa, Robyn 2469
Kállay, Dušan 434, 1444
Kang, Johanna 2263, 4986
Karas, G. Brian 5192
Karrebæk, Dorte 1186, 1191
Kaya, Ismail 1736
Kehr, Karoline 1404
Kellenberger, Martin 1580
Kelley, Gary 4126
Kellogg, Steven 3173, 4035, 4036
Kepezinskas, Rimvydas 1759
Kimber, Murray 682, 717
Kirby, Patrick 1554
Kirin, Vladimir 1434
Kiselova-Sitekova, Jana 2631
Kitami, Kakashi 2634
Kitamura, Satoshi 1951
Klages, Simone 429
Knox, Charlotte 2091
Koch, Hannie 1454
Konishi, Eiko 1782
Kontio, Tomi 1227
Konwicki, Tadeusz 2651
Kovalski, Maryann 639
Krahn, Fernando 1624
Kramer, Hilde 2535
Kreutzmann, Nina Spore 1702
Kristensen, Jens 1704
Krüll, Dieter 1407
Krykorka, Vladyana 937
Kuhlman, Andrew 2403
Kulot-Frisch, Daniela 1581
Kunnas, Mauri 1232
Kupesic, Rajka 842
Kveta, Pacovska 417

L'owta, Sief Edeen 2271
La Marche, Jim 2262
Labrosse, Darcia 1565
Laden, Nina 4598
Laffon, Marine 3059
Lagarde, Marc 592
Lagercrantz, Rebecka 1436
Lago, Alexis 1113
Lai, Ma 1548
Lalev, Dimitar 1445
Laliberté, Louise-Andrée 724
Landström, Olof 2976
Langlois, Suzane 1682
Launis, Mika 1231, 1237
Lausche, Katherina 1401
Lauter, Richard 3319
Lavalee, Barbara 3815
Lawrence, Jacob 3390
Lee, Alan 1876
Lee, Dom 4559, 5072
Legge, David 116, 145
Lelooska, Chief 3103
Lemieux, Michele 687, 762
Lemmens, Riske 546
Lemmetty, Jukka 1559
Lempinen, Erja 1699
Lengheim, Wolfgang 373
Lepp, Mati 2982
Levert, Mireille 712
Levola, Kari 1226
Lewin, Betsy 4357, 4594
Lewin, Ted 3364, 4698, 4985
Lewis, Anthony 1978
Lewis, E.B. 919
Lhoták, Kamil 1526
Life, Kay 3696
Lightburn, Ron 625, 679, 710, 822
Lindenbaum, Pija 2977
Lindström, Eva 2979
Lippincott, Gary A. 3187, 4384, 5056
Littlechild, George 3998
Liu, Zonghui 1459
Llana, Dindo A. 1449
Llorach Ramos, Esteban 1071
Lloyd-Jones, Karen 191
López, Domínguez 1718
López, Nivio 2792
López Escrivá, Ana 2794
Lord, John Vernon 2087
Louchard, Antonin 1284
Louhi, Kristiina 1241
Lucas, Cedric 4585
Lucht, Irmgard 1330
Luetke, Joachim 449, 1524
Lumme, Mika 1236
Lundell, Margo 4485
Lundkvist, Ulf 2971
Lusted, Ian 2776
Lynch, P.J. 1878, 1880, 2238, 3367, 3472, 3479, 3488

Macaulay, David 2392, 4549, 4688
Magallon, Jordi 2852
Maigné, Claire 1439
Majaluoma, Markus 1213, 1235, 1242
Malekos, Andreas 1763
Mancek, Marjan 1427
Manna, Giovanni 1540
Marais, Christine 1457
Marcellino, Fred 4531, 4686
Marchand, Barbara 1687
Marschall, Ken 750, 966
Martchenko, Michael 867, 1686
Martínez, Enrique 1509
Martinez, Raul 1065
Martinez Blanco, Enrique 2269
Martínez Gómez, Eddie 2293
Martínez Torres, Leovigildo 2289
Mathers, Petra 4198
Mattotti, Lorenzo 2628
Matysiak, Gunnar 1328
McCarty, Peter 3483
McClelland, Linda 2505
McCue, Lisa 4864
McCully, Emily 3760, 4694
McDermott, Gerald 4699, 5020
McDonnell, Flora 1928
McEwen, Keith 142
McGaw, Laurie 824, 963
McGee Kvasnosky, Laura 3853, 3854
McGraw, Deloss 4656
McKissack, Fredrick L. 4755
McKissack, Patricia 3527, 4107, 4755
McLaughlin, Wayne 5263
McNaughton, Colin 1888, 1973
McPhail, David 4122
Meade, Holly 4409, 4711
Medlock, Scott 4910
Meeuwissen, Tony 2093
Mehrem, Gisela 2788
Mela, Eva 2144, 2201
Melbye, Inni Karine 1564
Mellinette, Martine 1630
Mello, Roger 608, 621
Mendrinou, Anna 2114
Meza B., Mariluz 1441
Micich, Paul 4668, 5070
Mikolaycak, Charles 4124

Milano, Ed 1620
Milleli, Pascal 685
Miranda, Regina 1722
Miranda, Robin 1506
Mitchell, Rita Phillips 1964
Mobio, Claire 1622
Modesto, António 1499
Mölck-Tassel, Bernd 1419
Mollet, Charlotte 1311
Mombourquette, Paul 770, 832, 835
Moore, Inga 1957
Moore, Yvette 812
Morales Villanueva, Judit 2899
Moreno, Sergio 2287
Morgenstern, Christian 1388
Morimoto, Junko 81
Morin, Paul 624, 626, 678, 702, 1685
Morrill, Leslie 3651, 3687
Morris, Jackie 2075
Morris, Sandra 2501
Moser, Barry 3248
Most, Bernard 4306
Moyes, Lesley 2485
Muchanova, Elena 1429
Muhammaiyan, Hušang 1498
Müller, Jörg 1329, 3047
Muñoz Bachs, Eduardo 1069, 1114
Munsinger, Lynn 3322, 4135, 4330, 4567
Murdocca, Sal 5267
Murphy Tyrol, Adelaide 3101
Murphy, David 4573
Murphy, Jill 1971
Murphy, Jim 4377
Myers, Christ 4718

Nadaud, Claire 1283
Nakatsuji, Etsuko 2643
Narelle, Oliver 73
Nasmith, Ted 766
Nava Bouchaín, Francisco 1726
Nidasio, Grazia 1465
Nine, Carlos 1721
Nivola, Claire A. 4461
Njeng, Pierre Yves 1533
Njoya, Idrissou 1603
Nolan, Dennis 3805, 3837
Nordberg, Harald 2552
Nordqvist, Sven 1713
Nordström, Jockum 2983
Nöstinger, Christine 374

O'Connell George, Kristine 3860
Offen, Hilda 1962
Ohi, Ruth 921
Olsen, John Alexander 2286
Olsen, Keith 2482
Ondrejcka, Karol 1428
Orecchia, Giulia 1649
Oronte-Siantu, Theodora 1739
Örtengren, Lisa 2980
Osojnik, Mojca 454
Otaševic, Dušan 1432
Ousland, Ingrid Jangaard 2544
Overend, Jenni 266
Owens, Mary Beth 3467, 4193, 4196, 4653
Oxenbury, Helen 1882, 1891, 1896, 1959, 1968, 2006, 3246, 4596

Pacheco, Alma Rosa 2292
Pacheco, Luis Gabriel 2288
Pacovská, Kvéta 1335, 2402, 3045
Page, Denis 2477
Palmisciano, Diane 3704
Panek, Dennis 4304
Pasirayi, Thomas 1677
Passicot, Monique 3106
Pastor, Perico 2859
Paul, Korky 2011
Paunov, Viktor 1613
Pearson, Debora 845
Peet, Bill 4685, 4897, 5046
Peles, Les Chates 2633
Pellan, Alfred 1732
Pelletier, David 4713
Perez, Olga Marta 1058
Petrièiæ, Dušan 1683
Pfister, Marcus 3482
Philpot, Graham 1815
Pieper, Christiane 1403
Pilkey, Dav 3288, 4714
Pinkney, Brian 3096, 3266, 3537, 3811, 4709, 4720, 4988
Pinkney, Jerry 1659, 3097, 3102, 3262, 3476, 3531, 3754, 3806, 3842, 4109, 4131, 4333, 4347, 4529, 4568, 4681, 4701, 4725, 4822, 4867, 5190, 5195
Piotrowska, Malgorzata 2536
Pla, Imma 2783
Plöger, Juliane 1410
Podwal, Mark 3105
Pohrt, Tom 3104, 4517
Poiesz, Karin 1584
Pokorny, Vaclav 420
Polacco, Patricia 3660, 3819, 4033, 4824
Popescu, Vlad 1601
Pottie, Marjolein 532
Poulin, Stéphane 726, 831, 859, 1605
Pouttu, Riitta 1244
Pratt, Pierre 699, 718, 730, 808, 882, 2627
Priceman, Marjorie 4707, 4990
Primavera, Elise 3484, 3987, 4388
Prstec, Zeljko 1609
Psaraki, Vasso 2197
Pulles, Elisabeth 2778

Rabanal, Daniel 1518
Räder, Andréa 1537
Ramos, Mario 1631, 2405
Rand, Ted 3452
Rankin, Joan 2722, 2723, 2724
Ransome, James 3528
Raschka, Chris 4700
Rathmann, Peggy 4706, 4745
Rayevsky, Robert 3982
Rayyan, Omar 3387
Réber, László 1536
Reczuch, Karen 629, 768
Reichstein, Alexander 1224
Reid, Barbara 628, 631, 680, 729, 5029, 5043
Reloba, Juan Carlos 1048
Rendeiro, Charlene 3469
Rendle, Christiaan 3923
Reynolds, Adrain 2020
Ribic, Igor 2660
Ricci, Regolo 763
Riet, Samantha van 1678
Riff, Helene 2416
Rihu, Susanne 1411
Ringgold, Faith 3522, 3996, 4690
Rivera Ferner, Marta 1551
Robins, Arthur 1984
Rodari, Florian 1435
Rodríguez, Bonachea, Vicente 1052
Rodríguez Hernandez, David 1033, 1045, 1050, 1072
Rogers, Gregory 1877
Rogers, Jacqueline 4439
Rohmann, Eric 4704
Rolph, Mic 1693
Rondón, Javier 1728
Root, Kimberly Bulken 4349
Ross, Christine 2502
Ross, Tony 1835, 1952, 2409, 3648, 3708
Rossiter, Nan Parson 4353
Roth, Susan 3389
Rowe, John 424, 2619, 2632
Rubio, Gabriela 1752, 2889
Rudevics, Karlis 1589
Ruffu Manea, Lucia 1644
Ruhl, Greg 751

Sabuda, Robert 3834, 3848, 3849
Salgado, Rosa 1063
Salgado Hurtado, Rosa 1086
Salinas, Bobbi 5015
Sánchez, José Ramón 2793
Sánchez, Maria Teresa 1056
Saport, Linda 3135
Sato, Makiko 1778
Sauvant, Henriette 1415
Savadier, Elivia 4982, 4991
Savino, Irene 1440
Say, Allen 3258, 4695
Scheffler, Axel 1688, 1982, 3764
Schick, Joel 3694, 5139
Schindler, S.D. 3346
Schmidt, Jelka Godec 2659
Schneider, R.M. 4548
Schössow, Peter 1408
Schröder, Ron 1583
Schroeder, Binette 1397
Schubert, Dieter 1744
Sekiguchi, Shun 1591
Sekiya, Toshitaka 2642
Seligson, Susan 5163
Seltzer, Isadore 4430
Selznick, Brian 3201, 3358, 4407, 4437, 5077
Serrano, Javier 1753
Shannon, David 3206, 3211, 3755, 4307, 4337, 5078
Sharkey, Niamh 1932, 4593
Sharpe, Elaine 256
Sharratt, Nick 1822, 2017
Shearing, Leonie 2248
Shed, Gred 4920
Shiffman, Lena 3450
Shine, Andrea 3485
Shulevitz, Uri 3856, 4722, 4979
Siejkowski, Lech 1528
Sigurdardottir, Frida 2217
Sigurðardóttur, Erlu 1560, 2216
Silverstein, Shel 5212
Simmonds, Posy 1949
Simmons, Elly 3681
Sis, Peter 3355, 4524, 4712, 4723
Skidmore, Steve 1614
Slavin, Bill 1698
Slonim, David 5067
Small, David 3478, 4516, 4715
Smith, Lane 2622, 3181, 3287, 3656, 3758, 4427, 4691
Smith, Manu 2511
Sneed, Brad 4134
So, Meilo 3989
Soentpiet, Chris K. 3683, 4009
Sofilas, Mark 15
Sogabe, Aki 3839
Solé, Francisco 2797, 2803
Sollie, André 533
Sorensen, Henri 4588
Sormann, Christine 430, 1472
Spee, Gitte 1770
Spurn, Gennadij 407
Stalfelt, Pernilla 1711, 2981
Stammen, Jo Ellen MacAllister 4195
Stanley, Diane 3843, 4872
Starostin, A.G. 1773
Stefanidi, Fotini 2125
Stefanidis, Yannis 2138
Steig, William 2395, 4038, 4528, 4553
Stephens, Catrin 2060
Steptoe, Javaka 3534
Stevens, Janet 3175, 3847, 4381, 4705, 5069
Stevenson, James 4118
Stevenson, Sucie 3685, 3692, 3695, 3699, 3709
Stock, Catherine 2725
Stöllinger, Heide 452, 2646, 2648
Stupica, Marija Lucija 1479
Sung-Woan, Park 2270
Sutherland, Ralph 1510
Sylvada, Peter 3490
Szaligyi, Mary 4119

Taback, Simms 4717, 4724
Tait, Les 771, 1680
Talbott, Tedd 3752, 4374
Tan, Shaun 83, 130
Tang, Yongli 1503
Tanner, Jane 185
Tarlton, John 2490
Tauss, Herbert 4984
Tchen, Richard 1756
Teckentrup, Britta 1669
Teng, Jean 4426
Thau-Jensen, Cato 1708
Thé, Tjong-Khing 1576
Tibo, Gilles 708, 757, 760, 840
Tidholm, Anna-Clara 1712
Tiitinen, Tuula 1230
Timmers, Leo 537
Tjong-Khing, Thé 568
Tobin, Nancy 4561
Tomás González, Manuel 1095
Torseter, Øyvind 2568
Tsangares, Champes 1452
Tsuchida, Yoshiharu 1569
Tubau, Victòria 1748
Tuinen, Marianne van 1437
Tusa, Tricia 4201
Tyrrell, Robert 4908

Uchnár, Peter 2644
Unenge, Johan 2969
Urdiales, Alberto 2791

Vagin, Vladimir 3981
Vainio, Pirkko 1240
Valkanov, Venelin 1737
Valverde, M. 2806
van Allsburg, Chris 3280, 3753, 4115
van Haeringen, Annemarie 1771, 2419
van Leeuwen, Joke 1772
van Rompaey, Pierre 526
Vanden Broeck, Fabricio 2295
Vandenberk, Sonja 461
VanGenechten, Guido 1768
Várnai, György 1616
Velasco, Samuel 2890
Veldkamp, Tjibbe 2421
Velthuijs, Max 2399, 2401, 2414
Verplancke, Klaas 1767
Vervaeke, Geert 527
Vian, Enid 1111
Vila Declòs, Jordi 1632
Villeneuve, Anne 912
Vincent, Gabrielle 4590
Vitale, Stefano 3100
Vivas, Julie 56, 1661
Vlasova, Anna 1490
Voake, Charlotte 1976
Voigt, Anneliese 2777
Vos, Peter 2396
Vrede, Angela de 1425
Vuori, Julia 1238
Vuori, Pekka 1246

Wagenbreth, Henning 1636
Wagner, Friederike 383
Waipara, Manawa-Ote-Rangi 2491
Waldman, Neil 797, 3099, 3457, 4533, 5175, 5179
Waldschütz, Barbara 372, 378
Wallace, Ian 677, 769, 805
Wallace, Mary 1684
Walrod, Amy 3862
Ward, Helen 1950
Warhola, James 3756
Wechdorn, Susanne 447
Weihs, Erika 3093, 4978
Weller, Lucy 1948
Wells, Rosemary 4572
Westcott, Nadine Bernard 4114, 5065

Westerduin, Anne 531, 564
Westerskov, Kim 2468
Weve, Sylia 2397
White, Michael P. 3661
Wick, Walter 3268
Widener, Terry 3718
Wiesmüller, Dieter 1395, 1414
Wiesner, David 4689, 4727
Wijngaard, Juan 4909
Wild, Margaret 86
Wilkón, Jósef 1296
Williams, Vera B. 4687, 5028
Willis, Jeanne 1818
Willms, Russ 814
Wilson, Janet 683, 749, 767
Wilson, Sharon 4583
Wimmer, Mike 4376
Wirsén, Stina 2984
Wisenfeld, Alison 2036
Wisniewski, David 4710
Wojtowycz, David 1827
Wolff, Ashley 3209
Wolfsgruber, Linda 436, 460, 463, 465, 1640, 2641
Woloszyn, Marek 2558
Wood, Audrey 5121
Wood, Don 4373, 4904
Wood, Jakki 4657
Wood, Michele 3535
Woolman, Steven 70, 193
Wormell, Christopher 2089
Wynn, Gwyneth 1462

Xiao, Aozi 1788
Xu, Dungu 1787

Yalowitz, Paul 3453
Yerxa, Leo 627, 681, 815
Young, Ed 3239, 3252, 3316, 4591, 4684, 4692, 5059
Young, Noela 106
Young, Selina 2489

Zamani, Mihran 1743
Zawadzki, Marek 1406
Zdinak, William 3456
Zelinsky, Paul O. 4521, 4703, 4716
Zeman, Ludmila 720
Zhang, Ange 818
Zhou, Xiang 1786
Zimmer, Dirk 4425
Zorrilla, Daniel 1035
Zullo, Albertine 2647
Zupan, Dim 2658
Zwerger, Lisbeth 444, 2423, 2624, 3042

Title Index

101 Ways to Bug Your Parents 3205, 3875, 4807, 4968, 4969
2MUCH4U 2497, 2515
2150 yilina yolculuk 1745
22 wezen 2421
24 i sekundet 1703
26 Fairmount Avenue 4091
38 Weeks Til Summer Vacation 4280
45 + 47 Stella Street 342
48 Hours with Franklin 1885
48 Shades of Brown 87
92 Queens Road 2742

A Bad Case of the Stripes 3206, 3211, 5023, 5078, 5225
A Band of Angels 3861
A banda sen futuro 2901
A Bowl of Mischief 3300
A Bridge to Wiseman's Cove 76
A Cageful of Butterflies 2741
A cavallo della scopa 1646
A Chance Child 4648
A Child's Calendar 4728
A Child's Treasury of Nursery Rhymes 632, 686, 732
A Christmas Carol 2620
A Close Call 1924
A cuca vem pegar 1514
A Day, a Dog 4590
A. Diamantes. To taxidi tes mikres rozus 1739
A Dog Like Jack 3990
A Dog Named Sam 5192
A Drop of Water: A Book of Science and Wonder 3268, 5076
A expedición do Pacífico 2917
A Family Apart 5090
A Fence Away from Freedom: Japanese Americans and World War II 3385
A Fox Spirit in a Desolate Garden 2625
A Frog Prince 2265
A Ghost in the House 4876, 5257
A Girl Named Disaster 4079
A Godmother for Denada 2162
A Hand Full of Stars 4294
A Handful of Beans 4553
A Haunting in Williamsburg 5107
A Home Among the Gum Trees 210
A Job for Wittilda 5064
À la vie, à la mort 1281, 1656
A Leaf in Time 1693
A lenda do capitan Miñoca 2833
A Letter to Sunday 2282
A Little Bit Dead 3579
A Little Tiger in the Chinese Night 813
A Log's Life 3765
A Long Hard Journey: The Story of the Pullman Porter 3518
A Long Way from Chicago 4086
A Long Way from Verona 4641
A medida que nos vamos conociendo 1010
A Mouse Called Wolf 4511
A Négyszögletü Kerek Erdõ 1536
A noite das cabras do aire 2922
A Outra Enciclopédia Canina 612
A Perfect Pork Stew 4132
A Pioneer Story: The Daily Life of a Canadian Family in 1840 748, 817, 938
A pirata penamoura 2826
A Place of Safety 315
A Place to Claim as Home 4843
Å plukke en smørblomst 2574
A Prairie Alphabet 812
A propos d'un bateau a vapeur 883
A Rabbit Named Harris 278
A revolta das palavras 614
A Screaming Kind of Day 735
A sereiazinha 1464
A Slipper 2279
A Son Among Daughters 1643
A Sound of Chariots 4642
A Sudden Silence 3327, 4811, 5136
A Summery Saturday Morning 2489
A Taste of Salt: A Story of Modern Haiti 3995
A terra dos meninos pelados 621
A Time for Dancing 3308, 4891
A Time of Fire 2012
A Time of Troubles 4788
A Trail of Tears 4939
A través de los ojos 1070
A Tree in a Forest 744
A Visit to Oma 5185
A Visitor's Guide to Ancient Rome 2052
A Walk to the Beach 2499
A Winter's Tale 769
A Year on Monhegan Island 4197
Aan de overkant van de rivier 485
Aan de verkeerde kant van de aarde 2346
Aapelus 1612
Aasi ja Morso 1229
Abalone Summer 645
ABC doido 615
ABCD-boken 2982

Abe Lincoln for Class President 5191
Abigail Adams: Witness to a Revolution 3260, 3840
Abiyoyo 5128
Across America in an Emigrant Train 4015, 4479
Adam a Eva 2631
Adam and Eve and Pinch Me 670, 716, 939
Add It, Dip It, Fix It: A Book of Verbs 4548
Adventure on Thunder Island 986
Advice for a Frog 4916
Aesop and Company with Scenes from His Legendary Life 3094
Aesop's Fables 2087
Afdankertjes 2420
Afrika achter het hek 2410
After the War 847
Afternoon of the Elves 4055
Agapimene mou Noe 2111
Agnes in the Sheep 2442
Ahoj, pravеké jaštery 1482
Aida 3519
Airborne 4775
Ajeemah and His Son 3256
AK 2098
Akiak: A Tale from the Iditarod 3986, 4744, 5173
Älä ankka aivasta 1242
Albatross Adventure 2468
Alboum 1652
Alessandra: Alex in Rome 2443
Alex in Winter 2441
Alex, le petit joueur de hockey 1733
Alfred der Bär u. Samuel der Hund steigen aus dem Pappakarton 1408
Alguien borra las estrellas 1073
Alguien nos está observando 1042
Alice in Wonderland 2423
Alice's Adventures in Wonderland 1882, 1896, 4596
Aliens Ate My Homework 3158
Aliens for Breakfast 5000
Alitji in Dreamland 123
All About Sam 3325, 3396, 3741, 4227, 4663
All in the Blue Unclouded Weather 272
All Join In 1887
All Sorts 2033
Alla signorina Elle con tanto affetto 1497
Allemaal bedrog 2334
Allerleirauh 1415
Alles in Butter, liebe Mutter! 380
Allez! Allez! 1316
Almost the Real Thing 4776
Alone at Ninety Foot 675, 783
Alphabet Apartments 2485
Alphabet City 4708
Alphabetari tes Kypru 1579
Als die Steine noch Vögel waren 456
Als die Welt noch jung war 1347, 3076
Als je goed om je heen kijkt zie je dat alles gekleurd is 2320
Als Viktoria allein zu Hause war 429
Alwna's Garden 2077
Amada! Amanda 3009
Amazing Anthony Ant 1815
Amazing Gracie 5057
Amber Brown Is Not a Crayon 3708
Ami! Ami? 601
Amigos del Otro Lado 2293
Amigos 2859
Amos the Story of an Old Dog and His Couch 5163
Amy's Promise 925
An Alphabet of Animals 2090
An Autobiography by Bill Peet 4897
An Egyptian Pyramid 2037
An Extraordinary Life: The Story of a Monarch Butterfly 4483
An Indian Winter 3818
An Island Like You: Stories of the Barrio 4674
Ananse and the Golden Drum 1458
Anansi and the Talking Melon 5069
Anarkai 3016
Anastasia's Album 927, 968
And If the Moon Could Talk 3270
Anderkantland 2719, 2754
Anders 547
Aneesa Lee and the Weaver's Gift 4569
Angel's Gate 66
Angels Passing By 1674
Angels Without Wings 2252
Ängelungen/Enkelimuksu 1234
Animais de compañía 1777
Animals Have Many Faces 2269
Anna und die Wut 374
Anne Frank 1344
Anne Frank: Beyond the Diary 3462, 3725
Another Kind of Monday 1474
Ant Colony 5048
Antologia de la narrativa infantil cubana 1075
Antología poética de Vicente Huidobro 2886
Antti Puuhaara 1237
Aph'ste ton sticho na sas pareap'to cheri 1738
Apinakuninkaan juhlat 1231
Apo Stroph 452, 2646
Appalachia: The Voices of Sleeping Birds 3248, 4452
Appointment with a Stranger 4812
Aquila 2105
Arabella oder Die Bienen-Königin 1383
Ariel, Zed and the Secret of Life 5
Ark in the Park 71
Arkitektur med andre ord 1172
Armien's Fishing Trip 2725
Arnold Always Answers 4660
Art Dog 4743
Arthur and the Dragon 2500
Arthur's Chicken Pox 3506
Arthur's Reading Race 3713
Artworks on ... Interiors 2085
Arven etter Onkel Rin-Tin-Tei 1586
As cousas claras 2923
As I Grow Older 265
Asfalttisoturi 1256
Attaboy, Sam! 3400, 3701, 3960
Au Bonheur des ours 1302
Au Cinéma avec papa 852
Au cinéma Lux 1287
Au pied de mon arbre 1628
Auf der anderen Seite 371
Aufstand der Tiere 1329
Aunt Flossie's Hats and Crab Cakes Later 4545
Aunt Harriet's Underground Railroad in the Sky 3996
Aussie Bites Series 181
Australian Animal Series 186
Australian Guide to Endangered Animals 198
Australian Guide to Pondlife 196
Australian Guide to Seashores 197
Auszeit oder der Lowe von Kauba 446, 2612

Awake and Dreaming 727, 793, 928, 942
Azouz, der Junge vom Stadtrand. Eine algerische 3040

Baba 1562
Babe 143
Babushka's Doll 3295
Baby Bear Goes to the Zoo 131
Baby 4877
Baby-Sitter Blues 587
Back Home 5184
Back to Beyond 958
Bad Boy 665, 932
Bad, Bad Cats 2031
Báje a mýty starých Slovan 1428
Baje Ceského Pošumaví 1433
Bamboozled 41, 116, 145, 341
Bananenrot und himbeerblau 458
Bandit's Moon 4049
Bang in Beiroet 477
Bang of Boos 501
Banvaktsbarn, Fredrik Matsson blir kär 2978
Bara Tsatsiki 2961, 3017
Barco de sueños 1063
Bark, George 3434
Barnen från Tibet 2975
Barnens svenska historia 3012
Barquichuelo de papel 2792
Barrio: José's Neighborhood 3136
Baseball in April: And Other Stories 4041
Basket 4119
Bat 6 4006
Batter 2 1778
Beauty 4799, 5228
Because I Love You 3798
Been to Yesterdays 3469, 3836
Beep! Beep! 4573
Beetles, Lightly Toasted 5131
Begigorritarren erlojua 2814
Begin een torentje van niks 2355
Behind the Secret Window 3934
Being with Henry 800, 843
Belle Prater's Boy 4081
Belly Flop 108, 146
Ben Markis, oder die reise in das Abendland 1367
Benjamin dufa 2212
Benni und die sieben Löwen 375
Benno en het berekind 2405
Benny and Omar 1692
Bernardo y Canelo 1624
Berta la Modista 2786
Berts bokslut 2967
Besuch aus der Vergangenheit 389
Betty and Bala and the Proper Big Pumpkin 1483
Beware of Boys 5100
Beyond Mayfield 4582
Bi Bop et que ça saute 864
Big Bang 2049
Big Boy 919
Big Cats 3698
Big Dog 258
Big Fat Hen 3830
Bijna iedereen kon omvallen 2339
Bill Peet 4685, 5046
Billedtid 1175
Billy the Punk 109, 232, 343
Bingo Brown, Gypsy Lover 4515
Bip, the Snapping Bungaroo 121
Bird Boy 4575
Biscernica 2659
Biscuits in the Cupboard 827
Bitte eine neue Welt, Herr Ober 3090
Blabber Mouth 29, 138, 331
Blabla: pesmi in igre za male in velike tigre 1427
Black & White 4688
Black and British 2039
Black Cowboys, Wild Horses: A True Story 5195
Black Hands, White Sails: The Story of African-American Whalers 4859
Black Ships Before Troy 1876
Black Water Swamp 4962
Blaeberry Sunday 2237
Blij met mij 537
Blood and Chocolate 3737, 4893
Blosse Hände 1354
Blote handen 502, 554, 578, 2361
Blue Skin of the Sea 3439, 4098
Blue Skye 4905
Blueback 192
Blueprint 1364
Bob and Jack: A Boy and His Yak 4123
Bob the Builder and the Elves 118, 150
Bobute iš Paryziaus arba Lakštingala Zarasuose: Eilerašciais 1430
Bokutachi no Konnyaku sensei 1780
Bone Dance 673, 945
Bonizaz und der Räuber Knapp 3087
Boo Barney 2007
Boogie Woogie 1285
Boris Beer 2394
Borrequita and the Coyote 4187
Bouncing and Bending Light 4780
Box and Cox 4516
Box Turtle at Long Pond 3361
Boys, Pickel und andere Megasorgen 443
Boza majka: Knizka za dobri deca 1445
Bra Börje 2977
Braam en die engel 2674
Brændt jord 1623
Brak og brestir 2213
Brand in de Tikkebossen 559
Breaking Boxes 3356
Breathing Room 3229
Brewster Rooster 814
Brian Boru 2228
Brian's Winter 3733, 3975, 5160, 5222
Brief Garland 4473
Bring Back the Deer 5175
Bring Up Beauty 791, 964
Broc Môr 2061
Brokatna podoba, Pravljice kitajskih manjšin 2655
Broken Chords 4472
Brønden 1181
Brother Eagle, Sister Sky 3120, 4120, 5183
Bruder 1358
Bruin zonder zon 491
Brujas, hechizos y otros disparates 1026, 1030
Brunas de octubre 2842
Bud, Not Buddy 3538, 3951, 4088, 4584
Buffy 153
Bull Run 3303, 4791
Bum face 47, 112, 115, 348, 1574
Buns for the Elephant 2029
Buoy: Home at Sea 4552
Burning with Revenge 170, 303
Burnt Toast on Davenport Street 4926
Buster's World 4293
But I'll Be Back Again 4450
Button 1943
Buttons 4586
Buz 4630
By the Hanukkah Light 797
By the Light of the Halloween Moon 3825

By Truck to the North: My Winter Adventure 845
Byw a Bod yn y Bath 2081
Bzzz… 2889

Caballero Negro 1002
Cadillac 4253
Cages 4282
Caihui ben zhongguo minjian gushi 1503
Cakes and Miracles: A Purim Tale 4978
California Blue 3680
Call of the Wolves 4377
Calling the Doves 3644, 3681
Came Back to Show You I Could Fly 54, 96
Camels for Uncle Sam 4941
Can the Whales Be Saved? 3448
Can You Teach Me to Pick My Nose? 787
Canalla, traidor, morirás! 2818
Cando petan na porta pola noite 1508, 2930
Canto de lunas para un duende 1008
Canto Familiar 3307
Cantos de camino 1046
Capitol for the Nation 4464
Carabela, Calavera 994
Caretta Caretta 462
Carn i ungla 2781
Carrie's War 4683
Cartas a Julio Orlando 1057
Cartas al cielo 1104
Casa en las nubes 1094
Casey in the Bath 3663
Castor målar 2963
Cat of Artimus Pride 915
Cat Running 4045
Catherine and the Lion 1930
Catherine, Called Birdy 3306, 3831, 4070
Cautionary Tales and Other Verses 1949
Cavalhadas de Pirenópolis 608
Ce n'est pas de ma faute ! 1439
Celebration Song 1942
Cell Wars 1991
Cells Are Us 1992
Cendrillon, Un conte de Noël et Rose blanche 3057
Chandra 1905
Change the Locks 215
Changes in Latitude 3215
Chanson pour Frédéric 869
Charlie and the Chocolate Factory 27
Charlie Anderson 3979
Charlie's Eye 1937
Charlotte et l'île du Destin 734, 1731
Chato's Kitchen 4675, 5012
Cheerful Spirits 1668
Cherokee Summer 4467
Chicka Chicka Boom Boom 3247, 4116
Chicken Lady 990
Chicken Soup for the Teenage Soul 3222, 4839, 5124
Chicken Sunday 3301, 3819
Chikka 1679
Child of the Owl 3676
Children Just Like Me 2043
Children of the Dust Bowl 3677, 4014, 4043, 4478, 4935
Children of the Night 3722
Children of the River 3925
Chinese Fables 2629
Chocolatina 3170
Choose Your Grandmother 985
Choosing Up Sides 3948
Christina's Ghost 5084, 5129
Christmas in the Big House, Christmas in the Quarters 3527
Christopher Changes His Name 4133
Christopher Columbus: Voyager to the Unknown 4902
Chumba la cachumba 1501
Chumplufated… 2890
Chwedl Taliesin 2064
Chwedlau o 'r Gwledydd Celtaidd 2083
Cities in the Sea 2075
Claire's Gift 842
Class Clown 4862
Claude and Sun 4659
Close Encounters 4783
Clown 1945
Coffin on a Case! 3580
Coch yw Lliw Hunllef 2073
Cock-a-doodle-moo 4306
Cold Shoulder Road 3140
Color Zoo 4682
Columbeta, la isla libro 2795
Comme une peau de chagrin 721
Common Ground: The Water Earth and Air We Share 3763
Como el zunzun era su corazón 1086
Cómo escalar un pastel 1582
Companions of the Night 4403
Comptines á croquer 1467
Con los niños por la Habana Vieja 1103
Concert en sol major 2867
Consejos del Abuelo Conejo 1069
Contes a una cama trencada 2877
Contes du chat gris 900
Contes per a un món millor 2904
Contos por palabras 2883
Contra tu pecho desnudo 1109
Cool School: You Make It Happen 237
Copycat 5109
Coram Boy 2108
Counting on Frank 325
Coup de soleil 1634
Covered Bridge 756, 809
Cowboy: A Kid's Album 747
Cowboy Baby 1980
Cowboy with a Camera: Erwin E. Smith, Cowboy Photographer 4946
Cowboys, Indians and Gunfighters 4937
Coyote Steals the Blanket: A Ute Tale 3505, 4394, 5019
Crackling Brat 2096
Cranberries: Fruit of the Bogs 3599
Crash! 3919, 3976, 4259, 4272, 4287, 4402, 4438, 4635, 4880, 5118, 5224
Crashboomlove 3138
Crazy Lady 4067
Cristion Ydw I 2066
Croisière en meurtre majeur 1300
Crooked 3313
Crossfire 216
Crossroads 2447
Crow and Weasel 4517
Cry Wolf 2019
Cuchilla 1003
Cuenta, Cuenta 2287
Cuentos con alas y luz 1006
Cuentos del zorro 1721
Cuentos musicales 1090
Cuentos para no creer 1106
Cuentos sin edad 1100
Cul-Blanc 596
Cut from the Same Cloth: American Women in Myth, Legend, and Tall Tale 3096
Cymru Ddoe a Heddiw 2057

Da musst du durch, Lurch 3035
Daar is spore op die maan 2767

Daar's 'n spook in my kas 2697
Daddy's Chair 4977
Dafnis y Cloe 1105
Damjanovo jezero 1609
Dana se jaar duisend 2762
Dances with Wolves 4832
Dancing Elephants 2722
Dancing on the Bridge of Avignon 4987
Dancing on the Edge 4320
Danger Along the Ohio 4944
Danger in Quicksand Swamp 4244, 4496
Danger in the Desert 4288
Danger Zone 3204, 4351, 4819, 4922
Daniel's Story 790, 962
Daocaoren 1787
Dare Truth or Promise 1566, 2481
Dark Horses 2514
Dark Lord of Derkholm 4316
Das Bärenwunder 1339
Das geheime Wissen der Pinquine 2 432
Das Königsspiel 382, 1575
Das Land der Ecken 425
Das Lügennetz 428
Das Museum der gestohlenen Erinnerungen 1325
Das Schimpansen-Kinderbuch 402
Das Wunder von Jasina 1635
Dat komt er nou van… 1744
Daughter of the Stars 5113
Däumling 1387
Dawn Rider 914
Dawo'er zu 1511
Days of Awe: Stories for Rosh Hashanah and Yom Kippur 3093
De berggids vertelt 473
De blauwe stoel, de ruziestoel 2338
De brief die Rosie vond 512, 533
De eerste lente 2363
De eikelvreters 2304
De Frente Para o Sol 609
De genezing van de krekel 544
De huid van de beer 498
De kat en de adelaar 2373
De kleine koning 2402
De kwartjesclub 565
De meester is een schat 484
De o van opa 2317
De oma van Jules 519
De plant van Jan 2365
De prinses met de lange haren 2422
De prinses van de moestuin 2326, 2431
De reizen fan Tsjam 1494
De Roos en het Zwijn 510
De schaduw van skellig 2387
De schimmen van Pluckley 483
De sneeuwman die niet smelten wou 520
De storm 2325
De tijd is een cirkel 563
De tolbrug 2342
De Tunnel 2308
De veerpont 523
De verjaardag van alle anderen 2385
De verjaardag van de eekhoorn 2411
De verliefde prins 535, 2424
De visioenenvloek 561
De vlieger van opa 550
De voek van cornelia 2388
De vrolijke keuken 2375
De weg naar het noorden 2427
De wezen van Woesteland 2417
De wolk 475
De wraak van de marmerkweker 505
Deadly Deception 5152
Deadly Unna? 84, 133
Dear Mr. Sprouts 310
Dear Nobody 1800
December 3852
December Stillness 3320
Dedecek automobil 1526
Del-Del 99, 291
Demon Teddy 1833
Den plettede tiger 1168
Den store faktaboka om språk 2564
Den store røde hunden 2555
Dengang min onkel Kulle blev skor 1177
Denny and the Magic Pool 2065
Der blaue See ist heute grün 377, 441
Der dreckige Prinz 449, 1524
Der Frischkönig 1397
Der Gestiefekte Kater 1398, 2617
Der Hacht hat's gesagt! 407
Der Hund, der unterwegs zu einem Stern war 1340
Der Hund mit dem gelben Herzen oder die Geschichte vom Gegenteil 1392
Der Junge ohne Namen 409
Der Klavierling 1633
Der kleine Blumenkönig 417
Der Möhrenfresser 1403
Der Rabe Alfons 1386
Der Riese und die Erdbeerkonfitüre 3074
Der rote Nepomuk 1380
Der rote Wolf 1359
Der Sohn des Hauptlings 437
Der tapfere Theo 421
Der wind und der sterne 1379
Der Wolf ist tot 1638
Der Zauberer von Oz 444
Der zwerg base 2624
Der Zwerg im Kopf 3081
Der Zwerg Nase 1389
Desert Dan the Dunny Man 240
Desert Dog 317
Desperate Pursuit 4834
Destination: Moon 3768
Det mørke lyset 2576
Detective Donut and the Wild Goose Chase 49
Detour for Emmy 4889
Deucalion 92
Deux amis dans la nuit 910
Deux heures et demie avant Jasmine 703
Devil's Bridge 4667, 4960
Devuelve el anillo, pelo cepillo 2884
Dez Sacizinhos 610
Dezenove Poemas Desengonçados 611
Días de Reyes Magos 1753, 2898
Die avonture van Rodger, die renoster 2706
Die avonture van Ster en Polka 2694
Die breinwassers; Ouma Hester en die 2720
Die eiserne Lerche 1336
Die elfde hekkie 2693
Die engeltjie op die solder 2707
Die entstehung der Gurteltiere 2632
Die Erbsenprinzessin 1581
Die feetjietuin 2690
Die Fliege am Broadway 401
Die Früchte-u. Samenuhr 1400
Die geheim van Groukatlaagte 2702
Die Geheimnisse der Yingzi 3039
Die geschichte von der kleinen Gans, die nicht schnell genug war 2261
Die Guck-Gucks-Bande 406

Die Hexe zieht den Schlafsack enger 1466
Die Hexenkralle 411
Die huis met groen oë 2682
Die Insel der Möwen 1391
Die Kinder der Prärie 418
Die Konigin der Farben 1413
Die letzten Riesen 1390
Die meisie wat soos 'n botter-voël sing 2730, 2771
Die mieliestronkpop 2716
Die Mitte der Welt 365, 1326
Die optog van die aftjoppers 2755, 2768
Die Prinzessin auf dem Kürbis 379, 460
Die Prinzessin kommt um vier 1418
Die prinzessin mit dem dicken po 2637
Die pro 2737, 2759, 2769
Die Regentrinkerin 1382
Die somervakansie wat te lank was 2764
Die teken van die crux 2760
Die towersak en ander stories 2734
Die waterding 2709
Die Wette, wer zuerst wütend wird 1405, 2636
Die wilden Huhner 356
Die wit vlinder; Die towersak en ander stories 2675
Die Zeit ist kaputt 1345
Diego 4543
Dierenpraat 2389
Dimanche Diller 1967
Dina und der Zauberzwerg 373
Dinosaur Cousins? 5176
Dinosaur Dream 3805
Dinosaurier gibt es nicht 423
Dinosaurs, Dinosaurs 4658
Dinotopia 3502
Dirgelwch Loch Ness 2076
Discovering the Iceman: What Was It Like to Find a 5,300 Year Old Mummy? 824
Disteltage 448
Dit is het huis bij de kromme boom 1534, 2377
Ditsem Dawid! 2708
Dixie Storms 4900
Diyenkoroba ou Vieux-comme-le-monde 1611
Djavol, zmej, orisnici, mag'os-nici, samovili, vampiri 1715
Do Not Go Around the Edges 259
DO pour Dolorès 1729
Do You See Me, God? 3767
Doble joc 2843
Dockvandringen 2980
Dr. Kiss Says Yes 705
Doçura amarga 1535
Dödenboken 1711
Dodger 89
Dog Breath! 3349, 3759
Dogs Don't Wear Sneakers 4250
Dogzilla 3288, 5108, 5151
Dolphin Adventure 5052
Don't Check Your Brains at the Door 3776
Don't Fidget a Feather! 3346
Don't Laugh, Joe! 3429
Don't Look Back 5049
Don't Look Behind You 3969, 5089, 5137, 5141, 5243
Don't You Dare Read This, Mrs. Dunphrey 3202, 3941, 4355
Donde esté mi corazón 2805
Donna & Dario 450
Donne-moi la main, Arthur 1545
Doosje mon 546
Double Act 1820, 1970
Double Trouble in Walla Walla 5267
Dougy 217
Down Street 2729
Down the Road 4919
Downriver 3220, 3221, 3338
Dragon's Gate 3304, 4044, 4066
Dragonwings 4645
Dream Invader 2241
Dream on! 1614
Dreamcatcher 202
Dreamplace 3365
Driftwood Cove 960
Drive-By 3166
Driver's Ed 3727, 4506, 5155
Drôle de moineau 903
Drome op Duinebaai 2711
Droomwa 2673, 2718, 2748
Drop Dead 1893
Du groß, und ich klein 1350
Dúas bágoas por Máquina 2914
Duck for Cover 230, 338
Ducks Fly 4518
Duke Ellington: The Piano Prince and His Orchestra 4720
Duke, the Dairy Delight Dog 4826
Dustefjerten og den store mar-sipanfesten 2547
Dustefjerten og den store vårdagen 2577
Dyddiau Cŵn 2078
Earth Explained 4782
Earth Tales from Around the World 3101
Earthlings Inside and Out 1683
Earthquake at Dawn 3299
Earthquake Terror 5073, 5117
Earthshine 3441, 3679, 4913
Easter Egg Farm 3658, 4188
Eating Between the Lines 636, 655
Echoes for the Eye: Poems to Celebrate Patterns of Na-ture 3601
Echoes of the Elders: The Sto-ries and Paintings of Chief Lelooska 3103
Eddas lysthus 1727
Eddie och Maxon Jaxon 3011
Edmond et Amandine 888
Edmonia Lewis: Wildfire in Marble 3391
Een fruitje van zilver 553
Een koekje voor Blekkie 531
Een kuil om in te wonen 480
Een mond vol dons 2340
Een mondvol aarde 2300
Een pelikann op straat 2426
Een sok met streepjes. Leren lezen met plaatjes 1772
Een vijf met negen nullen 494
Een vlinder aan het raam 506
Een zeer geheime reiskist 2349
Eenders of anders 2739
Eenkantkind 2684
Eg greier meg 2549
Eg heiti Blidfinnur en pu matt kalla mig Bobo 2208
Eggg 2530, 2565, 2566
Eilandheimwee 2336
Ein Baum fur Mama 442
Ein fremdes Land 3031
Ein Meer voller Sterne 3089
Ein motorsykkel i natta 2524
Ein naken gut 2532
Ein Schmetterling aus Surinam 1381
Ein Sehnen nach etwas 414
Ein verrückter Tag 383
Eine Insel im Meer 1360
Eine Woche voller Samstage 3022
Eines Morgans was die Chom-reh leer 3030
Eines Tages war die Chromreh leer 426
Eins, funf, viele 1335
Eins zwei drei Tier 1362
El adivino. Cuento popular 1717
El alma en una nube 1034, 1039

El árbol inquieto 2856
El asunto de mis papás 2782
El capirote de Onofre 2858
El cartero llama tres veces 1066
El cuento Alas y luz 1007
El Dios de un Poeta 1012
El dueño de la luz 1440
El encargo de Fernanda 2290
El espejo en al agua 2296
El galió de les illes Cies 2866
El hombre, el árbol y el camino 2857
El huevo azul 2291
El imperio de las cinco lunas 1001, 1608
El león vegetaliano 1074
El libro de Antón Pirulero 1079
El libro de los pecesitos 1113
El libro del Minotauro 1011
El libro del orégano 1083
El malefici dels Da 2868
El Mar de las Maravillas 1606
El Mar dels Naufragis 2875
El mar i el desig 2864
El misterio de la mujer autónoma 2809
El misterio del eunuco 2844
El misterio Velázquez 2897
El mundo, septiembre adentro 2289
El niño que dejó de ser pez 2896
El oro de la edad 1024, 1108
El pais de los mil paraguas 1047
El pes de la carrega 2841
El pescador de la luna 1072
El príncipe de Blancanieves 1000
El rey Arturi cabalga de nuevo, más o menos 2831
El sapo que no quería comer 1726
El secreto de las 211 puertas 2888
El señor del Cero 2803
El sobreviviente 1573
El Sueño 1021
El temps felic 2848
El terror de sexto B 1518
El tresor de la Nit de Nadal 2909
El última Set 2798, 2837
El valle de la Pajara pinta 1110
El verano y sus amigos 2894
El viatge d'Alexandre 2788
El vuelo del señor Popol 2862
Eleanor Roosevelt 3824
Eleanor Roosevelt: A Life of Discovery 3257, 3670, 4065
Eleanor's Story: An American Girl in Hitler's Germany 3950
Elefantevangeliet 1705
Elfenmiddag 2335
Elizabeth and Larry 4527
Elizabeti's Doll 3645
Elk vir mekander 2686, 2731
Ella Enchanted 3167, 3203, 3359, 3560, 3977, 4084, 4211, 4740, 5269
Ella luokkaretkellä 1219
Els arbres passaven ran de finestra 2845
Els contes del llop 2907
Els gegants adormits 2852
Elsan ja Eetun erikoistapaukset 1222
Else-Marie och småpapporna 2986
Emile — Eine bunte Katzengeschichte 1417
Emily's Wonderful Pie 2507
Emma Bean 5188
Emma Pippifilippi 1523
En barkbåt till Eddie 2988
En busca de un tiempo perdido 1018, 1067
En Cosme i el monstre Menjamots 1749
En el cofre de un pirata 1096
En la última frontera 2295
En mi familia 3132
En o I havet 2614
En Zip i el xai de la son 2783
Ena dentro zitai avli 2116
Ena isitirio, parakalo! 2134
Ena saki malia 2135
Enchanted Journeys 1539
Enchanted Wood 5253
Enchantress from the Stars 4640
Enci benci na kamenci vol. 2. 2662
Encyclopedia of Australian Wildlife 203
Energij 2653
Engelen van het asfalt 2301
Engle græder ikke og andre historier 1188
Enkeliyöt 1249
Entre el juego y el fuego 2887
Eplasneplar 2215
Ernst stand auf und August blieb liegen 1404
Erzähler der Nacht 1385
Es busca portera 2879
Es war einmal von A bis Zett 387, 465
Escuelita de los horrores 1025, 1117
Ese niño de La Edad de Oro 1099
Esio Trot 1955
Espasa de constel lació 2869
Esperanza 2995
Este libro horroroso y sin remedio 1036
Etosha experience 1457
Eugenio 2628
Eva & Adam: fusk och farligheter 2962
Eva & Adam: jul, jul pinsamma jul 2969
Eva ou le pays des fleurs 2630
Eva 4495
Eventyret om Mozar 2558
Everywhere 3809
Evig flugt 1564
Exercícios de ser criança 616
Experiment in Terror 4372
Exploring the Titanic 5095
Extinction Is Forever 4781
Extra Innings: Baseball Poems 4910
Eye to Eye 79
Eyes of the Dragon 3316
Eyewitness Guide: Evolution 1998

Fábulas 1499
Fábulas salvajes 1505
Fafarraios 2913
Fair Is Fair: World Folktales of Justice 3098
Fairy Wings 3837
Fallen Angels 3413, 4884
Falling Up 4210, 5218
Fan hantsjeklap en sukerbak 1584
Fang Fang's Chinese New Year 128
Fangoso 1111
Fantasi-i šalgam wa 'aql 1742
Fantastic Mr. Fox 31
Far North 4942
Faraway Home 2242
Farmer Duck 1959
Fat, Four-Eyed and Useless 2449
Fear Street 4460
FeestVerHalen 2428
Feja Skazka. Izbrannye skazki dlja detej i vzroslych 1760
Felica y Odicia 2292
Félix Têtedeveau 598
Feuerland ist viel zu heiß! 1348
Fiddle-I-Fee: A Farmyard Song for the Very Young 4657
Fierce Milly 2248
Fietsen 577
Fig Pudding 5115

Figuring Out Frances 4095
Fil de fer, la vie 1297
Fili, fili, kardiofili 2128
Finders Keepers 57, 324
Finger hat es aufgeschrieben 440
Finis mundi 1706, 2835
Finn Inga 2572
Fire, Bed and Bone 1866
First Apple 3419
First in the Field: Baseball Hero Jackie Robinson 3947
First Light 69
Fishing for Islands: Traditional Boats and Seafarers of the Pacific 212
Five Days of the Ghost 786
Fiz voar o meu chapéu 618
Flags 1685
Flamingohøsten har begynt 1555
Flickan som inte ville kyssas 2951
Flight #116 Is Down 4246, 4338, 4389, 4735, 4815, 5103
Flight: The Journey of Charles Lindbergh 4477
Fliks en Flora 558
Flour Babies 1801, 2101
Flowers in the Attic 30
Fly Away Home 3297
Flyg, sa Alfons Åberg! 2959
Fog Cat 770, 832, 835
Folket i Birka. På Vikingarnas tid 1713
Follow That Hat! 2627
Footsteps of the Gods 2491
For the Love of a Fairy Tale 2153
For Your Eyes Only 4923
For Your Own Protection: Stories Science Photos Tell 5182
Forbidden City 933
Forever Amber Brown 3714
Forged by Fire 3533
Förr i tiden i skogen 3013
Forty Acres and Maybe a Mule 4796
Fourth Grade Rats 3190, 4866
Fox on the Job 3688
Foxspell 72
Frakk, a macskák réme 1616
Franklin Delano Roosevelt 3810, 4012, 4476
Fratz 1412
Fräulein Pop und Mrs. Up 1365
Freak the Mighty 3156, 3343, 3423, 4254, 4346, 4838
Fred Hollows. Leaving the World a Better Place 1446
Fredagsöverraskningen 1436
Freddrik 1707
Free as the Desert Wind 1553
Freedom Train North: Stories of the Underground Railroad in Wisconsin 3603
Freedom's Children: Young Civil Rights Activists Tell Their Stories 3997
Fremtiden. Hva skjer etter år 2000? 2569
Frida Maria 3678
Frindle 3201, 3404, 3475, 3748, 3874, 4273, 4286, 4407, 4437, 4510, 4637, 4671, 4739, 4767, 4771, 5077, 5236, 5265
Frippe lagar allt 2966
From the Beast to the Blonde 1870
From the Cherry Tree to the Internet 2169
Frontier Merchants 4927
Fruit 2091
Fu Ling's testamente i serien: Alex på Eventyr 1170
Fuffy und Max 1529
Fudge 3957, 4359, 4798, 4954, 5240
Fudge-a-Mania 3183, 3331, 3654, 3958, 4204, 4362, 4380, 4620, 4957, 5146
Fünf Minuten vor dem Abendessen 420
Funny You Should Ask 970
Furanchesuko 1448
Further Tales of Uncle Remus 4529
Fushigina yukidaruma 1569

G. A. Henty 1832–1902 1871
Gallows Hill 4408
Gamkab 2757
Gandhi. The Man of Peace 1460
Gans ganz groß 405
GASP! 48, 350
Gau, gau, gau (Oi zein ituna) 2827
Geen wonder dat moeder met de goudvissen praat 474
Gegnum thyrnigerdid 2211
Geheim Sacrament 517
Gehen wir heim, Kleiner Bär 415
Geiriadur Gomer i'r Ifanc 2069
George and Matilda Mouse … and the Floating School 2267
George's Monster 2506
Geraamtes dra nie klere nie 2765
Gerlong'er wang zhuanji 1607
Get More New Life 17
Getting Near to Baby 4089
Getting Physical 2042
Gevangen in de Andes 2315
Ghost Cadet 5104
Ghost Canoe 3589
Ghost of Sifty Sifty Sam 4439
Ghost Train 630, 684, 725, 943
Ghosts Don't Get Goosebumps 3192, 4967
Ghosts of Fourth Grade 4366
Gifts 628
Gina 1182
Gina je t'aime 1183
Ginger 1976
Gittan och gråvargarna 2956
Gizmo Again! 339
Gizmos & Gadgets 4785
Glennis, Before and After 3477
Go Away, Big Green Monster 3189
Goggle-Eyes 1857
Going for Kalta 211
Going to Sleep on the Farm 4909
Gold Dust 2102
Golem 4710
Gondwanan lapset 1224
Good Idea Gone Bad 638
Good Luck, Mrs. K.! 3487
Good Night, Mr. Tom 5087
Good-Bye Marianne 696
Goosebumps 4459
Gracey 268
Grandad's Prayers for the Earth 3488
Granddad's Teeth 50, 110, 113, 147, 171, 239
Grandfather's Journey 3258, 3302, 4695
Grandma Fina and Her Wonderful Umbrellas 3234
Grandma from Paris or Nightingale in Zarasai 2278
Grandma's Bill 2227
Grandmother Bryant's Pocket 4198
Grandpa's Slippers 2452
Grandpa's Teeth 3210, 3665
Grasshopper Summer 4241
Graveyard Girl 4469
Gravitation 3014
Greetings from Sandy Beach 58
Grilladir bananar 2217

Gröna rätter för unga kockar 1537
Growing Up in Coal Country 3368, 4002
Grutte Giele & Lytse Loer 1437
Grys Gomgommer 2689
Guaminiquinaje 1116
Guárdate de los idus 2802
Guess How Much I Love You 3124
Gulf 1901, 2010
Gulliverove Cesty I. 2644
Gunnar i granskogen 2979
Gurab-i pašmi 1498
Gurin med reverompa 2537
Gutenachtgeschichte für Maria Carolina 434, 1444
Gypsy Rizka 4579

Habibi 3232, 4004, 4100
Háblame del sol 2801
Hairy Maclary and Zachary 2493
Haïti, la perle nue 1629
Halastjarna 2207
Hallo-Weiner 5153
Han cremat el mar 2929
Hands On, Thumbs Up 743
Hanen og reven 1424
Hangman 1696
Hannah Plus One 78
Hanniel kommit in die Stadt 404
Hans mein Igel 1407
Hårboken 2981
Harlem: A Poem 4718
Haroun and the Sea of Stories 4309
Harriet's Hare 1817
Harris and Me 3974, 4890, 5214, 5255
Harry and the Bucketful of Dinosaurs 2020
Harry Potter à l'école des sorciers 1288
Harry Potter and the Chamber of Secrets 1829, 1981, 1989
Harry Potter and the Philospher's Stone 304, 364, 1825, 1977, 2015
Harry Potter and the Prisoner of Azkaban 1831, 1983, 2021, 2107
Harry Potter and the Sorcerer's Stone 3127, 3141, 3168, 3426, 3876, 3921, 4274, 4369, 4411, 4772, 5223
Harry's Mad 3321
Harvey Angell 2099
Harvey Potter's Balloon Farm 3162, 3191, 3208, 4127, 4398, 5170, 5260
Harvey Slumfenburger's Christmas Present 2095
Hasenmond 424
Hat Opa einen Anzug an? 1357
Hatchet 3279, 3647, 3740, 3967, 4269, 4277, 4810, 4837, 5082, 5227, 5241
Hattie and the Wild Waves 4192
Haus der Kunst — ein Gang durch die Kunstgeschichte 1355
Have You Seen Who's Moved in Next Door to Us? 1888
Havets djup 2964, 3018
Hear Me, My Son 2148
Heard It in the Playground 2023
Hearing Us Out 4850
Heart of a Champion 4345, 4627, 5147
Heart of a Tiger 4825, 5171, 5261
Heaven 3536
Heckedy Peg 4373, 5244
Hector 1552
Hee meneer Eland 2383, 2434
Heinähattu ja Vilttitossu 1235
Heinahattu, Vilttitossu ja vauva 1213
Heksenfee 1766
Helden op sokken 2384
Hélico et l'Iceburg 2618
Heljarstökk afturabak 2220
Hello Baby 1661
Hello God, It's Me 16
Help! I'm Trapped in My Teacher's Body 5154
Henas angelos mia phora 1763
Henry and Mudge and the Bedtime Thumps 3699
Henry and Mudge and the Best Day of All 3710
Henry and Mudge and the Careful Cousin 3709
Henry and Mudge and the Happy Cat 3695
Henry and Mudge and the Wild Wind 3705
Henry and Mudge Get the Cold Shivers 3692
Henry and Mudge in Puddle Trouble 3685
Henry and Mudge in the Family Trees 3716
Henry and the Long Weekend 3702
Henry Hikes to Fitchburg 3277
Her a reiki 2203
Her Stories 3529
Her Stories: African American Folktales, Fairy Tales and True Tales 4457
Her Story. Women Who Changed the World 1451
Here Comes Mother Goose 4572
Herman het kind en de dingen 2347
Hero 4471
Hero of Lesser Causes 709, 776
Herr der Diebe 3091
Herr Novak und die Mausfrau 455
Hershel and the Hanukkah Goblins 3498, 4683, 5165
Het avontuur 2413
Het bad van de zandloper 2397
Het beertje Pippeloentje 2408
Het beest van de Canigou 560
Het boek van Bod Pa 540
Het eiland klaasje 2352
Het geheim van meester Joachim 486
Het gouden oog 2322
Het huis van eb en vloed 515
Het ijzelt in juni 513
Het is de liefde die we niet begrijpen 522
Het is nacht, we gaan op jacht 2323
Het kleine geheim van Pieter 564
Het kleuterwoordenboek 1502
Het moment 2306
Het oma-komplot 495
Het wilhelmus 2343
Het wordt zomer, Kleine Beer 497
Het zout der aarde en het domme schaap 2360
Heviho ABC 1542
Hey! Get Off Our Train 4514
Hi, Pizza Man! 4305
High Valley 190
High Wire Henry 3332, 4243
Hije gusar 1602
Hilies kai mia nyhtes ton Valkanion 2115
Hillback to Boggy 4465
Hippity Hop, Frog on Top 4656
Hippo's River Café 1593
His Banner Over Me 779
Historia de Flechazo y la nube 1720

Historia de un amor exagerado 1443
Històries de sols 2787
Hitler's Daughter 85
Hjertebåndet 1171
Hjerte-smerte 1716
Ho peirates me ta alliotika matia 1538
Hodder 1363
Hoe papa zijn oude tante vermoordde 2416
Hola, Pep! 2829
Holes 3021, 3223, 3272, 3561, 3668, 4087, 4212, 4321, 4636
Hombres en juego 1092
Home Place 3806
Home Run 1450
Homme des vagues 592
Honey Girl 4933
Honghuli 1788
Hooway for Wodney Wat 4135, 4567
Horologiom 1305
Horrible Science: Blood, Bones and Body Bits 2002
Horrible Science: Ugly Bugs 2001
Horror at the Haunted House 4803, 5254
Hotel Hoteldebotel 489
Hotfoot 1447
How Animals Chose Their Colours 2271
How Can a Brilliant Detective Shine in the Dark 651
How Can a Frozen Detective Stay Hot on the Trail? 648
How Could You Do It Diane? 5099
How Nature Works 1994
How Smudge Came 822, 957
How Thopo became a great n'anga 1515
How to Fight a Girl 3650
How to Make an Apple Pie and See the World 3366
How to Make Pop-Ups 5043
How to Write Really Badly 1936
How Was It in Volos, Koataki? 2166
Hrestac in mišji kralj 1479
Hue Boy 1964
Hugh Glass, Mountain Man 4665, 4833
Hummingbirds: Jewels in the Sky 4908
Hunden som sprang mot en stjärna 3010
Hurricane City 3756, 4247
Hush! A Thai Lullaby 4711

I Am Mordred 3370
I Am Not Esther 1585
I Am Regina 3363
I Am the Cheese 4647
I Don't Remember Dropping the Skunk, but I Do Remember Trying to Breathe 3772
I ecogenia tou Iliou 2200
I et speil I en gate 359
I går var i dag i morgen 2540
I Hate English! 4539
I Have Lived a Thousand Years 3481, 4820
I Heard My Mother Call My Name 952
I Love Animals 1928
I Love You, Blue Kangaroo 3489
I miteroula mas i Rossia 2124, 2192
I peripetia mias karderinas 2144, 2201
I peripeties tou gatonou Niarniaouzen 2126
I pirates tis limnohoras 2199
I pokahorninu 2210
I Rode a Horse of Milk White Jade 3311
I See the Rhythum 3535
I taftotita mias iliahtidas 2188
I Was a Third Grade Science Project 3424
I Wish I'd Gone to the Moon with Neil Armstrong 125
I yaloussa 2119
I, Too, Sing America 3493
I'll See You When the Moon Is Full 3465
I'm in the Sky and I Can't Come Back 129
I'm Outta Here! Facing the Tough Choices After High School 3787
Ian and Fred's Big Green Book 2038
Ice-rink Music 2275
Ich schenk dir einen Ton aus meinem Saxofon 384
Ich und Jonna 408
Idjhil 314
Iep 541, 2367
If You Could Wear My Sneakers 740, 1565
If You Really Trust Me, Why Can't I Stay Out Later? 3773
Iira 1264
Ijsjes 525
Ik ben ik 2359
Ik maak nooit iets mee en andere avonturen 2358, 2362
Ik was de zee 2310
Ik wil die! 2327
Ikebana 1093
Ikkje gløym å klappe katten 2559, 2561, 2578
Il fantasma di Trastevere e altri racconti 1540
Iliada 2114
Ils dansent dans la tempête 858
Ilustrowane dzieje polski 1528
Im Pfirsich wohnt der Pfirsichkern 430
Imágenes 1023, 1084
In a Dark, Dark Room and Other Scary Stories 4425
In a Small, Small Pond 4454, 4696
In Daddy's Arms I Am Tall 3534
In de klauwen van de duivel 562
In de put 492
In der Nacht über die Berge 453, 3038
In die tyd van Esob 2756
In Flanders Fields: The Story of the Poem by John McCrae 749, 767
In het teken van de Ram 572
In My Family 3132, 5013
In My Father's House 5066
In the Night Kindergarten 2643
In the Rain with Baby Duck 3263
In the Time of the Drums 3537
In Two Worlds: A Yup'ik Eskimo Family 3372
Inciértico o La rica historia del Sexto Océano 1594
Incredible Jumbo 774
Indie Underground 451
Indio 4940
Inigo 11
Insect Metamorphosis: From Egg to Adult 3238
Inside the Whale and Other Animals 1925
Into the Mummy's Tomb 3721
Into the Wild 3732
Into Thin Air 3736
Inventarse un amigo 1081
Invisible Walls 2610
Ioannis Kapodistrias and His Age 2167

Ioshi i la pluja 1750
Ip bacakli uzayli çocuk 1615
Iqbal Masih and the Crusaders Against Child Slavery 3673
Ironman 3348
Irrepressible Spirit: Conversations with Human Rights Activists 3474
Is Anybody Listening? 1691
Is Anybody There? 4332, 4863
Is It Far to Zanzibar? 4594
Is It Larger? Is It Smaller? 4655
Is It True, Grandfather? 124
Is This a House for Hermit Crabs? 3927
Island on Bird Street 2608
Islands in My Garden 195
Ismaelillo 1078
Isojalkainen poika 1209
It 3217
It's a Frog's Life 187
It's a Jungle Out There 1620, 2247
It's a Spoon, Not a Shovel 5068
It's Our World, Too! Stories of Young People Who Are Making a Difference 3464
It's Time to Be Bold 3793
Izzy, Willy Nilly 3317

Jääsilmä 1257
Jack 1338
Jacob and the Stranger 4765
Jacob Two-two's First Spy Case 823
Jag Julia,Min läsebok 3015
Jag saknar dig, jag saknar dig! 2948
Jaguar 4356, 4970
Jakey 1547
Jakten på sannheten 2528, 2557
Jamela's Dress 1663, 2779, 3024
Jan, mein Freund 1331
Janey's Girl 674, 782, 848
Janjo and Shika 1554
Jannes 2345
Jardín de los Autómatas 2847
Järvihirviö 1208
Jay 1907
Jayhawker 3298
Jean Baptiste, coureur des bois 830
Jeder nach seiner art 1399, 2621
Jennifer Murdley's Toad 3347, 3555, 3743
Jenny Angel 86
Jeremiah Learns to Read 944
Jeremy Thatcher, Dragon Hatcher 3187, 3504, 3869, 4384, 5056
Jericho 4455, 4849
Jesse 307
Jetzt reicht's 1488
Jingo Django 605
Jip: His Story 4794
Jo vinc de tot arreu 1595
Joaquim, aixo no es fa! 2911
Jodie's Journey 139
Joel Tetralogie 369
John Henry 3097, 3262, 4347, 4701
John Willy and Freddy McGee 3431, 4409
Johnny Hart's Heroes 276
Jojofu 3985
Jonakin toisena päivänä 1253
Jonas, schilder of geus? 570
Jordi d'Urtx 2849
Jorsie 2683
Jose Smith and Eileen 1960
Josefine 2648
Joseph Had a Little Overcoat 4724
Josepha: A Prairie Boy's Story 682, 717
Journey of the Sparrows 3994
Juffrouw kachel 2398
Juffrouw Verdorie 566
Juan Ligero y el gallo encantado 1114
Jubeltenen 543
Juegos Infinitos 1014
Julius, the Baby of the World 3328
Jumanji 5211
Jumper Fables 3784
Jumping the Nail 5101
Junda's Fate 2281
Junie B. Jones and Her Big Fat Mouth 4393
Junie B. Jones and the Stupid Smelly Bus 3871, 5219
Junk 1805, 1865
Jurassic Park 40, 3216, 3972, 4382, 4835, 4887
Just Annoying 238, 349
Just Another Ordinary Day 3200, 4405
Just Crazy 154
Just in Case You Ever Wonder 3778
Just Like Martin 5105
Just Like New 629
Just Stupid 52, 241, 351
Just What the Doctor Ordered 3946, 4856
Jy en Toetenkat 2698
Kaarai el alcaraván. Literatura wayuu 1728
Kabalmysteriet 2534, 2571, 2611
Kærlighedens labyrint 1184
Kalinzu and the Oxpeckers 2726
Kaljander van die Karoo 2733, 2772
Kamer 13 2713
Kanaryamin öyküsü 1531
Kangaroos on Location 5187
Kannst du pfeifen, Johanna 1341
Kapote o kynigos 2132, 2194
Karel, Jarda und das wahre Leben 1353
Katie's War 3023
Katten på sjørøverøya 2548
Kattens skrekk 2541
Kdyz velci byli kluci 1765
Keeping a Christmas Secret 3450
Keeping Clean: A Very Peculiar History 2044
Keine Tiger in Afrika 3026
Keloglan 1489
Kensuke's Kingdom 1832
Keri 1478
Kerling vill hafa nokkuð fyrir snúð sinn 1617
Kesätukka ja muita juttuja Kukkulan korttelista 1263
Kevin and His Dad 4571
Key to the Kingdom 2093
Kids at Work: Lewis Hine and the Crusade Against Child Labor 3726, 3832, 3999
Kikker en het vogeltje 2324
Kikker in de kou 2330, 2401
Kikker is kikker 2414
Kikker is verliefd 2307
Killer Plants 209
Kinder im Dunkeln 445, 3036
Kinderbibel 419
Kindergedichte und Galgenlieder 1388
Kindheitshunger 3034
King of the Stable 3796
King Solomon and His Magic Ring 3105
Kirjolohikäärme 1216
Kirpun matka maailman ääriin 1221
Kiss the Dust 1811
Kivienkeli 1252
Klein verhaal over liefde 2357
Kleine Bever en de echo 2313
Klicketick 372
Klik, ik heb je 2354
Klonk, ou, Comment se

debarasser des adolescents 882
Knight's Wyrd 4310
Knights of the Kitchen Table 4172, 4961
Knjige lazu! 1525
Knocked for Six 2517
Knuffelkoe 548
Koch Eduard träumt 1410
Koirien Kalevala 1232
Koko's Story 3686
Komm mit, Moritz 1395
Komm, ich erzahl dir was vom Ferd 1416
Konfetoedenie 1762
Konig und Narr 436
Königskinder — eine wahre Liebe 1351
Korinthos 2196
Kort kjol 1714
Korvatunturi 1246
Košarkar naj bo! 2666, 2671
Koschka 1401
Kostkovaný ideály aneb breviár pro teenagery 1757
Kotten 2996
Kotuku: The Flight of the White Heron 2504
Koushi no haru 1779
Kou-Skelowh — We Are the People 1687
Kragevig-serien: Krageungen, Eddi, Tink og Alek 1185
Krindledrax 1958
Kronika wypodków mylosnych 2651
Kukel 2382
Kultamarja ja metsän salaisuudet 1225, 1245
Kun je fluiten johanna 2404
Kunst-Mal-Buch 416
Kurt — Quo vadis 2579
Kus me 481
Kuu taskussa 1265
Kvöldstund með pabba 1560
Kysset som fikk snøen til å smelte 2538

L'Arbre aux Corbeaux 1468
L'Albert i la menjabrossa 2822
L'amiga mès amiga de la formiga Piga 2932
L'attente des images 1504
L'autre vie de Noël Bouchard 1730
L'écharpe rouge 912
L'Enfant à l'étoile jaune 1274
L'enfant caché 1541
L'enfant océan 1289
L'Estret del Temps 2838
L'Hôtel du retour 1294
L'Infiniment petit 1298
L'Invention de la peinture 1303
L'Oeil du chat 1308
L'ourson qui voulait une Juliette 886
L'uomo della luna 1648
La Abuelita Fina y Sus Sombrillas Maravillosas 3234
La Bergère de chevaux 908
La Biblia contada a todas las gentes 2793
La casa de los diablos 2799
La casa pintada 2797
La Chanson de Hannah 3056
La cinquième saison 3062
La cruz de El Dorado 1632
La Dama Blanca i altres rondalles 2908
La Dama Blanca 1550
La Danse interdite 3065
La Deuxième Vie 862
La era del sueño 1516
La espada y la rosa 2800
La familia de Mic 2784
La Fille du canal 1306
La Grande Muraille des caractères 1292
La Guerre des marrons 1273
La liberté des loups 891
La Liberté? Connais pas... 737
La Ligne de trappe 887
La Lumière blanche 857
La Machine à bulles 760
La medalla 2816
La memoria dell'acqua 1649
La Noche 1053
La noia del temps 2828
La notte dei lupi 1642
La Nouvelle Maîtresse 863
La pequeña Wu-lli 2885
La petite annonce 597
La Pluma de Miguel: Una aventura en Los Andes 996
La Poudre magique 757
La princesa del retrato y el Dragon — Rey 1085
La promesse 1654
La Révolte d'Hop-Frog 1317
La rivière 1599
La Roca 2854
La rosa de Sant Jordi 2925
La route de Chlifa 714, 881
La ruse 1603
La sorcière de midi 590
La strada del guerriero 1653
La tienda de palabras 1681
La última vida de un gato y otrosa cuentos 2294
La Vallée des roses 1301
La venganza de la vaca 1723
La vida útil de Pillo Polilla 2285
La vieja que vuela 1043
La vraie historie du chien de Clara Vic 700
Laberinto 1089
Lady Muck 1894
Læse-let bøger 1167
Lägerhästarnas natt 2958
Land of Gray Wolf 5144
Landlocked 1695
Langston Hughes 3388
Langzaam, zo snel als zij maar konden 2311
Las alas de la pantera 2821
Las aventuras de Rosa se los vientos y Perico el de los palotes 1064
Las fotos de Sara 1752
Las horas largas 2804
Las lineas hablan y juegan 1098
Las sombras andan solas 1037
Läsa bok 1712
Lasiaurinko 1218
Last Leaf First Snowfall to Fall 627, 681, 815
Last of the Gold Diggers 1979
Later wil ik stuntman worden 476
Latviešu tautas teikas 1431
Lauf, Lilly, lauf! 1625
Laura Charlotte 4537
Laura's Poems 2471
Lausige Zeiten 3088
Lazniva Suzi 2667
Le chien bleu 3055
Le Chien invisible 1309
Le Collectionneur d'instants 3064
Le colosse machinal 2639
Le crocodile qui se prenait pour une fleur... 1641
Le cueilleur d'histoires 1732
Le défilé des innocents 1491
Le dernier des vampires 580
Le Domaine des Sans Yeux 906
Le fils de la sorcière et du loup 1657
Le Grimoire d'Arkandias 1276
Le jour où papa a tué sa vieille tante 1314
Le long silence 865, 1484
Le loup et la mésange 604
Le match des étoiles 868
Le monde salon Jean de... 711
Le monsieur de la rue d'a cote 3059
Le mystère de Greenwood 600
Le Parc aux sortilèges 859

Le pays du rêve 1495
Le Plus proche voisin 901
Le poète et la méchante humeur 1630
Le Procès des humains: comédie en deux actes 755
Le Rêve couleur d'orange 885
Le sixieme arret 884
Le Soleil de Diogène 1307
Le souffle de la Pierre d'Irlande 1279
Le sourire du loup 2623
Le temps s'enfuit 839
Le Train fantôme 3063
Le trouble-fête 1626
Le Voyage d'Orégon 909
Leah's Pony 3841
Leandie en die wonderklimtol 2691
Leaves for Mr. Walter 1568
Leaving Eldorado 4938
Leaving the Iron Lung 991
Leben und Leidenschaft von Pandonar dem Grausamen 3033
Leben! Leben! Leben! 3028
Legendás Váraink 1740
Legenede din tinuturi dobrogene 1644
Leikur a bordi 2221
Lejos como mi querer 998
Lelee, das Hirtenmädchen 3032
Lena vom Wolfsgraben 3083
Leo the Magnificat 3760
Leo Z 1559
Leonard 2381
Leonardo da Vinci 4482
Leon's Story 3271, 3389, 4019, 4557
Les Chocottes 2638
Les Compagnons de l'ombre 1270
Les Dents de la poule 904
Les Derniers Géants 1299
Les Etoiles cachées 1269
Les fantaisies d'Adèle 867
Les fantaisies de l'oncle Henri 699, 808
Les Grande peur sous les Etoiles 2263
Les Grands Sapins ne meurent pas 856, 907
Les històries perdudes 1748, 2832
Les joies de la princesa berber 2846
Les minuscules 594
Les mots ont des visages 1655
Les muntanyes de foc 2870
Les oubliés de Vulcain 1275
Les Quatre Fils de la terre 1296
Les Religions du monde 1313
Les secrets de Faith Green 603, 1278
Les yeux noirs 840
Lester 1667
Leteci mecki 2658
Letters from a Slave Girl 3820
Letters from Rifka 3459, 3932, 4981
Letters from the Inside 357
Letters to Henrietta 2050
Lettres d'amour 599
Lettres d'amour de 0 à 10 1312
Leyendas bajo la Cruz del Sur 1563
Library Lil 4176
Lidia e i turchi 1660
Lieblich klingt der Gartenschlauch 466
Liefdesbrieven van 0 tot 10 509
Lieve engerd, de groetjes 2329
Lieve kinderen hoor mijn lied 2396
Lieve oma pluis 2368
Liewe Heksie en die rekenaar 2774
Life of a Rotten Log 183
Lifelines Introductory Series (Booklets 1–4) 3769
Lili sin disfraz, libertad con disfraz 2825
Liliana bruja urbana 1509
Lille Pille og lille Fille i den dype skogs teater 2535
Lilly's Purple Plastic Purse 3125, 4130
Lily and Me 300
Lily and the Present 2502
Lily's Crossing 4085
Lintu ja poro 1230
Lisdalia 267
Liselotje gaat kamperen 1583
Lissi im Wunderland 385
Listen to the Dark 1965
Little Bo 3314
Little Dad 1830
Little Fireflies 2164
Little Lou 1293
Little Painter of Sabana Grande 5186
Little Sister 5079
Little Soldier 1665
Lives of the Musicians 3823, 4911
Livingstone Mouse 3354
Liza's Blue Moon 3230
Lizzie Zipmouth 1986
Lleuad yn Olau 2055
Lluvia de oro 1044
Llygedyn o Heulwen 2056
Lo único del mundo 999
Loch 3728, 4397
Locked in Time 5127
Lockie and Dadge 2245
Lockie Leonard, Human Torpedo 308, 340
Lockie Leonard, Scumbuster 218
Lon Po Po: A Red Riding Hood Story from China 3239, 4684
Long Hard Journey 3992
Longtime Waiting 2165
Look Out, Patrick 4385
Looking at the Moon 788
Looking for Alibrandi 37, 51, 65, 225, 262, 292
Looking for Jamie Bridger 3586
Los cosas del corazón 1059
Los cuatro amigos de siempre 1735
Los cuentos bobos 1065
Los cuentos de la casa del árbol 2286
Los cuentos del mago y el mago del los cuentos 1054
Los my uit, paloekas! 2751
Los pequeños prodigios 1061
Los sueños 1028, 1029, 1041
Los trapos sucios 2933
Los zapatos de murano 2895
Lost 3357
Lotte og Larsen på campingtur 1174
Lou Gehrig: The Luckiest Man 3718
Louisiana Sky 4997
Lov na zvezde 2656
Lov slov 1580
Love Flute 3095
Love Light 2256
Low Tide 1861
Lucie im Wald mit den Dingsda 464
Lucky Song 3428
Lui Lei Enzo 2406
Lullaby of the Little Perch 2276
Lumihanhi 1240
Lunar 1052
Lyle at Christmas 4574

Ma mère m'épuise 1627
Ma Nishkaf Behaloni 2254
Maaneiers 2705
Mabel Murple 639
Macker 1343
Madame Bigote-Gigote 589

Madame C. J. Walker 3379
Madame Trompette sort ce soir 582
Madisou 378
Magasin zinzin 3061
Magic Windows 4678
Magic with Everything 1884
Magica blanca 1076
Mágico Sur 2850
Mahogany the Mystery Glider 200
Mahpišani 1743
Mais que font les fées avec toutes ces dents 802
Maisa 1091
Maisy Goes to Bed 4654
Majed and His Friends 2273
Majken och skyddsängeln 2987
Majnice. Fulaste pesmi 1592
Make It Work! 4778
Make Lemonade 3440, 3828
Make or Break Spring 643
Malmok 2419
Mama and Papa Have a Store 3137
Mama, Do You Love Me? 3815
Maman! 1631
Maman, pourquoi tu m'aimes? 1650
Mambrú se fue a la guerra 1521
Mamma Mu gungar, Lillebror och Billan, Gunga lite grann 2989
Mammie! Mammie! 1426
Man kan inte säga allt 1710
Månefeen 2545
Maniac Magee 3240, 3284, 3362, 3412, 3553, 3652, 3802, 3913, 4056, 4169, 4229, 4267, 4365, 4383, 4498, 4619, 4733, 4761, 5094, 5230
Mansoor, of Hoe we Stina bijna doodkregen 504
Many Thousand Gone: African Americans from Slavery to Freedom 4848
Maphead 1863
Maraca 2288
Marama Tangiweto 2509
Marcel et André 1304
Marélie de la mer 899
Margt by í myrkrinu 2219
Maria Moll Cappero 1647
Maria Virginia está de vacaciones 1055
Marie Martin 588
Marie Pouceline of de nicht van de generaal 2333
Marieke, Marieke 1544
Mariken 542, 2379
Mario Loves Olimpia 2378
Marita Goes to School 1558
Market Day 3846
Markus og Diana 2526
Mart en de liefde 1769
Marta et la bicyclette 1719, 2647
Martha Calling 5158
Martha Graham: A Dancer's Life 3859
Martha Speaks 3339, 3416, 3757, 4341, 4624
Martin's Mountain 14
Marven of the Great North Woods 4199
Mary on Horseback: Three Mountain Stories 3483
Maska sto fengari 2195
Masques 895
Mästaren och de fyra skrivarna 2950
Mateo y los Reyes Magos 2791
Math Curse 3873, 4209, 5006
Matike, l'enfant de la rue 1480
Matilda 19, 43, 136, 144, 585, 2664, 2668, 2669, 3180, 3866, 3912, 4266, 4378, 4731, 5045, 5086
Matilda tänker bara på fotboll 2965
Matkalippu Mostariin 1261
Mattimeo 288, 1899
Maurits og den store barnålkrigen 2536
Max 1985
Max, der Unglücksrabe 410
Max en het vogeltje 2399
Max's Chocolate Chicken 5180
Maxie, Rosie, and Earl—Partners in Grime 4536
Mayfield Crossing 3744
Me harti kai kalamari 2201
Meanwhile Back at the Ranch 3143, 3648
Measuring Penny 4563
Mechanical Harry 2476
Med ilden i ryggen 1189
Mein Wienbuch 412
Meines Bruders Huter 1332
Meister Joachims Geheimnis 403
Melody for Nora 2244
Memorias de una gallina 2796
Memorias dun raposo 2921
Merlin Effect 5071
Messieurs Propres 1658
Mester, min lille hund i natten 1180
Met je rug tegen de muur 2337
Met mij gaat alles goed 507
Met weinig eerbied: een museumgids voor jongeren 526
Metis, the Octopus and the Olive Tree 264
Metro Manila 1449
Metsän poluilla: luontokirja lapsille 1244
Mev. Molle se hond 2695
Mevrouw Meijer, de merel 2418
Mi amigo Juan 1048
Mi amigo Mozart 1087
Mi bicicleta es un hada y otros secretos por el estilo 1020, 1080
Mi hermana Aixa 2806
Micí Agus An Rí 1462
Mick Harte Was Here 3159, 3558, 3662, 3746, 3963, 4285, 4447, 4738, 4766, 4879, 5235, 5262
Middelvoor 2681
Midnight Blue 1956
Midnite: The Wild Colonial Boy 33
Mig—en pige 358
Mig en pige Mig—bli'r kvinde 1173
Mighty Microbes 1995
Mijn botjes zijn bekleed met deftig vel 2314
Mijn Held 2260
Mijn oom gilbert 2415
Mijn tante is een grindewal 478, 551
Mijn tuin, mijn tuin 2370
Mijn vingers zijn niet lang genoeg 1492
Milo and the Magical Stones 3482
Min lille hund Mester 1179
Min syster är en ängel 2952
Minnie and Moo Go to the Moon 1600
Minty: A Story of Young Harriet Tubman 3476, 3531, 3842, 4131
Mipos idate ton Aorato? 2117
Mirakelman 500
Mirette on the High Wire 4694
Mirr Murr nyomoz Budapesten 1741
Mirre Marre 1402
Miss Bindergarten Gets Ready for Kindergarten 3209
Missing May 3241, 4062
Mission Impossible 918
Mississippi Bridge 3451

Mississippi Challenge 3378, 3458
Mistaken Identity 647
Mr. Bear to the Rescue 1824
Mr. Enigmatic 275
Mr. McGee and the Biting Flea 152
Mr. Plunkett's Pool 261
Mit dem Rücken zur Wand 3082
Mitt första år i riksdagen 1699
Model Boats That Really Go 2466
Moe the Dog in Tropical Paradise 4388
Moenie 'n mielie kielie nie 2676, 2735
Moenli en de moeder van de wolven 2298, 2309
Moho Wat: A Sheepeater Boy Attempts a Rescue 3917
Moja sobaka ljubit dzaz 1530
Molly Bannaky 3952, 4009
Mon affreux papa 602
Mon Chien est un éléphant 718, 820
Mond und Morgenstern. Eine Geschichte aus Afrika 1636
Monsieur Ilétaitunefois 730
Monster 4291
Monstermaan: Wat borrel in die pot? 2703
More About Anything Else 3940
More Bugs in Boxes 4535
More More More Said the Baby 4687
Morirás en Chafarinas 2926
Morning Girl 4790
Moro mu sagapo 1493
Morovers 2554
Mos më zgjoni 1572
Mossflower 286
Mote 3575
Mother Jones: One Woman's Fight for Labor 3470
Motley the Cat 1931
Motu-Iti, het meeuweneiland 2341
Mount Dragon 3734
Mountain Town 4595
Mouse in King Solomon's House 3785
Moving Mama to Town 3944
Mrs. Windyflax and the Pungapeople 1485
Mucho cuento! 1082
Mucky Pup 2013
Mufaro's Magic Blanket 2778
Muggie Maggie 3696
Muis en haar vriendjes 2407
Muis ging eens op wandel 1768
Mummies and Their Mysteries 5063
Music from a Place Called Half Moon 3443
Muslim Child 1689
Mustafa mit dem Bauchladen 427, 3085
Muu 532
My Brother Sammy 1671
My Daddy Was a Soldier 4534
My First Book of Time 2040
My Freedom Trip: A Child's Escape from North Korea 3949
My Girragundji 82
My Grandmother Maritsa 2159
My Grandmother's Stories 4975
My Kuia Is a Special Kuia 2510
My Land Sings: Stories from the Rio Grande 5016
My Life as a Fifth-Grade Comedian 4263
My Little Sister Ate One Hare 5119, 5264
My Louisiana Sky 4094
My Name Is Seepetza 954
My nic, my muzikanti 1758
My Rotten Red-Headed Older Brother 3660, 4824
My Teacher Fried My Brains 4431
My Teacher Is an Alien 4240, 4364, 4376, 4441, 4618
My Visit to the Aquarium 3706
Mystery at Lake Placid 792

Na Fogueira dos versos 2919
Nachts 1637
Nachtverhaal 2328
Nadando Contra a Morte 607
Nakusha, Femmes d'Asie opprimées 1315
Nanseli, waar ren je heen? 1770
Nasty, Stinky Sneakers 4505, 4805, 4964, 4965
Nathaniel Talking 3517
Native American Doctor: The Story of Susan LaFlesche Picotte 3377, 4903
Naughty Stories for Good Boys and Girls 346
Navratil 1311
Näytän hyvältä ilman paitaa 1259
Nejc in drobnozivke 2650
Nelli löytää kätkön 1217
Neptune's Children 1557
Nessa's Fish 4533
Neues ABC-Buch für Kinder 1420
Neun Leben 438
Neuzen in je oksel 1425
Never Spit on Your Shoes 3324
Never Take a Pig to Lunch and Other Poems About the Fun of Eating 5065
Never Trust a Dead Man 3593
New Faces: The Complete Book of Alternative Pets 207
Next Year in Jerusalem 3099
Ngoma and Click. Namibian Detective Stories 1500
Nibble, Nibble, Jerry Archer 3704
Nice Work, Little Wolf 1962
Nicht Chicago. Nicht hier 1639
Niet wiet, wel nel 2332
Nieuwsgierige Lotje 528
Night Golf 4585
Night Kites 3323
Night of the Full Moon 4847
Night Terrors 3193
Night Train 282
Nightjohn 5258
Nightmare 4956
Nightmare Mountain 3959, 4281, 4335, 5245
Nightmare Stairs 1826
Nighty-Nightmare 3687
Nigiyaka na okeiko 1781
Nijntje in de tent 2412
Nim and the War Effort 3945
Nine Spoons 4992
Ninette 2122, 2191
Ninina pesnika dva 2665
Niños del mundo 413
Nisse hos frisören 2976
No Bahamas 1423
No, David! 3667, 3761, 4307, 4721, 4928
No eres más que una pequeña hormiguita 2899
No es tan fácil saltarse un examen 2851
No Jumping on the Bed! 3649, 3751, 5134
No More Water in the Tub 4634
¡ No, no fui yo! 1724
No sé! 2861
No soy un libro 2928
No Star Nights 3926

No Such Thing 4357
No tinc paraules 1751
No todas las vacas son iguales 2900
No Turning Back: A Novel of South Africa 4093
No us podeu imaginar 2785
Noa 2560
Nobody's Son 669
Noémie: le secret de Madame Lumbago 724
Northern Lights 1804, 1864
Northern Lights: The Soccer Trails 937
Not a Nibble 77
Nothing But the Truth: A Documentary Novel 3150, 3415, 3720, 4059
Nothing Ever Happens on 90th Street 5197
Nothing to Fear 5060
Now Is Your Time! 3521, 3814
Nu trageti în … zîmbete! 1601
Nukas sommer 1702
Number the Stars 3397, 3411, 3552, 3801, 3868, 4053, 4203, 4732, 5217
Nur Ana 1747
Nurmi, der Bär 376
Nursery Tales Around the World 3100
Nyatiti: la Filla del Clan 2905
Nyfiken på naturvetenskap 2972
Nykytaide suurin piirtein 1238

O agosto que nunca esquecei 1588
O castron de ouro 2817
O conto dos sete medos 2811
O Ddawns i Ddawns 2058
O deus desaparecido 2808
O episkeptis tis nyhtas 2197
O gaiteiro e o Rato Pérez 2916
O Grande Tronante 1718
O hionanthropos pire ti mama 2142
O horos tis zois 2140
O keramidotrahalos 2190
O Loukoullos troei pygolambides 2133
O Mandolois 2125
O megalos belas 2110
O misterio dos fillos de Lúa 2820, 2931
O teatro 613
O, die stekels 557
Officer Buckle and Gloria 4128, 4432, 4629, 4706, 5216
Obuoliu pasakos 1759
Oceans, Grasslands, Wetlands and Coasts 199
Odysseus, een man van verhalen 2350
Of Love and Shadows 4828
Of Nightingales That Weep 4644
Of Things Not Seen 640
Ofrenda linca 1050
Oh, Freedom! Kids Talk About the Civil Rights Movement with the People Who Made It Happen 3672
Oh, tiempo! 1088
Okino und die Wale 1406
Old Elm Speaks: Tree Poems 3860, 4929
Old Hikoichi in Wilderness of Okhotsk 2642
Old Mother Hubbard: A Nursery Rhyme 4554
Old Turtle 3121, 3931
Olifant bly olifant 2685
Olinosters op die dak 2773
Oliver's War 637
Olivia 4599
Olympos. Diario di una dea adolescente 1465
On Board the Titanic: What It Was Like When the Great Liner Sank 750, 966
On ira à Mopti 1577
On the Devil's Court 4885
On the Far Side of the Mountain 5181
On the Shuttle: Eight Days in Space 746
Once Upon a Horse 4895
Once Upon a Place 1673
One Child 193
One Day in the Woods 5177
One Giant Leap: The Story of Neil Armstrong 4565
One Lonely Kakapo 2501
One Magic Moment 2736
One More River to Cross 3838
Oni no hashi 1789
Onion Tears 2
Oops! 1973
Ora 2687
Oro en la loma 1097
Orphan Train Rider: One Boy's True Story 3264, 4853
Os dez amigos no campo 1571
Os gritos das illas lobeiras 2824
Os Mornias 2915
Os naufragos de Malakadula 2815
Oscar y el León de Correos 2934
Ospatul lupilor 1546
Otonari wa majo 1591
Otto och Stures hemliga liv 2990
Ouma Hester met die blou hare wat so slim kan toor 2696
Our Endangered Planet: Atmosphere 4852
Our Only May Amelia 4090
Our Sixth Grade Sugar Babies 5142
Out of the Blue 778, 819
Out of the Dark 940
Out of the Darkness 1908
Out of the Dust 4082, 4795
Out of the Storm 4851
Over de werking van de kurketrekker en andere machines 2312, 2392
Over fjell over hav 2570
Owen 4697
Owl Babies 3418
Owl in Love 4313

P.S. Longer Letter Later 4555
Pagan's Scribe 281
Pagan's Vows 74
Paikea 2469
Painted Words/Spoken Memories: Marianthe's Story 4007
Pam fi, Duw, Pam Fi? 2070
Pam Fi Eto, Duw? 2082
Panna Nikt 361
Panther im Keller 3037
Papar 1619
Paper Faces 1859
Pappa! 2563
Para entonces 1058
Parallel Journeys 3471, 3671
Paratiisin lintu 1243
Parempi valita susi 1266
Paris-Hanoi 896
Parrot in the Oven: mi vida 3133, 4319, 4676
Parts 3513, 5159
Pas pismonoša 1578
Passage to Freedom: The Sugihara Story 4559, 5072
Pathki Nana: Kootenai Girl Solves a Mystery 3914
Paul Revere's Ride 3452
Paul Robertson 3378
Paul the Rascally Cake 1818
Paw Paw Chuck's Big Ideas in the Bible 3786
Paw Thing 321
Pecos Bill: A Tall Tale 4167

Pedro y su teatrino maravilloso 1005
People Might Hear You 95
Peppe the Lamplighter 4698
Peppino 2316
Perigo vexetal 2918
Personal 2147
Personlig tog jeg ikke skade af at vokse op 1438
Pet Sematary 3214
Pete's a Pizza 3432
Petey 4947
Petit Poil veut grandir 581
Petit zizi 1605
Petra kilisameni 2138
Phoenix Rising 3163, 3421, 4878
Phyllisia 3025
Pichenettes 1310
Pick-Up Sticks 706
Picture Book Magic 2477
Pien 728
Piepheini 1486
Pigen der krøb 1708
Pigen der var go' til mange ting 1186
Piggie Pie! 3176, 3198, 3509, 4129, 4742
Piggies 4904
Piggins 3409
Pigs and Honey 55, 120
Pigs Aplenty, Pigs Galore! 4122
Pikku sammakkoprinssi 1255
Pilgrim's Progress 1794
Pin Kaiser und Fip Hauar 1414
Pindorama terra das palmeiras 617
Pink and Say 3983, 4016, 4208
Pioneer Girl: Growing Up on the Prairie 4857
Pirate Pandemonium 2014
Piselli e farfalline … son piú belli i maschi o le bambine? 1651
Pit Pony 635
Plague 99 1898
Plague Year 4387, 5093
Platero y yo 1071
Playing Beatie Bow 101
Pleine crise 880
Plek van dolfyne 2747
Pobre corintiano careca 1442
Pode me beijar se quiser 1556
Pode 2568
Podposteljni škrat 1764
Poemas, tantanes y adivinanzas dificilísimas 1031
Poems for Children 2163
Poil de serpent, dent d'araignée 726, 831
Poison Ivy and Eyebrow Wigs 4252
Pojken som sov med snö i sin säng 2992
Polar, the Titanic Bear 44, 963
Pongwiffy 487
Ponolani 1056
Pontaro, den 1774
Pönttölän väki 1254
Poppa's New Pans 4546
Poppy 3265, 4175, 4255
Por los aires 2855
Por si las moscas 1107
Possum Come A-Knockin' 4532
Possum Magic 103, 177
Postcards from No Man's Land 1808
Potetboka 2546
Pourquoi les Vaches ont des taches? 854
Power and Glory 126
Pozor 1419
Praise and Worship 3788
Preacher's Boy 4021, 4578
Prikazki ot drevna Trakija 1737
Prikljucenija sdobnoj Lizy: Povest'-skazka 1429
Primeri detektiva Karla Loota 1543
Princes in Exile 355
Princesma 266
Princess Ashley 4375, 4830
Princess Ka'iulani: Hope of a Nation, Heart of a People 3393
Princesse Finemouche 583
Prins van de leegte 516, 573
Prinsessan siivet 1725
Printzesa Puzkertia 2834
Prišel je lev 2652
Prize in the Snow 3467, 4196, 4653
¡Prohibido Casar Papá! 1551
Project Kite 1838
Prophecy Rock 3585
Protecting Marie 3600
Prudence, la princesse téméraire 890
Psssst … It's Me the Bogeyman 3515
Pues señor, este era una circo 1095
Pumpkin Soup 1881
Punia and the King of Sharks: A Hawaiian Folktale 5024
Puntje puntje puntje 527
Pupos pasaka 1527
Pure Excitement 3790
Puss in Boots 4531, 4686
Put a Saddle on the Pig 2233
Putting on an Act 5126

Qu'est-ce que vous faites là? 860
Que farem, que direm? 2839
Què hi ha per a sopar? 1513
Que marinéro soy yo 1077
Quem faz o quê? 1722
Querido diario 1033, 1045
Qui vol un conte? 2906
Quién quiere a los viejos? 1517
Quin parell! 2878
Quin patarrabum! 2874
Quina nit de reis 2882
Quinze millions pour un fantôme 595
Quirky Tails 328

Raad een hoeveel ik van je hou 2351
Raben-Baby 431
Radical Take-Offs 313
Rainbow Bay 685
Raising Dragons 3484, 3987
Rakas Mikael 1258
Raketter 2581
Ramadan 3387
Ran Van: Magic Nation 798
Randall's Wall 4249
RanVan the Defender 816
Rapunzel 4716
Rascal 584
Ratona y Elefante 2794
Rats on the Roof and Other Stories 4541
Rått parti 2551
Rattlesnake Dance 4945
Raul, se abuela y los espiritus 1101
Raven 4699
Rebel 2700, 2753
Rebelle le loup 3058
Red Dirt Jessie 4466
Red Hugh 316
Red Leaf, Yellow Leaf 3596
Red Scarf Girl: A Memoir of the Cultural Revolution 4101, 4556
Red-Eyed Tree Frog 3274
Redwall 284, 287
Redwork 654, 701
Reënboogrant-studente: Eerstejaar blues 2701
Reg, kommandant 2763
Reise im August 3084
Reliable Friendly Girls 2478
Relic 3731
Remant cap al sol 2871
Rembrandt doe-boek voor kinderen 2390

Rennschwein Rudi Russel 1328
Resan till världens ände 2954
Rescue Josh McGuire 3337, 3664, 3916, 3929, 4342, 4934
Restless Spirit: The Life and Work of Dorothea Lange 3858
Rhian's Song 2080
Rice Without Rain 4530
Riding Freedom 3169, 3358, 4930
Riptide!... 4336
Risinn þjofotti og skyrfjallid 2218
River Boy 1806
Robin en god 2344, 2371
Robodad 4841
Rok smoka 2609
Romani chib ubeca 1589
Röndottir spoar 2214
Rooie 2321
Roosje kreeg een ballon 2305
Rosa Parks: My Story 4845
Rosalie s'en va-t-en guerre 804
Rosa's Famous Elbow 312
Rose Meets Mr. Wintergarden 63, 91
Rosebud and Red Flannel 4193
Roses Are Pink, Your Feet Really Stink 3172, 4434
Roses Sing on New Snow: A Delicious Tale 934
Rosie & the Yellow Ribbon 3460
Rosie Swanson 4542
Rot, blau und ein bißchen 439
Rotten Teeth 3425
Round the Twist 94, 251, 326
Rowan of Rin 67, 175, 334
Rozdestvo 1590
Rudi Renvarken 493
Rugby and Rosie 4353
Rules of the Road 3857
Rumpelstiltskin's Daughter 4872
Running Out of Time 3164, 3197, 4818
Rut och Knut ställer ut; Rut och Knut börjar träna 2984
Ryan White: My Own Story 3971
Rycari Kruglogo Stola 1481

's nachts op het dak 2353
S'ha de ser animal! 2813
Sabers udsendinge I & II 1166
Sadako 5059
Safari Beneath the Sea 4480
Safari ins Reich der Sterne 1337
Safran 1471
Sailor och Pekka 2994
Sakun lintukesä 1220
Salaisuuksia 1251
Salamandastron 298, 1902
Salamanderryttaren 2531, 2580
Sam and the Tigers 5190
Sam Plants a Sunflower 3764
Samfuni-i hammam 1532
Samira des quatres-routes 1272
Samlede Rim 1169
Sammy Keyes and the Hotel Thief 3592
Samotne wyspy i storczyk 1487
Sanctuary 2448
Sand Swimmers: The Secret Life of Australia's Dead Heart 201
Sanning eller konsekvens 2953, 2960
Santa Calls 3827
Santa Paws 4260
Santuary 2479
Saratoga Secret 5196
Sasscat to Win 2445
Saturnalia 3241
Sauve qui peut l'amour 853
Sauvetages 879
Sauvez ce fantôme 591
Saving Shiloh 3403, 3514, 3920, 3965, 4236, 5268
Saving Sweetness 3843
Say Cheese and Die 3285
Say Goodnight, Gracie 5088, 5130
Sbectol Inc 2072
Scared Silly: A Halloween Treat 3651
Scared Stiff 3333
Scary Stories 3: More Tales to Chill Your Bones 3282, 3501
Schaft gut, liebe Trere 1411
Schapenvellen en ganzenveren 521
School's Out 3700
Schräge Typen 3077
Science Play! 4784
Science with Weather 1997
Scooter 3259
Scooterboy 319
Scratch 2840
Se huset 2971
Se jubilan las hadas? 1035, 1062
Sea of Peril 1906
Seal Island School 4201
Secret City, USA 3437
Secretos de palacio 1049
Secrets 2028
Sector 7 3604, 4727
See Ya, Simon 1934
Seedfolks 3293, 3851
Seisho Monogatari 2634
Sekino seoce 1433
Selby Snowbound 242
Selby Spacedog 233
Selby Speaks 236, 285
Selby, Supersnoop 299
Selina and the Bear Paw Quilt 683
Seráse una vez 1549
Seven Blind Mice 3252, 4692
Seven Brave Women 4005
Seven Silly Eaters 4924
Seventh-Grade Weirdo 4963
Sex Education 4494
Shabanu Daughter of the Wind 4052
Shades of Gray 4011, 4787
Shades of Green 2025
Shadow Boy 3438
Shadow Catcher: The Life and Work of Edward S. Curtis 3833
Shadow of the Dragon 3340
Shadows 1909, 4396
Shadows and Reflections 3242, 4519
Shadows on the Wall 2470
Shalom, Haver: Goodbye, Friend 4989
Shape Up: Fun with Triangles 4561
Shape-Changer 4399, 4445
Share the Sky 1682
Sharon, Keep Your Hair On 243
Shiloh! 3151, 3286, 3399, 3554, 3655, 3803, 3870, 3915, 4058, 4170, 4205, 4230, 4268, 4363, 4386, 4442, 4499, 4621, 4666, 4734, 4802, 5003, 5231, 5251
Shiloh Season 3511, 3666, 3964, 4354, 4435, 4633, 5156
Shipwreck at the Bottom of the World: The Extraordinary True Story of Schackleton and the Endurance 4484
Shipwreck Season 3486
Shirley Chisholm 3375
Shiva's Fire 4597
Shizuko's Daughter 3598
Sho and the Demons of the Deep 722, 965
Sho et les dragons d'eau 722
Shortcut 4549

Show Me the Evidence 3574
Showtime! 318
Shrek 2395, 4528
Shylocks Tochter 368
Si les persones parlessin... 2903
Sierra 4042
Sikkas Fortælling 1187
Silfurkrossinn 2206
Silver 3968
Silverwing 661, 828, 930, 969
Silvia y la Máquina Qué 2812
Silvija 2670
Simone et la ville de carton 708
Sing noch einmal, mein Bruder 435
Sing to the Sun 4194
Siniala me kathreftes 2143
Sink or Swim 1675
Sink the Gizmo 172
Sins of the Father 650
Sir Walter Ralegh and the Quest for El Dorado 3276
¡ Sireno, Sireno! 2920
Sisters ... No Way! 2240
Sitti's Secrets 4000
Sitting Ducks 3312
Siwiti: A Whale's Story 953
Six Dinner Sid 1957
Skellig 1807, 2106
Skilpad en duif 2678
Skilpoppe 2738, 2761
Skjulte ærend 2525
Slam! 3532, 4892
Slate Mountain 1852
Sleep Tight, Mrs. Ming 712
Sleeping Dogs 280
Slinger-slinger 2758
Slot Machine 3730
Smaartie is skeel 2692
Small Steps: The Year I Got Polio 3559, 4235
Smarty Pants 799
Smoky Mountain Rose 4134
Smoky Night 3305, 4702, 4915
Snapshots from the Wedding 4677
Snater 2679
Sniper 3326, 4245, 5053
Snot Stew 4864, 5001
Snotty Bumstead 290
Snow 3430, 3856, 4722
Snow White and the Seven Aliens 1984
Snowflake Bentley 4200, 4719
Snowshoe Thompson 4907
Snow-White 2092
So eine lange Nase 3075
So Far from the Sea 3683
So Lonely 1352
So Much 1891, 1968
So Much to Tell You 104, 3449
Soap! Soap! Don't Forget the Soap! 3195, 4344, 4823, 5169
Sofies Welt 1342
Soft Child: How Rattle Snake Got Its Fangs 3157
Sojourner Truth: Ain't I a Woman? 3254
Sok of sprei 2380
Sol sin prisa 1115
Sola er en feit gud 2567
Sola—vår egen stjerne 2550
Soldier's Heart 4020
Solnce na patolkie 2613
Solo 1821
Sombres citrouilles 1290
Some of the Kinder Planets 657, 713, 3261
Somebody Loves You, Mr. Hatch 3453
Someone Is Hiding on Alcatraz Island 4829
Someone Like Me 80
Someone Was Watching 4668, 5070
Something Big Has Been Here 4118
Something from Nothing 935, 4980
Something Upstairs 3329, 4760, 4955
Somewhere in the Darkness 4064
Sommeren er ikke forbi 1165
Somnies, estimada? 2865
Song of the Buffalo 3227
Song Quest 1797
Songman 7
Songs and Wings 2149
Songs from Shakespeare 2094
Songs from the Loom: A Navajo Girl Learns to Weave 3384
Sopa de nit 2910
Sophie lance et compte 851
Sorani 1519
Sorrow's Kitchen: The Life and Folklore of Zora Neal Hurston 3374
SOS Titanic 4509, 5075
Sothach a Sglyfath 2067
Soul Looks Back in Wonder 3525
Space Demons 322
Space Station Science: Life in Free Fall 3864
Sparrow Hawk Red 3345
Sparrows in the Scullery 3590
Spasonosna odluka 1755
Speak 3863
Speed of Light 4994
Spelar död 2955, 3019
Spiders Spin Webs 191
Spinnekopsomer 2752
Spinners 1756
Spirit Seeker 5123
Spite Fences 3936
Splash, Splash 4304
SPLAT! 352
Splinters 567
Spooner of Later 335
Spotlight on Spiders 189
Spying on Miss Muller 4631
Stålborgen 1597
Star of Fear, Star of Hope 4986
Starbright and the Dream Eater 2486
Stargazers 4777
Starker Sohn und Schwester 3029
Starry Messenger 4712
STARS 967
Starting Home: The Story of Horace Pippin, Painter 3381
Stavnica 2660
Staying Fat for Sarah Byrnes 3344
Steal Away 3817
Stefano 1561
Stella etoile de la mer 841
Stella Louella's Runaway Book 3178
Stella Star of the Sea 948
Stellaluna 3122, 3341, 4912
Stephanie's Ponytail 3165
Stephen Biesty's Incredible Cross Sections 5055
Stephen Fair 662
Stephen's Feast 3454
Stepping on the Cracks 3185, 4339, 4789, 4875
Sterling 2699
Steweltjies na Wonderland 2714
Stiefland 2302
Stillemann—historien om et drap 2573
Stippe stappe stories 2704
Stone Cold 1802
Stone Water 4470
Stones in Water 3850, 4993
Stonewords 3243, 3336, 3576, 4538
Stony Heart Country 1672
Stop 2403
Stop Pretending 3494
Stopping for Death 2030
Stor og stærk 1178

Storebrorsan 2991
Stori Branwen 2079
Storia di Francesco il santo che sepava ridere 1621
Stories Jesus Told 3782
Stories of Little Rednose 2277
Stories South of the Sun 2743
Stories vir jong ore 2715
Stormy Night 687
Story Painter: The Life of Jacob Lawrence 3390
Stranded 4256
Stranded at Plimoth Plantation 1626 3935
Strandia 667
Strange Objects 3, 59, 271
Strange Orbit 1837
Strat and Chatto 1923
Strider 5249
Strikjes in de struiken 530
Strongbow 2235, 2251
Stroomversnelling 499
Suddenly! 5116
Sueño Aymará 995, 1441
Sueños y cuentos de la niña mala 1060
Sugemerket 2575
Sukey and the Mermaid 4822, 4867
Suma Went Walking 1510
Summer of Shadows 2513
Summer of the Mad Monk 658
Summer on Wheels 4046
Sun & Spoon 3602
Sun Dogs 992
Sunwing 663, 739, 838, 949
Suomen Lasten runotar 1236
Superfudge 21
Susan Laughs 1940
Susannah 4858
Suvi Kinos ja elämän eväät 1701
Suvi Kinos ja elämän kevät 1210
Svet zvírat 1610
Svorni gambusini a jine pribehy 1734
Swamp Angel 4628, 4703
Swashbuckler 75
Sweet Clara and the Freedom Quilt 3933
Sweet Clarinet 1939
Sworn Enemies 4983
Symphony of Whales 3490

T'he agafat caputxeta 2891
Ta asteria pou zilevan 2130
Ta dakrya tis Persephonis 2123
Ta fotismena parathyra digounte istories 2137, 2198
Ta Hristougenna tou tembeli 2139
Tacky the Penguin 3322, 3496, 4330
Tahdon 1226, 1700
Taily Po 5143
Taivaansavut-sarja 1248
Takes: Stories for Young Adults 672
Taking Hold: My Journey Into Blindness 3466
Tales from Gold Mountain 773, 951
Tales from Old Ireland 4593
Talking Eggs 5096
Talking with Artists 3253
Tamara 2712
Tangerine 3735, 4262, 4289, 4404
Tankenes reise 2539
Tanssi neljällä jalalla 1215
Tante Nans zat op een gans 529
Tanz in die Hölle 422
Tar Beach 3522, 3642, 4690
Tarot Says Beware 4401
Ta-Ta Tryweryn 2084
Tatari, la pandilla y yo 1051
Tatuaje Giratorio 1015, 1016
Taube Klara 1334
Taur 2487
Taxi! Taxi! 3643
Te Wao Nui A Tane 2496
Teacher's Pet 3689, 4951
Tears of a Tiger 5111, 5157
Teddie se geheim 2710
Tell Me a Story Mama 3641
Tell Me No Lies 1664
Tell Them We Remember: The Story of the Holocaust 3420
Ten Kids, No Pets 4493, 5097, 5242
Ten Little Dinosaurs 3510
Ten Little Rabbits 3930
Ten Minutes Till Bedtime 4745
Ten Small Tales 765
Tenk om...! 2542
Tereseta la bruixeta 2873
Terror at the Zoo 3961, 4171, 4502
Tesseris gigantes ki enas pemptos 2129
Teunis 2369
Teus Langneus 2393
Thank You, Mr. Falker 4558, 4769
Thanks to My Mother 4301
The 13th Floor: A Ghost Story 3199, 3355, 3403, 4547
The Abracadabra Kid: A Writer's Life 4921
The Absolutely True Story ... How I Visited Yellowstone Park with the Terrible Rubes 3584
The Adventures in Odyssey Bible 3783
The Adventures of Captain Underpants 3512, 3717, 4638, 4672, 4768
The Adventures of Sparrowboy 3266
The Adventures of Taxi Dog 4526
The All-Nite Cafe 2027
The Alphabet Parade 4540
The Always Prayer Shawl 4985
The Amazing Voyage of the Cucumber Sandwich 1993
The Apprentice 4296
The Araboolies of Liberty Street 3184
The Astonishing Armadillo 3228
The Baboon King 4302, 4577
The Baby Wouldn't Go to Bed 1879
The Ballad of Lucy Whipple 3682, 4047
The Bamboo Flute 64
The Bantam and the Soldier 2480
The Battle of Pook Island 2475
The Beautiful Lion 1974
The Beautiful Years 2155
The Beginner's Devotional 3775
The Best School Year Ever 3402, 3507, 3659, 3747, 3962, 4174, 4348, 4368, 4632, 4669, 4737, 4869, 5150
The BFG 23, 24, 141
The Big Book for Peace 3993
The Big Bug Book 3707
The Big Pets 2622
The Biggest Klutz in the Fifth Grade 4443
The Birchbark House 4580
The Blue Chamel 270
The Blue Horse 2234
The Blues of Flats Brown 4598
The Blunder of the Rogues 4564
The Body in the Basement 649
The Boggart 3556, 4099
The Bomb 4793, 4918
The Bone Talker 1698
The Borning Room 3813

The Boy in the Bubble 1813, 1903
The Boy Who Became a Frog 1775
The Boy Who Counted to a Million 1456, 2744
The Boy Who Lost His Belly-button 1952
The Boy Who Owned the School 4525
The Boy's War 3807
The Boys from St. Petri 4297
The Boys Start the War 4248, 4391, 4428, 4503, 4868
The Brooklyn Bridge 3943
The Bugalugs Bum Thief 344
The Buried City of Pompeii: What It Was Like When Vesuvius Exploded 751
The Burning Questions of Bingo Brown 3690
The Burnt Stick 15
The Butterfly Jar 4117
The Cabbage Patch Fib 97
The Candle Man 2068
The Car with Three Wheels 1455
The Case of the Mummified Pigs and Other Mysteries of Nature 3938
The Chanukkah Guest 4976
The Cheese Trap 2505
The Children's Daily Devotional Bible 3789
The China Coin 257
The China Garden 5120
The Choctaw Code 4468
The Christmas Alphabet 3834
The Christmas Miracle of Jonathan Toomey 1878, 2238, 3367, 3472
The Christmas of the Reddle Moon 4126
The Circuit 3134, 3269, 4048
The Clay Ladies 771, 1680
The Clearing 3587
The Client 3218
The Complete Entertainments 1947
The Cow Who Wouldn't Come Down 4125
The Cradle Will Fall 3213
The Creation 3528
The Crown of Dalemark 4313
The Crowstarver 1938
The Crystal Ball 3463
The Crystal Drop 916
The Cuckoo's Child 3444
The Damselfly 2467
The Dark and Deadly Pool 5239
The Dark Garden 795
The Dark Side of Nowhere 4925
The Dark-Thirty: Southern Tales of the Supernatural 3524, 4063
The Day Gogo Went to Vote 4583
The Day the Rabbi Disappeared: Jewish Holiday Tales of Magic 3106
The Dead Man in Indian Creek 4279, 4874, 5051, 5098, 5247
The Delmonico Two o Five 2732
The Devil's Arithmetic 4284
The Devil's Own 309
The Diamond Tree: Jewish Tales from Around the World 4979
The Dog That Dug 2011
The Dog Who Had Kittens 3500, 4381, 5167, 5250
The Do-It-Yourself House That Jack Built 4550
The Doll in the Garden: A Ghost Story 3742, 4228, 4239, 4664, 4800, 5092, 5229
The Doom Stone 4406, 5263
The Dorling Kindersley Guide to Space 1791
The Dragon New Year: A Chinese Legend 633
The Dragon's Pearl 626
The Dragon's Robe 4901
The Dream Carvers 693, 821
The Dream of Aengus 766
The Dust Bowl 768
The Dwellers Beneath 1476
The Ear, the Eye, and the Arm 3829, 4089, 5114
The Education of Little Tree 3119
The Electric Kid 1904
The Eleventh Hour 102, 135
The Emperor's Egg 2053
The Enchanted Wood 3980
The Exiles 1860
The Exiles at Home 1969
The Fabulous Fifty 3296
The Fabulous Song 825
The Face at the Window 3135
The Face on the Milk Carton 3219, 3970, 4497, 5145, 5248
The Faithful Friend 3309, 4709
The Falcon's Quest 1853
The Falcon's Wing 4453
The Famous Flying Fandinis 3942
The Farolitos of Christmas 5011
The Fat and Juicy Place 260
The Fat Man 2446
The Field (I Spy Wildlife) 2472
The Finders 1814
The Firework-Maker's Daughter 1975
The First Fleet: A New Beginning in an Old Land 208
The Fisherman and the Theefyspray 185
The Folk Keeper 3275, 4317
The Fortune Tellers 3255, 3821
The Friends 3267, 4299
The Frog Who Dreamed She Was an Opera Singer 2032
The Gardener 3478, 4715
The Gathering 68, 90
The Ghost Inside the Monitor 3398
The Ghost of Fossil Glen 5009
The Ghosts of Mercy Manor 4243, 4804, 5058, 5148
The Ghosts of the Plain 2152
The Gift of the Sun 2727
The Gigantic Turnip and Tales of Wisdom and Wonder 1932
The Girl Who Can and Other Stories 1785
The Girl Who Wanted to Hunt 5022
The Giver 3155, 3188, 3290, 3723, 3872, 4068, 4173, 4207, 4340, 4390, 4504, 4623, 4736, 4816, 5106, 5213, 5234
The Gizmo 105, 142, 250, 254, 336
The Gold Coin 3457
The Golden Bird 1935
The Grand Escape 4343, 4444
The Graphic Alphabet 4713
The Great American Goldrush 4040
The Great Elephant Chase 1963, 2100
The Great Fire 4017, 4073, 4481
The Great Kapok Tree: A Tale of the Amazon Rain Forest 3410
The Great Little Madison 3244, 4475
The Great Poochini 736

The Great Pumpkin Switch 3364
The Great Race 929
The Great White Man-Eating Shark 5091, 5166
The Gruffalo 1688, 1795, 1982
The Guns of Easter 2239, 2246
The Hallo-Weiner 5220
The Hare and Tortoise 1950
The Harlem Renaissance 3386
The Hat 3126, 3177
The Haunted Mask II 3289
The Haunting of Cabin 13 4238
The Haymeadow 4936
The Heart Is Big Enough 4458
The Hero of Bremen 4124
The Heroine of the Titanic 4844
The Hidden Forest 178
The Hidden House 2089
The Highwayman 5179
The Hired Hand 3102, 3310
The Hobbit 42
The Hollow Tree 733
The Hope Bakery 988
The Hosanna Bible 3779
The Hot Zone 3729
The Houdini Box 4762, 5002
The House Guest 4, 60
The House of Wooden Santas 642, 829
The House That Jack Built 2492, 2494
The Hundred-Mile-An-Hour Dog 1822
The Hunt 73
The Hunter 4591
The Hunter's Moon 936
The Illustrated Mum 1868
The Imp That Ate My Homework 3749
The Incomplete Book of Australian Mammals 194
The Inuksuk Book 1684
The Invisible Ladder: An Anthology of Contemporary American Poems for Young Readers 3492
The Iron Ring 1522
The Island of Ghosts 2229
The It-Doesn't-Matter Suit 1946
The Ivy Crown 1855
The Jolly Christmas Postman 1874
The Jolly Postman 3144
The Jubilee Family Illustrated Bible 3792
The Junkyard Dog 3350, 5122
The Keeper of the Isis Light 4650
The Kidderminster Kingdom Series — King Leonard's Celebration 3770
The Killer's Cousin 3591
The Killick: A Newfoundland Story 941
The Killing Freeze 5138
The King's Magic Drum 2776
The King's Shadow 3939, 4456
The Kingdom by the Sea 1858
The Kingdom of Kevin Malone 4311
The Kingfisher Book of Oceans 2003
The Know, Sow and Grow Kids' Book of Plants 2482
The Lady with the Alligator Purse 4114
The Lady with the Hat 4298
The Language of Doves 4920
The Last Innocent Summer 3225
The Last Noo-Noo 1971
The Last Polar Bears 362
The Last Princess: The Story of Princess Ka'Iolani of Hawai'i 3376
The Last Quest of Gilgamesh 720
The Last Safe House: A Story of the Underground Railroad 752
The Leaving 666
The Ledgerbook of Thomas Blue Eagle 3468, 3937
The Library Dragon 3661
The Life and Death of Crazy Horse 4943
The Life-Size Guide to Native Trees and Other Common Plants of New Zealand's Native Forest 2473
The Life-Sized Inflatable Whale 2490
The Lights Go on Again 692, 777
The Lion King 36, 107
The Lion Who Wanted to Love 1827
The Little Boat 1892
The Little Match Girl 4568
The Little Red Hen (Makes a Pizza) 3862
The Log Cabin Quilt 3473
The Long March 4560
The Long Road to Gettysburg 3822
The Loyal Cat 3839
The Maestro 671, 719, 759
The Magic Drum 1506
The Magic School Bus at the Waterworks 3408, 4328, 5132
The Magic School Bus Inside a Beehive 3715
The Magic School Bus Inside a Hurricane 3711
The Magic School Bus Inside the Earth 5081
The Magic School Bus: Inside the Human Body 3693
The Magic School Bus: Lost in the Solar System 3697
The Magic School Bus on the Ocean Floor 3703
The Magnificent Nose and Other Marvels 61, 122
The Man 1889
The Man from the Other Side 4295
The Man Who Loved Clowns 4231, 5232
The Man Who Tricked a Ghost 4430
The Man-eater 1754
The March on Washington 3380
The Mats 1587
The McIntyre Liar 917
The Mealie-cob Doll 1678
The Memory Prisoner 1854
The Mennyms 367, 1862
The Mermaid's Twin Sister 3130
The Middle Passage: White Ships Black Cargo 350
The Midnight Gang 45, 235
The Midnight Horse 4524
The Midwife's Apprentice 4075, 4507
The Million Dollar Shot 4448, 4808, 5161
The Monster Who Ate Australia 323
The Moorchild 3844, 4077
The Most Amazing Pop-Up Science Book 1999
The Mouse of Amherst 4461
The Mouse Rap 4523
The Music of the Dolphins 3845
The Mysterious Visitor: Stories of the Prophet Elijah 4991
The Mystery of the Missing Will 789
The Name of the Game Was Murder 3160, 3196, 3581, 4392

The Name of the Tree 677, 805
The Natural History of Make-Believe 1872
The Natural World of New Zealand 2488
The New Oxford School Atlas 2035
The Night Flyers 3594
The Night Is for Hunting 117, 305
The Nightingale 763
The Nose from Jupiter 833, 836
The Old Brown Suitcase: A Teenager's Story of War and Peace 956
The One-Minute Bible for Kids 3780
The Only Alien on the Planet 3352
The Origin of Life on Earth 3523
The Original Freddie Ackerman 4846
The Ornament Tree 4018
The Orphan Boy 624, 678, 702
The Other Side 1453
The Other Side of Dark 3318, 5047
The Outsiders 22
The Owl Tree 1978
The Oxford Children's A to Z of the Human Body 1477
The Pagemaster 35
The Paper Dragon 3848, 3849
The Paperboy 4714
The Parable Series 3791
The Party 631, 729
The Peddler's Gift 4995
The Perilous Journey of the Donner Party 4050
The Polar Bear Son 4261
The Polar Express 3280
The Power of One 227, 296
The Prince of Tarn 921
The Private Notebook of Katie Roberts, Age 11 4446
The Promise 2009
The Quicksand Pony 302
The Quiltmaker's Gift 3236
The Rabbits 83
The Race 127
The Rag Coat 3417
The Rainbabies 2262
The Rainbow Fish 3123, 3461, 4429
The Rainbow Serpent 256
The Raincatchers 3816
The Real Elephant 2272
The Rebellion: A Novel of Upper Canada 694
The Red Dress 2777
The Red King 222
The Red Racer 5121
The Rhyme Bible for Toddlers 3797
The Ring of Words 1951
The Rink 987
The River 3657
The River That Comes from the North 2158
The Road to Memphis 3520
The Robber and Me 4300
The Rooster's Gift 723
The Rough Face Girl 3755, 4337, 5102
The Runaway Settlers 2451
The Saturday Kid 4589
The Scarlet Pimpernel 1948
The School We Made 1454
The Seashell Song 1926
The Seasons Are Horses 989
The Sea-thing Child 1953
The Secret Diary of Adrian Mole, aged 13¾ 20
The Secret Funeral of Slim Jim the Snake 3401
The Secret Life of Amanda K. Woods 4562
The Secret of the Indian 3867
The Secret of the Ruby Ring 2230
The Secret Shortcut 4400, 5172
The Seven Chinese Brothers 4426
The Shadow Children 4984, 5189
The Shadow Club 5133
The Shadow of the Minotaur 1793
The Sign of the Scales 690
The Sign of the Seahorse 332
The Signmaker's Assistant 3653
The Silver Balloon 3480
The Silver Kiss 3182, 3330, 4813, 4886
The Silver Swan 4592
The Sky Is Falling 653, 689, 803
The Slayer of Shadows 2745
The Snake Scientist 3953
The Song of the Blackbird 2160
The Squeaky Wheel 4522
The Star Fisher 3455
The Star That Was Afraid of the Dark 2154
The Sterkarm Handshake 1867
The Stinky Cheese Man and Other Fairly Stupid Tales 3287, 3503, 3656, 3758, 4206, 4427, 4622, 4691, 4763, 5004, 5215
The Stolen 2516
The Stone Book 4646
The Story of Canada 745, 758, 764, 811
The Story of Creation 1961
The Story of Little Quack 807
The Story of Rosy Dock 188
The Story of Ruby Bridges 4870
The Stranger 4115
The Suitcase Kid 1812
The Summer I Shrank My Grandmother 4283, 4959
The Summer My Father Was Ten 3485
The Summer of Lily and Esme 2232
The Sweetest Fig 4626, 4764
The Taking of Room 114 4512
The Tale of Rabbit and Coyote 4914
The Tale of the Mandarin Ducks 3250
The Talking Eggs: A Folktale from the American South 3497, 3754, 4333, 4681
The Talking Walking Stick 1677
The Thief 4078
The Third Day, the Frost 111, 114, 301
The Third Planet: Exploring the Earth from Space 4779
The Three Little Javelinas 3152
The Three Little Pigs 3173, 5015
The Three Little Wolves and the Big Bad Pig 3153, 4625, 5149
The Tie Man's Miracle 5193
The Tiggie Tompson Show 2495
The Tiny Kite of Eddie Wing 659
The Toll Bridge Troll 3161, 4349
The Top of the World: Climbing Mount Everest 3273
The Topsy-Turvy Storybook 297
The Toy Horse 1567
The Trail North 3226
The Treasure Tree 3777
The Tree in the Field of Mathingamy Thame 3923

The Tree 2036
The Trolley 2503
The True Colors of Caitlynne Jackson 4352, 4881
The True Confessions of Charlotte Doyle 3249, 3808, 4057, 4097, 4270, 4958, 5054
The True Story of Spit MacPhee 277
The True Story of the Three Little Pigs by A. Wolf 3181
The Tuesday Cafe 920
The Tulip Touch 2104
The Twelve Days of Christmas 2724
The Twin in the Tavern 3582
The Twins: The Pirates and the Battle of New Orleans 4855
The Two Bullies 81
The Ugly Duckling 1659, 2270, 4725
The Ultimate Dinosaur Book 1996
The Uninvited Guest 4982
The Usborne Complete Book of the Microscope 2004
The Very Best of Friends 56
The Very First Christmas 3795
The Very Quiet Cricket 3148, 3283, 5140
The Video Shop Sparrow 1666
The View from Saturday 4080
The Viewer 130
The Volcano Disaster 4971
The Wall 4899
The War with Grandpa 3319
The Watertower 34, 70
The Watsons Go to Birmingham 3351, 3442, 3835, 4074, 4177
The Waves of the Aegean Sea 2157
The Way Home 1877
The Way Things Work 3407, 4774
The Web 2465
The Wednesday Surprise 4898
The Weirdo 3577
The Well: David's Story 4001
The Wheels on the Bus 4521
The Whipping Boy 4361
The Whitby Witches 1900
The White Guinea Pig 6, 274
The Wild Colorado 4949
The Wind Singer 1987
The Winter Room 4054
The Witches 28, 137
The Wood Wife 4314
The World of Shakespeare 2046
The World of Weather 2000
The Worst Band in the Universe 1676
The Wreck of the Zanzibar 1819, 2103
The Wreckers 697
The Wright Brothers 3812, 4013, 4060
The Year Without Michael 4883
The Years of Rebellion 2168
The Yellow Star 4588
The Young Green Consumer Guide 1835
The Young Merlin Trilogy: Passager, Hobby and Merlin 4315
The Zucchini Warriors 785
There Was an Old Lady Who Swallowed a Fly 4717
There Were Monkeys in My Kitchen! 810
There Will Be Wolves 668
There's a Boy in the Girls' Bathroom 3145, 3281, 3395, 3739, 3911, 3956, 4166, 4226, 4265, 4331, 4360, 4371, 4492, 4953, 4999, 5050, 5135
There's a Girl in My Hammerlock 3334, 3414
There's Another Way! 1618
Theseus & the Minotaur 1469
Think of an Eel 1890, 2041
This Big Sky 3233
This Island Isn't Big Enough for the Four of Us 4278, 4662, 5044
This Land Is My Land 3998
This Poem Doesn't Rhyme 2024
This Train 4570
Thomas and the Tonners 1972
Thomas' Snowsuit 3146
Thor 818, 3724
Threadbear 1810
Three Cheers for Catherine the Great 3433
Three Cheers for Tacky 5021
Three Collections in One 2146
Three Sacks of Truth 3982
Through My Eyes 3392, 3674, 4008, 4485
Throwing Shadows 4649
Tibet. Das Geheimnis der roten Schachtel 1361
Tibet Through the Red Box 4723
Ticket to Curlew 656, 691
Ticket to the Sky Dance 2483
Tickle, Tickle 2006
Tick-tack 1475
Tiden bor ingensteder 2543
Tiergeschichten 3067
Tiger 5168
Tiitiäisen pippurimylly 1250
Tiktala 796
Til All the Stars Have Fallen: Canadian Poems for Children 623
Till Victory Is Won: Black Soldiers in the Civil War 3383
Tim a la Lluna 2789
Time and the Universe 2048
Time Flies 839, 4704
Time for Andrew: A Ghost Story 3194, 3342, 3557, 3745, 4233, 4251, 5005, 5061, 5110, 5233
Tinus-in-de-war 2318
Tiputape 2280
'Tisio Tshipsan? 2063
Tita und Leo 3079
Titanic Crossing 4234, 4350, 4670, 4806
Tjarany Roughtail 205, 273, 311
To agalma pou kryone 2141, 2201
To athanato nero 2136
To basilopullon tes Benedias 1452
To Dance at the Palais Royale 641, 695, 780
To erotevmeno asteri 2112
To gefyri tis Anatolis 2127
To hamogelo tis Ekatis 2131, 2193
To Je Ernest 454
To kokkino tis anatolis 2189
To Market, to Market 3847
To og to 2562
To perasma tis gatas 2118
To phantasma tes Portitsas 1461
To taxidi pou skotoni 2113
To xehasmeno syrtari 2120
Toad Rage 180, 353
Toby 106
Toby's Riddle 13
Toc! Toc! Monsieur Cric-Crac! 2640
Toccata og fuge I D-moll — Rias krig 366
Toen de wereld nog jong was 508, 2366
Toen er nog bizons waren 2319
Toen onze daniel dood ging 2331

Tomás and the Library Lady 5014
Tomb Travellers 12
Tomorrow Series 173, 179
Tomorrow, When the War Began 46, 151, 155, 229, 249, 263, 294, 337
Tomppa tahtoo 1241
Tonight, by Sea 3131
Toning the Sweep 3526
Tonton René et Tante Gilberte 911
Too Much Magic 5178
Tops and Bottoms 3175, 4257, 4705
Torn Away 646
Tornado 4871, 4966
Tot de 13e maan 482
Totally Disgusting 3154
Toto la brute 855
Tough Cookie 4566
Toughing It 3583
Tout un monde 1284
Tragoudi yia tris 2121
Trapped 2484
Trapped Between the Lash and the Gun 4860
Trapped in Death Cave 4831, 4952
Trapped in Ice 971
Trauriger Tiger toastet Tomaten 1421
Treasure in an Oatmeal Box 3771
Tres historias de Sergio 2893
Tres lechuzas en un cuento 1040
Trickster and the Fainting Birds 3104
Trijntje Buskruit 479
Trois chiens pour courir 593
Trouble with Trolls 3186, 5018
Trucas 1570
True Stories 381, 457
Trying to Get the Toothpaste Back into the Tube 3781
Tsar of the Sea: A Russian Wonder Tale 946
Tsatsiki och kärleken 2968
Tsuki no fune 1783
Tub People 4186
Tuesday 4121, 4689, 5246
Tvillingbrødrene 2552
Tvillingbror 1470
Tvillingsøster 2527
Twisted Summer 3588, 5266
Two Bad Ants 3753, 4242, 5085, 5164
Two by Two 680
Two of Everything: A Chinese Folktale 5062
Two Weeks with the Queen 214
Two's Company 2026
Tyrannosaurus Rex and His Kin 4463

Uçmak isteyen kaplumbaga 1736
Ull d'ocell 2876
Ulldevellut 2880
Um fio de fumo nos confins do mar 1645
Un alt glob, va rog! 1463
Un champion 704
Un crime est-il facile? 1496
Un dimanche avec Cézanne 1435
Un dimanche avec Léonard de Vinci 1295
Un elefante en la cristalería 1022
Un Grand-père tombé du ciel 1277
Un hada y una maga en el piso de abajo 1112
Un llibre monstruós 2810
Un lugar posible 1102
Un monstruo en el armario 2927
Un nuit, un chat 3060
Un Prof extra 861
Una casa com un cabàs 2892
Una noche de colores 2860
Una Sombra en el Hielo 1013
Unbearable! 226, 293, 330
Unbelievable! 223, 246
Unbroken 1690, 4576
Uncanny 245, 289
Uncle Comanche 3231
Uncle Ronald 660, 826
Uncle Wizzmo's New Used Car 4520
Uncovered! 231
Under the Hawthorn Tree 2250, 3928
Under the Red-Blood Sky 3353, 4367, 4792
Under the Royal Palms: A Childhood in Cuba 4679
Underrunners 2444
Undone! 32, 140, 228, 247, 248, 295, 333
Une Amitié bleue outremer 1271
Une Belle Journée pour mourir 715
Une charlotte en papillote 892
Une histoire tirée par la queue 893
Unmentionable! 224, 327
Unreal! 26, 98, 220
V Is for Vanishing: An Alphabet of Endangered Animals 184, 206
V Is for Victory 4917
Vacances au village 1533
Valentine & Orsen 3245
Valldemuller 2830
Vallen 496, 539, 552, 2356
Vampiri — Gunduraci — Zmej 1613
Van de sneeuwman die niet smelten wou 1767
Var är Sailor och Pekka 2983
Vår gamle gudelære 2553
Variations sure un même & laqnot'aime 731
Vecerna sonata 2654
Ved kilden 2544
Veislan í barnavagninum 2216
Vejigante Masquerader 3129
Veldig blå 1704
Verboden toegang 1746
Verdi 3292, 4190, 4258, 4436, 5008
Veren 2348, 2432
Victor 707
Vif Argent 586
Vildvinter 1709
Vincent van Gogga 2680
Vinterviken 2949
Virtually Perfect 4410
Viva la musique 2633
Vladimir et compagnie 897
Vladimirin kirja 1207
Vlerkdans 2688, 2750
Voices in the Park 1895
Voices on the Wind 762
Volcanoes 3691
Volšebnyj vozok 1490
Von Gutenberg zum World Wide Web 388
... von wegen ... caminhos ... 459
Voor altijd samen, amen 2386
Voor altijd, altijd 490
Voor Paulien 503
Vos en Haas 518, 555, 568, 1576
Vra vir Frederika 2723
Vreemd land 2364, 2433
Vreng 2529
Vrienden van de maan 2430
Vuela, Ertico, Vuela 1068
Vull jugar 2823

Waarom niet 2400
Wadayaknow! 9
Wait Till Helen Comes 3955, 4276, 4329, 4730
Waiting for the Whales 625, 679, 710, 775

Wake Up, World! 1697
Walk Two Moons 360, 1816, 4071, 4817, 5112
Wanted ... Mud Blossom 3578
War Boy 2088
War Game 1966
War of the Eagles 947
Warabe-Uta 2635
Warum der Hase lange Ohren hat 386, 463, 1640
Was die alte Maiasaura erzählt 1472
Wat staat daar? 1771
Wat vliegt daar? Wat kruipt daar? Wat prikt daar? 2372
Watch Out! Big Bro's Coming! 5074
Watchdog and Coyotes 5067
Water van zout 511
Water Wings 234
Wayside School Gets a Little Stranger 3291, 3508, 3712, 4271, 4508, 5221, 5259
Wayside School Is Falling Down 3149, 3499, 3694, 4168, 5139
WC- Papier in den wind laten wapperen 2645
We All Fall Down 3335
We Have Our Dreams 1596
We Share Everything 1686
We're Back! A Dinosaur's Story 3752, 4374
We're Going on a Bear Hunt 3246
Weasel 4801, 4865
Well, a Crocodile Can! 1669
Wenn das Glück kommt muss man ihm einen Stuhl hinstellen 1346, 3086
Wenn das Licht ausgeht... 461
Wenn Jakob unterm Kirschbaum sitzi 447
What Daddy Did 4814, 4906
What Ever Happened to Janie 3973
What Hearts 4061
What I Had Was Singing: The Story of Marian Anderson 3382
What Jamie Saw 4072
What They Don't Know 849, 922
What Would Jesus Do? 3774
What! 1828
What's Inside? 4652
What's the Big Deal About Sex? 3799
What's Under the Bed? 2047
When I Left My Village 4988
When I Was Five 3422
When Jessie Came Across the Sea 1880, 3479
When Martha's Away 1929, 1944
When Sophie Gets Angry—Really, Really Angry 3435, 4726
When Stars Stop Spinning 2236
When the Persians 2150
When the Wind Changed 38
When Zachary Beaver Came to Town 1662
When Zaydeh Danced on Eldridge Street 4990
Where Does God Live? Questions and Answers for Parents and Children 3456
Where Does the Trail Lead? 3811
Where It Stops, Nobody Knows 3551
Where the Forest Meets the Sea 221
Where the Great Bear Watches 1927
Where the Sidewalk Ends 5212
Where's Waldo 3147
Where's Wally 25, 39
Which Way Is Home? 1823
Whirikoki and His Seal 2511
Whirligig 3855
Whispers from the Dead 4334, 4379, 4836, 5252
Whispers in the Graveyard 1803
White Jade Tiger 955
White Water 5237
Who Killed My Daughter? The True Story of a Mother's Search for her Daughter's Murderer 4501
Who Stole a Bloater? 2059
Who's Afraid of the Bwganwood? 2071
WICKED! 148, 168, 176, 252, 253, 347
Wicked Jack 3984, 4433
Wie 514
Wie kommt der Wald ins Buch? 1330
Wie se hart kan dit dan hou? 2749
Wieso das Känguruh so lange beine hat 2619
Wij zijn Koerdistan 2299
Wild Fox 4195
Wildflower Girl 2231
Wildwasser 363
Willa's New World 923
William and Grandpa 3447
Willy 536
Wilma Unlimited 4003
Wind Child 4581
Window 62, 100, 329
Wings to Fly 781
Winners and Losers 4395
Winterbucht 1349
Wir Kuckuckskinder 1333
Wish Me Luck 959
Witchcraft of Bony Hag 2283
With a Name Like Lulu, Who Needs More Trouble? 4451
With the Gaze Turned Towards 2161
Witnesses to War 2051
Witte Pijn 574
Wmffra 2062
Wo biancheng yi zhi pen huo long le! 1548
Wok van de Wilden 488
Wolf 1799, 4544
Wolf by the Ears 4500
Wolf Island 742
Wolf oder schaf bose oder brav? 2641
Wolf Rider: A Tale of Terror 5083
Wolfsaga 433
Wolfsjahre 1368
Wonders Never Cease! 1694
Woodsong 4842, 4932
Words of Stone 3597
Working Cotton 4693
Wormy Poems 2661
Would My Fortune Cookie Lie? 4854
Wow Canada! Exploring This Land from Coast to Coast to Coast 753
Wrango 4948
Wrestling with Honor 4896
Wringer 3369, 3445, 4083
Written on the Waves 2156
Wushi-de-chenchuan 1784
WWJD Today? 3794

Xiaoqingchong-de-meng 1786

Yang the Eldest and His Odd Jobs 4587
Yang the Third and Her Impossible Family 4551
Yao zu 1520
Yatto aeta 1782
Ydy Fe! 2074
Yksisarvinen ja sadepuu 1214
Yn y Dechreuad 2060
Yo! Yes? 4700
Yoko 5194
Yolonda's Genius 4076

Yön lintu ja siivetön 1212, 1262
Yonderbeyonder 10
Young Citizen's Passport 2045
Yuanyuan de facai meng 1459
Yumba Days 1670

Zack 834, 837, 1604
Zack Bumm! 390
Zagrebacka prica 1434
Zakázané holky 1473
Zak's Lunch 3988
Zamboni 806
ZAPT! 345
Zbirka povesti o Drekcu Pekcu in Pukcu Smukcu 2657
Zeg me dat het niet zal sneeuwen 534
Zelda and Ivy 3853, 3854
Zes maal één is zeven 571
Zhenzhu naicha de youhuo 1507
Zij is altijd de eerste 2409
Zin! Zin! Zin! A Violin 4707
Zizi & !Xau. The Eagle Calls 1512
Zizn' zamecatel'nych detej 1773
Zizn' zamecatel'nych zverej 1761
Zoë und Rea 1598
Zomer zeventien 576
Zomo the Rabbit: A Trickster Tale from West Africa 5020, 5256
Zoo 1875
Zorro heisst Fuchs 3027
Zorro. Im Jahr des Pferdes 1776
Zoum au jardin — Zoum au Zoo — Zoum au cirque 1283
Zwart als inkt 2374
Zwarte rugzak 2376
Zwischen Lenen, jazz und Harry Lime 2626
Zwischen zwei Scheiben Glück 1356
Zylindergeschichten 1396